Growing Up in the Ice Age

Growing Up in the Ice Age
Fossil and archaeological evidence of the lived lives of Plio-Pleistocene children

April Nowell

Oxford & Philadelphia

To Lena, James and Ailsa
with love

First published in the United Kingdom in 2021. Reprinted in 2023 and 2025 by
OXBOW BOOKS
81 St Clements, Oxford OX4 1AW

and in the United States by
OXBOW BOOKS
1950 Lawrence Road, Havertown, PA 19083

© Oxbow Books and April Nowell 2021

Paperback Edition: ISBN 978-1-78925-294-1
Digital Edition: ISBN 978-1-78925-295-8 (ePub)

A CIP record for this book is available from the British Library

Library of Congress Control Number: 2021934332

All rights reserved. No part of this book may be reproduced or transmitted in any form or by any means, electronic or mechanical including photocopying, recording or by any information storage and retrieval system, without permission from the publisher in writing.

Printed in the United Kingdom by CMP Digital Print Solutions

Typeset by Versatile PreMedia Services (P) Ltd.

For a complete list of Oxbow titles, please contact:

United Kingdom	United States of America
Oxbow Books	Oxbow Books
Telephone (0)1226 734350	Telephone (610) 853-9131, Fax (610) 853-9146
Email: oxbow@oxbowbooks.com	Email: queries@casemateacademic.com
www.oxbowbooks.com	www.casemateacademic.com/oxbow

Oxbow Books is part of the Casemate Group

Front cover: © Sculpture Elisabeth Daynes/Photo: S. Entressangle.
Back cover: Upper Paleolithic children playing with miniature weapons. Drawing: Marina Lezcano.

The Publisher's authorised representative in the EU for product safety is Authorised Rep Compliance Ltd., Ground Floor, 71 Lower Baggot Street, Dublin D02 P593, Ireland.
www.arccompliance.com

Contents

Acknowledgements vi
Foreword *by Jane Baxter* viii

1. Toward an archaeology of Paleolithic children..1

2. Birth and the Paleolithic 'family' 21

3. Toys, burials and secret spaces 46

4. Stone tools, skill acquisition and learning a craft.....................................78

5. Children, oral storytelling and the Paleolithic 'arts' 104

6. Adolescence in the Ice Age 146

7. Paleolithic children as drivers of human evolution............................... 164

Appendix 1. Chronology of the Paleolithic and timeline of fossil hominins 172
Appendix 2. Table of subadult fossils in the Plio-Pleistocene
 (perinatal–ca. 10 years) 173
Appendix 3. Table of subadult fossils from the Plio-Pleistocene
 (ca. 10 years–20 years)... 251
Bibliography.. 312
Index 363

Acknowledgements

The idea for this book began back in 2009 when I started throwing files into an electronic folder simply labelled 'Paleo kids'. It wasn't until a decade later that the writing of this book took shape but I had spent much of the intervening years, thinking, teaching and publishing on 'Paleo kids'. The majority of this book was written during the Covid-19 pandemic of 2020. I truly hope that as you read this you are thinking, that was awful, I am so glad that's *over*. As an academic, I was privileged to be able to continue doing my job, teaching and writing, from home. At the same time, limited access to my office and only online access to my university's library meant that many of the resources I needed were out of reach. This is where so many of my friends and colleagues stepped in to help. People generously sent me PDFs of their work and one friend, Anders Högberg, went so far as to photograph each page of a critical chapter with his phone and to email them to me one by one.

As Chair of the Department of Anthropology at the University of Victoria during the pandemic, my administrative load was heavier than usual. I had to oversee the shutdown of our department and transition to online teaching and the gradual return to work when it became safe to do so. In stepped more generous friends. Lisa Mitchell, Brian Thom, Daromir Rudnyckyj, Helen Kurki and Andrea Walsh each took on Acting Chair duties so that I could have nine weeks of mostly uninterrupted writing time. While this pandemic has brought with it many sadnesses, it has also brought home the kindness, good humor and supportive nature of those I am grateful to have around me.

In this context, I would like to thank the following people for sending me PDFs, commenting on earlier drafts, providing me with figures or generally being supportive of this endeavor and my sincere apologies to anyone who was inadvertently left out: Chris Ames, Traci Ardren, Paul Bahn, Stephanie Baker, Jane Eva Baxter, Gerhard Bosinski, Lisa Brown, Stephanie Calce, Maureen Carrol, Melanie L. Chang, Jean Clottes, Ben Collins, Amanda Cooke, Elizabeth Craig-Atkins, Dale Croes, Iain Davidson, Francesco d'Errico, Rebecca Farbstein, David Frayer, Carole Fritz, Khaled Hakami, Siân Halcrow, Anders Högberg, Helen Kurki, Liudmila Valentinovna Lbova, Mary Lewis, Marina Lezcano, Stuart Lipkin, Charlotte Mackie, Quentin Mackie, Lisa Mitchell, Mark Moore, Magen O'Farrell, Susan Pfeiffer, Frédéric Plassard, James Pokines, Felix Riede, Lisa Rogers, Aurora Skala, Dan Stueber, Meghan Strong, Nancy Tatebe, Gilles Tosello, Leslie Van Gelder and Alexei Vranich. Thank you also to Prof. Anne-Marie Tillier who first inspired me, through her publications, to start thinking about Neandertal children when I was still a graduate student. I thank Lisa Rogers for research assistance and Jeremy Beller for research assistance and masterful figure preparation.

Similarly, I especially thank Kirsten Blomdal for all of the hours she spent compiling data for many of the tables in this volume as well as for all of her work formatting and cross-referencing the bibliography and text. It was a massive undertaking and I am truly grateful for everything she has done. I thank Elisabeth Daynes (the Atelier Daynes) for the beautiful cover art and Jane Baxter for generously agreeing to write the foreword. Jane's pioneering work remains an inspiration for me. I would also like to thank my ever patient and kind editor at Oxbow, Jessica Scott, for believing she would eventually see a manuscript.

I thank my husband, Jon Miller, who was beginning to feel as if he was living through the writing of my dissertation a second time but continually encouraged me to put 'words on pages' and my children, Lena and James Miller, and my niece, Ailsa Miller, for being inspirations – it is no accident that I began with an interest in children and the evolution of play behavior and developed an interest in the unique contributions of teens as you all grew. Finally, I thank James Pokines, who back in 1999 suggested we write a paper together on children in the Paleolithic and to whom I replied, 'I am not sure we know enough to write anything'. You have never said 'I told you so'. Drinks are on me.

Foreword

Let me begin by simply saying that this book is an incredibly significant development in the trajectory of childhood studies in archaeology. With that proclamation made, let me explain why. The reasons are many.

Early scholarship on the archaeology of childhood focused on identifying traces of children and their lives in the skeletal and material records at archaeological sites. Children were often analyzed in isolation simply to demonstrate their presence could be identified, and that such an identification was useful in archaeological inquiry. These fundamentals were needed at a time when the archaeology of childhood was primarily invested in demonstrating the visibility and viability of children in the archaeological record to justify its pursuit by scholars. Chapter 1 of this book is a potent manifesto of why children traditionally have been understudied in archaeology, and why those reasons don't hold up to scrutiny. Dr Nowell makes a strong case for a reconfiguration of our archaeological approaches to the past to be more inclusive in our interpretations and understandings of those who lived before us. As a long-time scholar of children in archaeology, I found myself mentally applauding, fist pumping, and shouting, 'Amen' to the resounding declarations made in the first chapter: Children were present in the past. Children were important in the past. An archaeology without children is one that is fundamentally lacking in its interpretation of the past.

Taking such a view has resulted in more sophisticated understandings of children in human communities, and frequently involves an explicit or tacit focus on the relational nature of childhood. Relational approaches tell us that children belong to a category of person that is defined in relationship to other such categories. Children are understood as being different from adults, infants, adolescents, or others depending on the culture under study, and the boundaries between these categories are actively negotiated and regulated. Relational understandings of childhood demand an exploration of the relationships that create these categories and the boundaries between them. *Growing Up in the Ice Age* is a work that embraces the relational nature of childhood as a key underpinning, placing children as active agents in human communities through familial relationships, rituals in life and death, and communities of practice and artistic production. Chapter 6 focuses exclusively on adolescence – a category of personhood we are only beginning to appreciate and understand in archaeology, but one that also relies on a relational understanding of personhood. In this way, this book is definitely childhood archaeology 2.0 – one that assumes the presence of children and firmly situates them within human communities in rich and complex ways.

This book clearly illustrates how far the archaeology of childhood has come, although there is still a persistent myth in circulation that the archaeology of childhood is a new area of study. Certainly, it's not an area of scholarship with a deep history, but thirty years of thinking and writing by hundreds of authors makes this topic anything but new. A quick glance at the bibliography for this book points to the fact that Dr Nowell has been engaged in this community of scholars and thinkers for over a decade, and as such has produced a work that is deeply engaged with this literature and scholarship. Her understanding of the theoretical and methodological aspects of the archaeological study of childhood shine through in her work, particularly as she is able to make complex ideas so easily accessible to readers.

Being engaged in the literature shouldn't seem like a particularly distinctive feature of a scholarly work, but for the study of children in the deep past such an engagement is not always a given. Much of the early literature on the archaeology of childhood involved studies of children in the more recent past, where ethnographic and documentary sources could help build a case for children or aid in the interpretation of the material remains recovered. This has led some scholars to set aside this literature as largely irrelevant when dealing with the study of children in the more distant past, suggesting that studying childhoods that can be understood only through archaeology is a unique and particular enterprise. Some scholars also seem to be very selective in how they cite the works of their fellow archaeologists who work on childhood in the deep past. As someone who studies the recent past and is not a part of this particular community, I cannot account for these choices, but I can say it has been, in my observation, a detriment to the work of some scholars. The fact that Dr Nowell fully engages the methods and theories developed for the study of childhood in more recent periods and carefully considers and applies them as appropriate to children in the Ice Age makes this work a comprehensive and substantial interpretation of children and their worlds. Our understanding of these distant time periods is enriched and humanized because of this approach. For those seeking to know people in the past as fellow humans, this book is a very thoughtful and satisfying read about young people, their families and their communities.

The flip side of this particularism is that with the exception of some very notable and important insights from the oral traditions of indigenous peoples, the study of the Plio-Pleistocene peoples is one that relies solely on the archaeological record. In this way, *Growing Up in the Ice Age* is the realization of early works that claimed children were knowable through the archaeological record without direct context from other sources. An entire book on children that relies so thoroughly on archaeological evidence to recreate children's worlds is a fulfillment of earlier scholarship that theorized such potential.

This archaeological study of children in the deep past also involves considerable engagement with literature from evolutionary anthropology. The importance of interpreting the birth, care and successful rearing of children as an integral part of a species' strategy to perpetuate itself into the future is not a particular concern when one studies the more recent past, but it is central to the study of early human communities and their ancestors. Dr Nowell has elegantly woven this literature into the archaeological study of children with alacrity and skill that invites the reader to an understanding of the importance of children on multiple scales.

On the one hand, we are encouraged to see the intergenerational dynamics of human communities as an evolutionary imperative. As she recounts in Chapter 2, a former professor proclaimed to her class that the real message of evolution is, 'save the children'. Indeed, understanding the basic need to birth and raise healthy children generation after generation is central to understanding a vital concern of all human communities. If these fundamental aspects of childhood hadn't gone well at any time in the past, we wouldn't be here today. This particular understanding of childhood is particularly potent when we look at small communities of early humans.

Simultaneously, this book allows us to engage early humans as, well, humans. The same biological imperative to perpetuate the species theoretically applies to us today, but it is masked by our incredible evolutionary success and abundant population around the globe. Our concerns for children are still very real and are not unlike those of our ancestors if we think in contemporary economic terms. It is widely estimated that the average cost of raising a child in the United States today is just shy of a quarter of a million dollars, and that is exclusive of a college education. This estimate considers how families invest in their children from birth to age 18. Where does this money go? Well, a large chunk goes to providing food and medical care, and another large amount is accounted for by basic needs like clothing and shelter. The need to provide children with enrichment opportunities accounts for the lion's share of this budget. A child must have adequate toys and playthings to enhance cognitive, physical and social development; engage in activities and objects that enhance, amplify and augment formal education; and participate in activities like family vacations and travel to create lifelong memories, enduring family bonds and unique life experiences. It is this category of expenditure more than any other that has steadily raised the cost of having a child since 1960. This investment, now understood in terms of cost and capital, in practical terms helps to increase the likelihood of a child's successful future. Children should be healthy, happy and successful not just as children, but also as adults. Their success not only ensures intergenerational reproduction, but also serves as an illustration that the parents did a 'good job' in raising socially ideal citizens.

While the landscape of what constitutes a successful childhood has changed, the parallels between our aspirations and goals for children and those motivating Plio-Pleistocene communities are very real. By integrating evolutionary studies and concepts with those that focus on childhood across time and space, Dr Nowell illustrates the unique concerns of our early ancestors in raising their children while also creating a sense that they aren't so different from us after all.

Our desire to connect, to know and to appreciate the lives of our ancestors is a driving force behind our enduring interest in archaeology. There are many ways to make such a connection, but childhood in this way is special. Every human who has ever lived to become an adult was once a child. The details of their childhood may have been culturally determined, but childhood itself is a universal human experience. The ability to recognize the diversity of childhood experiences across time and space is an understanding that archaeology can give to us. The ability to feel a connection through the shared experience of childhood with those who lived long ago is a particular gift that *Growing Up in the Ice Age* gives to all of us, and is a celebration of the potentials and possibilities of a rigorous archaeology and the humanness of us all.

Jane Eva Baxter, PhD
Associate Professor and Chair of Anthropology
DePaul University
Chicago, IL USA

Chapter 1

Toward an archaeology of Paleolithic children

> Without children there is no inter-generational continuity of life and culture. As humans live on earth today, it is an empirical (and banal) fact that children must have been born, raised, grown into adults and had their own children throughout the deep time of human evolution and prehistory.
>
> (Anders Högberg 2018)

Where are all the children?

It is estimated that in prehistoric societies children comprised at least 40 to 65% of the population (Baxter 2005a; 2008), yet by default, in our collective imaginations, our ancestral landscapes are peopled by *adults* who hunt, gather, fish, knap tools and make art. But these adults were also parents, grandparents, aunts and uncles (however they would have codified these kin relationships) who had to make space physically, emotionally, intellectually and cognitively for the infants, children and adolescents around them. Nonetheless, the archaeological literature has largely been silent about the lives these children lived and the contributions they made because the economic, social and political roles of Paleolithic[1] children are often assumed to be negligible at best and unknowable at worst.

This is not a problem that is unique to those who study the Paleolithic period but is an issue that pervades archaeology more generally. Thirty years ago, the Norwegian archaeologist, Dr Grete Lillehammer (1989), published her seminal paper, 'A Child is Born', which many archaeologists saw as a call to arms to meaningfully integrate children into archaeological inquiries (Nowell *et al.* 2020). In the intervening decades, there has been a slow but steady uptake in child-focused studies in archaeology. But why were children understudied in the first place? It should be obvious that children existed in prehistory after all. In answer to this question, I think there are four main reasons that children have traditionally been understudied.

Living populations, archaeological populations and taphonomy

First, there are often fewer of them to study as the number of children uncovered in the archaeological record is not proportional to the number of children in living populations. Let's consider this in detail. Moving from a living population to an archaeological population is a winnowing process where there is a loss of information at each step of the way (Fig. 1.1) (Séguy and Buchet 2013). Let's imagine a census of all

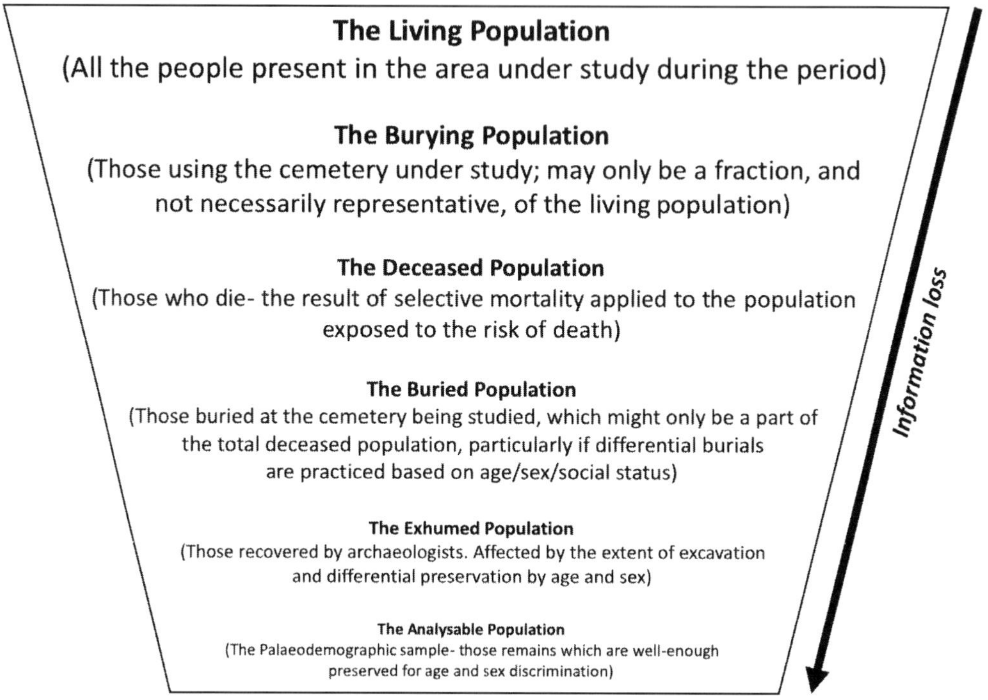

The Living Population
(All the people present in the area under study during the period)

The Burying Population
(Those using the cemetery under study; may only be a fraction, and not necessarily representative, of the living population)

The Deceased Population
(Those who die- the result of selective mortality applied to the population exposed to the risk of death)

The Buried Population
(Those buried at the cemetery being studied, which might only be a part of the total deceased population, particularly if differential burials are practiced based on age/sex/social status)

The Exhumed Population
(Those recovered by archaeologists. Affected by the extent of excavation and differential preservation by age and sex)

The Analysable Population
(The Palaeodemographic sample- those remains which are well-enough preserved for age and sex discrimination)

Information loss →

Figure 1.1: Diagram demonstrating the degree to which an archaeological population is representative of a living population (French, in press; reproduced with permission of J.C. French and redrawn by J. Beller).

those present in a particular region during a specific range of time, *i.e.* what paleodemographers call the 'living population'. It is possible, even likely, that not everyone in that population uses a particular cemetery or burial place. This is particularly true for people who practice a highly mobile hunter-gatherer lifestyle, which, until about 10,000 years ago, was the norm for virtually everyone on the planet (Bocquet-Appel *et al.* 2005; French 2015; French and Collins 2015; Kretschmer 2015; Maier and Zimmerman 2017; Schmidt and Zimmerman 2019). In this case, the remains of those who die in a given year from, for example, old age, illness, accident or childbirth are distributed over a larger geographic area relative to population density. Even in more sedentary populations, access to a burial ground can be defined based on socio-economic factors (*e.g.* a pauper's cemetery vs. Egypt's Valley of the Kings), religious factors (*e.g.* a Jewish or Catholic cemetery), ethnic factors (a Chinese cemetery or New York's historic African Burial Ground) or other determinants (*e.g.* a Leper's cemetery or a military cemetery such as Arlington National Cemetery). Those people who have access to a particular cemetery form the 'burying population'. A subset of the burying population is referred to as the 'deceased population'. These are the people who end up dying. The specific make-up of this population will vary based on age, sex, socio-economic status and individual pathological condition (Séguy and Buchet 2013, 16). We then move to the 'exhumed population'. The exhumed population is the proportion of the deceased population that is recovered through archaeological excavation. This number will vary based on whether the cemetery or burial ground is fully excavated or only selectively sampled. It also varies based on differential preservation. Finally, of the exhumed population, only a portion of these individuals will be amenable to analysis such as sex and age determination. This last group forms the 'analyzable population'. As Séguy and Buchet (2013, 17) observe, '[e]ven in optimal archaeological conditions it is never certain that the proportion exhumed is significantly representative of all the components of the buried population.' And I would argue even less so of the living population.

This winnowing process impacts all sex and age classes but the degree to which subadults are affected is still a matter of debate (Lewis 2007). The question is *exactly* how representative of the living population is the archaeological (*i.e.* analyzable) population of children. In an influential study, Schofield and Wrigley (1979) wrote that while mortality rates of individuals under 10 years of age are roughly 2.4% in modern industrial societies they are closer to 34% in modern non-industrial societies. According to Lewis (2007, 22), 'it is now common to cite this modern pre-industrial figure as the norm for child mortality in archaeological populations from many periods all over the World. That 30% of the sample should contain non-adults has become the gold standard by which under-representation is measured'. But in many cemetery samples and other forms of burial grounds, subadults represent less than 30% of the analyzable population (Lewis 2007).

This under-representation is usually assumed to be for taphonomic reasons. Taphonomy, from the Greek word *taphos* (τάφος) meaning 'burial' and *nomos* (νόμος) meaning 'law', is the study of burial processes (Efremov 1940). All things being equal, larger, denser bones preserve longer and in better condition in the archaeological record than do smaller, more porous bones – think elephant bones versus hollow bird bones or even a human femur vs. a middle ear ossicle. Not only are children's bones smaller but their epiphyses (*i.e.* the ends of their long bones) have not yet completely ossified or fused to the rest of the bone. Their bones are also highly porous, less mineralized and lack tensile and compressive strength. All of these characteristics render them particularly vulnerable to sedimentary pressure, bioerosion through contact with acidic soil and decomposing organic matter, and excavator bias (Nowell 2020; Nowell and Kurki 2020).

Excavator bias refers to the difference in recovery rates of materials based on a variety of factors including excavator experience and choice of methods employed. For instance, unless you screen excavated sediments using a fine mesh, you are much more likely to miss tiny remains such as deciduous teeth or fragments of vertebrae (Pokines and De la Paz 2016). At Drimolen, for example, a 2–1.5 million year old site in South Africa, excavators have uncovered the remains of 80 hominins[2] attributable to *Homo* sp. and *Paranthropus robustus*. Of the specimens that could be aged, infants (defined in this study as those under 5 years of age) accounted for just under 35%.

If those individuals aged between 6 and 10 years of age are included, then immature specimens account for almost half of the hominin sample (Riga *et al.* 2019). There are important behavioral reasons that likely explain this age distribution but another factor is the choices made by the site's project directors. Researchers there sieve and water screen all excavated materials including all medium and fine meshed finds. They then spread this material out on a table and meticulously sort through all of it (S. Baker personal communication 2020). This allows them to recover even the tiniest deciduous tooth that would likely have been missed if they did not follow such a rigorous protocol.

Another factor in the under-representation of children in the archaeological record is the fact that sometimes children may be subject to different funerary processes than older individuals due to cultural differences, for example, in attitudes towards 'personhood'. Differences in personhood mean variations in when (and on what basis) an individual is accorded the status of being a person and, in this case, a member of society requiring burial. Funerary differences associated with children may include interment in remote locations, shallower graves, the absence of grave markers and/or coffins, no interment at all or interment in burial containers such as jars or in ceramic vessels in caches (*e.g.* Lally and Ardren 2009; Carroll 2012; O'Reilly *et al.* 2019).

But questions of personhood are not always straightforward. Eileen Murphy (2011) studies 17th-century *cillíní* – or children's burial grounds in Ireland. These burial grounds were primarily for unbaptized infants but were also often the final resting place of 'other members of Irish society who were considered unsuitable by the Roman Catholic Church for burial in consecrated ground' (Murphy 2011, 409). *Cillíní* were often located in deserted church yards or other liminal spaces such as bogs – these spaces are the physical manifestation of being in 'limbo' or on the border between Heaven and Hell in the Roman Catholic tradition. More than 1300 *cillíní* have been identified throughout Ireland by archaeologists. Their location suggests that these infants were 'spiritually ambiguous'. Nonetheless, Murphy (2011) found expressions of parental grief such as simple grave markers (*e.g.* stones or stones bearing crosses) and grave goods such as white quartz, sea pebbles, and sea shells as well as an example of a figurine that resembles a baby in swaddling clothes and several 'jacks' – perhaps these mementos and toys were for the children to play with or to give them comfort while they waited in limbo. In other cases, neonates and infants were buried surreptitiously under church eaves so that they could be 'baptized' by dripping rainwater (Craig-Atkinson 2014). These examples underscore that differential burial doesn't necessarily mean lack of care and emotion but it can contribute to an under-representation of children in the archaeological record.

Children as 'distorters' of the archaeological record

The second reason that children have been understudied in the archaeological record is that children's play and their 'unconventional' use of material culture were, until recently, believed to introduce a randomizing and distorting element into the archaeological record (Baxter 2005a; see for example, Hammond and Hammond 1981). As Jane Baxter (2008) argues, for many archaeologists children were not only unknown, they were unknowable. Rather than trying to use material culture to reconstruct the lives of children, children were often used as a cautionary tale (David and Kramer 2001). Researchers would look to the ethnographic record to show how children's behavior might skew archaeological interpretations. For example, children might move 'items from their "proper" places or places of adult use and discard' (Baxter 2005b, 78 my emphasis). Children's play was also a way of explaining the unexplainable. For example, miniatures found in the archaeological record might be toys or a poorly constructed pot might have been made by a child. These were often ad hoc explanations rather than the basis for hypothesis testing and scientific inquiry.

But let's unpack this assumption a bit. What do we mean when we say children's play and unconventional use of material culture 'distorted' the archaeological record? The word 'distortion' has an interesting history in the study of archaeological theory. Approximately 40 years ago, there was a famous debate between Lewis Binford and Michael Schiffer, both professors of archaeology and both influential writers and thinkers in the realm of archaeological method and theory. The debate concerned the so-called 'Pompeii premise'. The Pompeii premise is a term that was first coined by Robert Ascher in 1961 in reference to the famous archaeological site of Pompeii, where everyday life was essentially frozen in time when the volcano, Mount Vesuvius, erupted in AD 79, burying the Roman city under layers of volcanic ash and pumice. This catastrophic event provided archaeologists with an unparalleled opportunity to reconstruct the lived lives of those ancient Romans and their relationships to objects with which they engaged and the spaces they inhabited. Everything was found '*in situ*' as we say, or 'in place'. Unfortunately, the vast majority of archaeological sites are not, as Binford (1981) observed, 'mini Pompeiis'. Only Cerén, a 1400-year-old Mayan village site in San Salvador that was also destroyed by a volcanic eruption, and Ozette, a 200-year-old water-logged Makah village site in Washington State, come close. All other sites (and even these 'Pompeiis') are subject to a variety of taphonomic processes.

Both Binford and Schiffer were well aware of the impact of taphonomic processes on an archaeologist's ability to reconstruct the everyday lives of people in the past. Schiffer (1975) referred to them as N-transforms (natural transformation processes such as wind, earthquakes and rodents burrowing) and C-transforms (cultural transformation processes such as looting, the human re-use of building materials or humans digging a basement that breaks through a previous occupation layer). Schiffer was interested in how artifacts moved from their 'systemic context' (use in people's everyday lives) to their 'archaeological context' (in which they are discovered and excavated by archaeologists). Further, artifacts could be in either primary context or secondary context. Artifacts in use-related primary context were recovered from the place they were acquired, made or used, while artifacts in transposed primary context were deposited by human activity outside where they were acquired, made or used, for example, middens or historic latrines that doubled as garbage dumps (Fig. 1.2).

Figure 1.2: A profile wall of a latrine at Fort Wellington, Prescott, Ontario, a 19th-century military fort. This latrine was divided into three sections – one for officers, one for enlisted men and one for women and children. Not only was the latrine used as a toilet but it doubled as a garbage dump. Its water-logged/anaerobic environment facilitated the preservation not only of ceramics and children's slate boards but of organics too, such as a delicate tablecloth and a woman's boot. The artifacts in this location would be in transposed primary context according to Schiffer (Photo: April Nowell).

Most of the objects uncovered by archaeologists at Pompeii, Cerén and Ozette were in primary use-related context.³ According to Schiffer, artifacts are in secondary context when the provenience, associations between objects and features and the sedimentary context (matrix) have been altered by natural or cultural transformational processes.

This particular debate centered around whether C-transforms 'distorted' the archaeological record or more precisely, the archaeologist's ability to make inferences from static artifacts existing in the present (archaeological context) about dynamic cultural systems in the past (systemic context). For example, does sweeping up flaking debris after an episode of stone tool making and moving the debris to a midden constitute a 'distortion' of the archaeological record? Schiffer (2010, 40) would say it depends on your research question. You can look at sweeping, a cultural transformation process, as a 'distortion' because it removes the material from its use-related primary context and is thus a 'consequential [source] of variability in the evidence'. Conversely, you can use sweeping to study the social and demographic factors influencing refuse management in that society and it is therefore, not a distortion. However, for Binford (1981, 200), 'a pattern or arrangement among artifacts at an archaeological site can only be viewed as distorted *if one is not interested in the cultural system as manifest*, but rather in some property of a cultural system chosen *a priori to receive special inferential attention*' (my emphasis). In other words, in our case, children's play is a 'distortion' of the archaeological record only if we are trying to reconstruct *adult* behavior, not *human* behavior more broadly in the past. Re-use is a natural part of the life history of an object whether we are talking about using broken glass in a mosaic floor, a book to prop open a window or goat vertebrae as toy soldiers. As Binford (1981, 206) notes, 'the challenge is how to use the "distorted" stuff, not how to discover the rare and unusual Pompeiis' or in our case the adult-only behavior. Material culture moved or modified by children can still be considered in use-related primary context, only now the object's use has been changed or redefined; the life history or biography of that object has now been added to (see Crawford 2009). This is where hypothesis testing can begin.

Children as pawns vs. children as social agents

The third reason children have been understudied in the archaeological record has to do with their perceived lack of agency. Agency is a term that refers to the strategies used by individuals in a society. From this perspective, 'women and men are not passively duped by the system around them' into 'blindly following social rules' (Johnson 2020, 114). Rather, they understand these rules and negotiate their relationships to them. While not fully autonomous, individuals can creatively bend these rules to a greater or lesser extent to advance their own agendas. There has been considerable debate in archaeology about the role of the individual and the degree to which they exercise agency (Johnson 2020), with consensus in the field coalescing around the importance of agency as a factor in understanding the dynamics of past cultural systems. However, these debates have overwhelmingly focused on adults, as children are more often assumed to be 'pawns' in adult strategies and 'empty vessels' waiting to be filled with knowledge rather than as social beings with agency in their own right (Van Gelder 2015b; Halstad McGuire 2019). This assumption is important because it leads to the conclusion that the archaeological record is the product of adults alone and thus that it speaks to the lived lives of adults only. This assumption, then, contributes to the perceived invisibility of children in the archaeological record even though the agency of children producing, 'collecting and depositing material may have a significant impact on the nature of the deposited assemblages' (Crawford 2009, 64; see also Lillehammer 2011). This assumption is tied to our expectations of children and childhood.

For more than a decade, I have taught a class on the archaeology of children. Each year, I begin by asking students what adjectives they associate with the words 'child' and 'childhood'. Without fail, they supply words and phrases such as 'innocent', 'playful', 'happy', 'naïve', 'dependent' and 'lack of responsibility'. These words and phrases either describe their own experiences as children or, more likely, their ideal of childhood. These words and phrases are rife with nostalgia for a real or imagined time in their lives. I then show a slide of the photograph in Figure 1.3 taken from a book chapter called *Material Culture Shock: Confronting Expectations in the Material Culture of Children* by Joanna Sofaer Derevenski (2000b, 3). In this photograph, we see a young Afrikaans girl in camouflage clothing receiving training in how to discharge a firearm. The original caption reads, 'A week in the life of the "new" South Africa'.

Figure 1.3: Sofaer Derevenski (2000b) uses this image of a young girl learning to fire a gun as an example of when the roles and material culture associated with children and childhood come into conflict with Western perceptions of this life stage (Photo: Ian Berry, Magnum Photos).

This image is 'shocking' to many of my students because it is in direct conflict with the narrative of children and childhood they had just constructed. Sofaer Derevenski (2000b, 3) writes,

> The photograph is a record of a real contemporary event, rather than the fiction of a book or film. The child is not playing; the gun is a lethal weapon, the girl is being trained to kill. The photograph creates a disjunction between the enculturated expectations of the modern Western reader and material reality. Connections which we hold with concepts of 'child' (innocent, passive, protected, happy and young) and 'weapon' (worldly, aggressive, violent, suffering and adult) are mutually exclusive oppositions. The juxtaposition of the child with a lethal weapon creates incongruity; the material culture of the gun ought to be held in a different hand, the uniform of battle should be worn by another body.

There is further disjunction caused by the fact that the girl is depicted using a traditionally 'male' object (*i.e.* we have different expectations of male and female children) and by the fact that children are supposed to be apolitical and yet here is a child engaged in what is arguably an emotionally charged and racialized political act (Sofaer Derevenski 2000b).

As Kohut (2011, 153) has observed, 'Western notions of childhood as an innocent, carefree period … may have hindered alternative views of the experience of childhood throughout space and time.' Kamp (2001b, 18) has argued that in addition to biases around what are 'appropriate' behaviors and occupations for children, a further hindrance to seeing agency in children is that archaeologists often assume that children are 'incapable of performing complex tasks or assuming responsibility'. But she counters (2001b, 18), 'it might be argued that a child who is able to learn to read, do arithmetic, and follow the rules of the classroom would also be able to perform a wide range of economically productive activities, some of them fairly complex.' I think of my own children at 5 and 6 years of age memorizing long, complex names of dinosaurs and their associated biological characteristics.

A growing body of data demonstrates that contemporary and archaeologically known children were actively engaged in the social, political, economic and religious spheres of the world around them. First, children did and do contribute to the work force, often in substantial numbers making a real difference to the economic well-being of those in their households and communities. Many tasks such as herding, fetching water, harvesting vegetables, collecting firewood, tending animals, cleaning and sweeping and caring for younger siblings are primarily associated with children and are important because they free adults to take on other tasks (Lillehammer 1989; Kamp 2001b). Children can also be key economic providers outside the home by working in factories and markets or as farm laborers and entrepreneurs (Kamp 2001b). Furthermore, children are often responsible for collecting and processing their own and younger siblings' food (see, for example, Bird and Bird 2000), which has been argued to reduce subsistence stress on mothers (Zeller 1987). The amount of work engaged in by children varies cross-culturally from 0 to more than 40 hours a week and is often dependent on expectations around gender, age and socio-economic class (Kamp 2001b). Archaeologically, Ancient Mayan children engaged in weaving (Kohut 2011); in Iron Age Austria children worked as miners (Pany-Kucera *et al.* 2019); urns from Ancient Greece depict young boys tending chickens and young girls spinning cloth and caring for younger children (Sommer and Sommer 2015); in Rome caring for pigeons was often left to children (Huntley 2016); while Ancient Egyptian tombs are decorated with scenes of boys plowing, sowing, tending cattle and chasing birds from crops and girls gleaning fields (Baxter 2005a).

Second, in many societies, children were actively engaged in the production of textiles, ceramics, stone tools and beads among other craft items (*e.g.* Kamp 2001a; Smith 2005; Högberg 2008; Kohut 2011; Arnold 2012; Lancy 2017). A particularly interesting example comes from Bronze Age Britain. In 2014, archaeologists revealed that children and teenagers were responsible for the intricate gold work decorating the handles of 4000-year-old Bronze Age daggers (Lorenzi 2014). One such dagger (Fig. 1.4) from the site of Bush Barrow, just under a kilometer from the famous site of Stonehenge, was decorated with 140,000 tiny gold studs, each thinner than a human hair (Lorenzi 2014). Hundreds of them together would be dwarfed by a sewing needle (Lorenzi 2014). Arranged in straight lines, the studs were designed to overlap like fish scales. This intricate work would have taken its toll on children as '[t]he ultra-fine craftwork entailed extremely tiny components such as microscopic gold pins and gold

Figure 1.4: (Left) Close up of individual gold pins used to decorate the wooden handle of an early Bronze Age dagger from Bush Barrow (UK). Each pin is less than the width of a human hair (Photo: © Wiltshire Museum, Devizes); (Right) Watercolor painting of the dagger when it was first discovered in 1808 (Drawing: Philip Crocker, © Wiltshire Museum, Devizes).

wires. According to optic experts, only children and teenagers, and those adults who had become myopic naturally or due to the nature of their work as children, would have been able to create and manufacture such tiny objects. The eye-stressing work would have blinded most child workers' (Ronald Rabbetts quoted in Lorenzi 2014).

Third, in addition to participating in the work force generally and craft production more specifically, children were also active in religious, political and military realms in some archaeologically known cultures. Among the Classic Maya, for example, 'to some extent, age did not prove to be a factor limiting children's ability to assume political or religious roles' (Kohut 2011, 154). In fact, a number of child kings, some as young as 5 years of age figure prominently in Classic Mayan history (T. Ardren personal communication 2020). Mayan children also worked as musicians in rituals associated with funerals, weddings, accession ceremonies and battles (Kohut 2011). In Ancient Egypt, the famous Tutankhamun became pharaoh around age 8 or 9, and Pepi II, likely ascended to the throne at the tender age of 6 (Baker and Baker 2001; Eaton-Krauss 2015). Children participating in military conflicts is not a modern phenomenon. Throughout history they have acted as messengers, spies, musicians (*e.g.* drummers), soldiers and human shields. In ancient Sparta, for example, boys began military training at the age of 7. Sofaer (2015, 82) observes that to be involved in combat you have to 'know how to hold, swing, and sheath a weapon, simultaneously developing endurance, musculature, and neuronal and motor pathways'. This training takes place within a particular cultural context that encourages, values and legitimizes these roles and behaviors. Some young people were even military leaders. In 1429 at the age of 17, Joan of Arc led the French royal army to its first victory over the English in the Hundred Years' War at the Siege of Orleans (DeVries 1999).

It is clear from all of the examples described above that children contributed to the material culture and patterning of the archaeological record. But to what degree did children exercise agency in their own lives? The extent to which children's actions were controlled or circumscribed would have varied over space and time. For example, Park (2005) writes that among the Canadian Inuit, infants are considered to be the reincarnation of deceased ancestors. In this context, children are given a great deal of latitude and the task of adults is to help the children 'remember' how to be responsible members of society. By contrast, for Tongan children, 'the process of child socialization is closely tied to cultural ideas about the "nature" of children and the way this must be accommodated, transformed or replaced in order for them to be regarded as fully adult persons' (Morton 1996, 70). For children to become adults and functioning members of society, adults must 'mold' and 'manage' their children's nature, behavior, heart and mind (Morton 1996).

Cross-culturally, children are taught the values, traditions and expectations of their culture from the adults around them through words, deeds and, most importantly for archaeologists, material culture. Let's consider toys in this regard. It is important to understand the inferences we make from toys about the lived lives of children. First, toys often reflect the values of the gift-giver to a greater degree than the gift-receiver. In this regard, Baxter (2016) discusses the example of the Fisher-Price Chatter Phone and the notion of nostalgia. First marketed in 1961, this pull toy, with its moving eyes and bell ringing rotary dial, was likely a cherished toy for many of you reading this book. Fisher-Price continues to sell more than 250,000 of these toys each year despite the fact that most people under 25 today have never used or even seen a rotary phone other than on television. The toy's continued popularity is directly related to its ability to tap into a strong sense of adult nostalgia. Re-releases in the 2000s of the 1980s Cabbage Patch dolls, Strawberry Shortcake figures and Smurfs speak to this same phenomenon. In 2019, Fisher-Price released a well-received commercial featuring the actor John Goodman. In it, Goodman strolls through a life-sized version of its popular toy farm, hand-in-hand with a young girl. He invites adults to buy these favorite toys and rediscover a world they once knew, a world where they were happy, a world they 'had to' leave once they grew up. The tag line of the commercial is: If you can't remember how to be a kid again, 'don't worry ... everything is exactly where you left it'.

Second, toys are often used to teach children about appropriate roles and behaviors particularly as they relate to age, gender and socio-economic class (Baxter 2005a). Park (2005) describes how modern Inuit children borrow their parents' snow knives to make miniature snow houses and girls use miniature stone lamps to cook tiny portions of meat to share with friends (*i.e.* the Inuit equivalent of an Easy Bake® oven). Archaeologically, Thule Inuit children may have played with miniature sledges, kayaks, umiaks, cooking pots, snow knives, dolls, lamps and weapons such as bows and arrows (Park 2005). These toys were essential to helping children 'remember' the knowledge they possessed as adults in their previous lives.

In his study of Victorian toys, Somerville (2015) demonstrates how toys were used as a means of reinforcing gender-specific roles and boundaries. Boys' toys (*e.g.* mechanical banks and train sets) were greater in number and variety than girls' toys and were made from durable materials like metal and wood that could withstand rough and tumble play (Somerville 2015). They were designed to 'develop leadership, courage, teamwork, and competitiveness' (Somerville 2015, 279). By contrast, girls' toys consisted of tea sets, dolls and stuffed animals. Made of delicate materials such as wax or paper, they were designed to 'impart fashion, etiquette, and a sense of style' (Somerville 2015, 279). They also constrained girls' bodily movements. The 'Miss Jewel' doll, for example, was adorned with a necklace of '30 glass lenses, each holding a miniature photograph ... [and] a cutout in its back that allows light to enter the doll's body making the miniature photographs viewable' (Somerville 2015, 281). She also had a kaleidoscope at the back of her head that children could use by peering through a hole in her mouth and she wore beautiful, finely made clothing. This type of toy required gentle, indoor (and thus close to home) play.

But while not fully autonomous, children are not fully constrained either. As Halstad McGuire (2019, 14) notes, 'children have agency and may subvert adult activities and material culture for their own purposes'. For example, Viking children may have created versions of adult games but with their own set of rules. She writes (2019, 24), 'the children of Scandinavian Scotland were not passive recipients of adult structured play. They made their own games and defined their own places within their worlds.' Similarly, Somerville (2015) points to agency among Victorian girls. In their diaries, girls write about purposefully breaking their dolls and using them to attack boys. Similarly, Baxter (2005a and references therein) lists historical accounts of girls nailing spikes into their dolls, breaking their limbs, forcing them to eat rocks, coal or dirt as punishment or 'killing' their dolls in order to hold funerals for them. While these ways of engaging with dolls would have run counter to the desires and hopes of their parents, children's motivations for doing so were complex. The doll funerals likely reflect the fact that most children in 19th-century America would have experienced the death of one or more siblings (Baxter 2019b). Play in this case would have been a way of mirroring rituals of mourning and grief and coming to terms with death and their own mortality (Baxter 2019b). Similarly, in reference to a study of children's toys on a 19th-century American slave plantation (Wilkie 2000), Baxter writes (2005a, 22), '[i]n this analysis, toys are not just the tools of parents or ways to enculturate children into adult roles. They become contentious objects in dialogues of control and resistance, reflections of a child's fears and anxieties as she grows older, and symbolic expressions of race and gender on a southern plantation.' In other words, even something as 'simple' as toys are much more nuanced, complex and negotiated and speak to the agency of children once we consider them more deeply.

Other material culture may have functioned in similar ways. Smith (2005), found in her study of prehistoric Huron 'juvenile pots' that are believed to have been made by children, that children followed the manufacturing processes taught to them by their mothers and grandmothers but they created their own unique design motifs. She

(2005, 72) argues that these innovative motifs were a means of 'identity negotiation'. This example is important because it demonstrates that while children directly or indirectly learn the values, mores and norms of the society in which they live, they also learn the range of tolerance or play (pun intended) within these boundaries and how to enact agency within and beyond these tolerated limits.

The marginalization of children as a research topic and a reimagining of the past

Finally, the fourth reason children have been understudied by archaeologists may be that they have been marginalized as a research topic. In 2007, Margaret Conkey, a pioneer in the archaeology of gender, published a provocative article titled 'Questioning theory: Is there a gender of theory in archaeology?'. In it, Conkey demonstrated that female archaeologists were primarily published in readers (*i.e.* edited volumes) in archaeological theory when they published on gender and closely related issues. As a consequence, she argued that the selection of articles reproduced in readers was not representative of the number of women in the field, that the theoretical work of women was consistently under cited and that papers by female authors in these readers were segregated, compartmentalized and easy to avoid, if desired. While this situation is now changing, it may go some way to explaining why the archaeology of children has been neglected as a research area. Because most authors writing about the archaeology of children are women, the topic may not have been seen as 'weighty' or 'serious' enough to become mainstream. While this is changing with more and more men making important contributions to this area of study, a survey of articles published in the journal *Childhood in the Past* since its inception a decade ago, shows that of the 88 authors listed on journal articles and editorial essays, only 27 are male, less than one third, and a close look reveals that this ratio has not changed much over time.

The 'rediscovery' of children in the archaeological record is also part of a larger reimagining of the past. This reimagining has taken many forms. For example, archaeology is perceived as largely a daytime activity. Professionals excavate during the day, the public visits sites and museums during the day, and we often picture ancient people going about their lives during the day. For the most part, we have forgotten that humans are also nocturnal beings. I recently co-edited a book with Nancy Gonlin titled *The Archaeology of Night: Life After Dark in the Ancient World*. In it, we invoke the 'parallax perspective', which essentially involves viewing one's subject from a different angle. The change in the position of the observer in this case was an explicit orientation toward nightly practices rather than daily practices (Gonlin and Nowell 2018a; 2018b). This proved to be extremely productive with chapter authors writing about ancient peoples navigating by the stars (Van Gilder 2018), crime after dark in Ancient Rome (Storey 2018), Mayan kings and queens performing sacred rituals under full moons (Gonlin and Dixon 2018) and iron smelters (Chirikure and Moffet 2018) and agriculturalists (Nathan 2018) profiting from a drop in temperature by working in the cooler evenings.

Conkey (2018) compared this shift in perspective from day to night as akin to the revolution in archaeology that she and her colleagues started in the 1970s. At that time, they developed robust methods and theories for exploring the lives of women in the past (*e.g.* Conkey and Spector 1984; Gero and Conkey 1991) and these approaches have since been extended to the study of children and anyone else who does not fit within the narrow confines of being adult, male, heterosexual, able-bodied and white (*e.g.* Prine 2000; Watkins 2000; 2016; Voss 2008; Southwell-Wright 2013; Cave and Oxenham 2016; Matić 2016; Appleby 2018). Throughout our history as a discipline, we have largely assumed that the archaeological record did not speak to the lived experiences of women, children, the elderly, the differently abled, non-binary genders, different sexualities, different ethnicities or Indigenous peoples,[4] when in fact it always has, we have just not been listening or more precisely we have not been asking the right questions.

From this discussion it is clear that the reasons for understudying children are many and complex. A survey of articles published in 14 mainstream journals in anthropology produced in the first 25 years since Lillehammer's (1989) article found that of the more than 14,000 articles published, only just under 400 could be considered 'child-focused'. Close to 60% of these articles centered on growth and development, morphology, the identification of disease, breastfeeding and weaning; 15% concerned burial practices and aging and sexing skeletal material; and 10% derived primarily from the nonhuman primate literature. Only a few percentages of the articles were devoted to archaeological perspectives on the lived lives of children. However, these numbers are misleading in that the past decade has witnessed an exponential growth in child-focused archaeological studies (*e.g.* Sofaer Derevenski 2000a; Kamp 2001a; 2001b; 2006; Baxter 2005a; 2006; 2008; 2019a; 2019b; Wileman 2005; Thompson *et al.* 2014; Coşkunsu 2015). So much so that in November 2017, Dr Jane Baxter from DePaul University, who is a pioneer in the study of the archaeology of children, delivered an inspirational keynote address to an audience of archaeologists at the annual meeting of the Society for the Study of Childhood in the Past. She began by telling those assembled there that they no longer had to apologize for studying children. It was no longer necessary to explain that children were alive in prehistory, likely comprised 40–65% of the population and likely were responsible for a significant amount of the material culture we all studied. In other words, we had come a long way since Lillehammer's foundational publication (Nowell *et al.* 2020). Now that we see that the archaeology of children has become an important subject of study in its own right, it is important to define what exactly we mean when we say we study 'children'.

What is a child?

What researchers mean when they use the terms such as 'infant', 'child' and 'adolescent' can vary considerably. For example, in Chapter 3, I consider infant burials in the Paleolithic but exploring this topic is complicated by the fact that not all researchers use the term infant in the same way. For example, for Zilhão (2005), an infant is an individual under the age of 4, whereas for Riel-Salvatore and Gravel-Miguel (2013), the category of 'infant' (or 'baby') only includes individuals 2 years of age or younger. Pettitt (2010, tables 6.2 and 7.1) does not explicitly define 'baby' and 'infant', but it is possible to infer from his tables that babies for Pettitt are under 12 months old and infants are between 1 and 3 years old. Formicola (2007) in his study of Upper Paleolithic burials does not distinguish between 'infants' and 'children' at all.

Similarly, researchers often use terms such as 'child', 'juvenile', 'non-adult' and 'subadult' or 'infant' and 'baby' interchangeably (Halcrow and Tayles 2008). In a sense, they are using these terms in a more colloquial fashion than in a scientific manner. In other words, it is assumed that we all *know* what a child is or what a baby is but as we have just seen understandings can vary widely. Furthermore, many authors have argued that terms such as 'subadult' and 'non-adult'[5] are problematic (Rothschild 2002; Baxter 2005a; Sofaer 2006; Lewis 2007; Halcrow and Tayles 2008). 'Subadult' suggests that children are 'less than' or inferior in some way to adults while 'non-adult' defines children by what they are not. Halcrow and Tayles (2008) describe this as a form of marginalization and 'othering' of children where they are seen as deviant from the norm (*i.e.* adults). Following Baxter (2005a), they argue (2008, 193), 'this mimics the modern Western cultural construction of children, where they are often perceived as incomplete beings compared with adults'. While acknowledging these issues, 'subadult' is a convenient term to describe a broad age category and will be used in this book.

Human biologists (*e.g.* Bogin 2003; 2009) normally divide human life history (see Chapter 2) into five stages – infancy (from birth to weaning), childhood (from weaning to the eruption of M1, the first permanent molar), juvenile (from M1 to puberty and the onset of the adolescent growth spurt), adolescence (from the onset of the adolescent growth spurt to the cessation of the growth and maturation) and adulthood, with the stages of childhood and adolescence being unique to humans. In this book, the terms 'child' and 'adolescence' are used as biologically defined stages of human development dependent on anatomical markers that permit comparisons between hominin species and between humans and other primates. At the same time, it is important to acknowledge that cross-culturally and over time what it means *phenomenologically* to be a 'child' varies greatly (*e.g.* Kamp 2001b; Baxter 2008; Konner 2010). Biological age is not the same as social age and this distinction is where we turn next.

Ageing and sexing subadults

How do we know that we are studying a child in the broadest sense of that word? One of the clearest ways to identify a subadult specimen is through reference to age. According to Lewis (2007, 38), age at death is key to understanding 'mortality rates, growth and development, morbidity, weaning ages, congenital conditions and infanticide'. During ontological development, subadults undergo tremendous change and for these reasons, bioarchaeologists can be more precise when ageing them compared to adult specimens. However, estimating how old an individual is, is not always a straightforward process. Halcrow and Tayles (2008) identify three different types of age that are often confounded – biological age, chronological age and social age (see also Séguy and Buchet 2013). I will briefly consider each of these age types here before turning to the sexing of subadults.

Biological age

Biological or physiological age is sometimes referred to as 'skeletal age' or 'dental age' and is inferred from biological changes observed in the body (Halcrow and Tayles 2008). A detailed discussion of the methods involved in aging subadults is beyond the scope of this book and for that I would refer readers to two excellent volumes by Mary Lewis: *The Bioarchaeology of Children: Perspectives from Biological and Forensic Anthropology* (2007) and *Paleopathology of Children: Identification of Pathological Conditions in the Human Skeletal Remains of Non-Adults* (2017). The following discussion is based on these sources. Age based on dental development (*e.g.* mineralization and eruption) is the most reliable means of establishing age in subadults, provided that the appropriate reference population is used. Fortunately, the developmental sequences for many ancient and modern populations is known. The most important factor introducing variation into dental sequences is sex. Females can be 1–6 months ahead of males in overall dental development and as much as 11 months ahead when just the canine, the most sexually dimorphic of all of the teeth, is considered (Lewis 2007). I return to sexual dimorphism in traits below.

Some researchers have tried to use dental wear to assess age – for example, if an individual's M1 has significant wear on it but her M2 has little to no wear it might be reasonable to suggest that the individual is close to age 12 when, on average, the M2 erupts. However, it has been shown that type of food and quality of dental enamel affect the degree of wear observable on a specimen. It may be most useful for distinguishing infants from children by establishing whether weaning foods have been introduced (Lewis 2007). I discuss weaning further in Chapter 2.

Microscopic ageing techniques of teeth are 'based on the incremental markings within the dental microstructure' (Lewis 2007, 42). In this sense, teeth are like trees. Many tree species add a growth ring every year they are alive and when you look at a horizontal cross-section of a tree you can count its rings and get an age in years for that tree. Similarly, in teeth, cross-striations represent a daily variation in enamel matrix secretion while striae of Retzius (or perikymata on the surface of the tooth) reflect almost weekly variations (ranging from 4 to 11 days) (Lewis 2007). Some researchers use the neonatal line, a characteristic band of incremental growth that corresponds with birth, as a base line and then count the cross-striations from there to achieve an age in days for an individual. While there are factors that complicate this process (see discussion in Lewis 2007), it is considered a reliable method (for an example of this method applied to hominin fossils, see Smith *et al.* 2010 and Chapter 2).

Skeletal age assessment is the next most reliable way of ascertaining biological age in subadults and can be used when teeth are not available or in conjunction with dental assessments. Subadult long bones are composed of a diaphysis (shaft), a metaphysis or 'growing zone' at the proximal and distal ends of the diaphysis, and epiphyses that are separated from the metaphyses by cartilaginous growth plates, an area of soft bone, that allows for longitudinal growth (Lewis 2007). Over time, these plates mature, decrease in width and eventually disappear once puberty is complete (Emons et al. 2011). Growth plates can be scored as open, partially fused or completely fused. Bioarchaeologists use epiphyseal fusion of different joints to estimate age (Lewis 2007; White et al. 2012). In addition to assessing these maturational markers, another method for estimating age based on the skeleton is diaphyseal length. This is used on fetal remains as well as older children with the caveat that length is affected by the mother's health, genetics, disease and access to nutrition among other factors (Lewis 2007). Finally, bioarchaeologists can use the appearance of fontanelles for ageing a specimen. At birth, a fetus's cranial vault is not completely rigid. Instead there are six fontanelles or 'soft spots' between the cranial bones that are covered with cartilaginous membranes. At the time of birth the fetus's cranium can be molded, reducing its diameter to facilitate passage through the birth canal (see Chapter 2). Eventually these membranes harden into bone (White et al. 2012).

Chronological age

According to Lewis (2007, 38) age estimation is reliant upon 'an accurate conversion of biological age into chronological age'. Chronological age is the amount of time that has elapsed since an individual's birth (Halcrow and Tayles 2008) and it is usually what we mean when we ask someone how old they are. Chronological age is not necessarily the same as biological age because individuals can grow and develop at different rates due to genetics, individual variation, disease, the environment, secular changes and other factors such as access to nutritious food and health care. The microscopic techniques for assessing dental age discussed above are the most direct way of converting biological age into chronological age but these only apply to dental formation.

Social age

Finally, the third type of age is social age. Social age is based on culturally constructed norms for what is appropriate behavior and knowledge associated with a particular age category (Halcrow and Tayles 2008). In the West, social age tends to be tied to chronological age – we accord certain latitudes or rights and responsibilities to individuals at a particular chronological age – but in more traditional societies, social age may be more related to when an individual has developed particular skills, personality and abilities (Kamp 2001b; Halcrow and Tayles 2008). Age categories are not neutral. As Séguy and Buchet (2013, 21) observe, 'For both adults and children, every age in life is characterized, in social, political, economic and legal terms, by the power it confers or denies, which distinguishes it from other ages.' These researchers argue that age is not merely a measure of time but also a state of being.

Social age categories are a way of marking continuities and discontinuities in the life course (Séguy and Buchet 2013). Cross-culturally, the number of age categories can differ and can even vary by gender. As Kamp (2001b, 4) notes:

> like gender, age categories and roles are culturally defined and must be investigated rather than assumed. It is not tenable to assume that specific age categories derived from modern Western models will correspond to socially significant stages for cultures, past or present. In fact the reverse is true. It should be expected that every society will have its own age categories and its own definitions for childhood.

Clearly, all three age types are related. There is a sociocultural component to chronological age as some societies, for example, begin counting at the moment of birth while others include time the fetus spent in the womb and thus an infant is considered to be a year old at the time of birth. As noted, biological age is influenced by many sociocultural and environmental factors (Gowland 2006). For example, do boys and girls have equal access to protein rich foods? While clear relationships exist, the fit between these types of ages is not always a comfortable one. As Sofaer (2006, 127) notes, '[t]he desire to turn biological categories into social ones by creating implicit and direct links between the two, causes problems by trying to turn a process (ageing) ... into a class (age)'. In sum, there are many different ways to assign age to remains and researchers need to be as explicit as possible in their publications about the choices they have made in order to allow for comparisons between studies. This includes not only specifying what type of age is being presented but the methods by which this age estimate was achieved.

Sexing

While it is easier to age subadults than adults, the reverse is true when it comes to assigning sex. Sexually[6] dimorphic characteristics of the skeleton generally do not appear before puberty. Lewis (2007) refers to accurately sexing subadults as the 'holy grail' of bioarchaeology because it would help archaeologists understand the lived lives of boys and girls in greater detail. Furthermore, since biological sex is an important determinate in maturation rates, knowing an individual's sex would increase the accuracy of any age assessment. There have been a number of attempts including looking at overall size of deciduous teeth with males having larger teeth than females, canine size, and different markers on the skull and pelvis. Some methods have met with mixed success, only marginally better than flipping a coin, while other methods appear to be more promising. Wilson *et al.* (2008), for example, were able to accurately sex skeletons more than 96% of the time based on the greater sciatic notch on the ilia (but see Vlak *et al.* 2008). Many studies found that reliability of sex determination increases with age.

Beginning in the 1990s, researchers have used aDNA to sex individuals in both forensic and archaeological contexts (see, for example Sikora *et al.* 2017; and Chapters 5 and 6) and Braga *et al.* (2019) have been able to sex subadults based on cochlear (a hollow tube in the inner ear) shape. One of the most exciting developments in the area of sexing subadults is new research involving tooth enamel peptides. Using a method based on the identification of sex chromosome-linked variants of the peptide amelogenin from human tooth enamel, researchers correctly sexed 28[7] of the 29 individuals in their archaeological sample of subadults ranging in age from 40 gestational weeks to 19 years of age (Gowland *et al.* 2021; see also Stewart *et al.* 2017). Not only does the method appear to be highly accurate but it is minimally destructive and less expensive than aDNA. In sum, sexing subadults is more difficult than ageing them as sexually dimorphic traits are less apparent before puberty. As with ageing, using the appropriate reference sample and assessing multiple traits will produce results in which one can have greater confidence. Again, genetics, individual development, pathology and environmental factors all introduce variation.

Ageing and sexing fossil subadults

Ageing subadult fossil hominins brings with it its own particular challenge. It was noted above that having the correct reference population is key for making accurate age and sex determinations. With fossil subadults, it can be difficult to know whether humans or non-humans serve as the best model. Each hominin species is unique and often there is no single, obvious modern analogue. For example, consider *Homo naledi*, a South African hominin species with a known temporal range of 335,000–226,000 BP. When DH7, a juvenile *Homo naledi*, is compared to *Australopithecus sediba* (1.98 mya) and *Homo erectus* (1.6 mya) subadults of the same skeletal (developmental) age, DH7 is estimated to have been 9–11 years old when it died (Bolter *et al.* 2020). However, when DH7 is compared to later *Homo* (*e.g.* Neandertals and early modern humans) who mature more slowly, its age at death is closer to 11–15 years of age because it would take these species that much longer to reach the same developmental age (Bolter *et al.* 2020). There are valid reasons for using each of these models but the results say something quite different about its length of childhood and concomitant opportunities for learning (Chapters 2 and 3).

Sexing of subadult fossil hominins is a relatively new area of research and is based primarily on aDNA (*e.g.* Teschler-Nicola *et al.* 2020, see Chapter 3) which has in some cases served to overturn previous sex determinations based on associated material culture and/or skeletal pathologies, for example, at the sites of Sunghir (Chapter 5) and Dolní Věstonice (Chapter 6). Sexing methods such as the one based on variants of tooth enamel peptides have the potential to revolutionize our understanding of social relationships in the Paleolithic.

Seeing children in the archaeological record of the Paleolithic

As we have seen in this chapter, until recently children were an understudied subject in archaeology generally. With notable exceptions, this is true in Paleolithic archaeology and paleoanthropology as well. Many fossil studies focused on what a colleague once referred to as dead 'dead children' rather than dead 'living children'. But in the last 20 years, there has been a concerted effort to reconstruct Paleolithic children's lives through new fossil and archaeological discoveries, new technologies and, perhaps most importantly, new questions.

In Chapter 2, I outline the evolutionary context for studying Paleolithic subadults and discuss what taking a life history approach can tell us about their lives and the societies of which they were a part. In Chapter 3, I detail the archaeological evidence for Paleolithic children by focusing on possible candidates for 'toys', visual representations of Paleolithic subadults, burials and finally children's use of space including handprint and footprint data. Chapters 4 and 5 focus on studying children through stone tools and the Paleolithic arts (*e.g.* oral storytelling, ceramics, music, painting and textiles), respectively. Chapter 6 considers what it might have meant to be a 'teenager' in the Ice Age and why this life history stage is so important. Finally, in Chapter 7, I argue that studying children contributes to a more holistic understanding of our prehistoric past and to a more robust model of human cultural evolution.

By the end of this volume what I hope to have imparted is that while we do not have written records, we do have evidence-based stories of Paleolithic children's lives – drawing under a ledge in a cave in Spain, creating a 'club house' in France, being carried hurriedly across a dry river bed in a mother's arms, or, bathed in ochre, gently placed in a shallow grave far too soon. In some ways, these narratives are more compelling than those we might tell of historic children because there is something about them that is unexpectedly familiar, and in that familiarity we rediscover our shared humanity.

Notes

1. Approximate date ranges for archaeological periods and hominins mentioned in this volume are found in Appendix 1. Archaeological periods are based on material culture. For this reason, they vary regionally (sometimes considerably) and do not map neatly onto the temporal ranges of hominin species. Lower, Middle and Upper Paleolithic are used for sites and stone tool industries located outside of Africa while Early, Middle and Late Stone Age are roughly equivalent terms employed inside Africa. The subdivisions within the Upper Paleolithic are confined to Europe except for the Aurignacian that has a wider geographic distribution. The use of these archaeological terms is not unproblematic but they are employed here as a heuristic. Regional variants for these gross periods are not used in this volume. Please note as little is known about the temporal range of hominins such as the Denisovans they are not included on the timeline (timeline drawn by Jeremy Beller, modified after https://humanorigins.si.edu/evidence/human-evolution-timeline-interactive).
2. Hominin is a term used to describe extant humans and their extinct ancestors including members of the genera *Ardipithecus*, *Australopithecus*, *Paranthropus* and *Homo*.
3. In Paleolithic archaeology we use the term 'living floor' to refer to artifacts found on an occupation surface in more or less primary use-related context (see discussion in Dibble *et al.* 1997).
4. It could be argued that all pre-Columbian archaeology of North and South America is about studying the material culture of Indigenous peoples but this is not the same as studying the lives of Indigenous people, particularly from an Indigenous perspective and incorporating Indigenous knowledge and ways of understanding the world (see, for example, Steeves 2019 and references therein).
5. Nowell and Van Gelder (2020) use the term 'non-children' to refer to adults in their study.
6. In using the term 'sex', I am specially referring to biological sex and not gender which is how cultures parse and assign certain characteristics and values to biological sex.
7. One sample of tooth enamel was not sufficiently mineralized to permit analysis (Gowland *et al.* 2021).

Chapter 2

Birth and the Paleolithic 'family'

> Do we need an archaeology of mothering? For prehistoric periods, I would argue, we need to challenge notions of parenting and child care that may subconsciously shape archaeological interpretations. The organization of child care and supervision would have been an ongoing consideration in any society, and it therefore deserves our consideration as much as do other prehistoric economic activities.
>
> (Wilkie 2003)

Introduction

In the mid-1990s when I was a doctoral student at the University of Pennsylvania, I had the privilege of participating in a graduate seminar on human evolution taught by one of the greatest human paleontologists of all times, the late Professor Phillip Tobias from the University of Witwatersrand. He was a spellbinding lecturer who seemingly never forgot a face or a name. One of the things that I remember most from that seminar was a pronouncement he made in relation to subadults. He looked at all of us seated around the table, pens poised in the air, and said in his elegant South African accent, 'the message of evolution is ... *save the children!*' Of course, he was right. In Darwinian terms, success is not measured by 'survival of the fittest', but rather differential reproduction of the fittest. Natural selection acts on an individual's phenotype (the physical characteristics that interact with the environment) thereby increasing or decreasing the contributions of their genotype (the underlying genetic basis of these characteristics and behaviors) to the population's genepool. From this perspective, in order to be successful, an individual must survive to reproductive age, find a mate and ensure that the resulting offspring also survive to pass on their genes. In this chapter, I will discuss hominin life histories, the birthing process and the evolution of infant care. I will then discuss what we know about social structure and the Paleolithic 'family'.

Evolving hominin life histories

What did a 'family' look like in the Paleolithic? The answer to that question literally evolves over time and to address it we need to understand changing hominin life history strategies. Life history is defined as 'the allocation of an organism's energy for growth, maintenance and reproduction ... [and is] a life strategy adopted by an organism to maximize fitness in a world of limited energy' (Dean and Smith 2009, 115). Life history is also defined somewhat more poetically as the 'speed of life' (Stearns 1992), which refers to the amount of time it takes for an individual to reach sexual maturity – it is the rate of reproductive turnover. Following this metaphor, primates have the slowest life history of all of the mammals (Harvey and Cluton-Brock 1985; Zimmermann and Radespiel 2007; Robson and Wood 2008) and in some ways, humans have the slowest life history of all of the primates. In reality, however, the situation is more complex (Nowell 2010; 2016).

Paleoanthropologists think in terms of r-strategists and K-strategists. Species that follow an r-strategy are ones that give birth to a large number of offspring but invest little in their upbringing with offspring relying more on instinct than learned behavior (*e.g.* fish and sea turtles). Only a small percentage of these offspring live to reproduce but enough do that the species remains viable. By contrast, K-strategists, including all primates, produce fewer, more 'expensive' offspring and invest heavily in their upbringing. While K-strategists produce high quality offspring, the drawback to being a slow reproducer is that you risk dying before you reproduce (Robson and Wood 2008; Dean and Smith 2009; Nowell 2016). Humans have solved this by living fast in some respects within an overall pattern of living slow (Nowell 2016) (Fig. 2.1).

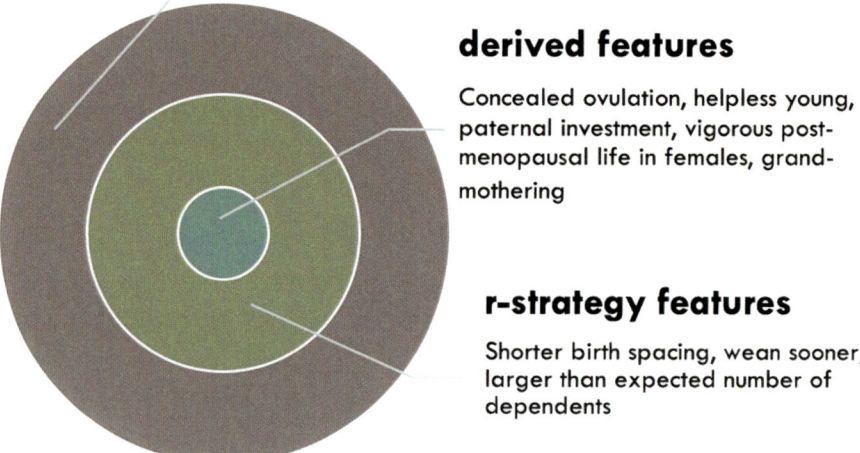

Figure 2.1: Hominin life histories are a unique combination of r-strategy, K-strategy and derived features that allow them to produce high quality offspring while at the same time mitigating the risks associated with being a slow reproducer.

Specifically, they are characterized by a long gestation period, a large brain relative to their body size, slower maturation with females reaching the age of reproduction later, an extended dependency period and increased longevity – these are all K-strategy features. At the same time, they have evolved shorter birth spacing, they wean their young sooner, and have more offspring than expected for an ape that matures at the age humans do (Robson and Wood 2008). Thus humans are characterized by a reproductive pattern that works in double time compared to the Great Apes (Dean and Smith 2009). Wood (1994) describes this pattern as secondary r-selection. Humans also have a unique set of derived features including concealed ovulation, helpless young, rapid post-natal brain growth in infants, continued dependency after weaning, paternal care and a vigorous post-menopausal life in females, which may explain a unique feature known as grandmothering (see below) (Bogin 1997; Kaplan 2002; Hawkes *et al.* 2003; Leigh 2004; 2012; Zimmerman and Radespiel 2007; Robson and Wood 2008; Dean and Smith 2009; Nowell 2016).

This slowing of hominin maturation rates relative to other primates has resulted in the insertion of two unique life history stages into the typical primate pattern (see Chapter 1) – childhood (from weaning to the eruption of M1) and adolescence (from the onset of the adolescent growth spurt to the cessation of growth and maturation). This slowed growth allows subadults more time to learn from the adults around them and from their peers. In their study of non-human primates, Street *et al.* (2012) found that longevity and social learning are positively correlated. Species with a greater emphasis on social learning also tended to live longer, suggesting that there was selection for not only increased time for learning but for opportunities to make the most of that learning.

Not all of the features of the hominin life history pattern appeared at once, thus we can envision this as a transition (and not always a linear one) from an ape-like to a human-like strategy over time. In these next sections, I will consider the fossil evidence for the appearance of some of these important features of hominin life histories and consider what they can tell us about the lives of subadults in the Pleistocene.

The birth process

There are six things that are often said to differentiate human from non-human primates in relation to the birth process: (1) the length and difficulty of human labor; (2) rotational births; (3) occiput anterior births (*i.e.* a neonate who is facing its mother's buttocks when it exits the birth canal); (4) assisted delivery; (5) the small brain size of human infants at birth relative to adult brain size; and by extension (6) an unusually high degree of neonate dependency.[1] The dominant model to explain these unique features has been the Obstetrical Dilemma (OD) (Washburn 1960). The OD posits that there was an evolutionary trade-off between the need to give birth to large brained infants and the constraints imposed upon the pelvic region by bipedalism. The model argues that the pelvis could only widen so much before significantly reducing energy efficiency during bipedal locomotion, thus human neonates are born underdeveloped

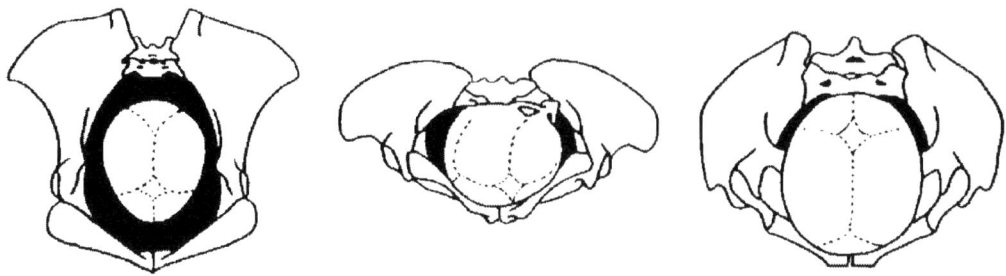

Figure 2.2: Comparison of infant skull size to pelvic outlet in a chimpanzee (Pan troglodytes), Australopithecus afarensis and Homo sapiens (without soft tissue). CC BY-SA 4.0, https://commons.wikimedia.org/w/index.php?curid=44884807.

relative to other primates (Fig. 2.2). While the uniqueness of these features or at least the uniqueness of this *combination* of features remains largely true, as we will see below new fossil finds and more data on non-human primate births have necessitated a rethink of this model.

In the transition from quadrupedal to bipedal locomotion 7 to 8 million years ago, the hominin pelvis underwent many anatomical changes in bony structure and musculature to support the upper body, and maintain balance, particularly while on one leg during the swing phase of bipedal locomotion. The resulting human pelvis, described as basin shaped, developed from an anteroposteriorly (*i.e.* front-to-back) elongated opening to an opening that is anteroposteriorly shortened and mediolaterally (*i.e.* side-to-side) oblong (Dunsworth and Eccleston 2015). This radical transition has had important implications for the birth mechanism in hominins. The human birth canal is divided into three planes – the pelvic inlet, the midplane and the pelvic outlet. The pelvic inlet is widest in the mediolateral dimension. The pelvic midplane, formed by the ischial spines that support the muscles of the pelvic floor, is the narrowest of the three planes. The pelvic outlet is widest in the anteroposterior dimension, perpendicular to the pelvic inlet (Dunsworth and Eccleston 2015). With few exceptions,[2] non-human primate fetuses enter and exit the birth canal in the same orientation, as the canal does not change shape or dimension (Laudicina *et al.* 2019). By contrast, human fetuses navigate a longer, more 'twisted' canal, and must rotate twice to align the long axis of their heads and their broad, rigid shoulders with the changing width and orientation of the three planes (Dunsworth and Eccleston 2015; Trevathan 2015; Laudicina *et al.* 2019). This rotation is one reason why human births are longer and more difficult and also explains the high percentage of injuries suffered by neonates (Dunsworth and Eccleston 2015). The tight fit between neonate head size and birth canal is mitigated somewhat by the fact that the cranial vault bones of an infant do not fuse until several years after birth (see Chapter 1). This allows the circumference of the fetus's head to be temporarily reduced during delivery as the cranial vault bones can slide past each other. The fetus's shoulders, however, are not nearly as flexible and actually present the biggest challenge to a safe delivery (Trevathan 2015). Dunsworth and Eccleston (2015) suggest that having a more malleable cranium began with *Australopithecus africanus*.

Human neonates are almost always born occiput anterior (*i.e.* face down) necessitating assisted births. It is difficult, if not impossible, for a woman to reach down and safely guide a neonate out of the birth canal because she would be essentially forcing it to bend backwards in the process. Furthermore, she is not able to easily clear mucus from the neonate's airway as it attempts to breathe or, if necessary, remove the umbilical cord from around its neck before a contraction pushes it forward, leading to possible strangulation (Dunsworth and Eccleston 2015; Trevathan 2015). While most non-human primates are born occiput posterior (face up), occiput anterior may be the norm for chimpanzees. In three observed cases, the chimpanzee neonate first presented face down but then rotated its head and body after the head had emerged (Hirata *et al.* 2011). In two of these cases, these neonates exited the birth canal with no guidance from the female. In fact, the newborns of many non-human primate species have the motor skills to assist in the delivery process by using their hands to help themselves exit the birth canal and make their way onto their mother's stomach (Trevathan 2015). While non-human births often attract attention from conspecifics, particularly in pair bonded primates, it is uncommon for females to receive assistance with the delivery. What is interesting though is that in some cases the presence of conspecifics may act to protect the birthing females from predators or from males intent on infanticide (Trevathan 2015). Bonobos (*Pan paniscus*) form particularly strong female bonds. In captive settings, researchers observed three deliveries in which females kept both males and flies away from the female giving birth and helped 'during the expulsive phase by performing manual gestures aimed at holding the infant' (Demuru *et al.* 2018, 502). It could be these forms of sociality that were selected for and augmented early on in hominin evolution.

By at least 195,000 years ago, we have evidence of the modern pelvic anatomy. Omo 1 (Ethiopia) is the earliest known pelvis of *Homo sapiens* and based on the features that are preserved, it falls comfortably within the range of modern human variation (Hammond *et al.* 2018). However, there is no agreement on exactly when rotated births emerged in hominin evolution as the fossil evidence for pelves is rare and fragmentary. In total, there are approximately 20 fossil pelves (Dunsworth and Eccleston 2015). The difficulties of making inferences from such a scant record is compounded by the variation introduced by a time scale of millions of years, vast geographic distances, individual variation in age and development, and the challenges of correctly sexing specimens.

Ardipithecus and Australopithecus

The oldest pelvis (ARA-VP-6/500) currently known belongs to the 4.4 mya *Ardipithecus ramidus* (Lovejoy *et al.* 2009; White *et al.* 2009). This pelvis is more similar to apes than humans and given that the neonate brain size of this species is also pongid like, it is unlikely that the human birth mechanism (*i.e.* a rotated birth) was in place at this time

(Nowell and Kurki 2020). Most of what we know about the pelvis of *Australopithecus* comes from the 3.2 mya A.L. 288-1 ('Lucy'), an *Au. afarensis,* and the 2.5 mya Sts 14, an *Au. africanus* (Johanson *et al.* 1982a; Berge and Goularas 2010). While these fossils have been interpreted variously by different researchers, 'recent interpretations of obstetrical implication of these pelves in relation to newborn size suggest that australopiths would have experienced elevated cephalopelvic proportions relative to apes, and at least semi-rotation, largely to accommodate the shoulders, but perhaps not the full rotation of modern human childbirth' (Nowell and Kurki 2020, 177–178 and references therein). Interestingly, new modeling of the pelvis of a 1.98 mya female *Au. sediba* (MH2), revealed that this species' obstetric planes more closely resembled *Homo* than other australopiths (Laudicina *et al.* 2019). In this species, the fetus would have entered the pelvic inlet transversely as with *Homo* but according to Laudicina *et al.* (2019, 15), the 'lack of bony impingement into the birth canal, combined with a small neonatal head size would not necessitate further rotation of the fetus as it descended through the canal, though [anteroposterior] expansion of the maternal pelvis still indicates that rotational birth may have occurred'. Based on this evidence, it may be that the capacity to give birth to larger brained infants preceded encephalization and that the morphology of the human pelvis is primarily the result of adaptions for bipedal locomotion, contra predictions of the OD model (Laudicina *et al.* 2019; see also Dunsworth and Eccleston 2015).

Homo

The earliest pelves of the genus *Homo* are associated *H. erectus* specimens. There is general consensus that it is with *H. erectus* that you first see the more human-like pattern of life history (Nowell 2010). The pelves derive from KNM-WT 15000, an 8–13 year old from Kenya (1.6 mya) known as Nariokotome Boy (or Turkana Boy) (Fig. 2.3), BSN49/P27a–d from Gona, Ethiopia (1.4–0.9 mya), and UA 173/405, (1.07–0.99 mya) from Buia, Eritrea. These three pelves tell very different stories of the hominin birth process with Nariokotome closely resembling that of later *Homo* while the specimen from Gona is much more australopithecine like and the Buia partial pelvis falls within the range of modern human variation for all the variables that could be analyzed (Simpson *et al.* 2008; Hammond *et al.* 2018). It is quite possible that the fossil pelvis from Gona does not belong to a *H. erectus* at all (its attribution to this species is based on the date and location of the find rather than on dental or crania remains) and may, in fact, be a member of the genus *Paranthropus* (Ruff 2010). Until its taxonomic affiliation is settled it is difficult to know how to interpret the implication of its morphology for understanding the evolution of the human birth mechanism. Similarly, there are three potential explanations for the Buia specimen. According to Hammond *et al.* (2018), either Buia is incorrectly assigned to *H. erectus* or modern human pelvic morphology evolved much earlier than expected (and thus other specimens are incorrectly assigned to this taxon) or *H. erectus* is a polytypic species. In my opinion, it is the last of these three explanations that is most likely (see Nowell 2010).

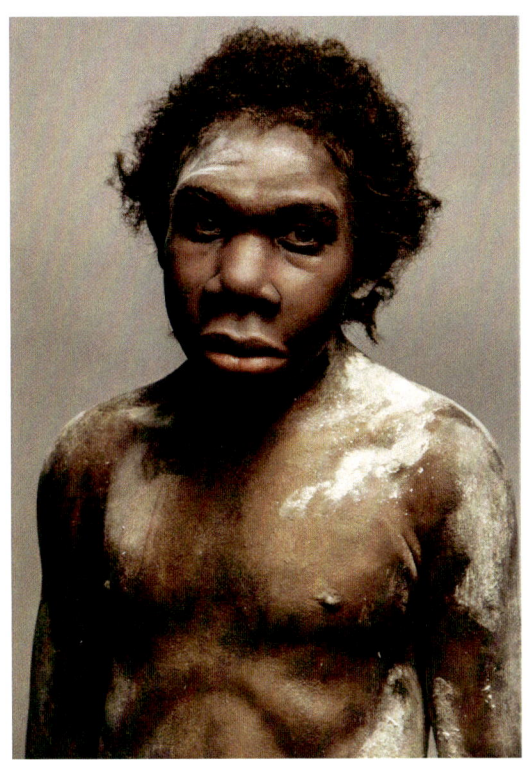

Figure 2.3: Reconstruction of KNM-WT 15000, the specimen known as Nariokotome Boy or Turkana Boy. This boy's remains consist of an almost complete fossil skeleton, and date from approximately 1.5 million years ago. He was found in 1984 near Lake Turkana in Kenya. Reconstruction by Elisabeth Daynes of the Daynes Studio, Paris, France; courtesy Science Photo Library.

The pelves of later *Homo*, *H. heidelbergensis* and Neandertals, are known primarily from male specimens such as the Sima de los Huesos Pelvis 1 from Spain at 430 kya (Arsuaga *et al.* 2015; Bonmatí *et al.* 2010) for the former and the Kebara 2 pelvis from Mount Carmel (Israel) at 60 kya (Rak and Arensburg 1987; Adegboyega *et al.* 2021) for the latter and a partial pelvis (Tabun 1) from a Neandertal female from Tabun (Israel). Again, there is a lack of consensus regarding important aspects of canal shape and whether Neandertals experienced fully *H. sapiens*-like rotational childbirth (*e.g.* Ponce de León *et al.* 2008; Weaver and Hublin 2009; see also Nowell and Kurki 2020). Other small brained, small bodied *Homo* species such as *H. naledi* (ca. 335–236 BP) and *H. floresiensis* (ca. 100–60,000 BP) exhibit a mosaic of australopithecine and *Homo* features in their skeleton (Berger *et al.* 2015; Sutikna *et al.* 2016) and while the implications of this anatomy for obstetrics is not clear, it does reinforce the non-linearity of the human birth mechanism. In sum, Nowell and Kurki (2020, 179) write,

> While disagreements persist concerning the reconstructions of these fossil hominin pelves, and whether and to what degree rotation of the newborn needed to occur during childbirth in these species, the evidence in general suggests that the plesiomorphic [*i.e.* ancestral] state is that of a medio-laterally broad pelvis relative to antero-posterior length, with varying degrees of antero-posterior expansion in *Homo* (and *Au. sediba*). *Homo sapiens* are the odd species out. We have relatively reduced canal breadth and further expanded antero-posterior length, within the constraints of the hominin pelvis. Some fossil reconstructions also include a degree of 'twisting' of the long axes of the planes of the canal, but none does so to the degree seen in *Homo sapiens*. Further, evidence is increasingly pointing to the fact that even *Australopithecus* faced a more difficult birth [than non-human primates], with a relatively broad-shouldered, if not large-brained newborn for maternal pelvic capacity.

The data that we have suggest that there was great diversity of birth mechanisms among Pleistocene hominins with some forms that were neither exactly ape-like nor exactly human-like, but for which we do not have a modern analogue.

Gestation, brain growth, and dependent young

Humans have a longer gestation period than expected for an ape of our size (Dunsworth and Eccleston 2015) and yet evolutionary models such the OD depict human neonates as underdeveloped or premature. There is some truth to this characterization in that they are born with only 28–30% of their eventual adult brain size (versus 40% in non-human primates) and it would take an additional 7 months gestation (!) for them to meet the threshold set by their non-human primate relatives (Dunsworth and Eccleston 2015). This has resulted in neonates that are secondarily altricial. Human infants are not able to support the weight of their heads initially nor are they able to locomote on their own, and during the first year of life their brains experience a fetal-like rate of growth (Nowell and Kurki 2020). At the same time, unlike other mammals, they are born with their ears and eyes open (Dunsworth and Eccelston 2015; Trevathan 2015). While the maternal birth canal sets an absolute limit on fetal brain size, gestation likely ends and birth begins when the mother can no longer support the growing fetus (Dunsworth and Eccelston 2015). As Trevathan (2015, 6) notes, 'the mother's metabolism simply cannot keep pace with the increasing demands of the infant body and brain growth towards the end of pregnancy. The deeply invasive human placenta and compromised immune system of the mother during pregnancy also likely play roles in determining the nine-month gestation period and relatively undeveloped brain.'

One significant advantage of this extra uterine brain growth, is that the developing brain is shaped by experiences in infancy and early childhood (Nowell 2016). In the first two years of life, brain growth in infants is uniquely growth in white matter, tissue that is responsible for connections between different parts of the brain, highlighting the importance of an infant's interaction with its social, cultural and physical environments (Cofran and DeSilva 2015). Liu et al. (2012) studied post-mortem brain samples from humans, chimpanzees and macaques at all stages of life. They found that there were significant differences in the developmental trajectories of synaptogenesis (formation of new connections in the brain) between these three species (Cohen 2012). Specifically, in the pre-frontal cortex (PFC), a region of the brain implicated in social behavior, abstract thinking and reasoning, the genes responsible for synaptogenesis are turned on in humans slightly after birth, peaking at 5 years of age. By contrast, in non-human primates the expression of these genes peaks during the last few months of fetal development and are turned off just after birth. Furthermore, there are 12 times the number of genes involved in the development and functioning of synapses in the PFC in humans than in chimpanzees. Similarly, researchers counted more than 7000 synapses in the three species at different ages and found that in non-human primates they dramatically increase in number just after birth whereas in humans they peak around 4 years of age. Similar results were found when the researchers studied gene expression and synapse formation in the lateral cerebellar cortex (CBC), a region associated with language, attention and manual abilities (Liu *et al.* 2012). What this research suggests is that even when corrected for differences in lifespan, humans have much more time to form synapses and that synapse formation is particularly influenced by experiences garnered during the first five years of life (Cohen 2012; Liu *et al.* 2012; Nowell 2016).

When in hominin evolution do we see the emergence of this more human-like pattern of life history? For taphonomic reasons the fossil record of infants and young children is quite fragmentary with only 200 to 300 specimens estimated to be 5 years of age or less at time of death (Appendix 2).[3] Nonetheless, an examination of these remains reveals two interesting patterns. First, over time, as adult hominin brain sizes increase hominin infants are born with a decreasing proportion of adult brain size followed by two years of rapid brain growth (Cunnane and Crawford 2014; Dunnsworth 2018) and second, even though the percentage of adult brain size at birth lessens, absolute brain size increases contributing to overall larger body mass in infants (DeSilva 2011; Nowell and Kurki 2020). In fact, human infant body mass is relatively large, approximately 6% of maternal body mass, compared to chimpanzee newborns that are about 3% of maternal body mass (DeSilva 2011). Both of these trends have important implications for the evolution of infant care and the lived lives of Plio-Pleistocene subadults.

Australopithecus

The earliest hominin infant remains belong to the 3.3 mya Dikika (DIK 1-1) specimen (Fig. 2.4) and the 3.2 mya specimen A.L. 333–105 from Hadar (Ethiopia) (Alemseged *et al.* 2006; Gunz *et al.* 2020). Dubbed 'Lucy's Child', even though she lived 200,000 years earlier than Lucy, DIK 1-1 is a largely complete *Au. afarensis* female with a mostly intact cranium, natural endocast (imprint of the outer regions of the brain), complete set of deciduous dentition (except the crown of the left lower incisor) and post-crania including the most complete foot of a fossil juvenile yet discovered (DeSilva *et al.* 2018). While clearly bipedal, she has an ape-like hyoid bone and a lunate sulcus in an anterior (ape-like) position (both are important for inferring language capabilities), an ape-like cranial organization, gorilla-like scapula and long, curved phalanges suggesting some remnant arboreal adaptation. Dunsworth and Eccleston (2015) argue that her ape-like shoulder joints may have made delivery easier. DIK 1-1's cranial capacity is 275 cm^3 while A.L. 333–105's brain size is slightly larger at 310–317 cm^3. Based on synchrotron microtomographic data, DIK 1-1 is 2 years and 4 months old and development of the mandibular dentition in A.L. 333–105 suggests both infants were the same age when they died (Gunz *et al.* 2020). The brain size of these infants is the same as extant apes of comparable age and yet, if they had survived into adulthood, they would have attained a larger adult brain size. Because we know that these infants grew at the same rate as apes do, the only way this can work is if the time they had to grow and develop was extended (Gunz *et al.* 2020). Thus there is evidence for the insertion of the childhood

Figure 2.4: Reconstruction of the 3-year-old Australopithecus afarensis *female known as Selam or the Dikika baby. The remains of this youngster date to 3.3 million years ago and were found in Dikika, Ethiopa in 2000. Photographed at The Ethiopian National Museum, Addis Ababa, Ethiopia; courtesy Science Photo Library.*

stage into the hominin life history pattern with these australopithecines even if it is not as long in duration as it is with later hominins.

The sample of *Au. africanus* infants includes two or three specimens from Sterkfontein from South Africa but the best studied infant is the 3.0 mya Taung child, also from South Africa. Based on dentition, age at death estimates of Taung range from 3.73 (LaCruz *et al.* 2005) to 6.1 years old (Skinner and Sperber 1982) depending on whether an ape or hominin model of dental development is used with a more recent estimate narrowing its age to between 3.02–4.4 years of age. The specimen consists of a partial skull, mandible and maxilla, deciduous dentition, permanent first molars and a natural endocast. Its cranial capacity ranges from 402–407 cc.

Homo

The oldest *Homo* infants and juveniles belong to *H. erectus* (Nowell and Kurki 2020). Based on known specimens, the range of *H. erectus* neonatal cranial capacities runs from 225 cc in the 1.7 mya Dmanisi fossils (Republic of Georgia) to 236.5–309.6 cc in the 1.5 mya Mojokerto infant (Indonesia) (DeSilva 2011), representing approximately 35% of adult brain size. This estimate falls between the chimpanzee average of 40% and the human average of 30%. The revised age of 0.5–1.5 years old for the Mojokerto child (Coqueugniot *et al.* 2004; see also Cofran and DeSilva 2015) led Simpson *et al.* (2008) to conclude that *H. erectus* prenatal cranial growth followed a human-like pattern while its post-natal cranial and somatic growth was intermediate between apes and humans.

In 2020, researchers published a spectacular find from the South African site Drimolen (Herries *et al.* 2020). DNH 134 is a *H. erectus* subadult partial cranium. Its cranial sutures are still open and in an early stage of fusion characterizing it as an infant. Its metopic suture is fused externally and its anterior and posterior fontanelles are absent suggesting that it was between 2 and 3 years old when it died, making it older

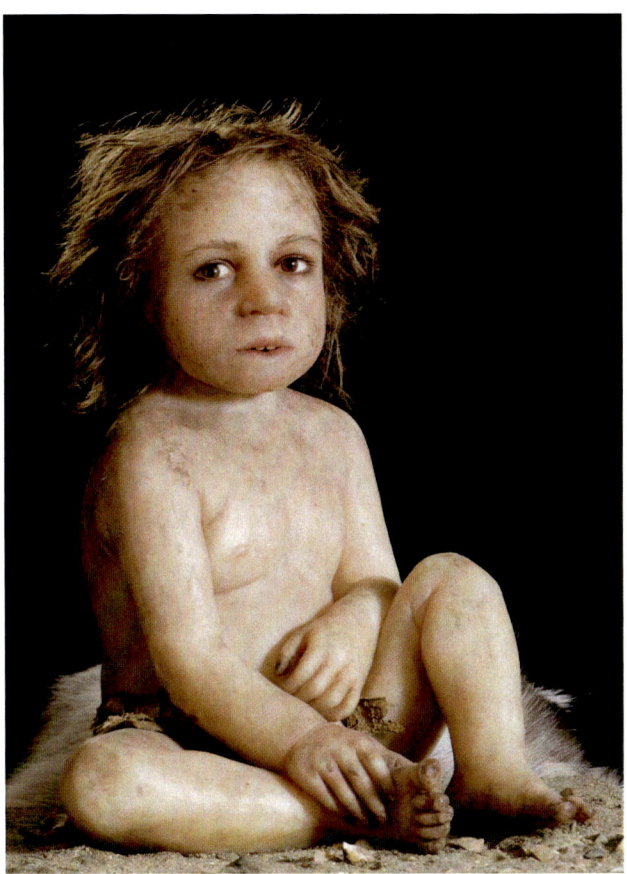

Figure 2.5: Reconstruction of a Neandertal child based on the Roc de Marsal fossils by Elisabeth Daynes of the Daynes Studio, Paris, France; courtesy Science Photo Library.

than the Mojokerto infant. DNH 134's cranial capacity is estimated to be 514 to 564 cm^3, exceeding the known range of *Australopithecus* infants.

There is general consensus that the life history of *H. erectus* included either a childhood stage for the first time or, particularly in light of the recent study by Gunz *et al.* (2020), a significantly expanded childhood (Bogin 2003; Krovitz, *et al.* 2003; Nowell 2010) with concomitant implications for learning. *H. erectus* may have also experienced a limited adolescent growth spurt but there is as yet no agreement on this assessment (Tardieu 1998; Antón and Leigh 2003; Dean and Smith 2009; Nowell 2010). The adolescent growth spurt will be discussed in more detail in Chapter 6.

The number of infants assigned to a particular taxon increases with Neandertals, perhaps due to the fact that intentional burial or 'funerary caching' may have begun with this species (Pettitt 2010) (see Chapter 3). Not only have paleoanthropologists uncovered a Neandertal fetus (La Ferrassie 4) and neonates (*e.g.* Saint-Césaire 2 and 3, and Le Moustier 2 from France, Mezmaiskaya 1 from Russia, Kiik-Koba 2 from Crimea), but the larger sample of subadults over the age of 2 years (*e.g.* Gibraltar 2, La Ferrassie 6) has allowed researchers to study Neandertal growth and development in detail (Weaver *et al.* 2016 and references therein).

Despite the larger sample size or, perhaps because of it, there is debate concerning the rate of maturation of young Neandertals (Fig. 2.5) with most researchers concluding that they experienced mosaic growth (*e.g.* Trinkaus *et al.* 2016). For example, anatomical features of the brain, mandible and thorax that distinguish Neandertals from modern humans are already present at birth (García-Martínez *et al.* 2020) but Neubauer and Hublin (2012) (see also Coqueugniot and Hublin 2007; 2012; Ponce de León *et al.* 2016) estimate that Neandertal neonates had brain sizes that slightly exceeded those of modern human neonates. This is indicative of greater prenatal brain growth than is found in humans. Postnatal brain growth in Neandertals was also more accelerated. While shorter in duration, this accelerated brain growth led to larger overall adult brain sizes in Neandertals and to the attainment of adult brain size at younger ages (Neubauer and Hublin 2012). Recent experimental findings support this characterization of accelerated brain growth. Scientists comparing Neandertal and *H. sapiens* genomes found an allele (*i.e.* gene variant) difference in the *NOVA1* gene that controls the functioning of many other genes and is important in early brain development. In the lab, they took human stem cells and replaced their *NOVA1* genes with the Neandertal variant. The modified cells grew into cortical organoids ('mini brains'). They discovered that not only did these mini brains look different (Neandertal ones were more popcorn like in comparison to the *H. sapiens* spherically shaped ones) but importantly their neurons fired sooner (*i.e.* matured much more quickly) (Trujillo *et al.* 2021). Further research is needed to fully explore the implications for understanding Neandertal growth, development and behavior. Similarly, while Neandertals matured more slowly than previous hominins including *H. erectus*, they may have experienced a compressed adolescence and adolescent growth spurt relative to early modern humans (Smith *et al.* 2010; Thompson and Nelson 2011; Nowell 2016; see Chapter 6). The maturation rate of Neandertals is further supported by the recent study of the ribcages of four young Neandertals (Mezmaiskaya 1, Le Moustier 2, Dederiyeh 1 and Roc de Marsal) ranging in age from a newborn to approximately 3 years old at time of death, that demonstrates faster thoracic growth than exhibited by early modern humans (García-Martínez *et al.* 2020; but see Rosas *et al.* 2017). Overall, more robust limbs and wider torsos would have made Neandertal infants appear stockier than their *H. sapiens* counterparts (García-Martínez *et al.* 2020). The dental evidence is more equivocal with Smith *et al.* (2010) arguing that Neandertals developed more quickly than their modern human counterparts and Macchiarelli *et al.* (2006) countering that they fall within the range of modern humans.

The earliest *H. sapiens* infant remains with cranial material include Qafzeh 13 (neonate), Amud 7 (10 months), and Skhul 1 (ca. 3 years old) from Israel, dating to between 90,000 and 115,000 years ago (Tillier 2008). A re-evaluation of hominin remains from Cro-Magnon, a 33,000 year old site in southwest France, revealed the presence of four *H. sapiens* infants represented by cranial fragments and limb bones (Partiot *et al.* 2020). The authors note (Partiot *et al.* 2020, 2), 'given maternal morphological constraints and the similarity of Gravettian and recent human female pelvic dimensions ... it is unlikely ... that the size of Gravettian newborns differed substantially from those of recent individuals'. Analysis of the remains demonstrated, unsurprisingly, that they fall within the range of recent human neonates and infants in size and patterns of maturation.

Evolution of infant care

Human infants require 24-hour care in the form of breastfeeding/eating, toileting, regulating body temperature and transport (Halcrow *et al.* 2020). Human infants have an underdeveloped immune system, which in conjunction with accelerated growth leaves them vulnerable to environmental stress (Halcrow *et al.* 2020 and references therein). In fact, infants and children carry a disproportionate amount of the disease burden in a society necessitating a great deal of care (Halcrow 2020). Unlike other forms of caregiving (*e.g.* for the elderly, differently abled or chronically ill), mothering behaviors are often assumed to be unskilled and instinctual (Halcrow *et al.* 2020). However, multiple studies of maternal behavior in human and non-human primates strongly support the argument that infant care is the result of learned behavior (*e.g.* Maestripieri 2005). Many parenting skills such as breastfeeding require instruction and practice (Palmquist 2020).

Infant carrying

One way we can estimate the relative amount of care fossil hominins invested in their infants is to look at the Infant to Mother Mass Ratio (IMMR). DeSilva (2011) created this index by comparing adult and neonate brain mass to neonate body mass in anthropoids to estimate birthweight in fossil hominin infants. According to DeSilva (2011), *Ardipithecus* infants, 4.4 million years ago, had a low IMMR, similar to extant apes, suggesting this was the ancestral condition (*i.e.* the last common ancestor of apes and hominins likely had a low IMMR). Australopithecine females, however, gave birth to notably heavier babies who weighed in at 5% of their mothers' body mass. DeSilva (2011) suggests the weight of these infants would have limited a female's ability to travel through the trees during pregnancy and after birth. *Paranthropus robustus*, *P. boisei* and early *Homo* exhibit IMMR's similar to that of australopithecines suggesting that a grade shift in body mass ratio occurred between *Ardipithecus* and later hominins (DeSilva 2011).

DeSilva (2011) estimates that australopithecine infants would have been unable to walk on their own until around 6 or 7 months of age. While non-human primate infants are able to cling to their mothers' fur, moving a hominin youngster around was more complicated. The secondary altriciality of hominin infants, and the upright posture of a bipedal hominin, in combination with thinning body fur and eventual hairlessness with early *Homo* sometime around 2 million years ago (Dávid-Barrett and Dunbar 2016) mean that it would have been impossible for females to carry their infants on their backs. Juvenile foot fossils are extremely rare but a study of the Dikika foot (DIK 1-1F), the most complete foot of a fossil juvenile yet known, found that while this 2.5 year old was fully able to walk on her own, she and other little ones clearly spent more time in the trees than adults did, perhaps for safety; she may also have used her feet to cling to her mother while the adult foraged for food (DeSilva *et al.* 2018). DeSilva *et al.* (2018, 4) observe that 'the Dikika child was similar in size to a chimpanzee of comparable age and was likely still dependent on and perhaps often actively carried by adults. Given the energetic costs of infant carrying, both adults and juveniles may have benefitted from the [range of mobility] present [in the big toe] in the juvenile foot of [*Au.*] *afarensis*.'

Infant carriers such as slings and cradleboards were likely in use for thousands of years but because they are made of perishable materials (*e.g.* wood, fiber, textiles), the earliest examples have been lost to time. There is no evidence of fiber technology before Neandertals (see Chapter 5) and certainly nothing about early hominin material culture suggest carriers were in use before *H. erectus* at the earliest. Therefore, beginning with *Australopithecus*, hominin infants were almost certainly carried by females and other caregivers on the front of their bodies. This change in positioning from the ape pattern allowed for greater interaction between infants and their caregivers (see discussion in Nowell 2020). Infants were better able to track parental gaze and to monitor, engage in and learn from social interactions. According to Tomasello (2014), the main difference between human and non-human primate infants is that human infants experience shared intentionality and engage in triadic interactions. For Hrdy (2011), this means that there has been selection for infants that are proficient at 'mind-reading' (*i.e.* ascertaining intentionality) and integrating themselves with potential caregivers.

Breastfeeding and weaning

The human brain is an expensive organ. Although it makes up only 2% of adult body weight, it demands about 20–25% of our metabolic energy even when we are at rest. This figure jumps to 60% in developing infants (Cofran and DeSilva 2015). Hominin females had to consume enough food to support themselves and the infants they were nursing or weaning. These nutritional demands would only have grown over time, particularly with the emergence of *H. erectus*. Body size for this species as a whole increased by 55% but female *H. erectus* body size increased by 70%, primarily as a result of gestating and breastfeeding larger-brained infants (Aiello and Key 2002; Aiello and Wells 2002; Antón 2003). The nutritional demands of both mother and infant would have necessitated a higher-quality diet, specifically, one rich in essential fatty acids and amino acids (Antón 2003; Cunnane and Crawford 2014).

In addition to consuming a high quality diet, another strategy for early hominins to follow would be to wean their infants sooner. Weaning is when infants cease breastfeeding and instead rely on solid foods. This is normally a gradual process with weaning foods used to supplement a decreasing intake of breast milk. As Nava *et al.* (2020, 1) note, 'the high nutritional demands of the human brain during the first years of life has been identified as the main reason for early weaning onset in modern humans'. While it is clear that many socioculture factors impact weaning decisions, from a biological point of view, the process of weaning is initiated when the nutritional requirements of infants (calories, protein, micronutrients) outstrip what mothers can provide through breast milk (Nava *et al.* 2020). In contemporary non-industrial societies and in archaeologically known populations (*e.g.* Dunne *et al.*

2019) weaning most commonly begins when an infant is 6 months old and this mirrors current WHO recommendations (Nava *et al.* 2020).

To identify weaning in fossil hominins, some human paleontologists have used the presence of dental enamel hypoplasia (*e.g.* Olgilvie *et al.* 1989; Bermúdez de Castro and Pérez 1995) which, depending on when in the life course they developed, can be indicators of stress related to weaning. For example, researchers studied a sample of eight Neandertals from El Sidrón in Spain (one infant, one juvenile, two adolescents and four young adults). The highest incidence of dental hypoplasia occurred around 4 years old. Four of these Neandertals also exhibited hypoplasia at 12 years old, prompting researchers to characterize 'weaning and adolescence as the life-history events [most] prone to nutritional stress in the El Sidrón sample' (Rosas *et al.* 2006, 19268).

Skinner (1997b) has argued that wear on deciduous teeth can be taken as an indicator of the age at which weaning foods were introduced. Others have measured nitrogen levels in bone as nitrogen is an indicator of trophic level. Breastfeeding infants are at a higher trophic level than their mothers but once weaning foods are introduced into their diet their nitrogen signatures decrease toward the maternal signature (Nowell *et al.* forthcoming). Thus, ^{15}N levels decrease during weaning and the decreasing reliance on maternal milk (Bocherens *et al.* 2001). Similarly, Humphrey *et al.* (2008) and Nava *et al.* (2020) have measured strontium/calcium (Sr/Ca) ratios in teeth to document dietary transitions associated with weaning. In infants that are exclusively breastfed, enamel Sr/Ca rates are significantly lower than prenatal rates because human milk is rich in calcium (Nava *et al.* 2020). Austin *et al.* (2013) have proposed a method for identifying weaning based on barium levels in teeth because they argue that barium is less susceptible to diagenetic change than Sr/Ca. Because barium is introduced through the mother's milk (the placenta acts as a barrier to barium transfer), barium levels in the developing teeth of nursing infants are high but they drop as the infant is weaned (Austin *et al.* 2013; Smith *et al.* 2018 but see Nava *et al.* 2020). This has proven to be a highly effective means of discerning the dietary transitions of non-human primate infants as well as those of extant and fossil hominins. More recently, Tacail *et al.* (2019), have developed a method based on calcium isotope levels ($\delta\ ^{44/42}$Ca) in dental enamel. Because the levels are low in modern Western breastmilk, a rise in levels detected in hominin infant dental enamel can be an indicator of weaning. While non-human primate infants are weaned at around 5.3 years (Smith *et al.* 2013), the age at which infants in non-industrial human societies are weaned varies among extant cultures with an average age of between 2 and 5 years with most infants weaned between 2 and 4 years of age (Humphrey 2010).

While we can make inferences based on non-human primates and the brain and body size of fossil hominins, it is only recently that we have direct evidence of weaning patterns among fossil hominins before Neandertals. Tacail *et al.* (2019) sampled teeth of 12 *Au. africanus*, 18 *P. robustus*, and 7 early *Homo* specimens from South Africa for a total of 84 enamel samples. What is interesting about this study is that they were able to sample multiple teeth of the same individual and where possible link the different calcium isotope signatures to change over time. For example, in the early *Homo* specimens, they sampled the deciduous incisor, first molar and canine and found ^{44}Ca levels were depleted relative to teeth that develop later in ontogeny such as the third premolar and third molar. In these later forming teeth, there was a marked increase in δ $^{44/42}$Ca values suggesting that around age 4 breastfeeding had completely or largely ceased. By contrast, *Au. africanus* and *P. robustus* are not characterized by low ^{44}Ca levels, which suggests to Tacil *et al.* (2019) that the early diet of youngsters in these taxa was primarily composed of adult solid foods with bouts of breastfeeding that were infrequent and/or shorter in duration. This is compatible with non-human primate data (Tacail *et al.* 2019). The researchers do not think it is likely that australopithecine and *P. robustus* breastmilk had elevated ^{44}Ca levels that could explain the observed signatures. The caveat when evaluating these results, however, is that Tacail *et al.* (2019) did not have access to incisor or premolar data for these two taxa so it is possible that their interpretations may change as more data are collected but currently it appears that early *Homo* infants in South Africa enjoyed a significantly longer and/or more intense period of breastfeeding than *Au. africanus* and *P. robustus* little ones did.

Most of what we know about weaning comes from studies on Neandertals. Smith *et al.* (2018) studied two Neandertals from France and concluded, based on barium levels, that Neandertal infants initially experienced a period of exclusive breastfeeding followed by a gradual transition to solid foods at ca. 2.5 years of age. A previous study (Austin *et al.* 2013) had detailed the early life of a Neandertal infant from Belgium. Breastfeeding for this infant ended abruptly around 1.2 years of age but the marked disruption of enamel formation and the sudden drop in barium levels suggest this is an anomaly perhaps as a result of a separation of the infant from the mother rather than the norm for Neandertal offspring (Austin *et al.* 2013; Smith *et al.* 2018). Smith *et al.* (2018) were further able to document that Neandertals in their small sample, following a generalized mammalian pattern, were born in the spring when food was more abundant and weaned in the fall, which suggests that Neandertal mothers became pregnant in the late summer or early fall. It follows that Paleolithic peoples would have mated during this time when the animals they hunted were at their fattest (Mussi 2007) as Neandertal females would have had to exceed a certain minimum threshold of body fat in order to be fertile. It is important to remember that this pattern is based on a very small sample and future research may uncover variations based on region/latitude, time period and cultural practices.

What we also know from the Smith *et al.* (2018) study is that Neandertal weaning was completed before the eruption of M1. In non-human primates, weaning follows the eruption of permanent dentition to facilitate the transition to solid foods but Neandertals, like modern human infants today, wean early (Humphrey 2010). This is likely a pattern that extends back to *H. erectus* given the increased nutritional demands on nursing mothers. Early weaning decreases birth spacing and reduces lactation-related costs for the mother but may lead to riskier outcomes for the infant (Humphrey 2010) if not mitigated in some way (Nowell and Kurki 2020).

Nava et al. (2020), studied deciduous teeth from three Neandertals[4] (Nadal 1, Fumane 1 and Riparo Broion 1) and one anatomically modern human subadult (Fumane 2) from three Italian sites in close proximity to each other. They recorded Sr/Ca levels to discern the onset of weaning and maternal diet and mobility. The neonatal line (Chapter 1) was visible in all four individuals, allowing them to conclude that the rate of tooth formation in Nadal 1, Riparo Broion 1 and Fumane 2 fell within the modern human range while Fumane 1 developed more quickly. In Fumane 1 and Riparo Broion 1, there was a marked drop in Sr/Ca levels immediately following birth (when breastfeeding would be beginning) followed by a slope change in levels as weaning was introduced at 115 days (3.8 months) and 160 days (5.3 months) respectively and an even stronger signal of food transition at 200 days (6.6 months) for Fumane 1 (Nava et al. 2020). By contrast, Nadale 1 was still being exclusively breast fed at 5 months old suggesting there is some individual or group level variability in breast feeding and weaning practices among Neandertals. There was not enough postnatal enamel growth available to detect the onset of weaning in Fumane 2 but this infant was clearly being breastfed based on a drop in Sr/Ca at birth (Nava et al. 2020).

Nava et al. (2020) then compared prenatal $^{87}Sr/^{86}Sr$ ratios in the subadults' deciduous teeth (which is a reflection of what their mothers ate while pregnant) to that of local micromammals to establish the chemical signature associated with eating local foods. Their results demonstrate that all the Neandertal mothers resided locally during the last part of their pregnancy and when they were breastfeeding their littles one. By contrast, Fumane 2, the modern human mother, gave birth away from the site and did not return to Fumane until her infant was 23 days old. This difference in group mobility patterns is suggestive but more research needs to be done. For instance, could this pattern be the result of seasonal differences in birth? In other words, if Smith et al.'s (2018) finding can be extrapolated to other Neandertals, is it possible that they tended to hunker down in one location in the winter months, giving birth in the spring?

Cooperative breeding, alloparenting and the Grandmother Hypothesis

Given the demands of caring for and feeding large, dependent offspring, many researchers believe that cooperative breeding, a social structure characterized by alloparenting, evolved early in hominin evolution as a way of relieving the energy burden on mothers (Barrickman et al. 2008; DeSilva 2011; Hrdy 2011; Isler and van Schaik 2012; 2014; Cofran and DeSilva 2015; Kramer and Otárola-Castillo 2015; Nowell and Kurki 2020). In primates, alloparenting allows for more rapid postnatal growth, reduced weaning ages and shorter birth intervals leading to what is sometimes referred to as 'infant stacking' (Humphrey 2010; DeSilva 2011; Kramer and Otárola-Castillo 2015; Halcrow et al. 2020; Nelson et al. forthcoming). Among apes it is normally juvenile females who engage in alloparenting, which can grade into a type of play known as play mothering (Smith 2010) (see Chapter 3) but among hominins, pair-bonded males, 'aunts' and older siblings may have all played a role in caregiving (Nowell and Kurki 2020). We know that in many extant societies older children provide food not only for themselves but for their younger siblings as well and the role of juveniles in the evolution of cooperative breeding in hominins remains an understudied area of research (Kramer and Otárola-Castillo 2015). It is hard to gauge male biological contributions to reproduction as there are no corresponding skeletal markers (Nowell *et al.* forthcoming) but fathers likely acted as alloparents by sharing food, and otherwise investing in their offspring through protection, transportation and the like depending on the degree of certainty of paternity (Gray 2013). Human males are capable of breastfeeding and in some extant societies they contribute to infant care by doing so (Palmquist 2020).

But what about the role of grandmothers? Fertility declines at roughly the same age in chimpanzee and human females but most chimpanzee females die soon after their period of fecundity ends while human females live on (Hawkes and Blurton Jones 2005). From an evolutionary perspective, even though these post-menopausal women are no longer fertile, they continue to play a role in the reproductive success of their group by subsidizing the fertility of their daughters (Kim *et al.* 2012). For example, among the Hadza, a foraging group in East Africa, weaned children are able to provide a lot of their own food depending on the season but they lack the physical strength to collect deeply buried tubers that are the year-round staple in these communities (Hawkes and Blurton Jones 2005). Weaned children depend on their mothers to provide tubers for them until their mothers give birth to a new baby – then it is the grandmothers who step in to ensure their well-being. Grandmothers in this society are excellent foragers who are just as productive as younger women and because they are able to spend more time foraging than their daughters, their overall economic contribution is greater (Hawkes and Blurton Jones 2005).

The contributions made by these grandmothers might explain human longevity and the vigorous post-menopausal lives that are unique to human females. From what we can see, australopithecines followed a more ape-like life history. Accordingly, weaned australopithecine juveniles likely foraged for themselves but the increasing aridity and seasonality of eastern and southern Africa during the late Pliocene/early Pleistocene might have meant that they increasingly relied on underground resources such as tubers that they could not collect themselves (Hawkes and Blurton Jones 2005). Hawkes and Blurton Jones (2005) in formulating the Grandmother Hypothesis, propose that vigorous australopithecine females who lived even just a little longer and who actively provisioned/shared food would have increased the overall fertility of their daughters and nieces. By extension, these 'grandmothers' would have a larger number of 'grandchildren' and 'grand-nieces' than females who did not engage in such behavior (Hawkes and Blurton Jones 2005). Over time there would have been selection for delayed maturation, larger maternal body size and extended life expectancy. Hawkes and Blurton Jones (2005, 120) write, 'maternal provisioning would create a novel opportunity for older females whose declining fertility made them less likely to have a newborn of their own: feeding their just-weaned grandchildren would allow childbearing-aged daughters to have shorter interbirth intervals without reductions in offspring survivorship'.

DeSilva (2011), argues that grandmothering as a strategy is more likely to have developed with *H. erectus* because of the evidence for female transfer and low life expectancy among australopithecines and early *Homo*. It is difficult to know for sure because there are no known skeletal markers associated with the cessation of fertility in females. While the 'onset of deterioration in bone quality (*e.g.*, trabecular bone thinning) may be indicative of older age, particularly in women ... it does not directly coincide with menopause' (Nowell *et al.* forthcoming). Either way, it is clear that grandmothers as alloparents were critical to infant survival (relatively) early in hominin evolution. In a mathematical simulation, Kim *et al.* (2012), started with a population characterized by chimpanzee-like life expectancy. They assumed that in this population females remained fertile until 45 years of age, which is roughly the cut-off for modern human and non-human primates. The model dictated that only females who were no longer fertile were eligible to be grandmothers. Furthermore, these grandmothers could only provision one offspring at a time with the default being the oldest juvenile ('grandchild') still dependent on its mother. According to the model's parameters, infants less than 2 years old were not eligible to be provided for in this way. The model's default assumptions are consistent with 'weak grandmothering' because, for example, in a real life scenario, grandmothers could provision multiple dependent juveniles simultaneously.

Initially, in the simulation, there were few females eligible to be grandmothers and therefore their impact on their daughters' fertility and on overall life expectancy was minimal. However, Kim *et al.* (2012) found that in less than 60,000 years, grandmothering doubled life expectancy in this simulated population. The model assumed nothing about changes in brain size, subsistence, learning capabilities etc. The impact of grandmothers alone was enough to transition a population from an essentially ape-like life history where most females die while still cycling into a human-like life history where most females survive into their post-reproductive years (Kim *et al.* 2012). By increasing overall longevity, grandmothering also increased male reproductive success as well (Kim *et al.* 2012).

Family and social structure

The preceding discussion brings us back to the question posed at the beginning of this chapter – what might a family have looked like in the Plio-Pleistocene? The term family implies a number of assumptions about relationships between individuals and how they might have codified these relationships. For this reason, Cooney (2018, 2), in her study of the Upper Paleolithic, defines family 'as the broader kinship group of the child's immediate community and would include those who are responsible for its wellbeing but also those with whom it shared social values'. It is in Cooney's sense that I will use the term family in this volume. I will also discuss hominin social structure to look at issues of demography and group organization more broadly.

Archaeologists reconstruct social structure by estimating group size from the size of the overall archaeological or fossil site or more specifically from sleeping areas when these can be reconstructed. When using this type of data, researchers often assume that archaeological remains are the result of a single occupation, which may not always be the case (Duveau *et al.* 2019). Paleoanthropologists have also tried to predict group size and structure from neocortex size (Dunbar 1992; 1998; Aiello and Dunbar 1993). This model proposes that the number of neocortical neurons is related to the brain's information processing capacity and by extension the number of stable relationships an individual can maintain at any one time. In modern humans, this number, sometimes referred to as Dunbar's number, is around 150 people and is described as 'the number of people you would not feel embarrassed about joining uninvited for a drink if you happened to bump into them in a bar' (Dunbar 1998, 77). Beyond this number, modern human groups need to rely on laws, restrictive rules, taboos etc. to maintain a cohesive, stable group.

We can strengthen estimates of group size and gain insights into sex and age categories by drawing on ethnographic analogies, non-human primate data (as appropriate), and footprint, handprint and finger fluting data (see Chapters 3 and 5). Although rare, we can also make inferences from catastrophic mortality events, for example, where an entire group of hominins is killed during a flashflood (Duveau *et al.* 2019). In these cases, researchers have a snapshot of a population of individuals who were interacting with each other at one moment in time.

Data concerning the social lives of the earliest hominins is scarce, forcing us to rely primarily on life history data and analogies with non-human primates. Chimpanzees are often used as a base model[5] for early hominin social structure and capabilities. This is because they are our closest relatives genetically. In addition, many of the behaviors that we thought made humans unique (*e.g.* tool use, cooperative/social hunting) are now known to be shared with them. Furthermore, the behavioral repertoires of non-human primates are incredibly complex (*e.g.* extensive plant use, creation of social alliances). Variations in many behaviors documented in chimpanzee populations are not related to environmental differences but appear to be the result of intergenerational learning and learning from peers; thus we can legitimately talk about chimpanzee 'cultures' (*e.g.* Whiten *et al.* 1999; 2009).

Australopithecines and early Homo

Using chimpanzees as analogies, we can infer that australopithecines lived in multi-male, multi-female groups. It is also very likely that male residence and female transfer between groups was the norm (Foley and Gamble 2009). Strontium-calcium ratios in a sample of *A. africanus* and *P. robustus* specimens from Swartkrans and Sterkfontein demonstrate that females were more likely to disperse from their natal group than males (Copeland *et al.* 2011). Seasonally, australopithecines would have broken into smaller groups or come together in larger ones based on availability of resources while on a daily basis they might have sought refuge in the trees to sleep or for protection. This may have been particularly true for little ones. Data from studies of DIK 1-1's gorilla-like scapula, curved phalanges and ape-like ankle are compatible with this model (DeSilva *et al.* 2018).

Brain growth in *Au. afarensis* suggests the insertion of the childhood stage in hominin life history for the first time approximately 3 million years ago (Gunz *et al.* 2020). While childhood was likely not as extended as it is in *Homo*, even a limited period of slowed growth would have allowed developing australopithecine subadults more time to learn from those around them (see the benefits of learning through play in Chapter 3). The correlate of an extended childhood is extended parenting wherein adults create the appropriate niche for social and cognitive development before offspring reach sexual maturity (Uomini *et al.* 2020; see Chapter 7). Given the evidence of secondary altriciality beginning with this genus and a grade shift in neonate body mass, australopithecine infants and juveniles were likely carried for at least 6 or 7 months on the front of their mother's body (or by other caregivers) again allowing for greater social interaction. Much like other non-human primates, the diet of *Au. africanus* and *P. robustus* was primarily composed of adult foods supplemented with bouts of breastfeeding (Tacail *et al.* 2019). Less is known about the lives of early *Homo* subadults but it seems reasonable to infer that patterns identified among australopithecines were amplified in this genus, including slowed brain growth, limited childhood and increased social interaction with caregivers. Compared to earlier hominins, early *Homo* youngsters were breastfed for longer and/or more intensely and that may also have created more opportunities for these little ones to engage in and track social interactions.

Homo erectus

With *Homo erectus*, we see a shift toward the human life history pattern with a significantly expanded childhood stage and increased opportunities for learning. *H. erectus* is the first obligate biped (*i.e.* first fully committed ground dweller), with no traces of an apelike dependence on trees. Its larger adult brain size, barrel-like chest, narrowing pelvis, and constricted birth canal (at least for some populations of this polytypic species) suggest increased infant dependency. *H. erectus* infants were likely weaned early (Humphrey 2010) allowing for decreased interbirth spacing. Early weaning depends on the availability of appropriate weaning foods. In the Neolithic, archaeologists have uncovered evidence of small spoons made from cattle bone that bear children's teeth marks on them. This suggests 'gruel' was a newly important weaning food (Stefanović *et al.* 2019). Unfortunately, we do not have that kind of evidence with *H. erectus* but we do know from its streamlined digestive tract that this species is consuming higher quality foods such as ones rich in essential fatty acids and amino acids. Furthermore, Wrangham (2017) argues that *H. erectus* regularly cooked its food which likely expanded the weaning foods available to infants. He notes (2017, S310), 'early weaning is clearly hard to reconcile with a raw diet unless it predictably included such elusive foods as brain and fat-rich marrow'. Early weaning is also facilitated by increased alloparenting. Grandmothering was likely in place with this species by 2.0 mya, if not earlier.

H. erectus social structure appears to have included a sexual division of labor. The second oldest set of hominin footprints in the world (see Chapter 3) is associated with an all-male group of adult *H. erectus* and date to 1.5 million years ago at Ileret in northern Kenya (Bennett *et al.* 2009; Dingwall *et al.* 2013; Hatala *et al.* 2016). According to Hatala *et al.* (2016), among primates, male alliances tend to form in circumstances when they provide an advantage in acquiring mates or food and therefore these footprints may be the oldest evidence of this behavior in hominins. In modern foraging societies, cooperation among males is particularly important in high risk activities such as hunting large game animals. Animal tracks at Illeret document their movement to and from waterways. By contrast, the *H. erectus* footprints show that these individuals were moving along the waterway as a foraging/hunting party would (Hatala *et al.* 2016).

At Engare Sero, a Late Pleistocene (ca. 11,000 BP) site in Tanzania, researchers uncovered 408 footprints attributed to early modern humans. Seventeen trackways belonging to 14 adult females, 1 adult male and 1 juvenile male tell the story of a group of hominins walking together, with the adult females all walking at the same pace. Based on ethnographic data, these trackways also capture a unique snapshot of cooperative and sexually divided foraging behavior (Hatala *et al.* 2020). This group of mostly adult female *H. sapiens* stands in contrast to the all-male group of adult *H. erectus* from Ileret. The near absence of children in both these cases may reveal something about the lives of these hominins that is not obvious at first glance. Hatala *et al.* (2020, 8) write, '[m]odern human foragers are unique among primates in that they typically forage together, and in that they typically divide labor between the sexes. In modern human groups such as the Ache and Hadza, groups of adult females will cooperatively forage, with occasional visits or accompaniment from adult males. Aside from nursing infants (who are likely to be carried), children are typically excluded from these types of group foraging activities and left behind in camp'. A sexual division of labor among *H. erectus* adults implies that subadults took on sex-based roles as they grew to be full members of their community.

Neandertals

Neandertals lived in small, isolated family groups of 10 to 30 individuals (Layton and O'Hara 2010; Lalueza-Fox *et al.* 2011; Hayden 2012; Prüfer *et al.* 2017; Duveau *et al.* 2019) (Fig. 2.6). Their social structure was likely egalitarian with a sexual division of labor (cf. Kuhn and Stiner 2006). Neandertal groups were quite mobile and young Neandertals already had robust muscle markings on their arms and legs attesting to the high levels of activity they engaged in beginning early in childhood (Wragg Sykes 2020). Similarly, a number of these subadults sustained injuries possibly through activity related accidents. Examples include broken jaws in Le Moustier 1 (11-15 years old)) and in Gibralter 1 (ca. 5 years old) a few years before their deaths. Gibralter 1 also experienced significant, possibly fatal blows to the skull (Wragg Sykes 2020).

2. Birth and the Paleolithic 'family'

Figure 2.6: Reconstruction of a Neandertal family in a cave in the Neanderthal Museum in the town of Krapina (Croatia), 25 February 2010. Photo courtesy: Nikola Solic/Reuters/Newscom.

As noted above, the number of fossil infants available for study increases dramatically with this species. One explanation for this trend might be a change in treatment of the dead. Neandertals are often described as the first species to bury members of their communities (Chapter 3). In fact, Zilhão (2005) has argued that Neandertals buried their infants more often than later modern humans did because Neandertal societies were more egalitarian than Upper Paleolithic ones and infants, as a result, were accorded personhood (see Chapter 1). While Neandertal burial practices are explored more fully in Chapter 3, it is worth looking at the question of the prevalence of infants in more detail here.

In their study, Nava *et al.* (2020) found that Neandertal mothers began introducing weaning foods into the diets of their infants when they were approximately 5 months old. This suggests that Neandertal females resumed post-partum ovulation at roughly the same pace as modern humans. Thus the proposition that Neandertal extinction was at least partly due to extended post-partum infertility (*e.g.* Skinner 1997b) is not supported. Yet while modern human population size increased (Mellars and French 2011), aDNA studies demonstrate that contemporary Neandertal population growth was restricted and that genetic variability within Neandertal populations was low (Prüfer *et al.* 2017). In fact, some Neandertal groups were highly inbred. For example, the parents of a Neandertal woman from Siberia were half-siblings (Prüfer *et al.* 2014).

How can these two lines of evidence be reconciled and how do they related to Zilhão's (2005) characterization of Neandertal societies? As Nava *et al.* (2020, 6) writes, 'other factors such as cultural behavior, shorter lifespan, and high juvenile mortality rate might have played a focal role in limiting Neandertals' group size'. Booth (2016; 2020; Booth *et al.* 2016) has demonstrated that stillborn infants are more likely to survive in the archaeological record because they are born without the gut bacteria that is largely responsible for post-mortem decomposition in full-term infants who died shortly after birth or as older subadults. It is possible that the prevalence of infants at Neandertal sites is related not to a higher valuation[6] of infants but rather to higher infant mortality (including stillbirths) than known for early modern humans. *H. erectus* and earlier hominins may also have experienced similar mortality rates but since they did not practice the same mortuary behaviors as Neandertals we do not have the same number of fossil infants. Given their small group size and their isolation, it is possible that they did not always have the same social supports in place that early modern humans did. Bergström and Tyler-Smith (2017, 587) observe that 'demographic modeling has suggested that whereas Neandertal groups might have been small and poorly connected, modern human groups had the sizes and network structures that allowed technology and culture to disseminate and persist over generations … Previous work has also shown that, as a genetic by-product of their long history of small group sizes, Neandertals suffered from a larger number of harmful mutations.' Low genetic variability leading to the increased prevalence of harmful mutations, care of large brained infants with an extensive post-natal growth period and the lack of a wider social network on which to depend could explain both the elevated rate of infant mortality and eventual Neandertal extinction. Through mathematical modeling, Degioanni *et al.* (2019, 10) demonstrate that 'a decline of less than 1.5% in survival for the youngest children [<1.0 year old] leads to rapid extinction (less than 2,000 years), while a reduction of survival rate as small as 0.4% provokes an extinction time of 10,000 years'.

Homo sapiens

The oldest known modern human fossils date to at least 200,000[7] BP in Africa and the Levant (McDougall *et al.* 2005; Hershkovitz *et al.* 2018) but less is known about their earliest social structure. Using *H. erectus* and Neandertals as a baseline, it is likely that even the earliest modern humans lived in small, egalitarian groups with a sexual division of labor. Much like modern foraging peoples, by at least 35,000 years ago in Europe, modern humans lived in small groups that consisted mostly of distantly related people that were connected to other similar groups of people though extensive social networks (Bergström and Tyler-Smith 2017). These social networks facilitated an exchange of mates, goods and ideas over vast geographic expanses. None of the individuals in these demes were 3rd degree relatives or closer (*e.g.* great-grandparents, great-grandchildren or first cousins). Genetic studies confirm that early modern humans regularly practiced exogamy (*i.e.* the tradition of marrying outside your community) (Sikora *et al.* 2017) and archaeological evidence suggests that Upper Paleolithic modern humans were highly mobile (Mellars and French 2011). Nava *et al.*'s (2020) finding that Fumane 2 gave birth and breastfed her infant for three weeks away from the site of Fumane supports the characterization of modern humans as highly mobile. Sikora *et al.* (2017, 4) write that, 'Human hunter-gatherer social structure of low levels of within-band relatedness, complex family residence patterns and relatively high individual mobility and multi-level social networks were already in place among UP societies 34,000 years ago. This social structure may have affected the development of cooperation and information transfer that underlie the evolution of culture in humans.' Similarly, Vanhaeren and d'Errico (2006) based on their study of patterning in personal ornaments identify the existence of diverse ethnolinguistic populations at this time.

In this chapter, I considered evolving hominin life history strategies and the implications for infant care, alloparenting including grandmothering, and early hominin 'family' or social structure. It is clear that all hominins faced obstetrical dilemmas of one sort or another and yet they survived and flourished as a species, many for a lot longer than modern humans have to date; these hominins learned ways to 'save the children' in spite of these dilemmas (Nowell and Kurki 2020) and many of these strategies depended on increasingly complex social networks. In the next three chapters, I consider in detail what the material culture and other traces of subadults in the archaeological record can tell us more specifically about the lived lives of later Paleolithic children and their families.

Notes

1. For a detailed review of obstetrics in fossil hominins see Wall-Scheffler *et al.* forthcoming.
2. See examples in Trevathan 2015.
3. While extensive, data presented in Appendices 2 and 3 are not exhaustive due to access to publications and variations in the way in which subadult remains (particularly isolated teeth) are reported.
4. These deciduous teeth fell out naturally in the process of being replaced by permanent teeth (*i.e.* these teeth did not belong to individuals who died as subadults).
5. See Sayers and Lovejoy 2008 for a critique of using chimpanzees as a model for early hominin evolution.
6. I am not arguing that Neandertals cared for their infants less than early modern humans did, simply that there is no evidence to suggest that they cared for them more.
7. Hublin *et al.* (2017) present evidence of the emergence of key modern anatomical features in fossils dating to 300,000 BP from Jebel Irhoud in Morocco. They do not consider these fossils to be anatomically modern humans, however, as they evince a mosaic of modern and primitive features.

Chapter 3

Toys, burials and secret spaces

> As long as archaeology continues to regard archaeological finds as the main barrier to approaching the subject, the possibilities of tracing the child's world are few. The potentialities increase when archaeology starts to focus directly upon the child and her ancient world.
>
> (Lillehammer 1989)

In her seminal 1989 article 'A Child is Born', Grete Lillehammer identifies three important child-centered relationships – a child's relationship to the environment, to adults and to other children. She argues that these relationships are related to core concepts in archaeology such as adaptation, intergenerational knowledge transmission and enculturation and can be studied through traditional methods in our field. In order to develop models of past cultures, archaeologists routinely investigate subsistence strategies, technology, ritual and ceremony, health and illness, social structure, sexual division of labor, and laws and taboos. As we saw in Chapter 1, when archaeologists study these facets of society they are of necessity studying children. While not all of these societal variables are knowable in a Paleolithic context, many are. Accordingly, in this chapter, I explore how children can be studied through toys, visual imagery, burials, and their use of space while Chapters 4 and 5 focus on seeing Paleolithic children through stone tools and the Paleolithic arts respectively. Together, these three chapters debunk the assumption that children are invisible in the archaeological record of the Paleolithic. Furthermore, they situate Paleolithic children as active and significant contributors to the economic, cultural and social wellbeing of the communities of which they were a part.

Evolution of play behavior and Paleolithic 'toys'

Lillehammer (1989, 95) argues that play 'directly expresses the everyday life of children. It reflects their challenges and corrections, their adaptations to growing up'. Building on Chapter 2, in this first section, I continue exploring the evolutionary context of hominin behavior by presenting an overview of the evolution and the benefits of play. I then consider the evidence for toys and games in the Paleolithic.

Play

Humans, like most mammals, spend a great deal of their dependency period in play. While approximately 60 attributes of play have been identified (see Pellegrini *et al.*

2007), following Smith (2010, 5), play is defined here as familiar behaviors (*e.g.* running, climbing, and manipulating objects) that are fragmented, repeated, exaggerated or reordered in some fashion (Nowell 2016 and references therein). Behaviors are normally identified as play if they have positive affect (*i.e.* there is enjoyment as indexed by play signals such as laughter); are flexible in form and content; are intrinsically motivated (*i.e.* performed for their own sake); if they are a means to an end (*i.e.* children are often more interested in the performance of the behavior than its outcome) and non-literal (Smith 2010, 6). The importance of play is supported by the fact that it will rebound in frequency and intensity in offspring deprived of play (Smith 2010) and the lack of play experience can seriously disadvantage an animal later in life (Bateson 2005). Pellis and Pellis (2009) found that play-deprived ratlings (juvenile rats) encountered the same difficulties in decision making and social interaction that rats with intentionally damaged pre-frontal cortices experience. The evolutionary benefits of play include the ability to practice behaviors that hominins will use once they reach adulthood and to learn from their mistakes safely (Bateson 2005, 17). Play also increases physical fitness (Smith 2010). Furthermore, there is a positive relationship between the frequency of social play and cerebellum size across species (Smith 2010) and play can also have a significant effect on learning in general. Individuals in a playful mood are more open to learning new things and learn more quickly.

Play increases steadily as 'young become more mobile and begin to interact with litter mates and other young ones in a group or herd and then decreas[es] as sexual maturity approaches, stable dominance positions are being acquired and the animal is typically engaged in serious competition for mates and resources' (Smith 2010, 54). Play forms part of a bio-behavioral package involving prolonged immaturity, opportunities for learning and parental investment in such learning and is characteristic of more encephalized species (*i.e.* those with a larger brain to body ratio), particularly K-strategists (Chapter 2) (Konner 2010; Smith 2010). Play is an almost universal mammalian characteristic with 17 of 19 orders of placental mammals engaging in play (Burghardt 2005). These behaviors include locomotor, object, social and sexual play.

Let's consider social play in more detail. Social play provides opportunities for individuals to cement social relationships (Bateson 2005), evaluate competitors, develop behavioral flexibility and coping skills and improve motor skills necessary for fighting (Bateson 2005; see also Ragir and Savage-Rumbaugh 2009). Furthermore, during social play, human children socialize and enculturate each other and this may be at least as important if not more so than parental nurturing. In fact, researchers argue that the 'vertical transmission of knowledge from older to younger children parallels, complements or undermines adult-child transmission' and thus children can be seen as significant 'agents of cultural change' (Konner 2010, 661) (see detailed discussion in Chapter 7). Furthermore, peaks in social play activity correlate with the development of neural networks that serve as the basis for shared systems of communication (Ragir and Savage-Rumbaugh 2009 and references therein). Taken together, for hominins this means that social play provides the evolutionary context within which meanings can be generated and shared by convention, hence the emergence of symbols and with them creativity.

Of all the mammals, primates engage in play the most, with the apes adding 'play mothering' to the aforementioned mammalian repertoire of play behaviors. Play mothering mostly refers to juveniles who pick up and 'mother' infants (Smith 2010) but there may be instances where this behavior involves the transference of species-specific mothering behaviors to inanimate objects such as sticks or logs (see, for example, Kahlenberg and Wrangham 2010). Object play, more generally, is well documented among primates (Smith 2010) as they use a large number of objects in their natural environment for food extraction, prey catching, agnostic displays and for a variety of other tasks. Thus, during play these animals are able to practice and explore tool behavior (Smith 2010).

As you might expect, of all the primates, humans play the most. While adults of most species stop playing once they reach sexual maturity and competition for mates and resources takes a more serious turn, adult humans continue to play (*e.g.* think of everything from card games to video games to seniors' hockey). As Lillehammer (1989, 94) writes, '[i]n its broadest sense, play is not restricted to the child's world. Play has a social function in rituals and in adult life. Games and play are part of the social strategy to maintain a cultural identity'. Studies show that adults continue to reap the benefits of play with synaptogenesis (see Chapter 2) continuing, if at a slower rate (Nowell 2016 and references therein).

Another way in which human primates are different is that they are the only species to engage in fantasy play, or imaginative/pretend ('what if') play. Fantasy play is part of a package of symbol-based cognitive abilities that includes self-awareness, language, and theory of mind (Smith 2010). These are all key for storytelling (see Chapters 4 and 5 for the social and pedagogic value of storytelling), sequential planning and the thinking through of the consequences of actions and decisions *before* enacting them. Researchers argue that fantasy play has been sustained evolutionarily because of its contribution to human psychological development and growth. The benefits of fantasy play include the development of creativity (Carruthers 2002), behavioral plasticity and imagination, as well as apprenticeship and planning (Nowell 2016). The clear evolutionary importance of play and the evidence of its rich and varied nature among mammals begs the question of what data we have of play behavior in Paleolithic children.

Toys and games

As discussed in detail in Chapter 1, toys are one of the most obvious ways archaeologists can identify children in the archaeological record. A toy can be as simple as a leaf 'boat' or cardboard box repurposed as a house or rocket ship. According to the Strong National Museum of Play,[1] the stick may be the oldest toy as even animals are known to play with them. Many toys are made of perishable materials such as clay, straw, fiber, animal skin and wood (see ethnographically known examples described in Langley 2018). Some toys require context or cultural knowledge to interpret them as such as might be the case with found or repurposed objects. This makes identifying toys in the Paleolithic somewhat challenging. Here, I discuss a few examples of possible categories of objects that have been suggested to be toys.

Thaumatropes and rondelles

The first category of objects that may have been intended for play in the Paleolithic is the thaumatrope (Nowell 2015b; Riede *et al.* 2018). Traditionally, thaumatropes are thought to date to the 19th century (Azéma and Rivière 2012 and references therein) but they may, in fact, have originated in the Upper Paleolithic only to be re-invented at a later date. Thaumatropes are circular disks with an image on both faces and a cord that passes through a perforation in the center. When the cord is pulled or twisted, the disk flips back and forth, revealing the image on each face in rapid succession (Azéma and Rivière 2012; Nowell 2015b). Because of retinal persistence, the images 'blend', causing the viewer to perceive a single image in motion. Modern-day equivalents are children's 'flip books', which are short, thick books with a slightly modified drawing on each page. An entire story unfolds as one rapidly flips through the book. Paleolithic thaumatropes are part of a larger category of portable art objects known as rondelles (Bahn 2016; Riede *et al.* 2018). Rondelles are circular disks often cut from bone (usually a scapula (shoulder blade) because of its thin, flat surface) or from stones such as slate, or from mammoth ivory (Bahn 2016). They are often engraved with abstract designs, animals and humans. Many rondelles have perforations in the center, while some more elaborate examples have perforations all around the circumference.

While some rondelles may have functioned as spindle whorls as part of a sophisticated textile industry dating back to at least 30,000 years ago (see Chapter 5), some rondelles functioned as thaumatropes. Riede *et al.* (2018) argue that there may have been a blending of these two technologies with the thaumatrope-like images contributing a playfulness or whimsy to the work of weaving. It is not an unreasonable suggestion given that there are spearthrowers (or atlatls) from the Upper Paleolithic sites of Le Mas d'Azil and Bédeilhac (France), that each have a young ibex carved at the distal end. In each case, the animal is looking back at a piece of excrement protruding from its anus.[2] Two birds sit atop the emerging turd at Le Mas d'Azil while only one is perched on the excrement extruded by the Bédeilhac Ibex. These spearthrowers may be an example of humor/visual play that is not unusual in the Upper Paleolithic (see Chapter 5 for other examples). Certainly, many other tools and weapons from this time period are decorated/incised beyond what is necessary for function so it may also be the case for the possible thaumatrope/spindle whorl.

A beautiful bone thaumatrope was uncovered at Laugerie-Basse, a Magdalenian (18,000–11,000 BP) site in southwest France. It is 31 mm in diameter and has a doe

Figure 3.1: Each face of this 'Paleolithic thaumatrope' from Laugerie-Basse (France) depicts a doe. When a string threaded through the hole in the center of this disk is manipulated, the disk flips back and forth creating the illusion of a doe springing. Thaumatropes such as these may have functioned as toys in the Upper Paleolithic. Diameter: 31 mm (Drawing: Holly Cecil).

engraved on each face (Fig. 3.1). On one face, the doe's legs are extended; on the other, they are folded under her. While some have interpreted these drawings as a representation of a dying doe that has fallen to the ground (Azéma and Rivière 2012), a more plausible explanation (Nowell 2015b; Riede *et al.* 2018), is that she is exhibiting the springing gait of a doe. When springing, does keep their backs horizontal and pull their legs up underneath their body. When you look at the thaumatrope, you can see that the doe's spine remains in the same plane on both faces of the disc, while her legs move up and down (Nowell 2015b). If the doe was falling to the ground, her hooves would remain on the ground while her body dropped down. Furthermore, a wounded doe would likely have her ears back, whereas on the disc the doe's ears remain pricked forward, which is characteristic of deer when they are running or feeling energetic (Nowell 2015b, Riede *et al.* 2018). Springing is a dynamic and distinctive deer behavior and thus ideally suited for visual play.

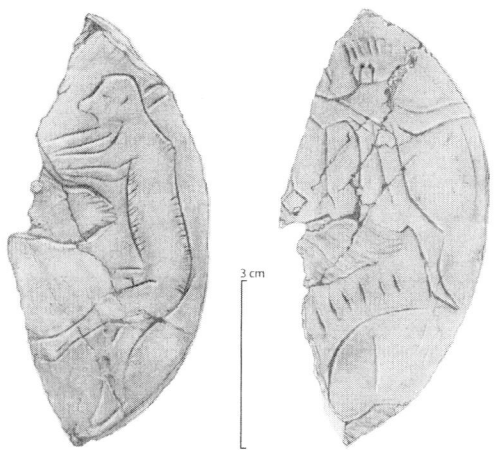

In Chapters 4 and 5, I discuss the importance of storytelling as a pedagogic device in foraging societies. There are rondelles that have a narrative quality and may have functioned as children's play objects, pedagogic tools or both

Figure 3.2: A partial bone rondelle from Mas d'Azil depicting a confrontation between a man and a bear. While not technically a thaumatrope, this rondelle exhibits a narrative quality. Maximum diameter: 78 mm (Drawing: Jenifer Gustavsen, redrawn after Duhard 1992).

simultaneously. For example, a rondelle recovered from the Magdalenian site of Mas d'Azil illustrates a man confronting a bear (Fig. 3.2). On one face, the man is standing with his left leg raised, his penis erect and a large stick over his right shoulder. Because the rondelle is broken, only the forelimb of the bear, with its claws extended, can be seen. On the other face, the man is shown lying face down on the ground, apparently having been attacked by the bear (Bahn 2016). It is not technically a thaumatrope because there is neither a visual illusion of motion nor a blending of images (*e.g.* a hat and a man's head where, with sufficient manipulation of the string, the man appears to be wearing the hat) but its narrative quality is suggestive (Riede *et al.* 2018). In Chapter 5, the point is made that stories are particularly important evolutionarily as teaching tools in cases where direct learning and experimentation are dangerous (Sugiyama 2001) and bear behavior would seem to fit the bill.

Human and animal figurines

The oldest ceramics date to approximately 25,000 years ago during the Gravettian at sites such as Dolní Věstonice (Czech Republic), Pavlov (Czech Republic), Předmostí (Czech Republic), Kostenki I (Russia) and Vela Spila Cave (Croatia) where researchers have uncovered multiple ceramic fragments and in some cases even kilns. While we normally associate ceramic technology with agricultural societies and assume early ceramicists made vessels for storing grain and other food items, it appears that the first ceramics were figurines – mostly small animal statuettes with a smaller number of human figures. Some of these animal figurines may have been made by or for children but there is little evidence to support this interpretation (Chapter 5) because little systematic work has been undertaken to study this possibility (but see Langley 2018). However, as Riede *et al.* (2018, 54) note, 'Upper Paleolithic mobiliary art ... may be another example of how play objects were supplied to children in order for them to learn and explore vital aspects of ecologically and hence adaptively relevant knowledge about animal behavior.' Kamp (2001b) emphasizes that children often enter communities of practice centered on ceramics through play and by making simple animals and pots (see Chapter 5).

Over 200 anthropomorphic (human like), mostly female, figurines are known from the Upper Paleolithic record (Beck 2000; Nelson 2004; Nowell and Chang 2014). They are made from a variety of materials, including stone, bone, ivory and fired loess, and have been recovered from sites from France to Siberia with temporal ranges between roughly 40,000 BP and 9,000 BP. These figurines have been interpreted variously as educational aids, personal ornaments, sexual imagery, markers of special places and/or time, markers of status, tokens of economic status and, of course, as toys or dolls (see Tringham and Conkey 1998 and references therein). For example, Filippov (2005) has argued that some of the Mal'ta figurines (see below) are unclothed and thus may have been dressed or colored like dolls. Again there is very little evidence one way or the other to evaluate the claims that these artifacts functioned as toys.

My personal feeling is that the figurines are so variable that it is unlikely that there was *one* function for all of them. They vary in terms of size, style, raw material, depositional location (*e.g.* burials, ceremonial pits, refuse piles) and whether they were worn/strung, hafted or none of these things. It is very possible some of them were made for and/or by children but we have not yet undertaken the research that would clearly show this one way or the other.

Tools and weapons

As discussed in Chapter 1, in foraging societies, children often play with miniature versions of tools, weapons and other objects routinely in use in their communities and thus, these items form a common category of 'toy' (Fig. 3.3). This type of play allows children to experiment with and learn the properties of some of the most important objects in their societies as well as the appropriate social behaviors and expectations that accompany their use. In the Paleolithic, candidates hypothesized to be this type of toy are generally small and/or poorly made stone tools. For example, Johansen and Stapert (2008; Stapert 2007a) identified a miniature handaxe (approximately 4.4 cm in length) at an early Middle Paleolithic site that they suggest was made for a Neandertal child, perhaps as an instructional tool. Similarly, Wragg Sykes (2020) suggests that the smaller sized 350,000-year-old wooden spears from Schöningen (Germany) may have been used by subadult Neandertals. She argues that this lakeside location may have been an ideal place to practice hunting in relative safety. Given the importance of tools for survival, evolutionarily, there was likely strong selection for this type of learning through play. Riede *et al.* (2018, 48) write,

> In an evolutionary context, technology-assisted hunting is the hunter-gatherer subsistence activity that requires the longest period of teaching and learning. Reaching the necessary levels in skill and technology production requires time, energy, and strong commitment. This extended learning phase, during which productivity is low, is compensated for by higher productivity during the adult phase and an intergenerational flow of high-quality food from old to young.

The topic of children and stone tools is further explored in Chapter 4.

Musical instruments

In many cultures, musical instruments are associated with children, particularly in societies in which they participate as musicians in ritual or battle (*e.g.* Kohut 2011). In other cases, instruments may simply have functioned as toys. The topic of children and music in the Upper Paleolithic is discussed in Chapter 5 but I will briefly consider three types of instruments that Lillehammer (1989) suggests may have functioned as toys – bullroarers, rattles and bird whistles. A bullroarer is a 'flat, perforated piece of wood, stone, bone, antler, or ivory tied onto the end of a cord, which creates a whirring sound when swung in a circular motion' (Morley 2013, 105). The sound varies based on the size of the bullroarer, the length of string, and the rate of rotation (Morley 2013). Several examples have been uncovered at Upper Paleolithic sites in France and Spain (Fig. 3.4a).

3. Toys, burials and secret spaces

Figure 3.3: Upper Paleolithic children playing with miniature weapons. Drawing: Marina Lezcano.

Percussive instruments have been found at the Upper Paleolithic sites of Mezin and Mezirich in the Ukraine. At Mezin, for example, in what has been described as a non-residential hut, researchers uncovered mammoth bones that had been struck multiple times and were found in association with reindeer-antler mallets and possible rattles (Morley 2013). There are also rasps. A rasp or scraped idiophone is a piece of 'wood, bone or stone with grooves cut into it perpendicular to its length, which are then rubbed with another object to create a staccato vibration' (Morley 2013, 109–110). Some researchers have argued that the so-called 'Venus' of Laussel, from France, is holding a rasp (Huyge 1991) (Fig. 3.4b).

Whistles are more difficult to define with certainty in the Paleolithic. For example, there are multiple punctured reindeer phalanges that have been described as whistles at Combe Grenal, a Middle Paleolithic site in France. While it is possible to produce a sound when blowing across the phalange, much like you can make a sound when you blow across a Coke bottle or empty jug, a detailed taphonomic study demonstrated that the holes were either of natural (*e.g.* carnivore punctures) or ambiguous origin (Chase 1990; 2001; but see Morley 2013). Of course, the phalanges could have still been used as instruments, in much the same way that a Coke bottle or jug can be repurposed for that function but there is no evidence to suggest that these Middle Paleolithic objects were employed that way. There is more convincing evidence

Figure 3.4: (a) Replica of a bullroarer from the Upper Paleolithic of Spain (Photo: April Nowell); (b) Venus of Laussel, holding what may be a rasp (Photo: Wikimedia Commons, https://commons.wikimedia.org/wiki/File%3AVenus-de-Laussel-vue-generale-noir.jpg).

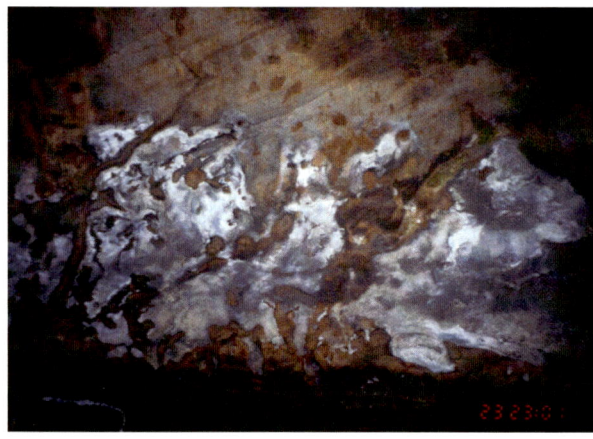

Figure 3.5: One of the best examples of play and toys in the Paleolithic are clay pellets adolescents threw at targets and sometimes at each other. The ones pictured here are from the 13,000-year-old site Toirano in Italy (Photo courtesy: Paul Bahn).

of bird bone whistles in the Upper Paleolithic of Siberia and Western Europe (*e.g.* Lbova *et al.* 2013; Ibáñez *et al.* 2015). While these whistles were made *of* bird bone (likely because they are hollow) they are not thought to be bird whistles (*i.e.* an instrument that produces sound reminiscent of a bird chirping). Ibáñez *et al.* (2015) argue that the limited range of sounds producible by the whistles at their site preclude their use as hunting decoys.

Clay pellets

At Fontanet, a 13,000 year old cave site in southern France, there are traces (*i.e.* footprints, see below) of adolescents playing by throwing clay balls at each other (Bahn 2015). At a similarly dated cave in Italy, Toirano (Fig. 3.5), dozens of these clay balls were thrown at the back wall as well as at a stalagmite, many of them missed their target and remain on the floor of the cave (Bahn 2015). We do not know who threw the balls of clay at Toirano but the similarity between this site and Fontanet suggests this may have been a common game played by young people.

Images of children in the Paleolithic

The most direct way of actually 'seeing' children in the Paleolithic is through imagery of them. Unfortunately, images of humans are rare in the corpus of Paleolithic art; images of subadults are rarer still and convincing images of subadults are the rarest of all. Possible examples of images of children and infants are engraved plaquettes (stone slabs) from Gönnersdorf and La Marche (France). At Gönnersdorf, a Magdalenian site in Germany, artists engraved stylized female figures (plaquette #87). In the example in Figure 3.6, we see four women with a possible infant or child in the center. The identification of this figure as a subadult is based on size alone as none of the figures have a head. D'Errico (2009) argues that the infant is being carried in a baby carrier on the back of the woman to its right. There are engraved lines connecting the two figures that support this interpretation. On plaquette 59 from this site researchers have identified a small anthropomorphic figure attached to a female figure by several lines. This has been interpreted as a fetus attached to its mother by an umbilical cord (Marshack 1975; d'Errico 2009; Bahn 2015).

The 14,280 BP site of La Marche is known for hundreds of animal and human engravings on plaquettes. According to Bahn (2015 and references therein), on plaquette 35-I, researchers have identified what looks to be an infant based on the large size of its head relative to its body and on plaquette 27, there are five heads that could belong to infants or young children (Fig. 3.7).

The only other examples of representations of Paleolithic children I can think of are clothed Gravettian figurines made from mammoth ivory from the sites of Mal'ta and Buret' (Lbova and Volkov 2015; 2017) in Siberia (Figs 3.8 and 3.9). In Schmidt's (2010) study of 32 figurines from these sites, he found that one third of them had head to body ratios approximate to that of infants and young children (*i.e.* heads that were one fourth to one third the size of their bodies). He argues that given the degree of realism noted in other figurines from these sites, the proportion is the result

Figure 3.6: Four stylized female figures from the Magdalenian site Gönnersdorf in Germany. Based on size alone, the figure in the center is suggested to be a small child or infant (Photo: Paul Bahn; courtesy Paul Bahn and Gerhard Bosinski).

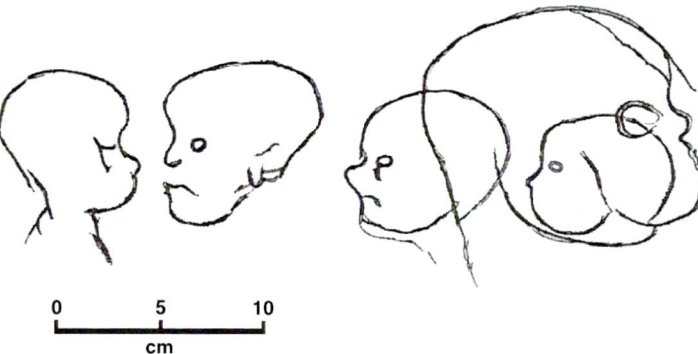

Figure 3.7: Plaquette 27 from La Marche, a 14,000-year-old site in France, with five engravings of possible infants and children (non-figurative lines have not been reproduced here in an effort to make the figurative drawings more visible) (Drawing: Jeremy Beller; redrawn after L. Pales 1976).

Figure 3.8: This figurine of a child from the Gravettian site Mal'ta (Siberia) is interpreted as wearing 'overalls' (Photo courtesy: Lyudmila Lbova).

Figure 3.9: At the Gravettian site Mal'ta (Siberia), archaeologists uncovered a figurine of a child wearing a fur parka (Photo courtesy: Lyudmila Lbova).

of the intentional representation of subadults. Interestingly, some of the figurines have traces of pigment on them. A purported figurine of a 'teenager' has remnants of vermillion while other figurines show traces of green and dark blue coloring. Could this be an indicator of what these people's clothing looked like in life? This find is particularly astounding because blue and green dyes are notoriously difficult to produce and we have always assumed that Upper Paleolithic peoples did not manufacture these colors. But this assumption is largely based on the range of colors typical of cave art. These parietal (wall) images are created with pigments that occur naturally in the environment (red, yellow and brown ochre, sometimes heat treated to extend the range of hues, black charcoal and manganese and white calcite). Lbova and Volkov (2017, 173) note that the adolescent 'appears to be dressed in a one-piece garment with hood, which covers the entire body and head. The front and back show long engraved triangles, probably representing the tails of furs from which the clothing was made. The presence of scarlet pigment has been detected in the area under the tail, on the right thigh and on the right arm'. Preliminary analyses show that the red pigment is composed of iron (Fe), strontium (Sr), zinc (Zn) and zirconium (Zr) while the blue is a blend of strontium (Sr), calcium (Ca), iron (Fe), zinc (Zn) and bromine (Br). The green is similar to the blue but with the addition of chromium (Cr) (Lbova and Volkov 2017; Lbova *et al.* 2017).

Seeing children through burials

Along with visual representations, one of the most direct ways of seeing prehistoric children is through their burials. Often with stone tools or other kinds of artifacts we have to infer that we are studying the products of children. Burials, however, are less ambiguous. In most cases, we can be certain that we are working with the remains of subadults and that the artifacts found within the delimited space of a burial are in some way associated with them, whether they speak to the lived life of the child directly or more broadly to the society in which they lived. As Cooney (2018) notes, the vast majority of material culture confidently associated with Paleolithic subadults derives from a burial context but this may be because our methods for seeing children outside burial contexts have been insufficiently robust. Subadults' skeletons are useful sources of data on mortality, growth and development, growth disruption, patterns of health and disease, subsistence, weaning patterns and inherited disorders (Halcrowe and Tayles 2008). Children are often the proverbial 'canary in a coal mine'; as changes in morbidity among children can be an important indicator of overall health in a community (Halcrowe and Tayles 2008).

There are more than one hundred burials associated with subadults in the Paleolithic (Table 3.1). Estimates vary due to different methods employed for determining an individual's age at death and because of disagreement over whether or not the remains are considered to be purposefully interred. To be a true burial, there must be evidence that a pit or hole of some kind was excavated for the deceased. For

Table 3.1. A listing of Paleolithic subadult burials.

Species	Countries	Approximate no. of burials/possible burials	Associated 14C dates (uncal BP)/estimated absolute date
Neandertals	Bulgaria, France, Iraq, Israel, Russia, Spain, Syria	45	183,000±14,000–33,000 BP
Homo sapiens	Austria, Chile, Czech Republic, France, Hungary, Israel, Italy, Poland, Portugal, Russia, United Kingdom, United States	70	115,000±15,000–6000 BP
Contested species designation	France, Israel, Italy	7	115,000±15,000–13,190 BP

example, Pettitt (2018, 2; see also Pettitt 2010) makes a distinction between 'burial' and 'funerary caching' with the latter defined as 'deliberate disposal of the dead in specific places of the landscape'. Funerary caching can be an interment at the back of a cave or under a natural overhang at a rock shelter, for example. Pettitt (2010) argues that with caching there is a desire to protect the deceased and to recognize a special status or transition in status for them. An example is the Sima de los Huesos (Pit of Bones) at the site of Atapuerca in Northern Spain. At this ca. 430,000-year-old site, archaeologists recovered the remains of 28 individuals including 1 child and 13 adolescents at the bottom of a natural cave shaft 13 m (43 ft) deep. No artifacts were found in association with them other than one handaxe that likely fell in by accident, but the completeness of the remains and the lack of occupation material suggests this was intentional disposal of the dead (Bahn 2015). In some ways, the primacy of burials versus other forms of mortuary behavior in archaeological literature could be seen as the result of a cultural bias on the part of archaeologists. However, it can be more difficult to demonstrate that funerary caching and similar behaviors are intentional and if the goal to is find the origins of mortuary behavior (and all of the assumption about symbolic behavior that go with that), it is easy to see why a focus on burials might be legitimate. In this section, I present a few examples of Neandertal and modern human infant, child and juvenile burials, while in Chapter 6 burials associated with adolescents are considered.

Neandertals

It is frequently said that Neandertals are the first hominin species to bury their dead. While I do not support the extreme thesis that there are *no* Neandertal burials (*e.g.* Gargett 1989; 1999), I do think this characterization of Neandertal behavior is an overstatement. As Pettitt (2010) notes, it is probably more correct to say that *some* Neandertals *at some times and places* buried their dead. The status of some Neandertal subadult burials are the subject of intense debate, such as the Roc de Marsal Child, with Sandgathe *et al.* (2011) suggesting the interment is natural and Gómez-Olivencia and García-Martínez (2019) calling into question some of the evidence Sandgathe and colleagues relied on to come to that conclusion. By contrast, the infant burials of Le Moustier 2 (France) and Mezmaiskaya 1 (Russia) are more widely accepted as intentional (Weaver *et al.* 2016).

Amud (Israel)

The provenience of the Amud 1 infant suggests that this may be an example of Neandertal funerary caching. According to Hovers *et al.* (1995, 52), 'A natural niche in the rock face of the cave wall served as burial structure, [with] the body laid down directly on the bedrock.' Lying on the infant's pelvis was part of a cervid's maxilla which has been described as an offering (Tillier 2008). For taphonomic reasons, it is difficult to know if the maxilla was deliberately placed on the infant.

La Ferrassie (France)

The largest number of Neandertal subadult burials have been uncovered at La Ferrassie in southwest France. In addition to two adults, archaeologists identified the remains of three children, two fetuses and one neonate. Of particular note is the double burial of La Ferrassie 4 and 4b because of the rarity of double burials in the Middle Paleolithic, and the single burial of La Ferrassie 6 because of its possible ritual dimension. La Ferrassie 6 is a 3-year-old child, interred in a pit in a tightly flexed position along an east–west orientation. Three stone tools were found in the association with the child and a triangular limestone block caps the burial (Pettitt 2010; Bahn 2015). The block is described as being decorated with cupules (small, intentionally hollowed out pits sometimes found in Upper Paleolithic art). It is possible, however, that these cupules are natural in origin.

In 2020, the burial of La Ferrassie 8, a 2-year-old child, was reanalyzed. Balzeau *et al.*'s study combined archival research (field notes from the original excavation that allowed for the precise location of the hominin remains), aDNA analysis of the original remains and a newly excavated bone belonging to the child's skeleton, and a ZooMS (Zooarchaeology by Mass Spectrometry) analysis of the paleontological material, which is a non-destructive way of identifying animal remains. Based on their results, they argue convincingly for the intentionality of this child's burial. According to these researchers, ca. 41,000 years ago, a small pit was dug into sterile sediment and the young Neandertal child's remains were placed within it. The pit was then refilled with surrounding sediment. While animal remains associated with the child in the archaeological layers above the pit were fragmented, scattered and weathered and exhibited stone tool produced cutmarks, the child itself was relatively complete,[3] in good condition and spatially contained. The preservation of the skeleton suggests that the body was not left out in the open and the fact that the surrounding sediment is sterile, *i.e.*, devoid of any other archaeological remains, argues against this layer having been part of a living floor (Chapter 1). La Ferrassie 8's remains are younger in age than the surrounding sediment and the overlying paleontological material, which makes sense if the child's community dug down into (older) sediment to create a burial pit. The child's body is oriented east–west in the same manner of other Neandertal remains at the site. Not following the natural slope of the layer, its head is higher than its pelvis. The orientation and positioning of the body suggests that care was taken when the child was placed in the pit.

Teshik-Tesh (Uzbekistan)

At the Middle Paleolithic site of Teshik-Tesh, a child of 8–11 years old was buried encircled by five horn cores belonging to Siberian ibex. Because the excavation was conducted in 1938 and few details are known regarding the original positioning of the remains and the horn cores it is hard to know how to evaluate this example. Chase and Dibble (1987) have argued that grave goods associated with Neandertal burials tend to be utilitarian in nature (*e.g.* stone tools or faunal remains that could have been swept into a burial by accident as a body was being covered with sediment). On the one hand, this begs the question of what kinds of objects we should expect to see in graves dating to the Middle Paleolithic but on the other, the contrast with modern human Middle and Upper Paleolithic grave goods couldn't be more striking (see below and in Chapters 5 and 6).

Modern humans and 'hybrids'

Skhul and Qafzeh Caves (Israel)

The Middle Paleolithic cave sites of Qafzeh and Skhul in Israel are the locations of the earliest intentional burials of subadults in the Paleolithic (Tillier 2008). Dating to approximately 100,000 years ago, subadults account for 30% of interments at Skhul and 60% of those at Qafzeh. The three subadults at Skhul fall within the ages of 1–4 years and 5–9 years old at death, while the range of ages of the nine subadults at Qafzeh is broader, from neonate to mid–late adolescence (Tillier 2008). The evidence for a ritual dimension to these burials is uneven. At Skhul, archaeologists uncovered shell beads, red ochre and colored flints near the burials but no direct association with the burials can be established (Tillier 2008). By contrast, Qafzeh 11, a 13-year-old adolescent, was interred on their back in a pit. Their arms are tightly flexed with their hands near their face (Tillier 2008). The teen was found with a large limestone block on their pelvis, red deer antlers in their hands and several pieces of ochre scattered throughout the burial (Tillier 2008; Bahn 2015).

Lagar Velho Rockshelter (Portugal)

At the back of the Gravettian Lagar Velho Rockshelter in the Lapedo Valley in Portugal in a shallow pit, archaeologists recovered the remains of what some have called a Neandertal and modern human 'love child' or, more correctly, a child of mixed Neandertal and modern human ancestry based on studies of its dentition, cranial and post-cranial skeleton (Bayle *et al.* 2010). Four red deer canines and two *Littorina obtusata* shells were found in association with the child (Vanhaeren and d'Errico 2002) (Fig. 3.10). The personal ornaments and the child's remains are bathed in ochre but the spatially delimited distribution of the ochre suggests that he or she was wrapped in a shroud. A young rabbit was carefully placed on the child's lower legs while two red deer pelves were placed at his/her shoulders and feet (Bahn 2015). A lens of charcoal underneath the child's right leg suggests there may have been a small ritual fire (Zilhão and Almeida 2002).

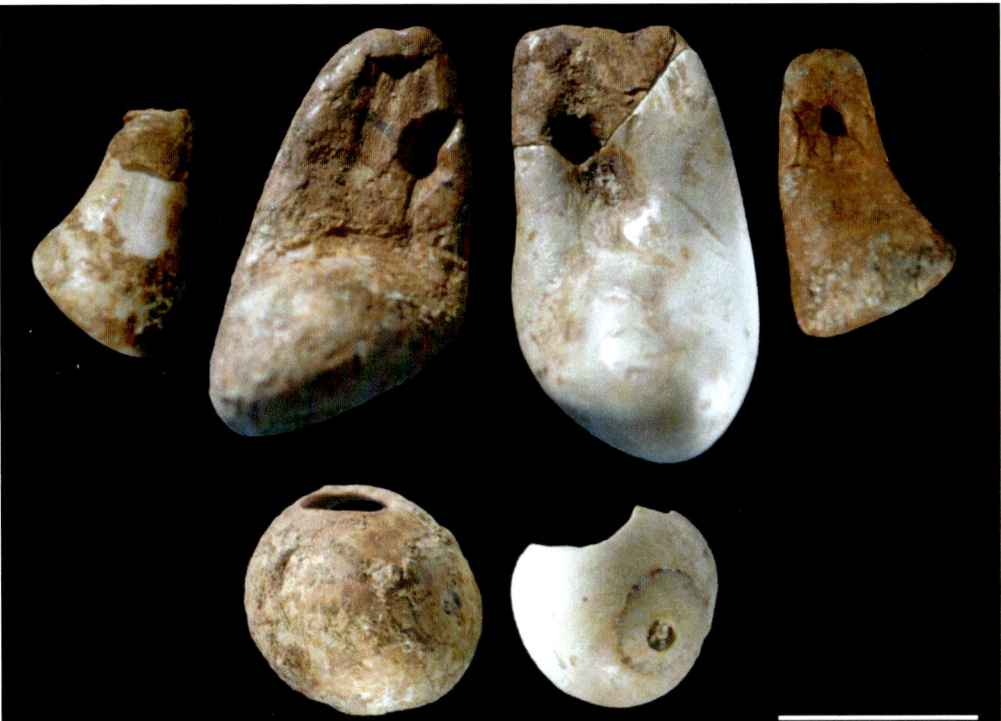

Figure 3.10: Personal ornaments associated with the Lagar Velho hybrid child from Portugal. Top row: Red deer canines; bottom row: Littorina obtusata shells (Photo courtesy: Francesco d'Errico).

Mal'ta (Siberia)

The Gravettian site of Mal'ta is perhaps best known for its numerous female figurines and other portable art objects, including 15 bird figurines (ducks, geese and swans), 12 of which are shown in flight (Medvedev 1998). Mal'ta contains the most spectacular of the infant burials assigned to the Gravettian. The double burial contains the remains of two infants laid one on top of the other, although it is likely that they were interred at different times given their differing degrees of erosion (Alekseev 1998). One infant has been aged to between 3 and 4 years; the other, covered in ochre, to approximately 1 year old (Alekseev 1998; Derev'anko 1998). The burial was capped with a flat stone. Associated with the burial is a necklace composed of 12 single- and four double-holed mammoth ivory beads and a bird pendant (possibly an owl in flight) manufactured from the same material, as well as a bracelet, a carved rectangular disk and stone and bone tools (Derev'anko 1998; Kirrilov and Derev'anko 1998).

Schmidt (2010) argues based on local ethnography that a special relationship between infants and birds in this region may reach back into prehistoric times. For example, the Nenets, Siberian reindeer herders, 'used maxillae of waterfowl with a piece of forehead skin to manufacture the heads of dolls for children. The heads of male dolls were made of goose beaks, while duck beaks were employed in making the heads of female dolls. A small rag roll or a swaddled beak represented "baby"-dolls and were put into toy cradles' (Schmidt 2010, 54). Furthermore, infants are sometimes dressed in clothing made from diving birds (teals) for warmth and protection from moisture but in some senses they are also seen as equivalent to birds (Schmidt 2010).

Krems-Watchberg (Austria)

At the Gravettian site of Krems-Watchberg, two infant burials were recovered by excavators (Einwögerer *et al.* 2006; 2009). Burial 1 contains the remains of male monozygotic (identical) twins (Teschler-Nicola *et al.* 2020). They are both highly flexed with their heads oriented north. They have been bathed in ochre, and 53 highly standardized mammoth ivory beads were found on the pelvis of one of the infants (Individual 1). The beads were likely on a string around his waist and the infant's tiny hand was found resting on top of the string. Unlike beads found with older Gravettian children (see Chapters 5 and 6), these beads showed no sign of wear. It is quite possible that these beads were made specifically for the burial or for the infant to wear in life but he never had the chance to. The second twin (Individual 2) wore three pierced mollusk shells (*Theodoxus* sp.) and a pierced fox incisor around his neck as pendants. While initially aged to between 9 and 10 months based on tibial size (Einwögerer *et al.* 2006; 2009), a detailed dental analysis demonstrates that they were born full-term (somewhere between 36 and 40 prenatal weeks) but died shortly thereafter (Teschler-Nicola *et al.* 2020, 3). Individual 2 died at birth followed by his brother 50 days later. The burial was initially created for Individual 2 but space was later made for Individual 1 who is described as 'huddled against the grave pit's edge' (Teschler-Nicola *et al.* 2020, 3).

Located approximately 1.5 m away is Burial 2. This burial contains the remains of a third male infant who was the twins' third-degree relative[4] (in this case probably a first cousin). This boy was also covered in ochre, but because the pigment is highly delimited in space, researchers have argued that the infant was wrapped in a shroud. A mammoth ivory pin was found above his head, suggesting that the shroud was closed at the top. Similar to the other two, he is in a highly flexed position, but his head is oriented south (Einwögerer *et al.* 2006; 2009). He died between 91 and 98 days after birth (Teschler-Nicola *et al.* 2020, 3).

While the cause of death for these young ones is unknown, researchers noted several pathologies. These observations include severe tibial periostitis (inflammation of the tissue covering the tibia) in Individual 1 and unusual accentuated lines in all three infants' dental enamel. They write, 'the non-specific stress symptom of subperiosteal newly built bone formations at the tibia of individual 1 ... in conjunction with the atypical accentuated lines observed in the enamel emphasise severe stress episodes and/or insufficient supply that might have contributed to the early death of the perinates' (Teschler-Nicola *et al.* 2020, 5).

Grotte des Enfants (Italy)

At Grotte des Enfants, in Italy, two infants (1 and 2 years of age) were buried side by side in a shallow grave. The little ones were laid to rest in an extended position with their hands at their sides and their heads carefully turned to the right. Around their waists and pelvic regions, archaeologists uncovered several hundred perforated shells arranged in rows. A fragment of a triangular shaped point was embedded in the thoracic vertebra of one infant. This was likely the cause of death as there is no sign of healing (Pettit 2010). Both children suffered from periostitis (Pettitt 2010), which is an inflammation of the connective tissue around the bone that can be caused by too much vitamin A, among other factors.

Burial data

In sum, despite the poverty of associated artifacts, there does appear to be a handful of intentional subadult Neandertal burials (*e.g.* La Ferrassie 8, Le Moustier 2 and Mezmaiskaya 1) or funerary caches in Pettitt's (2010) sense of the term (*e.g.* Amud 1). According to one study (Defleur 1993; see also Bahn 2015), of 47 Neandertals of known age, subadults accounted for 38% of them and 55.5% of these individuals were between 1 and 10 years of age at time of death. Because most of the Neandertal burials were excavated decades ago, it is not always clear that these are intentional interments. Nonetheless, I would argue that something different is happening, some change in behavior had to have occurred – whether this is true burial or simply funerary caching

– for there to be such a dramatic increase in the preservation of little ones with this hominin species compared to *Homo erectus* and earlier taxons among whom we have no credible evidence of mortuary behavior.

By contrast, there is a much larger number of unequivocal burials attributable to *Homo sapiens* subadults beginning in the Middle Paleolithic. I have only presented a handful of burials here but more examples will be discussed in Chapter 5 in relation to clothing and in Chapter 6 in relation to lives (and deaths) of Ice Age teens. While not all *Homo sapiens* interments have grave goods and a clear ritual dimension to them, enough do to be able to make some generalizations. First, research at La Vergre (France) and Arene Candide (Italy), both sites described as Upper Paleolithic 'cemeteries', revealed that adults and subadults, regardless of sex, were equally likely to be associated with the same categories of personal ornaments (Vanhaeren and d'Errico 2003). Other researchers have similarly found greater differences between regions with regards to interments than within regions (Riel-Salvatore and Gravel-Miguel 2013) meaning that subadults appear to have been as valued as other members of society. Second, material culture associated with subadults is often smaller in size (Cooney 2018); this is particularly true of personal ornaments such as beads that were sewn or embroidered onto clothing (*e.g.* at sites such as Sunghir, La Madeleine and Grotte des Enfants). Third, double and triple burials of subadults occur with more frequency in the Gravettian. Finally, as will be elaborated upon in Chapter 6, many of the interred individuals, including subadults, during the Gravettian/EpiGravettian suffered from a wide range of pathologies including exceedingly rare congenital abnormalities, or they seem to have died violent deaths.

Seeing Paleolithic children through the use of space

Until about 30 years ago, archaeologists studied landscapes primarily as physical backdrops to human activity, focusing on the ways in which the environment constrained or allowed for certain forms of subsistence. In the 1990s, there was a shift to understanding the ways in which landscapes both shape and are shaped by human experience. This phenomenological approach has allowed archaeologists to explore ways in which natural and built environments create a sense of identity and way of being in the world. According to Baxter (2005a; 2005b), the ways in which children are enculturated includes the use of space. She observes that children are taught acceptable locations for different behaviors such as sleeping, working and playing and that these locations vary based on age, gender and social status, with age being the most important factor in determining how far children roam from the adults in their lives. In this sense, landscapes are not 'culturally neutral'. Places that are out of direct view of adults, where children can exert some autonomy, take on the status of a 'special' or 'secret space' (Baxter 2005b). As such, Lillehammer (2000, 21) urges archaeologists to 'look for the spaces in which children learn to behave outside the adult world'.

Secret spaces

Based on the work of Sobel (1993), Wilke (1994), Baxter (2005b), Moore (2015) and others, Langley (2020 and references therein) proposes several criteria for identifying children's playhouses or secret spaces in the Paleolithic. She describes these spaces as being in locations that are at least partially out of direct sight of adults, ephemeral in nature although they can sometimes include a more built structure, are similar in style to housing types in the communities in which the children live and contain material culture associated with children, including what Baxter (2005b) refers to as 'low value items', *i.e.*, objects often collected and/or repurposed by children. These spaces often contain food refuse as well because as Sobel (1993) argues, food can enhance the 'specialness' of a place.

At the Late Magdalenian site, Étiolles, in the Paris Basin, researchers uncovered evidence of master and novice flintknappers and the relationships that existed between them (Pigeot 1987; Olive 1988; 1992; Olive *et al.* 2019) (see Chapter 4). On one living floor (see Chapter 1), dating to between 13,160 BP–12,800 BP, these researchers identified six archaeological features that relate to different habitation or activity areas (Fig. 3.11). Based on a detailed analysis of the materials found in association with these features, they have interpreted them as follows. U5 and P15 are large (>70 m square) tents that functioned as habitation centers with dense concentrations of lithics and a central hearth (Olive *et al.* 2019). There is evidence for the working of bone and hide, preparation and consumption of meals and the repairing of hunting weapons. It is likely that this is where people slept, ate and spent a great deal of their time socializing,

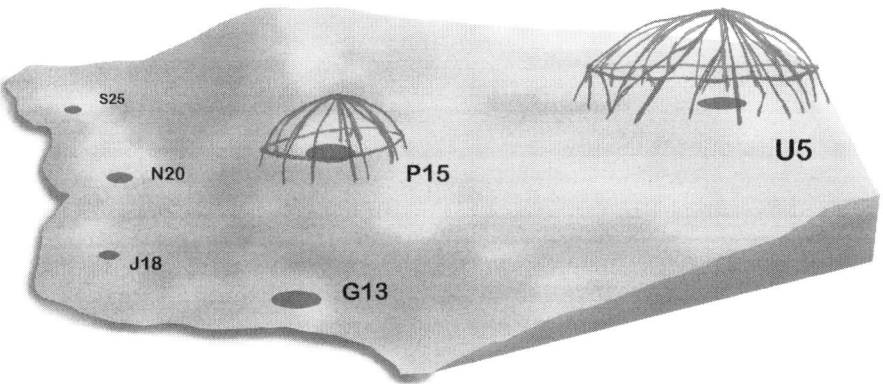

Figure 3.11: A drawing of Étiolles, a late Magdalenian site in France. Locales J18 and G13 are suggested to be Upper Paleolithic children's 'secret spaces' based on location and material culture uncovered there. Less dense lithic scatters have not been included in this drawing in order to focus on the relationship between the smaller and larger locales at the site (Drawing: Charlotte Mackie after drawing by Y. Le Jeune and N. Pigeot in Langley 2020 and after Olive et al. 2019, fig. 6).

perhaps engaging in storytelling, song and dance (see Chapter 5). By contrast, the four remaining features are smaller with S25 and N20 measuring approximately 30 m^2 while G13 and J18 varied between 10–16 m^2 each. S25 is described as a location for butchering animals and preparing stone tool cores while N20, an extensive outdoor area, is interpreted as a zone of more diverse activity focused around a hearth. At N20 there is evidence of meal preparation and consumption, stone tool manufacture and hide working (Olive 1992; Olive *et al.* 2019; see also Langley 2020).

But it is the two remaining features, J18 and G13 that are of most interest here. According to Olive *et al.* (2019), these two locales are the smallest of the six features. They have the lowest concentration of artifacts but the highest amount of knapping products associated with novices who are assumed to be subadults (see Chapter 4 for a detailed discussion of why). The results of Olive *et al.*'s (2019) meticulous excavation and analysis beg the question of whether these two features may be best interpreted as the remnants of children's secret spaces. Langley (2020) argues that they do fit the criteria listed above in the following ways. First, both J18 and G13 are located along a stream bank. The steeply sloped hill would have at least partially obscured these locales from the view of adults residing at U5. Second, as mentioned they are the smallest features, reaching a maximum of 16 m^2 each. Third, there are similarities between these two outdoor locales and the larger tents. For example, at U5 and P15 people were careful to knap on one side of the hearth and to prepare meals on the other (Olive *et al.* 2019) and a similar designated use of space is found at J18 and G13 (Langley 2020). In addition, the hearths at J18 and G13 are constructed in a similar fashion to those at U5 and P15 but are smaller in size. Fourth, the small size, low density artifact scatter and limited evidence of hearths suggests these features were ephemeral in nature. Finally, the evidence for child focused material culture is more equivocal. Preservation at the site is such that there is little evidence of organics. At G13, there are three bovine rib fragments and a few remains of reindeer while at J18 there are unidentifiable bone fragments in relation with blades near a hearth (Langley 2020). Olive *et al.* (2019) suggest these are consistent with meal preparation and consumption. What is notable, however, is that the lithic assemblage contains recycled materials, which is often associated with children/novices (see Chapter 4). Children moved well-worked cores and flakes produced at U5 and elsewhere to these spaces to continue knapping them. Furthermore there is an absence of 'high value objects' such as personal ornaments, projectile points, ochre and retouched tools such as burins and scrapers (Olive 1992; Langley 2020).

Small places

In addition to the evidence for possible secret places, we can look for children through the evidence of human activity in places too small to have accommodated adult bodies. According to Bahn (2015), these 'small places' include a 35 cm wide decorated gallery in Fronsac (southwest France), a narrow passageway in La Pasiega that is covered in geometric signs (see Chapter 5), and similarly narrow passageways at Bédeilhac (southern France) and Les Combarelles I (southwest France). However, Bahn (2015, 180) notes, 'the mastery of technique and form displayed in the figures made even in these difficult places strongly suggests that adults were responsible [for their creation]'. At Las Chimeneas in Spain, there is a low ledge under which Paleolithic children drew with their fingers in soft sediment (see more about finger fluting in Chapter 5). I can say from experience that this is not a place that adults can reach easily or comfortably, as such it is not surprising that this locale has only traces of children's activities. Similarly, at Koonalda in Australia, there is a region of this Paleolithic cave known as 'The Squeeze'. As its name suggests, this is a particularly narrow passageway. Given that there is substantial evidence of children's finger flutings in other parts of the cave (Van Gelder 2015c), this locale is the focus of future research.

Footprints

Another way in which we can look at Paleolithic children's use of space is through a study of their footprints (*i.e.* ichnofossils). Not only can they give us a sense of the height, weight and even sex of the track makers but we can often infer behavior as well – how fast someone was walking or running, whether they were carrying something or someone, and whether they were in the company of others. The oldest known hominin footprints are those belonging to *Australopithicus afarensis*. They were uncovered at the famous 3.7 million year old site Laetoli in Tanzania. The footprints were created when a volcanic eruption followed by a rain storm turned their terrain into an ashy mud. Several hominins and a variety of other animals crossed this landscape leaving behind traces of their journey. A second volcanic eruption then buried these prints, preserving them for millions of years. At Laetoli, researchers identified trails belonging to three individuals – G1 (1.10–1.15 m/3.6 to 3.75 feet), G2 (1.52 m/4.98 ft) and G3 (1.32 m/4.33 ft) (White and Suwa 1987). G1 and G2 walked side by side while G3 followed behind walking over and in the footprints of G2. It has been suggested that G3 may have been carrying a child or a foraging load on their hip (Wall-Scheffler *et al.* 2015) because of the uneven weight distribution noted in the footprints.

There are literally thousands of Paleolithic footprints (Lockley *et al.* 2008; Hatala *et al.* 2016; 2020; Duveau *et al.* 2019) but in this chapter I will focus on examples attributable to subadults (Table 3.2). At the 700,000 year old site, Gombore II-2, one of a complex of sites at Melka Kunture in Ethiopia, researchers uncovered 12 footprints belonging to *Homo heidelbergensis* who ranged in age from 12 months to adult (Altamura *et al.* 2018). The tracks are associated with a rich archaeological record of stone tools and faunal remains including butchered hippopotami. A taphonomic study of the site revealed that the prints, tools and butchered remains were produced

Table 3.2. Examples of Paleolithic sites with subadult footprints (modified after Duveau et al. 2019).

Site	Country	Date	Type	Substrate	Species	Description	References
Calvert Island	Canada	13.3–12.6 Ka	Open air	Clay	H. sapiens	29 footprints made by at least three individuals, including one juvenile. Several toe impressions are evident.	McLaren et al. 2018
Chauvet	France	37–28 Ka	Cave	Clay	H. sapiens	A trackway of about 20 footprints attributed to a juvenile.	Bahn and Vertut 1988; Harrington 1999; Garcia 2001; Quilles et al. 2016
Ciampate de Diavolo (Devil's Footprints)	Italy	349 Ka	Open air	Tuff	H. heidelbergensis	Several trackways composed of 81 human traces, mainly footprints. Trackways A, B and C are ascribed to 'adult individuals no taller than 1.56 m'.	Mietto et al. 2003; Panarello 2005; De Angelis 2009; Panarello et al. 2020
Fontanet	France	12 Ka	Cave	Clay	H. sapiens	Several isolated footprints. One footprint was possibly made by a shod foot. Some footprints were interpreted as a child following an animal, possibly a fox or puppy.	Delteil et al. 1971; Clottes and Simonnet 1974; Clottes 1975; Bahn and Vertut 1988
Gombore II-1	Ethiopia	700 Ka	Open air	Sand/silt	H. heidelbergensis	11 footprints made by adults and juveniles, including a trackway of two footprints. Their morphology is consistent with other footprints attributed to the Homo genus.	Altamura et al. 2018
Grotta Della Basura (Basura Cave)	Italy	14 Ka	Cave	Clay	H. sapiens	107 human traces of partial and complete footprints and knee prints. Traces are made by a 3-year-old child, a 6 year old, a pre-adolescent of 8–11 years old, and two adults. These likely represent exploration of the cave by five individuals who were crouched over.	Blanc 1960; Citton et al. 2017; Romano et al. 2019; Avanzini et al. 2020

(Continued)

Table 3.2. (Continued)

Site	Country	Date	Type	Substrate	Species	Description	References
Grotto Tuc d'Audoubert	France	13.9 Ka	Cave	Clay	H. sapiens	Several trackways and isolated footprints, some of which are attributed to juveniles. Toe impressions are still visible.	Begouen and Vallois 1927; Begouen et al. 2009; Pastoors et al. 2015
Jeju Island	South Korea	25–3.7 Ka (?)	Open air	Tuff	H. sapiens	A total of 505 footprints made by adults and juveniles, including at least nine trackways.	Kim et al. 2004; 2009; 2010; Cho et al. 2005; Sohn et al. 2015
Laetoli	Tanzania	3.7 Ma	Open air	Tuff	Au. afarensis	Four trackways and an isolated footprint made by individuals of different stature, including adults and juveniles. The footprints are broad with an abducted hallux. These are the first secure evidence of human bipedalism.	Clarke 1979; Hay 1979; Crompton et al. 2011; Masao et al. 2016
Lascaux	France	17 Ka	Cave	Clay	H. sapiens	Several footprints created by adolescents.	Barriere and Sahly 1964; Bahn 1995;
Le Rozel	France	80 Ka	Open air	Sandy muds	H. neanderthalensis	257 footprints from multiple age classes. Largest known Neanderthal ichnological assemblage. Indicative of Neanderthal social group size (10–30 individuals).	Duveau et al. 2019; Mercier et al. 2019
Monte Verde	Chile	14.6 Ka	Open air	Clay	H. sapiens	Three footprints made by a young individual or an adolescent.	Dillehay 1989; Meltzer 1997; Dillehay et al. 2008
Niaux	France	12.9–12.4 Ka	Cave	Clay	H. sapiens	Around 40 footprints. Some tracks were possibly made during children's game.	Pales and De Saint-Pereuse 1976; Clottes et al. 1992; Valladas et al. 1992

(Continued)

Table 3.2. Examples of Paleolithic sites with subadult footprints. (Continued)

Site	Country	Date	Type	Substrate	Species	Description	References
Pech Merle	France	25–15 Ka	Cave	Clay	H. sapiens	12 footprints made by adults and juveniles. Some associated tracks have been identified as those of a walking stick.	Duday et al. 1983; Pastoors et al. 2015; 2017
Tana della Basura	Italy	12.3 Ka	Cave	Clay	H. sapiens	30+ footprints made by adults and juveniles. These were initially attributed to Neanderthals before new dating associated them with H. sapiens.	Chiapella 1952; Pales 1954; 1960; de Lumley and Vicino 1984; Citton et al. 2017
Theopetra	Greece	130 Ka	Cave	Clay	H. neanderthalensis	Four footprints were made by young individuals (2–4 years old). One footprint is interpreted as made by a shod foot.	Manolis et al. 2000; Valladas et al. 2007
White Sands National Park Locality-3	USA	14.5–10 Ka	Open air	Mud and sand	H. sapiens	Double trackway (bidirectional) of unshod individual, likely an adolescent or small adult female. These are occasionally associated with child tracks (<3 years old). Larger contact area of left foot on the north-bound trip may indicate that the child was carried for a longer duration on that side.	Bennett et al. 2020

over a relatively short period of time and certainly within one season (Altamura *et al.* 2018). The footprints underlie and overlie stone tools suggesting that hominins were standing around or walking short distances within the site. The association of the footprints with butchering and knapping activities demonstrates that children were incorporated into all aspects of daily life from a very young age and that space was made for them to learn skills from others in their community that would have been key to their survival (Altamura *et al.* 2018).

Two hundred and fifty-seven Neandertal footprints were uncovered at Le Rozel, an 80,000-year-old Middle Paleolithic site in Normandy (France) (Duveau *et al.* 2019). Based on individual dimensions, at a minimum the footprints represent 10–13 individuals. The smallest footprints were also the shallowest ones, which makes sense given that, all things being equal, depth is a function of body weight. What this observation highlights is that while subadults were responsible for 90% of the footprints at the site, the youngest children may, in fact, be under-represented in the sample (Duveau *et al.* 2019). Archaeologists recovered Middle Paleolithic stone tools and more than 8000 faunal remains at the site. They also identified hearths and knapping areas. In combination with the footprint data, these finds further demonstrate that space was made for children to participate in and/or observe the making of tools and processing of animals.

The largest collection of Paleolithic footprints in the world was uncovered in the Willandra Lakes Region of Australia. Dating to between 23,000 BP and 17,000 BP, many of these footprints were made by a 4- or 5-year-old child (Franklin and Habgood 2009; Bahn 2015). Two crescent-shaped grooves associated with the footprints were identified by local people as marks children make with their fingers when playing in the mud but it is also possible that these ancient marks were made with a digging stick or stone tool (Franklin and Habgood 2009; Bahn 2015; Nowell 2015b).

The longest and most continuous set of Pleistocene human tracks was uncovered at White Sands National Park in New Mexico (USA). Here, sometime between 13,000 and 11,550 years ago, a woman[5] walked quickly for 1.5 km across a slick, muddy playa before turning around and walking back the way she came (Bennett *et al.* 2020). On the outward journey, the woman was carrying a 2-year-old child that she occasionally set down on the ground in order to take a moment's rest or to shift the child from one hip to the other. Researchers know this because the child's footprints are visible at different points in the journey and the adult's footprints are broader and more varied (*i.e.* 'banana shaped') due to the differential weight distribution of carrying a load on one hip (Bennett *et al.* 2020; Bennett and Reynolds 2020). Two additional observations make this vignette even more compelling. First, both a Giant Sloth and several mammoths (including a large bull) crossed over the human tracks. According to the researchers the sloth was aware of the humans as it appears to have reared up on its hind legs before turning and leaving (Bennett and Reynolds 2020), while the mammoths, by contrast, continued their journey unconcerned. Second, on the return trip, the adult female is alone, no child in her company this time. Her tracks crossover the sloth and mammoth prints (Bennett and Reynolds 2020).

While the preceding examples are in open-air locales, many Paleolithic footprints have been found in caves and the majority of these ones were made by subadults (Bahn 2015). That the prints are primarily known from caves is not surprising for taphonomic reasons but neither is the fact that most of the tracks belong to children and adolescents. Children are natural explorers, often choosing the 'path less travelled', and for that reason their tracks are less likely to be obliterated by subsequent traffic (Garcia 2001). At Chauvet (France), an 8- or 9-year-old boy, 1.3–1.4 m in height (just under 4'6"), left a 50 m trail of footprints. The ceiling in that part of the cave was low and there are torch wipes on it suggesting he carried a torch with him as he made his way through the passage. Bahn (2015) argues that he was likely heading toward a source of water. The young boy may have also left two clay-covered prints of his right hand at the base of a decorated panel (Garcia 2001; Bahn 2015). Researchers think the handprints belong to him as their size is in keeping with the footprints. At Réseau Clastres (France), researchers have documented three trails of children's footprints for a total 500 prints that likely date to the Upper Paleolithic. The youngsters, walking side by side, appear to be around 8 to 10 years old (Bahn 2015). At nearby Niaux, there is a greater evidence of play behavior. Niaux is a vast underground decorated cave with no natural source of light and yet children's footprints are found a kilometer from the entrance near a part of the cave known as the Galerie Profounde. Two children approximately 8 and 11 years in age, weighing between 27 and 30 kg (59–66 lbs) and standing between 1.33 and 1.39 m (again just under 4'6") tall, left behind 24 complete footprints and 15 heal or toe imprints that look fresh even today (Pales 1976; Lockley *et al.* 2008; Bahn 2015). Their tracks show that they visited this low, muddy area at least twice and spent time carefully making perfectly formed footprints (Bahn 2015) (Figs 3.12–3.13).

At Fontanet, in the same region as Réseau Clastres and Niaux, there is further evidence of play. In this cave, researchers identified two trails of footprints – one set made by a child of approximately 5 years old and the other created by a puppy or young fox. It appears that the child, who also left knee prints and handprints, followed along after the animal deep into the cave (Bahn 2015). At Tuc d'Audoubert (France), the footprints of a 4 year old were found in the Galerie des Petits Pieds while in the Salle des Talons researchers uncovered 183 heel prints initially believed to

Figure 3.12: Children of 8 and 11 years of age playfully made footprints in the mud 11,000 to 17,000 years ago in Niaux, a vast underground decorated cave in southern France (Photo: Jean Vertut, P. Bahn Collection).

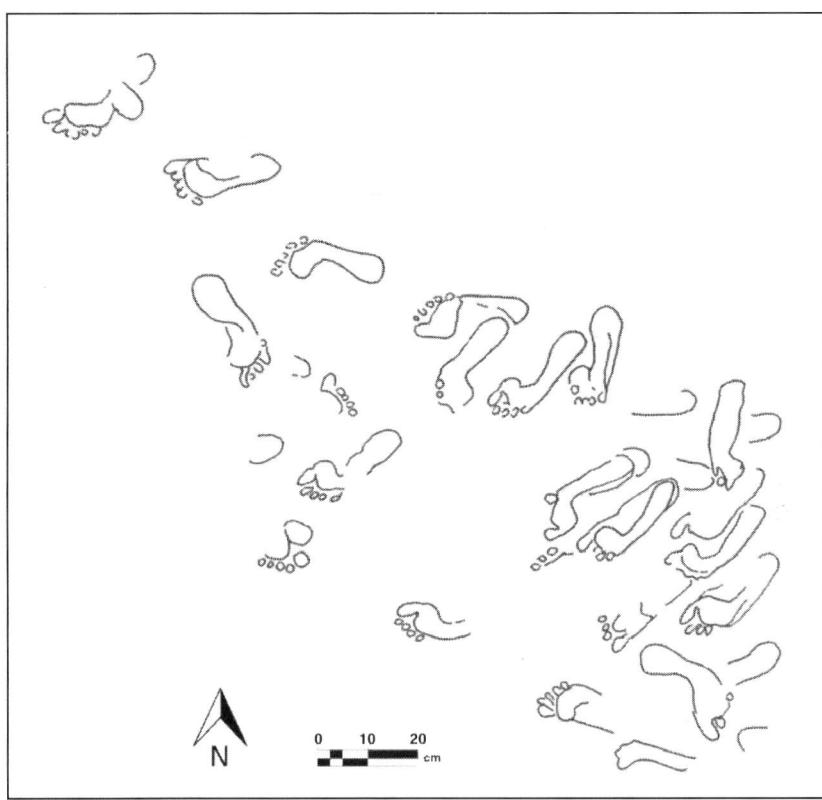

Figure 3.13: Drawing of footprints of children at play at Niaux (France) (Drawing: Jeremy Beller, redrawn after Lockley et al. 2008).

have been created by multiple children and adolescents during a ritual or dance but as discussed in Chapter 5, modern trackers reanalyzed these heel prints and have reinterpreted them as the normal stride of a man and adolescent boy collecting clay from a pit located 15 m away from a pair of beautiful clay bison. The trackers noted that a knowledgeable tracker can recognize an individual from a complete footprint and suggested that the main reason to walk on your heels is to remain anonymous (Pastoors *et al.* 2015).

A final example of Paleolithic subadult footprints in a cave is perhaps one of the best snapshots of Paleolithic family life. At Grotta della Bàsura, a 14,000-year-old cave site in Italy, a group of five individuals made their way through a deep cave. Based on 3D modeling of 180 overlapping footprints, archaeologists have deduced that the group consisted of two adults, one adolescent and two children, aged 6 and 3. To illuminate their way, the group carried with them lit bundles of resin covered pine branches. Sticking close together, the tallest adult led the way while the toddler, on unsteady feet, brought up the rear (Smith 2019). At one point, the passageway narrowed and the ceiling dropped to 80 cm (2.6 ft) in height. According to the archaeologists, the tallest adult paused, rocked back on their heels, perhaps considering the difficulty posed by this change in terrain, before pressing onward (Smith 2019). The group stayed close to the wall. Charcoal covered handprints attest to the adults feeling their way through the narrow passage. Highly detailed knee and tibia prints reveal that this family was lean and athletic. The family was barefoot and wore no clothing on their arms or legs (Romano *et al.* 2019). These prints along with digit and handprints on the floor are the first evidence of sustained crawling – it is not that it is a surprise that early modern humans could crawl, of course – but rather that this is unique evidence of that type of locomotion. Once they were able to stand again they were forced to wade through a pond leaving deep, muddy prints as they went. Finally, they reached a large inner chamber. The adults left handprints on the ceiling while the children playfully covered stalagmites with wet clay and then drew curving lines in it with their fingers. The drawings are at three different heights, corresponding to the ages of the three different children. On the return trip, the group understandably chose an upper chamber that was drier and with higher ceilings than the route they followed into the cave. Canid tracks suggest they may have had a dog in their company as they explored the cave (Romano *et al.* 2019) (see more about dogs in Chapter 6).

Handprints and hand stencils

Another way in which Paleolithic children quite literally made their mark was by leaving traces of their hands on cave walls. These traces include handprints (a positive impression of the hand), hand stencils (a negative impression of the hand), and finger flutings (tracings made with fingers in soft sediment on caves walls and ceilings – discussed in detail in Chapter 5). Handprints are made by pressing a paint covered hand directly onto a surface while hand stencils were made by blowing pigment around the hand using a tube or one's mouth. While there are hundreds of subadult handprints and stencils at cave sites and rock shelters in Europe and Australia dating to the Paleolithic, including a possible gloved hand at Altamira in Spain (Freeman *et al.* 1987) (Table 3.3), I will briefly consider examples from two French sites – Cosquer Cave and Gargas Cave. Chapter 5 considers different methods for sexing and aging these markings.

Cosquer Cave, located near Marseilles in France, was discovered by Henry Cosquer, a professional diver, in 1991 as he was in the process of guiding a tour. The entrance to this cave is 37 m (121 ft) below the Mediterranean Sea. Because sea levels were at least 100 m (300 ft) lower during the Late Pleistocene than they are today, the cave would have been dry when it was in use. There are more than 100 images dating to around 18,500 BP of animals including horses, bison and ibex as well as unique examples of possible jelly fish and an extinct flightless seabird knows as the Great Auk. Hand stencils, dating to 27,000 BP, are found on the cave's walls and on stalactites with some of the stencils decorated with black or red dots (Clottes 2010). At this site,

Table 3.3. Examples of Paleolithic sites with handprints, hand stencils and finger flutings of subadults.

Site	Country	Date	Site Type	Substrate	Species	Art type	Description	References
El Castillo	Spain	40.8 Ka	Cave	Clay	H. sapiens	Finger fluting	Several long multi-fingered streams, smaller flutings attributed to children.	Freeman 2009; Pike et al. 2012; Van Gelder 2015
Altamira	Spain	35–15 Ka	Cave		H. sapiens	Handprints	Black handprint, possibly gloved, attributed to a child.	Roveland 2000; Garcia-Diez et al. 2013; Handpas Project
Grotte Cosquer	France	27 Ka	Cave		H. sapiens	Handprints	Handprints attributed to very young children.	Clottes 2010
Grotte de Gargas	France	27 Ka	Cave	Clay	H. sapiens	Finger fluting	Made by seven individuals, of which three are children, one of which is male. The smaller children were held up to make some flutings.	Barriere 1982; Clottes et al. 1992; Van Gelder and Sharpe 2009; Van Gelder 2015; Nowell and Van Gelder 2020
						Handprints	250+ hand stencils. Many are attributed to adolescents and children, likely under 7 years old.	Barriere 1975; 1982; Leroi-Gourhan and Michelson 1986; Groenen 1988; Clottes et al. 1992
Grotto de Rouffignac	France	27–13 Ka	Cave		H. sapiens	Finger fluting	500 square meters of finger fluting made by eight individuals. Three individuals were children and a fourth was a female youth. One of the children was 2–3 years of age.	Plassard 1999; Van Gelder and Sharpe 2009; Van Gelder 2015
Pech Merle	France	25–15 Ka	Cave		H. sapiens	Finger fluting	Finger drawings attributed to adolescents or small females. Located on panel C on the ceiling.	Pastoors et al. 2017

(Continued)

Table 3.3. Examples of Paleolithic sites with handprints, hand stencils and finger flutings of subadults. (Continued)

Site	Country	Date	Site Type	Substrate	Species	Art type	Description	References
Fuente del Trucho	Spain	25 Ka	Cave		H. sapiens	Handprints	Three black hand stencils with small dimensions have been attributed to children.	Utrilla et al. 2012; Handpas Project
La Lastrilla	Spain	Gravettian	Cave		H. sapiens	Handprints	At least one red positive hand attributed to a juvenile.	Handpas Project
Fuente del Salín	Spain	22 Ka	Cave		H. sapiens	Handprints	Black hand stencil attributed to a child. Note that this is one of the only known black hand stencils on the Cantabrian Coast. Other red stencils attributed to children and adults.	Clottes 2010; Utrilla et al. 2012
Gorham's Cave	Gibraltar	21–20 Ka	Cave		H. sapiens	Handprints	Black hand stencil found in a rock hollow. Due to the small size of the wrist it is believed to have been most likely made by a child or youth.	Simón-Vallejo et al. 2018
Las Chimeneas	Spain	18–12 Ka	Cave		H. sapiens	Finger fluting	Found on wall faces and made by children under 7 years old and by one youth.	Moure et al. 1996; Van Gelder 2015
Bédeilhac	France	14 Ka	Cave		H. sapiens	Handprints	Presence of handprints attributed to infants.	Clottes 1997; Van Gelder 2015
Fontanet	France	12 Ka	Cave		H. sapiens	Handprints	Handprint attributed to a 5-year-old child.	Clottes 1997; Van Gelder 2015

a small child, either lifted up or sitting on an adult's shoulders, pressed their hand in the soft surface of the cave wall 2.2 m (7 ft) above the floor (Clottes *et al.* 2005). According to Bahn (2015, 179), 'there is another one nearby, 2.4 m [7.9 feet] up, with an engraving of a possible sea animal between them'.

The hand stencils at Gargas, a cave site located in Aventignan in the Hautes-Pyrénées (France) are similar in age to those at Cosquer. What is unique, however, is that of the 124 best preserved stencils of adults, adolescents, younger children and babies, only 10 are whole (Bahn 2016) – the others have been described as 'mutilated'. The mutilated stencils are all missing at least one finger and 30% are missing at least two. It is not clear whether the fingers were purposefully bent to create stencils of hands that are communicating a message using a form of sign language. It is also possible that the fingers are missing due to frostbite[6] or disease, or were intentionally mutilated (Bahn 2016 and references therein). At Gargas, there is an infant's hand that was stenciled by an adult, we know this because the adult's wrist is partially visible (see Chapter 5). There is also an infant's hand stenciled in black but the fingers are blurred (could the child have been moving their hand impatiently during the process?). Other markings include two complete stencils in black of infant hands, two identical child's hands stenciled in red, a child's hand stenciled in black in a niche approximately 5 m (16.4 ft) above the floor and possibly one handprint in clay, belonging to a boy of 10 or 11 years of age or girl of 12 to 13 years of age, where the fifth digit ('little finger') is missing (Bahn 2015).

In this chapter I explored ways in which we can see Paleolithic children through a study of toys, visual imagery and burials. I also considered their use of space and 'place making' through the establishment of possible 'club houses' away from the adult gaze and the exploration of caves with family or friends. These data provide snapshots of children adventuring, playing, making stone tools and art and processing food. It is clear that space was made for children to learn about and participate in all aspects of community life. Furthermore, the subadult burial data speak to the depth of emotion members of their community felt at their passing and provide a window onto how subadults were seen and valued in their societies (Nowell 2020).

Notes

1. The Museum of Play can be found at https://www.museumofplay.org/.
2. See Bandi 1988 for an alternative explanation.
3. While not all of the child's skeleton was found, the bones that were uncovered were mostly intact (Balzeau *et al.* 2020).
4. Examples of third-degree relatives are great-grandparents, great-grandchildren, great aunts and uncles, grandnieces and nephews and cousins.
5. Because of the overlap in size, it is also possible that the footprints represent an adolescent male.
6. Similarly, there are small 'mutilated' hand stencils found at the Upper Paleolithic site Fuente del Trucho (Spain) belonging to children around 4 years of age. Utrilla (2021; see also Utrilla and Bea 2015) argues that these little ones may have 'lost some of their fingers due to frostbite when passing [through] the glaciated mountain passes of the Pyrenees'.

Chapter 4

Stone tools, skill acquisition and learning a craft

> Children's activities have been seen by ethnographers as economically inconsequential. It is increasingly clear that this assumption is wrong, and that children's activities are often of vital consequence to their parents' and siblings' reproductive success.
>
> (Shea 2006, 213)

In Chapter 1, I made a distinction between biological, chronological and social age. Social age reflects the categories that cultures use to mark continuities and discontinuities in the life course (Séguy and Buchet 2013). In non-industrial societies, social age is often defined based on the development of certain skills or the acquisition of sacred knowledge. For example, an adolescent may be considered an adult only once they have shown that they can contribute to the hunt or perform certain rituals expertly. In this chapter, I will explore what we know about skill acquisition and craft learning by subadults in the Paleolithic with regards to flintknapping. I will begin by discussing why stone is a particularly good medium for studying skill acquisition. Then I will evaluate how we can identify subadults as novices in the archaeological record. Finally, the social and cognitive contexts of learning to knap will be presented. In Chapter 5, I will consider ceramics, textile production and image making in the Upper Paleolithic. The evidence presented in this and the subsequent chapter supports the assertion that Paleolithic children's participation in craft production was key to the economic and social wellbeing of their communities.

Stone tools as a vehicle for studying Paleolithic subadults

It is no surprise that stone tools are ubiquitous at Paleolithic sites. They are, of course, the material that defines this time period. They also happen to be an excellent way of tracking novices in the archaeological record. As Shea (2006, 212) observes, 'by the time they achieved competence, every flintknapper who ever lived had probably already littered the landscape with thousands of virtually indestructible stone artifacts'. The oldest stone tools date to approximately 3.4 million years ago (Harmand *et al.* 2015) and from this perspective, the likely contribution of children to the totality of the archaeological record is staggering (Bamforth and Finlay 2008; Högberg 2018). Because most knappers learn through trial and error (see below), novices produce copious amounts of lithic debitage that may overwhelm the archaeological signatures of adult expert knappers (Shea 2006).

There are a number of properties of stone that make it ideal for tracking novices. First, stone is an abundant natural resource and it is often easy to obtain. Second, it is durable and for the most part easy to work. Finally, unlike ceramics and metallurgy, stone tool making is a subtractive technology (*i.e.* you take away material to form the tool) and thus, in a sense, each stone tool is a fossilized record of the decision making and learning processes that were followed to produce it (Grimm 2000; Bamforth and Finlay 2008; Ferguson 2008). With ceramics, you can fix (and thus erase) a mistake before firing an object or in the case of metallurgy you can recast the metal and start again but stone tools perforce carry their life history with them (see van der Leeuw 2000 for a discussion of the difference between making tools from stone and other materials). In this chapter, I look at how that unique characteristic allows archaeologists to ask questions about apprenticeship, learning through play, embodied cognition, acculturation, skill acquisition and the social context within which learning takes place (Bamforth and Finlay 2008; Högberg 2008; Hildebrand 2012).

How to make a stone tool

As we will see below, one way to identify children in the Paleolithic record is to recognize errors that are typical of a novice knapper. In order to understand why these knapping behaviors are errors we have to review the fundamentals of stone tool making.[1] At its most basic, the making of a stone tool requires parent material (a core) such as flint, obsidian or quartzite and a hard or soft hammer percussor such as a rounded cobble or antler, respectively (Fig. 4.1). Flakes can be removed through direct percussion, indirect percussion or pressure flaking. With direct percussion, the core is normally held in one hand and the percussor is struck against the core with a glancing blow to remove a flake or blade (a blade is a flake that is at least twice as long as it is wide). The force used to remove the flake travels from the percussor into the core until it terminates at an edge, detaching the flake. The core then preserves a negative flake scar of that removal. With indirect percussion, a punch, *i.e.*, another stone or an antler, is used as an intermediary between the percussor and the core. This is useful in situations where you want to concentrate the force of the blow in a specific location. Finally, pressure flaking involves direct contact between the indentor[2] (usually an antler tine or a sharpened bone) and the core but instead of a glancing blow, the knapper applies pressure inwards, then downward, to detach the flake. This technique gives you the most control over a flake removal but isn't appropriate for all types of tool making strategies.

Archaeologists distinguish stone tools from natural stone based on the existence of characteristic landmarks on flakes and cores. Landmarks on flakes (Fig. 4.2) include the striking platform (a natural or prepared surface at the proximal end of the flake), a point of percussion on the striking platform which is specifically where the core was struck, and a bulb of percussion on its ventral or interior surface as a result of the force travelling through it. Sometimes ripples can be seen on the interior surface, particularly in fine grained materials like obsidian. These radiating waves are a deformation of the

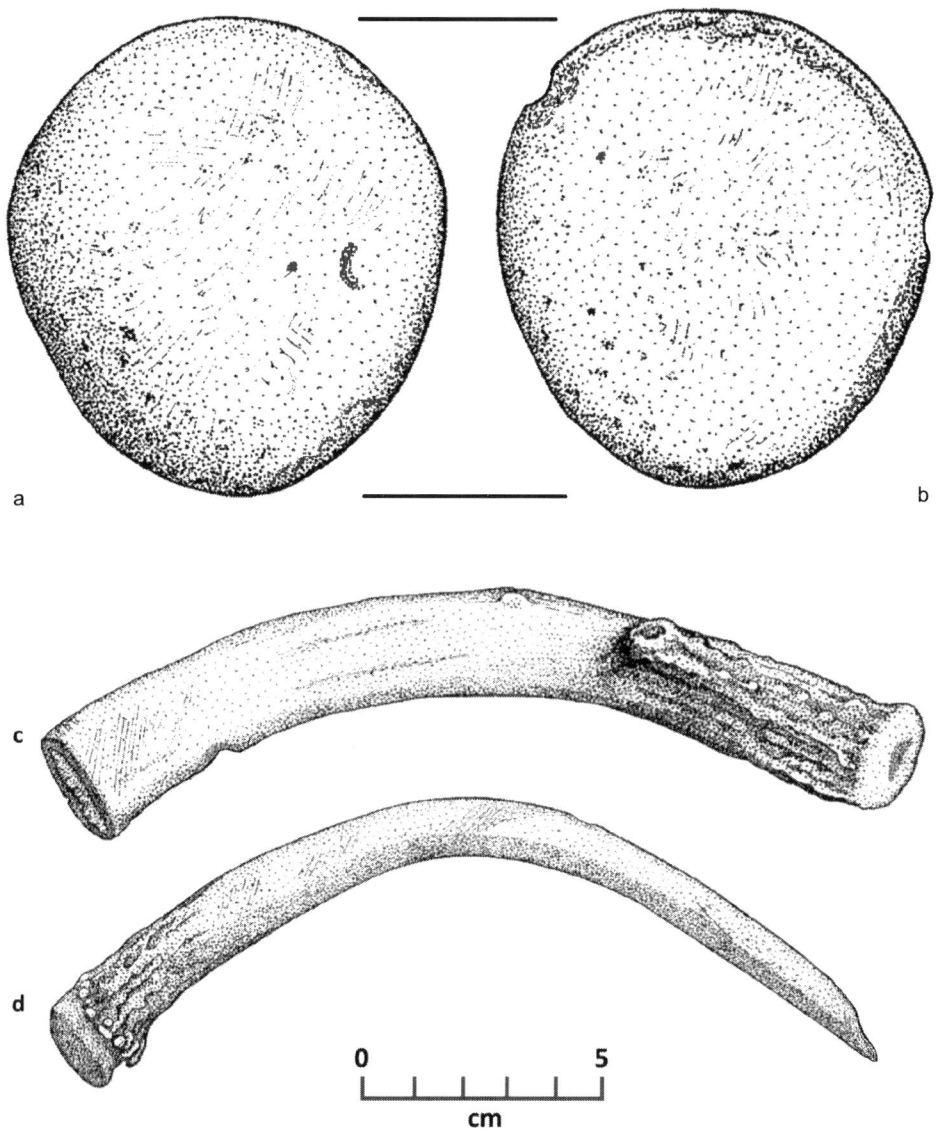

Figure 4.1: Percussors used in flintknapping include (a–b) a hammerstone, (c) an antler for soft hammer percussion, and (d) an antler tine for pressure flaking (Drawing: Jeremy Beller, after Andrefsky 2005).

rock as the force moves through the material. Sometimes hackle lines or radial striations are apparent as well. Hackle lines are microfractures in material that can occur when extreme force is used (Tsirk 2014). On a flake's dorsal or exterior surface (*i.e.* what used to be the outer surface of the core) there may be old flake scars attesting to previous

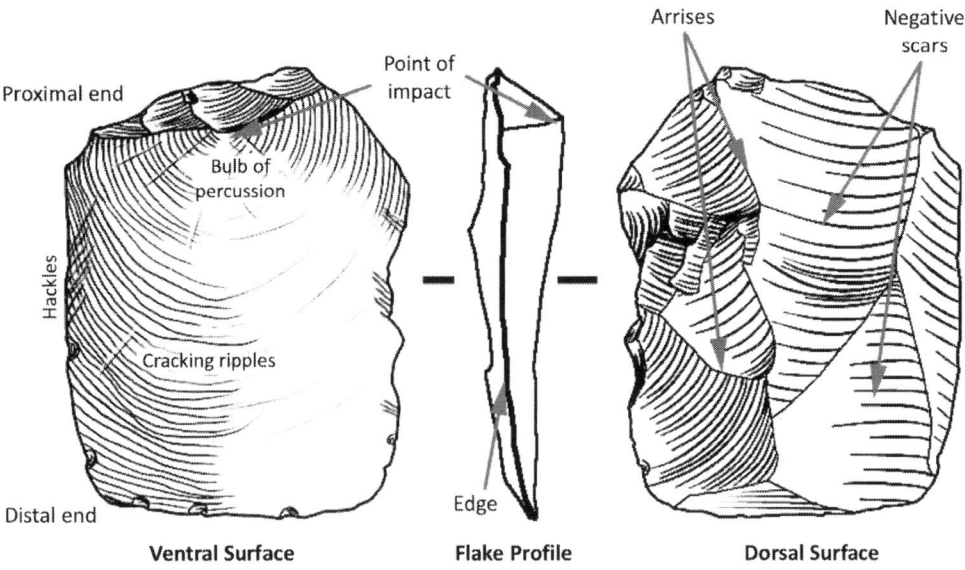

Figure 4.2: Landmarks on flakes (Drawing: Jeremy Beller after José-Manuel Benito Álvarez, CC BY-SA 2.5, https://commons.wikimedia.org/w/index.php?curid=827254).

flake removals as well as remnants of cortex (the weathered outer surface of the stone). Archaeologists distinguish between primary, secondary and tertiary flakes based on the amount of cortex apparent on the exterior surface. Primary flakes are fully cortical, secondary flakes preserve some cortex, and tertiary flakes have no cortex at all. All things being equal, primary flakes are removed before secondary and tertiary flakes, and archaeologists can use this information when reconstructing reduction sequences (see refitting and the chaîne opératoire approach below).

The key to removing a flake successfully is to apply just the right amount of force with a glancing blow to the edge of the core. The flake that is detached can have one of several types of terminations or distal end shapes (Fig. 4.3) (Debénath and Dibble 1993; Andrefsky 2005). Flake terminations are described as feathered, hinged, stepped or plunging (the latter is sometimes referred to as overshot or outrepassé). Normally, when a knapper strikes a core the force travels through the material, gradually exiting it. The result is a sharp, feathered edge flake. When too little force is applied relative to the platform angle and shape of the core mass, the propagating flake loses energy and stalls. This results in a step or plunging termination. Step terminations result when a flake prematurely breaks or snaps during removal, leaving a distal end that is often squared off. Plunging flakes are the result of the force moving back towards the core (Andrefsky 2005). This can result in the partial removal of the core's distal or opposite edge. When too much force is applied relative to the mass of the flake that you are trying to remove then a hinged termination is produced. This phenomenon

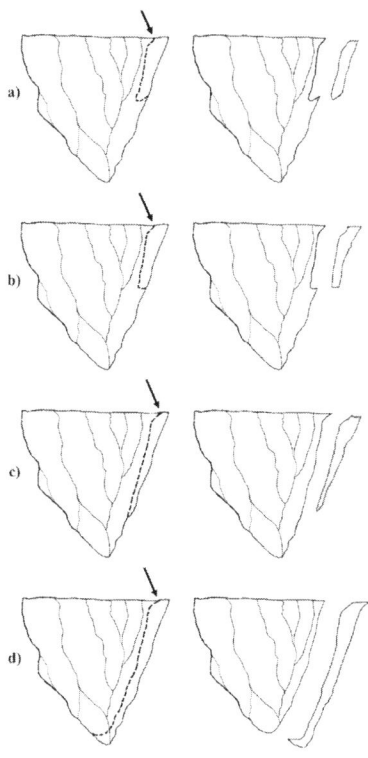

Figure 4.3: Profile of a core showing different types of flake terminations: (a) feathered; (b) hinge; (c) step; and (d) plunging (Drawing: Jeremy Beller, redrawn after Andrefsky 2005).

is a result of the force moving away from the core, resulting in a rounded distal end (Andrefsky 2005). Hinge, step and plunging terminations are called abrupt terminations. Abrupt terminations are sometimes deliberately controlled by the most skilled knappers but are normally considered to be errors. Abrupt terminations can also be the product of an internal flaw in the material but normally are a reflection of the skill of the knapper.

Unmodified flakes and blades can be used for a variety of tasks or they can be retouched (*e.g.* edges sharpened or blunted using a percussor) into desired shapes and used as they are or hafted onto wooden or bone shafts to create composite tools such as spears.

Ways to 'see' novices through stone tools in the archaeological record

What is a 'novice'? A novice is often defined as someone who is new or inexperienced in a field or situation.[3] The term novice does not necessarily denote a non-adult but in a culture where stone tools are key to survival, it is likely that most, and probably all, people learned to knap as children (Grimm 2000; Petraglia *et al.* 2005; Shea 2006; Lancy 2017; Shipton and Nielson 2018). Archaeologists study novice flintknappers primarily through three means: (1) replications studies, (2) refitting studies and the chaîne opératoire approach, and (3) ethnoarchaeology. I will consider each of these in turn before looking at the archaeological signatures of novices.

Replication studies

For more than a century, professional archaeologists and other experts in traditional technologies have engaged in experimental replication of stone tools. Pioneering knappers include people like Bruce Bradley, Errett Callahan, Don Crabtree, Jacques Pelegrin and Gene Titmus. The work of these and other experimental knappers has provided 'a sophisticated and detailed body of knowledge that helps us to make sense out of data provided by the archaeological record' (Bamforth and Finlay 2008, 3). In other words, because of their experimental research, we know what mistakes look like and we know what it looks like when knappers tried to work around or correct mistakes. We also know what *kinds* of mistakes are characteristic of learners versus experts. My friend and colleague, Dan Stueber, is an excellent flintknapper. When we work together on 300,000-year-old stone tools from Jordan (Nowell *et al.* 2016), he will sometimes stare at a tool for a minute and then start laughing or shaking his head because he can see that the knapper made an error in the final steps of manufacturing this tool. He can easily imagine their frustration and chagrin because he has been there. In effect, through his years of practice, he has learned to 'read' a tool in this way. Common errors made by novices include stacked step scars, hinge terminations, multiple hammer marks on core faces (*i.e.* 'face battering'), wasteful or ineffectual use of raw material and irregular products (Shelley 1990; Bamforth and Finlay 2008; Takakura 2013). Stacked step scars result when a knapper removes a series of flakes in roughly the same area of the core that all terminate in hinge or step terminations (Shelley 1990, 188). Face battering refers to the fact that to remove a flake from a core you normally look for an acute angle, and with a hammerstone, apply just the right amount of force there. Novices will sometimes strike too far in on a core or misjudge the amount of force needed and then keep hitting the core until a flake is dislodged or they give up. I remember seeing several cores like this at the Middle Paleolithic site of Combe-Capelle in southwest France. Johansen and Stapert (2008) have made similar observations of core battering at Maastricht-Belvédère, a Middle Paleolithic site in the Netherlands.

Refitting studies and the chaîne opératoire approach

The second way in which archaeologists study and document novices is through refitting studies. Refitting involves taking all of the debitage (flaking debris) and usable products (flakes, blades, retouched pieces, etc.) produced during the process of making stone tools and fitting them back together onto the core or parent material. Essentially, it is a reverse engineering of Paleolithic technologies. The process is time consuming and resembles working on a 3D puzzle with more than half of the pieces missing as archaeologists have yet to devise a satisfactory method of automating this process (but see López-Ortega *et al.* 2020 for a promising approach). Despite the time investment, refitting, when possible, helps us to understand the decision making process of ancient knappers in the most direct way possible – we can see the order in which decisions were made and actions taken. The underlying assumption of refitting studies is that we are seeing the product of one person's work and therefore this method is one way of seeing the individual in the remote past (Grimm 2000).

French archaeologists developed a robust body of theory around refitting studies known as chaîne opératoire (*e.g.* Boëda *et al.* 1990; see also Schlanger 1994; Kerry and Henry 2000; Finlay 2015). A chaîne opératoire is the 'operational sequence' or sequence of decisions made by a flintknapper from the initial procurement of raw material to the production and (re)use of a stone tool to its eventual discard. In North America, it is sometimes referred to as 'reduction sequence analysis'. Initially developed within Paleolithic archaeology, the chaîne opératoire approach is now routinely applied to lithics of more recent time periods and has been extended to the analysis of other sorts of artifacts, including Paleolithic figurines (Farbstein 2010; 2011a; 2011b).

In addition to addressing decision making, refitting can also be used to trace the movement of individuals within and between sites. Furthermore, refitting can offer clues to a site's taphonomy as refits between lithics (or other artifact types) uncovered at significantly different vertical depths within a site may be an indication that a site has been disturbed by water, rodents or other processes (*e.g.* Dibble *et al.* 1997).

Pincevent, a 12,000-year-old Magdalenian site in north-central France, is a great example of the usefulness of refitting studies. At this site, archaeologists documented three levels of knapping skill from novice to expert (Bodu *et al.* 1990; see also Shea 2006). Ten hearths of different shapes and sizes were located across a 500 m^2 area of the site. Approximately 3000 stone tools were found in association with these hearths. Most of these artifacts were classified as chipping debris while usable tools made up about 15% of the lithic assemblage. Archaeologists also uncovered 20 cores. Bodu *et al.* (1990) painstakingly refit the lithic assemblage together and drew on the chaîne opératoire approach to identify different individual knappers. For example, one knapper, who was very skilled and, therefore, presumed to be an adult, made highly standardized prismatic blades. These blades were widely distributed for use throughout the site – in fact, only 10 of the 50 blades and bladelets this individual crafted were found where they were knapped. Most of the others were brought to hearths 10 to 30 m away while some were taken from the camp, possibly on hunting trips because they were so well made (these are sometimes referred to as 'ghost artifacts' after Morrow 1996). Based on refitting studies, Bodu *et al.* (1990) was also able to trace the movement of other materials (and thus people) between hearths and to identify varying skill levels of average and novice knappers whom he identified as adults and children, respectively.

A similar study was conducted at Hattoridai 2, an Upper Paleolithic site in Japan. Here archaeologists were able to refit four contemporary sets of lithic assemblages. Two sets (No. 130 and 153) were knapped by highly skilled knappers while two other sets (No. 128 and 203) were made by novice knappers. Takakura (2013) noted that the cores produced by novices were less prepared; their flaking products exhibited hinge or step terminations and strongly marked bulbs of percussion; and the reduction sequence that they followed was unsystematic, minimally productive and resulted in irregularly shaped blades. Whereas the tools knapped by the expert knappers were missing and likely transported away for use, all of the novice knappers' artifacts were found where they had been knapped.

Ethnoarchaeology

Finally, the third method for studying novice flintknappers is ethnoarchaeology. Ethnoarchaeology is the study of living cultures through the eyes of an archaeologist. Traditionally, these studies have focused on technology, decision making and the archaeological signatures certain behaviors might leave behind and by extension what behaviors leave no traces in the archaeological record (*e.g.* Binford 1978; 1980). Dietrich Stout (2002) spent time with adze makers in the village of Langda in Indonesian Irian Jaya to learn about apprenticeship, social scaffolding (see below), technological strategies and the perceptual-motor and cognitive skills associated with adze making in this community. While modern hunter-gatherers are in no way 'living fossils' or direct analogues for prehistoric peoples, for those archaeologists who did not grow up in these sorts of economies and have never been reliant on stone tools for survival, working and studying with these communities of people can provide archaeologists with a great deal of insight about the archaeological record.

Archaeological signatures of novices

Through replication studies, refitting and ethnoarchaeology, archaeologists have identified a variety of archaeological signatures of novice flintknappers. I will briefly consider seven of them here – errors, non-productivity and morphological variability, location, quality of raw material, recycled materials, knapping strategies and size.

Errors

Novices tend to make errors in both the conception and execution of making a tool because they have limited knowledge of the basic principles of flintknapping (Grimm 2000). In studying novice knappers, Grimm (2000) observed that the reduction strategies they follow are often incomplete as novices tend not to think through fully or plan out what they are going to do in advance. In other words, they often forget to keep an eye on the 'bigger picture' and fail to worry about overall core maintenance and organization (Grimm 2000; Sternke and Sørensen 2009). Flake removals often end prematurely in hinge or step fractures rather than in sharp-edged feather terminations because novices apply too much force. Other times, they hesitate and do not apply enough force (Grimm 2000). Often bulbs of percussion are more strongly marked, and flakes carry thick remnants of striking platforms. Both of these variables suggest a novice is using hard hammer percussion and applying excessive force (see also Shelley 1990; Takakura 2013; Lancy 2017). When it comes to making blades, novices often are unsuccessful in maintaining either the proper platform angle or they fail to differentiate the striking platform and the blade production face (Grimm 2000). Flakes knapped by novices tend to be less standardized (Sternke and Sørensen 2009). Finally, a further indicator of a novice is the premature abandonment of a core (Grimm 2000), which can happen when novices encounter a problem that only a more expert knapper can work around. Unable to solve the problem, they eventually give up and abandon the core.

At Solvieux, a large Upper Paleolithic open-air site in southwest France, Grimm (2000) encountered many of these types of errors in her analysis of 27 lithics found across three locations at the site. For example, she observed that a novice used excessive force to remove flakes as evidenced by pronounced bulbs of percussion. She also noted invasive thick and broad flake removals, and that the flakes carried remnants of the striking platform and ended in hinge terminations. Furthermore, these lithics were made using poorer quality flint compared to other lithics on the site suggesting these tools were being knapped for practice (see below).

Through practice, novices begin to make fewer of these kinds of errors as they develop the appropriate muscle memory and their hand-eye coordination and overall strength[4] improve (Bamforth and Finlay 2008). And, of course, not all mistakes are the result of the novices at work as even experts can have a bad day (Bamforth and Finlay 2008; Högberg 2018). However, experts don't tend to make the same kinds of mistakes that novices make. In this regard, Lohse (2011) makes a distinction between 'savoire-faire' (know how) and 'performance'. Savoire-faire is all of the conceptual knowledge that is required to make a stone tool – understanding the properties of your materials and the goals and the processes of tool making – while performance is defined as the ability to *consistently* execute these processes. When experts make mistakes, they tend to make errors of performance, not errors of savoire-faire.

Non-productivity and morphological variability

In addition to these typical mistakes, Grimm (2000) argues that novices create products that are not useful even with subsequent modification. For this reason, novice lithics will normally be found near where knapping took place in contrast to the products of expert knappers that are more widely distributed throughout a site. Shelley (1990; see also Karlin and Julien 1994; Högberg 2008; Takakura 2013) makes a similar point when he argues that novices knap for practice, *i.e.*, that there is no intention to ever use this material. To my mind, virtually any lithic artifact with a sharp edge can be used for a variety of tasks so the idea that these products are never used is likely incorrect. At the same time, Shea (2006) notes that his novice flintknapping students produced highly variable by-products that differed significantly from those produced by expert knappers. In fact, he observed that many of these artifacts had no archaeological analogue. So while I believe that novices' knapping products were used on occasion, particularly for their own purposes, the supposition that on the whole novice knapping products will be found close to where they were made seems well founded. As Högberg (2008) notes, we are looking primarily at episodes of practice rather than tool production. The novice assemblages from Hattoridai 2 are a prime example of this behavior (Takakura 2013).

Location

Building on these observations, location within a site can often be a clue to who is knapping. Sometimes the products of novices will be found on the periphery of adult knapping spaces and hearths (Grimm 2000) while at other times novices seem to work where they can observe and perhaps receive help from expert knappers. What is most remarkable about Grimm's (2000) study at Solvieux, is that she was able to track a novice's movements across the site. First, the novice picked up a core that had been previously tested and abandoned by a more expert knapper (Grimm 2000).

Then the novice began knapping flakes on the periphery of the site's main activity area, but subsequently seems to have encountered some difficulty and decided to bring the core to a more expert knapper for help. The expert knapper corrected the stacked step terminations (Grimm 2000). After that, the novice continued knapping in this central area until the core was eventually exhausted and discarded. The chipping debris of both the novice and the expert are found together in this second location. This fine, detailed spatial and technological analysis allows the archaeologist to reconstruct the relationship between two people thousands of years ago. This is what Leslie Van Gelder (2015a) has called an 'archaeology of intimacy' (see also Nowell and Van Gelder 2020).

Similarly, at Étiolles, a 14,000-year-old Magdalenian site in northern France, meticulous refitting work and a detailed study of the spatial distribution of knapping debris (Pigeot 1990; Karlin and Julien 1994; Högberg 2018) revealed that expert knappers worked in the center of the site closest to the hearth (perhaps for better light if knapping was taking place in the evening) while less productive knappers were situated further away. The least experienced knappers, likely the youngest children, were located on the periphery where they could practice knapping and play without being in the way of the adolescents and adults (Pigeot 1990; Lancy 2017). By contrast, a more intimate space was created for children at the Upper Paleolithic site of Oldeholtwode in the Netherlands where novices were seated much closer to the hearth while more experienced knappers took a back seat (Johansen and Stapert 2004; 2008). At Hattoridai, novices and experts worked in spatially distinct locales that were in close enough proximity for each to observe the work of the other (Takakura 2013). On a regional level, novices may be more likely to be found at residential sites such as caves and rock shelters where they can knap safely (Shea 2006) or at quarry sites where raw material is abundant (Bamforth and Finlay 2008; Ferguson 2008; Jalbert 2011).

Quality of raw material

If high quality raw material is abundant (*i.e.* material that is the right size and shape, easy to knap, fractures in a predictable way, free of inclusions, etc.), there may be no difference in the type of raw material used by novices and experts (Takakura 2013). However, in places where high quality raw material is more limited, novices may be relegated to using lower quality materials (Pigeot 1990; Shelly 1990; Högberg 1999; Grimm 2000; Shea 2006; Ferguson 2008; Hildebrand 2012). As Shea (2006, 214) argues, '[o]ne might reasonably expect adults would take measures to keep high quality raw materials procured from great distances, or ones that are available locally but scarce, out of children's hands'. As noted above, knapping is a reductive technology and for the most part errors cannot be fixed the way they can be when working with other kinds of materials. For this reason, available quantities of lithic material may also impact the degree to which novices are permitted to experiment and explore the properties of various raw materials (Ferguson 2008). In this situation, there may be a greater dependence on scaffolding as a learning and teaching strategy (see below). Similarly, it was noted above that a common mistake made by novices is using a hammerstone to apply too much force – essentially bashing your way through the core to produce a flake. Johansen and Stapert (2008; see also Pigeot 1990) have observed this phenomenon on lithics from their study sites, prompting them to suggest that children were not allowed to use antler as a percussor because it might have been a material that was in more limited supply than hammerstones.

Recycled materials

Recycling of materials is a common way of identifying the work of novice flintknappers in the archaeological record (Olive 1988; Ferguson 2008; Johansen and Stapert 2008). Particularly in times and places of raw material scarcity, novices may have been encouraged to use discarded cores and knapping by-products to practice on. For example, novice knappers at Étiolles almost exclusively practiced on recycled cores (Olive 1988; Pigeot 1990; Johansen and Stapert 2008; Högberg 2018; Olive *et al.* 2019). It was also a common practice at Oldeholtwolde (Johansen and Stapert 2008). Similarly, at Pincevent, Bodu *et al.* (1990) documented examples of cores being picked up, transported around the site and reworked, often by less experienced knappers. Differences in patina (chemical weathering) and in skill level are indicators of the recycling of materials.

Knapping strategies

Most often the errors we attribute to novices are ones that are made in the process of following standardized knapping strategies. However, another archaeological signature of novices can be a deviation from these standard strategies, for example, when a young knapper tries to imitate the final product (say an axe or projectile point) without the conceptual knowledge (or savoire-faire) of how to get there (see, for example, Högberg 2008 discussed below). Other times, a simpler knapping strategy is employed. At Maastricht-Belvédère, the Middle Paleolithic site in the Netherlands mentioned above, cores displaying typical novice errors such as stacked steps and face battering, were reduced following a simple discoidal strategy rather than the more complex Levallois method (Stapert 2007b). Taken together, the errors and the simpler knapping strategy suggest that the cores were the product of someone with only basic knapping skills.

Size

Another indicator that stone tools may be the product of children and juveniles, or that the tools were made for them by an adult is size, but this variable needs to be approached with caution. Small tool (microlithic) assemblages are not uncommon in the Middle Stone Age of Africa and throughout the Paleolithic and Mesolithic periods in Europe. There are a variety of possible explanations for them including raw material availability (in times or places of scarcity you will likely use and rework tools until they are no longer viable), ease of transport, and size of the raw material from which the tool was made. Function is another explanation for small size. For example, microblades can be hafted into wooden handles to create highly effective composite tools. Furthermore, depending on their absolute size, small tools can easily be used in the hand with a firm grip on the tool using the index finger, or both the index and middle fingers, and the thumb. Small tools may also have been selected for their suitability for precise work as many tasks require small tools, particularly when working on smaller materials.

For these reasons, Shea (2006) suggests that archaeologists need to look at microlithication that is not correlated with raw material scarcity, increased mobility or task related needs. In other words, if there is no 'obvious' reason for the existence of small tools then their existence may be an archaeological signature of novices and/or children more broadly. This is particularly true if we return to the importance of play (Chapter 3). Lillehammer (1989, 95) writes, 'child's play functions as a mediator between the child's world and the adult world. Children imitate the adult world by playing biological and social roles which often reflect and adapt roles which adults have in the community … The child's play is not a question of leisure and spare time away from a daily routine; it is an expression of the child's labouring to grow up'. In Park's (2005) study of contemporary and prehistoric Inuit artifacts, discussed in Chapter 1, many of the artifacts associated with children were miniaturized tools such as child-sized bows and arrows (see also Högberg 2018). Similarly, among Kalahari hunter-gatherers, Lombard (2015) describes examples of adults and older children providing scaled-down versions of adult weapons for younger children. As the children age, they are provided with larger, more powerful versions of these same weapons and tools (Lombard 2015). Johansen and Stapert (2008; Stapert 2007a) identified a miniature handaxe (approximately 4.4 cm in length) at an early Middle Paleolithic site that they suggest was made for a Neandertal child, perhaps as an instructional tool. It is interesting to note that fewer studies of children as novices are undertaken at Lower and Middle Paleolithic sites because there is an assumption that the 'simple' technologies of these time periods render novices less visible (Shea 2006; Johansen and Stapert 2008) but, in fact, handaxe production and the Levallois method, for example, require a great deal of practice and there is, in fact, wide scope for child-focused studies of these periods (see for example, Nowell and White 2010).

Who made the tools?

While there is clear evidence of novices in the archaeological record, answering the more specific question of who made the tools is trickier. In the Mesolithic, archaeologists uncovered what Lillehammer (1989, 99) describes as '[t]he chewing gum of the past'. A child's teeth marks were found on a piece of resin used to make a composite tool (Bang-Andersen 1976; 1979). Unfortunately, nothing similar has been found in the Paleolithic – there is no smoking gun when it comes to lithic manufacture. However, as noted above, while the term novice does not necessarily denote a non-adult in a culture where stone tools are key to survival, it is likely that all people learned to knap as children (Grimm 2000; Shea 2006; Lancy 2017; Shipton and Nielson 2018). This may be particularly true in Pleistocene societies where the average age of death was significantly lower than in contemporary societies (Shea 2006). Even if they did not go on to become master knappers, it is clear that a general knowledge of flintknapping would have been essential for anyone living in the Paleolithic. At Pincevent, for example, the presence of so many knappers of varying skill suggests that everyone learned to make tools for their own day-to-day needs (Bodu *et al.* 1990). But can we get a more precise window within which children may have begun to flintknap and thus contribute to the archaeological record? And what do we know about the sex of toolmakers?

Age

In traditional societies, learning a craft begins informally and is often related to learning through play (Kamp 2001a; Högberg 2008; Nowell 2015b) (see discussion in Chapter 3). Learning a craft involves both understanding new concepts and developing new motor skills and new muscle memory (Kamp 2001a). These cognitive and physical demands place absolute limits on when children can participate in a craft. Scaffolding, however, may lower these age limits. Scaffolding is a way of providing enough support to someone learning a new craft to ensure a successful outcome – we can think of the scaffolding of a building that is dismantled once construction is complete. In the case of learning a craft, scaffolding is gradually removed as a skill is mastered. More or less scaffolding may be warranted depending on the complexity and risk associated with a task. A simple example, familiar to many of us, is the act of teaching young children to tie their shoes. By setting up the 'bunny ears' so that all the child has to do is pull them to create a perfect bow, a parent teaches the concept of shoe tying and the child begins to develop the muscle memory associated with the task well before they could master it on their own. Scaffolding may be particularly important when raw material is scarce and you want to allow for learning without wasting materials (Ferguson 2008).

Ferguson (2008) has argued that children 4 years of age and younger are incapable of flintknapping safely regardless of the amount of scaffolding provided, whereas 4 year olds are perfectly capable of working with clay. However, what is appropriate and considered safe for a child is often culturally defined. For example, among the Efe of the Democratic Republic of Congo, infants safely handle machetes and among the Fore of New Guinea infants and children use knives and fire safely by the time they are able to walk (Rogoff 2003) (see a further example in Fig. 4.4). In contrast to Ferguson, Grimm (2000), argues that under normal circumstances novices can work with stone without risk of injury. The truth likely lies somewhere in between Ferguson's and Grimm's perspectives. Speaking from personal experience, cuts and

4. Stone tools, skill acquisition and learning a craft

Figure 4.4: A young Maniq girl, in the rainforest, Satun province, Southern Thailand, in the Summer of 2014, carefully holding a large knife (Photo courtesy: Khaled Hakami).

even more grievous injuries from sharp edges, flying debitage and misjudged hammerstone strikes are inevitable as you learn to knap proficiently but I know many colleagues whose young children have engaged in knapping without serious incident.

Stone tool production requires a basic understanding of core geometry. A knapper has to be able to recognize an acute angle on the surface of the core and, using a hammerstone, apply the right amount of force to remove a flake successfully. Even very intelligent non-human primate species, such as the bonobo (*Pan paniscus*), a close relative of the chimpanzee (*Pan troglodytes*), have difficulty with the concept of core geometry. Archaeologists Nick Toth and Kathy Schick and their colleagues (Toth *et al.* 1993; Schick *et al.* 1999; Savage-Rumbaugh *et al.* 2007; Toth and Schick 2009) worked with Kanzi, a bonobo housed at the Language Research Center in Atlanta, Georgia. Despite extensive training, Kanzi was unable to learn to knap with the degree of precision noted in even some of the oldest known stone tools from Gona, Ethiopia. Savage-Rumbaugh and colleagues (2007, 279) have made the point that Kanzi was not raised in a society where knapping was the norm and thus he began knapping with a 'profound cultural disadvantage'.

While Savage Rumbaugh *et al.*'s (2007) observation is undoubtedly true, contemporary adult and subadult humans can eventually learn to knap with precision even with no prior experience with stone tools, but it takes practice. Lancy (2017) has argued that subadults under the age of 8 or 9 may not have sufficient muscle mass and the necessary sensorimotor skills to produce certain types of tools. Finlay (2015) agrees, noting that juveniles under the age of 10 are incapable of producing pressure flakes long enough to thin a tool blank. She further argues that ethnoarchaeological and replication studies have demonstrated that juveniles between 6 and 11 have short attention spans, and limited conceptual awareness of surface and plane orientations – all essential skills for stone tool production, especially secondary tool modification. Johansen and Stapert (2008), similarly found that until the age of 10, juveniles have difficulty with 3D knapping (*i.e.* being able to consider the entire volume of a core at once) and suggest that expert knappers include adolescents over the age of 12 to 14 years. A similar finding was reported by Sternke and Sørensen (2009). Stout (2002) in his ethnoarchaeological study of adze makers found that adolescents apprenticed for five years beginning at age 12 or 13 years. By contrast, Shea (2006) argues that by age 10, juveniles are potentially competent knappers. He cites in support of this point of view, a study by Hawcroft and Dennell (2000) that found that modern children between the ages of 7 and 11 years old have both the physical strength and cognitive skills necessary to manufacture stone tools.

Growing up in a society where one's livelihood depends on using stone tools for protection, to create other tools and to process plants and animals for food, medicines, pigments, cordage, clothing and shelter, it is likely that even as infants, children were accustomed to using stone tools, observing others make them and eventually learning to make them themselves. Children's stone tool usage likely began very simply with the use of unmodified stone and simple flakes – both of which can be put to multiple uses. Later, as they approached 8 or 9 years of age they developed to a greater extent the cognitive and physical abilities necessary to undertake more complex knapping, increasing in proficiency as they entered adolescence.

Sex

Now, let's talk about sex. So far, I have been careful to use sex/gender neutral language to describe both adult and subadult flintknappers because archaeologists do not know the sex or the gender of Paleolithic knappers. Historically, there has been an assumption in the archaeological literature that males predominantly or exclusively made the stone tools that we study (*e.g.* Keeley 1980; Kohn and Mithen 1999; Johansen and Stapert 2008; see also discussion in Finlay 2015). This assumption is part of the continued dominance of the larger caveman trope where males hunted, made stone tools and created art, while women stayed at home and tended children – a 1950s Western understanding of a 'natural' sexual division of labor (Conkey 2013; Zihlman 2013).

Unlike with cave art (see Chapter 5) where we do have some forensic evidence that can offer clues to which sex(es) engaged in the production of images, we cannot determine the sex of toolmakers based on the archaeological data we have (Nowell and Chang 2009). However, based on ethnohistoric, ethnographic and ethnoarchaeological data, it is clear that while many studies have focused on men's knapping (*e.g.* Murdock and Provost 1973), women 'made and used stone tools for shaving hair, tattooing, woodworking, fighting sticks, digging sticks, cutting tools, spear points, incising/decorating, and scraping hides' among other activities (Weedman 2006b, 270 and references therein; see also Gero 1991; Bird 1993; McKell 1993; Torrence 2001; Frink and Weedman 2005; Weedman 2005; 2006a). Furthermore, in a detailed ethnoarchaeological study of hide scraping across a number of small scale, traditional societies, Weedman (2005; 2006a; 2006b) found no difference by gender in the use of space, manufacturing process, resulting tool morphology or raw material (Nowell and Chang 2009). In other words, the tools produced by men and women were archaeologically identical. Similarly, among tropical foragers, Roosevelt (2002, 365) notes, 'the handaxe's descendants, the hafted stone axe or the steel-head hatchet or machete, are owned and used by women as well as men as everyday tools for cutting wood, digging and dispatching animals'.

Finally, it is worth noting that in non-human primate societies, females make and use tools more often than males and for a wider variety of purposes (Roosevelt 2002; Gruber *et al.* 2010). For example, chimpanzees (*Pan troglodytes*) have been observed using a stone hammer and a tree root as an anvil to crack nuts (Boesch and Boesch-Achermann 2000) and similar behaviors have been noted among bonobos (*Pan paniscus*) in the Democratic Republic of the Congo (Fig. 4.5). According to Zihlman (2012, 37), 'the adult females engage in tool using activities more frequently than males, and in processing hard shells, adult females reach the highest level of skill, measured in hits per nut and nuts processed per minute ... Social dimensions seem to be the difference: females are less distracted while cracking nuts than are males'.

Another aspect of female chimpanzee tool use is particularly relevant here and that is the occurrence of scaffolding as a teaching strategy. In addition to nut cracking, chimpanzees engage in a variety of other tool-using behaviors such as using leaves as sponges to collect water or to wipe away feces, blood or semen and the use of sticks, rocks or tree branches to augment displays to appear more fierce. The degree to which chimpanzees use tools varies from population to population and in most cases does not seem to be related to environmental differences, prompting some primatologists to refer to these populations as different chimpanzee 'cultures' (Whiten *et al.* 1999). Musgrave *et al.* (2020) studied termite fishing among chimpanzees at Gombe in Tanzania and at Goualougo in the Republic of Congo. Gombe chimpanzees are considered to be 'low-tech' (Whiten 2020). They fish for termites in aboveground termite mounds using a flexible probe such as a grass stem, twig or piece of bark. By contrast, Goualougo chimpanzees fish in deep, subterranean termite nests and are considered to be 'high-tech'. Their termite fishing depends on a toolkit. The first tool in their kit is a stick that can be up to a meter in length and chosen from a specific species of plant. Using both the hand and foot, a chimpanzee thrusts the stick deeply into the underground nest, creating a tunnel. The stick is pulled out of the nest several times and sniffed to see if they have hit a concentration of termites. Once it is satisfied, the chimpanzee discards the stick. Whiten (2020, 803) describes the next steps in the process:

Figure 4.5: Bonobo (Pan paniscus) using a rock to break open nuts. Sanctuary Lola Ya Bonobo Chimpanzee, Democratic Republic of the Congo (Photo: Martin Harvey; copyright Getty Images).

the chimpanzee works with a second tool, a fresh stem (often one of several) that it has picked en route and held in the mouth. The stem is trimmed in length, leaves are stripped off, and the tip is then pulled through part-closed teeth several times to create a brush-like tip … which, as experiments show, is particularly effective for picking up termites in the nest. The tip is then moistened with saliva, and the fibers are compressed together to form a neat end, then efficiently threaded down the tunnel. Termites gathered are picked off the tool using the lips or swept off manually.

While both Gombe and Goualougo chimpanzees use more than 20 different kinds of tools, toolkits associated with Goualougo chimpanzees are more complex. For example, even when they fish for termites in aboveground mounds, Goualougo chimpanzees will often use a perforator to break the termite mound's hard casing, if necessary (Musgrave *et al.* 2020; Whiten 2020). At Gombe, 5 year olds are considered to be proficient termite fishers, while at Goualougo, proficiency is achieved closer to adulthood (Musgrave *et al.* 2020).

Interestingly, Musgrave *et al.* (2020) noticed that the prevalence of scaffolding is significantly higher among the high-tech Goualougo chimpanzees than among chimpanzees living at Gombe. Scaffolding in this case involves 'tool transfer'. Tool transfer is when a juvenile chimpanzee snatches away or is given a ready-made tool in which to complete a task. Juveniles in both populations watch their mothers fishing and learn through observation how to complete this task but it appears that making the right tool is a lot more difficult than the actual job of fishing itself (Musgrave *et al.* 2020; Whiten 2020). According to Whiten (2020, 803), '[t]ransfers of manufactured tools from mother to offspring occur at Goualougo at over 3 times the rate seen at Gombe, and the probability of transfer after the youngster requests a tool (usually by reaching for it and whimpering) can be 5 to 8 times higher at Goualougo'. Furthermore, at Goualougo, mothers do something that is never seen at Gombe, they actively share their tools. When a juvenile requests a tool, the mother will move out of the way to allow the youngster to take it or they will sometimes split a stick or stem down the middle so they each have a functioning tool (if they split it in half in the other direction, it would be too short to be of any use for either of them). Based on this research, Musgrave *et al.* (2020, 969) argue that 'these population differences in tool-transfer behavior may relate to task complexity and that active helping plays an enhanced role in the cultural transmission of complex technology in wild apes'.

So while it would be incorrect to argue that females made all or even most of the stone tools we study, based on all of the evidence presented here, it would be equally incorrect to assume the opposite. In fact, females play a pivotal role in the cultural transmission of technology. Based on all of the data presented here, the sex(es) of Paleolithic flintknappers should be a starting point for hypothesis testing rather than a question that we assume has already been answered.

The social context of learning a craft

The practice of scaffolding and the cultural transmission of knowledge leads to our next question – how did children learn to make stone tools? Learning a craft and learning generally in hunting and gathering societies differ from the classroom-based style of learning and teaching that many are familiar with in the West. However, this difference has often been mischaracterized by anthropologists as an absence or rarity of verbal teaching in foraging societies (*e.g.* MacDonald 2007; Lancy 2010; Hewlett and Roulette 2016). In fact, teaching of children in hunting and gathering societies takes many forms, including storytelling and conversation (a point to which we will return in Chapter 5) (Lombard 2015; Sugiyama 2017). What these forms of teaching have in common is a strong social underpinning. In fact, many authors have emphasized the importance of the social milieu within which craft learning takes place (*e.g.* Stout 2002; Ferguson 2003; 2008; Shea 2006; Crown 2007; Bamforth and Finlay 2008; Lombard 2015; Lancy 2017; Högberg 2018). In this section, I will discuss what is meant by skill, the evidence for communities of practice in the Paleolithic and the importance of embedded learning, before turning to embodied cognition and an example of learning through play.

Skill acquisition

Most archaeologists would agree based on personal experience that it takes years to become a highly skilled flintknapper. Beyond anecdotal evidence, skill has also been addressed through the experimental recreation of the learning conditions under which knapping skills were acquired in the Paleolithic as well as investigating the skills needed to knap a tool (Pargeter *et al.* 2019). These studies include exploring the role of verbal vs. non-verbal instruction (Putt *et al.* 2014; Morgan *et al.* 2015; Cataldo *et al.* 2018); documenting the neural correlates of stone tool making (Stout and Chaminade 2007; Stout *et al.* 2008); highly controlled knapping experiments, sometimes using machines, to gauge how individual variables impact knapping outcomes (Dibble and Pelcin 1995; Pelcin 1997a; 1997b; Schillinger *et al.* 2016); and teaching both human and non-human primates to knap (*e.g.* Toth and Schick 2009).

Anders Ericsson, a Swedish cognitive psychologist and someone who has studied what it means to be an 'expert', defines skill as 'an extended series of gradual psychological and cognitive changes that affect the performer's observable performance and are acquired through long term repetitive practice' (2006, 694). Ericsson's work has been mislabeled in the popular media as the '10,000 hour rule' which was interpreted to mean that it takes 10,000 hours of practice to become an expert in a field. What he is actually arguing is far more interesting. Ericsson (2006, 696) identifies three stages of skill acquisition:

> At the first encounter with a task people focus on understanding it and carefully generating appropriate actions … With more experience, individuals' behaviors adapt to the demands of performance and become increasingly automatized, people lose conscious control over the production of their actions and are no longer able to make specific intentional adjustments to them … When the behaviors are automatized, mere additional experience will not lead to increased levels of performance. In direct contrast to the acquisition of everyday skills, expert performers continue to improve their performance with more experience as long as it is coupled with deliberate practice … By actively seeking out demanding tasks – often provided by their teachers and coaches – that force the performers to engage in problem solving and to stretch their performance, the expert performers overcome the detrimental effects of automaticity and actively acquire and refine cognitive mechanisms to support continued learning and improvement.

While we intuitively feel that an individual's innate ability must be a determining factor in ultimate skill level, that somehow an individual's maximum potential is largely predetermined, Ericsson's research argues against this. He (2006, 690) notes, 'there is no objective evidence that a child or adult is able to exhibit a high level of performance without any relevant prior experience and practice … When the performance of child prodigies in music and chess are measured against adult standards, they show gradual, steady improvement over time'. Ericsson (2006) emphasizes that it is practice and specifically 'deliberate practice' that is key to skill acquisition. Deliberate practice involves dividing tasks into chunks, identifying specific goals, focusing on technique and receiving feedback from a teacher or mentor. It is not simply 10,000 hours of 'general' practice; rather, skill acquisition is about pushing yourself beyond your comfort zone. It's about focusing on a task that you are currently unable to perform consistently but one that 'can be mastered within hours of practice by concentrating on critical aspects and by gradually refining performance through repetitions after feedback' (Ericsson 2006, 694). What we can take away from this body of research is that while individual practice is absolutely crucial to skill acquisition, setting the right kinds of goals and receiving timely feedback are what transform someone from an acceptable knapper into a master knapper and for this kind of support, you need a 'community of practice'.

Paleolithic children as members of communities of practice

In their review of the ethnographic literature, Shennan and Steele (1999) found that people in non-industrial societies learn their crafts from their families with boys learning from their fathers and other male relatives and girls from their mothers and other female relatives (see also Bamforth and Finlay 2008). Bamforth and Finaly (2008, 10) noted that 'this learning is often integrated, formally or informally, into the flow of everyday community life'. In fact, children enter into established communities of practice and their participation within these communities increases over time. A community of practice includes all of the people who are engaged in the production of a particular craft. But it is more than just people – it is their knowledge of materials and symbols, their practices, their values, their traditions and all of the objects with which they engage. Essentially, it is a 'network of relations among people and objects mediated by [the] actions they conduct' (Joyce *et al.* 2012, 150). Communities of practice research employs a 'biography of things' perspective whereby objects have histories in their own right and in which their relationships, importance and roles change over time (Gosden and Marshall 1999). It also focuses on the role that learning and apprenticeship play in the cycle of the social reproduction of knowledge and practice (Nowell 2015a; 2017). In her study of potters, Crown (2007, 687) describes the value of communities of practice in this way: 'As children, budding artisans were guided by experienced community members, who were models for observations and imitation, critics of finished products, and sometimes collaborative partners in the creation of artifacts. Such collaborative work raised the skill level of the child artisan, while reproducing community standards for how to create.'

A communities of practice approach provides the necessary vocabulary and theoretical tools for archaeologists to pursue questions about knowledge production, apprenticeship, social decision making and social participation, and how these might have changed over time and space (Nowell 2017). It is likely that there were many entangled communities of practice in the later Paleolithic centered on the embodied production of ceramics, textiles, stone and bone tools, personal ornaments ('jewelry') and portable and parietal art, including finger flutings (*e.g.* Nowell and Van Gelder 2020; Van Gelder and Nowell 2021; see Chapter 5). Because these activities and ways of engaging are 'learned and practiced by community members' (Joyce *et al.* 2012, 150), they persist over time and that means archaeologists should be able to infer the existence of these communities of practice in the archaeological record.

One way to study communities of practice is to identify archaeologically visible standardized means of production or 'traditions' of which there are many in the Upper Paleolithic. Many stone tools are highly standardized. There are multiple variables that influence stone tool morphology, including the shape and size of the original parent material, the degree to which a tool is used and resharpened, and the degree to which function necessitates a specific shape (Nowell 2000). However, without a doubt, there are tools such as the Solutrean Laurel Leaf point from the Upper Paleolithic that are highly standardized and speak to the existence of a community standard. Another way to identify communities of practice is to look for points of disjuncture or discontinuity in the archaeological record that might reflect changes in social practice. For example, between 80,000 and 35,000 years ago during the Middle Stone Age (MSA) in South Africa, archaeologists have documented episodes of innovativeness followed by what looks like return to more conventional technologies at the site of Rose Cottage Cave. Around 66,000 years ago there is a transition from an MSA flake-based technology to the Howieson's Poort Industry, which is defined by its backed pieces and predominance of blades (Soriano *et al.* 2007). While we do not as yet have a satisfactory explanation for this transition, it speaks to community level decision making. Approximately 57,000 years ago, there is a return to flake-based technologies while raw material use shows continuity (Soriano *et al.* 2007). Finally, all of the work identifying the archaeological signatures of novices and the case studies discussed above speak to the existence of apprentices and thus communities of practice centered on lithics in the Paleolithic.

Communities of practice are important because they provide opportunities for varying degrees of embedded learning. Embedded learning is a form of scaffolding. It involves 'hands-on' or experiential learning, where you learn by 'doing'. Ferguson (2003; see also Högberg 2018) experimented with teaching novice knappers how to make pressure-flaked projectile points using embedded learning. Whenever the novice encountered a difficulty Ferguson would take over knapping, solve the problem or work around the obstacle and then return the material to the novice who resumed working on the core or projectile point. In so doing, Ferguson was able to help them overcome the difficulty while simultaneously teaching them solutions to common problems (Högberg 2018). In the end, the points produced by novices were virtually indistinguishable from those of an expert knapper.

It would be hard for us to know if the form of embedded learning with which Ferguson (2003) experimented was employed in the Paleolithic because the knapping products would be difficult to identify as the work of novices – for the most part everything would look like the work of skilled knappers. My reading of the archaeological evidence, however, leads me to believe that a less 'micromanaged' form of embedded learning strategy was employed. For example, at sites such as Hattoridai,

Oldeholtwolde, Trollesgave and Solvieux, we have evidence of novices, advanced learners and expert knappers sitting near each other (Fischer 1990a; 1990b; Johansen and Stapert 2008; Takakura 2013; Donahue and Fischer 2015). At Solvieux, we have evidence of the correction of stacked step terminations while at Pincevent we know that novices working on the periphery of an encampment moved to the site's main activity area to receive instruction of some sort from more skilled knappers. At Kamishirataki 2, a late Upper Paleolithic site in Japan, a skilled knapper executed with precision every step necessary to produce high quality blades and yet none of these blades was removed from the knapping site – each remained *in situ*. Takakura (2013) interprets this assemblage as the result of an expert knapper instructing novice knappers in a fairly formal setting. Following Johansen and Stapert (2008), he refers to these as 'academic' cores and flaking products.

These examples of frequent and intensive interaction between learners and experts are common when learning a craft (Bamforth and Finlay 2008) and there is no reason to believe it would have been different in prehistory. Paleolithic children living in these communities had the opportunity to learn through observation, imitation and experimentation. They learned by doing and, when necessary, they received direct instruction, which Ericsson (2006) argues is essential to progressing one's mastery of a craft. This engagement is what Lave and Wegner (1991) refer to as situated learning and legitimate peripheral engagement (see Chapter 7). By interacting with expert knappers, children's own skill levels deepen, allowing them to move from being on the periphery of these communities of practice to fully participating in them (Lave and Wegner 1991).

Embodied cognition and Paleolithic children learning the affordances of stone

As Paleolithic children began to flintknap, they would have explored the properties of stone and developed the necessary muscle memory to become an expert knapper until the 'doing' became effortless and they engaged in an intimate and recursive relationship with their materials. 'Affordances' are an important concept in this regard (Nowell and Gonlin 2020; Nowell and Van Gelder 2020). Affordance is a term most often attributed to psychologist James Gibson (1979). According to Gibson (1979), objects have properties that lend themselves to specific uses, allowing human agents to take possible actions. In what Carl Knappett (2004) refers to as 'orthodox' psychology, objects are said to be interpreted based on pre-existing categories. For example, a human agent perceives the properties of a chair (for instance, four legs, flat surface) and then fits that object into the pre-existing category of 'chair'. This process is referred to as indirect perception. Gibson (1979), however, argues that human agents *directly* perceive properties, or as he termed them 'affordances', and the potential for acting in relation to them. To keep with the same example of a chair, a chair's affordances mean that it can be sat on, stood on, used to hold open a door or employed as a weapon (Knappett 2004). These affordances, however, are not limitless in that they depend on the situation. If the chair is too low, it cannot be sat upon by someone with mobility issues. Conversely, if it is too high, it is out of reach of a small child (Knappett 2004). Thus, affordances are a more nuanced way of thinking about objects and their properties. The relationship between them is not static but 'fundamentally dynamic in nature, working on the plausible assumption that human perception is geared toward tracking possibilities for action in the world' (Knappett 2004, 44).

Knappett (2004) describes three key aspects of affordances that each have useful implications for thinking about craft learning in the Paleolithic. The first concept is relationality. Knappett argues that an affordance is neither an independent property of the object nor solely in the mind of the human agent engaging with it, but it is a 'relational property' shared between them. The chair that can be both too high and too low is an example of this property.

This interplay between object and agent is strongly related to embodied, extended cognition. Malafouris (2013) argues that archaeologists mistakenly situate all cognitive processes inside the human mind, *i.e.*, literally within our skulls, because they hold a Cartesian understanding of the mind/body divide. He stresses that by denying the role of things in the constitution of cognition, archaeologists rob the discipline of its potential to contribute in a meaningful way to the study of human cognition. The human brain is characterized by plasticity, with many studies documenting the influence of social, cultural and environmental factors as well as individual experiences on the shaping of human cognitive processes and behavioral outcomes. Because of this recursive relationship between the internal and the external, Malafouris (2013) emphasizes that it is more correct to speak of an extended cognition – one that extends beyond the skull into the material world of artifacts. Using a classic example, Malafouris (2013) asks where a blind man's mind ends and his world begins – is it at the tip of his cane where the tactile is transformed into the visual?

This brings us to the knapping of a stone tool. As we know, a tool is made by striking a core with a percussor. The affordances of the core – its shape, color, texture, chemical composition – allow for certain possibilities. When an unexpected inclusion or impurity in the rock is struck, the core may shatter, or, at the very least, there will be auditory and perceptual cues that will change what the knapper knows about this core and will impact the knapper's subsequent actions. As Bamforth and Finlay (2008, 4) phrase it, 'skill in flintknapping is found in the intersection between knowledge and practice; the relationship between them changes in terms of experience and the complex interplay of mind and material as each flake is struck'. Thus, there is a dynamic, fluid relationship between cognition, perception and action (Knappett 2004); between object, affordances and the human agent; between the lithic toolkit, the possibilities of stone and antler and the knapper. It is this full embodiment of the toolmaking process that transforms a novice into an expert, and in the Paleolithic, perhaps an adolescent into an adult.

The second aspect of affordance is transparency. Gibson (1979) argues that affordances of an object may be self-evident through direct perception. Knappett (2004), however, counters that some affordances or limits to an object's affordances may be apparent only with cultural knowledge. He gives the example of a mailbox and a garbage bin that look similar in size and shape – only one will result in your letter being delivered to it its desired destination.[5] Cultural knowledge is clearly fundamental to archaeological considerations of affordance. For example, Carroll (2016) found that children often use the wrong end of antler when first attempting soft hammer percussion but that this error does not occur if they are first able to watch an expert knapper. In other words, they required cultural knowledge in order to take full advantage of the affordances of antler as a percussor.

The final aspect of affordance is sociality. Gibson (1979) focuses on the object-agent as a fixed dyad (Costall and Richards 2013), but Knappett (2004) counters that sociality is an essential element to consider, as in many situations, there will be more than one human involved (see also Ingold 2000). Keller and Keller (1996) refer to this situation as a 'constellation' of relationships. Similarly, Tomasello (1999) emphasizes the ability of objects to be the subject of joint attention or the 'pivot' around which social activity ensues. This complexity of relationships means that there can be shared affordances or contested affordances (Knappett 2004). In the examples presented above, we see novices and experts knapping together and mistakes corrected; we see the co-creation of lithic products and examples of embedded learning. In fact, Pincevent, Oldeholtwolde, Gramsbergen (Johansen and Stapert 2008) and Trollesgave (Fischer 1990a; 1990b; Donahue and Fischer 2015) are described as 'teaching sessions'.[6] In this way, the archaeological evidence allows researchers to begin to reconstruct some of the social context in which children learned to knap stone tools in the Paleolithic.

Learning through play and imitation vs. emulation

In Chapters 2 and 3, we looked at the significance of the slowing of the maturation process in humans. The point was made that childhood is crucial in adding four years of relatively slow growth that allows for experiential learning and behavioral plasticity (Bogin 2003, 32). Similarly, adolescence further extends this period of growth and development with additional years to learn, practice, transmit, modify and innovate upon aspects of their culture (Nowell 2016). In particular, the importance of learning through play was discussed. In this section, I present an example of learning through play with lithics before turning to imitation versus emulation.

One of the best examples of a prehistoric child learning to knap through play is Högberg's (2008) study of a Neolithic[7] youngster at a knapping area in Sweden. It is a great study because of the story it tells and the elegance of the evidence used to tell it. At this knapping area, Högberg recovered 400 flint artifacts. Most of the lithics were made from high quality Danian flint and were related to the manufacture of a Neolithic square-sectioned axe but the rest of the flakes were made from a lower quality raw material called morainic flint. Also made from morainic flint was an artifact that had the rough shape of a Neolithic square-sectioned axe but was not an authentic example of this type of tool. The process for making a square-sectioned axe is well known today and the person knapping in the Danian flint was clearly an expert knapper who was following this well-established sequence. Högberg (2008) interpreted the other knapper as a child who attempted to create the correct final product but who lacked the savoire-faire, *i.e.* the conceptual knowledge, of how to go about it. They also lacked the performance ability. The child followed a completely different, non-standardized knapping strategy, making errors typical of a novice in the process. The faux axe was left in place while the true square-sectioned axe was moved to another location, presumably to be put to use in some task. While the adult knapper remained in one location while he or she knapped, the child's knapping debris shows that they were much more dynamic, moving around the adult while he or she worked (Fig. 4.6). Högberg (2008) interprets this as the child watching the more expert knapper, emulating his or her actions, while playing.

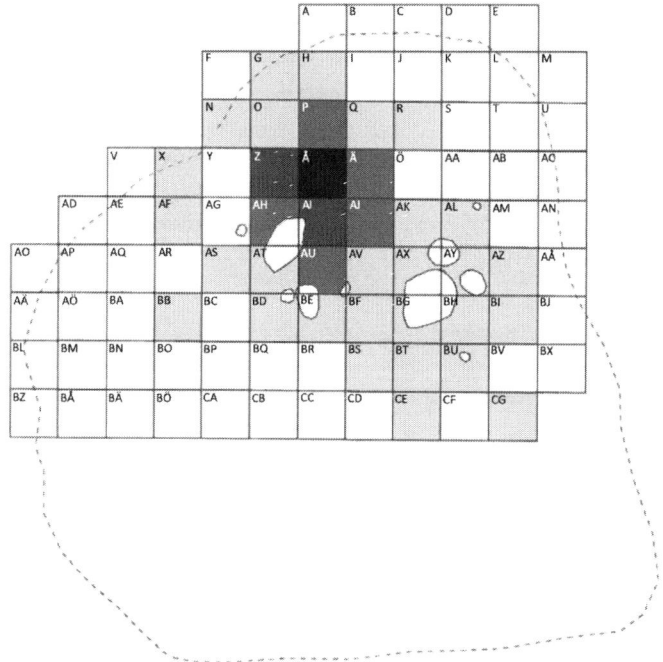

Figure 4.6: Map showing the different distribution of flakes at a Neolithic knapping area in Sweden. The color of the squares indicates the density of flakes with darker grey indicating a higher concentration of flakes and lighter grey indicating a lower density. Based on Högberg's (2008) interpretation of the site, in the center is a dense concentration of flakes produced by an adult as he or she sat knapping a Neolithic square-sectioned axe. By contrast, flakes of a poorer quality material produced by a child in the process of emulating the adult knapper are found encircling this dense concentration. The child's flakes are much more dispersed, scattered around two stones, without any clear clustering (Drawing: Jeremy Beller after Högberg 2008, 128).

Högberg's interpretation supports Shea's (2006) observation that most knappers learn through trial and error; through observation and imitation. Younger children are consistently drawn to older, more competent individuals (Lancy 2017) and they learn from observing them. In this regard, Högberg (2018; see also Högberg and Gärdenfors 2015; Gärdenfors and Högberg 2017) makes a distinction between imitation and emulation. For Högberg (2018, 64), '[e]mulation is when the learner observes the outcomes of the model's actions and tries to reach the same outcome ... imitation is when the learner observes the sequence of the model's actions and tries to perform the same actions'. While emulation is goal oriented learning, imitation is process oriented learning. I think of my own son at the age of 3 who, sitting in the back seat of our car, shook a roadmap and yelled 'damn it' because he thought that was an integral part of the wayfinding process. It is normal for young children to over-imitate (Lyons *et al.* 2007) but in the case of Högberg's Neolithic child we see a clear example of emulation and learning through play.

In this chapter, focusing on flintknapping, I discussed the role of Paleolithic sub-adults in the communities of practice of which they were a part. I began by arguing that stone is a particularly good medium for studying skill acquisition. Then I explored the ways in which children as novice knappers can be identified in the archaeological record. Finally, I presented a discussion of the social and cognitive contexts of learning to knap. In the next chapter, we will continue this discussion by looking at the evidence for the participation of Paleolithic children in communities of practice focused on ceramics, textiles and image making. In Chapter 7, I will return to a consideration of children's economic, social and cultural contributions within an evolutionary model.

Notes

1. This discussion focuses on chipped stone tools and not ground stone tools, as the latter are characteristic of the Neolithic period, which is not the subject of this book. For more detailed discussions of flintknapping, stone tool typologies and lithic analysis, the reader is directed to sources such as Debénath and Dibble 1993; Whittaker 1994; and Andrefsky 2005.
2. In the case of pressure flaking, some people prefer the term indentor or compressor to percussor as the latter denotes percussion (Crabtree 1972).
3. Oxford dictionary, https://www.lexico.com/en/definition/novice.
4. This is particularly relevant to growing children.
5. According to a colleague, this used to be a large problem at Yellowstone National Park, where the garbage cans were armored and immobile, with a swinging lid, all to deter bears. They also had 'litter' written on them. Many foreign tourists would put mail in them, thinking that it said 'letter' (James Pokines personal communication, 26 October 2020).
6. 'Teaching' may not be the best word because it brings with it certain Western assumptions. Perhaps 'knowledge sharing' is a better way to encapsulate the interaction these archaeologists are describing.
7. As noted, this book is focused on the Paleolithic but I am including this example here because it nicely illustrates learning to flintknap through play.

Chapter 5

Children, oral storytelling and the Paleolithic 'arts'

> To rethink not the value of individual studies of pottery, stone and metal, but rather the way in which the agendas arising from these artifacts have dominated material culture studies discourse is not to negate what has been achieved, but rather to augment and integrate perishable material culture as a fundamental act of enrichment.
> (Hurcombe 2014, 1)

In Chapter 4, I considered the evidence for subadult novices in the archaeological record of the Paleolithic by focusing on lithic artifacts and the skills needed to flintknap. In this chapter, I turn to activities and materials that are less archaeologically visible – ones that rely more on inferences from ethnographic data and that have benefited from new approaches to, or reinterpretations of, existing archaeological data, as well as the discovery of new data through the use of innovative technologies and nuanced theoretical frameworks. I begin by exploring the evolutionary importance of oral storytelling, music and dance and the archaeological evidence for these activities in the Paleolithic. Next, I consider the role of subadult novices in the Paleolithic 'arts', defined here as engraving, painting, sculpting and ceramics. In particular, I discuss ways in which we may be able to identify novices, the evidence for extensive communities of practice in relation to the arts and children's entry into these communities. Finally, I look at fiber technologies and textile and cordage production and what plant-based taskscapes can tell us about the lived lives of Paleolithic children.

Oral storytelling, music and dance in the Upper Paleolithic

To begin, in this section, I consider the archaeological and ethnographic evidence supporting the role of oral storytelling, dance and music in the lives of Paleolithic children.

Children, firelight and the evolutionary importance of oral storytelling

Five hundred thousand years ago, hominins learned to make and control fire on a regular basis[1] (Roebroeks and Villa 2011). This technological innovation led to wide ranging biological, cultural and social transformations. The creation of artificial light allowed hominins to extend the number of 'daylight' hours. This in turn impacted hominins' circadian rhythms. Our daily lives are regulated by a 'biological clock' or circadian cycle. This 24-hour cycle relies primarily on the hormone melatonin to convert external light cues into biological rhythms (Burton 2009). All life forms, from single-celled organisms to humans, respond to sequences of light and darkness (Burton 2009). This response, referred to as photoperiodicity, is a function of the amount of the light hitting the earth at a particular time and place and it underlies species' specific patterns of activity, growth and reproduction (Burton 2009). It also influences our sleep patterns.

All things being equal, an adult in synchronicity with the sun will naturally fall asleep a few hours after sunset but sitting around a campfire changed all that (Nowell 2018; see Chapter 6 for a discussion of adolescent sleep patterns). Compared to non-human primates, humans sleep less but more intensely with a significantly higher proportion of our TST (total sleep time) spent in REM sleep than is predicted for a primate of our brain size, body mass, diet, foraging needs and predation risk (Nunn and Samson 2018). During NREM (*i.e.* non-REM) sleep, your body temperature lowers, your breathing slows and your body redirects its energy toward repairing bone and tissue. By contrast, during REM sleep, you brain is more active, causing you to experience intense and vivid dreams and, most importantly, areas of the brain related to memory, learning and the rehearsal of stressful situations are stimulated (Nunn and Samson 2018 and references therein). The evolutionary importance of imagination, planning, thinking through the consequences of a situation, innovating and adapting to novel situations is attested to by the fact that the benefits of REM sleep were selected over the significant benefits of NREM sleep. In fact, almost all of the TST we 'lost' can be accounted for by a three-hour reduction in NREM sleep (Nunn and Samson 2018).

Imagination, memory and the ability to sequence events are all integral components of effective oral storytelling. As noted in Chapter 4, one of the primary ways in which children learn in hunting and gathering societies is through oral storytelling. In foraging societies, storytelling normally takes place around a campfire in the evening. Artificially produced light did not simply add more 'daylight' hours; it opened up a new and distinct space for hominins to inhabit (Wiessner 2014). During productive daylight hours most conversations in foraging societies center on matters of economics, politics and gossip, while nighttime is reserved for singing, dancing, ritual and storytelling (Wiessner 2014) – the kinds of activities that promote social cohesion and transmission of knowledge from one generation to the next (Sugiyama 2001; Boyd 2009; Dunbar 2014; Lombard 2015; Smith *et al.* 2017; Nowell 2018).

Storytelling is a universal feature of human groups (Sugiyama 2001; Smith *et al.* 2017) and in foraging societies it performs a crucial pedagogic function. Sugiyama (2017) argues that storytelling has all of the features of direct teaching, which, as noted in Chapter 4, is often suggested to be rare in foraging societies. These features include a person signaling that they intend to share information, the identification of intended recipients of this information and the transmission of knowledge that has applicability beyond the immediate context. Signaling that one is about to share a story occurs through eye contact, pointing and other visual and auditory cues (Sugiyama 2017). A storyteller might say, 'here is something you need to know after I am gone' or they might ask if the audience is listening or whether people want 'more' of a story (Sugiyama 2017). Thus there is engagement and investment in the telling of the story on the part of both the expert (storyteller) and the novice (audience). Storytellers vary the timbre of their voices, pause for effect, use onomatopoeia, include redundancy and predictable patterning in the telling of the story, create anthropomorphized animals and objects as models for human behavior and mimic animal sounds and atmospheric noises (Sugiyama 2017). In fact, some people have compared the rhythm and tempo of expert storytellers to 'motherese' and 'motionese' used by parents to communicate effectively with infants (Sugiyama 2017). The audience responds by filling in names of places or people when prompted and laugh, gasp or scream as appropriate.

As humans, we often retain information presented in narrative form better than other formats. The use of redundancy and patterned elements in stories as well as the other devices mentioned above help to create narrative fluency in older children (Sugiyama 2017). These practices reinforce the pedagogic nature of storytelling. Sometimes these stories have an even more obvious visual dimension. For example, among the Yupik, Indigenous people of south-central Alaska and Eastern Russia, older girls use 'story knives' or snow knives to draw stories for younger girls in the snow or earth that teach them about their social and ecological environments (Lew-Levy *et al.* 2018).

Forager stories are a source of generalized historical, social and ecological knowledge (Sugiyama 2017) communicated in a lively and engaging manner. For example, before they begin to participate in a hunt, 'young hunters have listened to countless hunting and tracking encounters, described in minute detail during storytelling around the campfire' (Lombard 2015, 883). Often very detailed environmental information that is incidental to the plot is shared (Sugiyama 2017). Listening intently, through these stories, children and adolescents learn about their history, tool-use and manufacture, plants, natural resources, fishing, where to find patches of food, weather patterns, warfare, wayfinding, topography and place names, ecological disasters, famine, gender roles, marriage, taboos, how to behave appropriately towards non-kin and kin (including in-laws!) and the consequences of bad behavior (Sugiyama 2001; 2017; Boyd *et al.* 2011; Lombard 2015; Smith *et al.* 2017; Lew-Levy *et al.* 2018). The body of knowledge transmitted through these stories forms part of a foraging society's intangible culture that is key to their survival. As Sugiyama (2017, 2) notes, '[i]ndividuals incapable of acquiring sufficient local knowledge by early adulthood would have been at elevated risk of starvation, exposure, predator attack and a host of other hazards'. Stories are an economic way of communicating large bodies of knowledge to children and adolescents without requiring the listener to acquire this information first hand, thus reducing potential dangers (*e.g.* consumption of poisonous plants or encounters with dangerous animals) (Sugiyama 2001).

Direct evidence for storytelling in the Paleolithic is, of course, scarce as these people's stories have been lost over the generations that separate us from them. However, for the remainder of this section, I will present aspects of cave art that I believe relate to a tradition of oral and/or visual storytelling in the Paleolithic. In this regard, Clottes (1996) has argued that the changing subject matter of prehistoric art over time may reflect changes in peoples' stories and myths. For example, images of dangerous animals such as mammoths and cave lions are more common in caves dating to 20,000 to 40,000 years ago, such as Chauvet and even Rouffignac[2] in France. But over time, these animals begin to drop out of artists'[3] repertoires. Similarly, it has been observed that over time there is a divergence between the animals Upper Paleolithic peoples consumed and the ones they depicted (Bahn 2016), suggesting that these images were not simply iconic representations of the world around them but may have held symbolic meaning(s) as well. For example, at Lascaux (France), 60% of the painted and engraved figures are horses but there is only one reindeer depicted in the art, and yet this species accounts for 90% of the faunal remains in the cave. As Meg Conkey once said (2004), these Magdalenian people may have had reindeer in their stomachs but they had horses on their minds!

Azéma and Rivère (2012) have further developed this notion of storytelling by arguing that Upper Paleolithic images of single animals depicted with multiple horns, legs or tails (Fig. 5.1) should be interpreted not as a herd of animals but rather as one animal in motion – a type of primitive animation. The cinematic effect is enhanced by changes in shadow and color saturation (see discussion below). Other attempts to depict motion from still images include breaking up a narrative over several panels or 'scenes', such as the Panel of Lions at Chauvet Cave, where artists depicted cave lions stalking and then lunging after fleeing bison (Azéma and Rivère 2012).

With a single viewpoint the viewer only sees one moment in time but motion can still be conveyed if a subject is in the process of movement. It is particularly effective if the depicted moment differs significantly from when the subject is at rest, for example, the swing phase in bipedal walking (Nowell 2015b). A subject depicted in profile, as the vast majority of Paleolithic figurative images are, is most effective in this regard and, in fact, Paleolithic artists accurately depicted quadrupedal walking more often than later artists (Horvath *et al.* 2012). Movement may also be inferred by the image's content as there is no such thing as a still waterfall or a bird frozen in mid-air (Friedman and Stephenson 1980). One example of this that comes to mind are the possible 'jelly fish' from Cosquer Cave on the Mediterranean (Fig. 5.2a) (Nowell 2015b). Projectile points 'flying' toward the so-called 'Chinese' horse from Lascaux (Fig. 5.2b) might be another example, although it has also been suggested that these weapons might be better interpreted as waving grass – either way motion is suggested.

As noted, storytelling as described by Wiessner (2014), Sugiyama (2017) and Smith *et al.* (2017), normally takes place in the evening around campfires. The archaeological examples described above relate to the interior of caves and viewing the art would have required artificial lighting. Campfires are only one form of artificial light in

Figure 5.1: This drawing of a bison with eight legs from the Panel of Horses at Chauvet (France) is an example of how Upper Paleolithic artists depicted motion in two dimensional images. Images such as these may have played a role in oral as well as visual storytelling (Photo courtesy: J. Clottes, Chauvet Scientific team).

the Paleolithic. By at least the beginning of the Upper Paleolithic, early humans also used lamps and torches and these may have played an important role in storytelling. There are at least 300 probable lamps from more than 100 sites concentrated mainly in southwest France. Lamps were carved from limestone or sandstone (Fig. 5.3), and residue analysis conducted on a sample of lamps indicates that Upper Paleolithic peoples used animal fat, particularly from suids and bovids (de Beaune 1987), as fuel. Wicks tended to be made from mostly conifer, juniper, grass and 'non-woody' organics, such as lichen or moss, based on ethnographic analogy and experimental archaeology (de Beaune 1987). Not all lamps were portable, however, as some were fixed points of light. In Nerja Cave, a Solutrean site in southern Spain, researchers uncovered five lamps created from natural concavities in the cave (Medina-Alcaide et al. 2019). In at least one case, they were able to confirm its use as a lamp based on the presence of ash and the residue of smoke and charcoal.

When the exact provenience of the lamps is known, they were often found overturned in pairs at cave entrances, where cave galleries intersect and along walls, possibly for reuse at a later date (de Beaune 1987). Upper Paleolithic stone lamps cast very little light, approximately 2 lumens per m^2. This is less light than is generated by a standard candle but it would have been enough to find your way around a cave

Figure 5.2: Two examples of motion cues due to content: (a) possible jellyfish at Grotte Cosquer (France) (Photo courtesy: J. Clottes); and (b) a horse moving through waving grass or feathered darts projected at a the horse (Deuxième cheval chinois, the Axial Gallery, Lascaux Cave, Montignac (Dordogne, France). Photo: © N. Aujoulat MCC/Centre National de Préhistoire).

or even to create art requiring fine detail, provided that the lamps were placed close enough to the image (De Beaune 1987; De Beaune and White 1993).

Torches are a third source of artificial light in the Upper Paleolithic. Functionally, torches are equivalent to lamps, since both are portable sources of light, but there may be as yet untested differences in longevity, reliability and maneuverability between them (Nowell 2018). Archaeological evidence for torches include rubbings, burnt wood and branch impressions. The practice of 'rubbing' a torch along a cave wall functions to increase the amount of oxygen available, allowing the torch to burn more brightly. These marks are sometimes used in AMS dating of painted caves, most famously at Chauvet Cave (Quiles *et al.* 2016). Archaeologists have identified burnt bundles of resin-covered pine sticks used by a Paleolithic family for light as they explored a deep cave in Italy 14,000 years ago (Romano *et al.* 2019) (see Chapter 3). Another line of evidence for torches is the impression of branches on cave walls at Chauvet. These imprints may have been made when early humans fixed a torch to the wall to free their hands (Medina-Alcaide *et al.* 2018).

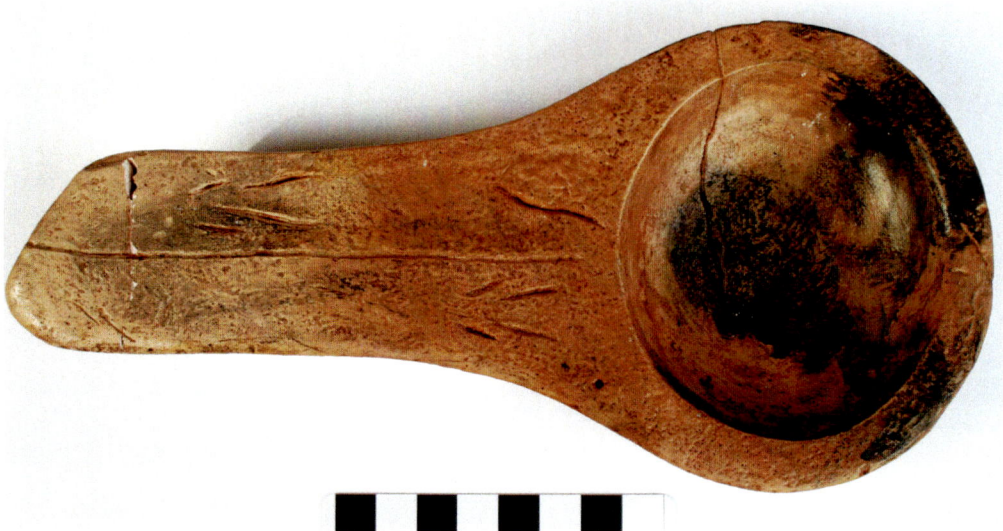

Figure 5.3: Replica of a ca. 17,500-year-old Upper Paleolithic stone lamp from Lascaux, France (Photo: April Nowell).

Lamps, torches and hearths have all been found inside Upper Paleolithic painted caves. At Chauvet, hearths inside the cave produced charcoal that was used in the creation of some of the parietal (*i.e.* wall) art. In fact, a recent study estimates that 170 kg of wood was burned at Chauvet (Salmon *et al.* 2020). Hearths such as those as Chauvet, were likely also a source of heat in a damp and chilly cave (caves can be cold even during the summer) as well as a source of light for creating art. Lamps and torches would have been important for wayfinding. All three light sources likely served another function as well. Observing images by lamplight in the cave of Le Mouthe (France), Edward Wachtel (1993, 137) writes, 'In the space of a few moments, I saw cuts and dissolves, change and movement. Forms appeared and disappeared. Colors shifted and changed. In short, I was watching a movie.' Flickering flames, dancing shadows, the fire's warm glow, all transform a cave's interior into theater. I remember visiting the cave of Pech Merle in southwest France for the first time. I had always read that if you hold a torch (or, in this case, a flashlight) at just the right angle, an animal image would 'project' from the cave wall, *i.e.*, it would appear three-dimensional. But it wasn't until I was in the company of an excellent guide and saw this projection for myself that I really understood the power of this effect.

Cave artists routinely took advantage of the cave's natural topography to lend three dimensionality to their art (Nowell 2006). A natural recess became an eye, a concavity an auroch's flank. One of my favorite examples, is the use of natural flowstone to depict an ibex's shaggy coat at the French site of Cougnac. Artists at Chauvet Cave often further enhanced this effect by using a thick charcoal paste to paint an animal's contour. Because our visual system relies on a 'nearest neighbor' approach to visual data (Livingstone 2014), the slight difference in depth between the contour and the rest of the animal has a greater visual effect than it should, giving the impression that the animal is projecting from the wall (Nowell 2015b). Another technique is to blur just enough detail so that our visual system is not able to detect that an image is flat and by default it focuses on other depth cues such as perspective and shading (Livingstone 2014). At Chauvet artists employed a stump-tool to blur contours and for shading and blending (Clottes 2010). In addition, Paleolithic artists used a variety of other techniques to create three dimensionality in their paintings and drawings, such as occlusion (*e.g.* overlapping spotted horses at Pech Merle), perspective (*e.g.* at Chauvet a herd of rhinos is suggested by decreasing sizes of their horns), shading and luminance variance. In the physical world the magnitude of luminance difference can be in the thousands and while Paleolithic peoples experimented with color not even modern paints can achieve more than 20 times the luminance between the 'whitest white' and the 'blackest black' (Livingstone 2014; Nowell 2015b). Again, because our visual system is more attuned to local changes rather than global ones, it only measures the luminance difference between 'nearest neighbors' (Livingstone 2014). Paleolithic artists took advantage of this through their use of color. At Chauvet, artists learned to scrape a surface before painting it (Clottes 2010) as the white color of the newly exposed surface exaggerated the luminance difference.

The illusion of three dimensionality and the importance of what I call 'visual play' in Paleolithic art was brought home to me on a visit to the Upper Paleolithic site El Castillo in Spain. During our tour, our guide pointed out various animal images, including the painted lower body of a bison. He then drew our attention to a rock a few feet from the wall that resembled a bison's head. Holding his flashlight just so, he projected the rock's shadow onto the cave wall. We were all astonished to see that the bison's shadow 'head' fit neatly on its painted body. Visual play is not unusual in Paleolithic art. We tend to think of Paleolithic peoples as serious, as always on the verge of starvation, with no time for anything frivolous. Yet there are numerous examples of humor and playfulness in their art. There are animals with mischievous smiles (Fig. 5.4) at Rouffignac in France and a purple horse at Tito Bustillo in Spain. Another one of my favorite caves is Pair-Non-Pair in France. Here engraved animals are grouped on the walls of a circular gallery that has a hole in the roof allowing for natural light. There are five ibex including two facing each other, two horses side by side facing right, a second grouping of two horses that are looking backward, and two bison or aurochs facing each other. The only animal on these first two panels that seems forlorn is a single mammoth. It is not until you look across the gallery that you spy a tiny mammoth looking directly at its much larger companion. In Covalanas in Spain, a row of painted deer look toward the cave's entrance as if startled by your sudden appearance and at Altamira, also in Spain, eerie stone 'masks' with eyes that seem to follow you, peer out from corners of the cave (Fig. 5.5).

Figure 5.4: An artist chose to depict this bison from Rouffignac with an expressive eye and 'eyebrow' and an almost knowing grin. This image is one of several 'smiling' animals in Paleolithic art and is an example of the humor and visual play that is characteristic of this corpus of art (Photo: Jean Plassard, courtesy Frédéric Plassard).

The use of techniques to create a sense of three dimensionality in their art, the properties of artificial light, the examples of motion and these examples of visual play suggest to me that these images were at least sometimes involved in storytelling. This supposition is further supported by the existence of fantastical creatures. While human figures as a category are rare in Paleolithic art, there are a small number of examples of therianthropic (half-human, half-animal) or fantastical creatures. In Europe, examples of these include the 'Birdman' and the 'Unicorn' (with two horns, oddly enough, which some people believe is a human wearing an animal hide or mask) from Lascaux, and 'The Sorcerer' from Les Trois Frères (France), while in Sulawesi in Indonesia the

Figure 5.5: One of several 'masks' from Altamira Cave (Spain). This natural convexity in the cave wall resembles a human face. Its human features are enhanced by charcoal drawn pupils in natural concavities (Face Mask, © Cave of Altamira Museum of Altamira. Photo P. Saura).

44,000-year-old site of Leang Bulu' Sipong 4 boasts several human figures with animal features (Aubert *et al.* 2019). These figures from Paleolithic art 'are consistent with the ritual use of masks and transformational capacities assigned to ritual practitioners in many small-scale cultures' (Culley 2021, 188). In European Paleolithic cave art, there are also 'wounded men' – men with lines interpreted as spears protruding from their torsos (*e.g.* at Cougnac, France) and 'bison-women' (*e.g.* at Pech Merle, France). As Culley (2021, 188) notes, '[b]oth the sorcerer and wounded man are recurring motifs frequently depicted with bent postures as seen in ritual dance and with erect penises'. The bison-women are similarly bent forward, possibly in dance.

Additionally, there are multiple scenes with narrative quality in Paleolithic art. Art from this time period is typically described as having few if any scenes (*e.g.* Delport 1984; Halverson 1992; Clottes 2001; White 2003). Certainly what constitutes a scene in rock art is complicated (see discussion in Davidson and Nowell 2021) but if we define a scene minimally as one figure involved in an activity such as a human hunting or a horse whinnying or as two engaged figures (*i.e.* where there is evidence of mutual interaction/mutual influence, see Culley 2021), then there are true scenes in Paleolithic art. For example, in Leang Bulu' Sipong 4, the therianthropic figures are holding ropes or spears and appear to be hunting pigs (*Sus celebensis*) and dwarf buffaloes (*Bubalus* sp.) (Aubert *et al.* 2019). At Chauvet, two rhinoceros appear locked in conflict, demonstrating aggressive behavior that is typical of mating season (Fritz and Tosello 2007); while in this same cave the Panel of Lions depicts a hunt. At Lascaux, a line of deer swim or wade through water, at Cueva del Niño (Spain) two fawns are engaged in play (Davidson 2021), while at Font-de-Gaume (France), a standing male reindeer bends his head to gently lick the forehead of a smaller, female reindeer lying on the ground. At the cave of Lagrave (France), an engraved herd of horses walks along a clearly defined ground line with their manes overlapping and multiple vertical lines representing their legs (Fritz *et al.* 2016). One horse, slightly apart from the others, is larger suggesting it is closer to the viewers (Fritz *et al.* 2016). Furthermore, all of the examples of animals and artifacts in motion described above would similarly qualify as scenes.

One of the most famous scenes in Paleolithic art is the 'Shaft Scene' in Lascaux (Fig. 5.6). The elements of this scene are the therianthropic 'Birdman' (possibly dead, falling backwards, with an erect penis and 4-fingered hands that more closely resemble a bird's feet), a charging disemboweled bison with a spear through its flank, a second spear lying abandoned near the birdman and a 'bird on a stick', which is likely an atlatl or spear thrower with a bird carved on the end (there are archaeological examples of these weapons, see Chapter 3). As Davenport and Jochim (1988, 560) write, '[t]he majority of authors ... agree that the close association of the wounded bison and the humanoid indicates *a single artist with a story to tell*; it seems apparent that the bison has given the humanoid a [wound inflicted with its horn]. The close relation of the abandoned spear-thrower below the humanoid and the long, eviscerating spear surely indicates that the two were used together' (my emphasis). Whether this narrative

Figure 5.6: The 'Shaft Scene' from Lascaux Cave (France), dating to approximately 17,500 years ago, is one of the most famous scenes in Paleolithic art. Its narrative quality attests to a rich oral and visual storytelling tradition (Photo: La scène du Puits, Grotte de Lascaux, Montignac (Dordogne, France), © N. Aujoulat/CNP/MC).

scene refers to an actual historical event (*i.e.* a hunter/shaman in regalia being gored by a bison), a shamanistic vision (some have pointed to the fact that the anthropogenic figure mirrors the bird's head on the spearthrower, see Davenport and Jochim 1988), an allegorical tale or a teaching tool for young hunters is unknown.

Dance

In addition to oral storytelling, Upper Paleolithic children likely participated in dance. Among foraging people, it is common for children to imitate 'traditional dances, which typically have significant associations with critical values around gender, egalitarianism, and sharing' (Boyette 2018, 309). Archaeological evidence for dance, however, is much less robust than for storytelling. Once again, possible evidence comes from the site of Chauvet. At this site, there is a panel of 'dots' that form the figure of a bison, rhinoceros (Mohen 2002) or mammoth (Clottes 2010). The dots are in fact palm prints made when Aurignacian peoples pressed their palms in an ochre paste and then pressed them against the cave wall. Forensic studies of the palm prints (and associated portions of fingers that were also imprinted) suggest that there was a performative dimension to the production of the animal figure, as a number of different people's hands were involved in its creation (Clottes 2003). Another possible line of evidence for dance may be finger flutings (see below). Leslie Van Gelder (personal communication, May 2016) has suggested that perhaps some finger flutings, lines drawn in soft sediment on cave walls and ceilings (quite literally the residue of touch), may have been created during dance. Finally, at one time it was thought that 183 heel prints in the French cave Tuc D'Audoubert were the product of young individuals dancing, perhaps as part of an initiation ritual (Bégouën et al. 2009). A recent study that relied on the expertise of three professional trackers from the Ju/'hoan San failed to corroborate this initial interpretation (Pastoors et al. 2015). Instead, the heel marks have been reinterpreted as the normal stride of a man and adolescent boy collecting clay from a pit located 15 m away from a pair of beautiful clay bison. The trackers noted that the main reason to walk on your heels is to remain anonymous, as a knowledgeable tracker can recognize an individual from a complete footprint (Pastoors et al. 2015).

Music

As archaeologists, we often privilege the visual and the tactile over the auditory; it is an understandable bias given the nature of our work. However, music is believed to be ubiquitous in human cultures (Fukui and Toyoshima 2014) and is a highly potent means of communicating emotion (Nowell 2018). We know, for example, that humans are particularly sensitive and susceptible to both positive and negative emotion in music (Blood and Zatorre 2001; Andrade and Bhattacharya 2003; Marin and Bhattacharya 2009) and that music-generated emotion can have residual effects. Studies have shown that listening to 'positive' music impacts people's sense of taste, how they interpret emotion in the faces of others (particularly in drawings and photographs of 'neutral' faces) and even their sensitivity to false memory production (Storbeck and Clore 2005; Logeswaran and Bhattacharya 2009; Marin and Bhattacharya 2009). Furthermore, listening to music that people preferred made them more altruistic, whereas listening to music they disliked had the opposite effect (Fukui and Toyoshima 2014). As Mark Changizi (2009) notes, 'the lion's share of emotionally evocative stimuli in the lives of our ancestors would have been the faces and bodies of other people'. One possible implication of these cross-model studies of music and emotion is that positive or negative emotion perceived in and generated through music in Upper Paleolithic societies could have been redirected or manipulated to influence how individuals perceive others within or outside their groups and to modify subsequent action (Nowell 2018).

Much as with dance, Upper Paleolithic children likely began to learn the songs of their people and to learn *through* the songs of their people from an early age. In foraging societies, music is produced primarily through voice and the use of the body as a percussive instrument (clapping of hands, stomping of feet, etc.) and thus music in these societies is very much an embodied experience (Morley 2013). When instruments are used they are often percussive instruments made of perishable materials such as gourds and animal skins as drum heads (Morley 2013). Nonetheless, in the Upper Paleolithic there is a substantial amount of material evidence for music in the form of instrumentation, including more than 144 fragments of technologically sophisticated flutes, whistles and pipes (Lawson and d'Errico 2002; Conard *et al.* 2009; Morley 2013) and now even a decorated and modified conch shell horn (Fritz et al. 2021). It has been suggested that the large avians used to create these flutes do not arrive in Europe prior to the Upper Paleolithic, which may explain why there are no flutes yet known from the Middle Paleolithic and earlier (Tyrberg 1998).

The flutes, many dating to the Aurignacian (ca. 40,000–30,000 BP), are particularly striking. Most derive from the sites of Geißenklösterle, Vogelherd and Hohle Fels in Germany (Conard *et al.* 2009; Conard 2011), and from Isturitz in France (Lawson and d'Errico 2002; d'Errico *et al.* 2003). The instruments are made from bone (swan and vulture radii) and mammoth ivory. The ivory flutes are especially remarkable for their complexity. To fashion a flute from ivory one must cut a tube from the ivory, split it in half, hollow out each half and then seamlessly fit the two pieces back together. The flute makers incised small notches in each piece to guide themselves and they manufactured a sealant to make the flute air tight (Conard *et al.* 2009). Experimental work demonstrates that these ancient instruments were capable of producing a wide range of tones (Conard 2011).

In Chapter 3, I discussed whistles and percussive instruments in relation to children's toys and children's roles as musicians. There is no evidence to suggest who made or used instruments in the Upper Paleolithic. As noted in Chapters 1 and 3, there are examples of child musicians in military and ritual contexts in later time periods but this doesn't tell us anything about the Paleolithic per se. What we do know from ethnographic data is that in foraging societies children participate in song and dance at an early age, often first through play and observation of adult activities and then more formally (Lewis 2016; Boyette 2018). It is reasonable to hypothesize that Upper Paleolithic children did too given the evolutionary significance of music (Morley 2013).

In sum

According to Lewis (2016, 147–148 and references therein) 'cultural knowledge, or any expert knowledge, must be acquired, stored, and recovered in mostly non-linguistic ways if it is to be used efficiently'. Storytelling, dance and music are ubiquitous in human societies, suggesting that these behaviors have deep roots that reach back into Paleolithic times. Amongst foragers, these behaviors most often take place at night around a campfire (Wiessner 2014). Stories, in particular, serve both pedagogical and galvanizing functions. They transmit sacred and practical knowledge from one generation to the next and, along with song and dance, bring people together to renew and strengthen social bonds. In the Paleolithic, direct evidence for storytelling is scarce, however, we do know that the regular use of fire began at least 500,000 years ago, changing our circadian rhythms and opening up a new space for hominins to inhabit. In the Upper Paleolithic, there are multiple lines of evidence that suggest that at least some of the images produced during that time were used in storytelling. These lines of evidence include the changing subject matter of Paleolithic art over time and space, the decoupling of dietary fauna from depicted fauna, the rendering of fantastical creatures, therianthropes and other hominioids, many in ritualized positions, the existence of narrative scenes, and examples of visual play including the use of shadow, motion and three dimensionality. Like Conkey (1997, 344), I dislike grand, overarching schemes that try to explain all of Paleolithic art by reference to one interpretation such as hunting magic or fertility magic where all the art is about ritually ensuring the hunt or the fecundity of animals and people, respectively (see also Conkey 1989; Nowell 2006; Bahn 2016). At the same time, given the ethnographic and archaeological evidence, it is likely that some of the art in some times and places was used in storytelling, primarily to educate Paleolithic children and adolescents. Throughout our evolution, the ability to tell compelling stories was selected because it transmitted information key to survival without requiring individuals to acquire this information first hand, potentially exposing themselves to perilous situations (Sugiyama 2001). Storytelling also brought Paleolithic people together by having them invest in a real or imagined past as well as in their joint future. Perhaps it is not surprising that Smith *et al.* (2017, 1) found that in foraging groups with effective storytellers, group cooperation increased, skilled storytellers were preferred social partners and these same storytellers enjoyed greater reproductive success, indicating individual-level selection for a behavior that so greatly benefits the larger group.

Children and the making of images in the Upper Paleolithic

Over at least 1200 generations, Upper Paleolithic peoples engaged in the production of thousands of figurative and non-figurative drawings, engravings and paintings in the caves and rock shelters of France and Spain (Conkey 2010). In addition, thousands of decorated and shaped tools, sculptures, plaquettes (engraved slabs of stone) and personal ornaments circulated within and between culture groups with specific artifact types and artistic styles waxing and waning in popularity throughout the Upper Paleolithic period (Nowell 2015b). Upper Paleolithic peoples may have also engaged in forms of body decoration, including temporary or permanent tattooing and scarification (Nowell and Cooke 2020). They used natural pigments such as charcoal, ochre and calcite to create these images and applied them using their fingers and the palms of their hands. They also blew pigment through hollow bird bones and may have used animal hair brushes as well. They even employed scaffolding to ceilings and places on walls that would have been otherwise out of reach. Post holes and remnants of the cordage used in constructing the scaffolding have been found in caves in France and Spain.

We know that one way in which children in foraging societies learn is simply by observing adult behavior and listening to adult conversations taking place around them (Lombard 2015). Upper Paleolithic children, as social actors, would have learned to decode, reproduce and perhaps even innovate upon the images that circulated within their communities – some of these images they must have encountered on a daily basis while others were likely only rarely seen (Nowell 2015b). Based on archaeological evidence, we know that at times infants as well as older children witnessed or actively participated in the production of Upper Paleolithic art. Finger-holes in clay, handprints, hand stencils (the negative imprint or outline of a hand) and footprints have been recorded in a number of Upper Paleolithic Australian, French and Spanish decorated caves including Aldène, Bédeilhac, Chauvet, Cosquer, Font-de-Gaume, Fontanet, Gargas, Montespan, Niaux, Ojo Guareña, Pech Merle, Réseau Clastres and Tuc d'Adoubert (see Chapter 3), and their finger flutings are known from El Castillo, Gargas, Las Chimeneas, Koonalda and Rouffignac (Roveland 2000; Clottes 2013; Van Gelder 2015b; 2015c; Bahn 2016). Particularly poignant for me are the children's handprints in Gargas that are lower down on the wall (see Chapter 3 for examples of where children were lifted up to make their marks at Gargas).

Figurative and non-figurative image production

Within the social space that was created for and by children, children produced both figurative and non-figurative images including geometric signs. Non-figurative signs

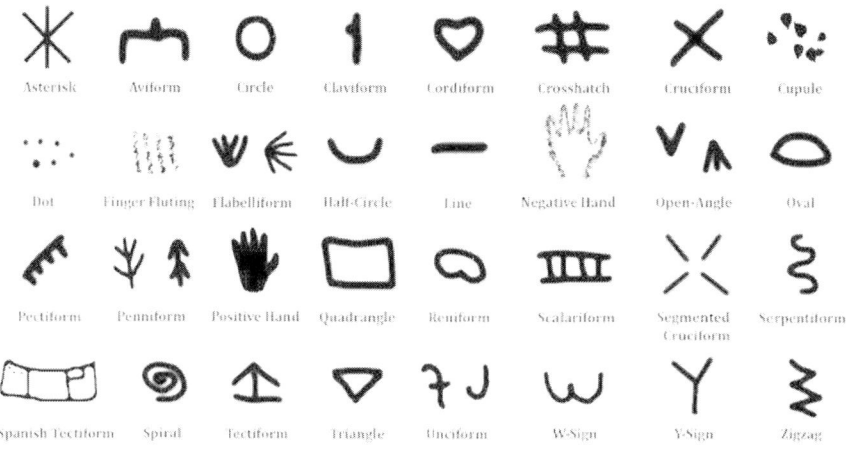

Figure 5.7: Thirty-two different non-figurative signs have been identified in the imagery at Upper Paleolithic decorated caves in Europe including tectiforms (bottom row, third from the left), a sign found finger fluted by children and an adult at Rouffignac Cave (Drawing: Jeremy Beller, redrawn after Von Petzinger 2017).

include circles, lines, dots, zigzags and a variety of other geometric shapes. There is debate over whether these figures are iconic representations of, for example, water, lightning or weapons, or whether they are some kind of abstracted graphic communication (Von Petzinger 2017). At Rouffignac Cave in France, children produced 'tectiforms' or 'roof-shaped' signs (Figs 5.7–5.8) (Van Gelder 2015b). This is an incredible discovery as these are the only known examples of subadults creating non-figurative signs. We know they were created by children because these tectiforms were finger-fluted. To 'flute' means to create a surface that is grooved, channeled or ribbed, and thus, the term 'finger fluting' captures the three-dimensional shape of these lines (Nowell and Van Gelder 2020). Upper Paleolithic peoples sometimes used their fingers to trace (flute) images in soft sediments that lined the walls, floors and ceilings of limestone caves. In Rouffignac, children used their small fingers to flute tectiforms on the walls of the cave.

In most cases, non-figurative signs are painted or engraved and thus we don't normally have recourse to the same kind of forensic data that we do when images are fluted. In the early 2000s, Leslie van Gelder and her late husband, Kevin Sharpe, pioneered a method for estimating age and sex from the flutings (*e.g.* Sharpe and Van Gelder 2004; 2005; 2006a; 2006b; 2006c; Van Gelder and Sharpe 2009; Van Gelder

Figure 5.8: Tectiform in Rouffignac Cave (France) finger fluted by a child whose three-fingered width measures 31 mm (France) (Photo courtesy: Leslie Van Gelder).

2010a; 2010b; 2012; 2015b; 2015c). Their method is based on measuring the combined width of the three middle fingers of a person's hand (*i.e.* the index, middle and ring fingers). This method has the advantage that it works for either hand as the three middle fingers remain the same. Experimental data indicate three-finger widths of 33 mm and smaller belong to children 7 years of age and younger while widths of 30 mm and smaller belong to children 5 years of age and younger. Flutings 34 mm and larger overlap with adult widths making it difficult to distinguish large older children and adolescents from small adults (Sharpe and Van Gelder 2004; 2006a; 2006c; Van Gelder 2015b; 2015c). Using calipers, Sharpe and Van Gelder measured the widths of three-fingered flutings at the narrowest point of the fluting from several caves in France and Spain. Flutings where fingers were splayed were not measured. Individuals were identified using a 2 mm margin of error to compensate for possible asymmetry between a person's left and right hand. In addition, individual profiles were further refined by collecting data on 'fluting preferences' such as three-fingered vs. two-fingered fluting, one handed vs. two handed fluting, depth and even the 'speed' of fluting. Through experimentation they determined that faster fluting produces a greater buildup of residue at the end of the fluting stream (Sharpe and Van Gelder 2005). At Rouffignac, these researchers identified the second most prolific fluter in the cave as a girl (5 years of age or younger) whose three-finger width was 28 mm. She fluted in all but one chambers of the cave, and is unusual in that she consistently fluted with two hands. Her tectiform in Chamber H1 is next to two more tectiforms created by a slightly older child (Van Gelder 2015b).

We also have examples of Paleolithic children co-creating a figurative image at Rouffignac. In a chamber known as the Grande Fosse, 0.94 km from the entrance of the cave, at the furthest point in which finger flutings are found in the cave, three individuals collaborated to create what has been interpreted as an image of a saiga (a now endangered antelope that inhabits the Eurasian steppe). The fluters' finger widths are 31 mm, 34 mm and 38 mm. While 31 mm is clearly the three-finger width of a child, Van Gelder (2015b), thinks that the individual with the 34 mm width is likely a girl of 7 or 8 years of age given the height at which she flutes and her interaction with other children in the cave. While the 34 mm and 38 mm individuals created most of the saiga together, the child with the 31 mm width fluted one of the lines (Van Gelder 2015b). Another possible example from Rouffignac, is a mammoth drawn with one finger measuring 8 mm in width. It is located near flutings by the possible child with the 34 mm width and across from flutings created by the child with the 28 mm width.

Children's engagement in art

Another observation that can be made in relation to children's engagement with Upper Paleolithic images is that their participation never occurred in isolation (Roveland 2000; Van Gelder 2015b). For example, children's footprints are always found in association with adult footprints. We also know that children were held up to make handprints and fluting streams high above the caves' floors. At Gargas, an adult held an infant's hand steady against the cave wall while making a stencil of it (*i.e.* blowing pigment such as charcoal or ochre around the hand leaving behind a negative imprint of it) and in the process stenciled his or her own wrist as well. At Rouffignac, the approximately 5-year-old girl with the 28 mm width discussed above normally fluted at a height that a child of her age could comfortably reach but in some areas of the cave it is clear she is given a little help. For example, in Chamber E, her flutings appear in a depression on the ceiling at a height of 2.2 m suggesting she was lifted up or sitting on someone's hip (Van Gelder 2015b). There are many other such examples. As Van Gelder (2015b) notes, there is no evidence to suggest the children were ever left alone in these caves.

Children, in the company of adults, visited the furthest recesses of the caves, sometimes over difficult terrain and following branching galleries and corridors (Van Gelder 2015b). For example, at Rouffignac, a 2- or 3-year-old child whose three-fingered width measures 22 mm fluted in three chambers including one that is 700 m from the cave's entrance. Given the terrain, including cave bear (*Ursus spelaeus*) pits[4] that would have to be crossed, it is likely the child would have had to be carried for at least part of the journey (Van Gelder 2015b). Characteristically, this child's flutings are in short strokes, which is typical of the limited motor control displayed by young children (Van Gelder 2015b). Similar flutings were made by a child with a 22 mm three-finger width at Gargas.

The young girl with the 28 mm three-finger width at Rouffignac was described as using both her hands when she fluted. For Van Gelder (2015b), this posed an interesting question with regards to social engagement – who was holding her light? There is no natural light in Rouffignac and in order to flute she would have required either light from a hearth or someone else would have had to hold a torch or lamp for her.

Children often engaged in co-creating fluted panels not only with other children but with male and female adults as well. This can be seen in the crisscrossing of fluted lines or the close association of fluted lines created by different sized hands. In one particularly poignant example, Van Gelder (2015b) describes one panel at the 26,000-year-old cave site of Gargas (France) where a female adult is fluting with her left hand on the left side of the panel while a 5-year-old boy, presumably on her hip, flutes on the right side of the panel. Their flutings are at the same height – well above where a 5 year old could reach on his own. Other co-created panels include the saiga from Rouffignac and a panel in the chamber known as G4 in this same cave. Here (Fig. 5.9), we find seven arced flutings. Six of these arcs are spaced closely together, decreasing in size as you move toward the ceiling. At first glance, because they are all angled the same way, you might assume they were made by the same hand but, in fact, five different people made these arcs, including the possible child with the 34 mm width and a definite child with a 31 mm width. The fluting by the younger child is one of the highest in this panel and would be far higher than they could reach

Figure 5.9: Arced flutings created by five different people, including one definite child (31 mm) and one probable child (34 mm), attest to the inclusion of children in Upper Paleolithic image making at Rouffignac Cave (France), Chamber G4 (Photo courtesy: Leslie Van Gelder).

without being lifted by an adolescent or adult (Van Gelder 2015b; Van Gelder and Nowell 2021). Another interesting example concerns two more tectiforms, this time in the Voie Sacré in Rouffignac. One is created by the possible child with a three-finger width of 34 mm and the other by an older individual with a three-finger width of 38 mm. The 38 mm individual drew a large tectiform of about 70 cm in length, then a 7- or 8-year-old child (with the 34 mm finger width) drew a second tectiform of approximately 50 cm in length. We know this was the sequence in which the tectiforms were created because the upper right flutings of the child crossover the bottom left flutings of the older individual. It is tempting to imagine that the child was practicing how to create a tectiform or learning when it is appropriate to create such a sign. It is possible that if these fluters were standing side by side that their flutings reflect their respective heights (Van Gelder 2015b; Van Gelder and Nowell 2021).

Finally, in each of the four European caves that Van Gelder (2015b) studied that contained the flutings of children, she also found animals drawn with one finger, and often poorly so! Measurements of the single fingers indicate that the images might have been drawn by adults. Whether these animals were drawn for the amusement of children as they are often found in close association with children's flutings is unknown but the suggestion is compelling. Overall, the work of Sharpe and Van Gelder gives archaeologists a glimpse of intimate moments in the lives of Ice Age people, allowing us to connect with them in ways that would otherwise be impossible.

Communities of practice and evidence of apprenticeship in Upper Paleolithic art

In Chapter 4, I discussed the importance of communities of practice for children and evidence for the existence of these sorts of communities centered around lithic technologies in the Paleolithic. A similar case can be made for communities of practice focused on the Paleolithic arts. I am defining 'arts' in the broadest sense here to include paintings and engravings on the walls, ceilings and floors of caves and rock shelters, engraved and incised bone, antler and stone and ivory and clay sculptures of animal and human figures (Nowell 2006). As noted, one way to study communities of practice is to identify archaeologically visible standardized means of production or 'traditions'. Well-known examples in the Paleolithic include thousands of tiny Aurignacian (ca. 35,000 BP) basket-shaped, mammoth ivory beads (White 2007), highly standardized animal head cutouts known as 'contours découpés', animal-ended spear-throwers (Conkey 1993; Dobres 2001), and feline-human statues from sites in Germany (Conard 2011). Over the years, many other instances of conventions (both local and regional) for depicting animals have been documented by researchers (see detailed examples in GRAPP 1993).

Another way to identify communities of practice is to look for points of disjuncture or discontinuity in the archaeological record that might reflect changes in social practice. For example, as discussed above, over time there was a diverging relationship between fauna chosen to be consumed and fauna chosen to be painted and engraved on cave walls (Gonzales-Morales 1997). A second example is the change in recipe used to make the pigments employed in the production of images in caves. While artistic style remained the same over generations, there is a clear regional change in southern France in pigment recipe at 13,000 BP with the addition of biotite as an extender[5] (Clottes 1993).

Another example of a discontinuity is the change of practice in engraving between the Magdalenian and Azilian periods in Europe. Farbstein and Davies (2017, 6 and references therein) observe that 'the gestures craftspeople use when making art are particularly important points of reference because they relate to Marcel Mauss' (1934) "techniques du corps" or culturally-variable, learned and prescribed bodily behaviours and gestures'. According to Fritz *et al.* (2016), it was standard practice in the Magdalenian to begin engraving an animal from the head and to work backward toward the tail. They know this because they used a scanning electron microscope to document the order in which different components were engraved. They write (2016, 1319),

> [t]he training of young engravers went even further as the manner in which drawings that were accomplished followed certain rules ... The head systematically came first, starting with

the horns or antlers, then the chest, the line of its back, the front legs, the stomach line, the back legs, and finally its rear end and tail. Once the outline was complete, the engraver made its internal attributes (fur, signs, eyes, nostrils) but always after the outline.

They also note that geometric patterns were created following a similar set of rules. They studied engravings from multiple Magdalenian sites and found very little deviation in mode of execution over time and space. By 13,000 BP at the beginning of the Azilian, however, engravers abandoned these rigid rules (Fritz *et al.* 2016). Instead, there is greater gestural variability, emphasizing simplicity, efficiency and visibility of the engraved lines (d'Errico 1994, 1319). Fritz *et al.* (2016) argue that this discontinuity and shift in approach 'between the two periods is rooted in a new cultural setting, in changing parameters for the making of engraved objects, and in a different community of practices'. These changes in practice mirror thematic and stylistic changes also noted in the Azilian (Fritz *et al.* 2016 and references therein).

Finally, one further line of evidence in support of communities of practices in Paleolithic arts may be the findings of engraved plaquettes. Clottes (2010; see also Russell 1989) has observed that many of the engravings on these portable artifacts are not as skilled as engravings on cave walls, suggesting they may be the work of apprentices. In fact, the idea that there were centers or 'art schools' for apprentices is an old one (*e.g.* Cartailhac and Breuil 1907; Capitan and Bouyssonie 1924) but these early suppositions were largely based on intuition rather than hard evidence.

The integration of children into these communities of practice would depend to some degree on age-related physical (*e.g.* motor-control and endurance) and cognitive constraints (*e.g.* ability to conceptualize and execute designs and forms) (Kamp 2001a) as well as specific cultural conventions related to childhood. There are many ways in which younger children and novices can participate in activities associated with craft production (Grimm 2000; Kamp 2001a). These tasks could have included collecting and grinding ochre and other minerals necessary for pigment production, collecting firewood to make charcoal, collecting bird bones or slabs of rock suitable for use as palettes, and holding a torch or lamp to facilitate image production in caves (Nowell 2015b). In the process, they would learn about the properties of raw materials (*e.g.* where to find them, how to process them, what qualities to look for), and the social conventions for producing images and decoding meanings.

As we saw in Chapter 3, learning may have begun through play. Clay in particular lends itself to early experimentation. It can be manipulated by the youngest of children with little fear of injury. It is easy to work, even for small hands with minimal physical strength and limited motor control. It is a forgivable material – until it is fired it can be reshaped repeatedly. Its malleability means that it can be pinched and stretched into a variety of forms, unlike bone and ivory that, to some degree, can dictate the shape of the final product, particularly in novices' hands. Farbstein and Davies (2017, 3) argue that the 'introduction of this innovative material and the associated technologies used to make ceramic art proved to be an important catalyst for more experimentation and play in the production of art, which led to innovations in artistic expression'. Exploring and 'playing' with the affordances of clay is something that can begin at an early age and likely did for Paleolithic children.

The role of practice in the production of art
Apprenticeship is a topic that was discussed at length in Chapter 4 in relation to flint-knapping but far less research into apprenticeship in the production of Paleolithic art has been undertaken. I think there are three reasons for this. The first reason is the sheer number of archaeologists who study lithics. These individuals vastly exceed the number of Paleolithic art specialists and thus the scope of studies in the area of lithics is broader.

Second, there is a long history of archaeologists studying the technical aspects of lithic production through experimentation, refitting and the chaîne opératoire approach and ethnoarchaeology. The study of Paleolithic art traditionally dates back to the discovery of the Spanish decorated cave site Altamira in 1879. In subsequent decades there was primarily a focus on interpreting the images (Conkey 1999) – what does this bison *mean*? It is only in the last 30 years or so that the emphasis has shifted toward a more forensic approach to understanding the production of cave art – what can be characterized as a move from 'artwork' to the 'work of art' (Nowell and Van Gelder 2020). Drawing on ethnography, ethnoarchaeology, taphonomic science, experimental archaeology and replicative studies, researchers now study the chemical makeup of pigments (Chalmin *et al.* 2003; Roldán *et al.* 2016); the heat treating of pigments; techniques of pigment application (Clottes 2010; Nowell 2015b); the preparation of wall surfaces (Clottes 2010); footprints, handprints and hand stencils in association with the art (Chazine and Noury 2005; Wang *et al.* 2010; Pastoors *et al.* 2015; Nelson *et al.* 2017); the use of artificial lighting in the Paleolithic (de Beaune 1987; Nowell 2018); acoustic properties of painted caves (Díaz-Andreu and Matiolli 2015); and the embodied use of space in the production of art panels (Fritz and Tosello 2007). I believe this relatively recent interest in the forensic approach to art as well as a growing body of literature on practice, embodied cognition and the like (see Chapter 4) create a space for Paleolithic art specialists to consider apprenticeship, skill and the social context of learning (*e.g.* Fritz 1997; 1999a; 1999b; Rivero; 2016; Fritz *et al.* 2016).

The third reason I believe apprenticeship has been understudied in Paleolithic art is because there is a belief on the part of both the general public and the scientific community that artistic skills are somehow more innate than the abilities needed for making stone tools – essentially you are 'gifted' or you are not (see discussion in Gustavsen 2014). In a Western context, there is an assumption that 'works of "true" art are the product of individual genius' (White 2003, 23) and that practice may not have a large role to play. The well-known rock art specialist, David Whitley, for example, argued in a 2008 book that the corpus of Paleolithic art is a series of masterpieces created by shamans who are in effect 'tortured geniuses'. There are too many faulty assumptions in that statement to unpack here but I mention it because it highlights this deep-seated assumption that skilled art somehow springs fully formed from the soul. But in a recent study of the relationship between hours of practice and skill level in representational (*i.e.* 'realistic') drawing, Gustavsen (2014) found that close to 70% of variance in skill level could be accounted for by hours of practice. This is directly relevant for the study of Upper Paleolithic imagery as much of the art is considered representative art. Through a regression analysis, Gustavsen (2014) observed a rapid acquisition of skill during the first 5000 hours of practice with a deceleration in skill acquisition after that, mostly tapering off close to the 10,000 hour mark. Between 10,000 and 34,000 hours (the most any artist in her study had practiced) skill level nonetheless increased, albeit more slowly, as artists continued deliberate practice (see Ericsson 2006 and Chapter 4 for a discussion of deliberate practice).

Gustavsen (2014) also explored the relationship between drawing practice in childhood specifically (defined as under the age of 12 years) and skill as an adult. She found a strongly positive correlation between the two variables. She (2014) further observed that at some point children realize their representative drawings are not truly realistic and, without encouragement, many stop drawing as a result. This usually occurs around the age of 9 or 10 (Edwards 2012). Those that push through by continuing to practice become more skilled. Adults who stopped drawing as children when asked to draw a figure later in life find they are still at the skill level of their younger selves (see Edwards 2012). Interestingly, Gustavsen notes (2014) that historically, guilds required young representative artists to complete a 10-year apprenticeship.

Representative artists produce large quantities of practice art during their lifetime. The implication for archaeologists studying children is somewhat equivocal. Theoretically, as with lithics, a significant portion of the total corpus of Paleolithic art ever produced could be the work of child and adolescent novices. Unlike with lithics, however, these practice images were not necessarily all created on or with durable and thus archaeologically visible materials.

Identifying novices in the Paleolithic arts
Errors

Engraving. In much the same way as with lithics, we can look for mistakes commonly made by novices. In the European Upper Paleolithic, artists used tools such as stone burins and projectile points to engrave bone, antler and ivory. Through experimentation, Fritz *et al.* (2016) determined that there are three angles that are key to engraving bone – the angle of a tool when it is first applied to the bone, the front-working angle and the side-working angle. All of these need to be at 45 degrees. They observe (Fritz *et al.* 2016, 1317–1318) that if this is not the case, 'errors can be seen on the bottom and the edges of the groove (*e.g.* scratches, side markings, irregular lines). The skill and hence the technical know-how of the engraver may be inferred by the frequency with which these mistakes were made'. These researchers observed that it is easier to engrave following the direction of the bone fibers as there is less resistance and most often this is what Upper Paleolithic engravers did but at times they needed to engrave a line perpendicular to the bone fibers. This change in direction, for example when engraving a curved line, is particularly challenging for novices – it requires more force and more control (Fritz et al. 2016). Similarly, Rivero (2016) argues that even deepening a line can be challenging for novices. Deeply engraving a line can require a minimum of six passes and it is often hard for a novice keep the tool in the groove. He (2016, 90) also notes that a lack of control of the tool can result in what he refers to as involuntary 'hookings ... which appear as sudden changes of direction or small elevations in the interior of the incisions'. Other novice errors include superficial engravings, tool 'slips', multiple corrections, a poor appreciation of the resistance of the bone, simplified designs and 'stick-slip oscillations', which are noticeable variations in the bottom of a groove as a result of a variation in the amount of pressure that is being exerted on the engraving tool (Fritz et al. 2016; Rivero 2016; Bello et al. 2020). Stick-slip oscillations are more common in curved lines and are identifiable by small transverse ripples (Rivero 2016, 90).

By contrast, Rivero (2016, 91) identifies six characteristics of master engravers. The first indicator is incision depth. This is when a tool is moved back and forth within a groove to create a deep incision without the tool slipping out. Next is profile combination. This is when the artist, for aesthetic reasons, creates different forms of incisions (*e.g.* the grooves have 'V', left or right asymmetrical 'V', straight angle, flat or 'W' profiles). The third characteristic is differential relief. According to Rivero (2016, 91), this is a very difficult technique to master. It involves 'progressively lowering the external edge of an incision to create different visual planes in the case of overlapping figures or different parts of a single figure' (Rivero 2016, 91). Fourth, skilled engravers often combine technologies such as cutting, engraving and perforating. Finally, gesture precision and surface preparation (*i.e.* smoothing the surface) are two more ways of identifying a master craftsperson. In their separate studies of Magdalenian engraved objects, Fritz et al. (2016), Rivero (2016) and Bello et al. (2020) all noted a wide range of skill levels.

Ceramics. Upper Paleolithic ceramics were limited to the production of figurines and similar objects, or at the very least we can say we have yet to find evidence of vessel production for storage of food. Nonetheless, observations drawn from the study of novices in vessel production in more recent periods are relevant as they can be extrapolated to ceramic work more broadly. Based on her study of Sinagua ceramicists in the US southwest (1100–1250 AD), Kamp (2001a) identifies several variables that can be used to identify novice ceramic artisans. The first variable is size. Novices tend to make smaller pots than experts because they are easier to work with, particularly in the case of young children. Second, novice vessels can be less symmetrical than ones made by more skilled artisans. The third variable is vessel thickness. Novices tend to create pots that are of uneven thickness in comparison to pots shaped by master craftspeople. Furthermore, novice pots tend to be roughly finished while expertly made vessels are smooth and often burnished. Experts employ more complicated techniques in the making of their vessels. For example, they create coiled or paddle and anvil pots while novices are more likely to make 'pinch pots'. Finally, novice produced pots are often characterized by small drying cracks, which is something you would not observe on expertly made pots. Uneven thickness in the wall of a pot causes cracking as thicker sections dry more slowly than thinner ones. In sum, Kamp (2001a, 430–431) writes, novice ceramicists

> may not have the requisite knowledge to control necessary production variables, leading to errors in tempering, drying, or firing. Similarly, their understanding of the standard range of ceramic shapes or designs may be incomplete, leading to the production of unusual forms or decoration. Alternatively, novices may be able to visualize the ideal vessel but be unable to produce it because they lack the motor skill to form large, symmetrical, or even vessels.

Vandiver *et al.* (1989, 1007) argue that fragments of figurines found in kilns at sites in the Czech Republic were 'ritually exploded'. They assert that the properties of the material (a loess paste) make accidental thermal shock 'improbable' and instead they believe that it required *'intentional effort and practice'* to explode these figurines into small fragments (my emphasis). Certainly, this is a possibility but it is also possible that we are looking at the work of novices (and the occasional expert having an off-day). The ceramic human and animal figures from the Upper Paleolithic are solid pieces and according to modern ceramic experts, it is quite easy for solid (vs. hollow) pieces to explode if too wet or there is air trapped in the clay even at very low temperatures. Another point of weakness may be the manner in which heads or limbs were attached to a figure's torso (Farbstein and Davies 2017). A reanalysis of the fragments with an eye to looking for the work of novices might produce a new understanding of these archaeological remains. Farbstein and Davies (2017) note that some figurines are so soft that it is clear that they were not fired but rather left to air dry. Thus, another interesting study would be to compare the fired to the air dried figurines in the context of the investigation novice ceramic production.

Raw material

Fritz *et al.* (2016) noted in their study that novices (identified by errors typically made by learners) often worked with poor quality raw materials, and scraps of raw material, for example antlers where discs had already been cut out. Again, this is an avenue that should be explored in relation to other Paleolithic arts media.

Image quality

Drawing in a broad sense, used here to include painting and engraving, involves mastery of both technical and artistic skills (Fritz *et al.* 2016). In paintings and engravings on both parietal and portable art, there are a number of variables that can suggest the work of novices including (1) line quality, (2) use of positive and negative space, (3) shading, (4) perspective, (5) proportion and (6) gestalt. First, according to Gustavsen (2014), a skilled line is one that is executed in a single motion creating either a smooth or tapered line. Following Eisner and Poplaski (2008), she characterizes skilled lines as expressive, precise and descriptive. Novices show greater hesitation than experts when drawing a line. The resulting line is made up of multiple overlapping strokes, some of which may have been erased (Edwards 2012). By contrast, younger children often draw from memory rather than in front of a subject. In this case, their lines tend to be solid (*i.e.* made up of stroke) and of even thickness, but 'wobbly' and with few or no corrections (Edwards 2012; Gustavsen 2014).

In their fine and detailed analysis of each individual gesture of the artist who drew the two rhinoceros locked in conflict at Chauvet (Fig. 5.10), Fritz and Tosello (2007, 64) documented hesitations, erasures and corrections. They write,

> The rhinoceros on the right exhibits more complex gestural sequences primarily due to the number of corrections expressed by the artist. As with the rhinoceros on the left, the nasal and frontal horns are drawn first but with a significant correction made to the nasal horn (phase 1). The initial rectangular shape of the horn is transformed into a curved appendage approaching anatomical reality. With the horns in place, the artist draws the mouth and a first phase of the mandible/chest with a certain hesitation. The chest is redrawn with a firm, broad stroke then a second version of the mandible is drawn slightly higher than the first. The artist then erases the original line of the mandible and using his or her fingers modifies the contour of the redrawn mandible (phase 2).

It is important to note that the medium (engraving, painting, drawing) and the uneven surface of the cave wall or ceiling can have an impact on the quality of a line. For example, through experimentation, Aujoulat (2005) found that charcoal 'crayons' could produce a line of 35 cm in length before needing to be changed. This could be a factor when evaluating many of the larger drawings. Farbstein and Davies (2017) make a similar observation in relation to poorer quality clay.

The next variable is the use of positive and negative space. Positive space is the space occupied by an object or figure in a drawing while negative space is the background and the space between objects (Carson 2012). According to Gustavsen (2014, 18), '[n]ovice artists often do not consider the distribution of space, and generally focus on the most representative aspects of the figure's positive space while ignoring its negative space. This can lead to a crooked and disproportionate figure. In contrast, skilled artists are aware of the importance of accurate negative space, and execute their drawings accordingly'.

Shading, or what Edwards (2012, 204) refers to as 'light logic', is a third important variable as it defines much of a subject's form (Edwards 2012). Its accuracy depends on both the placement of the shadows and their tonal value (*i.e.* lightness or darkness) (Gustavsen 2014). Natural light casts shadows on a figure in ways unanticipated by a novice artist (Gustavsen 2014). Novices typically shade the contour of a figure rather than correctly assessing the direction of light on a subject and shading where the shadows fall (Gustavsen 2014). This flattens the figure, undermining the desired effect of realism (Edwards 2012). In a sense, novices are drawing what they *think* rather than

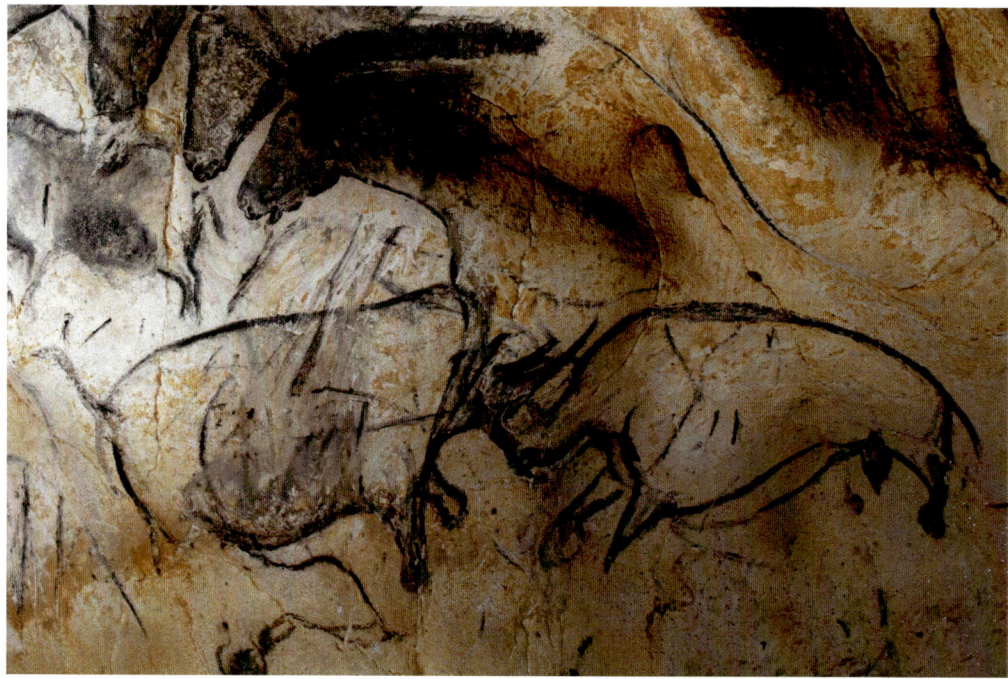

Figure 5.10: Two rhinoceros locked in conflict on the walls of Chauvet Cave (France). Fritz and Tosello's (2007) detailed study of this scene reveal the individual gestures and bodily movements of the artist, including numerous attempts to correct or redraw the figures (Photo courtesy: Carole Fritz/Ministère de la Culture).

what they *see* – part of becoming an expert is learning to see (Nowell 2015b). Novices also typically fail to accurately reproduce the range of tonal variation in an image, rendering the subject too light or too dark (Gustavsen 2014).

Perspective, or the way in which a three dimensional subject is depicted on a two dimensional surface, is a fourth variable. Expert artists draw an imaginary line ('vanishing line') that depicts the angle at which a three-dimensional object recedes into space. These lines converge on a spot on the horizon known as the vanishing point (Edwards 2012). If these lines do not converge the illusion of three dimensionality is shattered. This can prove challenging for novice artists.

A fifth variable is proportion. Proportion is the relative size of different components of a figure or composition and it work in conjunction with perspective to maintain the illusion of three dimensionality (Gustavsen 2014). A head that is out of proportion to its body, for example, fails to achieve the desired effect.

The final two variables considered here are balance and 'gestalt'. Physical balance is a figure's mass and structure while focal balance refers to how an artist draws the viewer's eye to a figure (Edwards 2012; Gustavsen 2014). According to Gustavsen

(2014, 26), '[o]ne of the most frequent mistakes new artists make is not correctly utilizing the focal point by applying equal attention to detail throughout the entire figure'. Gestalt refers to the overall appeal of the drawing and can be more difficult to teach but it is a 'feel' or aesthetic sensibility that develops with practice (Edwards 2012).

Who made the art?

Much like with flintknapping the question of who made the art needs to be explored. In this section, I will briefly consider what we know about the age and sex of the makers of Paleolithic arts.

Age

In Chapter 4, I argued that while a novice is not necessarily the same thing as a child, it was very likely that Paleolithic children learned flintknapping from a young age; I further argued that it was reasonable to use the evidence of novices as a proxy for the evidence of children and adolescents in the archaeological record of this period. A similar argument can be made for the arts but with some caveats. From the ethnographic record, it is clear that children in traditional societies enter communities of practice at a young age and learn through play and by observing and listening to the adults around them. We also know from the size[6] of handprints, finger holes, finger fluting and footprints that children witnessed and engaged in the production of Paleolithic arts. At the same time, while at least basic flintknapping was likely key to survival in the Paleolithic, it is not clear that the ability to produce images and figurines played as crucial a role in the lives of all members of these societies although perhaps being able to interpret them did (Nowell 2015b). I think what we can reasonably say is that while perhaps not all members of society learned to draw, paint, engrave and sculpt, those that did began their apprenticeship at a young age. This begs the question of how much of the archaeological record of the Paleolithic arts is the result of children. With lithics, I argued that the children's archaeological signatures likely 'swamp' adult contributions to the archaeological record. But can the same be said of children's contribution to Paleolithic arts? Probably not. Gustavsen (2014) has argued that during the first 9000 hours of practice, novice artisans in the Upper Paleolithic conservatively produced two drawings per practice hour. However, because painting, drawing, engraving and sculpting can be practiced on perishable materials (unlike flintknapping that, by definition, is practiced on stone) and because clay work can be remodeled prior to firing, it is more difficult to judge just how much of the surviving archaeological examples of Paleolithic arts are the result of novices.

Further impeding our ability to see children in the production of Paleolithic arts is the tendency of textbooks, popular media and even researchers to publish photographs of the more striking examples of Paleolithic art. This choice gives the false impression that the entire corpus is the work of master craftspeople. Clottes (2010) and Guthrie (2005), have suggested that some of the cruder drawings in cave art may be the work of children but what is needed is a systematic (rather than anecdotal or impressionistic) study of the art, with an eye to the contributions of children. This could be done using the criteria outlined above in conjunction with a set of criteria drawn from developmental psychology as the sequence and timing of representational capacities in children cross-culturally is well-documented. For example, cross-cultural studies (Kellogg 1969; Di Leo 1970; Goodnow 1978; see also Huntley 2010) demonstrate that all physically and cognitively able children progress through six specific stages (Huntley 2010 and references therein) when it comes to drawing, although the pace at which they progress through these stages can depend on access to materials and other variables such as degree of encouragement (*e.g.* Alland 1983). According to Huntley (2010), these stages are: (1) *Scribbling*, which begins at age 2 cross-culturally (interestingly this is also when children begin to engage in imaginative play; see Nowell 2016); (2) *Pre-Schematic*, which is when children begin to draw 'diagrams' by combining six basic shapes or 'diagrams' to make representational figures (rectangle/square, circle/oval, triangle, Greek cross, diagonal cross and a closed irregular shape); (3) the *Schematic* stage when drawings become more complex as children combine several of these diagrams to make aggregate figures; (4) the *Pre-visual realism* stage when children create more objective representations with figures pointing outward because of the importance of face-to-face interactions; and (5) finally, the *Visual realism* stage (sometime between the age of 7 and 10 years) when greater realism emerges. There can still be some confusion in the drawing, for example, a figure in profile may have two eyes facing out! Using these criteria, Huntley (2010; 2016; 2018) studied children's graffiti at Pompeii and similar studies have been undertaken on pottery in the US southwest (*e.g.* Crown 2001). This kind of work is yet to be undertaken in the Paleolithic and would be instrumental in helping us to understand the nature and degree of children's participation in Upper Paleolithic arts.

Finally, it is worth noting that fingerprints in clay have been studied by archaeologists as a way of estimating the age of the pottery maker in more recent periods (*e.g.* Kamp 2001a). To my knowledge, the only fingerprint that has been observed on an Upper Paleolithic clay object is on an artifact from the site of Dolní Věstonice. Initial studies of a fingerprint on the back of the Dolní Věstonice ('venus') figurine suggest it belongs to a subadult between the ages of 7 and 15 years (Králík *et al.* 2002). It may be possible in the future, using a technique called RTI (Reflectance Transformation Imaging), to look for fingerprints in clay fingerholes, painted images where the paint is digitally applied such as at Niaux (France) and, of course, in the flutings.[7] RTI relies on multiple images and mathematical modeling to produce highly detailed three dimensional images. Bennison-Chapman and Hager (2018) have used RTI to image fingerprints and palm prints on Neolithic clay tokens to explore sex-based division of labor at the site of Boncuklu Höyük in Turkey, while Díaz-Guardamino *et al.* (2015)

have used it to study manufacturing techniques in Late Bronze Age engraved rock art in Spain. Initial applications of RTI to the study of Paleolithic art include Porter *et al.*'s (2016) research on portable art.

Sex

Identifying young fluters at Rouffignac as Upper Paleolithic *girls* or *boys* brings us to the question of sex (but, as discussed in Chapter 3, not necessarily gender). Much like with lithics (Chapter 3) there has been an assumption, beginning at the turn of the last century with the renowned prehistorian, Abbé Breuil, that most Paleolithic art was created by men (see discussion in Russell 1991; Hays-Gilpen 2004; Nowell and Chang 2009; Fritz *et al.* 2016). Hays-Gilpen (2003, 90) writes,

> Abbé Breuil was convinced that making art was a religious activity, so rock art had to have been done by priests and shamans, who would have been male only, because in his experience, only men were priests. Leroi-Gourhan, Guthrie, Onians, and others thought art was made by hunters, and in their understanding of world ethnography, only men were hunters. Many believed that caves were too deep, dark, and difficult to get into, and so would have been too frightening for women.

Arctic biologist Dale Guthrie (2005), for example, characterizes the overwhelming majority of Paleolithic art as 'sexually charged images' and violent hunting scenes and argues that the images are best interpreted as graffiti created by sexually excited teenage boys based on handprints in cave art (Nowell and Chang 2009). This is an inaccurate assessment of the corpus of Paleolithic art, not only because, as will be discussed in Chapter 6, specialists are hard-pressed to identify any unambiguous examples of 'violent hunting scenes' or 'sexually charged' images (Bahn 1986; 2006; Jonaitis 2007) but also because subsequent studies of handprints and finger flutings in European caves such as Rouffignac, Pech Merle and El Castillo (Sharpe and Van Gelder 2004; 2006a; 2006b; 2006c; Snow 2006; 2013) and at Upper Paleolithic cave sites in Borneo (Chazine 1999; Chazine and Fage 1998; 1999; Chazine and Noury 2005) attribute these markings to men and women, adults and subadults. Furthermore, the low sexual dimorphism exhibited by subadults, discussed in Chapter 1, means that we can't sex their hands based on size alone (Nelson *et al.* 2006; Snow 2006; Cooke 2014).

Flutings. When fingertips are visible and the fluting hand (right or left) can be established, Van Gelder and Sharpe (2009) determine the sex of individual fluters using what is known as the 2D:4D ratio (see detailed discussion of this ratio in Cooke 2014). This ratio, also sometimes referred to as Manning's ratio, describes the relationship between the length of a person's second digit (or index finger) and his or her fourth digit (or ring finger). The 2D:4D ratio is predetermined in utero through exposure to estrogen and testosterone (Koehler *et al.* 2004). Ratios of less than 1.0 (*i.e.* the index finger is shorter than the ring finger) reflect greater testosterone exposure and thus are typical of males, while ratios of or greater than 1.0 (*i.e.* the index finger is the same size or greater than the ring finger) are typical of females (Manning *et al.* 1998). The ratio is calculated by measuring from the palmer proximal crease to the finger tips along the midline without compressing the finger pads. Sharpe and Van Gelder had to modify how this ratio is calculated because these lengths cannot be measured in flutings as individuals used only their fingertips to flute (Cooke 2014). Instead, they measured the lengths of the second finger (2F), third finger (3F) and fourth finger (4F) of each fluting and compared the extension of each fingertip to each other. In this case, a shorter 2F than 4F is found in males while the reverse is true for females (Cooke 2014).

Handprints. Another way to infer the sex of Paleolithic artists is by applying the 2D:4D ratio to handprints and hand stencils (also known as positive and negative handprints, respectively) that are found at Paleolithic sites throughout Europe, Australia and Indonesia (Chazine and Noury 2005; Snow 2006; 2013) (see Chapter 3). While positive handprints are created by pressing a hand into pigment and then onto the cave's surface, a negative handprint is created by spitting pigment directly around the hand or by blowing pigment through a hollow bird bone.

While the 2D:4D ratio is more or less established in adults, it is more equivocal in children. Male hands develop at a faster rate than female hands in utero until birth. By contrast, from birth until adolescence, female hands develop more quickly than male hands and at an increasing rate, resulting in female hands achieving their adult size two years earlier than male hands (Cooke 2014). It is conceivable that this difference in growth and development between males and females could impact the reliability of the 2D:4D ratio – *i.e.* could it settle earlier in females (Cooke 2014)? Williams *et al.* (2003) studied the ratio in 196 Scottish children between the ages of 2 and 5 and found that the ratio did not settle until middle childhood (normally defined as somewhere between 5 and 12 years old). Similarly, Manning *et al.* (2004) studied sex and ethnic differences in the presentation of the 2D:4D ratio in 798 children between the age of 5 and 14 cross-culturally. They concluded that sexual dimorphism in the 2D:4D ratio is apparent by age 2, cross-culturally applicable although population variation does exist, and increases in reliability with age, settling in place sometime between the ages of 5 and 14. Cooke (2014) applied the 2D:4D ratio to a sample of 318 children and adolescents in Canada, ranging in age from 5 to 16 in order to study the presentation of this ratio in subadults before and during puberty. In contrast to Manning *et al.* (2004), in Cooke's (2014) study, more than 75% of male participants presented with a male patterned 2D:4D ratio but less than 25% of female participants presented with a typically female patterned ratio. In other words, most of the female participants patterned as males. These results were consistent throughout her sample, regardless of age, and she found that the onset of puberty was not a factor in the settling of this ratio (Cooke 2014). This doesn't mean that the ratio cannot be used to sex children's hand stencils but it does underscore the need to draw on the correct reference population. Snow's (2013) study of adult subjects in Pennsylvania found a similarly masculinized sample suggesting this patterning could be a North America-wide phenomenon but more research is required (Cooke 2014).

While the first mention of the potential of Manning's ratio for sexing handprints in archaeology can be found in the work of Mavis and John Greer (1999), to my knowledge the first actual application of this ratio was published seven years later. Chazine and Noury (2005), used software to capture the size and shape of hand stencils on a panel at the Paleolithic site of Gua Masri II in Borneo. Applying the 2D:4D ratio to these stencils, they discovered 17 male and 16 female hands. Also in 2006, Snow published a study based on scans of more than 100 students at Penn State University. He found that absolute length of the hand and of each of the 2D, 3D, 4D and 5D correctly determined sex 79% of the time. Using the 2D:4D ratio and a 2D:5D ratio, his success rate dropped to 59% leading him to advise using both absolute length and the ratio together for greater accuracy. He applied that two step method to six hand stencils at four decorated caves in France (Les Combarelles, Font-de-Gaume, Abri du Poisson and Pech Merle). He concluded that four of them represented female hands, one a male hand and one a subadult male hand. In 2013, he expanded his archaeological sample to 32 hand stencils at seven cave sites (Abri du Poisson, Bernifal, El Castillo, Font-de-Gaume, Gargas, Les Combarelles and Pech Merle). Using his two step method, he concluded that 75% of the hands in his archaeological sample were female. Interestingly, Snow (2013) found less continuity (*i.e.* there was a wider gap) between the male and female patterned ratio in his Upper Paleolithic sample than he found in his North American sample. This suggests that Upper Paleolithic peoples may have been more sexually dimorphic and thus rendering the results of these methods more reliable (Cooke 2014).

While these applications of the 2D:4D ratio to archaeological samples are compelling, there are some challenges with its direct application that should make us cautious. First, there is the difficulty of locating and measuring the required anthropometric landmarks on handprints and stencils. Positive handprints are not a faithful reproduction of the entire hand. Through experimentation, Cooke (2014) found that because of the way pressure is applied during the making of a positive handprint, the tops of fingertips are often missing and more importantly, the palmer proximal crease of the fourth digit is often missing as well. The length of the fourth digit can still be inferred but this can introduce a source of error (Cooke 2014). With hand stencils, we are looking at an outline of the hand and thus the palmar proximatal creases are not reproduced at all. Instead, the creases are located in reference to wedges (spaces between digits) on either side of the digits (Snow 2013; Cooke 2014). When the wedges are visible with a clear delineation of the lowest point, which in life corresponds with the anatomical hand, then the creases can be inferred with accuracy (Cooke 2014) (Fig. 5.11).

Second, the archaeological sample of measurable hands for any age is small and even smaller when only subadult hands are considered. Additionally, as Fritz *et al.* (2016) note, there are surprisingly few skeletal remains of hands that can be used as a direct reference population. Furthermore, the existing 2D:4D ratio studies have focused on adult hand stencils (*e.g.* Snow 2006; 2013).

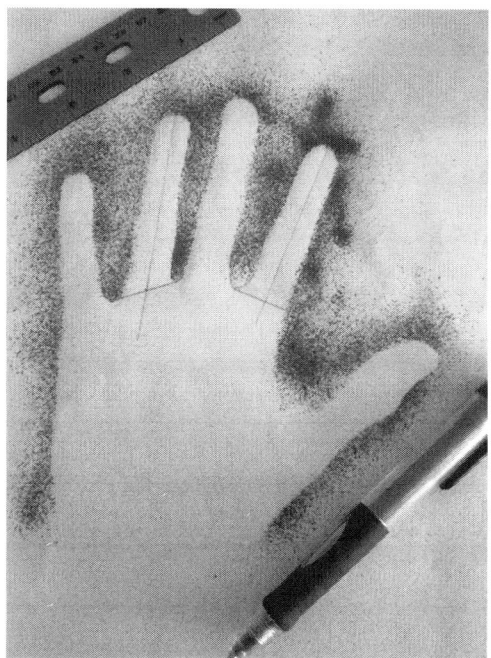 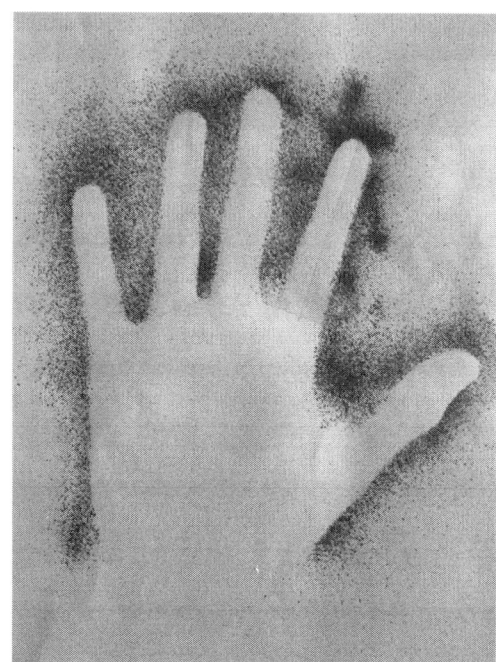

Figure 5.11: Hand stencils created by modern subadults using a BloPen on white paper taped to a wall. The stencil on the left was created by a 5-year-old male while the one on the right was created by a 15-year-old male. Pencil lines indicate the midline and the palmer creases as inferred from wedges on either side of the second and fourth digits (Photos courtesy: Amanda Cooke).

Third, the topography of the cave's ceilings and walls introduces another variable. Unlike in a lab setting where participants make handprints and hand stencils under ideal conditions, caves have many natural convexities and concavities. Depending on the projection angle of the pigment and whether the individual's hand is flat against a wall, the hand can be distorted, in particular, fingers can be lengthened (Cooke 2014; Fritz *et al.* 2016). If the hand is placed higher than the mouth, it can be difficult to blow the pigment around the tips of the fingers, while if the hand is placed lower than the mouth, pigment may be sprayed downward below the fingertips (Cooke 2014). Differing lengths of fingernails are another source of potential error (Cooke 2014). These issues may be especially important for interpreting stencils made by subadults as children exhibit more diversity in the stenciling process (Fig. 5.12) due to motor control, motivation or comprehension of the goals of the exercise. In her study of modern child-produced hand stencils, Cooke (2014) found that the percentage of measurable hand stencils increased dramatically by age 8, with little difference between 8 and 16 years. Whether you have help or not may be another factor, particularly for children. Spit painting requires that enough ground pigment (*e.g.* charcoal

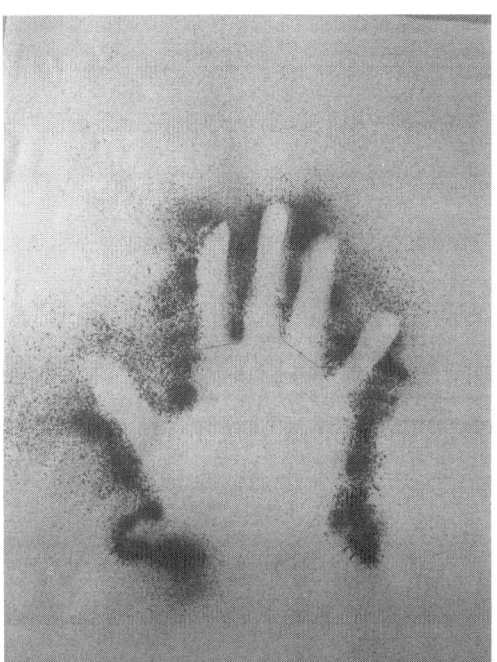 

Figure 5.12: Hand stencils made by children using a BloPen and white paper taped to a wall. The stencil on the left was made by a 5-year-old female while the one on the right was created by a 6-year-old male. This demonstrates the range in variability exhibited by children particularly up to age 7 (Cooke 2014). Clearly, only the left stencil could be measured (Photos courtesy: Amanda Cooke).

or manganese) be readily available for spitting following secondary grinding in the mouth. In experiments conducted by my undergraduate students, it was found that even with practice it was difficult to keep your hand in a fixed location if you had to reach for additional pigment. Even a slight movement of the hand impacted the length and shape of the resulting stencil.

Finally, it is not clear how faithful a reproduction of the soft-tissue hand a hand stencil is. Because the 2D:4D ratio works sufficiently well to differentiate males from females in living populations, there is an assumption that it can be applied directly to an archaeological hand stencil. In the study referenced above, Cooke (2014) asked 318 children between the ages of 5 and 16 to create hand stencils using plain white paper taped to a wall and BloPens. Measurements were taken of their hands as well as from the stencils they created. Setting aside non-measurable stencils such as the one in Figure 5.12, Cooke (2014) found a degree of error in every one of the stencils produced. In one third of the stencils, the 2D or 4D were smaller than the anatomical digits that produced them while in two thirds of the cases, the stenciled digits were larger. The error ranged between 1 mm and 13 mm with a mean error of 2.6 mm, with most errors under 4 to 5 mm. Paired-t tests showed that the error for both 2D and 4D were highly significant with a P-value of <0.001. An error of 2.6 mm might be negligible, particularly if the error is impacting both the 2D and the 4D equally but that wasn't always the case in her study sample. Furthermore, these results were produced under ideal conditions and the degree of error is likely to be greater under 'real world' conditions (*i.e.* in caves and rock shelters).

Fiber technologies

The last body of evidence for the lived lives of Paleolithic children to be considered in this chapter is fiber technology. I begin with a discussion of the evidence for clothing and textiles and then turn to cordage before considering how plant-based technologies shape our understanding of late Pleistocene children.

Clothing, ornaments and textiles

The human body lies at the interface between the individual self and the group (Kosut 2015). As a product of both nature and culture, it can be modified to fulfill, challenge or rebel against ideals of beauty (Perper *et al.* 2017) and expectations related to age, gender, social status, kinship, ethnicity, group membership, sexuality, religion and occupation (Nowell and Cooke forthcoming). One of the ways in which humans culturally modify their bodies is through clothing and personal adornment. While there is no direct evidence of clothing prior to the Upper Paleolithic, there is considerable data to suggest that some of our earlier hominin relatives engaged in fiber production and wore clothing.

The loss of body hair in hominins, probably around 2.0 mya (Chapter 2), presented a problem of how to stay warm at night and during chillier times of year. Keeping warm would also have been a concern as hominins migrated into cooler climates. Researchers such as Ian Gilligan (2010) suggest that clothing was one of the solutions to that problem. Natural fibers trap pockets of warm air near the skin, maintaining warmth while allowing perspiration to dissipate. A study of head and body lice deviation suggests that the regular wearing of clothing began around 200,000 years ago among anatomically modern humans in Africa. There are two forms of the human louse (*Pediculus humanus*) – the head louse and the body louse. They are distinguishable from each other by how they look, how they behave and where they live. Hairlessness confined *P. humanus* to the head, but sometime between 83,000–170,000 years ago, body lice evolved to live in clothing and bedding, most often laying their eggs in the seams of clothes (Toups *et al.* 2010).

Based on the location of cutmarks on faunal remains that are associated with pelt removal, and usewear and residue on stone tools related to skinning animals and scraping hides, archaeologists argue that Neandertals (and possibly even earlier hominins) wore clothing (see Nowell and Cooke forthcoming and Nowell and Skala forthcoming). However, disagreement remains over the exact nature and design of these items of apparel, whether or not they were tailored and their role in Neandertal extinction and survival (*e.g.* Aiello and Wheeler 2003; Trinkaus 2005; Wales 2012; Collard *et al.* 2016; Hosfield 2016).

By the early Upper Paleolithic, there is considerable evidence of textile production. Archaeologists have uncovered hundreds of fine bone and ivory needles too fragile to be used to sew hides and skin (Soffer *et al.* 2000a; 2000b). Another technological innovation may be the rondelles/spindle whorls discussed in Chapter 3 (see Riede *et al.* 2018). A third line of evidence of textile production comes from impressed clay tablets. People making clay figurines in the vicinity of kilns sometimes sat or kneeled down on wet clay, imprinting the weave of their clothing in the process. Many of these accidental imprints were fortuitously fired leaving archaeologists with an incomparable record of the types of weaves and knots in use at the time (Adovasio *et al.* 1996; Soffer 2004; see also Nowell and Cooke forthcoming). In total, there are roughly 100 imprints of textiles on clay from Dolní Věstonice I and II and Pavlov in the Czech Republic, Kostienki I and II and Zaraisk in Russia and Gönnersdorf in Germany; as well as a textile imprint on a bone from France (Adovasio *et al.* 1996; Soffer and Adovasio 2010 and references therein). In addition, clothing details, including head gear can be discerned on many female figurines in Europe, primarily from the Gravettian (Soffer *et al.* 2000a; 2000b; 2002). Specifically, we have evidence of caps, bandeaux, belts, bracelets and necklaces of plant fiber and string skirts (Soffer and Adovasio 2010). In Siberia, at the Gravettian sites of Mal'ta and Buret', fully dressed figurines of women, men and children have recently been reanalyzed (Lbova and Volkov 2015). According to researchers, they are wearing hooded, full-length garments sewn from animal fur, hide (leather) and seal or fish guts (Lbova and Volkov 2015; 2017). Many of the garments are similar to clothing worn by present-day Indigenous people in Siberia. Altogether, Lbova and Volkov (2015; 2017) have identified different types of hats and hoods, fur overalls, hooded parkas, belts, fur boots, bracelets, bags and even one backpack with two straps. As noted in Chapter 3, some of the figurines exhibit traces of colorful pigments. Other details include leather braided straps, fur, shells and fabric (Lbova and Volkov 2017).

Another line of evidence for textile production are 30,0000-year-old wild flax fibers archaeologists uncovered in the Republic of Georgia that were spun, dyed and knotted (Kvavadze *et al.* 2009; but see Bergfjord *et al.* 2010). Finally, Trinkaus (2005; Trinkaus and Shang 2008), based on a comparative study of the proximal pedal phalanges (the part of the toes closest to the foot) of a sample of Middle and Upper Paleolithic populations, argues that humans wore supportive footwear by at least the Gravettian in Europe and perhaps closer to 40,000 BP in China at the site of Tianyuan 1.

Other than the figurines of children in Siberia (Chapter 3), the only (in)direct evidence we have of children's clothing in the Upper Paleolithic comes from burials (Chapter 3). This evidence is in the form of personal ornaments such as mammoth ivory beads and perforated teeth that we assume were sewn onto clothing such as caps, tunics and pants (Taborin 2004). For example, at Sunghir, a Gravettian site in Russia, two boys were buried head to head. One boy (Sunghir 3) was approximately 10 years of age when he died while the other was closer to 12 years of age (Sunghir 2) (Sikora *et al.* 2017; Trinkaus and Buzhilova 2018). A 35- to 45-year-old male (Sunghir 1) was buried next to them (Trinkaus and Buzhilova 2018). Approximately 13,000 mammoth ivory beads were associated with the interred individuals, with Sunghir 3 having the greatest number – approximately 5400 beads (Soffer 1985; Trinkaus and Buzhilova 2018). The beads, likely sewn onto clothing, are highly standardized, and the ones associated with the children are two-thirds the size of those associated with the adult male. According to Soffer (1985), the beads represent more than 2500 person-hours of investment. Testart (2012), however, argues that children often outgrow their clothing before they are worn out completely and that the beads found with the Sunghir children may have been added to their clothing over time to make them 'good as new' as they were patched and passed on to a new generation. For this reason he believes that we should not be surprised at a child having twice the number of beads as an adult. It is clear from use-wear studies that the beads on the children's clothing show evidence of wear (d'Errico and Vanhaeren 2016) and this could support Testart's (2012) argument.

At the 10,000-year-old site of La Madeleine (France), a young child of 3–7 years of age was laid to rest on their back in an extended position with their head oriented south and their arms laid out straight along their body. Arranged around their head are three limestone slabs forming a protective barrier (Bahn 2015). The only drawing made by archaeologists during the excavation shows hundreds of *Dentalium* shell beads (Figs 5.13 and 5.14) at the child's head, elbows, wrists, knees and ankles and around their neck but the exact location of each individual bead is unknown (Vanhaeren and d'Errico 2003). These highly standardized beads were between 6 and 7 mm in length (Cooney 2018). Based on the size of unbroken *Dentalium* shells, each shell could have produced two to a maximum of three beads. Therefore, it is estimated that it would have taken 15 to 20 hours to collect a sufficient number of shells to manufacture all of the beads found in the burial. Some beads were snapped while others were sawn to the right size. The natural pointed end of each shell was removed to create a larger aperture so a thread could be passed through each tiny tube-shaped bead (Vanhaeren and d'Errico 2003). Based on wear patterns, we know that the beads were embroidered onto the child's clothing rather than having been strung together. In total, there were 9 m of beads requiring at least that much thread to attach them to the garment with needles as thin as 1.5 mm, corresponding to the smallest diameter of the beads. To attach all of the beads would have required 2400 holes in either very soft leather or textile. Depending on the skill of the garment maker, this clothing would have required 30 to 50 hours to complete (Vanhaeren and d'Errico 2003).

A final example of clothing comes from Grotte des Enfants in Italy. At this 11,130-year-old site, two children were buried side by side. GE1 was 2–4 years old at death while GE2 was closer to 1–2 years old. It is not known how GE1 died, but GE2

5. Children, oral storytelling and the Paleolithic 'arts'

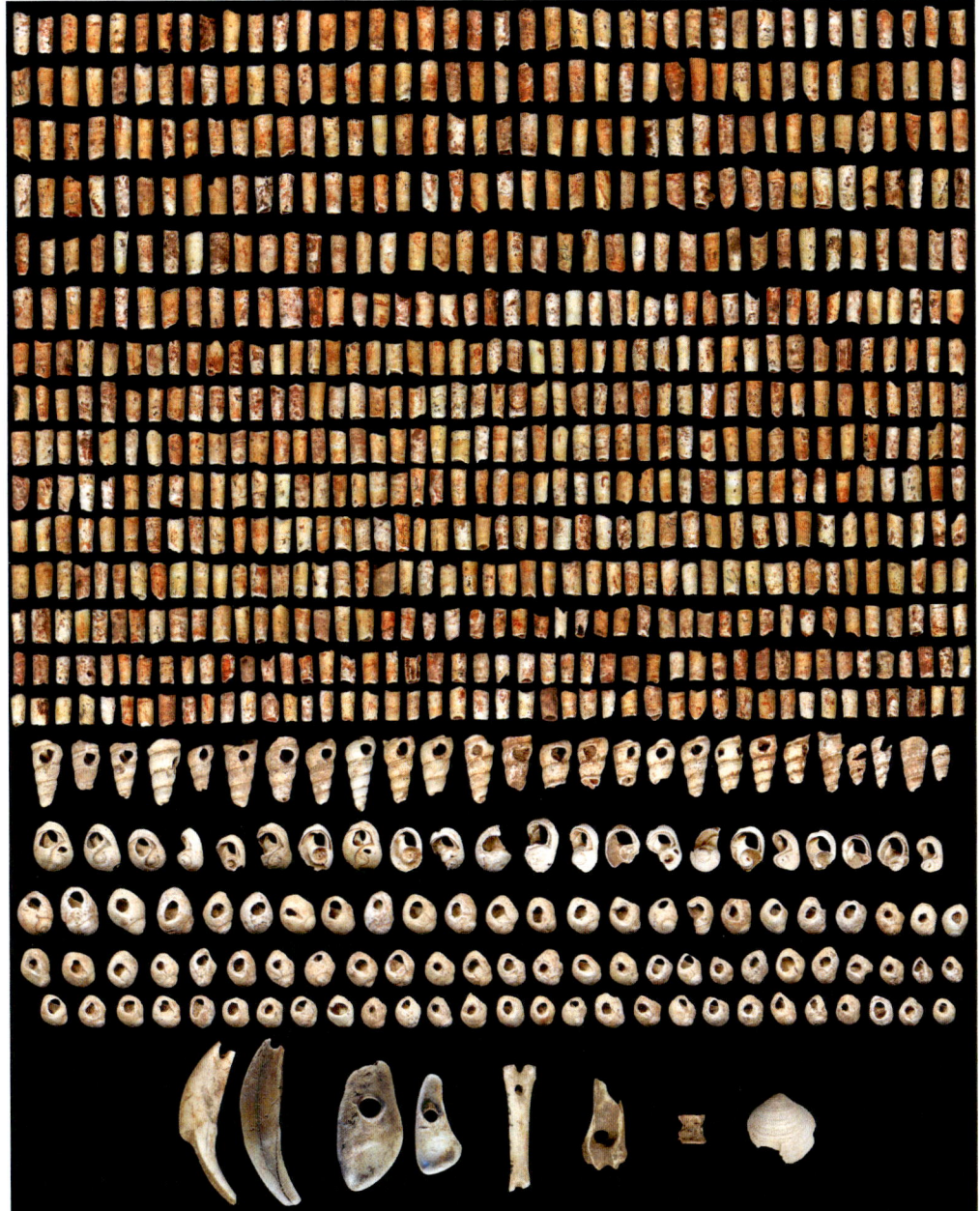

Figure 5.13: A portion of the shell beads found in the La Madeleine child burial. Each bead was sawn to between 6 and 7 mm in length and was likely embroidered onto clothing worn by the child. The beads are heavily worn suggesting they were not made specifically for the burial (Photo courtesy: Francesco d'Errico).

Figure 5.14: An artist's reconstruction of what the bead work on clothing associated with the La Madeleine child burial might have looked like (Drawing: Marina Lezcano).

had a flint projectile point embedded in one of its thoracic vertebrae, which was the likely cause of death (Vanhaeren and d'Errico 2003). Close to 1500 *Cyclope* sp. shells were found around the children's pelves. The shells chosen were so tiny that if the distribution of shells was the same in the Pleistocene as it is now, it would have taken at least 30 hours of searching to gather the ones found in the burial. Each bead bears a 2–4 mm perforation. Since no beads were found under the bodies, researchers suspect the beads were applied to clothing requiring a substantial investment of time (Vanhaeren and d'Errico 2003).

As with the Sunghir beads, these beads from La Madeleine and Grotte des Enfants were worn in life and were deliberately made smaller than those associated with adults in burials of the same period (Vanhaeren and d'Errico 2001; 2003). It is possible that children may have helped in the collection of some of these beads by 'beachcombing' or wading through shallow waters (Walshe forthcoming; see also Bednarik 1998; 2019). They may have even made some of the tiny perforations as with the work on the Bronze Age dagger mentioned in Chapter 1. Either way, these tiny beads would not have been reused on adult garments and thus it 'is clear is that [Upper Paleolithic] people invested a surprising degree of attention, time and specific skills into the manufacture of ostentatious beadwork for children. This effort is comparable to that observed in more recent societies' (Vanhaeren and d'Errico 2001, 504).

Cordage

Recently, evidence for fiber technology has been uncovered at Abris du Maras in France. At this Neandertal site, dating to 41,000–52,000 years ago, a 6.2 mm fragment of 3-ply baste fiber was found adhering to a Levallois flake (Hardy *et al.* 2020). At Ohalo II, a waterlogged site in Israel, three fragments of fiber dating to 19,000 years ago were uncovered, while at Lascaux researchers found remnants of 17,000-year-old 6-ply cordage (Bahn 1995). Finally, at Hohle Fels Cave in southern Germany, archaeologists discovered a 20 cm strip of mammoth ivory with four holes drilled into it that was used for making rope (McKie 2020). Early modern humans would have threaded plant fibers through the holes, twisting them into strong ropes (McKie 2020). As Hardy *et al.* (2020, 1) note, '[t]wisted fibres provide the basis for clothing, rope, bags, nets, mats, boats, etc. which, once discovered, would have become an indispensable part of daily life'.

Implications for the lived lives of Upper Paleolithic children

In archaeology, it is common to discuss how prehistoric foragers scheduled their lives around animal migrations and the procurement of lithic resources but we sometimes forget that plants accounted for a significant percentage of hominin diets and were used as medicines, dyes, tinder, bedding and adhesives and in fiber technologies including textiles and cordage. Plants and other organics form part of what Hurcombe (2014, 2) refers to as the 'missing majority' in the archaeological record. This reliance on plants reminds us of the importance of seasonality in the lives of foraging peoples. Finlay (2015, 107) notes that cultural knowledge and values would prescribe 'the timing and scheduling of activities and the responsibilities and ages of participants'. Working with plants requires deep, intergenerational knowledge of their properties, how, when and where to gather them, and how to properly store them so they last and are kept safe from animals (Nowell and Skala forthcoming). It also requires great flexibility[8] as, for example, an unusually dry season or a cold snap and climate change can alter plant availability and distribution from year to year or over the longer term as well as the integrity of that material. If flax is not available one year, an individual may need to use bast fibers or tanned hides instead; if tansy needs to be used as medicine one winter, then lichen may have to be used for dying textiles in its place. If you do not collect high quality bast fibers, your resulting thread will not be strong no matter how skilled you are at cordage (Nowell and Skala forthcoming).

Given the sheer importance of plants, Paleolithic children must have learned about their individual properties through guided experimentation, oral storytelling and listening to the adults around them. They would have learned what plants were edible, what ones could heal you, what ones could be made into textiles or other useful objects and what ones were to be avoided. While not everyone may have engaged in cordage or textile production on a regular basis, it is probable that by the Upper Paleolithic basic sewing and cordage skills would be knowledge possessed by everyone. At the very least being able to repair your own clothing would have been key to survival. For example, Ötzi, the famous Bronze Age 'Iceman', is believed to have repaired and possibly made his own clothing while trekking in the mountains (Khaleeq 2016). Aurora Skala argues, if you grow up 'observing skilled weavers, carvers, hunters, trackers, painters, cordage makers, dyers, plant harvesters, [and] bead makers ... you are likely to have a general knowledge on these topics and an ability to troubleshoot and transfer these skills because of your knowledge base' (Skala personal communication, June 2020).

As we saw with lithics and with the Paleolithic arts, social context is key. In this regard, Ingold's (1993) concept of the 'taskscape' is relevant. Ingold (1993, 158) writes, '[e]very task takes its meaning from its position within an ensemble of tasks, performed in series or in parallel, and usually by many people working together'. To create an item of clothing, for example, one has to gather plants at the right time of year for both the garment and the dye (perhaps integrating this task with other ones), and draw on intergenerational knowledge for its physical and aesthetic design and execution. Even maintaining a prized garment and keeping it safe from getting damaged by fire, insects and moisture while living an active, outdoor lifestyle could be considered part of a fiber's taskscape (Nowell and Skala forthcoming).

In this chapter, I considered the impact of intangible culture (oral stories, dance and music) and less archaeologically visible material culture than lithics (*e.g.* ceramics,[9] sculpting, engraving, painting and fiber technologies) on our understanding of the lived lives of Paleolithic children and adolescents. For more than two centuries, our thinking about Paleolithic societies has been dominated by the 'stones and bones' we find in abundance at our sites – and arguably for good reason. As scientists, we privilege the tangible, this is the very heart of positivism. But a blind adherence to positivism is a very narrowly defined definition of science (Johnson 2020) and this privileging has become what I would describe as a 'tyranny of the tangible'. Hurcombe (2014, 2) reminds archaeologists that, 'the majority of material culture is made up of organic raw materials, that most of those are highly perishable materials, and that their absence has severely affected our interpretation of their significance'. She (2014, 2) further cautions that these facts '[do] not and should not preclude them from being an essential aspect of archaeological thinking'. The pedagogic role, the galvanizing potential and the complex taskscapes and chaîne opératoires of the activities and crafts discussed in this chapter strongly support Hurcombe's assertions and contribute to a more holistic understanding of Paleolithic peoples generally and Paleolithic subadults specifically.

Notes

1. The oldest evidence for fire use dates back to at least 1 million years ago in South Africa (*e.g.* Berna *et al.* 2012).
2. Rouffignac has never been officially dated. Van Gelder 2015(b) argues that stylistically this cave, nicknamed the 'cave of a hundred mammoths', could be as old as 20,000 years.
3. The use of terms such as 'art' and 'artist' in the context of the Paleolithic is problematic given that they carry with them modern Western assumptions about what constitutes art, its function(s) or purpose(s) and who makes art (White 2003; see also Conkey *et al.* 1997; Davidson 2013; Robb 2017). Following, Soffer and Conkey (1997), I normally prefer to use terms such as 'Pleistocene visual cultures' and 'image makers' or 'mark makers' (Nowell 2006; 2015a; 2015b; 2017). In the context of this chapter, however, I am discussing the 'arts' more broadly and thus I will continue to use 'art' and 'artist' because they are convenient terms despite their conceptual shortcomings, a decision archaeologists make that Robb (2017, 589) refers to as 'art plus disclaimer'.
4. Cave bears and humans would not have occupied the cave at the same time but cave bear pits, created when the bears hibernated, would have to be crossed.
5. An extender is a substance that an artist adds to paint to give it a more workable consistency, for example, it can be used to dilute the paint or make it thicker.

6. Absolute size of footprints and handprints can be used within reason to infer the presence of children but there is an overlap between larger children, adolescents and smaller adults (see Chapter 6).
7. This would work only for finger flutings in clay that are not covered by calcite as fingerprints in mondmilch are unlikely to survive. Mondmilch is organic and constantly growing, thus fingerprint data would likely be covered over (Van Gelder personal communication, September 2020).
8. My discussion of plant-based knowledge and fiber technologies is a direct result of conversations and consultation with Aurora Skala, MA.
9. Most archaeologists would consider ceramics a highly visible archaeological material because it is more durable than organics. I consider it here as 'less visible' because it appears rather late in hominin prehistory, we don't have a clear idea of its origins and some of the figures have not been fired rendering them more vulnerable to taphonomic processes.

Chapter 6

Adolescence in the Ice Age

> The reason teens are doing all of this exploring and novelty seeking is to build experience so that they can do a better job in making the difficult and risky decisions in later life.
>
> (Romer 2017)

While Paleolithic children, in the broadest sense of that term, have been understudied by archaeologists, the situation is particularly pronounced when it comes to adolescents. The reason for this reluctance on the part of archaeologists may be the presumed difficulty of studying this age group (Nowell and French 2020). In some sense, it feels more straightforward to distinguish 'children' (*sensu lato*) from 'adults' based on size, developmental age and associated artifacts. Adolescence, by contrast, is often seen as more ambiguous and a more liminal category. In other words, how do we decide when a 'teen' became an adult in in the Paleolithic? Yet by studying adolescents, we have an opportunity to enrich our understanding of Upper Paleolithic lifeways as a whole. Adolescence is marked by intensive biological, cognitive and psycho-social changes that have prompted psychologists to describe this stage of life as a time of increased creativity, flexibility, exploration and risk taking (Barbot and Heuser 2017) – all behaviors that could have had an enormous impact on the course of hominin biological and cultural evolution (Nowell and French 2020). In this chapter, I first discuss several biological markers of adolescence (*e.g.* adolescent growth spurt, sexual maturation and shifting sleep patterns) within an evolutionary context. Then, I explore the adaptive nature of cognitive changes associated with adolescence. Next, I look at what it means to be an adolescent socially and culturally. I then review examples of adolescent burials. Finally, I examine the archaeological evidence for behaviors and tropes often associated with teens to see if they have roots that reach back into the Paleolithic.

Biological markers of adolescence and their evolutionary significance

Growth spurt

From a biological point of view, the advantage of studying adolescents is that it is relatively straightforward to assign an individual to this category. As noted in Chapter 1, along with childhood, adolescence is one of two stages that is unique to the human life course (Bogin 2003). Adolescence is typically defined as the period from the onset of the adolescent growth spurt to its cessation. This growth spurt, when teens seem to grow overnight, refers to the acceleration and deceleration of growth that impacts virtually the entire skeleton (Bogin 2003). By contrast, non-human primates experience a growth spurt in body mass but not in the skeleton (Bogin 2003) and it is with *Homo erectus* that we may see the first evidence of at least a limited human-like adolescent growth spurt, but this remains controversial (Tardieu 1998; Antón and Leigh 2003; Dean and Smith 2009; Nowell 2010). By contrast, researchers agree that Neandertals experienced a prolonged childhood (Chapter 2) and adolescence, although they may have reached adulthood more quickly than modern humans (see below). In modern humans and likely Neandertals, it is during adolescence that individuals gain 50% of their weight and 20% of their final adult stature.

Sexual maturity

Adolescence encompasses puberty (*i.e.* sexual maturation) and fortunately for archaeologists, there are skeletal markers associated with particular phases of puberty (Nowell *et al.* forthcoming). For example, about one year after peak height velocity (PHV) (the period of maximum growth rate that occurs during the adolescent growth spurt, *i.e.* when teens are growing their fastest) is reached, menstruation begins in females (Bogen 2003). Shapland and Lewis (2013; 2014; cf. Doe *et al.* 2019) have developed a system of assessing puberty status from skeletal indicators associated with phases of the growth spurt including cervical vertebrae maturation, ossification and fusion of the iliac crest, fusion of the distal radius and hand phalangeal epiphyses, ossification of the hook of the hamate and mineralization of the mandibular canine. This system allows them to gauge whether puberty and sexual maturity occurred early or late, as well as the speed and duration of PHV (Nowell *et al.* forthcoming). According to recent genetic studies, Neandertal females reached menarche earlier than modern humans (Chintalapati *et al.* 2017; Kuhlwilm and Boeckx 2019). Studies of the Le Moustier 1 male (France) suggest that Neandertal males also reached puberty earlier than modern humans, experienced faster growth during adolescence and reached adulthood sooner (Thompson and Nelson 2011; Hublin *et al.* 2015; Day *et al.* 2017) but other studies have concluded they fall within the range of modern humans (Rosas *et al.* 2017; see also Nelson *et al.* forthcoming). Given the sample size paleoanthropologists have to study this difference may be related to individual variation or environmental factors.

While a boy is fertile before he develops any secondary sexual characteristics (*e.g.* enlargement of the larynx and a deepening of his voice, growth of facial and body hair including pubic hair, and increased stature), a girl 'develops nearly all of her secondary sexual characteristics [*e.g.* breasts, underarm and pubic hair, increased stature] to their fullest extent before acquiring her fertility' (Lancaster 1986, 21). In fact, most girls experience one to three years of anovulatory menstrual cycles following menarche (Bogin 2003). In addition, girls only achieve adult pelvic dimensions at the very end of puberty (Lancaster 1986). While the adolescent growth spurt impacts virtually the entire skeleton in girls, the female pelvis follows its own trajectory of slow but steady growth (Bogin 2003).

Figure 6.1: An Upper Paleolithic adolescent female experiencing her first pregnancy (Drawing: Marina Lezcano).

What this difference in patterning between boys and girls suggests is that, evolutionarily, there has been selection for delaying fertility in human females until they have had time to function socially as adults (Lancaster 1986; Bogin 2003; Nowell and French 2020). There was likely strong evolutionary selection for this delay in fertility. Pfeiffer *et al.* (2014) studied 246 skeletons of Later Stone Age (LSA) foragers of the South African Cape including 40 late adolescents/very young adults (26 female, 14 male). These researchers did not find any evidence of difference in levels of interpersonal violence, access to resources or burial practices that could explain the observed sex bias in mortality. Their research led them to conclude that risks associated with a woman's first pregnancy best explained why more young women were dying, making first pregnancy a significant life history factor. Pfeiffer *et al.* (2014, 16) note that 'compared to subsequent births, first time childbirth is a risky undertaking, prone to complication by cephalopelvic disproportion, fetal presentation, and potentially by other complications'. Furthermore, in the US, 1.7%–3.6% of deaths in young women are attributable to pregnancy, child birth and puerperium (the first six weeks after pregnancy during which a woman's organs return to their pre-pregnancy state). That figures rises to 37% in young Bangladeshi women (Pfeiffer *et al.* 2014 and references therein). In a forthcoming publication, Jennifer French and I studied age at death in a sample of 35 Gravettian teens and found a similar pattern. While teens of both sexes tended to die in late adolescence, males were more evenly distributed with 19% of males dying between the ages of 9 and 13, 30% between roughly 14 and 18 years of age and 50% between 19 and late 20s. By contrast, all except 2 females in our sample died in late adolescence (83%).

While double burials in the Paleolithic are relatively rare,[1] there are at least two examples of modern human late adolescent women in association with fetuses and neonates. Twenty-seven thousand years ago, at Abri Pataud (France), a 16-year-old teen was buried with a newborn in her arms (Pettitt 2010; Bahn 2015). At Ostuni, a contemporary site in Italy, archaeologists uncovered the well-preserved skeletal remains of a heavily pregnant 20-year-old woman (Ostuni 1; Fig. 6.1) (Nava *et al.* 2017). Hundreds of perforated shells, some caked in ochre, adorned the young woman's wrists and head. She was lying on her left side in a flexed position (knees bent) with her right arm across her abdomen. The remains of a fetus, (Ostuni 1b) estimated to be 31–33 gestational weeks, were found within her pelvic cavity in the position the fetus would have been when alive (Nava *et al.* 2017). Researchers documented three episodes of severe physiological stress in Ostuni 1b's prenatal dental enamel that they believe could have been the cause of death for both mother and fetus (Nava *et al.* 2017).[2]

As Bogin (2003) notes, giving birth is only one aspect of reproduction, as mothers also need to learn to care for infants to ensure they survive to eventually reproduce (Chapter 2). In studies of non-human primates, infant mortality rates decrease with each subsequent birth. This trend is attributable, at least in part, to females accumulating mothering experience over time (Bogin 2003). In many human cultures, juvenile and adolescent girls are responsible for caring for their younger siblings and in the process they learn a lot about children's needs (Weisner 1987; Kamp 2001a; Bogin 2003). Early in adolescence, human females begin to look and act like adults. This allows them to participate in adult behavior and create alliances that are key to reproductive success long before they are fertile and have an infant of their own to care for (Bogin 2003, 35; Hochberg and Konner 2020). Taken together this 'human advantage may seem small, but it means that up to 21 more people than baboons or chimpanzees survive out of every 100 first-born infants – more than enough over the vast course of evolutionary time to make the evolution of human adolescence an overwhelmingly beneficial adaptation' (Bogin 2003, 214).

These factors offer plausible explanations for why the outward (phenotypic) signs of sexual maturity precedes fertility in adolescent females but it does not explain why the reverse pattern is true for adolescent males. Bogin (2003) argues that in the case of boys, the developmentally timed release of androgen and endocrine hormones prompts them to begin thinking and acting like adults. This motivates them to participate in the world of men, and learn the skills they will need as adults, but since they still look like children they are not perceived as a threat, *i.e.* competition with adult males for resources and potential mates. While boys are fertile by around age 11 or 12, they normally do not become fathers until their 20s as, cross-culturally, fertile women generally do not perceive them as viable mates (Bogin 2003). If adolescent Neandertal males reached puberty earlier than modern humans and its duration was shorter due to accelerated growth rates then as Nelson *et al.* (forthcoming) write, 'males [may have] entered the mating arena early, which may have affected learning of adult skills and behavior. Increasing vulnerability, due to male-male competition and high-risk hunting, may have contributed to high mortality rates in adolescents and younger adults'. In small, highly dispersed populations (Chapter 2), the loss of these young men would have had a disproportionate effect on the well-being and overall viability of their communities. This may have been an important biocultural difference between early modern humans and other hominins including Neandertals.

In sum, Bogin (2003, 38) argues that there was selection for the insertion of adolescence into the hominin life history pattern 'because it conferred significant reproductive advantages to our species, in part, by allowing the adolescent to socially integrate into the economic, sexual, and political world of adults'. Adolescents were able to build social networks and practice being adults before taking on the responsibilities traditionally associated with this phase of the life course.

Shifting sleep patterns

With the onset of puberty, a significant shift in sleep patterns occurs (Nowell and French 2020). Alterations to circadian and homeostatic systems lead to increasingly later releases of melatonin throughout puberty (Galván 2020). This means that teens feel the need to sleep later and wake later than others do (Nowell and French 2020). While this shift in sleep patterns can sometimes drive the parents of teens to distraction, they can take comfort in the fact that staying up late and sleeping in late may have been particularly adaptive evolutionarily. Samson *et al.* (2017) studied the relationship between chronotype variation (the times of day that a person feels the most alert or the greatest need for sleep) and group sleeping among the Hadza, a people who practice a foraging lifestyle in Northern Tanzania. Over a 20-day period, they found that there were only 18 one-minute episodes in which everyone was simultaneously asleep, while 99.8% of the time one person or more was awake. Interestingly, chronotype varied by age only and not by sex, co-sleeping, nursing or study day. The researchers argued that when it comes to group sleeping, variation in age helps to generate variation in chronotype, which facilitates sentinel-like behavior, which evolutionarily would have been key to group survival (*e.g.* for detection of danger from predators, other humans and the environment). This variation in sleeping patterns is particularly important for the small groups in which foragers usually live and camp (12 or fewer). In models where they controlled for chronotype variation (*i.e.* they assumed that all members of a group fell asleep and woke at roughly the same time), groups had to be significantly larger for individual variation (*e.g.* someone waking up because they are too hot, had a nightmare, are hungry, or need to urinate) to produce the same 'sentinel effect' (Samson *et al.* 2017). Thus, as teens enter puberty, they begin to play an increasingly important role in overall group safety (Nowell and French 2020).

The teenage years

The biological changes associated with adolescence are universal but the timing of them varies based on sex, nutrition and other environmental factors. From a biological perspective, in a 21st-century context, adolescence begins around age 10 but when it ends is less clear (Sawyer *et al.* 2018). In living populations, researchers can use Tanner staging to document and track sexual maturity in adolescents. This clinical classification system focuses on visible characteristics related to the size and appearance of the penis and breasts as well as the length and texture of pubic hair. According to this scale, adolescence is complete by Tanner Stage V when testicular volume exceeds 20 ml and the penis is more than 14 cm in length, breasts are adult sized with a darkened areola and protruding nipple, and pubic hair for both sexes extends beyond the crease between the abdomen and thigh and onto the thigh itself (Emmanuel and Bokor 2020;

Hochberg and Konner 2020). Unfortunately this scale relies on soft tissue markers and is not directly applicable to fossil populations. Another abrupt shift in sleeping patterns occurs at age 20 and for some (*e.g.* Roenneberg *et al.* 2004), this is a useful marker for the end of adolescence but again it is not directly applicable to fossil hominins. Turning to the skeleton, the adolescent growth spurt is complete by approximately 16–17 years old but skeletal growth often continues until around age 25. Drawing on Arnett (2000), Hochberg and Konner (2020) propose that late adolescence, *i.e.* between the ages of 18 and 25, differs fundamentally from early adolescence, so much so that this period should be considered as a separate life history stage called 'emerging adulthood'. They argue that emerging adulthood is a period of physiological, cognitive and social development that includes 'brain maturation, learning about intimacy and mutual support, intensification of pre-existing friendships, family-oriented socialization, and the attainment of those social skills that are needed for mating and reproduction' (Hochberg and Konner 2020, 1). They suggest that the transition from adolescence to emerging adulthood takes place at the end of Tanner Stage IV (not V), and that during this final period of subadulthood, individuals require protection and nurturing as they continue to grow and develop. From the perspective of the skeleton, in this scheme, adolescence ends when growth velocity returns to a pre-puberty level (Hochberg and Konner 2020).

My view on when adolescence ends is that whether researchers call the years between roughly 18 and 25 'late adolescence/young adulthood' or 'emerging adulthood', they are identifying the same patterns of cognitive, physiological and social development and there is a general recognition that parental investment in offspring continues throughout this period (Hochberg and Konner 2020). The question is whether or not the changes taking place during these years are so different that they constitute a new life history stage, and I would argue that they do. An adolescent at 10 or 12 years of age is not the same person at 18 or 25 years old and because we divide the rest of subadulthood (infancy, childhood and juvenility) into chunks of two to six years depending on the hominin, it seems out of step to lump together these final 10 to 12 years particularly when an individual is undergoing so many profound changes.

Among the !Kung, the adolescent stage of the life course for girls is defined as the period between the onset of menstruation and the birth of their first child, meaning that adolescents are those between approximately 16 and 21 years of age (Howell 2010). The period of adolescence is longer for boys, lasting on average from 16 to 27, and similarly ending with the birth of their first child (Howell 2010). If, as argued below, contemporary foraging societies are a valid model for adolescents in ancestral foraging societies, then these age ranges can be taken as a guide for archaeologists studying adolescence and/or emerging adulthood in the Paleolithic (Nowell and French 2020).

Cognitive markers of adolescence and the evolutionary significance

As Arain *et al.* (2013, 451) observe, 'adolescence is one of the most dynamic events of human growth and development, second only to infancy in terms of the rate of developmental changes that occur in the brain'. During adolescence, there is a gradual decrease in synaptic density. In a process described as 'use it or lose it' (O'Rourke *et al.* 2020), excess neurons and synaptic connections no longer needed by the brain are pruned to improve the transmission efficiency of remaining neurons (Khundrakpam *et al.* 2016). Pruning is the behavioral and physiological suppression of competing behaviors that are no longer considered relevant (Casey *et al.* 2000). This process demonstrates how both biology and environmental experience shape the maturing adolescent brain (Nowell and French 2020; O'Rourke *et al.* 2020).

Adolescents are often described as risk takers given to impulsivity and emotionally driven decision making. The reason for this is that different parts of the brain mature at different rates. During adolescence, there are significant changes in the subcortical limbic system governing emotion and mood. However, the prefrontal cortex, governing executive functions such as attention, inhibition, cognitive flexibility and the ability to plan and think through the consequences of an action, is the last region of the brain to fully mature at around age 25 (Khundrakpam *et al.* 2016; O'Rourke *et al.* 2020). This can lead to greater risk taking behavior without the necessary checks and balances needed to constrain that behavior being fully available (Nowell and French 2020).

While this behavior can be worrisome to parents, the delayed development of the PFC may have been evolutionarily important. What is often described as 'impulsivity' in teens is actually a reflection of their desire to explore and learn about the world in which they live (Romer *et al.* 2017). Positive risk taking activates the brain's reward centers and by comparison with adults, teens are more sensitive to these rewards. This means that adolescents experience greater activation of reward centers when learning a new task than adults. Taken together, this makes teens better adapted to efficiently learn from their environment (Murdock 2017). This is enhanced by the fact that the overall plasticity of the adolescent brain renders teens more open to learning new tasks (O'Rourke *et al.* 2020).

The emotional life of adolescents is equally complex. During puberty, activation of the amygdala leads to an increased ability to read emotions in the faces of others (O'Rourke *et al.* 2020) and in taking on other emotional perspectives – what Burnett and Blakemore (2009, 52) describe as the ability to 'step into someone else's shoes'. It is easy to see how increased empathy would be important for social cohesion particularly among small foraging groups (Nowell and French 2020). Additionally, during puberty, gonadal hormones, implicated in reorganizing neural circuitry in males and females, lead to greater interest in romantic and sexual partners (O'Rourke *et al.* 2020). In studies of fMRIs, researchers found that adolescents use different regions of their brain to process social situations than adults. However, overtime, as they garner more life experience, processing these situation becomes more automatic. Burnett and Blakemore (2009, 54–55) suggest that 'an unexplored implication of this could be that the period of life [during which these] social brain regions are still developing– the teens and early 20s – might be a period of particular open mindedness to new ideas and different types of people'. Psychologists argue that emotion plays a key role in learning in that situations that produce strong emotional reactions are more likely to be remembered. Situations with positive affect are likely to be repeated while those with negative affect are more likely to be avoided in the future (Murdock 2017).

Social markers of forager adolescence

Adolescence is not only a distinct period biologically and cognitively but socially as well (Schlegel and Barry 1991; Nowell and French 2020). As noted in Chapter 1, social age is based on culturally constructed norms for what is appropriate behavior and knowledge associated with a particular age category (Halcrow and Tayles 2008). While biological age and social age are different ways of dividing up the life course, they are interrelated. As Nowell and French (2020, 2) observe, 'social and environmental factors such as degree of physical activity, access to nutritious food, familial stress, life expectancy and socioeconomic stress can impact the onset and duration of puberty'. Furthermore, as noted above, the development of secondary sexual characteristics (for example, breasts and rounded hips in females; increased muscle mass, facial hair and deepening of the voice in males) can signal readiness to take on adult roles and responsibilities (Nowell and French 2020; see for example, Lewis *et al.* 2016).

Foraging societies as a source of analogy

While biological and cognitive markers of adolescence are human universals, social adolescence is more variable. Without implying that modern hunter-gatherers are anything other than present-day populations with their own unique historical trajectories and cultures, Nowell and French (2020) argue that these societies are the best analogues for Upper Paleolithic adolescence. This is because many of the features of social adolescence in foraging societies are driven by demographic factors such as low population density and small group size. Based on archaeological evidence, we know that these variables also characterize Upper Paleolithic hunter-gatherers. How much further back in the Paleolithic these similarities can be inferred is a matter of debate but at least it gives us a model from which to start.

In their comprehensive study of hunter-gatherer adolescence, Hewlett and Hewlett (2012) identify adolescent behaviors common to higher primates broadly (*e.g.* increase in time spent learning complex behaviors and in sexual activity) and to humans more specifically (*e.g.* marriage and sexual division of labor). They also discuss features of adolescence that they describe as being unique to foraging societies, such as those outlined in Table 6.1. I will consider each of them briefly.

Physical and emotional intimacy, autonomy and the adolescent 'identity crisis'

Foraging societies are characterized by low population sizes with a mean of 25–30 people and fluid group composition often dictated by seasonally available resources. In addition,

Table 6.1. Key characteristics of adolescence that are unique to Foragers (Nowell and French 2020, table 2 after Hewlett and Hewlett 2012).

Characteristics of forager adolescence
Relatively high sexual freedom
Long distance exploration
Autonomy and self-directed social learning
Minimal and non-obligatory responsibility for subsistence and infant care
Physical and emotional intimacy with parents and other adults
Female initiation ceremonies
Lack of adolescent identity crisis
High levels of cultural energy, creativity and play

infant and child mortality rates can be high, with 43–49% of subadults dying before the age of 15. Taken together this means that, by default, adolescents in these communities socialize in mixed age and sex groups. As Nowell and French (2020, 13–14) write,

> This combination of small group sizes and high childhood mortality means that, in contrast to many other societies, adolescents are rarely spending their time only with other adolescents; there are simply too few of them for this to occur. Adolescent socialisation and maturation thus occurs in an intergenerational context, alongside both younger children and adults, a factor that contributes notably to the 'physical and emotional intimacy with parents and other adults' that characterises hunter–gatherer adolescence.

This physical and emotional intimacy and a collective world view promotes individual autonomy and a strong sense of self and belonging in foraging teens (Hewlett 2017). Teenage rebellion and identity crises that are often argued to be part of the universal (*i.e.* cross-cultural) adolescent condition (*e.g.* Blakemore 2018) simply do not exist among foraging societies (Hewlett and Hewlett 2012). This observation is important for rethinking social dynamics and social relations during the Upper Paleolithic.

Sexual freedom and long distance exploration

Foraging societies often exist at very low regional densities with approximately 0.25 people per km^2 (Marlowe 2005). Low populations and low densities mean that adolescents often have to travel far to seek out sexual and marriage partners (MacDonald and Hewlett 1999; Nowell and French 2020). Sexual selection theory posits that the sex with the higher reproduction rate will compete more strongly for mates (MacDonald and Hewlett 1999), thus perhaps it is not surprising that males travel further than females in search of suitable partners. The absence of adolescent males from foraging encampments is a common observation in ethnographic studies (*e.g.* Milner *et al.* 2014;

Nowell and French 2020). Furthermore, there may have been selection for navigation skills in adolescent males (Nowell and French 2020). In a study of male and female West Point cadets, Munion *et al.* (2019, 1933) note that 'traveling longer distances without changing course, pausing less, and fewer returns to previously visited locations were significantly related to the ability to locate the correct target ... [and] the significant relationship between gender and navigational success is fully accounted for by men and women producing different wayfinding behaviors, which in turn predict differences in navigational success'.

Cultural energy, creativity and play, adolescent responsibilities and innovation

According to Hewlett and Hewlett (2012), foraging teens have a great deal of free time due to their 'minimal and non-obligatory responsibility to participate in subsistence tasks and infant care'. Furthermore, as noted above, adolescence is a period of particular creativity, flexible learning, exploration and risk taking (Nowell and French 2020). While subadults learn from their parents (vertical teaching) and their peers (horizontal teaching), during adolescence, forager teens increasingly turn to non-parental adults (oblique teaching) to learn complex skills and social norms (Dira and Hewlett 2016; Garfield *et al.* 2016). The evolutionary importance of oblique teaching is discussed in more detail in Chapter 7. In their cross-cultural study of the social context in which forager teens learn subsistence skills, Lew-Levy *et al.* (2017) found that while adolescents are not the innovators in this regard, they 'preferentially seek out adults identified as innovators from whom to learn. They are also the main group to whom these innovations are transmitted' (Nowell and French 2020, 17). Thus while they are not the prime innovators, they are the prime recipients of innovations (Nowell and French 2020) and they often use these innovations to help in their search for sexual and/or marriage partners (Lew-Levy *et al.* 2017).

Female and male initiation rituals and 'testosterone-fueled' graffiti art

In all cultures, human groups mark the transition from subadult to adult with some form of ritual or ceremony. For this reason, one explanation for the presence of children in decorated caves (Chapters 3 and 5) is that they may have been participating in initiation rites (*e.g.* Breuil 1952; Leroi-Gourhan 1967; Pfeiffer 1982; Bednarik *et al.* 1990; Owens and Hayden 1997; see also Ucko and Rosenfeld 1967; Bahn 2012). Hewlett and Hewlett (2012) note that female initiation rites, in particular, are typical of foraging societies. Unfortunately, there is no archaeological evidence for these sorts of ceremonies among Paleolithic teens of either sex. In her study of finger flutings, Van Gelder (2015b) noted that the largest number of individuals making marks in any one of the caves was eight and the smallest number was two. In caves without children, the number was never higher than four. Clottes *et al.* (1992) recorded a similarly limited number of individuals in painted caves. Van Gelder (2015b, 136) argues that given the small number of children 'it seems unlikely that the flutings are evidence of society-wide rituals such as initiations'.

By contrast, Guthrie (2005) has argued based on his study of handprints that much of cave art was created by adolescent boys with sex and violence on their minds. He bases this opinion on his attribution of the handprints to teenage males, and the supposed prevalence of 'naked' women and violent hunting scenes on cave walls. But, as noted in Chapter 5, attributing handprints to adolescents based on size alone is highly problematic and his characterization of the corpus of cave art as primarily being about hunting and sex is equally so. Bahn (2006, 575) writes:

> Unfortunately, [Guthrie's] reading of the images is extremely literal, excessively so in my view. In his quest for 'clear expressions of the artists' hunting preoccupations', he thinks he can recognize depictions of 'males with hunting weapons such as spears or spear-throwers', of hunting parties with men 'being attacked by wounded game or dangerous carnivores', of nosebleeds and defecations, and even of bleeding puncture wounds without weapons. People often see what they want to see in rock art, and I think it is safe to say that few of Guthrie's interpretations would be readily accepted by most specialists in Ice Age art.

As Bahn (2006) notes, in the tens of thousands of Paleolithic art images there is not one unambiguous hunting scene and often Guthrie relies on his selectively modified redrawings of these 'scenes' to support his arguments. Furthermore, the notion that 'images of rotund women, vulvae, and men with erections are found at many sites' or that 'giant penises ... occur throughout Paleolithic art' (Guthrie 2005, 8) is puzzling. Finally, Guthrie's interpretation makes assumptions about age-specific ways of thinking and acting in the world that may not be appropriate for the Upper Paleolithic (Jonaitis 2007).

We know from their footprints (Chapter 3) that adolescents visited these caves, sometimes with family, sometimes with friends. We know that they sometimes played games such as throwing clay pellets at each other. It is likely that they produced some of the art we observe in caves and rock shelters, but their specific contribution in this regard is harder to detect. It is also highly probable that Paleolithic peoples marked the transition to adulthood in some manner as this behavior is ubiquitous today, including among recent foragers (Hewlett and Hewlett 2012). However, it may be that this change in the life course was marked by some type of modification of soft tissue (*e.g.* circumcision, scarification, piercing, tattooing, body painting) or some other form of intangible culture (dance, trance or vision quests), that leave behind no traces for the archaeologist to discover.

Stressed out teens

The multitude of biological, cognitive and social changes experienced by adolescents as they move through puberty and the shifts in socio-cultural status that accompany these changes may have rendered Paleolithic adolescents particularly vulnerable to nutritional stress and pathogens. As noted in Chapter 2, at El Sidrón (Spain), four Neandertals had multiple episodes of dental hypoplasia corresponding to the 4th year and 12th year of life, prompting researchers to identify 'weaning and adolescence as the life history events more prone to nutritional stress' (Rosas *et al.* 2006, 19268). At this same site, one Neandertal teen suffered from a painful dental abscess and a chronic gastrointestinal pathogen causing diarrhea (Weyrich *et al.* 2017). Through an analysis of his dental calculus (plaque), researchers discovered that the adolescent consumed plants that contained salicylic acid, which is a natural pain killer, similar to the active ingredients in aspirin (Barras 2017; Weyrich *et al.* 2017). They also found traces of the *Penicillium* fungus from which we derive penicillin. Consumption of this antibiotic may have been accidental as this fungus grows naturally on plants but it was only found in the mouth of this teenager and not in the mouths of healthy individuals at the site (Barras 2017).

Burial evidence

Another way in which we can reconstruct the lived lives of Paleolithic teens is through a study of their burials. In addition to the examples of interments at Abri Pataud, Ostuni and Sunghir discussed in this and earlier chapters, a number of other adolescent burials are known. Four examples dating to the Gravettian/EpiGravettian will be discussed here. While each burial is unique, there are some traits that characterize interments from these periods (Formicola 2007; Pettitt 2010). Double and triple burials are more common during this period than any other time in the Paleolithic. In some cases, individuals in triple burials are placed side by side in a common shallow grave, with one person disengaged, and other two 'engaged', *i.e.* interacting with each other in some way – for example, intertwined or facing one another (Pettitt 2010). Furthermore, these burials are often richly adorned with ochre and personal ornaments.

While burial data is compelling, it is comparatively rare, and only provides 'snap shots' of the experience and roles of some adolescents in these societies (Nowell and French 2020). These adolescents were likely those who were in some way unusual or special enough to warrant a formal (and often richly furnished) burial (Nowell and French 2020). Frequently, interred individuals during the Gravettian and EpiGravettian, including teens, suffered from a congenital pathology or died as a result of violence, prompting some researchers to describe these burials as the interments of people who suffered 'bad deaths' (Formicola 2007; Pettitt 2010; Sparacello *et al.* 2018; see also Nowell 2020).

Dolní Věstonice II (Czech Republic)

Approximately 30,000 years ago (Fewlass *et al.* 2019), three adolescent males were buried side by side in a shallow grave (Formicola 2007). DV15 in the center and DV14 on the right were closely related, probably brothers, while DV 13 on the left did not share this close relationship (Mittnik *et al.* 2016). Each was adorned with personal ornaments consisting of pierced beads made from mammoth ivory and arctic fox and wolf teeth (Formicola 2007). Their upper bodies were stained with ochre, most likely from clothing that has long since rotted away or from body paint. Ochre was caked onto the head of DV 13 suggesting he wore some kind of headgear or mask (Pettitt 2010). Other grave goods include a flint knife and flakes. Once the bodies were placed into the grave, a thick branch or wooden pole was thrust deep into the hip of DV 13, perhaps to stake down his body. Then the young men were covered with branches or a wooden structure that was set on fire and then quickly extinguished by throwing silt on the flames (Pettitt 2010). DV 13 and DV 15 were buried on their backs and DV 13 has his arm outstretched and his hand on the pubic region of DV 15 which is caked in ochre. By contrast DV 14 was buried on his chest with his head looking away from the other two. A piece of burnt reindeer pelvis had been placed in DV 15's mouth (Bahn 2011).

Researchers have long speculated about what human drama might have taken place as it is clear that this is a carefully designed tableau. Initially, based on a morphological analysis, DV 13 and 14 were designated male but DV 15 was tentatively described as female (Formicola 2007) because the pathology of his pelvis made it difficult to sex the skeleton with certainty. Under this scenario, archaeologists suggested we might be witnessing a love triangle 'gone wrong'. However, in 2016 Mittnik *et al.* performed an aDNA analysis (see Chapter 1) and discovered all three were adolescent males. Of course, this could still be a 'love triangle' but more often the burial is now described as a mishap that took the lives of 'three friends' (!) or simply an unknown tragedy. DV 15 was encumbered with a number of pathologies that would have been evident in life including arms and legs that were uneven in length and bowed, enamel defects and an unusual number and position of his teeth (Formicola *et al.* 2001; Trinkaus 2018).

Barma Grande (Italy)

Twenty-five thousand years ago, an adolescent male (BG4), an adolescent female (BG3) and an adult male (BG2) (from left to right) were buried side by side in a shallow grave at the site of Barma Grande in Italy

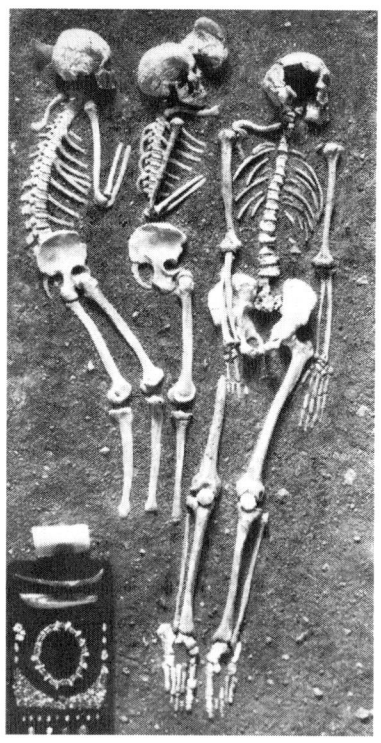

Figure 6.2: Reconstruction of the triple burial from the Barma Grande in the caves of the Balzi Rossi, near Ventimiglia, Liguria, Italy, ca. 20,000 BP. Ventimiglia, Museo Preistorico Dei Balzi Rossi (Prehistorical Museum) (Photo: DeAgostini/ Getty Images).

(Pettitt 2010) (Fig. 6.2). All three skeletons were stained with red ochre, possibly from clothing or body painting. While no photos exist of the interment at the time of discovery, drawings completed during excavation show that the adult male was placed on his back in an extended positon, with his head facing left and a long flint blade in his left hand. The adolescents were placed on their left sides with their legs bent, facing into the grave (Pettitt 2010). A bovid femur had been placed under the head of BG3 while a large flint scraper was tucked under BG4 (Pettitt 2010). The body of the teenage girl was partly covered by the other two, which suggests that her body had been placed in the grave first but the tightly constrained distribution of the ochre suggests they were all interred at the same time (Pettitt 2010). All three were adorned with ornaments consisting of incised deer canines, fish vertebrae, perforated shells and bone pendants (Pettitt 2010).

Il Principe (Italy)

Sometime between 20,000 and 23,500 years ago, an adolescent male was placed in a shallow grave on a bed of ochre, in an extended position, with his head turned to the left and a long flint blade in his right hand. He is known as 'The Prince' because of the extraordinary richness of his burial. He appears to have been wearing a hat or mask as his head is surrounded by hundreds of perforated deer canines and shells (Pettitt 2010). On his torso were mammoth ivory pendants and pierced shells, and four perforated batons of elk antler. Interestingly, part of his left mandible is missing with a mass of yellow ochre in its place. Archaeologists speculate that although the wound had begun to heal by the time of his death, the yellow ochre was placed there to 'fill in' the missing bone (Pettitt 2010).

Romito Cave (Italy)

Eleven to twelve and a half thousand years ago, during the final EpiGravettian in Italy, a 17-year-old boy (R2) was buried wrapped in the arms of an adult female (R1) in Romito Cave (Frayer *et al.* 1987; 1988) (Fig. 6.3). Based on a morphological analysis (Frayer *et al.* 1987; 1988), the woman is likely the boy's mother but aDNA tests have not been carried out to confirm this conclusion (Tilley 2015). At a height of 144 cm (ca. 4'9"), the teen represents the oldest known chondrodystrophic dwarf in the archaeological record. According to researchers, the skeleton exhibits all of the typical features of this condition including a high domed skull, and extremely shortened arms and legs (Frayer *et al.* 1987; 1988). In fact, they were about 45% to 58% of the average length of limbs in that population (Frayer *et al.* 1987; 1988) and with severely deformed hand bones, R2 would have had restricted mobility and limited use of his forearms and hands (Tilley 2015). According to Tilley (2015, 64), 'Romito 2's skeletal dysplasia limited his participation in typical economic and ... cultural activities undertaken by his cohort, and anomalies in [his] appearance [would have] distinguished him from

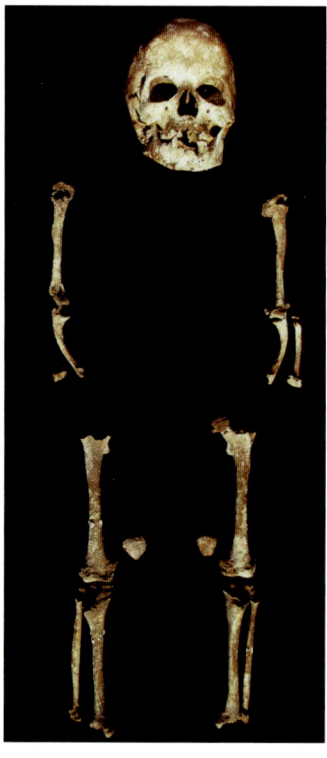

Figure 6.3: Skeletal remains of Romito 2 (Romito Cave, Italy). This 17-year-old boy is the earliest known chondrodystrophic dwarf. Buried in the arms of a woman who was likely his mother, his survival is a testament to the care and support he received from his family and community (Photo courtesy: David Frayer).

his peers from infancy onwards'. As Tilley (2015) notes, this contrast between Romito 2 and his peers would have taken on added significance as he entered adolescence and he was unable to assume the roles and responsibilities associated with this phase of life. In contrast with The Prince, Romito 2's burial was very meager indeed with only a couple of auroch horns as grave goods. Nonetheless, in life, the teen seems have been treated like everyone else. He ate the same meat rich diet as other members in his clan even though he could not have hunted with his peers. 'In a small, often stressed, subsistence group, meeting Romito 2's needs would require the cooperation of all economically productive members; this suggests a cohesive community with the willingness, intellectual flexibility and organisational skills necessary for managing a constant demand on scarce resources' (Tilley 2015, 70). Without wanting to overinterpret this burial, I feel there is something about the intimacy of being held in his mother's arms for eternity that speaks to this enduring affection for him; after all, it was members of the teen's community who chose to carefully arrange their bodies in this manner.

A boy and his dog?

Finally, in this chapter I would like to explore one trope of adolescence. The classic tale of the relationship between an adolescent boy and his dog is a popular theme in many novels and films. Stories set in the Paleolithic are no exception. From Justin Denzil's (1988) *Boy of the Painted Cave* to the 2018 Columbia Pictures film *Alpha* (Fig. 6.4), the unique friendship that develops between two outsiders is a plot line that never fails to pull on our heart strings. But how accurate is this portrayal? According to experts, dog domestication began somewhere between 40,000 and 15,000 years ago (Prassack *et al.* 2020). By 16,000 to 12,000 years ago domesticated dogs are present at sites in Europe, Asia and North America including the first dog burials (Janssens *et al.* 2018; Prassack *et al.* 2020) and dogs are in Australia by at least 3450 BP (Shipman 2020).

Genetic evidence suggests that domesticated dogs and modern-day wolves last shared a common ancestor approximately 27,000 years ago (Skoglund *et al.* 2015).

Figure 6.4: A scene from the 2018 film Alpha, *in which a teenage boy (actor Kodi Smit-McPhee) living during the Aurignacian befriends a wolf. The film follows their growing dependence on each other as they begin a long and perilous journey back to the boy's family encampment (© 2018 Studio 8, LLC. All Rights Reserved. Courtesy of Columbia Pictures).*

But speciation is not the same thing as domestication, of course (Freedman and Wayne 2017). Fossil evidence documents diagnostic skull changes from wolf to dog beginning about 33,000 years ago (Ovodov *et al.* 2011). These physical changes include a foreshortening of the snout and skull, and a widening of the palate and braincase relative to wolves (Germonpré *et al.* 2012), a process known as neoteny whereby juvenile features are retained in the adults of a species. These changes came about through the process of domestication as early humans selected for behavioral traits such as lowered aggression. Multiple regions have been suggested for the origin of dog domestication, with Europe or Asia being the most likely candidates (Janssens *et al.* 2018). We now know that people transitioned to agriculture at different times and different places around the globe between 12,000 and 2,000 years ago, and similarly, it is likely that dog domestication occurred more than once over the millennia.

While the remains of wolves have been uncovered at Acheulian sites up to 400,000 years ago (Clutton-Brock 2016), pinpointing the earliest domesticated dog is challenging as domestication is a gradual process and the earliest dogs would have closely resembled their now extinct ancestor, the prehistoric Eurasian grey wolf (Morey and Jeger 2015). In fact, researchers studying canid fossils at the Gravettian site, Předmostí, in the Czech Republic, use the term 'protodogs' to describe what are generally considered to be the oldest domesticated dogs in Europe (Prassack et al. 2020; see also Germonpré et al. 2012). These researchers combined osteology, isotope analysis and dental microwear texture analysis to see if they could distinguish between dog morphotypes and wolf morphotypes based on diet. They discovered that the dog-looking animals primarily ate deer bones while the animals that looked more like wolves more often ate mammoth. They hypothesize that the former subsisted on scraps given to them by humans, while the latter hunted (or scavenged) their food (Prassack et al. 2020). This is a promising approach as changes in behavior, including diet, precede changes in biology and thus can be early indicators that the process of domestication is under way before it is apparent osteologically. In Asia, the oldest dog remains were recovered in the Altai mountains in Russia, dating to approximately 33,000 years ago (Druzhkovka et al. 2013) while in East Asia and North America domesticated dogs are Neolithic in origin (Freedman and Wayne 2017). At the 14,000-year-old site Grotta della Bàsura (Italy) evidence suggests a dog may have accompanied a family as they explored the cave (Romano et al. 2019; see Chapter 3).

There are many utilitarian reasons why early humans may have wished to domesticate the dog, including help in hunting, protection, transportation, waste disposal, pest control, warmth (bed warmers), clothing (pelts) and food (canophagy), although the rarity of cutmarks on dog bones does not support their regular use for pelts or meat according to Janssens et al. (2018). Archaeologists working at Bonn-Oberkassel, a 14,000-year-old Magdalenian site in Germany, think there may be another reason. One of two dogs found at this site was between 27 and 28 weeks old when it died. It was buried with two adult humans and grave goods. What is most notable about this puppy is that it was extremely ill for most of its short life (Janssens et al. 2018). Researchers observed severe periodontal disease, oral cavity lesions and multiple dental hypoplasias. As previously noted, hypoplasias are defects in the enamel due to malnutrition, stress or illness that can only occur as teeth are developing. Researchers conclude that at 19 weeks of age the puppy suffered from morbillivirus (canine distemper), an infection that impacts a dog's respiratory, gastrointestinal and central nervous systems. This puppy was gravely ill between 19 and 23 weeks of age. Given the high mortality rate associated with morbillivirus infections, the dog could not have survived its illness without extensive human care and intervention. Because the dog would have been of no utilitarian value to the people living at Bonn-Oberkassel before and during its illness, archaeologists argue that at 'least some Late Pleistocene humans regarded dogs not just materialistically, but may have developed emotional and caring bonds for their dogs' (Janssens et al. 2018). A similarly evocative example comes from Předmostí, where one of the three (proto) dogs uncovered there was buried with a mammoth bone in its mouth. It could only have been placed there after death by a human perhaps as food for its journey to the afterworld (Prassack *et al.* 2020). While the trope of the adolescent boy and his dog may or may not be completely accurate in the Upper Paleolithic, it is likely that the deep bond of companionship felt between many people and their dogs today has a deep history.

In sum, life for Upper Paleolithic teens meant spending most of their time in small extended family groups socializing with their younger siblings and cousins as well as with the adults around them from whom they learned the skills they needed to survive in an often challenging environment. They particularly would have sought the company of those who they perceived to be innovators and would have been quick to adopt new technologies. Much like teens today, they likely lay awake long into the night after others were asleep, listening to the crackling fire, cries of wolves in the distance or just the silence punctuated by the occasional wail of an infant. Perhaps the family's dog lay nearby. Their days were spent hunting, foraging, learning about plants, honing their tool making skills and helping to care for the little ones in their group while their nights were spent learning (through) the stories and songs of their people. Their growing sense of empathy and compassion may have led them to offer support to those who were differently abled in their communities. Occasionally, they explored caves with their friends or family; they may have even created some of the art archaeologists have documented there. Boys were likely away from camp more often than girls in search of romantic or sexual partners but all Upper Paleolithic teens would have used this protected time as an opportunity to explore new relationships and cement existing ones before assuming their prescribed roles as parents and eventually as elders in their communities.

In this chapter, I discussed the biological, cognitive and social markers of adolescence within an evolutionary context. I then considered what adolescent burials might be able tell us about the lived lives of at least some Paleolithic teens. Finally, I examined the archaeological evidence for behaviors and tropes often associated with teens. It is clear from the data presented in this chapter, that while understudied, adolescence is an exceedingly important stage of the human life course that stands to enrich our understanding of Paleolithic lifeways as a whole.

Notes

1. The oldest known double burial dates to approximately 100,000 years ago in Qafzeh (Israel). At this site, Qafzeh 9, an adolescent who is presumed to be female, is buried with Qafzeh 10, a 5- or 6-year-old child (Tillier 2008).
2. de Castro and Nicolàs (1997) have suggested that premature maternal deaths may explain some aspects of Neandertal demography.

Chapter 7

Paleolithic children as drivers of human evolution

> Children (like adults) are not passive recipients of biological and cultural inheritance but active agents, influencing what is learnt through changes in their cognitive development, and their active pursuit of knowledge.
>
> (Flynn *et al.* 2013, 308)

In Chapter 1, I asked why archaeologists were slow to study children. I argued that taphonomy, the assumption that children introduce a randomizing and distorting element into the archaeological record, children's perceived lack of agency and the marginalization of children as a research topic were all key factors. In this concluding chapter I want to address why we *should* study children. It is clear that children are worthy subjects in their own right and that a study of Paleolithic children, in particular, contributes to a richer and more holistic understanding of a period that conservatively represents 99.83% of humanity's time on Earth. But perhaps more importantly, evolutionary biology suggests that children were and are drivers of human evolution. In this final chapter, I discuss Niche Construction Theory as a framework for understanding the role Paleolithic children played in shaping hominin evolution.

The Modern Synthesis, Extended Evolutionary Synthesis and Niche Construction Theory

According to the Modern Synthesis (MS) (the integration of neo-Darwinian principles of variation, inheritance, differential reproduction and natural selection with Mendelian population genetics (Müller 2017)), spontaneous mutations are the source of all novel biological variation in living organisms and it is upon this variation that the other forces of evolution – genetic drift (random fluctuations in gene frequency from one generation to the next), gene flow (mating within and between populations) and natural selection – act. Given the natural variation in populations some individuals are better adapted to surviving in their ecological niche. As discussed in Chapter 2, these individuals, all things being equal, produce more offspring who then carry these traits with them into the next generation, altering the population's gene pool in the process. Environmental change impacts organisms by altering their niche and by extension the traits best suited for inhabiting it. Thus, in conventional biological narratives, even though natural section acts on behavior, organisms are framed as lacking agency, as passive vehicles for gene transmission, and 'victims' of selection (Flynn *et al.* 2013). For instance, the classic example in evolutionary biology of Darwinian selection is the case of the peppered moths (*Biston betularia*). Before the Industrial Revolution in England the dominant color of this species was white allowing them to alight on light colored trees unnoticed. Most of the few darker colored moths in the population were easily picked off by birds. After the Industrial Revolution began, the trees inhabited by these moths were covered with soot and other forms of pollution rendering the white moths highly visible and, by extension, vulnerable to predation, while at the same time effectively camouflaging the darker colored ones. In a few short generations the predominant color (phenotype) of the peppered moth was black. Thus, in a very simplistic way of framing things, conventional narratives characterize evolution as something that *happens to organisms.* While there is considerable evidence to support the processes that MS describes, many researchers argue that this paradigm does not account for all observable data and that, in fact, it fails to integrate many phenomena, prompting them to advocate for an Extended Evolutionary Synthesis (EES) (Laland et al. 2015; Müller 2017). EES focuses on reciprocal rather than unilinear causation and 'emphasizes the role of constructive processes, ecological interactions, and system dynamics in the evolution of organismal complexity as well as social and cultural conditions' (Müller 2017, 1). While EES encompasses many different concepts, I will discuss Niche Construction Theory (NCT) in relation to the role of subadults in hominin evolution.

In contrast to classic models of evolution, NCT focuses on organisms as *active* constituents of their own evolution (Prince-Buitenhuys and Bartelink 2020). Through their actions, they modify patterns of selection acting on themselves and other organisms (Odling and Smee *et al.* 2003; Laland and Sterelny 2006; Creaza *et al.* 2013; Prince-Buitenhuys and Bartelink 2020). As Lewontin *et al.* (1983, 280) write, 'organisms do not adapt to their environments, they construct them out of the bits and pieces of the external world'. NCT is defined as the 'modification of both living and non-living components in environments through the metabolic, physiological and behavioral activities of organisms as well as through their choices' (Flynn *et al.* 2013, 296).

From the perspective of NCT, evolution is the result of a *reciprocal* relationship between organisms and the environment that does not depend on genetic mutations, fluctuations in gene frequencies or natural selection (Prince-Buitenhuys and Bartelink 2020). While NCT is not in opposition to Darwinian concepts, it adds a missing piece of the puzzle and for many researchers the strength of its explanatory power means it should be considered a force of evolution in its own right (Lewontin *et al.* 1983; Odling and Smee *et al.* 2003; Creaza *et al.* 2013; Müller 2017; Prince-Buitenhuys and Bartelink 2020 and references therein). According to Flynn *et al.* (2013, 298), by modifying selection, Niche Construction (NC) results in new evolutionary outcomes, facilitates range expansion, and generates 'self-perpetuating acceleratory niche-constructing capabilities … In other words, the feedback that niche construction generates in evolution makes a difference to how organisms evolve'. NC modifies selection at the phenotypic,[1] ontogenetic (*i.e.* within an individual's life) and cultural (*e.g.* technological innovations) levels.

There are two key concepts of NCT. The first is 'environmental modification' or Selective Niche Construction (SNC), where an organism alters their own or others' local environment (Flyn *et al.* 2013; Stotz 2017; Prince-Buitenhuys and Bartelink 2020). For example, a tree growing taller casts a wider shadow altering what plants and organisms can survive in its vicinity and thus the chemistry and nutrient content of the soil its roots inhabit. Beavers build dams on rivers creating an ideal home for themselves. The pool of water behind the dam also results in a new habitat for fish and aquatic plants. Second, 'ecological inheritance', or Developmental Niche Construction (DNC), is inheritance through niche construction of resources and their associated modified selection pressure (Odling and Smee 2003). Humans are considered to be the ultimate niche constructors. While genetic drift, gene flow and natural selection act on genetic variation (mutations), NC modifies natural selection through ontogenetic and cultural mechanisms and 'it is this reliance on learning, plasticity and culture that lends Human Niche Construction a special potency' (Flynn *et al.* 2013, 298). For example, processes initiated by *Homo sapiens* roughly 300,000 years ago have had a global impact. The dispersal of modern humans from Africa resulting in landscape modification, hunting and the translocation of species; the emergence and spread of agriculture and pastoralism; island colonization[2] and the rise of cities and elaborate trade networks have accelerated to such a pace that some scientists argue that the planet has entered a new geological epoch – the Anthropocene (Boivin *et al.* 2016). This name reflects the dramatic impact humans have exerted and continue to exert on the planet, altering their own and other organisms' evolutionary trajectory in the process.[3]

Another feature of NC is that acquired characteristics play a key role in modifying selection (Flynn *et al.* 2013; Müller 2017). In the early 1800s, French naturalist Jean-Baptiste Lamarck proposed a theory that physical characteristics acquired during an individual's lifetime could be passed on to their offspring. The often cited example is that of a giraffe. A growing subadult giraffe possesses a certain length of neck based on a combination of genes and the environment (*e.g.* access to food). By the time it reaches adulthood its neck length is fixed. Lamarck, however, argued that by reaching for leaves on ever higher branches, the giraffe would eventually elongate its neck and this elongation would be passed on to its offspring. The theory was eventually discredited through the development of an awareness of the genetic basis of phenotypic traits (*i.e.* Modern Synthesis) but Lamarck was onto something. It is true that individuals die with the same genes with which they were born. However, population level adaptions for learning and development mean that if the environment changes, species can adapt. Under glacial conditions, plants and animals can migrate south. Humans can also migrate south but, in addition, they can alter their hunting strategies, create fire, sew warm clothing, as detailed in Chapter 5, and build shelters. These adaptations can happen within a lifetime and be passed on to future generations. Crucially, these adaptations allow for further learning opportunities, knowledge creation and information transfer that ultimately lead to expanded niche construction and modified selection.

Developmental niche construction

It is the symbolically-mediated, material-based transmission of culturally relevant information that has allowed humans to occupy even the most hostile of environments (Boyd *et al.* 2011; Creaza *et al.* 2013; Müller *et al.* 2017). Drawing on developmental psychology, Flynn *et al.* (2013) outline four processes that are key to the construction of a learning environment that permits transmission of this information between individuals, 'with infants and children being directed, *and directing*, their development' (my emphasis). These processes are natural pedagogy, activity theory, distributed cognition and situated learning. I will briefly consider each of these in turn.

Natural pedagogy

Infants are born into cultural niches surrounded by people who are performing cultural behaviors (Flynn *et al.* 2013). As novices, they need to acquire this knowledge but it can be difficult to discern what is relevant. Flynn *et al.* (2013) argue that it would be impractical for subadults to attempt to learn everything they need to through observation alone, emphasizing points made in Chapters 4 and 5 concerning the importance of direct teaching in foraging societies. They write, 'humans have a social communicative learning mechanism, "natural pedagogy", in which culturally knowledgeable individuals (usually adults) assist novices in acquiring cultural behavior through ostensive-referential demonstrations of the relevant aspects of the behaviour' (Flynn *et al.* 2013, 300; see also Gergely *et al.* 2006). Parents often use eye-contact, gestures (motionese) and speech (motherese) to direct infants' attention. Many of these are features of oral storytelling (Chapter 5). As noted in Chapter 2, the main difference between human and non-human primate infants is that human infants experience shared intentionality and engage in triadic interactions (Tomasello 2014). The shift beginning with australopithecines to carrying infants on the front of their bodies means that infants were better able to track parental gaze and to monitor, engage in and learn from social interactions. Through natural pedagogy, cultural experts construct a cultural niche that facilitates the acquisition of culturally relevant information that novices can then rapidly apply and generalize to a variety of situations (Flynn *et al.* 2013).

Activity theory

In Chapter 1, I detailed the growing body of data that demonstrates that contemporary and archaeologically known children were (and are) actively engaged in the social, political, economic and religious spheres of the world around them. This means that while they remain cultural novices, children are not passive learners or empty vessels for expert (adult) knowledge. In fact, they often direct their own learning (*i.e.* shape their own cultural niche) by setting goals and initiating interactions (Flynn *et al.* 2013). In a society, knowledge may not be shared evenly. Children make choices around their learning and these choices are not 'random but biased toward a preference for what will most likely lead to the most advantageous skills or knowledge' (Boyette 2016, 160). As children develop emotionally, cognitively and socially the forms of learning that are most relevant and effective change (Flynn *et al.* 2013). This includes who they learn from, as not all instructors are adults (Flynn *et al.* 2013). Children learn through vertical (parent-to-child), horizontal (peer-to-peer) and oblique transmission (from non-parental adults). In Chapter 3, I discussed the importance of learning through play throughout the hominin life course but particularly during childhood and adolescence. As children grow, peers take on greater importance but as noted in Chapter 6, adolescents actively seek out adults they perceive to be innovators, thus engaging in oblique knowledge transfer. Based on extensive modelling, Creaza *et al.* (2013, 219) argue that 'teaching of any kind (vertical *or* oblique) can allow cultural traits to fix more rapidly in a population but this effect is more pronounced and stronger when teaching is oblique' (emphasis in the original). In Chapter 5, I argued that oral storytelling was an important form of direct teaching by at least the Upper Paleolithic. Oral storytelling is also a form of oblique teaching par excellence. Therefore, a transition to deliberate teaching and an emphasis on oblique information transfer may have allowed early modern humans and subadults in particular 'to spread useful knowledge more rapidly and with greater fidelity than previously possible' (Creaza *et al.* 2013, 219).

Activity theory focuses on learning and knowledge transmission through socially organized activities (Flynn *et al.* 2013) such as bead making or many of the other activities discussed in Chapters 4 and 5. In Chapter 4, I discussed scaffolding as a way of providing enough support to someone learning a new task to ensure a successful outcome. Vygotsky's (1978) Zone of Proximal Development (ZPD) is relevant here. The ZPD is 'the distance between the actual development level as determined by independent problem solving and the level of potential development, as determined through problem solving under adult guidance or in collaboration with more capable peers' (Vygotsky 1978, 86). Scaffolding effectively lowers the age at which a child is able to master a task and allows the child to direct their learning through what Wood *et al.* (1978) refer to as 'contingent tutoring'. More help is offered to a child who is struggling with a task while less help is offered to one who is mastering it.

Distributed cognition and the cognitive niche

In Chapter 2, I discussed how the human brain is characterized by plasticity, with social, cultural and environmental factors as well as individual experiences shaping human cognitive processes and behavioral outcomes, particularly during the first five years of life. In Chapter 4, I discussed embodied cognition, extended cognition and the affordances of material culture. I argued that the mind is not limited to the skull of an individual but extends into the material world of artifacts (Malafouris 2013). In that context, I emphasized the importance of the recursive and embodied relationship between agent and object by giving the example of a stone toolmaker. Each blow of the hammerstone against a core revealed something new about the stone, which then influenced the subsequent behavior of the craftsperson. Building on these concepts, distributed cognition looks at cognition that is shared among individuals, artifacts and internal and external representations within a particular activity or cognitive niche (see Wheeler and Clark 2008). Flynn *et al.* (2013, 302) write, 'distributed cognition is critical in developmental niche construction as it allows children to work with others to learn, undertake and develop cultural practices, relying on coordination across a group'.

Distributed cognition is related to another concept that is key in understanding Paleolithic children's contribution to human cultural evolution and that is cumulative culture. To return to the above example of human adaptations to living in a glacial environment, the cultural knowledge required to not only survive but thrive in these niches is beyond the capacity of one individual mind but is instead the collective knowledge of many minds that is augmented over time and transmitted through ecological inheritance (Mesoudi and Thornton 2018; see also Creaza *et al.* 2013). In this context, researchers talk about the 'ratchet effect' of cumulative culture (*e.g.* Tennie *et al.* 2009; Haidle *et al.* 2015). A ratchet is a tool with angled teeth that engages in such a way as to allow for motion in only one direction. Tomasello (1999, 512) writes, 'The major part of the ratchet in the cumulative cultural evolution of human societies takes place during childhood. That is, each new generation of children develops in the "ontogenetic niche" characteristic of its culture ... mastering the artifacts and social practices that exist at that time.' Distributed cognition and the ratcheting of culture are what make complex technologies, cultural institutions and symbol systems that characterize human niches possible. Oral storytelling and the storage of information outside the body in the form of Upper Paleolithic imagery and non-figurative signs (Chapter 5) are examples of ways in which cumulative culture was shared and built upon. According to Creaza *et al.* (2013), teaching, and again, particularly oblique teaching, lessens the fitness benefits required for a trait to be maintained in a population through intergenerational knowledge transfer. Thus, the rich cumulative culture that is characteristic of modern humans is likely the result of oral storytelling and other forms of direct teaching that reach back at least into the Upper Paleolithic. If the data presented in Chapter 6 are correct, then adolescents are particularly important consumers and 'influencers' of cumulative culture.

Situated learning

The ontological niche into which organisms are born in part dictate what they learn. As Flynn *et al.* (2013, 305) observe, 'niche construction not only affects *what* we should learn but also provides an opportunity for learning something more general, the ability to learn *how* to learn' (emphasis in the original). In Chapters 4 and 5, I discussed Paleolithic communities of practice and Lave and Wegner's (1991) concept of legitimate peripheral practice. I argued that by interacting with expert knappers, children's own skill levels deepened, allowing them to move from being on the periphery of these communities of practice to fully participating in them. Similarly, children participating in communities of practice centered around the Paleolithic arts might begin by collecting and grinding ochre and other minerals necessary for pigment production, firewood to make charcoal, bird bones and slabs of rock suitable for use as palettes, and holding a torch or lamp to facilitate image production in caves (Nowell 2015b). In the process, they would learn about the properties of raw materials (*e.g.* where to find them, how to process them, what qualities to look for), and the social conventions for producing images and decoding meanings.

Thus situated learning involves novices and experts together with material culture, cultural symbols and social norms that support novices in the appropriation of cultural knowledge within a community of practice. As we saw in Chapters 4 and 5, however, communities of practice can lead to change as well. These decisions were recognizable through discontinuities in the archaeological record (*e.g.* new tool technologies, alterations in pigment recipes, stylistic innovations, etc.).

In sum, through natural pedagogy and activity theory, culturally knowledgeable people (sometimes but not always adults) transmit information critical to flourishing in a particular niche to culturally naïve individuals (most often children and adolescents) with subadults actively making critical choices about what to learn and whom to learn from (Flynn *et al.* 2013). Distributed cognition and situated learning govern behavior within that niche. Flynn *et al.* (2013, 308) write,

> human infants become part of a community (a niche) and can draw from many different sources (peers, adults, constructed opportunities within the environment, cultural tools such as books or artefacts) to become an active member of that community. Children (like adults) are not passive recipients of biological and cultural inheritance but active agents, influencing what is learnt through changes in their cognitive development, and their active pursuit of knowledge.

Culture can be thought of as a multigenerational system of information transfer (see Riede *et al.* 2021). Within the context of NC, it is clear that Paleolithic children were the ultimate consumers, producers and transmitters of hominin cumulative culture. Because cumulative culture is the foundation of the elaborate artifacts, symbol systems, cultural institutions, moral and belief systems and technical competencies that typify human and hominin niches, children are arguably the prime drivers of hominin cultural and biological evolution.

In Chapter 1, I began by observing that Paleolithic children were understudied in the archaeological record. However, the sheer wealth of data presented in this volume undermines this assertion. As noted in Chapter 1, it may be more accurate to say that we, as researchers, have until recently focused on 'dead' Paleolithic children rather than living Paleolithic children. In other words, we have traditionally documented their fossil remains, pathologies and burials but not necessarily how they lived their lives. We have been engaging in an excavation of children rather than an archaeology of children. By bringing together data from archaeology, primatology, ethnography, evolutionary biology, paleontology, genomics and evolutionary psychology, I hope I have shown that we can begin to know these children in ways once never thought possible. It is clear from the evidence presented in Chapters 2–6 that Paleolithic children loved and were loved; experienced hunger and pain but also joy; played games, made art and occupied 'secret spaces'; listened to stories and made music; learned to hunt, gather and fish; made medicines and textiles; and produced ceramics and stone tools. In so doing, they contributed to the economic, cultural and social wellbeing of their communities. Furthermore, they were drivers of hominin evolution. The evolutionary model presented in this final chapter demonstrates why we should be studying Paleolithic children for who they were and not just for the adults they would become. The writing of this book has brought me closer to understanding what growing up in the Ice Age might have been like but it has also highlighted the many gaps in our knowledge, particularly of the lives of Paleolithic children outside of Upper Paleolithic Europe. Expanded research, new discoveries, innovative technologies and re-analyses of existing data will no doubt begin to fill in these gaps and at the same time uncover new questions. The next decade of research into Paleolithic children promises to be an exciting one.

Notes

1. Selection has genotypic consequences but they do not map directly one to one from selection on phenotype although one could argue that gene therapy is selection on genotype and thus represents the ultimate in human NC.
2. Island ecosystems are often more vulnerable to extinctions. Furthermore, humans brought with them so many plants and animals that archaeologists sometimes refer to these as 'transported landscapes'.
3. While 'impact' in this context carries with it a negative connotation, humans also use technology to create vaccines, grow crops in the Arctic and remove plastic from the oceans, for example.

Appendix 1. Approximate date ranges for archaeological periods and hominins mentioned in this volume.

Archaeological period	Approximate date range (years before present)
Lower Paleolithic	2,500,000–300,000
Middle Paleolithic	300,000–45,000
Upper Paleolithic	45,000–10,000
Châtelperronian	45,000–40,000
Aurignacian	45,000–31,000
Gravettian	31,000–21,000
Solutrean	21,000–18,000
Magdalenian	18,000–10,000

Appendix 2. Table of subadult fossils in the Plio-Pleistocene (perinatal-ca. 10 years).

Specimen name	Species	Country	Context	Age estimate (years at death)	Associated artifacts	Associated ^{14}C dates (uncal BP)/estimated absolute date	References/sources
A.L. 333-105	Australopithecus afarensis	Ethiopia	Part of multi-individual hominin assemblage.	3.2 years		3.2 mya	Johanson et al. 1982b; Alemseged et al. 2006b; Ward et al. 2012
A.L. 333-111	Australopithecus afarensis	Ethiopia		Immature		3.2 mya	Lovejoy et al. 1982
A.L. 333-140 (AL 333-140, -142, -162/110 may represent same individual)	Australopithecus afarensis	Ethiopia	Part of multi-individual hominin assemblage.	Subadult		3.2 mya	Ward et al. 2012
A.L. 333-142 (AL 333-140, -142, -162/110 may represent same individual)	Australopithecus afarensis	Ethiopia	Part of multi-individual hominin assemblage.	Subadult		3.2 mya	Ward et al. 2012
A.L. 333-162/110 (AL 333-140, -142, -162/110 may represent same individual)	Australopithecus afarensis	Ethiopia	Part of multi-individual hominin assemblage.	Subadult		3.2 mya	Lovejoy et al. 1982; Ward et al. 2012
A.L. 333-39	Australopithecus afarensis	Ethiopia		Juvenile		3.2 mya	

(Continued)

Appendix 2. Table of subadult fossils in the Plio-Pleistocene (perinatal–ca. 10 years). (Continued)

Specimen name	Species	Country	Context	Age estimate (years at death)	Associated artifacts	Associated ^{14}C dates (uncal BP)/estimated absolute date	References/ sources
A.L. 333-43	Australopithecus afarensis	Ethiopia	Part of multi-individual hominin assemblage.	Juvenile		3.2 mya	Lovejoy et al. 1982; Ward et al. 2012
A.L. 333-86/99/104	Australopithecus afarensis	Ethiopia	Part of multi-individual hominin assemblage.	Juvenile		3.2 mya	Lovejoy et al. 1982; Ward et al. 2012
A.L. 333-95	Australopithecus afarensis	Ethiopia		Immature		3.2 mya	Lovejoy et al. 1982
A.L. 333n-1	Australopithecus afarensis	Ethiopia		Possible subadult		3.2 mya	
A.L. 333w-43/120	Australopithecus afarensis	Ethiopia		Subadult		3.2 mya	Lovejoy et al. 1982
A.L. 333x-6/9	Australopithecus afarensis	Ethiopia	Part of multi-individual hominin assemblage.			3.2 mya	Ward et al. 2012
KNM-MO 26	Afropithecus turkanensis	Kenya		2–3 years		17.5 mya	Kelley and Smith 2003
Amud 10	Homo neanderthalensis (assumed)	Israel		Infant		70–50 kya	Hovers et al. 1995; Valladas et al. 1999; Tillier et al. 2003

(Continued)

Appendix 2. Table of subadult fossils in the Plio-Pleistocene (perinatal–ca. 10 years) 175

Appendix 2. (Continued)

Specimen name	Species	Country	Context	Age estimate (years at death)	Associated artifacts	Associated ¹⁴C dates (uncal BP)/estimated absolute date	References/ sources
Amud 11	*Homo neanderthalensis* (assumed)	Israel		7 years		70–50 kya	Hovers et al. 1995; Valladas et al. 1999
Amud 12	*Homo neanderthalensis* (assumed)	Israel		Infant		70–50 kya	Hovers et al. 1995; Valladas et al. 1999; Tillier et al. 2003
Amud 15	*Homo neanderthalensis* (assumed)	Israel		Infant		70–50 kya	Hovers et al. 1995; Valladas et al. 1999
Amud 16	*Homo neanderthalensis* (assumed)	Israel		16 months		70–50 kya	Hovers et al. 1995; Valladas et al. 1999
Amud 18	*Homo neanderthalensis* (assumed)	Israel		Infant		70–50 kya	Hovers et al. 1995; Valladas et al. 1999
Amud 5	*Homo neanderthalensis* (assumed)	Israel		6–9 months		70–50 kya	Hovers et al. 1995; Valladas et al. 1999

(Continued)

Appendix 2. Table of subadult fossils in the Plio-Pleistocene (perinatal–ca. 10 years). (Continued)

Specimen name	Species	Country	Context	Age estimate (years at death)	Associated artifacts	Associated ^{14}C dates (uncal BP)/estimated absolute date	References/ sources
Amud 6	Homo neanderthalensis (assumed)	Israel		Neonate		70–50 kya	Hovers et al. 1995; Valladas et al. 1999
Amud 7	Homo neanderthalensis (assumed)	Israel	Intentional burial.	10 months	Almost complete red deer maxilla, lying on pelvis.	70–50 kya	Hovers et al. 1995; Valladas et al. 1999
Amud 8	Homo neanderthalensis (assumed)	Israel		8 years		70–50 kya	Hovers et al. 1995
Amud 3	Homo neanderthalensis (assumed)	Israel		4 years		70–50 kya	Hovers et al. 1995; Valladas et al. 1999
Amud 4	Homo neanderthalensis (assumed)	Israel		3 years		70–50 kya	Hovers et al. 1995; Valladas et al. 1999
Anzick infant	Homo sapiens	USA	Pit burial. Found alongside Anzick child.	1–2 years	Found directly below roughly 100 stone tools and fragments of 15 bone tools. 8 fluted projectile points, 4 uniface tools, 3 flake tools, 69 large heat-treated ovoid and lanceolate chert bifaces, 6 complete and partial bone foreshafts made from large mammal	10,915±50 BP	Owsley et al. 2001; Lepper 2014; Rasmussen et al. 2014; Becerra-Valdivia et al. 2018

(Continued)

Appendix 2. (Continued)

Specimen name	Species	Country	Context	Age estimate (years at death)	Associated artifacts	Associated ¹⁴C dates (uncal BP)/estimated absolute date	References/ sources
Anzick child	Homo sapies	USA	Possible burial. Remains may have washed into pit at a later time. Found alongside Anzick infant.	6–8 years	Found alongside Anzick infant, no ochre staining on skeleton.	8,600 BP	Owsley et al. 2001
Archi 1	Homo neanderthalensis/ Archaic Homo sapiens	Italy		3–6 years		Middle Paleolithic; Early last glacial, OIS 4 or early stage 3	Ascenzi and Segre 1971; Giacobini et al. 1984; Faerman et al. 1994; Tompkins 1996; Mallegni and Trinkaus 1997; Bailey and Hublin 2006
Arene Candide 11	Homo sapiens	Italy		1–4 years		9,925±50 – 10,735±55 BP	Tompkins 1996; Formicola et al. 2005; Formicola 2007; Gazzoni and Fontana 2011; Shackelford et al. 2012

(Continued)

Appendix 2. Table of subadult fossils in the Plio-Pleistocene (perinatal–ca. 10 years). (Continued)

Specimen name	Species	Country	Context	Age estimate (years at death)	Associated artifacts	Associated ^{14}C dates (uncal BP)/estimated absolute date	References/ sources
Arene Candide 15	Homo sapiens	Italy	Part of double burial with Arene Candide 14 & 15.	Child	Part of double burial with Arene Candide 14 & 15.	10,585±55 BP	Formicola et al. 2005; Formicola 2007;
Arene Candide 5	Homo sapiens	Italy	Part of double burial with Arene Candide 5 & 6.	2–3 years	Part of double burial with Arene Candide 5 & 6.	9,925±50 BP	Formicola et al. 2005; Shackelford et al. 2012
Arene Candide 6	Homo sapiens	Italy	Part of double burial with Arene Candide 5 & 6.	4–5 years	Part of double burial with Arene Candide 5 & 6.	9,925±50 BP	Formicola et al. 2005; Formicola 2007; Gazzoni and Fontana 2011
Arene Candide 8	Homo sapiens	Italy		5–7 years		10,655±55 BP	Tompkins 1996; Formicola et al. 2005; Formicola 2007; Gazzoni and Fontana 2011; Shackelford et al. 2012
Arene Candide 9	Homo sapiens	Italy		Immature		Upper Paleolithic – Byzantine	Gazzoni and Fontana 2011

(Continued)

Appendix 2. Table of subadult fossils in the Plio-Pleistocene (perinatal–ca. 10 years) 179

Appendix 2. (Continued)

Specimen name	Species	Country	Context	Age estimate (years at death)	Associated artifacts	Associated ¹⁴C dates (uncal BP)/estimated absolute date	References/sources
Aubesier site	Homo neanderthalensis	France		5–10 years			Trinkaus 1995
Aveline's Hole	Homo sapiens	UK		Subadult		Mesolithic	Bailey and Hublin 2006
Bacho Kiro Cave		Bulgaria		Child		43 kya	Tillier et al. 2017
Badegoule 3	Homo sapiens	France		3–4 years		Upper Pleistocene	Tompkins 1996; Shackelford et al. 2012
Badger Hole 226 30	Homo sapiens	UK		Subadult		Upper Pleistocene	Tompkins 1996
Badger Hole 227 31	Homo sapiens	UK		Subadult		Upper Pleistocene	Tompkins 1996
Balla child 68147-5	Homo sapiens	Hungary		1 year	Lithic artifacts.		Tillier et al. 2009
Balma Guilanya E3998	Homo sapiens	Spain		Child		11,095±195 BP; 10,195±255 BP	Gazzoni 2011
Baousse-Rousse 1969–9	Homo sapiens	Italy		Subadult		Upper Pleistocene	Tompkins 1996
Barakai 1	Homo neanderthalensis	former Soviet Union		3 years		Mousterian context, found in lower part of Upper Pleistocene level	Faerman et al. 1994; Mallegni and Trinkaus 1997

(Continued)

Appendix 2. Table of subadult fossils in the Plio-Pleistocene (perinatal–ca. 10 years). (Continued)

Specimen name	Species	Country	Context	Age estimate (years at death)	Associated artifacts	Associated ¹⁴C dates (uncal BP)/estimated absolute date	References/ sources
Barma Grande child	Homo sapiens	Italy		9–11 years			Shackelford et al. 2012
Borsuka Cave	Homo sapiens	Poland	No evidence of pit. Possible burial.	12–18 months	112 pendants made from the teeth of ungulates – 78 specimens from incisors and canines of steppe wisent or aurochs (B. priscus/ B. primigenius), and 34 from incisors and canines of European elk (A. alces) Deciduous and permanent teeth of both taxa used for pendants.	25,150± 160 BP; 27,350± 450 BP; 26,430± 180 BP	Wilczynski et al. 2012; 2016
Brillenhohle 2	Homo sapiens	Germany		6–7 years		Upper Pleistocene	Tompkins 1996; Shackelford et al. 2012
Bruniquel	Homo sapiens	France		Subadult		Upper Pleistocene	Bailey and Hublin 2006
Bruniquel II EM 536	Homo sapiens	France		Subadult		Upper Pleistocene	Tompkins 1996
Bruniquel II EM 538	Homo sapiens	France		Subadult		Upper Pleistocene	Tompkins 1996
Bruniquel II EM 541	Homo sapiens	France		Subadult		Upper Pleistocene	Tompkins 1996
Bruniquel Lafaye 25	Homo sapiens	France		Subadult		Upper Pleistocene	Tompkins 1996

(Continued)

Appendix 2. Table of subadult fossils in the Plio-Pleistocene (perinatal–ca. 10 years) 181

Appendix 2. (Continued)

Specimen name	Species	Country	Context	Age estimate (years at death)	Associated artifacts	Associated ¹⁴C dates (uncal BP)/estimated absolute date	References/ sources
Buca de Taso site	*Homo neanderthalensis*	Italy		5–10 years			Trinkaus 1995
Capelle	*Homo sapiens*	France		Subadult			Bailey and Hublin 2006
Capo di Leuca	*Homo neanderthalensis*	Italy		5–10 years			Trinkaus 1995
Carihuela/ Cariguela site	*Homo neanderthalensis*	Spain		6 years			Giacobini et al. 1984
Caverna del Fate	*Homo neanderthalensis*	Italy		1–5 years			Trinkaus 1995
Caverna del Fate	*Homo neanderthalensis*	Italy		5–10 years			Trinkaus 1995
Chateauneuf-sur-Charente (second child)	*Homo neanderthalensis*	France		5–10 years			Trinkaus 1995
Chateauneuf-sur-Charente 2	*Homo neanderthalensis/ Archaic Homo sapiens*	France		5–6 years		Upper Pleistocene	Tillier 1979
Chez Leix	*Homo sapiens*	France	Isolated element	5–9 years	Possible association with Aurignacian industry.	Aurignacian	Gambier 2000
Cisterna 3				Subadult			Wilczynski et al. 2016

(Continued)

Appendix 2. Table of subadult fossils in the Plio-Pleistocene (perinatal–ca. 10 years). (Continued)

Specimen name	Species	Country	Context	Age estimate (years at death)	Associated artifacts	Associated ¹⁴C dates (uncal BP)/estimated absolute date	References/sources
Combe-Grenal 1	Homo neanderthalensis	France		5–7 years		75–65 kya	Tompkins 1996; Garralda et al. 2005; Shackelford et al. 2012;
Combe-Grenal 24	Homo neanderthalensis	France		Child-Adolescent		75–65 kya	Garralda et al. 2000
Combe-Grenal 31	Homo neanderthalensis	France		3 years±12 months	No associated artifacts. Found amongst fauna and a meridional Acheulean industry.	130 kya	Bayle et al. 2009a; Maureille et al. 2011
Combe-Grenal IX	Homo neanderthalensis	France		9–14 years		75–65 kya	Garralda et al. 2000
Combe-Grenal XIII	Homo neanderthalensis	France		5–9 years			Garralda et al. 2000
Coupe-Gorge (symphyse)	Homo neanderthalensis	France		3–5 years			Granat and Heim 2003
Cova Negra Femur I Specimen CN 42168 & 42169	Homo neanderthalensis	Spain	Possible disturbed burial.	5 years		OIS 3	Arsuaga et al. 2007

(Continued)

Appendix 2. Table of subadult fossils in the Plio-Pleistocene (perinatal–ca. 10 years) 183

Appendix 2. (Continued)

Specimen name	Species	Country	Context	Age estimate (years at death)	Associated artifacts	Associated ¹⁴C dates (uncal BP)/estimated absolute date	References/sources
Cova Negra Specimen CN 42164a	*Homo neanderthalensis*	Spain	Possible disturbed burial. MNI = 2 out of Specimens: CN 42164a, CN 42164b, CN 42170-7310, CN 42170-7312, and CN 42174, 42174a, 42174b	5–8 years		OIS 4	Arsuaga et al. 2007
Cova Negra Specimen CN 42164b	*Homo neanderthalensis*	Spain	Possibly disturbed burial. MNI = 2 out of Specimens: CN 42164a, CN 42164b, CN 42170-7310, CN 42170-7312, and CN 42174, 42174a, 42174b	5–8 years		OIS 4	Arsuaga et al. 2007
Cova Negra Specimen CN 42165	*Homo neanderthalensis*	Spain	Possible disturbed burial.	5 years		OIS 4	Arsuaga et al. 2007
Cova Negra Specimen CN 42166 & 42167	*Homo neanderthalensis*	Spain	Possible disturbed burial.	5–8 years		OIS 4-3	Arsuaga et al. 2007
Cova Negra Specimen CN 42170-7310	*Homo neanderthalensis*	Spain	Possible disturbed burial.	5–8 years		OIS 4-3	Arsuaga et al. 2007

(Continued)

Appendix 2. Table of subadult fossils in the Plio-Pleistocene (perinatal–ca. 10 years). (Continued)

Specimen name	Species	Country	Context	Age estimate (years at death)	Associated artifacts	Associated ¹⁴C dates (uncal BP)/estimated absolute date	References/sources
Cova Negra Specimen CN 42170-7312	Homo neanderthalensis	Spain	Possibly disturbed burial. MNI = 2 out of Specimens: CN 42164a, CN 42164b, CN 42170-7310, CN 42170-7312, and CN 42174, 42174a, 42174b	5–8 years		OIS 4-3	Arsuaga et al. 2007
Cova Negra Specimen CN 42171	Homo neanderthalensis	Spain	Possible disturbed burial.	<6 years		OIS 3	Arsuaga et al. 2007
Cova Negra Specimen CN 42174, 42174a, 42174b	Homo neanderthalensis	Spain	Possibly disturbed burial. MNI = 2 out of Specimens: CN 42164a, CN 42164b, CN 42170-7310, CN 42170-7312, and CN 42174, 42174a, 42174b	2 years		Unknown Found in Mousterian sediments	Arsuaga et al. 2007
Cova Negra Specimen CN 7755	Homo neanderthalensis	Spain	Possible disturbed burial.	5 years		OIS 5b	Arsuaga et al. 2007
Cranium 14	Homo	Spain		5–12.5 years		530 kya	Gracia et al. 2009

(Continued)

Appendix 2. Table of subadult fossils in the Plio-Pleistocene (perinatal–ca. 10 years)

Appendix 2. (Continued)

Specimen name	Species	Country	Context	Age estimate (years at death)	Associated artifacts	Associated ¹⁴C dates (uncal BP)/estimated absolute date	References/sources
Cro-Magnon 5	Homo sapiens	France	Burial. Found near female CM2	1 year	Shell and ivory pendants and ochre found in immediate vicinity of bones.	Aurignacian	Gambier 2000
Cro-Magnon neonate 1	Homo sapiens	France	Burial. Found near female CM2	Neonate	3 ivory pendants found in immediate vicinity of skeleton. Ochre on bones.	27,680±270 BP	Irish et al. 2008; Henry-Gambier et al. 2013; Nava et al. 2017
Cro-Magnon neonate 2	Homo sapiens	France	Burial. Found near female CM2	Neonate	Shell and ivory pendants and ochre found in immediate vicinity of bones.	Aurignacian	Gambier 2000
Cro-Magnon 3	Homo sapiens	France	Burial	0–6 months		Aurignacian	Gambier 2000
Croze de Dua	Homo neanderthalensis	France		5–10 years			Trinkaus 1995
Cuckvati site	Homo neanderthalensis	Georgia		5–10 years			Trinkaus 1995
Dederiyeh Cave burial 1 (serial no. 8) Dederiyeh child 1	Homo neanderthalensis	Syria	Burial	17–24 months	Lithic assemblage: Prepared core flakes, Levallois points. 9 Levantine Mousterian flints. Scrapers – Most made on waste flakes from preparation of Levallois type cores. Assemblage matches phase B or phase C of sequential model of the Levantine Middle Palaeolithic.	70–50 kya	Akazawa et al. 1999; Pettitt 2002; Tillier et al. 2003; Gómez-Olivencia et al. 2015

(Continued)

Appendix 2. Table of subadult fossils in the Plio-Pleistocene (perinatal–ca. 10 years). (Continued)

Specimen name	Species	Country	Context	Age estimate (years at death)	Associated artifacts	Associated ^{14}C dates (uncal BP)/estimated absolute date	References/ sources
Dederiyeh Cave burial 2 (serial no. 10) Dederiyeh child 2	Homo neanderthalensis	Syria	Pit burial. Primary deposition.	2 years	Lithic assemblage: Prepared core flakes, Levallois points. 14 Levantine Mousterian flints. Scrapers – Most made on waste flakes from preparation of Levallois type cores. Assemblage matches phase B or phase C of sequential model of the Levantine Middle Palaeolithic. 100 pieces of debitage and numerous animal bone fragments including large piece of tortoise shell. Context of numerous hearths preserving plant remains. Hackberry (Celtis sp.) dominant.	70–50 kya	Akazawa et al. 1999; Pettitt 2002
Dederiyeh Cave Infant	Homo neanderthalensis	Syria	Deliberate burial.	1–3 years	Sub-rectangular limestone slab at the top of the head Triangular piece of flint on heart	70–50 kya	Smith 1991; Akazawa et al. 1995b; 1995a
Dederiyeh serial no. 13	Homo neanderthalensis	Syria		Subadult			
Dederiyeh serial no. 14	Homo neanderthalensis	Syria		Subadult			
Dederiyeh serial no. 15	Homo neanderthalensis	Syria		Subadult			

(Continued)

Appendix 2. Table of subadult fossils in the Plio-Pleistocene (perinatal–ca. 10 years) 187

Appendix 2. (Continued)

Specimen name	Species	Country	Context	Age estimate (years at death)	Associated artifacts	Associated ¹⁴C dates (uncal BP)/estimated absolute date	References/ sources
Dederiyeh serial no. 5	*Homo neanderthalensis*	Syria		Newborn			Akazawa et al. 1999
Dederiyeh serial no. 9	*Homo neanderthalensis*	Syria		Child			Akazawa et al. 1999
Denisova 2	*Homo sp.*	Russia	Specimen (tooth) likely fell out of living child.	10–12 years		122,700–194,400 BP	Slon et al. 2017; Douka et al. 2019;
Denisova 3	*Homo sp.*	Russia		Child		48,650± 2,380 BP; >37,235 BP; 29,200± 360 BP	Krause et al. 2010 suppl.
Devil's Tower 1; Gibraltar 2; Gibraltar child	*Homo neanderthalensis*	Gibraltar		3–5.8 years		47–30 kya	Buxton 1928; Skinner and Sperber 1982; Tillier 1983a; 1988; Dean et al. 1986; Smith 1986; 1994; Stringer et al. 1990; Faerman et al. 1994;

(Continued)

Appendix 2. Table of subadult fossils in the Plio-Pleistocene (perinatal–ca. 10 years). (Continued)

Specimen name	Species	Country	Context	Age estimate (years at death)	Associated artifacts	Associated ¹⁴C dates (uncal BP)/estimated absolute date	References/ sources
							Smith and Tompkins 1995; Antón 1997; Mallegni and Trinkaus 1997; Stringer and Dean 1997; Shackelford et al. 2012
Dolní Věstonice 10	Homo sapiens	Czech Republic	Specimen (tooth) likely fell out of living child.	9–10 years		27–25 kya	Hillson et al. 2006; Svoboda 2007
Dolní Věstonice 17	Homo sapiens	Czech Republic		6–10 years		27–25 kya	Trinkaus et al. 2000; Hillson et al. 2006; Svoboda 2007
Dolní Věstonice 27	Homo sapiens	Czech Republic		6–10 years		27–25 kya	Hillson et al. 2006; Svoboda 2007
Dolní Věstonice 36	Homo sapiens	Czech Republic		10–12 months		26,970±200 BP	Trinkaus et al. 2000; 2010; Svoboda 2007

(Continued)

Appendix 2. Table of subadult fossils in the Plio-Pleistocene (perinatal–ca. 10 years) 189

Appendix 2. (Continued)

Specimen name	Species	Country	Context	Age estimate (years at death)	Associated artifacts	Associated ¹⁴C dates (uncal BP)/estimated absolute date	References/ sources
Dolní Věstonice 4	Homo sapiens	Czech Republic	Possible burial.	<5 years	Bones found below a fragment of an incomplete mammoth scapula and within an extended concentration of charcoal and red-burnt clay. Skull covered by red ochre. 42 fox canines, ordered in a pattern of opposite-oriented pairs. Some teeth damaged and some partly burnt.	25,950±630 BP	Hillson et al. 2006
Ehringsdorf G	Homo neanderthalensis/ Archaic Homo sapiens	Germany		7–13 years		150–120 kya	Tompkins 1996; Shackelford et al. 2012
El Castillo	Homo sapiens	Spain		4–5 years		40,000±2,100–37,000±1,800 BP	Gambier 2000
El Sidrón Infant 1	Homo neanderthalensis	Spain		2–3 years		49 kya	Lalueza-Fox et al. 2011; Rosas et al. 2017
El Sidrón J1/ Juvenile 1	Homo neanderthalensis	Spain		5–7.7 years		49 kya	Lalueza-Fox et al. 2011; Rosas et al. 2017
El Sidrón J2/ Juvenile 2	Homo neanderthalensis	Spain		8–9 years		49 kya	Lalueza-Fox et al. 2011

(Continued)

Appendix 2. Table of subadult fossils in the Plio-Pleistocene (perinatal–ca. 10 years). (Continued)

Specimen name	Species	Country	Context	Age estimate (years at death)	Associated artifacts	Associated ^{14}C dates (uncal BP)/estimated absolute date	References/ sources
Engis 2	Homo neanderthalensis	Belgium		3–7 years		> 30–50 kya	Tillier 1983b; Radovcic et al. 1988; Stringer et al. 1990; Maureille and Bar 1999; Smith et al. 2010; Shackelford et al. 2012
Eshkaft-e Gavi A11-2096	Homo sapiens	Iran		3–8 years	Bone displays evidence of cutmarks and is burnt. 161 other fragments of mammal bone in feature (mostly bovids and/or cervids), 31% of all fragments are burned. Many lithic artifacts.	18 kya – >28 kya	Scott and Marean 2009
Eshkaft-e Gavi B21-5615	Homo sapiens	Iran		3–10 years		18 kya – >28 kya	Scott and Marean 2009
Font-de-Gaume	Homo sapiens	France	Isolated element	2–4 years		Aurignacian	Gambier 2000
Fontechevade 1957-53	Homo sapiens	France		4–5 years	Possible association with possible Aurignacian material	Upper Pleistocene	Gambier 2000; Bailey and Hublin 2006; Shackelford et al. 2012

(Continued)

Appendix 2. Table of subadult fossils in the Plio-Pleistocene (perinatal–ca. 10 years) 191

Appendix 2. (Continued)

Specimen name	Species	Country	Context	Age estimate (years at death)	Associated artifacts	Associated ^{14}C dates (uncal BP)/estimated absolute date	References/sources
Fossellone 3/ Circeo IV	*Homo neanderthalensis*	Italy		9–10 years	Remains of *Hyaena crocuta spaela*, *Panthera pardus*, *Rhinoceros Merkii*, and *Cervus elaphus*.		Giacobini et al. 1984; Mallegni 1992
Gargas Cave	*Homo sapiens*	France	Possible burial	2–5 years	Faunal remains with anthropogenic marks, several lithic elements – tools and debitage in flint and quartzite, used pebbles and coloring materials. Human clavicle fragment, in higher spit, 30 cm from mandible.	25,050±170 – 26,960±460 BP	Foucher et al. 2012; San Juan-Foucher 2005
Gran Dolina ATD6-116	*Homo antecessor*	Spain		2–4 years		MIS 21	Bermúdez de Castro et al. 2020
Gran Dolina ATD6-118	*Homo antecessor*	Spain		Immature		MIS 21	Bermúdez de Castro et al. 2020
Gran Dolina Hominid 1		Spain		Early adolescent			
Gran Dolina Hominid 2	*Possible Homo heidelbergensis*/ *Homo antecessor sp.*	Spain		Child	Aurora stratum assemblage: 100 lithic objects (limestone, sandstone, quartzite, and 2 varieties of flint) – flakes (primarily), retouched flakes, cores and heavy duty tools, 2 choppers. Faunal remains and fragments of hominin bones.	> 780 kya	Carbonell et al. 1995; Pares and Perez-Gonzalez 1995; Bermúdez de Castro et al. 1997

(Continued)

Appendix 2. Table of subadult fossils in the Plio-Pleistocene (perinatal–ca. 10 years). (Continued)

Specimen name	Species	Country	Context	Age estimate (years at death)	Associated artifacts	Associated ^{14}C dates (uncal BP)/estimated absolute date	References/ sources
Gran Dolina Hominid 3		Spain		10–11.5 years			Bermúdez de Castro et al. 1997
Grotta del Cavallo	Homo sapiens	Italy		baby		43–45 kya	
Grotte de la Masque	Homo neanderthalensis	France		5–10 years			Trinkaus 1995
Grotte de Rigabe	Homo neanderthalensis	France		1–5 years			Trinkaus 1995
Grotte des Abeilles	Homo sapiens	France		4±12 months	Associated with Aurignacian split bone points industry.	Aurignacien ancient	Gambier 2000
Grotte des Enfants 1	Homo sapiens	Italy	Part of double burial with Grotte des Enfants 1 & 2.	2–3 years	Part of double burial with Grotte des Enfants 1 & 2. Numerous pierced *Cyclope neritea* shells covering abdominal region.	11,130±100 BP	Tompkins 1996; Vanhaerne and d'Errico 2001; Formicola 2007; Gazzoni and Fontana 2011; Formicola and Holt 2015

(Continued)

Appendix 2. Table of subadult fossils in the Plio-Pleistocene (perinatal–ca. 10 years)   193

Appendix 2. (Continued)

Specimen name	Species	Country	Context	Age estimate (years at death)	Associated artifacts	Associated ^{14}C dates (uncal BP)/estimated absolute date	References/sources
Grotte des Enfants 2	Homo sapiens	Italy	Part of double burial with Grotte des Enfants 1 & 2.	1–2 years	Part of double burial with Grotte des Enfants 1 & 2. Numerous pierced *Cyclope neritea* shells covering abdominal region. Retouched bladelet embedded in T4 vetebral body.	11,130±100 BP	Tompkins 1996; Vanhaerne and d'Errico 2001; Formicola 2007; Gazzoni and Fontana 2011; Formicola and Holt 2015
Grotte des Hyènes 2	Homo sapiens	France	Isolated element	1±4 months		Aurignacian	Gambier 2000
Grotte des Rois 1955-148-1	Homo sapiens	France		Subadult		Upper Pleistocene	Tompkins 1996
Grotte du Renne Specimen no. 26, 27, 28, 34 Specimen label C7	Homo neanderthalensis	France	Remains found in 15 stratigraphic layers ranging from Gravettian to Mousterian cultural attribution.	7–18 months	Found in association with Châtelperronian assemblage. Assemblage includes: Personal ornaments, rings, awls, pierced animal teeth, ivory pendants, perforated fox canine, perforated reindeer phalange, and grooved fox canine, marmot incisor, bovid incisor, and fossil *Rhynchonella* sp. Colorants bearing facets produced by grinding, Châtelperronian points, convergent sidescrapers.	Layer Xb: 33,820±720 BP; 34,450±75 BP; 33,400 BP	David et al. 2001; Bailey and Hublin 2006; Higham et al. 2010; Caron et al. 2011

(Continued)

Appendix 2. Table of subadult fossils in the Plio-Pleistocene (perinatal–ca. 10 years). (Continued)

Specimen name	Species	Country	Context	Age estimate (years at death)	Associated artifacts	Associated ¹⁴C dates (uncal BP)/estimated absolute date	References/sources
Grotte du Renne Specimen no. 17 Specimen label C7	Homo neanderthalensis	France	Remains found in 15 stratigraphic layers ranging from Gravettian to Mousterian cultural attribution.	>7 years			Bailey and Hublin 2006
Grotte du Renne Specimen no. 18, 19, 20 Specimen label D10	Homo neanderthalensis	France	Remains found in 15 stratigraphic layers ranging from Gravettian to Mousterian cultural attribution.	4–7 years	Found in association with Châtelperronian assemblage. Assemblage includes: Personal ornaments, rings, awls, pierced animal teeth, ivory pendants, perforated fox canine, perforated reindeer phalange, and grooved fox canine, marmot incisor, bovid incisor, and fossil *Rhynchonella* sp. Colorants bearing facets produced by grinding, Châtelperronian points, convergent sidescrapers.	38–33 kya	Bailey and Hublin 2006; Higham et al. 2010; Caron et al. 2011;
Grotte du Renne Specimen no. 21 Specimen label A11.1916	Homo neanderthalensis	France	Remains found in 15 stratigraphic layers ranging from Gravettian to Mousterian cultural attribution.	7–9 years			Bailey and Hublin 2006

(Continued)

Appendix 2. Table of subadult fossils in the Plio-Pleistocene (perinatal–ca. 10 years) 195

Appendix 2. (Continued)

Specimen name	Species	Country	Context	Age estimate (years at death)	Associated artifacts	Associated ^{14}C dates (uncal BP)/estimated absolute date	References/sources
Grotte du Renne Specimen no. 22, 23, 24 Specimen label B5/B6.1506/B6	Homo neanderthalensis	France	Remains found in 15 stratigraphic layers ranging from Gravettian to Mousterian cultural attribution.	4–8 years	Found in association with Châtelperronian assemblage. Assemblage includes: Personal ornaments, rings, awls, pierced animal teeth, ivory pendants, perforated fox canine, perforated reindeer phalange, and grooved fox canine, marmot incisor, bovid incisor, and fossil *Rhynchonella* sp. Colorants bearing facets produced by grinding, Châtelperronian points, convergent sidescrapers.	Layer Xb: 33,820±720 BP; 34,450±75 BP; 33,400	David et al. 2001; Bailey and Hublin 2006; Higham et al. 2010; Caron et al. 2011;
Grotte du Renne Specimen no. 25 Specimen label B11.3191	Homo neanderthalensis	France	Remains found in 15 stratigraphic layers ranging from Gravettian to Mousterian cultural attribution.	5–7 years	Found in association with Châtelperronian assemblage. Assemblage includes: Personal ornaments, rings, awls, pierced animal teeth, ivory pendants, perforated fox canine, perforated reindeer phalange, and grooved fox canine, marmot incisor, bovid incisor, and fossil *Rhynchonella* sp. Colorants bearing facets produced by grinding, Châtelperronian points, convergent sidescrapers.	Layer Xb: 33,820±720 BP; 34,450±75 BP; 33,400	David et al. 2001; Bailey and Hublin 2006; Higham et al. 2010; Caron et al. 2011

(Continued)

Appendix 2. Table of subadult fossils in the Plio-Pleistocene (perinatal–ca. 10 years). (Continued)

Specimen name	Species	Country	Context	Age estimate (years at death)	Associated artifacts	Associated 14C dates (uncal BP)/estimated absolute date	References/sources
Grotte du Renne Specimen no. 29, 30, 31, 33 Specimen label C8	*Homo neanderthalensis*	France	Remains found in 15 stratigraphic layers ranging from Gravettian to Mousterian cultural attribution.	6–18 months	Found in association with Châtelperronian assemblage. Assemblage includes: Personal ornaments, rings, awls, pierced animal teeth, ivory pendants, perforated fox canine, perforated reindeer phalange, and grooved fox canine, marmot incisor, bovid incisor, and fossil *Rhynchonella* sp. Colourants bearing facets produced by grinding, Châtelperronian points, convergent sidescrapers.	Layer Xb: 33,820±720 BP; 34,450±75 BP; 33,400	David et al. 2001; Bailey and Hublin 2006; Higham et al. 2010; Caron et al. 2011
Grotte du Renne Specimen no. 32 Specimen label C8	*Homo neanderthalensis*	France	Remains found in 15 stratigraphic layers ranging from Gravettian to Mousterian cultural attribution.	>5 years	Found in association with Châtelperronian assemblage. Assemblage includes: Personal ornaments, rings, awls, pierced animal teeth, ivory pendants, perforated fox canine, perforated reindeer phalange, and grooved fox canine, marmot incisor, bovid incisor, and fossil *Rhynchonella* sp. Colourants bearing facets produced by grinding, Châtelperronian points, convergent sidescrapers.	Layer Xb: 33,820±720 BP; 34,450±75 BP; 33,400	David et al. 2001; Bailey and Hublin 2006; Higham et al. 2010; Caron et al. 2011

(Continued)

Appendix 2. Table of subadult fossils in the Plio-Pleistocene (perinatal–ca. 10 years) 197

Appendix 2. (Continued)

Specimen name	Species	Country	Context	Age estimate (years at death)	Associated artifacts	Associated ^{14}C dates (uncal BP)/estimated absolute date	References/sources
Grotte du Renne Specimen No. 35 Specimen label A7.806	*Homo neanderthalensis*	France	Remains found in 15 stratigraphic layers ranging from Gravettian to Mousterian cultural attribution.	6–9 years			Bailey and Hublin 2006
Grotte du Renne Specimen no. 37 Specimen label Z6.2085	*Homo neanderthalensis*	France	Remains found in 15 stratigraphic layers ranging from Gravettian to Mousterian cultural attribution.	3–7 years	Found in association with Châtelperronian assemblage. Assemblage includes: Personal ornaments, rings, awls, pierced animal teeth, ivory pendants, perforated fox canine, perforated reindeer phalange, and grooved fox canine, marmot incisor, bovid incisor, and fossil *Rhynchonella* sp. Colorants bearing facets produced by grinding, Châtelperronian points, convergent sidescrapers.	38–33 kya	Bailey and Hublin 2006; Higham et al. 2010; Caron et al. 2011
Grotte du Renne Specimen no. 38 Specimen label C9	*Homo neanderthalensis*	France	Remains found in 15 stratigraphic layers ranging from Gravettian to Mousterian cultural attribution.	4–8 months	Found in association with Châtelperronian assemblage. Assemblage includes: Personal ornaments, rings, awls, pierced animal teeth, ivory pendants, perforated fox canine, perforated reindeer phalange, and grooved fox canine, marmot incisor, bovid incisor, and fossil *Rhynchonella* sp.	38–33 kya	Bailey and Hublin 2006; Higham et al. 2010; Caron et al. 2011

(Continued)

Appendix 2. Table of subadult fossils in the Plio-Pleistocene (perinatal–ca. 10 years). (Continued)

Specimen name	Species	Country	Context	Age estimate (years at death)	Associated artifacts	Associated ^{14}C dates (uncal BP)/estimated absolute date	References/sources
					Colorants bearing facets produced by grinding, Châtelperronian points, convergent sidescrapers.		
Grotte du Renne Specimen no. 36 Specimen label A7 or RXb2 B5	Homo neanderthalensis	France	Remains found in 15 stratigraphic layers ranging from Gravettian to Mousterian cultural attribution.	Birth	Found in association with Châtelperronian assemblage. Assemblage includes: Personal ornaments, rings, awls, pierced animal teeth, ivory pendants, perforated fox canine, perforated reindeer phalange, and grooved fox canine, marmot incisor, bovid incisor, and fossil Rhynchonella sp. Colourants bearing facets produced by grinding, Châtelperronian points, convergent sidescrapers.	38–33 kya	Bailey and Hublin 2006; Higham et al. 2010; Caron et al. 2011
Grotte du Renne AR-7	Homo neanderthalensis	France	Possible burial	<2 years	Found in close spacial association with a hominin temporal bone from square C7, layer Xb (assigned to infant of 1 year), and 10 dental specimens from squares C7 and C8. Found in association with Châtelperronian assemblage.	38–33 kya	Higham et al. 2010; Caron et al. 2011; Welker et al. 2016

(Continued)

Appendix 2. Table of subadult fossils in the Plio-Pleistocene (perinatal–ca. 10 years) 199

Appendix 2. (Continued)

Specimen name	Species	Country	Context	Age estimate (years at death)	Associated artifacts	Associated ^{14}C dates (uncal BP)/estimated absolute date	References/ sources
					Assemblage includes: Personal ornaments, rings, awls, pierced animal teeth, ivory pendants, perforated fox canine, perforated reindeer phalange, and grooved fox canine, marmot incisor, bovid incisor, and fossil *Rhynchonella* sp. Colorants bearing facets produced by grinding, Châtelperronian points, convergent sidescrapers.		
Grotte du Renne Specimen no. 11 Specimen label Z11.451	*Homo neanderthalensis*	France	Remains found in 15 stratigraphic layers ranging from Gravettian to Mousterian cultural attribution.	>8 years	Found in association with Châtelperonian assemblage. Assemblage includes: Personal ornaments, rings, awls, pierced animal teeth, ivory pendants, perforated fox canine, perforated reindeer phalange, and grooved fox canine, marmot incisor, bovid incisor, and fossil *Rhynchonella* sp. Colorants bearing facets produced by grinding, Châtelperronian points, convergent sidescrapers.	38–33 kya	Bailey and Hublin 2006; Higham et al. 2010; Caron et al. 2011

(Continued)

Appendix 2. Table of subadult fossils in the Plio-Pleistocene (perinatal–ca. 10 years). (Continued)

Specimen name	Species	Country	Context	Age estimate (years at death)	Associated artifacts	Associated ¹⁴C dates (uncal BP)/estimated absolute date	References/sources
Grotte du Renne temporal bone C7	Homo neanderthalensis	France	Possible burial	1 year	Found in association with Châtelperronian assemblage. Assemblage includes: Personal ornaments, rings, awls, pierced animal teeth, ivory pendants, perforated fox canine, perforated reindeer phalange, and grooved fox canine, marmot incisor, bovid incisor, and fossil *Rhynchonella* sp. Colorants bearing facets produced by grinding, Châtelperronian points, convergent sidescrapers.	38–33 kya	Hublin et al. 1996; Higham et al. 2010; Caron et al. 2011; Welker et al. 2016
Grotte du Rousset		France		4–5 years			Shackelford et al. 2012
Grotte Simard/Grotte Rene-Simard	Homo neanderthalensis	France		1–5 years			Trinkaus 1995
Grub/Kranawetberg 1		Austria	Deciduous teeth	Subadult		24,400–25,400 BP	Teschler-Nicola et al. 2004; Wilczynski et al. 2016
H. naledi Dinaledi chamber	Homo naledi	South Africa		Immature		335–236 kya	Dirks et al. 2017; Hawks et al. 2017

(Continued)

Appendix 2. Table of subadult fossils in the Plio-Pleistocene (perinatal–ca. 10 years)   201

Appendix 2. (Continued)

Specimen name	Species	Country	Context	Age estimate (years at death)	Associated artifacts	Associated ¹⁴C dates (uncal BP)/estimated absolute date	References/sources
H. naledi Locality 102a	Homo naledi	South Africa		Immature		335–236 kya	Dirks et al. 2017; Hawks et al. 2017
H. naledi Locality 102b	Homo naledi	South Africa		Immature		335–236 kya	Dirks et al. 2017; Hawks et al. 2017
HCM 1	Unconfirmed	Israel		2–6 years	Levallois technology, short thin flakes, retouched flakes. Lithics which show centripetal core preparation.	220–115 kya	Tillier 1995; Tillier et al. 2011
HCM 2 (Possibly same individual as HCM 2, 3, and 4)	Unconfirmed	Israel		<6 years	Levallois technology, short thin flakes, retouched flakes. Lithics which show centripetal core preparation.	220–115 kya	Tillier et al. 2011
HCM 20	Unconfirmed	Israel		6–8 years	Levallois technology, short thin flakes, retouched flakes. Lithics which show centripetal core preparation.	220–115 kya	Tillier et al. 2011
HCM 3 (Possibly same individual as HCM 2, 3, and 4)	Unconfirmed	Israel		<6 years	Levallois technology, short thin flakes, retouched flakes. Lithics which show centripetal core preparation.	220–115 kya	Tillier et al. 2011
HCM 4 (Possibly same individual as HCM 2, 3, and 4)	Unconfirmed	Israel		<6 years	Levallois technology, short thin flakes, retouched flakes. Lithics which show centripetal core preparation.	220–115 kya	Tillier et al. 2011

(Continued)

Appendix 2. Table of subadult fossils in the Plio-Pleistocene (perinatal–ca. 10 years). (Continued)

Specimen name	Species	Country	Context	Age estimate (years at death)	Associated artifacts	Associated ^{14}C dates (uncal BP)/estimated absolute date	References/ sources
HCM 5	Unconfirmed	Israel		7–14 years	Levallois technology, short thin flakes, retouched flakes. Lithics which show centripetal core preparation.	220–115 kya	Tillier et al. 2011
HCM 6	Unconfirmed	Israel		14–17 years	Levallois technology, short thin flakes, retouched flakes. Lithics which show centripetal core preparation.	220–115 kya	Tillier et al. 2011
HCM 7	Unconfirmed	Israel		Juvenile	Levallois technology, short thin flakes, retouched flakes. Lithics which show centripetal core preparation.	220–115 kya	Tillier et al. 2011
HCM 8	Unconfirmed	Israel		2–6 years	Levallois technology, short thin flakes, retouched flakes. Lithics which show centripetal core preparation.	220–115 kya	Tillier et al. 2011
Hoedec H12		France	Possible burial	3–5 years	Necklace made up of: 12 Cardium edule, 1 Cardium norvegicum, 2 Chlamus varia, 1 Cardita, 1 Pecten, and 8 Patella. On clavicles: 2 Haliotis tubercolata.		Gazzoni 2011
Hoedic H4	Homo sapiens	France		Infant			Gazzoni 2011
Hohlenstein infant 1	Homo neanderthalensis	Germany		1–2 years			Shackelford et al. 2012

(Continued)

Appendix 2. Table of subadult fossils in the Plio-Pleistocene (perinatal–ca. 10 years)   203

Appendix 2. (Continued)

Specimen name	Species	Country	Context	Age estimate (years at death)	Associated artifacts	Associated ^{14}C dates (uncal BP)/estimated absolute date	References/sources
Hortus 2/3	Homo neanderthalensis	France	Cave site	6–10 years		Upper Pleistocene	Giacobini et al. 1984; Tompkins 1996; Shackelford et al. 2012; Williams et al. 2018
Istallosko	Homo sapiens	Hungary		Subadult			Tillier et al. 2009
Isturitz III	Homo sapiens	France		4.6–5.9 years			Skinner 1997a; Bailey and Hublin 2006
Isturitz III (1937) 1950-7		France		1–2 years			Shackelford et al. 2012
Isturitz III 1937	Homo sapiens	France		Subadult		Upper Pleistocene	Tompkins 1996
Isturitz III 1937-5-1		France		4–6 years			Shackelford et al. 2012
Isturitz III 1950-5-1	Homo sapiens	France		Subadult		Upper Pleistocene	Tompkins 1996
Isturitz III 1950-6	Homo sapiens	France		4–5 years		Upper Pleistocene	Tompkins 1996; Shackelford et al. 2012

(Continued)

Appendix 2. Table of subadult fossils in the Plio-Pleistocene (perinatal–ca. 10 years). (Continued)

Specimen name	Species	Country	Context	Age estimate (years at death)	Associated artifacts	Associated ^{14}C dates (uncal BP)/estimated absolute date	References/ sources
Jebel Irhoud 3	Homo sapiens/ Homo neanderthalensis	Morocco		6–9 years		160,000± 16,000 BP	Giacobini et al. 1984; Garralda et al. 2000; Smith et al. 2007b; Shackelford et al. 2012
KB 5223 (Possibly same individual as KB 6067)	Paranthropus robustus	South Africa		>2–3 years		Dating remains problematic	Grine 1982; Braga et al. 2013; 2017
KB 6067 (Possibly same individual as KB 5223)	Unconfirmed Possible Paranthropus robustus	South Africa		<5 years		Dating remains problematic	Braga et al. 2013; 2017
Kebara 1	Homo neanderthalensis	Israel	Burial	<1 year	Three stones and rhinoceros tooth nearby.	61.6±3.6 kya– 64±6 kya	Trinkaus 1995
Kiik-Koba 2	Homo neanderthalensis	Ukraine		4–7 months		Lower Mousterian	Vlcek 1973; Cowgill et al. 2007
KMH 1 – Kebara 1	Homo sapiens/ Homo neanderthalensis	Israel		7–12 months	Found in small area close to 3 stones and a rhinoceros tooth.	64–59 mya	Akazawa et al. 1995a; Tillier et al. 2003
KMH 12	Homo	Israel		8–10 years		64–59 mya	Tillier et al. 2003

(Continued)

Appendix 2. Table of subadult fossils in the Plio-Pleistocene (perinatal–ca. 10 years)

Appendix 2. (Continued)

Specimen name	Species	Country	Context	Age estimate (years at death)	Associated artifacts	Associated ¹⁴C dates (uncal BP)/estimated absolute date	References/sources
KMH 13	Homo	Israel		<6–12 months		64–59 mya	Tillier et al. 2003
KMH 15	Homo	Israel		12 months		64–59 mya	Tillier et al. 2003
KMH 16	Homo	Israel		unknown – Specimen (tooth) likely fell out of a living child at 6 years.		64–59 mya	Tillier et al. 2003
KMH 21 (KMH 21, 22, and 23 Possibly same individual)	Incertae sedis	Israel		5 years		64–59 mya	Tillier et al. 2003
KMH 22 (KMH 21, 22, and 23 Possibly same individual)	Incertae sedis	Israel		5–6 years		64–59 mya	Tillier et al. 2003
KMH 23 (KMH 21, 22, and 23 Possibly same individual)	Incertae sedis	Israel		5 years		64–59 mya	Tillier et al. 2003

(Continued)

Appendix 2. Table of subadult fossils in the Plio-Pleistocene (perinatal–ca. 10 years). (Continued)

Specimen name	Species	Country	Context	Age estimate (years at death)	Associated artifacts	Associated ^{14}C dates (uncal BP)/estimated absolute date	References/sources
KMH 25 (KMH 25, 26, and 29 Possibly same individual)	Homo	Israel		6–12 months		64–59 mya	Tillier et al. 2003
KMH 26 (KMH 25, 26, and 29 Possibly same individual)	Homo	Israel		6–12 months		64–59 mya	Tillier et al. 2003
KMH 29 (KMH 25, 26, and 29 Possibly same individual)	Homo	Israel		6–12 months		64–59 mya	Tillier et al. 2003
KMH 30	Homo	Israel		8–10 years		64–59 mya	Tillier et al. 2003
KMH 4 (KMH 4 and 8 Possibly same individual)	Homo	Israel		9–12 months		64–59 mya	Tillier et al. 2003
KMH 5 (KMH 5 and 7 Possibly same individual)	Homo	Israel		2 years		64–59 mya	Tillier et al. 2003

(Continued)

Appendix 2. Table of subadult fossils in the Plio-Pleistocene (perinatal–ca. 10 years) 207

Appendix 2. (Continued)

Specimen name	Species	Country	Context	Age estimate (years at death)	Associated artifacts	Associated ^{14}C dates (uncal BP)/estimated absolute date	References/ sources
KMH 7 (KMH 5 and 7 Possibly same individual)	Homo	Israel		3–5 years		64–59 mya	Tillier et al. 2003
KMH 8 (KMH 4 and 8 Possibly same individual)	Homo	Israel		6–12 months		64–59 mya	Tillier et al. 2003
KNM-ER 1477	*Paranthropus boisei*	Kenya		2.5–3 years			Bromage 1987; Dean 1987
KNM-ER 1507	Early *Homo*	Kenya		5 years			Bromage 1987; Dean 1987
KNM-ER 1590	Early *Homo*	Kenya		5.7 years			Smith 1986; Bromage 1987; Antón 1997
KNM-ER 1820	*Paranthropus boisei*	Kenya		2.5–3.1 years			Smith 1986; Bromage 1987; Dean 1987
KNM-ER 812	*Paranthropus boisei*	Kenya		2.5–3 years			Bromage 1987; Dean 1987

(Continued)

Appendix 2. Table of subadult fossils in the Plio-Pleistocene (perinatal–ca. 10 years). (Continued)

Specimen name	Species	Country	Context	Age estimate (years at death)	Associated artifacts	Associated ¹⁴C dates (uncal BP)/estimated absolute date	References/sources
KNM-ER 820	Early Homo	Kenya		5.3 years			Bromage and Dean 1985; Bromage 1987
Kostenki 15 (Gorodstov) N3	Homo sapiens	Russia		5–7 years		Gravettian	Henry-Gambier 2008a; Shackelford et al. 2012
Kostenki 18 (Khvoiko) N4	Homo sapiens	Russia		9–10 years		Gravettian	Henry-Gambier 2008a
Kostenki 3	Homo sapiens	Russia		Child		Gravettian	Tompkins 1996; Wilczynski et al. 2016
Kostenki 4	Homo sapiens	Russia		Child		Gravettian	Tompkins 1996; Wilczynski et al. 2016
Kostenki neonate	Homo sapiens	Russia		Neonate		23–29 kya	Nava et al. 2017

(Continued)

Appendix 2. Table of subadult fossils in the Plio-Pleistocene (perinatal–ca. 10 years) 209

Appendix 2. (Continued)

Specimen name	Species	Country	Context	Age estimate (years at death)	Associated artifacts	Associated ¹⁴C dates (uncal BP)/estimated absolute date	References/sources
Kozarnika infant	*Homo neanderthalensis*	Bulgaria		3–6 months	Level contained East Balkan Levallois Mousterian debitage with bifacial leaf points. Retouched forms include: Simple and convergent side scrapers, Mousterian points, piercers, retouched levallois blades and flakes, and denticulated and truncated flakes. Many burnt flints. Anvil on a long bone shaft fragment from a large ungulate; Retoucher on a fragment of unidentified bone; Long bone shaft fragment that has been 'retouched' and partly polished. Small fragment of rib body with traces of scraping and polishing (unconfirmed if anthropic origin).	128,000± 13,000 – 183,000± 14,000 BP	Tillier et al. 2017
Krapina 45	*Homo neanderthalensis/ Archaic Homo sapiens*	Croatia		6–8 years		Upper Pleistocene	Tompkins 1996; Shackelford et al. 2012
Krapina 46	*Homo neanderthalensis/ Archaic Homo sapiens*	Croatia		5–7 years		Upper Pleistocene	Tompkins 1996; Maureille and Bar 1999; Shackelford et al. 2012

(Continued)

Appendix 2. Table of subadult fossils in the Plio-Pleistocene (perinatal–ca. 10 years). (Continued)

Specimen name	Species	Country	Context	Age estimate (years at death)	Associated artifacts	Associated ¹⁴C dates (uncal BP)/estimated absolute date	References/ sources
Krapina 47	Homo neanderthalensis/ Archaic Homo sapiens	Croatia		9–11 years		Upper Pleistocene	Tompkins 1996; Shackelford et al. 2012;
Krapina 51	Homo neanderthalensis/ Archaic Homo sapiens	Croatia		4–7 years		Upper Pleistocene	Tompkins 1996; Shackelford et al. 2012;
Krapina 52	Homo neanderthalensis/ Archaic Homo sapiens	Croatia		7–8 years		Upper Pleistocene	Tompkins 1996; Shackelford et al. 2012;
Krapina 53	Homo neanderthalensis/ Archaic Homo sapiens	Croatia		9–12 years		Upper Pleistocene	Tompkins 1996; Shackelford et al. 2012;
Krapina 55	Homo neanderthalensis/ Archaic Homo sapiens	Croatia		10–13 years		Upper Pleistocene	Tompkins 1996; Shackelford et al. 2012;
Krems-Wachtberg – adolescent rib	Homo sapiens	Austria	Isolated, from horizon with dislocated material (AH 4.11)	Adolescent		26,580±160 BP	Simon et al. 2014

(Continued)

Appendix 2. Table of subadult fossils in the Plio-Pleistocene (perinatal–ca. 10 years)   211

Appendix 2. (Continued)

Specimen name	Species	Country	Context	Age estimate (years at death)	Associated artifacts	Associated ¹⁴C dates (uncal BP)/estimated absolute date	References/sources
Krems-Wachtberg A	*Homo sapiens*	Austria	Double burial with Krems-Wachtberg A & B.	Perinatal: 9th–10th month gestation	Double burial with Krems-Wachtberg A & B. Bodies overlaid with an adult mammoth scapula, supported by part of a tusk. Bodies embedded in red ochre. Decorated with >30 ivory beads, placed near pelvis.	26,580±160 BP	Einwogerer et al. 2006; Händel et al. 2008; Henry-Gambier 2008a
Krems-Wachtberg B	*Homo sapiens*	Austria	Double burial with Krems-Wachtberg A & B.	Perinatal: 9th–10th month gestation	Double burial with Krems-Wachtberg A & B. Bodies overlaid with an adult mammoth scapula, supported by part of a tusk. Bodies embedded in red ochre.	26,580±160 BP	Einwogerer et al. 2006; Händel et al. 2008; Henry-Gambier 2008a
Krems-Wachtberg C	*Homo sapiens*	Austria	Possible burial	0–3 months	Body embedded in red ochre. Ivory pin 2 cm above skull in same orientation.	26,580±160 BP	Einwogerer et al. 2006; Händel et al. 2008; Henry-Gambier 2008a
Ksar Akil – second child		Lebanon		Subadult			
Ksar Akil 1	*Homo sapiens*	Lebanon		7–9 years		35 kya?	Bergman and Stringer 1989

(Continued)

Appendix 2. Table of subadult fossils in the Plio-Pleistocene (perinatal–ca. 10 years). (Continued)

Specimen name	Species	Country	Context	Age estimate (years at death)	Associated artifacts	Associated ^{14}C dates (uncal BP)/estimated absolute date	References/sources
La Chaise 13 (S5-10)	Homo neanderthalensis	France		3.5–5 years		150–100 kya	Tillier and Genet-Varcin 1980; Faerman et al. 1994; Mallegni and Trinkaus 1997; Tillier et al. 2003
La Chaise 14	Homo neanderthalensis	France		4–5 years		150–100 kya	Tillier and Genet-Varcin 1980
La Chaise de Vouthon / Charente – Dupont Cave	Homo sapiens	France		8–10 years	Split bone points	Aurignacian	Gambier 2000
La Crouzade CIII	Homo neanderthalensis	France		3 months		(49,776–44,805) – 42,000±3000 BP	Saos et al. 2020
La Crouzade CIX	Homo neanderthalensis	France		3 months	Assemblage dominated by Levallois production. Unconfirmed association of artifacts.	(49,776–44,805) – 42,000±3000 BP	Saos et al. 2020
La Ferrassie 3	Homo neanderthalensis	France	Deposited in deliberately excavated pit.	5–10 years		50 kya	

(Continued)

Appendix 2. Table of subadult fossils in the Plio-Pleistocene (perinatal–ca. 10 years)

Appendix 2. (Continued)

Specimen name	Species	Country	Context	Age estimate (years at death)	Associated artifacts	Associated ^{14}C dates (uncal BP)/estimated absolute date	References/sources
La Ferrassie 4	Homo neanderthalensis	France	Deposited in deliberately excavated pit.	Foetus		50 kya	Pettitt 2002
La Ferrassie 4-4bis	Homo neanderthalensis	France		12–15 days – 3 months		50 kya	Granat and Heim 2003; Tillier et al. 2003
La Ferrassie 4a	Homo neanderthalensis	France	Deposited in deliberately excavated pit.	Neonate		50 kya	Pettitt 2002
La Ferrassie 5	Homo neanderthalensis	France	Deposited in shallow depression.	Foetus – 7 months gestational age	Several beautiful flint scrapers found nearby. 3 flint scrapers deposited in proximity.	50 kya	
La Ferrassie 6	Homo neanderthalensis	France	Possible burial	3–5 years	Skeleton covered with limestone block engraved with small cuplike depressions on one surface.	50 kya	Pettitt 2002; Cowgill et al. 2007
La Ferrassie 8	Homo neanderthalensis	France	Burial	23–24 months		50 kya	Shackelford et al. 2012; Gómez-Olivencia et al. 2015; Balzeau et al. 2020

(Continued)

Appendix 2. Table of subadult fossils in the Plio-Pleistocene (perinatal–ca. 10 years). (Continued)

Specimen name	Species	Country	Context	Age estimate (years at death)	Associated artifacts	Associated ¹⁴C dates (uncal BP)/estimated absolute date	References/sources
La Geniere #3	Homo sapiens			5–6 years		Upper Pleistocene	Tompkins 1996; Shackelford et al. 2012
La Madeleine 4 (LM4)	Homo sapiens	France	Burial	2–4 years	Head surrounded by 3 stones. Burial covered in ochre. Ornamentation on head, neck, elbows, wrists, knees, and ankles: many small shells and pierced teeth. Inventory of ornamentations: 1275 Dentalium, 86 Neritina, 24 Cyclope, 42 Turritella, 1 Glycymeris, 2 stag teeth ('croche de cerf'), 2 fox canines and 1 perforated phalange of a lagomorph. Other: Crown of human pre-molar (covered in ochre), lagomoph humerus, and fish vertebra (both also covered in ochre).	9990 – 10,390 BP	Vanhaeren and d'Errico 2001; Bayle et al. 2009b; 2010; Shackelford et al. 2012
La Quina H18	Homo neanderthalensis	France		5–8 years			Giacobini et al. 1984; Shackelford et al. 2012
La Quina Q-761 (child)	Homo neanderthalensis	France		5–6 years			Shackelford et al. 2012

(Continued)

Appendix 2. Table of subadult fossils in the Plio-Pleistocene (perinatal–ca. 10 years)

Appendix 2. (Continued)

Specimen name	Species	Country	Context	Age estimate (years at death)	Associated artifacts	Associated ^{14}C dates (uncal BP)/estimated absolute date	References/sources
Laetoli juvenile				Subadult			
Lagar Velho 1	Homo sapiens	Portugal		2–5 years	Pierced shell (Littorina obtusata) near cervical vertebrae. Red ochre. Vertically oriented animal bones and stones outline ochre-stained sediment around skeleton. Non-artifacts directly associated with burial: Charcoal, and Cervus elaphus remains; Vertebra from a semiarticulated section of a Oryctolagus cuniculus vertebral column immediately overlying the legs. Pierced deer teeth (?)	24.5 kya	Zilhao and Trinkaus 2002; Zilhao 2006; Henry-Gambier 2008a; Bayle et al. 2010
Lapedo child	Homo sapiens	Portugal		Subadult		24 kya	
Laterite baby	Archaic Homo sapiens	India		<5 months		0.166±30 M Middle Pleistocene	Rajendran et al. 2003; 2006
Laugerie-Basse 1	Homo sapiens	France		4–6 years		Upper Pleistocene	Tompkins 1996; Shackelford et al. 2012
Laugerie-Basse 2	Homo sapiens	France		2–4 years		Upper Pleistocene	Tompkins 1996; Shackelford et al. 2012

(Continued)

Appendix 2. Table of subadult fossils in the Plio-Pleistocene (perinatal–ca. 10 years). (Continued)

Specimen name	Species	Country	Context	Age estimate (years at death)	Associated artifacts	Associated ^{14}C dates (uncal BP)/estimated absolute date	References/ sources
Laugerie-Basse 3	Homo sapiens	France		4–6 years		Upper Pleistocene	Tompkins 1996; Shackelford et al. 2012
Laugerie-Basse 5	Homo sapiens	France		Subadult		Upper Pleistocene	Tompkins 1996
Laugerie-Basse 6	Homo sapiens	France		2–3 years		Upper Pleistocene	Tompkins 1996; Shackelford et al. 2012
Laugerie-Basse teen	Homo sapiens	France		9–10 years		Upper Pleistocene	Tompkins 1996; Shackelford et al. 2012
Le Fate I	Homo neanderthalensis	Italy		8–10 years		75,000–82,000 + 36,000/–14,000 years BP	Giacobini et al. 1984
Le Fate II	Homo neanderthalensis	Italy		6–10 years		75,000–82,000 + 36,000/–14,000 years BP	Giacobini et al. 1984; Tompkins 1996; Shackelford et al. 2012
Le Figuier 1	Homo sapiens	France		2–4 years		Gravettian	Henry-Gambier 2008a

(Continued)

Appendix 2. Table of subadult fossils in the Plio-Pleistocene (perinatal–ca. 10 years) 217

Appendix 2. (Continued)

Specimen name	Species	Country	Context	Age estimate (years at death)	Associated artifacts	Associated ^{14}C dates (uncal BP)/estimated absolute date	References/sources
Le Moustier 2	*Homo neanderthalensis*	France	Le Moustier. Lower rock shelter, archaeological level J.	4 months	Flint flakes.	40 kya	Maureille 2002
Le Mura 1 Grotta delle Mura 1	*Homo sapiens*	Italy	Possible burial	16 months	2 flat elongated stones perpendicularly stacked over each other placed over post-cranial skeleton, 2 smaller stones supported skull.	11,420±100 BP	Formicola 2007; Gazzoni 2011; Gazzoni and Fontana 2011
Le Peyrat child (1)	*Homo sapiens*	France		Subadult		Upper Pleistocene	Tompkins 1996; Wilczynski et al. 2016
Le Piage 1	*Homo sapiens*	France		Perinatal	Associated with Aurignacian industry.	Aurignacian	Gambier 2000
Le Placard 56029 (68098)	*Homo sapiens*	France		6–7 years		Upper Pleistocene	Tompkins 1996; Shackelford et al. 2012
Le Placard 61401 (DG#31/32)	*Homo sapiens*	France		8–10 years		Upper Pleistocene	Tompkins 1996; Shackelford et al. 2012
Le Placard 61401 (DG#40)		France		3–4 years			Shackelford et al. 2012

(Continued)

Appendix 2. Table of subadult fossils in the Plio-Pleistocene (perinatal–ca. 10 years). (Continued)

Specimen name	Species	Country	Context	Age estimate (years at death)	Associated artifacts	Associated 14C dates (uncal BP)/estimated absolute date	References/sources
Le Placard 61401-61397	Homo sapiens	France		6–8 years			Shackelford et al. 2012
Le Roc de Sers 11-3	Homo sapiens	France		Subadult		Upper Pleistocene	Tompkins 1996
Le Roc de Sers 75113	Homo sapiens	France		Subadult		Upper Pleistocene	Tompkins 1996
Les Fees 1	Homo sapiens	France		Subadult		Upper Pleistocene	Tompkins 1996
Les Rois I	Homo sapiens	France		6±24 months	Found in direct association with Aurignacian I and II industries without split bone points.	Aurignacian	Gambier 2000
Les Rois J	Homo sapiens	France		8±24 months	Found in direct association with Aurignacian I and II industries without split bone points.	Aurignacian	Gambier 2000
Les Rois K	Homo sapiens	France		5–17 years	Found in direct association with Aurignacian I and II industries without split bone points.	Aurignacian	Gambier 2000
Les Rois C	Homo sapiens	France		4±12 months –5±16 months	Found in direct association with Aurignacian I and II industries without split bone points.	Aurignacian	Gambier 2000

(Continued)

Appendix 2. (Continued)

Specimen name	Species	Country	Context	Age estimate (years at death)	Associated artifacts	Associated ¹⁴C dates (uncal BP)/estimated absolute date	References/sources
Les Rois E	Homo sapiens	France		9±24 months	Found in direct association with Aurignacian I and II industries without split bone points.	Aurignacian	Gambier 2000
Les Rois D	Homo sapiens	France		2±8 months	Found in direct association with Aurignacian I and II industries without split bone points.	Aurignacian	Gambier 2000
Les Rois Mandible A	Homo sapiens	France		10±30 months	Found in direct association with Aurignacian I and II industries without split bone points.	Aurignacian	Gambier 2000
LH 2	Australopithecus afarensis	Tanzania		3.25–3.6 years			Bromage 1987
LH 3	Australopithecus	Tanzania		4.6 years			Bromage 1987
LH 6	Australopithecus	Tanzania		4.9 years			Bromage 1987
Magrite 2426 Indiv #5	Homo sapiens			Subadult		Upper Pleistocene	Tompkins 1996
Magrite 2678 Indiv #6	Homo sapiens			Subadult		Upper Pleistocene	Tompkins 1996
Malladetes occipital bone	Homo sapiens	Spain	Bone found in small niche along the interior wall of the cave.	5–7 years	Bone found below a large block. Fragments of charcoal and abundant osseous remains.	25,120±240 years BP	Arsuaga et al. 2002

(Continued)

Appendix 2. Table of subadult fossils in the Plio-Pleistocene (perinatal–ca. 10 years). (Continued)

Specimen name	Species	Country	Context	Age estimate (years at death)	Associated artifacts	Associated ¹⁴C dates (uncal BP)/estimated absolute date	References/sources
Mal'ta (older child)	Homo sapiens			1–2 years		Upper Pleistocene	Tompkins 1996; Shackelford et al. 2012
Mal'ta (younger child)	Homo sapiens			6–24 months			Shackelford et al. 2012
Mal'ta 1	Homo sapiens			3–4 years		Gravettian	Henry-Gambier 2008a
Maritza 1	Homo sapiens	Italy		8 years		14,488±800 BP	Formicola 2007; Gazzoni 2011; Gazzoni and Fontana 2011
Maritza 2	Homo sapiens	Italy		Possible subadult		Final Epigravettian	Formicola 2007; Gazzoni 2011
Marmes F2	Homo sapiens	USA	Possible cremation	6 years		9,870±50 BP	Lepper 2014
Marmes H4	Homo sapiens	USA	Possible cremation	8–14 years		9,430±40 BP	Lepper 2014
Marmes H5	Homo sapiens	USA	Possible cremation	8–14 years		9,430±40 BP	Lepper 2014
Marmes H6	Homo sapiens	USA	Possible cremation	8–14 years		9,430±40 BP	Lepper 2014

(Continued)

Appendix 2. Table of subadult fossils in the Plio-Pleistocene (perinatal–ca. 10 years) 221

Appendix 2. (Continued)

Specimen name	Species	Country	Context	Age estimate (years at death)	Associated artifacts	Associated ¹⁴C dates (uncal BP)/estimated absolute date	References/sources
Mas d'Azil	Homo sapiens	France		4–5 years		Upper Pleistocene	Tompkins 1996; Shackelford et al. 2012
Mezmaiskaya 1	Homo neanderthalensis	Russia		Newborn/Perinatal – < 2 months	No artifacts of faunal debris in immediate area. No traces of a burial pit. Small charcoal fragments recovered from sediment surrounding the skeleton.	29,195±965 years BP	Golovanova et al. 1999; Barriel and Tillier 2002; Pettitt 2002
Mezmaiskaya child	Homo neanderthalensis	Russia	Burial pit	1–2 years	Pit overlain by a limestone block.	Upper Middle Paleolithic	Golovanova et al. 1999; Pettitt 2002
Miesslingtal (site)	Homo sapiens	Austria		Subadult			Bailey and Hublin 2006
Miesslingtal 22034 (73577)	Homo sapiens	Austria		Subadult		Upper Pleistocene	Bailey and Hublin 2006; Wilczynski et al. 2016
Mladec 3	Homo sapiens	Czech Republic	Possible burial	2 years			
MLD 11/30	Australopithecus	South Africa		5–9 years			Mann 1975; Bromage 1987
MLD 2	Australopithecus	South Africa		6–11 years			Bromage 1987

(Continued)

Appendix 2. Table of subadult fossils in the Plio-Pleistocene (perinatal–ca. 10 years). (Continued)

Specimen name	Species	Country	Context	Age estimate (years at death)	Associated artifacts	Associated ^{14}C dates (uncal BP)/estimated absolute date	References/ sources
MLD 5	Australopithecus	South Africa		1–2.5 years			Skinner and Sperber 1982; Bromage 1987
Mojokerto child/Perning I	Homo erectus Possible Asian Homo erectus	Indonesia		4–6 years		1.81±0.04 mya 0.97–1.07 mya Contention that dated material directly correlates with date of fossils	Hyodo et al. 1993; 1998; Storm 2002; Swisher 1994; Swisher et al. 1994; Antón 1997; Huffman 2001
Molare 1	Homo neanderthalensis/ Archaic Homo sapiens	Italy		3–4 years	Lithic industry = 57 tools. Mostly points and side-scrapers. A Quinson piece, a few demi-Quina elements.	Early phase of Last Glacial Middle Paleolithic	Mallegni and Ronchitelli 1987; 1989; Tompkins 1996; Mallegni and Trinkaus 1997
Monsempron	Homo neanderthalensis	France		5–10 years			Trinkaus 1995

(Continued)

Appendix 2. Table of subadult fossils in the Plio-Pleistocene (perinatal–ca. 10 years) 223

Appendix 2. (Continued)

Specimen name	Species	Country	Context	Age estimate (years at death)	Associated artifacts	Associated ¹⁴C dates (uncal BP)/estimated absolute date	References/ sources
Montgaudier 3	Homo sapiens	France		6–8 years		Upper Pleistocene	Arsuaga et al. 2002; Tompkins 1996; Shackelford et al. 2012
Mother Grundy's Parlour EN 1.7.1	Homo sapiens	UK		Subadult		Upper Pleistocene	Tompkins 1996
Mugharet el-'Aliya 1	Homo sapiens	Morocco		9 years			Minugh-Purvis 1993
Nariokotome male Specimen KNM-WT 15000	Homo erectus	Kenya		8 years		1.5 mya	Dean et al. 2001
Nataruk		Kenya		Fetus		10.5–9.5 kya	Nava et al. 2017
Nazlet Khater		Egypt		Fetus		37 kya	Nava et al. 2017
Nazlet Khater 2		Egypt		Subadult			
Nerja infant		Spain		3 year		Solutrean	Lalueza-Fox, 1995
Neuwied-Irlich		Germany		Fetus/ neonate		12 kya	Nava et al. 2017

(Continued)

Appendix 2. Table of subadult fossils in the Plio-Pleistocene (perinatal–ca. 10 years). (Continued)

Specimen name	Species	Country	Context	Age estimate (years at death)	Associated artifacts	Associated ^{14}C dates (uncal BP)/estimated absolute date	References/ sources
Noisetier Cave	*Homo neanderthalensis*	France		6–7 years		MIS 3	Becam and Chevalier 2019
Obi-Rakhmat Neanderthal	*Homo neanderthalensis*	Uzbekistan		6–9 years			Smith et al. 2010; Shackelford et al. 2012
Obristvi – 4 child		Czech Republic				Mesolithic	
OH 30	*Paranthropus boisei*	Tanzania		2.5–3.2 years			Bromage 1987
OH-7	*Homo habilis*	Tanzania		Subadult		1.8 mya	Antón 1997; Spoor et al. 2015
Olduvai Hominid 8		Tanzania		Possible subadult			DeSilva et al. 2010
Olerdola twins		Spain		Perinatal			
Ostuni 1b/Os1b fetus	*Homo sapiens*	Italy	Burial. Primary deposition within pelvic region of Os1.	31–36 gestational weeks	>600 perforated shells around wrists and covering head of mother (Os1). Shells covering her head were pasted together with red ochre. Shells mostly *Cyclope neritea*. Shells of Cypraeidae are single, not paired. Presence of remains of ungulate skull fragments (mainly *Equus ferus*).	24,410±320 – 27,000 BP	Giacobini 2006; Nava et al. 2017

(Continued)

Appendix 2. Table of subadult fossils in the Plio-Pleistocene (perinatal–ca. 10 years) 225

Appendix 2. (Continued)

Specimen name	Species	Country	Context	Age estimate (years at death)	Associated artifacts	Associated ^{14}C dates (uncal BP)/estimated absolute date	References/sources
					Other shells (*Columbella*, cowries, *Nassarius*) grouped together near the 2 forearms and in front of the chest and belly of mother. Pierced deer canine lay near right parietal bone of mother. A few flint tools. Shells (perforated) identified as: *Tritia neritea, Tritia mutabilis, Trivia monacha,* and *Columbella rustica*. Red ochre mainly limited to mother's skull.		
Paglicci adolescent 2	*Homo sapiens*	Italy		10–14 years		Epigravettian	Shackelford et al. 2012
Paria a Mare 2				Newborn			Gazzoni and Fontana 2011
Pataud 2		France		0–6 months		Gravettian	Henry-Gambier et al. 2005; Henry-Gambier 2008a
Pataud 26.230B		France		4–6 years			Shackelford et al. 2012
Pataud 26.236	*Homo sapiens*	France		5–7 years		Upper Pleistocene	Tompkins 1996; Shackelford et al. 2012

(Continued)

Appendix 2. Table of subadult fossils in the Plio-Pleistocene (perinatal–ca. 10 years). (Continued)

Specimen name	Species	Country	Context	Age estimate (years at death)	Associated artifacts	Associated ^{14}C dates (uncal BP)/estimated absolute date	References/sources
Pataud 4		France		0–1 years		Gravettian	Henry-Gambier et al. 2005; Henry-Gambier 2008a
Pataud 6		France		4–5 years		Gravettian	Henry-Gambier et al. 2005; Henry-Gambier 2008a
Pataud 7		France		Subadult			Wilczynski et al. 2016
Pataud baby	Homo sapiens	France		Newborn		Epigravettian	
Pavlov 11	Homo sapiens	Czech Republic		Subadult			Wilczynski et al. 2016
Pavlov 16	Homo sapiens	Czech Republic		6–10 years		29–33 kya	Hillson et al. 2006; Svoboda et al. 2016; Wilczynski et al. 2016
Pavlov 17	Homo sapiens	Czech Republic		6–10 years		29–33 kya	Hillson et al. 2006; Svoboda et al. 2016

(Continued)

Appendix 2. Table of subadult fossils in the Plio-Pleistocene (perinatal–ca. 10 years) 227

Appendix 2. (Continued)

Specimen name	Species	Country	Context	Age estimate (years at death)	Associated artifacts	Associated ¹⁴C dates (uncal BP)/estimated absolute date	References/sources
Pavlov 18	*Homo sapiens*	Czech Republic		6–10 years		29–33 kya	Hillson et al. 2006; Svoboda et al. 2016
Pavlov 30	*Homo sapiens*	Czech Republic		8–16 years		27–25 kya	Trinkaus et al. 2010
Pavlov 32	*Homo sapiens*	Czech Republic		5–12 years		27–25 kya	Trinkaus et al. 2010
Pech de l'Aze 1	*Homo neanderthalensis*	France		18.5 months–3.6 years	Unconfirmed due to history of excavation. Possibly skeleton placed above bifaces, possibly skull placed above "belles haches du type Saint-Acheul". Unable to confirm from excavation notes which exact level remains belonged to.	41–51 kya	Minugh-Purvis 1988; Tillier 1988; Antón 1997; Mallegni and Trinkaus 1997; Maureille and Soressi 2000; Granat and Heim 2003; Soressi et al. 2007
Pech de l'Aze IVa	*Homo neanderthalensis*	France		1–2 years		49–56 kya	Turq et al. 2004
Pech de l'Aze IVb	*Homo neanderthalensis*	France		4–9 years		49–56 kya	Turq et al. 2004
Petit Marais 4/Marais 4	*Homo sapiens*			3 years			Gazzoni 2011

(Continued)

Appendix 2. Table of subadult fossils in the Plio-Pleistocene (perinatal–ca. 10 years). (Continued)

Specimen name	Species	Country	Context	Age estimate (years at death)	Associated artifacts	Associated ¹⁴C dates (uncal BP)/estimated absolute date	References/sources
Portel-Ouest Individual 3 LP-22, LP-28	Homo neanderthalensis	France	Cave site	6–11 years	Associated with reindeer, horse, and bison remains, as well as Mousterian artifacts, within the archaeological levels.	44 kya	Becam and Chevalier 2019
Portel-Ouest Individual 4 LP-24	Homo neanderthalensis	France	Cave site	6–8 years	Associated with reindeer, horse, and bison remains, as well as Mousterian artifacts, within the archaeological levels.	44 kya	Becam and Chevalier 2019
Portel-Ouest Individual 6 LP-26 & LP-31	Homo neanderthalensis	France	Cave site	9–10 years	Associated with reindeer, horse, and bison remains, as well as Mousterian artifacts, within the archaeological levels.	44 kya	Becam and Chevalier 2019
Portel-Ouest Individual 7 LP-6, LP-19	Homo neanderthalensis	France	Cave site	9–11 years	Associated with reindeer, horse, and bison remains, as well as Mousterian artifacts, within the archaeological levels.	44 kya	Becam and Chevalier 2019
Portel-Ouest Individual 8 LP-20	Homo neanderthalensis	France	Cave site	9–11 years	Associated with reindeer, horse, and bison remains, as well as Mousterian artifacts, within the archaeological levels.	44 kya	Becam and Chevalier 2019
Portel-Ouest Individual 9 LP-21, LP-23, LP-30	Homo neanderthalensis	France	Cave site	6–11 years	Associated with reindeer, horse, and bison remains, as well as Mousterian artifacts, within the archaeological levels.	44 kya	Becam and Chevalier 2019

(Continued)

Appendix 2. Table of subadult fossils in the Plio-Pleistocene (perinatal–ca. 10 years) 229

Appendix 2. (Continued)

Specimen name	Species	Country	Context	Age estimate (years at death)	Associated artifacts	Associated ^{14}C dates (uncal BP)/estimated absolute date	References/ sources
Praia a Mare 1	Homo sapiens	Italy		1 year		9,070±80 BP	Gazzoni 2011; Gazzoni and Fontana 2011
Praia a Mare 2	Homo sapiens	Italy		Neonate			Gazzoni and Fontana 2011
Předmostí 11		Czech Republic		6 months		25–27 kya	Henry-Gambier 2008a
Předmostí 12		Czech Republic		4 months		25–27 kya	Henry-Gambier 2008a
Předmostí 13		Czech Republic		2 months		25–27 kya	Henry-Gambier 2008a
Předmostí 15		Czech Republic		Infant		25–27 kya	Henry-Gambier 2008a; Svoboda 2008
Předmostí 16		Czech Republic		Infant		25–27 kya	Henry-Gambier 2008a
Předmostí 17		Czech Republic		Infant		25–27 kya	Henry-Gambier 2008a
Předmostí 2		Czech Republic		6–7 years		24–27 kya	Henry-Gambier 2008a; Svoboda 2008

(Continued)

Appendix 2. Table of subadult fossils in the Plio-Pleistocene (perinatal–ca. 10 years). (Continued)

Specimen name	Species	Country	Context	Age estimate (years at death)	Associated artifacts	Associated ¹⁴C dates (uncal BP)/estimated absolute date	References/ sources
Předmostí 20		Czech Republic		9–10 years		25–27 kya	Henry-Gambier 2008a
Předmostí 22		Czech Republic		9–11 years		25–27 kya	Henry-Gambier 2008a
Předmostí 24		Czech Republic		6–10 years		25–27 kya	Henry-Gambier 2008a
Předmostí 25		Czech Republic		6–10 years		25–27 kya	Henry-Gambier 2008a
Předmostí 6		Czech Republic		2–4 years		25–27 kya	Henry-Gambier 2008a; Svoboda 2008
Předmostí 8		Czech Republic		4 years		25–27 kya	Henry-Gambier 2008a; Svoboda 2008
Putride	Homo neanderthalensis	France		1–5 years			Trinkaus 1995
Qafzeh ?b	Homo sapiens	Israel		3–7 years		92–115±15 kya	Schwarcz et al. 1988; Courtaud and Tillier 2005; Tillier 2008

(Continued)

Appendix 2. Table of subadult fossils in the Plio-Pleistocene (perinatal–ca. 10 years)

Appendix 2. (Continued)

Specimen name	Species	Country	Context	Age estimate (years at death)	Associated artifacts	Associated ^{14}C dates (uncal BP)/estimated absolute date	References/sources
Qafzeh 10	Homo sapiens	Israel	Double burial with Qafzeh 9	5–6 years		92–115±15 kya	Schwarcz et al. 1988; Tillier et al. 2003; Tillier 2008; Smith et al. 2010; Shackelford et al. 2012
Qafzeh 11	Homo sapiens	Israel	Burial. Primary deposition.	8–13 years	Parts of fallow deer antlers placed directly in contact with hands.	92–115±15 kya	Tillier 1984; Schwarcz et al. 1988; Shackelford et al. 2012
Qafzeh 12	Homo sapiens	Israel		3–4 years		92–115±15 kya	Schwarcz et al. 1988; Tillier et al. 2001
Qafzeh 13	Homo neanderthalensis	Israel	Burial	Fetus/Neonate	Found under a stone.	92–115±15 kya	Schwarcz et al. 1988; Tillier et al. 2003; Tillier 2008; Tillier 2011
Qafzeh 14		Israel		Infant		92–115±15 kya	Schwarcz et al. 1988; Tillier et al. 2003; Tillier 2008

(Continued)

Appendix 2. Table of subadult fossils in the Plio-Pleistocene (perinatal–ca. 10 years). (Continued)

Specimen name	Species	Country	Context	Age estimate (years at death)	Associated artifacts	Associated ^{14}C dates (uncal BP)/estimated absolute date	References/sources
Qafzeh 15	Homo sapiens	Israel		6–8 years		92–115±15 kya	Schwarcz et al. 1988; Tillier et al. 2003; Tillier 2008; Shackelford et al. 2012
Qafzeh 22	Homo sapiens	Israel		Immature		92–115±15 kya	Schwarcz et al. 1988; Courtaud and Tillier 2005; Tillier 2008
Qafzeh 4	Homo neanderthalensis	Israel		5–8 years		92–115±15 kya	Schwarcz et al. 1988; Mallegni and Trinkaus 1997; Maureille and Bar 1999; Tillier 2008; Shackelford et al. 2012
Qafzeh 21	Homo sapiens	Israel		3 years		92–115±15 kya	Schwarcz et al. 1988; Tillier et al. 2003; Courtaud and Tillier 2005; Tillier 2008

(Continued)

Appendix 2. Table of subadult fossils in the Plio-Pleistocene (perinatal–ca. 10 years) 233

Appendix 2. (Continued)

Specimen name	Species	Country	Context	Age estimate (years at death)	Associated artifacts	Associated ^{14}C dates (uncal BP)/estimated absolute date	References/sources
Quirhuac	Homo sapiens	Peru	Burial	Subadult		9,020±650 – 10,650±180 BP	Powell 2005
Ranis infant		Germany		1 year		Early Magdalenian	Irish et al. 2008
Rebenley Oberkassel	Homo sapiens			Subadult			Bailey and Hublin 2006
Riparo Bombrini	Homo sapiens	France	Isolated element	6±24 months	Associated with Aurignacian industry	Aurignacien ancien	Gambier 2000
Roc de Marsal 1	Homo neanderthalensis	France	Possible burial	2–4 years	Limestone blocks covering over skeleton, a number of Mousterian flints, faunal remains. Debate re. grave goods or natural taphonomic dispersal.	Upper Pleistocene	Tillier 1983a; Madre-Dupouy 1992; Faerman et al. 1994; Mallegni and Trinkaus 1997; Maureille and Bar 1999; Bayle et al. 2009a; 2010; Sandgathe et al. 2011; Shackelford et al. 2012

(Continued)

Appendix 2. Table of subadult fossils in the Plio-Pleistocene (perinatal–ca. 10 years). (Continued)

Specimen name	Species	Country	Context	Age estimate (years at death)	Associated artifacts	Associated ^{14}C dates (uncal BP)/estimated absolute date	References/ sources
Rochereil III	Homo sapiens	France	Possible burial	2–4 years	Skull deposited and resting on 2 stones.	11,255±50 BP	Vallois 1971; Tillier et al. 2001; Marfart et al. 2007
Rochereil 1945-18		France		1–2 years			Shackelford et al. 2012
Romanelli 2		Italy		Child			Formicola 2007
Romanelli 3		Italy		Child			Formicola 2007
Saint Germain La Rivière 1970-8 B3	Homo sapiens	France		5–7 years		Upper Pleistocene	Tompkins 1996; Shackelford et al. 2012
Saint Germain La Rivière 1970-8 B4	Homo sapiens	France		6–8 years		Upper Pleistocene	Tompkins 1996; Shackelford et al. 2012
Saint Germain La Rivière 1970-8 B5	Homo sapiens	France		4–6 years		Upper Pleistocene	Tompkins 1996; Shackelford et al. 2012
Saint Germain La Rivière 1970-8 B6	Homo sapiens	France		4–6 years		Upper Pleistocene	Tompkins 1996; Shackelford et al. 2012

(Continued)

Appendix 2. Table of subadult fossils in the Plio-Pleistocene (perinatal–ca. 10 years) 235

Appendix 2. (Continued)

Specimen name	Species	Country	Context	Age estimate (years at death)	Associated artifacts	Associated ^{14}C dates (uncal BP)/estimated absolute date	References/sources
Saint Germain La Rivière 1970-8 B7	Homo sapiens	France		4–6 years		Upper Pleistocene	Tompkins 1996; Shackelford et al. 2012
Salemas	Homo neanderthalensis	Portugal		1–5 years			Trinkaus 1995
Sangiran S7-37	Homo erectus	Java		8–9 years			Dean and Liversidge 2015
Sarstedt 1	Homo neanderthalensis	Germany		2–4 years		117–25 kya	Street et al. 2006
Scladina juvenile	Homo neanderthalensis	Belgium		8–11 years		127–80 kya	Smith et al. 2007a; Shackelford et al. 2012
Sediba infant	Australopithecus sediba	South Africa		12–18 months		1.977 mya	
Selam (DIK-1/1)	Australopithecus afarensis	Ethiopia	Burial. Primary deposition.	3 years		3.3 mya	Alemseged et al. 2006a
Sesselfelsgrotte	Homo neanderthalensis	Germany		Neonate		57–47 kya	Street et al. 2006
Shanidar 10	Homo neanderthalensis	Iraq		1–2 years		Middle Paleolithic – lower levels OIS 6-4	Cowgill et al. 2007

(Continued)

Appendix 2. Table of subadult fossils in the Plio-Pleistocene (perinatal–ca. 10 years). (Continued)

Specimen name	Species	Country	Context	Age estimate (years at death)	Associated artifacts	Associated ^{14}C dates (uncal BP)/estimated absolute date	References/sources
Shanidar 7	Homo neanderthalensis	Iraq		8 months			Tillier et al. 2003; Trinkaus 2014
Shanidar 9	Homo neanderthalensis	Iraq		8 months			Trinkaus 2014
Sima de los Huesos – Cranium 14	Homo neanderthalensis	Spain	Remains found in both disturbed and undisturbed deposits. Minimum number of individuals in pit together = 32.	5–12.5 years	Assemblage of hominin bones at site also includes hundreds of *Ursus deningeri* bones.	> 530 kya	Arsuaga et al. 1997a; 1997b; Bermúdez de Castro and Nicolas 1997; Gracia et al. 2009
Sima de los Huesos – Facial Bones AT-465 + AT-624 + AT-764 + AT-765 + AT-766 + AT-1159	Homo neanderthalensis	Spain	Remains found in both disturbed and undisturbed deposits. Minimum number of individuals in pit together = 32.	Late childhood/ Early adolescence Post-M1 emergence, post-M2 emergence & pre-M3 emergence	Assemblage of hominin bones at site also includes hundreds of *Ursus deningeri* bones.	> 530 kya	Arsuaga et al. 1997a; 1997b; Bermúdez de Castro and Nicolas 1997; Gracia et al. 2009

(Continued)

Appendix 2. Table of subadult fossils in the Plio-Pleistocene (perinatal–ca. 10 years)

Appendix 2. (Continued)

Specimen name	Species	Country	Context	Age estimate (years at death)	Associated artifacts	Associated ¹⁴C dates (uncal BP)/estimated absolute date	References/sources
Sima de los Huesos – Facial Bones AT-626 + AT-1150	Homo neanderthalensis	Spain	Remains found in both disturbed and undisturbed deposits. Minimum number of individuals in pit together = 32.	Child Post-M1 emergence & pre-M2 emergence	Assemblage of hominin bones at site also includes hundreds of Ursus deningeri bones.	> 530 kya	Arsuaga et al. 1997a; 1997b; Bermúdez de Castro and Nicolas 1997; Gracia et al. 2009
Sima de los Huesos – Parietal Bones AT-785 + AT-803 + AT-1196	Homo neanderthalensis	Spain	Remains found in both disturbed and undisturbed deposits. Minimum number of individuals in pit together = 32.	Juvenile	Assemblage of hominin bones at site also includes hundreds of Ursus deningeri bones.	> 530 kya	Arsuaga et al. 1997a; 1997b; Bermúdez de Castro and Nicolas 1997; Gracia et al. 2009
Sima de los Huesos – Zygomatic Bones AT-768 + AT-1170	Homo neanderthalensis	Spain	Remains found in both disturbed and undisturbed deposits. Minimum number of individuals in pit together = 32.	Juvenile	Assemblage of hominin bones at site also includes hundreds of Ursus deningeri bones.	> 530 kya	Arsuaga et al. 1997a; 1997b; Bermúdez de Castro and Nicolas 1997; Gracia et al. 2009

(Continued)

238 Growing Up in the Ice Age

Appendix 2. Table of subadult fossils in the Plio-Pleistocene (perinatal–ca. 10 years). (Continued)

Specimen name	Species	Country	Context	Age estimate (years at death)	Associated artifacts	Associated ^{14}C dates (uncal BP)/estimated absolute date	References/ sources
Sima de los Huesos Individual IX	Homo neanderthalensis/ Homo heidelbergensis	Spain	Remains found in both disturbed and undisturbed deposits. Minimum number of individuals in pit together = 32.	4–6 years	Assemblage of hominin bones at site also includes hundreds of Ursus deningeri bones.	> 530 kya	Arsuaga et al. 1997a; 1997b; Bermúdez de Castro and Nicolas 1997; Pettitt 2002; Gracia et al. 2009
Sima de los Huesos Individual XVIII	Homo neanderthalensis	Spain	Remains found in both disturbed and undisturbed deposits. Minimum number of individuals in pit together = 32.	9–11 years	Assemblage of hominin bones at site also includes hundreds of Ursus deningeri bones.	> 530 kya	Arsuaga et al. 1997a; 1997b; Bermúdez de Castro and Nicolas 1997; Pettitt 2002; Gracia et al. 2009
Sima de los Huesos Individual XXV	Homo neanderthalensis	Spain	Remains found in both disturbed and undisturbed deposits. Minimum number of individuals in pit together = 32.	7–9 years	Assemblage of hominin bones at site also includes hundreds of Ursus deningeri bones.	> 530 kya	Bermúdez de Castro and Nicolas 1997; Gracia et al. 2009
Sipka	Homo neanderthalensis	Czech Republic		8–9 years		Upper Pleistocene	Giacobini et al. 1984

(Continued)

Appendix 2. Table of subadult fossils in the Plio-Pleistocene (perinatal–ca. 10 years) 239

Appendix 2. (Continued)

Specimen name	Species	Country	Context	Age estimate (years at death)	Associated artifacts	Associated ^{14}C dates (uncal BP)/estimated absolute date	References/sources
SK 105	Paranthropus	South Africa		7–14 years			Bromage 1987
SK 13/14	Paranthropus	South Africa		8–15 years			Bromage 1987
SK 1524	Paranthropus	South Africa		8–15 years			Bromage 1987
SK 25	Paranthropus	South Africa		6–11 years			Bromage 1987
SK 27	Paranthropus	South Africa		5–8 years			Mann 1975; Skinner and Sperber 1982; Bromage 1987
SK 28	Paranthropus	South Africa		8–14 years			Bromage 1987
SK 37	Paranthropus	South Africa		6–12 years			Bromage 1987
SK 3978	Paranthropus robustus	South Africa		1–3.1 years			Skinner and Sperber 1982; Bromage 1987; Conroy et al. 1991 Part II
SK 438	Paranthropus robustus	South Africa		1–2 years			Mann 1975; Bromage 1987; Conroy et al. 1991 Part II

(Continued)

Appendix 2. Table of subadult fossils in the Plio-Pleistocene (perinatal–ca. 10 years). (Continued)

Specimen name	Species	Country	Context	Age estimate (years at death)	Associated artifacts	Associated ^{14}C dates (uncal BP)/estimated absolute date	References/ sources
SK 47	Paranthropus	South Africa		7–13 years			Bromage 1987
SK 55 & 55b	Paranthropus	South Africa		5–10 years			Bromage 1987
SK 6	Paranthropus	South Africa		8–14 years			Bromage 1987
SK 61	Paranthropus robustus	South Africa		3–6 years			Skinner and Sperber 1982; Bromage 1987; Conroy et al. 1991 Part II
SK 62	Paranthropus robustus	South Africa		2.5–5.8 years			Skinner and Sperber 1982; Bromage 1987; Conroy et al. 1991 Part II
SK 63	Paranthropus robustus	South Africa		3–6.1 years		1.8–1.5 mya	Skinner and Sperber 1982; Bromage 1987; Conroy et al. 1991 Part II

(Continued)

Appendix 2. Table of subadult fossils in the Plio-Pleistocene (perinatal–ca. 10 years) 241

Appendix 2. (Continued)

Specimen name	Species	Country	Context	Age estimate (years at death)	Associated artifacts	Associated ^{14}C dates (uncal BP)/estimated absolute date	References/ sources
SK 64	*Paranthropus robustus*	South Africa		1–3.1 years			Skinner and Sperber 1982; Bromage 1987; Conroy et al. 1991 Part II
SK 66	*Paranthropus*	South Africa		3.5–4.5 years			Mann 1975; Bromage 1987
SK 68	*Paranthropus*	South Africa		5–7 years			Mann 1975; Bromage 1987
SK 69/73	*Paranthropus*	South Africa		5–7 years			Mann 1975; Bromage 1987
SK 71	*Paranthropus robustus*	South Africa		3.5–5 years			Mann 1975; Bromage and Dean 1985; Bromage 1987
SK 73	*Paranthropus robustus*	South Africa		Infant			Bromage and Dean 1985
SK 74b	*Paranthropus/ Early Homo*	South Africa		5–6 years			Mann 1975; Bromage and Dean 1985; Bromage 1987

(Continued)

Appendix 2. Table of subadult fossils in the Plio-Pleistocene (perinatal–ca. 10 years). (Continued)

Specimen name	Species	Country	Context	Age estimate (years at death)	Associated artifacts	Associated ^{14}C dates (uncal BP)/estimated absolute date	References/sources
SK 75	Paranthropus	South Africa		8–14 years			Bromage 1987
SK 822	Paranthropus	South Africa		5.5–8 years			Mann 1975; Bromage 1987
SK 824	Paranthropus	South Africa		5.5–8 years			Mann 1975; Bromage 1987
SK 825	Paranthropus	South Africa		5.5–8 years			Mann 1975; Bromage 1987
SK 826	Paranthropus	South Africa		6–11 years			Bromage 1987
SK 839	Paranthropus	South Africa		1.9 years			Bromage 1987
SK 841a	Paranthropus robustus	South Africa		2 years			Mann 1975; Bromage 1987
SK 842	Paranthropus	South Africa		1.5–2.5 years			Mann 1975; Bromage 1987
SK 843	Paranthropus robustus	South Africa		7–12 years			Bromage 1987
SK 852	Paranthropus	South Africa		2.7 years			Bromage 1987

(Continued)

Appendix 2. Table of subadult fossils in the Plio-Pleistocene (perinatal–ca. 10 years) 243

Appendix 2. (Continued)

Specimen name	Species	Country	Context	Age estimate (years at death)	Associated artifacts	Associated ¹⁴C dates (uncal BP)/estimated absolute date	References/ sources
SK 856	*Paranthropus*	South Africa		6–7 years			Bromage 1987
SK 871	*Paranthropus*	South Africa		7–14 years			Bromage 1987
SK 93	*Paranthropus*	South Africa		7–9 years			Bromage 1987
SK 96	*Paranthropus*	South Africa		4–5 years			Mann 1975; Bromage 1987
Skhul I	*Homo neanderthalensis/ Homo sapiens*	Israel	Burial	1–5 years		40 kya	Mallegni and Trinkaus 1997; Tillier et al. 2003; 2011; Tillier 2008; Shackelford et al. 2012
Skhul 8	*Homo neanderthalensis/ Homo sapiens*	Israel	Possible burial	5–9 years		40 kya	Tillier 2008
Skhul 10	*Homo neanderthalensis/ Homo sapiens*	Israel	Possible burial	3–5 years		40 kya	Tillier 2008; Shackelford et al. 2012
SKW 33	*Paranthropus*	South Africa		8–14 years			Bromage 1987
Solutré	*Homo sapiens*			Subadult			Bailey and Hublin 2006

(Continued)

Appendix 2. Table of subadult fossils in the Plio-Pleistocene (perinatal–ca. 10 years). (Continued)

Specimen name	Species	Country	Context	Age estimate (years at death)	Associated artifacts	Associated ^{14}C dates (uncal BP)/estimated absolute date	References/ sources
Solutré 1956-49 (671, 1868)	Homo sapiens			Subadult		Upper Pleistocene	Tompkins 1996
Spy VI	Homo neanderthalensis	Belgium		1.5 years		32,970 +200/−190 BP; 33,950±550 BP	Crevecoeur et al. 2010
Starocelje	Homo neanderthalensis	Crimea		18–24 months		30 kya	Spitery 1980
Sts 1	Australopithecus africanus	South Africa		6–13 years			Bromage 1987
Sts 18	Australopithecus africanus	South Africa		4–7.2 years			Skinner and Sperber 1982; Bromage 1987; Conroy et al. 1991 Part II
Sts 2	Australopithecus africanus	South Africa		2.5–5.1 years			Skinner and Sperber 1982; Bromage 1987; Conroy et al. 1991 Part II
Sts 24a	Australopithecus africanus	South Africa		3.3–4 years			Bromage 1987; Conroy et al. 1991 Part II

(Continued)

Appendix 2. Table of subadult fossils in the Plio-Pleistocene (perinatal–ca. 10 years)   245

Appendix 2. (Continued)

Specimen name	Species	Country	Context	Age estimate (years at death)	Associated artifacts	Associated ^{14}C dates (uncal BP)/estimated absolute date	References/sources
Sts 28	Australopithecus africanus	South Africa		11–18 years			Bromage 1987
Sts 32a & b	Australopithecus africanus	South Africa		11–15 years			Bromage 1987
Sts 57	Australopithecus africanus	South Africa		3.4–7.9 years			Skinner and Sperber 1982; Bromage 1987
Sts 8	Australopithecus africanus	South Africa		7–13 years			Bromage 1987
StW 151	Australopithecus africanus	South Africa		4–5 years			Bromage 1987; Dean and Liversidge 2015
StW 327	Australopithecus africanus	South Africa		7–8 years			Conroy et al. 1991 Part II
Subalyuk 2	Homo neanderthalensis	Hungary		3–7 years			Bartucz 1940; Tillier 1988
Sunghir 3	Homo sapiens	Russia	Multiple burial with Sunghir 2 and 4.	9–10 years	>13,000 mammoth ivory beads. Mobilary art objects, hundreds of perforated arctic fox canines, ivory spears, ivory pins, disc-shaped pendants, ivory animal carvings, long spears of mammoth tusk. Burial covered in red ochre.	24,100±240 BP; 26,000±410 BP	Pettitt and Bader 2000; Pettitt et al. 2003; Formicola 2007;

(Continued)

Appendix 2. Table of subadult fossils in the Plio-Pleistocene (perinatal–ca. 10 years). (Continued)

Specimen name	Species	Country	Context	Age estimate (years at death)	Associated artifacts	Associated ^{14}C dates (uncal BP)/estimated absolute date	References/sources
Tabun		Israel		2–3 years			Henry-Gambier 2008a; Dobrovolskaya et al. 2012; Trinkaus et al. 2014 Tillier 1995
Tangiers 1 (Mugharet el'Aliya)	Homo sapiens	Morocco		Subadult		Upper Pleistocene	Tompkins 1996
Taramsa	Homo sapiens	Egypt		Possible subadult			
Taubach	Homo neanderthalensis	Germany		Subadult		Middle/Upper Paleolithic	Mallegni and Trinkaus 1997
Taung	Australopithecus africanus	South Africa		3.3–6.1 years			Skinner and Sperber 1982; Bromage 1987; Conroy et al. 1991 Part II
Teshik-Tash 1	Homo neanderthalensis	Uzbekistan		8–11 years		Middle/Upper Paleolithic	Mallegni and Trinkaus 1997; Arsuaga et al. 2002

(Continued)

Appendix 2. Table of subadult fossils in the Plio-Pleistocene (perinatal–ca. 10 years)

Appendix 2. (Continued)

Specimen name	Species	Country	Context	Age estimate (years at death)	Associated artifacts	Associated ^{14}C dates (uncal BP)/estimated absolute date	References/sources
Teviec T8	Homo sapiens	France	Double burial with T7 and T8. T8 placed in arms of T7.	2 months	Double burial with T7 and T8. T8 placed in arms of T7. Traces of ochre. Lithics: 5 blades, 1 grooved blade, 1 blade with traces of use, 2 scrapers, 1 fragment rock crystal, 1 pebble. Fauna: 38 *Littorina obtusata*, 24 *Trivia europea*, 1 *Dentalium*, 9 *Nassa reticolata*.		Gazzoni 2011
Teviec T10	Homo sapiens	France	Double burial with T9 and T10.	Child	Double burial with T9 and T10. Covered in ochre.	6,500–6,000 BP	Gazzoni 2011
Teviec T12	Homo sapiens	France		Child		6,500–6,000 BP	Gazzoni 2011
Teviec T22	Homo sapiens	France		Infant		6,515±65 BP	Gazzoni 2011
TM 1511	Australopithecus	South Africa		11–16 years			Bromage 1987
TM 1536	Paranthropus	South Africa		2.5–3 years			Mann 1975; Bromage 1987
TM 1601a	Paranthropus	South Africa		1.75–2 years			Skinner and Sperber 1982; Bromage 1987
TM 1601b	Paranthropus	South Africa		5.5–7.3 years			Skinner and Sperber 1982; Bromage 1987

(Continued)

Appendix 2. Table of subadult fossils in the Plio-Pleistocene (perinatal–ca. 10 years). (Continued)

Specimen name	Species	Country	Context	Age estimate (years at death)	Associated artifacts	Associated ^{14}C dates (uncal BP)/estimated absolute date	References/ sources
TM 1601c	*Paranthropus*	South Africa		5–7.3 years			Skinner and Sperber 1982; Bromage 1987
TM 1601d	*Paranthropus*	South Africa		5–7.3 years			Skinner and Sperber 1982; Bromage 1987
TM 1601e	*Paranthropus*	South Africa		3–5.4 years			Skinner and Sperber 1982; Bromage 1987
Trasacco TG 24a	*Homo sapiens*	Italy		Child			Gazzoni 2011
Trasacco TG 24b	*Homo sapiens*	Italy		Neonate			Gazzoni 2011
Trasacco TG 35	*Homo sapiens*	Italy		Child			Gazzoni 2011
Upward Sun River Individual 1	*Homo sapiens*	USA	Pit burial. Primary burial. Multiple burial with Individual 2, and below cremated remains of Individual 3	6–20 weeks	Ochre-rich matrix; possibly wrapped in shrouds. Buried with four antler rods and two projectile points, and a third biface, all covered in red ochre.	10,705±35 BP	Potter et al. 2014; Halffman et al. 2015; Tackney et al. 2015; Fiedel 2017

(Continued)

Appendix 2. (Continued)

Specimen name	Species	Country	Context	Age estimate (years at death)	Associated artifacts	Associated ^{14}C dates (uncal BP)/estimated absolute date	References/ sources
Upward Sun River Individual 2	Homo sapiens	USA	Pit burial. Possible secondary inhumation. Multiple burial with Individual 1, and below cremated remains of Individual 3.	Foetus 28–40 gestational weeks	Ochre-rich matrix; possibly wrapped in shrouds. Buried with four antler rods and two projectile points, and a third biface, all covered in red ochre.	10,705±35 BP	Potter et al. 2014; Halffman et al. 2015; Tackney et al. 2015; Fiedel 2017
Upward Sun River Individual 3	Homo sapiens	USA	Pit burial, cremated remains. Multiple burial above Invidual 1 and Individual 2	3 years	Charred wood fragments	11,500 BP (cal)	Potter et al. 2011; 2014
Uzzo 11/Uzzo IX	Homo sapiens	Italy		2–3 months		10,000 BP	Gazzoni and Fontana 2011
Uzzo 4/Uzzo III	Homo sapiens	Italy		4–6 months		10,000 BP	Gazzoni and Fontana 2011
Uzzo 8/Uzzo VI	Homo sapiens	Italy		5 years		10,000 BP	Gazzoni and Fontana 2011

(Continued)

Appendix 2. Table of subadult fossils in the Plio-Pleistocene (perinatal–ca. 10 years)

Appendix 2. Table of subadult fossils in the Plio-Pleistocene (perinatal–ca. 10 years). (Continued)

Specimen name	Species	Country	Context	Age estimate (years at death)	Associated artifacts	Associated ^{14}C dates (uncal BP)/estimated absolute date	References/sources
Vado all'Arancio B/Vado all'Arancio 2/ VA 2	Homo sapiens	Italy		18 months	No apparent purposeful artifacts. Epigravettian lithics, fauna, and perforated gastropods found in area.	11,330±50 BP	Formicola 2007; Gazzoni 2011; Gazzoni and Fontana 2011
Verberie VRB 1	Homo sapiens	France		1–2 years		8,740±50 BP	Gazzoni 2011
Vindija 76/232	Homo sapiens	Croatia		Subadult		Upper Pleistocene	Tompkins 1996
Wilczyce	Homo sapiens	Poland	Possible burial	34–38 gestational weeks	Bones identified amongst previously recovered fauna. Necklace of >80 drilled arctic fox teeth, several hundred sandstone slabs.	12,870±60 BP; 13,180±60 BP	Irish et al. 2008; Nava et al. 2017
Yamashita-cho I	Homo sapiens	Japan		6 years		40–32 kya	Trinkaus and Ruff 1996; Arsuaga et al. 2007
Zaskalynaya 6	Homo neanderthalensis	Ukraine		5–6 years		Upper Pleistocene	Vlček 1975; Tompkins 1996

Appendix 3. Table of subadult fossils from the Plio-Pleistocene (ca. 10 years–20 years).

Individual	Species	Chrono-cultural attribution	Country	Context	Age estimate (years at death)	Sex	Associated Artefacts	Associated 14C dates (uncal BP)/ estimated absolute date	References
Abri Dubalen (Brassempouy)	*Homo sapiens*	A	France	Isolated element (tooth)	12+30 months	?		31,520±360 (Gif/LSM-10657)	Gambier 2000
A.L. 200-1a	*Australopithecus afarensis*		Ethiopia		>11.3 years			3 mya ± 0.2mya	Johanson and Taieb 1976; Bromage 1987
A.L. 288-1 Lucy	*Australopithecus afarensis*		Ethiopia		>10.5 years			3 mya ± 0.2mya	Johanson and Taieb 1976; Bromage 1987
Arch Lake Woman	*Homo sapiens*		USA	Burial	17–19 years	F	Buried with a talc stone necklace, bone tool, stone tool, and a pouch filled with red ochre.	10,020 ± 50 BP	Owsley et al. 2010; Lepper 2014
Arene Candide I ("Il Principe")	*Homo sapiens*	G	Italy	Single burial Primary deposition	12–18 years	M	Head surrounded by 100's of perforated shells and canines of deer (shell cap). Shells (*Ciprea* sp.), 4 pendants of mammoth ivory, 4 perforated "Bâtons de Commandement" of elk antler (3 decorated with thin radial striations around hole), and 23 cm long flint blade held in right hand.	23,440 ± 190 (OxA-10700)	Pettitt et al. 2003; Giacobini 2007; Henry-Gambier 2008b

(Continued)

Appendix 3. Table of subadult fossils from the Plio-Pleistocene (ca. 10 years–20 years). (Continued)

Individual	Species	Chrono-cultural attribution	Country	Context	Age estimate (years at death)	Sex	Associated Artefacts	Associated 14C dates (uncal BP)/ estimated absolute date	References
Arene Candide 10	Homo sapiens	EG	Italy	Primary/ disturbed primary burial	20–29 years	M	Body positioned on a layer of red ochre. yellow ochre mass between left clavicle and mandible. Red ochre spread over skeleton.	11,605±445 (GX-16960-A)	Bietti and Molari 1994; Gazzoni and Fontana 2011; Sparacello et al. 2018
Arene Candide 13	Homo sapiens	EG	Italy	Secondary deposition	20–22 years	?	Deer canines, squirrel caudal vertebrae, sea shells, 2 moose antlers.		Formicola 2007; Gazzoni and Fontana 2011; Sparacello et al. 2018
Arene Candide 16/"Zona A"	Homo sapiens	EG	Italy	Primary/ disturbed primary burial	12–17 years	M		10,810±65	Sparacello et al. 2018
Atapuerca 2	Homo		Spain		11–14 years			780 kya	Shackelford et al. 2012
Baume des Peyrards	Homo neanderthalensis		France		10–20 years				Trinkaus 1995

(Continued)

Appendix 3. Table of subadult fossils from the Plio-Pleistocene (ca. 10 years–20 years) 253

Appendix 3. (Continued)

Individual	Species	Chrono-cultural attribution	Country	Context	Age estimate (years at death)	Sex	Associated Artefacts	Associated 14C dates (uncal BP)/ estimated absolute date	References
Baousso da Torre 2/Balzo della Torre 2 (BT 2)/Bausu da Ture 2	*Homo sapiens*	G	Italy	Single burial	20–29 years	M	Red ochre		Giacobini 2006; Gazzoni and Fontana 2011; Villotte et al. 2011; Formicola and Holt 2015
Baousso da Torre 3/Balzo della Torre 3 (BT 3)/Bausu da Ture 3	*Homo sapiens*	G	Italy	Primary deposition Single burial	10–18 years	M	Traces of ochre. Buried with 2 adult skeletons.		Giacobini 2007; Villotte et al. 2011; 2017; Formicola and Holt 2015; Villotte 2018
Barma Grande 3 (BG 3)	*Homo sapiens*	G	Italy	Primary deposition Multiple burial (with BG 2 & BG 4)	12–13 years	F?	*Nassa* and perforated fish vertebrae on her head, small hemispherical bone pendant. On her chest: bone pendant, shaped like a double olive (55 mm × 18 mm). In left hand: blade in zoned flint from Forcalquier (26 cm × 55 mm). Head supported on an ox femur, condyles protruded the frontal.	14,990±80 (Beta-6 3510/CMAS-7641)	Formicola 1988; Giacobini 2007; Henry-Gambier 2008a; 2008b; Gazzoni and Fontana 2011; Onoratini et al. 2012; Formicola and Holt 2015

(Continued)

Appendix 3. Table of subadult fossils from the Plio-Pleistocene (ca. 10 years–20 years). (Continued)

Individual	Species	Chrono-cultural attribu-tion	Country	Context	Age estimate (years at death)	Sex	Associated Artefacts	Associated 14C dates (uncal BP)/ estimated absolute date	References
							Purpura shell (pierced) found between the skulls of BG3 and BG4, attributed to the BG3 burial. Each individual had ornaments: collars made of marine shells, fish vertebrae, and deer teeth. Bone and ivory pendants with parallel incisions. All bodies in triple burial were buried on an ochre bed. Bodies covered with red ochre and powdered oligist.		
Barma Grande 4 (BG 4)	Homo sapiens	G	Italy	Primary deposition Multiple burial (with BG 2 & BG 3)	12–15 years	F?	Head against a large zoned flint blade (17 cm × 48 mm). Nassa and perforated fish vertebrae on his head. On the front several hemispheric pendants.	14,990±80 (Beta-6 3510/CMAS-7641)	Formicola 1988; Giacobini 2007; Henry-Gambier 2008a; 2008b; Gazzoni and Fontana 2011; Onoratini et al. 2012; Formicola and Holt 2015

(Continued)

Appendix 3. Table of subadult fossils from the Plio-Pleistocene (ca. 10 years–20 years) 255

Appendix 3. (Continued)

Individual	Species	Chrono-cultural attribution	Country	Context	Age estimate (years at death)	Sex	Associated Artefacts	Associated 14C dates (uncal BP)/ estimated absolute date	References
							Necklace: 2 rows of fish vertebrae, a row of Nassa (*Nassa neritea*). Rows were interspersed with deer canines ornamented with striae on the crown. Ornament shaped like a double olive near neck. Each individual had ornaments: collars made of marine shells, fish vertebrae, and deer teeth. Bone and ivory pendants with parallel incisions. All bodies in triple burial were buried on an ochre bed. Bodies covered with red ochre and powdered oligist.		
Buhl burial	*Homo sapiens*		USA		17–21 years	F	Presumed grave goods include an unused biface (found under the skull), a bone needle, a badger baculum (unmodified), and a bone awl or pin.	10,625±95 BP	Powell 2005; Jazwa et al. 2021

(Continued)

Appendix 3. Table of subadult fossils from the Plio-Pleistocene (ca. 10 years–20 years). (Continued)

Individual	Species	Chrono-cultural attribution	Country	Context	Age estimate (years at death)	Sex	Associated Artefacts	Associated 14C dates (uncal BP)/ estimated absolute date	References
Calascio	Homo neanderthalensis		Italy		10–20 years				Trinkaus 1995
Cavallo	Homo neanderthalensis		Italy		10–20 years				Trinkaus 1995
Caviglione 1/ Barma del Caviglione 1/"Dame du Cavillon"	Homo sapiens	G	Italy	Single burial	Young adult	F	Cap made of shells (genus Cyclope) and perforated deer canines, an awl fashioned from the radius bone of a cervid, 2 flint blades placed against the occiput and a 'leg bracelet' (of Cyclope shells) below the left knee. Cranial vault coated with red ochre. Groove filled by powdered oligist on front of face. Oligist powder spread over the skeleton.	22,400–26,700 BP (calibrated)	Giacobini 2007; Gazzoni and Fontana 2011; Formicola and Holt 2015; Chevalier 2019
Circeo IV	Homo neanderthalensis		Italy		10 years				Giacobini et al. 1984
Combe-Grenal 24	Homo neanderthalensis		France		Child-Adolescent			75–65 kya	Garralda and Vandermeersch 2000

(Continued)

Appendix 3. Table of subadult fossils from the Plio-Pleistocene (ca. 10 years–20 years) 257

Appendix 3. (Continued)

Individual	Species	Chrono-cultural attribution	Country	Context	Age estimate (years at death)	Sex	Associated Artefacts	Associated 14C dates (uncal BP)/ estimated absolute date	References
Combe-Grenal 32	*Homo neanderthalensis*		France		14–17 years			75–65 kya	Gómez-Olivencia et al. 2013
Combe-Grenal 33	*Homo neanderthalensis*		France		16–19 years			75–65 kya	Gómez-Olivencia et al. 2013
Combe-Grenal III–IV	*Homo neanderthalensis*		France		13–15 years			75–65 kya	Garralda and Vandermeersch 2000
Combe-Grenal IX	*Homo neanderthalensis*		France		9–14 years			75–65 kya	Garralda and Vandermeersch 2000
Cova Negra Specimen CN 42318	*Homo neanderthalensis*		Spain	Possibly disturbed burial.	Adolescent			OIS 4	Arsuaga et al. 2007
Cova Negra Specimen CN 7856	*Homo neanderthalensis*		Spain	Possibly disturbed burial.	18 years			OIS 3	Arsuaga et al. 2007
Cova Negra Parietal II	*Homo neanderthalensis*		Spain	Possibly disturbed burial.	Adolescent			OIS 4	Arsuaga et al. 2007

(Continued)

Appendix 3. Table of subadult fossils from the Plio-Pleistocene (ca. 10 years–20 years). (Continued)

Individual	Species	Chrono-cultural attribu-tion	Country	Context	Age estimate (years at death)	Sex	Associated Artefacts	Associated 14C dates (uncal BP)/ estimated absolute date	References
Cussac 1 (Locus 3)	Homo sapiens	G	France	Co-mingled remains of multiple individuals of which at least one is adolescent	Late adolescent	?		25,120±120 (Beta 156643)	Aujoulat et al. 2002; Formicola 2007; Peigneaux et al. 2019
Denisova 2	Homo sp.		Russia	Primary deposition Specimen (tooth) likely fell out of living child.	10–12 years			122,700-194,400 BP	Slon et al. 2017; Douka et al. 2019
Denny	Homo sp. Homo neanderthalensis/ Homo denisova hybrid		Russia		13 years	F		90,000 BP	Warren 2018
Dolní Věstonice 11/Dolní Věstonice 12	Homo sapiens		Czech Republic		Possible late-adolescent or adult			28–24 kya	Trinkaus et al. 2000; 2010; Svoboda 2007

(Continued)

Appendix 3. Table of subadult fossils from the Plio-Pleistocene (ca. 10 years–20 years) 259

Appendix 3. (Continued)

Individual	Species	Chrono-cultural attribution	Country	Context	Age estimate (years at death)	Sex	Associated Artefacts	Associated 14C dates (uncal BP)/ estimated absolute date	References
Dolní Věstonice 13 (DV II)	Homo sapiens	G	Czech Republic	Multiple burial (DV 13, DV 14, DV 15)	17–19 years	M	20 pierced carnivore teeth, 4 small oval-shaped perforated ivory pendants dispersed around skulls of DV 13 and DV 15. Perforated carnivore teeth ordered in three rows of 4, 5, and 11 teeth, partially selected according to size. Siltstone with regular engravings – found near triple burial. Found in general burial area – 4 other perforated fox canines, 6 lumps of burnt clay, nonperforated Tertiary shells, an assemblage of 116 lithic implements and 1 bone awl, and small fragments of bones, some of which were burnt. Mammoth ivory stake through pelvis. Ochre around skull.	27,660±80 (GrN-13692); 26,640±110 (GrN-14831); 24,000±900 (ISGS-1616); 24,970±920 (ISGS-1617)	Alt et al. 1997; Formicola et al. 2001; Riel-Salvatore and Clark 2001; Trinkaus et al. 2001; Hillson et al. 2006; Svoboda 2006a; Formicola 2007; Mittnik et al. 2016

(Continued)

Appendix 3. Table of subadult fossils from the Plio-Pleistocene (ca. 10 years–20 years). (Continued)

Individual	Species	Chrono-cultural attribution	Country	Context	Age estimate (years at death)	Sex	Associated Artefacts	Associated 14C dates (uncal BP)/estimated absolute date	References
Dolní Věstonice 14 (DV II)	Homo sapiens	G	Czech Republic	Multiple burial (DV 13, DV 14, DV 15)	16–17 years	M	Siltstone with regular engravings – found near triple burial. Found in general burial area – 4 other perforated fox canines, 6 lumps of burnt clay, nonperforated Tertiary shells, an assemblage of 116 lithic implements and 1 bone awl, and small fragments of bones, some of which were burnt. Ochre around skull.	27,660±80 (GrN-13692); 26,640±110 (GrN-14831); 24,000±900 (ISGS-1616); 24,970±920 (ISGS-1617)	Alt et al. 1997; Formicola et al. 2001; Riel-Salvatore and Clark 2001; Trinkaus et al. 2001; Hillson et al. 2006; Svoboda 2006a; Formicola 2007; Mittnik et al. 2016
Dolní Věstonice 15 (DV II)	Homo sapiens	G	Czech Republic	Multiple burial (DV 13, DV 14, DV 15)	20 years	M?	20 pierced carnivore teeth, 4 small oval-shaped perforated ivory pendants dispersed around skulls of DV 13 and DV 15. 4 pierced fox canines. In mouth area – piece of animal bone with cutmarks. Siltstone with regular engravings – found near triple burial.	27,660±80 (GrN-13692); 26,640±110 (GrN-14831); 24,000±900 (ISGS-1616); 24,970±920 (ISGS-1617)	Alt et al. 1997; Formicola et al. 2001; Riel-Salvatore and Clark 2001; Trinkaus et al. 2001; Hillson et al. 2006; Svoboda 2006a; Formicola 2007; Mittnik et al. 2016

(Continued)

Appendix 3. Table of subadult fossils from the Plio-Pleistocene (ca. 10 years–20 years) 261

Appendix 3. (Continued)

Individual	Species	Chrono-cultural attribution	Country	Context	Age estimate (years at death)	Sex	Associated Artefacts	Associated 14C dates (uncal BP)/ estimated absolute date	References
Dolní Věstonice 17	Homo sapiens	G	Czech Republic		6–10 years		Found in general burial area – 4 other perforated fox canines, 6 lumps of burnt clay, nonperforated Tertiary shells, an assemblage of 116 lithic implements and 1 bone awl, and small fragments of bones, some of which were burnt. Piece of deer or horse rib in mouth. Ochre around the skull. DV 15 has ochre in head and pelvic area.	27–25,000	Trinkaus et al. 2000; 2010; Hillson et al. 2006; Svoboda 2007
Dolní Věstonice 31	Homo sapiens	G	Czech Republic	Isolated element	21–25 years	?		27–25,000	Trinkaus et al. 2000; 2010; Hillson et al. 2006; Svoboda 2007

(Continued)

Appendix 3. Table of subadult fossils from the Plio-Pleistocene (ca. 10 years–20 years). (Continued)

Individual	Species	Chrono-cultural attribution	Country	Context	Age estimate (years at death)	Sex	Associated Artefacts	Associated 14C dates (uncal BP)/ estimated absolute date	References
Dolní Věstonice 32	Homo sapiens	G	Czech Republic	Isolated element	21–25 years	?		27–25,000	Trinkaus et al. 2000; 2010; Hillson et al. 2006; Svoboda 2007
Dolní Věstonice 33	Homo sapiens	G	Czech Republic	Isolated element	mid-Adolescent	?		27–25,000	Trinkaus et al. 2000; 2010; Hillson et al. 2006; Svoboda 2007
Dolní Věstonice 37	Homo sapiens	G	Czech Republic	Isolated element	16–20 years	?		27–25,000	Trinkaus et al. 2000; 2010; Hillson et al. 2006; Svoboda 2007
Dolní Věstonice 64	Homo sapiens	G	Czech Republic	Isolated element	<18 years	?		27–25,000	Trinkaus et al. 2000; 2010; Hillson et al. 2006; Svoboda 2007
Dolní Věstonice 9	Homo sapiens	G	Czech Republic	Isolated element	21–25 years	?		27–25,000	Trinkaus et al. 2000; 2010; Hillson et al. 2006; Svoboda 2007
Ehringsdorf G	Homo Neanderthalensis/ Archaic Homo sapiens		Germany		7–13 years			150–120 kya	Tompkins 1996; Shackelford et al. 2012

(Continued)

Appendix 3. Table of subadult fossils from the Plio-Pleistocene (ca. 10 years–20 years) 263

Appendix 3. (Continued)

Individual	Species	Chrono-cultural attribution	Country	Context	Age estimate (years at death)	Sex	Associated Artefacts	Associated 14C dates (uncal BP)/ estimated absolute date	References
El Sidrón Adolescent 1	*Homo neanderthalensis*		Spain		11–15 years	M			Estalrrich and Rosas 2015
El Sidrón Adolescent 2	*Homo neanderthalensis*		Spain		12–15 years				Estalrrich and Rosas 2015
El Sidrón Adolescent 3	*Homo neanderthalensis*		Spain		12–15 years	M			Estalrrich and Rosas 2015
El Sidrón Adult 1	*Homo neanderthalensis*		Spain		Young adult	M			Lalueza-Fox et al. 2011
El Sidrón Adult 2	*Homo neanderthalensis*		Spain		Young adult	M			Lalueza-Fox et al. 2011
El Sidrón Adult 4	*Homo neanderthalensis*		Spain		Young adult	F			Lalueza-Fox et al. 2011
Eshkaft-e Gavi A11-2098	*Homo sapiens*	B	Iran	Isolated element	>12–13 years	?	Bone displays evidence of cutmarks and is burnt. 161 other fragments of mammal bone in feature (mostly bovids and/or cervids), 31% of all fragments are burned. Many lithic artefacts.	>28,000–18,000	Scott and Marean 2009
Eshkaft-e Gavi A11-2099	*Homo sapiens*	B	Iran	Isolated element	>14–16 years	?	Bone displays evidence of cutmarks and is burnt. 161 other fragments of mammal bone in feature (mostly bovids and/or cervids), 31% of all fragments are burned. Many lithic artefacts.	>28,000–18,000	Scott and Marean 2009

(Continued)

Appendix 3. Table of subadult fossils from the Plio-Pleistocene (ca. 10 years–20 years). (Continued)

Individual	Species	Chrono-cultural attribution	Country	Context	Age estimate (years at death)	Sex	Associated Artefacts	Associated 14C dates (uncal BP)/estimated absolute date	References
Eshkaft-e Gavi A11-2208	Homo sapiens	B	Iran	Isolated element	>13–16 years	?		>28,000–18,000	Scott and Marean 2009
Fossellone	Homo neanderthalensis		Italy		9 years		Remains of Hyaena crocuta spaela, Panthera pardus, Rhinoceros merkii, and Cervus elaphus.		Mallegni 1992
Gran Dolina ATD6-118	Homo antecessor		Spain		Immature			MIS 21	Bermúdez de Castro et al. 2020
Gran Dolina Hominid 1	Homo antecessor		Spain		Early adolescent				
Gran Dolina Hominid 3 ATD6-69	Homo antecessor		Spain		10–11.5 years				Bermúdez de Castro et al. 1997
Grotta dei Fanciulli 4 (Enfants)	Homo sapiens	G	Italy	Primary deposition Burial	Adolescent				Henry-Gambier 2008b; Formicola and Holt 2015

(Continued)

Appendix 3. Table of subadult fossils from the Plio-Pleistocene (ca. 10 years–20 years) 265

Appendix 3. (Continued)

Individual	Species	Chrono-cultural attribution	Country	Context	Age estimate (years at death)	Sex	Associated Artefacts	Associated 14C dates (uncal BP)/estimated absolute date	References
Grotta dei Fanciulli 5 (Enfants)	Homo sapiens	G	Italy	Primary deposition Double burial with GF6	Adolescent	M	Double burial contains: shells (*Cyclope*), perforated deer canines, and flint tools.		Mallegni and Parenti 1973; Giacobini 2007; Henry-Gambier 2008a; Gazzoni and Fontana
Grotta dei Fanciulli 6 (Enfants)	Homo sapiens	G	Italy	Primary deposition Double burial with GF5	12–15 years	M	Double burial contains: shells (*Cyclope*), perforated deer canines, and flint tools. Little structure of assembled stones protected head.		2011; Riel-Salvatore and Gravel-Miguel 2013; Formicola and Holt 2015
Grotte des Hyènes 1 (Brassempouy)	Homo sapiens	A	France	Isolated elements	10±30 months	?		31,820±550 BP±510 (Gif 8568)	Gambier 2000
Grotte des Hyènes 3 (Brassempouy)	Homo sapiens	A	France	Isolated elements	9±24 months	?		31,940±160 (Gif/LSM-11035)	Gambier 2000

(Continued)

Appendix 3. Table of subadult fossils from the Plio-Pleistocene (ca. 10 years–20 years). (Continued)

Individual	Species	Chrono-cultural attribution	Country	Context	Age estimate (years at death)	Sex	Associated Artefacts	Associated 14C dates (uncal BP)/ estimated absolute date	References
Grotte du Renne Specimen no. 21 Specimen label A11.1916	Homo neanderthalensis		France	Remains found in 15 stratigraphic layers ranging from Gravettian to Mousterian cultural attribution.	7–9 years			38–33 kya	Bailey and Hublin 2006
Grotte du Renne Specimen No. 35 Specimen label A7.806	Homo neanderthalensis		France	Remains found in 15 stratigraphic layers ranging from Gravettian to Mousterian cultural attribution.	6–9 years			38–33 kya	Bailey and Hublin 2006

(Continued)

Appendix 3. Table of subadult fossils from the Plio-Pleistocene (ca. 10 years–20 years)

Appendix 3. (Continued)

Individual	Species	Chrono-cultural attribution	Country	Context	Age estimate (years at death)	Sex	Associated Artefacts	Associated 14C dates (uncal BP)/ estimated absolute date	References
Grotte du Renne Specimen no. 11 Specimen label Z11.451	*Homo neanderthalensis*		France	Remains found in 15 stratigraphic layers ranging from Gravettian to Mousterian cultural attribution.	>8 years		Found in association with Châtelperronian assemblage. Assemblage includes: Personal ornaments, rings, awls, pierced animal teeth, ivory pendants, perforated fox canine, perforated reindeer phalange, and grooved fox canine, marmot incisor, bovid incisor, and fossil. Colourants bearing facets produced by grinding, Châtelperronian points, convergent sidescrapers.	38–33 kya	Bailey and Hublin, 2006; Higham et al. 2010; Caron et al. 2011
Grotte du Renne Specimen no. 13 Specimen label Z13	*Homo neanderthalensis*		France	Remains found in 15 stratigraphic layers ranging from Gravettian to Mousterian cultural attribution.	15–18 years			38–33 kya	Bailey and Hublin 2006

(Continued)

Appendix 3. Table of subadult fossils from the Plio-Pleistocene (ca. 10 years–20 years). (Continued)

Individual	Species	Chrono-cultural attribution	Country	Context	Age estimate (years at death)	Sex	Associated Artefacts	Associated 14C dates (uncal BP)/ estimated absolute date	References
Grotte du Renne Specimen no. 17 Specimen label C7	Homo neanderthalensis		France	Remains found in 15 stratigraphic layers ranging from Gravettian to Mousterian cultural attribution.	>7 years			38–33 kya	Bailey and Hublin 2006
Grotte du Renne Specimen no. 4 Specimen label B7	Homo neanderthalensis		France	Remains found in 15 stratigraphic layers ranging from Gravettian to Mousterian cultural attribution.	12–18 years			38–33 kya	Bailey and Hublin 2006

(Continued)

Appendix 3. Table of subadult fossils from the Plio-Pleistocene (ca. 10 years–20 years) 269

Appendix 3. (Continued)

Individual	Species	Chrono-cultural attribution	Country	Context	Age estimate (years at death)	Sex	Associated Artefacts	Associated 14C dates (uncal BP)/ estimated absolute date	References
Grotte du Renne Specimen no. 5 Specimen label A6	*Homo neanderthalensis*		France	Remains found in 15 stratigraphic layers ranging from Gravettian to Mousterian cultural attribution.	>15 years			38–33 kya	Bailey and Hublin 2006
Grotte du Renne Specimen no. 7 Specimen label Z8	*Homo neanderthalensis*		France	Remains found in 15 stratigraphic layers ranging from Gravettian to Mousterian cultural attribution.	>12 years			38–33 kya	Bailey and Hublin 2006
Grotte Simard/Grotte Rene-Simard	*Homo neanderthalensis*		France		10–20 years				Trinkaus 1995

(Continued)

Appendix 3. Table of subadult fossils from the Plio-Pleistocene (ca. 10 years–20 years). (Continued)

Individual	Species	Chrono-cultural attribution	Country	Context	Age estimate (years at death)	Sex	Associated Artefacts	Associated 14C dates (uncal BP)/ estimated absolute date	References
HCM 5	Unconfirmed		Israel		7–14 years		Levallois technology, short thin flakes, retouched flakes. Lithics which show centripetal core preparation.	220–115 kya	Tillier et al. 2011
HCM 6	Unconfirmed		Israel		14–17 years		Levallois technology, short thin flakes, retouched flakes. Lithics which show centripetal core preparation.	220–115 kya	Tillier et al. 2011
Horn Shelter No. 2	Homo sapiens		USA	Double burial with 35–40 year old male	10–11 years		Covered in ochre and with grave goods including a flintknapping kit, marine shell beads, and perforated coyote canines. Head of adult resting on a turtle carapace.	9,690±50 BP	Young et al. 1987; Powell 2005; Jodry and Owsley 2014; Leper 2014
Hortus IV	Homo neanderthalensis		Italy		15–30 years	F			Giacobini et al. 1984; Estalrrich and Rosas 2015; Williams et al. 2018
Hortus V	Homo neanderthalensis		Italy		18–25 years				Williams et al. 2018

(Continued)

Appendix 3. (Continued)

Individual	Species	Chrono-cultural attribution	Country	Context	Age estimate (years at death)	Sex	Associated Artefacts	Associated 14C dates (uncal BP)/ estimated absolute date	References
Hortus VII	Homo neanderthalensis		Italy		15–30 years				Estalrrich and Rosas 2015
Hortus VIII	Homo neanderthalensis		Italy		15–30 years				Estalrrich and Rosas 2015
Hortus IX	Homo neanderthalensis		Italy		15–30 years				Estalrrich and Rosas 2015
KMH 12	Homo		Israel		8–10 years			64–59 mya	Tillier et al. 2003
KMH 30	Homo		Israel		8–10 years			64–59 mya	Tillier et al. 2003
Kostenki 18 (Khvoikovskaia)	Homo sapiens	G	Russia	Primary deposition Single burial	9–10 years	?	Mammoth bones possibly over grave.	23,440±150 (OxA-X 2666-53)	Henry-Gambier 2008a; 2008b; Reynolds et al. 2017
Krapina #47	Homo Neanderthalensis/ Archaic Homo sapiens		Croatia		9–11 years			Upper Pleistocene	Tompkins 1996; Shackelford et al. 2012
Krapina #53	Homo Neanderthalensis/ Archaic Homo sapiens		Croatia		9–12 years			Upper Pleistocene	Tompkins 1996; Shackelford et al. 2012
Krapina #54	Homo Neanderthalensis/ Archaic Homo sapiens		Croatia		12–14 years			Upper Pleistocene	Tompkins 1996; Shackelford et al. 2012

(Continued)

Appendix 3. Table of subadult fossils from the Plio-Pleistocene (ca. 10 years–20 years). (Continued)

Individual	Species	Chrono-cultural attribution	Country	Context	Age estimate (years at death)	Sex	Associated Artefacts	Associated 14C dates (uncal BP)/ estimated absolute date	References
Krapina #55	Homo Neanderthalensis/ Archaic Homo sapiens		Croatia		10–13 years			Upper Pleistocene	Tompkins 1996; Shackelford et al. 2012
Krems-Wachtberg	Homo sapiens	G	Austria	Isolated element	Adolescent	?		28,300±270 (VERA-3932); 27,420 +240/−230 (VERA-3933); 27,190 + 230/−220 (VERA-3934); 27,230 + 230/−220 (VERA-4533);	Simon et al. 2014

(Continued)

Appendix 3. Table of subadult fossils from the Plio-Pleistocene (ca. 10 years–20 years)   273

Appendix 3. (Continued)

Individual	Species	Chrono-cultural attribution	Country	Context	Age estimate (years at death)	Sex	Associated Artefacts	Associated 14C dates (uncal BP)/ estimated absolute date	References
								28,000 + 250/_240 (VERA-4534); 6800±220 (VERA-5196)	Simon et al. 2014
Kulna	Homo neanderthalensis		Czech Republic		10–20 years				Trinkaus 1995
La Chaise de Vouthon/ Charente – Dupont Cave	Homo neanderthalensis	A	France	Isolated element	8–10 years	?	Split bone points.	Aurignacian	Gambier 2000
La Chaud 3	Homo sapiens		France		14–17 years				Shackelford et al. 2012
La Crouzade CI	Homo neanderthalensis		France		Adolescent			49,776–44,805 BP	Saos et al. 2020
La Crouzade CII/CIV	Homo neanderthalensis		France	Possible evidence of anthropic interference with corpse.	10–20 years			(49,776–44,805) – 42,000±3000 BP	Trinkaus 1995; Henry Gambier and Sacchi 2008; Saos et al. 2020
La Crouzade VI	Homo sapiens		France		Young adult			31,200±400 BP	Saos et al. 2020

(Continued)

Appendix 3. Table of subadult fossils from the Plio-Pleistocene (ca. 10 years–20 years). (Continued)

Individual	Species	Chrono-cultural attribution	Country	Context	Age estimate (years at death)	Sex	Associated Artefacts	Associated 14C dates (uncal BP)/ estimated absolute date	References
La Ferrassie 3	Homo neanderthalensis		France	Deposited in deliberately excavated pit.	5–10 years			50 kya	
La Quina (Qui-A 2)	Homo neanderthalensis	A	France	Isolated element	12–15 years	?		31,170±350 (GRO-1493); 30,760±490 (GRO-1489); 32,650±850 (OxA-6147 (Ly-256)); 33,290±330 (OxA-15054)	Verna et al. 2012
La Quina (Qui-A 3)	Homo neanderthalensis	A	France	Isolated element	7–11.5 years	?		31,170±350 (GRO-1493); 30,760±490 (GRO-1489); 32,650±850 (OxA-6147 (Ly-256)); 33,290±330 (OxA-15054)	Verna et al. 2012
La Quina 5	Homo neanderthalensis		France		16–30 years	F	Spheroid, bone shards, sediment covering?	Aurignacian	Riel-Salvatore and Clark 2001

(Continued)

Appendix 3. Table of subadult fossils from the Plio-Pleistocene (ca. 10 years–20 years) 275

Appendix 3. (Continued)

Individual	Species	Chrono-cultural attribution	Country	Context	Age estimate (years at death)	Sex	Associated Artefacts	Associated 14C dates (uncal BP)/estimated absolute date	References
Laugerie-Basse teen	Homo sapiens		France		9–10 years			Upper Pleistocene	Tompkins 1996; Shackelford et al. 2012
Le Fate II	Homo neanderthalensis		Italy		9–10 years			75,000–82,000 + 36,000/−14,000 BP	Giacobini et al. 1984; Tompkins 1996
Le Moustier 1	Homo neanderthalensis		France	Possible burial	11–17 years	M	Bone shard and lithic "pillow".	40 kya	Riel-Salvatore and Clark 2001; Smith et al. 2010; Shackelford et al. 2012
Le Piage 2	Homo sapiens	A	France	Isolated element	15±36 months	?	Remains found associated with an Aurignacian industry.	Aurignacian	Gambier 2000
Le Placard 61397	Homo sapiens		France		14–17 years				Shackelford et al. 2012
Le Placard 61401 (DG#31/32)	Homo sapiens		France		8–10 years			Upper Pleistocene	Tompkins 1996; Shackelford et al. 2012
Le Portel	Homo neanderthalensis		France		10–20 years				Trinkaus 1995

(Continued)

Appendix 3. Table of subadult fossils from the Plio-Pleistocene (ca. 10 years–20 years). (Continued)

Individual	Species	Chrono-cultural attribution	Country	Context	Age estimate (years at death)	Sex	Associated Artefacts	Associated 14C dates (uncal BP)/ estimated absolute date	References
Les Rois A	Homo sapiens/ Homo neanderthalensis	A	France	Isolated element	10±30 months	?	Remains found in direct association with the Aurignacian I and II industries.	28,960±210 (KIA 25247); 30,440+290/ −280 (KIA 25248; 27,270+240/ −230 (KIA 25246)	Gambier 2000; Ramirez Rozzi et al. 2009
Les Rois B	Homo sapiens/ Homo neanderthalensis	A	France	Isolated element	12±30 months	?	Remains found in direct association with the Aurignacian I and II industries.	28,960±210 (KIA 25247); 30,440+290/ −280 (KIA 25248; 27,270+240/ −230 (KIA 25246)	Gambier 2000; Ramirez Rozzi et al. 2009
Les Rois E	Homo sapiens/ Homo neanderthalensis	A	France	Isolated element	9±24 months	?	Remains found in direct association with the Aurignacian I and II industries.	28,960±210 (KIA 25247); 30,440+290/ −280 (KIA 25248; 27,270+240/ −230 (KIA 25246)	Gambier 2000; Ramirez Rozzi et al. 2009

(Continued)

Appendix 3. Table of subadult fossils from the Plio-Pleistocene (ca. 10 years–20 years)

Appendix 3. (Continued)

Individual	Species	Chrono-cultural attribution	Country	Context	Age estimate (years at death)	Sex	Associated Artefacts	Associated 14C dates (uncal BP)/ estimated absolute date	References
Les Rois F	Homo sapiens/ Homo neanderthalensis	A	France	Isolated element	15±36 months	?	Remains found in direct association with the Aurignacian I and II industries.	28,960±210 (KIA 25247); 30,440+290/ −280 (KIA 25248; 27,270+240/ −230 (KIA 25246)	Gambier 2000; Ramirez Rozzi et al. 2009
Les Rois K	Homo sapiens	A	France		5–17 years		Remains found in direct association with the Aurignacian I and II industries.	Aurignacian	Gambier 2000
Les Rois Mandible A	Homo sapiens	A	France		10±30 months		Found in direct association with Aurignacian I and II industries without split bone points.	Aurignacian	Gambier 2000
Les Rois Mandible B	Homo sapiens	A	France		12±30 months		Found in direct association with Aurignacian I and II industries without split bone points.	Aurignacian	Gambier 2000
Macassargues	Homo neanderthalensis		France		10–20 years				Trinkaus 1995

(Continued)

Appendix 3. Table of subadult fossils from the Plio-Pleistocene (ca. 10 years–20 years). (Continued)

Individual	Species	Chrono-cultural attribution	Country	Context	Age estimate (years at death)	Sex	Associated Artefacts	Associated 14C dates (uncal BP)/ estimated absolute date	References
Malarnaud	Homo neanderthalensis		France	Mandible with 2 permanent molars preserved in situ.	14 years			50–100 kya	Garralda and Vandermeersch 2000; Becam and Chevalier 2019
Malarnaud 1	Homo neanderthalensis		France		11–12 years				Granat and Heim 2003
Manot Cave	Homo sapiens		Israel		13–17 years		Mixed archaeological assemblage of Levantine Aurignacian and Ahmarian artefacts. Includes 3 marine mollusks, 2 Cowries shells (*Erosaria sp.* and *Zanaria pyrum*), *Columbella rustica* shell, 4 el-Wad points (2 made of non-local flint).	Early Upper Paleolithic	Borgel et al. 2019
Marmes F1	Homo sapiens		USA	Possible cremation	15–20 years	F		9,870±50 BP	Lepper 2014
Marmes F3	Homo sapiens		USA	Possible cremation	15–25 years	M		9,870±50 BP	Lepper 2014
Marmes H4	Homo sapiens		USA	Possible cremation	8–14 years			9,430±40 BP	Lepper 2014

(Continued)

Appendix 3. Table of subadult fossils from the Plio-Pleistocene (ca. 10 years–20 years) 279

Appendix 3. (Continued)

Individual	Species	Chrono-cultural attribution	Country	Context	Age estimate (years at death)	Sex	Associated Artefacts	Associated 14C dates (uncal BP)/ estimated absolute date	References
Marmes H5	Homo sapiens		USA	Possible cremation	8–14 years			9,430±40 BP	Lepper 2014
Marmes H6	Homo sapiens		USA	Possible cremation	8–14 years			9,430±40 BP	Lepper 2014
Mladeč 1	Homo sapiens	A	Czech Republic	Secondary deposition	16 years	?	Difficult to ascertain due to early excavation practices. Ochre-coloured marks on walls.	31,190 +400/−390 (VERA-3073)	Frayer et al. 2006; Oliva 2006; Svoboda 2006b; Teschler-Nicola et al. 2006; Wild et al. 2006
Mladeč 2	Homo sapiens	A	Czech Republic	Secondary deposition	16 years	?	Difficult to ascertain due to early excavation practices. Ochre-coloured marks on walls.	31,320 +410/−390 (VERA-3074)	Frayer et al. 2006; Oliva 2006; Svoboda 2006b; Teschler-Nicola et al. 2006; Wild et al. 2006
Mladeč 10	Homo sapiens	A	Czech Republic	Secondary deposition	18–19 years	?	Difficult to ascertain due to early excavation practices. Ochre-coloured marks on walls.	34,160 +520/−490 (GRN-26333); 34,930 +520/−49 (GRN 26334)	Frayer et al. 2006; Oliva 2006; Svoboda 2006b; Teschler-Nicola et al. 2006; Wild et al. 2006

(Continued)

Appendix 3. Table of subadult fossils from the Plio-Pleistocene (ca. 10 years–20 years). (Continued)

Individual	Species	Chrono-cultural attribution	Country	Context	Age estimate (years at death)	Sex	Associated Artefacts	Associated 14C dates (uncal BP)/ estimated absolute date	References
Mladeč 47	Homo sapiens	A	Czech Republic	Secondary deposition	11–12 years	?	Difficult to ascertain due to early excavation practices. Ochre-coloured marks on walls.	34,160 +520/−490 (GRN-26333); 34,930 +520/−49 (GRN 26334)	Frayer et al. 2006; Oliva 2006; Svoboda 2006b; Teschler-Nicola et al. 2006; Wild et al. 2006
MLD 2	Australopithecus		South Africa		6–11 years				Bromage 1987
Montgaudier	Homo neanderthalensis		France		13 years				Garralda and Vandermeersch 2000
Montmaurin La Niche	Homo neanderthalensis		France		15–18 years				Granat and Heim 2003
Nazlet Khater 2 (NK 2)	Homo sapiens		Egypt	Primary deposition Single burial	20–29 years	M		33,000 BP	Pinhasi and Semal 2000; Vermeersch 2002; Crevecoeur 2012
OH 13	Early Homo		Tanzania		10–17 years				Bromage 1987
OH 5	Paranthropus		Tanzania		11–16 years				Bromage 1987
OH-16	Homo		Tanzania		Nearly adult, 3rd molar erupting				Tobias 1991

(Continued)

Appendix 3. Table of subadult fossils from the Plio-Pleistocene (ca. 10 years–20 years) 281

Appendix 3. (Continued)

Individual	Species	Chrono-cultural attribution	Country	Context	Age estimate (years at death)	Sex	Associated Artefacts	Associated 14C dates (uncal BP)/ estimated absolute date	References
Ostuni 1/Os1	Homo sapiens	G	Italy	Burial. Primary deposition With Os1b (foetus) within pelvic region.	20 years	F	>600 of perforated shells around wrists and covering her head. Shells covering her head were pasted together with red ochre. Shells mostly *Cyclope neritea*. Shells of Cypraeidae are single, not paired. Presence of remains of ungulate skull fragments (mainly *Equus ferus*). Other shells (Columbella, cowries, Nassarius) grouped together near the 2 forearms and in front of the chest and belly. Pieced deer canine lay near right parietal bone. A few flint tools. Shells (perforated) identified as: *Tritianeritea, Tritiamutabilis, Trivia monacha,* and *Columbella rustica*.	23,446±107 (MAMS-11449); 24,410±320 (Gif-9247)	Giacobini 2007; Ronchitelli et al. 2015; Fu et al. 2016; Nava et al. 2017; Chakroun et al. 2018

(Continued)

Appendix 3. Table of subadult fossils from the Plio-Pleistocene (ca. 10 years–20 years). (Continued)

Individual	Species	Chrono-cultural attribution	Country	Context	Age estimate (years at death)	Sex	Associated Artefacts	Associated 14C dates (uncal BP)/ estimated absolute date	References
							Shells covering her head were pasted together with red ochre. Red ochre mainly limited to skull.		
Paglicci 2	Homo sapiens	G	Italy	Burial. Primary deposition.	10–14 years	M	Fragment of manganese oxide bearing deep incisions – found between ankles. Tool kit: 11 lithics, 1 bone piercer (unused) Ornaments: 30 red deer canines close to skull, one on left wrist and one near right ankle. 2 specimens of *Luria lurida* (Cypraeidae) on left hemithorax, and block of manganese oxite (previously attributed as hematite) between ankles, close to right tibia.	24,720±420 (F-55)	Riel-Salvatore and Clark 2001; Giacobini 2007; Shackelford et al. 2012; Ronchitelli et al. 2015

(Continued)

Appendix 3. Table of subadult fossils from the Plio-Pleistocene (ca. 10 years–20 years) 283

Appendix 3. (Continued)

Individual	Species	Chrono-cultural attribution	Country	Context	Age estimate (years at death)	Sex	Associated Artefacts	Associated 14C dates (uncal BP)/ estimated absolute date	References
							Ochre cover, thick on head. Fine layer of haematite. Bones and grave goods are ochre soaked. Red pigment more abundant around skull. Ochre: Mixture of a clayey-silty sand with a natural earthy-micaceous hematite.		
Paglicci 15	Homo sapiens	G	Italy	Burial. Primary deposition.	14 years	?	Ochre present.	24,720±420 (F-55)	Riel-Salvatore and Clark 2001; Giacobini 2007; Shackelford et al. 2012; Ronchitelli et al. 2015

(Continued)

Appendix 3. Table of subadult fossils from the Plio-Pleistocene (ca. 10 years–20 years). (Continued)

Individual	Species	Chrono-cultural attribution	Country	Context	Age estimate (years at death)	Sex	Associated Artefacts	Associated 14C dates (uncal BP)/ estimated absolute date	References
Paglicci 25	Homo sapiens	G	Italy	Burial. Primary deposition.	18–25 years	F	Tool kit: 5 lithic artefacts (unused). Ornaments: 7 red deer craches on the front, 1 valve of *Pecten* close to left foot. Forehead: 7 deer canines with pierced roots turned towards the face, not towards skull vault. Ungulate skull fragments (mainly *Equus ferus*). Ochre cover, thick on head. Ochre bed, chunks of ochred stone over grave. Humerus soaked with red ochre. Grave strewn with ochre. Ochre concentrated on head, pelvis and feet. Smudge of ochre covering head and extending toward right side of skull – possibly corresponded to the hair. Ochre: Nanosized hematite-rich clayey natural material.	23,470±370 (F-57); 23,040±380 (F-58)	Riel-Salvatore and Clark 2001; Giacobini 2007; Shackelford et al. 2012; Ronchitelli et al. 2015

(Continued)

Appendix 3. Table of subadult fossils from the Plio-Pleistocene (ca. 10 years–20 years)

Appendix 3. (Continued)

Individual	Species	Chrono-cultural attribution	Country	Context	Age estimate (years at death)	Sex	Associated Artefacts	Associated 14C dates (uncal BP)/ estimated absolute date	References
Paglicci 3	Homo sapiens		Italy	Pit burial	18–20 years		Humerus and hip articulations soaked in red ochre. Tool kit: 5 lithic artefacts (unused). Ornaments: 7 red deer canines on the front and 1 Pecten close to the left foot. Ochre concentrated on head, pelvis and feet. Valve of Pecten near skull. Presence of remains of ungulate skull fragments (mainly Equus ferus).	23,470±379 BP 28,431–27,071 BP	Ronchitelli et al. 2015
Paglicci 12	Homo sapiens		Italy		Adolescent			Gravettian	
Paglicci 27	Homo sapiens		Italy		Possible subadult				
Pali Aike adolescent	Homo sapiens		Chile	Cremated remains. Bones scattered, associated with 2 subadults and 2 adults.	10–15 years			11,000 BP	Powell 2005

(Continued)

Appendix 3. Table of subadult fossils from the Plio-Pleistocene (ca. 10 years–20 years). (Continued)

Individual	Species	Chrono-cultural attribution	Country	Context	Age estimate (years at death)	Sex	Associated Artefacts	Associated 14C dates (uncal BP)/ estimated absolute date	References
Parpallo 1	Homo sapiens		Spain		13–15 years			Upper Pleistocene	Arsuaga et al. 2002; Tompkins 1996; Shackelford et al. 2012
Pataud 1	Homo sapiens	G	France	Primary deposition Double burial (with Abri Pataud 2)	20–29 years	F	Grave structure: 3 rocks over skull. Abundant ornaments, including shells, ivory beads. Ochre present.	22,000±600 – 21,980± 250 BP	Nespoulet et al. 2006; Henry-Gambier 2008b; Chiotti et al. 2015; Villotte et al. 2018
Pataud 3	Homo sapiens	G	France	Primary deposition Double burial (with Abri Pataud 4)	>20 years	F	Unknown.	21,800±90 (GrA-45013); 21,910±90 (GrA-45133); 22,360±90 (GrA-45132); 22,470±90 (GrA-45016)	Nespoulet et al. 2006; Henry-Gambier 2008b; Chiotti et al. 2015; Villotte et al. 2018
Pataud 5	Homo sapiens	G	France	Primary deposition. Bones dispersed	>20	M?	Unknown.	21,800±90 (GrA-45013); 21,910±90 (GrA-45133); 22,360±90 (GrA-45132); 22,470±90 (GrA-45016)	Nespoulet et al. 2006; Henry-Gambier 2008b; Chiotti et al. 2015; Villotte et al. 2018

(Continued)

Appendix 3. Table of subadult fossils from the Plio-Pleistocene (ca. 10 years–20 years)   287

Appendix 3. (Continued)

Individual	Species	Chrono-cultural attribution	Country	Context	Age estimate (years at death)	Sex	Associated Artefacts	Associated 14C dates (uncal BP)/ estimated absolute date	References
Pataud mother	*Homo sapiens*		France		16 years				
Paviland 1 ("Red Lady")	*Homo sapiens*	G	UK	Single burial Primary deposition	20–29 years	M	2 rocks at head/feet. Abundant ornaments including; shells and possibly ivory/bone pendants, flint tools, ivory or bone tools, and faunal remains. Ochre present.	28,870±180 (OxA-16412); 28,400±320 (OxA-16502); 29,490±210 (OxA-16413); 28,820±340 (OxA-16503); 25,850±280 (OxA-8025); 26,350±550 (OxA-1815)	Henry-Gambier 2008b; Jacobi and Higham 2008
Pavlov 5	*Homo sapiens*	G	Czech Republic	Isolated element	21–25 years			26,170±450 (GrN-20391)	Hillson et al. 2006; Trinkaus et al. 2010; Svoboda et al. 2016
Pavlov 16	*Homo sapiens*	G	Czech Republic	Isolated element	6–10 years			26,170±450 (GrN-20391)	Hillson et al. 2006; Trinkaus et al. 2010; Svoboda et al. 2016

(Continued)

Appendix 3. Table of subadult fossils from the Plio-Pleistocene (ca. 10 years–20 years). (Continued)

Individual	Species	Chrono-cultural attribution	Country	Context	Age estimate (years at death)	Sex	Associated Artefacts	Associated 14C dates (uncal BP)/ estimated absolute date	References
Pavlov 17	Homo sapiens	G	Czech Republic	Isolated element	6–10 years			26,170±450 (GrN-20391)	Hillson et al. 2006; Trinkaus et al. 2010; Svoboda et al. 2016
Pavlov 18	Homo sapiens	G	Czech Republic	Isolated element	6–10 years			26,170±450 (GrN-20391)	Hillson et al. 2006; Trinkaus et al. 2010; Svoboda et al. 2016
Pavlov 22	Homo sapiens	G	Czech Republic	Isolated element	21–25 years			26,170±450 (GrN-20391)	Hillson et al. 2006; Trinkaus et al. 2010; Svoboda et al. 2016
Pavlov 23	Homo sapiens	G	Czech Republic	Isolated element	21–25 years			26,170±450 (GrN-20391)	Hillson et al. 2006; Trinkaus et al. 2010; Svoboda et al. 2016
Pavlov 29	Homo sapiens	G	Czech Republic	Isolated element	early–mid 2nd decade			26,170±450 (GrN-20391)	Hillson et al. 2006; Trinkaus et al. 2010; Svoboda et al. 2016

(Continued)

Appendix 3. Table of subadult fossils from the Plio-Pleistocene (ca. 10 years–20 years) 289

Appendix 3. (Continued)

Individual	Species	Chrono-cultural attribution	Country	Context	Age estimate (years at death)	Sex	Associated Artefacts	Associated 14C dates (uncal BP)/ estimated absolute date	References
Pavlov 30	Homo sapiens	G	Czech Republic	Isolated element	8–16 years			26,170±450 (GrN-20391)	Hillson et al. 2006; Trinkaus et al. 2010; Svoboda et al. 2016
Pavlov 32	Homo sapiens	G	Czech Republic	Isolated element	5–12 years			26,170±450 (GrN-20391)	Hillson et al. 2006; Trinkaus et al. 2010; Svoboda et al. 2016
Petit-Puymoyen P.Pm I	Homo neanderthalensis		France	Cave site	14 years				Granat and Heim 2003
Petit-Puymoyen P.Pm II	Homo neanderthalensis		France	Cave site	15 years				Granat and Heim 2003
Petit-Puymoyen P.Pm IV	Homo neanderthalensis		France	Cave site	15 years				Granat and Heim 2003
Portel-Ouest Individual 1	Homo neanderthalensis		France	Cave site	13–15 years		Associated with reindeer, horse, and bison remains, as well as Mousterian artifacts, within the archaeological levels.	44 kya	Becam and Chevalier 2019

(Continued)

Appendix 3. Table of subadult fossils from the Plio-Pleistocene (ca. 10 years–20 years). (Continued)

Individual	Species	Chrono-cultural attribution	Country	Context	Age estimate (years at death)	Sex	Associated Artefacts	Associated 14C dates (uncal BP)/ estimated absolute date	References
Portel-Ouest Individual 2	*Homo neanderthalensis*		France	Cave site	Adolescent or Adult		Associated with reindeer, horse, and bison remains, as well as Mousterian artifacts, within the archaeological levels.	44 kya	Becam and Chevalier 2019
Portel-Ouest Individual 3	*Homo neanderthalensis*		France	Cave site	6–11 years		Associated with reindeer, horse, and bison remains, as well as Mousterian artifacts, within the archaeological levels.	44 kya	Becam and Chevalier 2019
Portel-Ouest Individual 5	*Homo neanderthalensis*		France	Cave site	10–11 years		Associated with reindeer, horse, and bison remains, as well as Mousterian artifacts, within the archaeological levels.	44 kya	Becam and Chevalier 2019
Portel-Ouest Individual 6	*Homo neanderthalensis*		France	Cave site	Adolescent		Associated with reindeer, horse, and bison remains, as well as Mousterian artifacts, within the archaeological levels.	44 kya	Becam and Chevalier 2019

(Continued)

Appendix 3. Table of subadult fossils from the Plio-Pleistocene (ca. 10 years–20 years) 291

Appendix 3. (Continued)

Individual	Species	Chrono-cultural attribution	Country	Context	Age estimate (years at death)	Sex	Associated Artefacts	Associated 14C dates (uncal BP)/ estimated absolute date	References
Portel-Ouest Individual 7	*Homo neanderthalensis*		France	Cave site	Adolescent		Associated with reindeer, horse, and bison remains, as well as Mousterian artifacts, within the archaeological levels.	44 kya	Becam and Chevalier 2019
Portel-Ouest Individual 8	*Homo neanderthalensis*		France	Cave site	Adolescent		Associated with reindeer, horse, and bison remains, as well as Mousterian artifacts, within the archaeological levels.	44 kya	Becam and Chevalier 2019
Portel-Ouest Individual 9	*Homo neanderthalensis*		France	Cave site	Adolescent		Associated with reindeer, horse, and bison remains, as well as Mousterian artifacts, within the archaeological levels.	44 kya	Becam and Chevalier 2019
Předmostí 1	*Homo sapiens*	G	Czech Republic	Burial. Partial skeletons in mixed burial/pit	20–25 years	F	Grave covered with 2 mammoth shoulder blades and a limestone layer.	25,820±170 (GrN-1286)	Klíma 1991; Ullrich 1996; Riel-Salvatore and Clark 2001; Svoboda 2008

(Continued)

Appendix 3. Table of subadult fossils from the Plio-Pleistocene (ca. 10 years–20 years). (Continued)

Individual	Species	Chrono-cultural attribution	Country	Context	Age estimate (years at death)	Sex	Associated Artefacts	Associated 14C dates (uncal BP)/ estimated absolute date	References
Předmostí 5	Homo sapiens	G	Czech Republic		12–16 years	F	Grave covered with 2 mammoth shoulder blades and a limestone layer.	25,820±170 (GrN-1286)	Klíma 1991; Ullrich 1996; Riel-Salvatore and Clark 2001; Svoboda 2008
Předmostí 7	Homo sapiens	G	Czech Republic		12–14 years	?	Grave covered with 2 mammoth shoulder blades and a limestone layer.	25,820±170 (GrN-1286)	Klíma 1991; Ullrich 1996; Riel-Salvatore and Clark 2001; Svoboda 2008
Předmostí 9	Homo sapiens	G	Czech Republic		20–25 years	M	Grave covered with 2 mammoth shoulder blades and a limestone layer.	25,820±170 (GrN-1286)	Klíma 1991; Ullrich 1996; Riel-Salvatore and Clark 2001; Svoboda 2008
Předmostí 10	Homo sapiens	G	Czech Republic		20–25 years	F	Grave covered with 2 mammoth shoulder blades and a limestone layer.	25,820±170 (GrN-1286)	Klíma 1991; Ullrich 1996; Riel-Salvatore and Clark 2001; Svoboda 2008

(Continued)

Appendix 3. Table of subadult fossils from the Plio-Pleistocene (ca. 10 years–20 years)

Appendix 3. (Continued)

Individual	Species	Chrono-cultural attribution	Country	Context	Age estimate (years at death)	Sex	Associated Artefacts	Associated 14C dates (uncal BP)/ estimated absolute date	References
Předmostí 18	Homo sapiens	G	Czech Republic		20 years	M	Grave covered with 2 mammoth shoulder blades and a limestone layer.	25,820±170 (GrN-1286)	Klíma 1991; Ullrich 1996; Riel-Salvatore and Clark 2001; Svoboda 2008
Předmostí 20	Homo sapiens	G	Czech Republic		9–10 years			25,820±170 (GrN-1286)	Klíma 1991; Ullrich 1996; Riel-Salvatore and Clark 2001; Svoboda 2008
Předmostí 22	Homo sapiens	G	Czech Republic		9–11 years	?	Hare teeth on forehead.	25,820±170 (GrN-1286)	Klíma 1991; Ullrich 1996; Riel-Salvatore and Clark 2001; Svoboda 2008
Předmostí 25	Homo sapiens	G	Czech Republic		<12 years	?		25,820±170 (GrN-1286)	Klíma 1991; Ullrich 1996; Riel-Salvatore and Clark 2001; Svoboda 2008
Qafzeh 9	Homo sapiens		Israel	Double burial with Qafzeh 10.	15–19 years				Tillier 2008

(Continued)

Appendix 3. Table of subadult fossils from the Plio-Pleistocene (ca. 10 years–20 years). (Continued)

Individual	Species	Chrono-cultural attribution	Country	Context	Age estimate (years at death)	Sex	Associated Artefacts	Associated 14C dates (uncal BP)/ estimated absolute date	References
Qafzeh 11	Undetermined		Israel	Burial. Primary deposition.	8–13 years		Parts of fallow deer antlers placed directly in contact with hands.	95–115±15 kya	Tillier 1984; Schwarcz et al. 1988; Tillier 2008; Shackelford et al. 2012
Romito 2 (Romito dwarf)	Homo sapiens	EG	Italy	Double burial (with Romito 1)	17 years	M?	Bodies buried lying parallel to a large stone with an engraving representing a bull. 2 bone cores of aurochs' horn between the femurs of Romito 1 and 2.	11,150±150	Formicola 2007; Giacobini 2007; Gazzoni and Fontana 2011
Scladina juvenile	Homo neanderthalensis		Belgium		8–11 years			80–127 kya	Smith et al. 2007; Shackelford et al. 2012

(Continued)

Appendix 3. Table of subadult fossils from the Plio-Pleistocene (ca. 10 years–20 years) 295

Appendix 3. (Continued)

Individual	Species	Chrono-cultural attribution	Country	Context	Age estimate (years at death)	Sex	Associated Artefacts	Associated 14C dates (uncal BP)/ estimated absolute date	References
Sima de los Huesos Cranium 3	*Homo neanderthalensis*		Spain	Remains found in both disturbed and undisturbed deposits. Minimum number of individuals in pit together = 32	Juvenile/adolescent Post-M2 emergence & pre-M3 emergence		Assemblage of hominin bones at site also includes hundreds of *Ursus deningeri* bones.	530–780 kya	Arsuaga et al. 1997a; 1997b; 2002; Bermúdez de Castro and Nicolas 1997; Gracia et al. 2009
Sima de los Huesos Cranium 7	*Homo neanderthalensis*		Spain	Remains found in both disturbed and undisturbed deposits. Minimum number of individuals in pit together = 32	Adolescent Post-M2 emergence & pre-M3 emergence		Assemblage of hominin bones at site also includes hundreds of *Ursus deningeri* bones.	530–780 kya	Arsuaga et al. 1997a; 1997b; 2002; Bermúdez de Castro and Nicolas 1997; Gracia et al. 2009

(Continued)

Appendix 3. Table of subadult fossils from the Plio-Pleistocene (ca. 10 years–20 years). (Continued)

Individual	Species	Chrono-cultural attribution	Country	Context	Age estimate (years at death)	Sex	Associated Artefacts	Associated 14C dates (uncal BP)/ estimated absolute date	References
Sima de los Huesos Cranium 14	Homo neanderthalensis		Spain	Remains found in both disturbed and undisturbed deposits. Minimum number of individuals in pit together = 32	5–18 years		Assemblage of hominin bones at site also includes hundreds of Ursus deningeri bones.	530–780 kya	Arsuaga et al. 1997a; 1997b; 2002; Bermúdez de Castro and Nicolas 1997; Gracia et al. 2009
Sima de los Huesos Individual I	Homo neanderthalensis		Spain	Remains found in both disturbed and undisturbed deposits. Minimum number of individuals in pit together = 32	19 years		Assemblage of hominin bones at site also includes hundreds of Ursus deningeri bones.	530–780 kya	Arsuaga et al. 1997a; 1997b; 2002; Bermúdez de Castro and Nicolas 1997; Gracia et al. 2009

(Continued)

Appendix 3. Table of subadult fossils from the Plio-Pleistocene (ca. 10 years–20 years) 297

Appendix 3. (Continued)

Individual	Species	Chrono-cultural attribution	Country	Context	Age estimate (years at death)	Sex	Associated Artefacts	Associated 14C dates (uncal BP)/ estimated absolute date	References
Sima de los Huesos Individual II	*Homo neanderthalensis*		Spain	Remains found in both disturbed and undisturbed deposits. Minimum number of individuals in pit together = 32	15 years		Assemblage of hominin bones at site also includes hundreds of *Ursus deningeri* bones.	530–780 kya	Arsuaga et al. 1997a; 1997b; 2002; Bermúdez de Castro and Nicolas 1997; Gracia et al. 2009
Sima de los Huesos Individual III	*Homo neanderthalensis*		Spain	Remains found in both disturbed and undisturbed deposits. Minimum number of individuals in pit together = 32	18 years		Assemblage of hominin bones at site also includes hundreds of *Ursus deningeri* bones.	530–780 kya	Arsuaga et al. 1997a; 1997b; 2002; Bermúdez de Castro and Nicolas 1997; Gracia et al. 2009

(Continued)

Appendix 3. Table of subadult fossils from the Plio-Pleistocene (ca. 10 years–20 years). (Continued)

Individual	Species	Chrono-cultural attribution	Country	Context	Age estimate (years at death)	Sex	Associated Artefacts	Associated 14C dates (uncal BP)/ estimated absolute date	References
Sima de los Huesos Individual X	Homo neanderthalensis		Spain	Remains found in both disturbed and undisturbed deposits. Minimum number of individuals in pit together = 32	16 years		Assemblage of hominin bones at site also includes hundreds of Ursus deningeri bones.	530–780 kya	Arsuaga et al. 1997a; 1997b; 2002; Bermúdez de Castro and Nicolas 1997; Gracia et al. 2009
Sima de los Huesos Individual XI	Homo neanderthalensis		Spain	Remains found in both disturbed and undisturbed deposits. Minimum number of individuals in pit together = 32	15 years		Assemblage of hominin bones at site also includes hundreds of Ursus deningeri bones.	530–780 kya	Arsuaga et al. 1997a; 1997b; 2002; Bermúdez de Castro and Nicolas 1997; Gracia et al. 2009

(Continued)

Appendix 3. Table of subadult fossils from the Plio-Pleistocene (ca. 10 years–20 years) 299

Appendix 3. (Continued)

Individual	Species	Chrono-cultural attribution	Country	Context	Age estimate (years at death)	Sex	Associated Artefacts	Associated 14C dates (uncal BP)/ estimated absolute date	References
Sima de los Huesos Individual XII	*Homo neanderthalensis*		Spain	Remains found in both disturbed and undisturbed deposits. Minimum number of individuals in pit together = 32	20 years		Assemblage of hominin bones at site also includes hundreds of *Ursus deningeri* bones.	530–780 kya	Arsuaga et al. 1997a; 1997b; 2002; Bermúdez de Castro and Nicolas 1997; Gracia et al. 2009
Sima de los Huesos Individual XIV	*Homo neanderthalensis*		Spain	Remains found in both disturbed and undisturbed deposits. Minimum number of individuals in pit together = 32	15 years		Assemblage of hominin bones at site also includes hundreds of *Ursus deningeri* bones.	530–780 kya	Arsuaga et al. 1997a; 1997b; 2002; Bermúdez de Castro and Nicolas 1997; Gracia et al. 2009

(Continued)

Appendix 3. Table of subadult fossils from the Plio-Pleistocene (ca. 10 years–20 years). (Continued)

Individual	Species	Chrono-cultural attribution	Country	Context	Age estimate (years at death)	Sex	Associated Artefacts	Associated 14C dates (uncal BP)/ estimated absolute date	References
Sima de los Huesos Individual XV	Homo neanderthalensis		Spain	Remains found in both disturbed and undisturbed deposits. Minimum number of individuals in pit together = 32	17 years		Assemblage of hominin bones at site also includes hundreds of Ursus deningeri bones.	530–780 kya	Arsuaga et al. 1997a; 1997b; 2002; Bermúdez de Castro and Nicolas 1997; Gracia et al. 2009
Sima de los Huesos Individual XVI Cranium 9	Homo neanderthalensis		Spain	Remains found in both disturbed and undisturbed deposits. Minimum number of individuals in pit together = 32	12–14 years		Assemblage of hominin bones at site also includes hundreds of Ursus deningeri bones.	530–780 kya	Arsuaga et al. 1997a; 1997b; 2002; Bermúdez de Castro and Nicolas 1997; Gracia et al. 2009

(Continued)

Appendix 3. Table of subadult fossils from the Plio-Pleistocene (ca. 10 years–20 years)

Appendix 3. (Continued)

Individual	Species	Chrono-cultural attribution	Country	Context	Age estimate (years at death)	Sex	Associated Artefacts	Associated 14C dates (uncal BP)/ estimated absolute date	References
Sima de los Huesos Individual XVIII	*Homo neanderthalensis*		Spain	Remains found in both disturbed and undisturbed deposits. Minimum number of individuals in pit together = 32	9–11 years		Assemblage of hominin bones at site also includes hundreds of *Ursus deningeri* bones.	530–780 kya	Arsuaga et al. 1997a; 1997b; 2002; Bermúdez de Castro and Nicolas 1997; Gracia et al. 2009
Sima de los Huesos Individual XIX	*Homo neanderthalensis*		Spain	Remains found in both disturbed and undisturbed deposits. Minimum number of individuals in pit together = 32	18 years		Assemblage of hominin bones at site also includes hundreds of *Ursus deningeri* bones.	530–780 kya	Arsuaga et al. 1997a; 1997b; 2002; Bermúdez de Castro and Nicolas 1997; Gracia et al. 2009

(Continued)

Appendix 3. Table of subadult fossils from the Plio-Pleistocene (ca. 10 years–20 years). (Continued)

Individual	Species	Chrono-cultural attribution	Country	Context	Age estimate (years at death)	Sex	Associated Artefacts	Associated 14C dates (uncal BP)/ estimated absolute date	References
Sima de los Huesos Individual XX Cranium 6	Homo neanderthalensis		Spain	Remains found in both disturbed and undisturbed deposits. Minimum number of individuals in pit together = 32	12–14 years		Assemblage of hominin bones at site also includes hundreds of Ursus deningeri bones.	530–780 kya	Arsuaga et al. 1997a; 1997b; 2002; Bermúdez de Castro and Nicolas 1997; Gracia et al. 2009
Sima de los Huesos Individual XXIII	Homo neanderthalensis		Spain	Remains found in both disturbed and undisturbed deposits. Minimum number of individuals in pit together = 32	17 years		Assemblage of hominin bones at site also includes hundreds of Ursus deningeri bones.	530–780 kya	Arsuaga et al. 1997a; 1997b; 2002; Bermúdez de Castro and Nicolas 1997; Gracia et al. 2009

(Continued)

Appendix 3. Table of subadult fossils from the Plio-Pleistocene (ca. 10 years–20 years) 303

Appendix 3. (Continued)

Individual	Species	Chrono-cultural attribution	Country	Context	Age estimate (years at death)	Sex	Associated Artefacts	Associated 14C dates (uncal BP)/ estimated absolute date	References
Sima de los Huesos Individual XXVIII	*Homo neanderthalensis*		Spain	Remains found in both disturbed and undisturbed deposits. Minimum number of individuals in pit together = 32	18 years		Assemblage of hominin bones at site also includes hundreds of *Ursus deningeri* bones.	530–780 kya	Arsuaga et al. 1997a; 1997b; 2002; Bermúdez de Castro and Nicolas 1997; Gracia et al. 2009
Sima de los Huesos Individual XXIX	*Homo neanderthalensis*		Spain	Remains found in both disturbed and undisturbed deposits. Minimum number of individuals in pit together = 32	14 years		Assemblage of hominin bones at site also includes hundreds of *Ursus deningeri* bones.	530–780 kya	Arsuaga et al. 1997a; 1997b; 2002; Bermúdez de Castro and Nicolas 1997; Gracia et al. 2009

(Continued)

Appendix 3. Table of subadult fossils from the Plio-Pleistocene (ca. 10 years–20 years). (Continued)

Individual	Species	Chrono-cultural attribution	Country	Context	Age estimate (years at death)	Sex	Associated Artefacts	Associated 14C dates (uncal BP)/ estimated absolute date	References
Sima de los Huesos Individual XXX	Homo neanderthalensis		Spain	Remains found in both disturbed and undisturbed deposits. Minimum number of individuals in pit together = 32	12 years		Assemblage of hominin bones at site also includes hundreds of Ursus deningeri bones.	530–780 kya	Arsuaga et al. 1997a; 1997b; 2002; Bermúdez de Castro and Nicolas 1997; Gracia et al. 2009
Sima de los Huesos Individual XXXII	Homo neanderthalensis		Spain	Remains found in both disturbed and undisturbed deposits. Minimum number of individuals in pit together = 32	12 years		Assemblage of hominin bones at site also includes hundreds of Ursus deningeri bones.	530–780 kya	Arsuaga et al. 1997a; 1997b; 2002; Bermúdez de Castro and Nicolas 1997; Gracia et al. 2009

(Continued)

Appendix 3. Table of subadult fossils from the Plio-Pleistocene (ca. 10 years–20 years) 305

Appendix 3. (Continued)

Individual	Species	Chrono-cultural attribution	Country	Context	Age estimate (years at death)	Sex	Associated Artefacts	Associated 14C dates (uncal BP)/ estimated absolute date	References
Sima de los Huesos AT-1100, AT-1111, AT-1197, AT-1198	*Homo neanderthalensis*		Spain	Remains found in both disturbed and undisturbed deposits. Minimum number of individuals in pit together = 32	16–18 years		Assemblage of hominin bones at site also includes hundreds of *Ursus deningeri* bones.	530–780 kya	Arsuaga et al. 1997a; 1997b; 2002; Bermúdez de Castro and Nicolas 1997; Gracia et al. 2009
Sima de los Huesos Facial Bones AT-465, AT-624, AT-764, AT-765, AT-766, AT-1159	*Homo neanderthalensis*		Spain	Remains found in both disturbed and undisturbed deposits. Minimum number of individuals in pit together = 32	Late childhood/ Early adolescence Post-M1 emergence, post-M2 emergence & pre-M3 emergence		Assemblage of hominin bones at site also includes hundreds of *Ursus deningeri* bones.	530–780 kya	Arsuaga et al. 1997a; 1997b; 2002; Bermúdez de Castro and Nicolas 1997; Gracia et al. 2009

(Continued)

Appendix 3. Table of subadult fossils from the Plio-Pleistocene (ca. 10 years–20 years). (Continued)

Individual	Species	Chrono-cultural attribution	Country	Context	Age estimate (years at death)	Sex	Associated Artefacts	Associated 14C dates (uncal BP)/ estimated absolute date	References
Sima de los Huesos Facial Bones AT-767, AT-963	Homo neanderthalensis		Spain	Remains found in both disturbed and undisturbed deposits. Minimum number of individuals in pit together = 32	14 years		Assemblage of hominin bones at site also includes hundreds of *Ursus deningeri* bones.	530–780 kya	Arsuaga et al. 1997a; 1997b; 2002; Bermúdez de Castro and Nicolas 1997; Gracia et al. 2009
Sima de los Huesos Occipital IV	Homo neanderthalensis		Spain	Remains found in both disturbed and undisturbed deposits. Minimum number of individuals in pit together = 32	Juvenile/Late adolescent Post-M2 emergence & pre-M3 emergence		Assemblage of hominin bones at site also includes hundreds of *Ursus deningeri* bones.	530–780 kya	Arsuaga et al. 1997a; 1997b; 2002; Bermúdez de Castro and Nicolas 1997; Gracia et al. 2009

(Continued)

Appendix 3. (Continued)

Individual	Species	Chrono-cultural attribution	Country	Context	Age estimate (years at death)	Sex	Associated Artefacts	Associated 14C dates (uncal BP)/ estimated absolute date	References
Sima de los Huesos Parietal Bones AT-785, AT-803, AT-1196	Homo neanderthalensis		Spain	Remains found in both disturbed and undisturbed deposits. Minimum number of individuals in pit together = 32	Juvenile		Assemblage of hominin bones at site also includes hundreds of Ursus deningeri bones.	530–780 kya	Arsuaga et al. 1997a; 1997b; 2002; Bermúdez de Castro and Nicolas 1997; Gracia et al. 2009
Sima de los Huesos Zygomatic Bones AT-768, AT-1170	Homo neanderthalensis		Spain	Remains found in both disturbed and undisturbed deposits. Minimum number of individuals in pit together = 32	Juvenile		Assemblage of hominin bones at site also includes hundreds of Ursus deningeri bones.	530–780 kya	Arsuaga et al. 1997a; 1997b; 2002; Bermúdez de Castro and Nicolas 1997; Gracia et al. 2009

(Continued)

Appendix 3. Table of subadult fossils from the Plio-Pleistocene (ca. 10 years–20 years). (Continued)

Individual	Species	Chrono-cultural attribu-tion	Country	Context	Age estimate (years at death)	Sex	Associated Artefacts	Associated 14C dates (uncal BP)/ estimated absolute date	References
SK 6	Paranthropus		South Africa		8–14 years				Bromage 1987
SK 13/14	Paranthropus		South Africa		8–15 years				Bromage 1987
SK 25	Paranthropus		South Africa		6–11 years				Bromage 1987
SK 28	Paranthropus		South Africa		8–14 years				Bromage 1987
SK 37	Paranthropus		South Africa		6–12 years				Bromage 1987
SK 47	Paranthropus		South Africa		7–13 years				Bromage 1987
SK 52	Paranthropus		South Africa		11–15 years				Bromage 1987
SK 55 & 55b	Paranthropus		South Africa		5–10 years				Bromage 1987
SK 75	Paranthropus		South Africa		8–14 years				Bromage 1987
SK 105	Paranthropus		South Africa		7–14 years				Bromage 1987
SK 826	Paranthropus		South Africa		6–11 years				Bromage 1987
SK 843	Paranthropus robustus		South Africa		7–12 years				Bromage 1987

(Continued)

Appendix 3. Table of subadult fossils from the Plio-Pleistocene (ca. 10 years–20 years)

Appendix 3. (Continued)

Individual	Species	Chrono-cultural attribution	Country	Context	Age estimate (years at death)	Sex	Associated Artefacts	Associated 14C dates (uncal BP)/ estimated absolute date	References
SK 871	*Paranthropus*		South Africa		7–14 years				Bromage 1987
SK 1524	*Paranthropus*		South Africa		8–15 years				Bromage 1987
SKW 33	*Paranthropus*		South Africa		8–14 years				Bromage 1987
Spy 2	*Homo neanderthalensis*		Belgium		16–30 years			36 kya	Riel-Salvatore and Clark 2001; Henry et al. 2011
Sts 1	*Australopithecus*		South Africa		6–13 years				Bromage 1987
Sts 8	*Australopithecus*		South Africa		7–13 years				Bromage 1987
Sts 28	*Australopithecus*		South Africa		11–18 years				Bromage 1987
Sts 52a & b	*Australopithecus*		South Africa		11–15 years				Bromage 1987
Sunghir 2	*Homo sapiens*	A/G	Russia	Multiple burial (with Sunghir 3 & 4)	12–13 years	M	>13,000 mammoth ivory beads. Mobiliary art objects, hundreds of perforated arctic fox canines, ivory spears, ivory pins, disc-shaped pendants, ivory animal carvings, long spears of mammoth tusk.	23,830±220 (OxA-9037); 27,210±710 (AA-36474); 26,200±640 (AA-36475); 30,100±550 (OxX-2395-6)	Formicola and Buzhilova 2004; Formicola 2007; Dobrovolskaya et al. 2012; Marom et al. 2012;

(Continued)

Appendix 3. Table of subadult fossils from the Plio-Pleistocene (ca. 10 years–20 years). (Continued)

Individual	Species	Chrono-cultural attribution	Country	Context	Age estimate (years at death)	Sex	Associated Artefacts	Associated 14C dates (uncal BP)/ estimated absolute date	References
							Sunghir 4 adult femur shaft filled with ochre – adjacent to left humerus. Burial covered in red ochre.		Trinkaus et al. 2014; Cowgill et al. 2015; Sikora et al. 2017; Trinkaus and Buzhilova 2018
Sunghir 3	Homo sapiens	A/G	Russia	Multiple burial (with Sunghir 2 & 4)	9–10 years	M	>13,000 mammoth ivory beads. Mobiliary art objects, hundreds of perforated arctic fox canines, ivory spears, ivory pins, disc-shaped pendants, ivory animal carvings, long spears of mammoth tusk. Burial covered in red ochre.	24,100±240 (OxA-9038); 26,190±640 (AA-36476); 30,000±550 (OxX-2395-7)	Formicola and Buzhilova 2004; Formicola 2007; Dobrovolskaya et al. 2012; Marom et al. 2012; Trinkaus et al. 2014; Cowgill et al. 2015; Sikora et al. 2017; Trinkaus and Buzhilova 2018

(Continued)

Appendix 3. Table of subadult fossils from the Plio-Pleistocene (ca. 10 years–20 years) 311

Appendix 3. (Continued))

Individual	Species	Chrono-cultural attribution	Country	Context	Age estimate (years at death)	Sex	Associated Artefacts	Associated 14C dates (uncal BP)/ estimated absolute date	References
Tagliente/ Tagliente 2	Possible *Homo neanderthalensis*	EG	Italy	Partially destroyed grave	20–29 years	M	2 decorated stones placed on legs (one with linear incisions, one with an outline of a lion's head and an aurochs horn). Another stone on body with traces of ochre. Fragment of the bone core of the horn of a large bovine (likely bison) next to right femur. Traces of ochre on a stone placed on body	13,190±90 (OxA-10672)	Hedges et al. 1993; Giacobini 2007; Gazzoni and Fontana 2011
Teshik-Tash 1	Undetermined		Uzbekistan		8–11 years		Circle of goat horns.		Mallegni and Trinkaus, 1997; Riel-Salvatore and Clark 2001
TM 1511	*Australopithecus*		South Africa		11–16 years				Bromage 1987
TM 1517	*Paranthropus*		South Africa		10–18 years				Bromage 1987
Vilhonneur 1	*Homo sapiens*	G	France	Single burial	15–25 years	M		27,010±210 (Beta 216141); 26,690±190 (Beta 216142)	Henry-Gambier et al. 2007

Bibliography

Adegboyega, Mayowa T., Peter A Stamos, Jean-Jacques Hublin, Timothy D Weaver (2021) Virtual reconstruction of the Kebara 2 Neanderthal pelvis. *Journal of Human Evolution* 151, 1-9. DOI: 10.1016/j.jhevol.2020.102922

Adovasio, James M., Olga Soffer, and Bohuslav Klíma (1996) Upper Paleolithic fiber technology: interlaced woven finds from Pavlov I, Czech Republic, ca. 26,000 years ago. *Antiquity* 70(269), 526–534.

Aiello, Leslie C., and Robin I.M. Dunbar (1993) Neocortex size, group size, and the evolution of language. *Current Anthropology* 34(2), 184–193.

Aiello, Leslie C., and Catherine Key (2002) The energetic consequences of being a *Homo erectus* female. *American Journal of Human Biology* 14(5), 551–565.

Aiello, Leslie C., and Jonathan C.K. Wells (2002) Energetics and the evolution of the genus *Homo*. *Annual Review of Anthropology* 31(1), 323–338.

Aiello, Leslie C., and Peter Wheeler (2003) Neanderthal thermoregulation and the glacial climate. In van Andel, Tjeerd H., and William Davies (eds) *Neanderthals and Modern Humans in the European Landscape during the Last Glaciation: Archaeological Results of the Stage 3 Project*, 147–166. Cambridge, McDonald Institute.

Akazawa, Takeru, Sultan Muhesen, Yukio Dodo, Osamu Kondo, Yuji Mizoguchi, Yoshito Abe, Yoshihiro Nishiaki, Shoji Ohta, Takashi Oguchi, and Jamal Haydal (1995a) Neanderthal infant burial from the Dederiyeh Cave in Syria. *Paléorient* 21(2), 77–86.

Akazawa, Takeru, Sultan Muhesen, Yukio Dodo, Osamu Kondo, and Yuji Mizoguchi (1995b) Neanderthal infant burial. *Nature* 377(6550), 585–586.

Akazawa, Takeru, Sultan Muhesen, Hajime Ishida, Osamu Kondo, and Christophe Griggo (1999) New discovery of a Neanderthal child burial from the Dederiyeh Cave in Syria. *Paléorient* 25(2), 129–142.

Alekseev, V. (1998) The physical specificities of Paleolithic hominids in Siberia. In Derev'anko, Anatoliy P. (ed.) *The Paleolithic of Siberia*, 329–335. Urbana, University of Illinois Press.

Alemseged, Zeresenay, Fred Spoor, William H. Kimbel, René Bobe, Denis Geraads, Denné Reed, and Jonathan G. Wynn (2006a) A juvenile early hominin skeleton from Dikika, Ethiopia. *Nature* 433(7109), 296–301.

Alemseged, Zeresenay, Fred Spoor, William H. Kimbel, René Bobe, Denis Geraads, Denné Reed, and Jonathan G. Wynn (2006b) A juvenile early hominin skeleton from Dikika, Ethiopia. *Nature* 443(7109), Suppl. S4b.

Alland, Alexander Jr. (1983) *Playing with Form: Children Draw in Six Cultures*. New York, Columbia University Press.

Alt, Kurt W., Sandra Pichler, Werner Vach, Bohuslav Klíma, Emanuel Vlček, and Jurg Sedlmeier (1997) Twenty-five thousand-year-old triple burial from Dolní Vestonice: an Ice-Age family? *American Journal of Physical Anthropology* 102(1), 123–131.

Altamura, Flavio, Matthew R. Bennett, Kristiaan D'Août, Savine Gaudzinski-Windheuser, Rita T. Melis, Sally C. Reynolds, and Margaret Mussi (2018) Archaeology and ichnology at Gombore II-2, Melka Kunture, Ethiopia: everyday life of a mixed-age hominin group 700,000 years ago. *Scientific Reports* 8(1), 2815.

Andrade, Paulo Estévão, and Joydeep Bhattacharya (2003) Brain tuned to music. *Journal of the Royal Society of Medicine* 96(6), 284–287.

Andrefsky, William (2005) *Lithics*, 2nd Edition. Cambridge, Cambridge University Press.

Antón, Susan C. (1997) Developmental age and taxonomic affinity of the Mojokerto child, Java, Indonesia. *American Journal of Physical Anthropology* 102(4), 497–514.

Antón, Susan C. (2003) A natural history of *Homo erectus*. *American Journal of Physical Anthropology* 122(S37), 126–170.

Antón, Susan C., and Steve R. Leigh (2003) Growth and life history in *Homo erectus*. In Thompson, Jennifer Louise, Gail E. Krovitz, and Andrew John Nelson (eds) *Patterns of Growth and Development in the Genus Homo (Volume 37)*, 219–245. Cambridge, Cambridge University Press.

Appleby, Jo (2018) Ageing and the body in archaeology. *Cambridge Archaeological Journal* 28(1), 145–163.

Arain, Mariam, Maliha Haque, Lina Johal, Puja Mathur, Wynard Nel, Afsha Rais, Ranbir Sandhu, and Sushil Sharma (2013) Maturation of the adolescent brain. *Neuropsychiatric Disease and Treatment* 9, 449–461.

Arnett, Jeffrey Jensen (2000) Emerging adulthood: a theory of development from the late teens through the twenties. *American Psychologist* 55(5), 469

Arnold, Jeanne E. (2012) Detecting apprentices and innovators in the archaeological record: the shell bead-making industry of the Channel Islands. *Journal of Archaeological Method and Theory* 19(2), 269–305.

Arsuaga, Juan Luis, Ignacio Martínez, Ana Gracia, and Carlos Lorenzo (1997a) The Sima de los Huesos crania (Sierra de Atapuerca, Spain). A comparative study. *Journal of Human Evolution* 33(2–3), 219–281.

Arsuaga, Juan Luis, Ignacio Martínez, Ana Gracia, José Miguel Carretero, Carlos Lorenzo, N. García, and Ana Isabel Ortega (1997b) Sima de los huesos (Sierra de Atapuerca, Spain). The site. *Journal of Human Evolution* 33(203), 109–127.

Arsuaga, Juan Luis, Valentín Villaverde, Rolf Quam, Ana Gracia, Carlos Lorenzo, Ignacio Martínez, and José-Miguel Carretero (2002) The Gravettian occipital bone from the site of Malladetes (Barx, Valencia, Spain). *Journal of Human Evolution* 43(3), 381–393.

Arsuaga, Juan Luis, Valentin Villaverde, Rolf Quam, Ignacio Martínez, José Miguel Carretero, Carlos Lorenzo, and Ana Gracia (2007) New Neandertal remains from Cova Negra (Valencia, Spain). *Journal of Human Evolution* 52(1), 31–58.

Arsuaga, Juan Luis, José-Miguel Carretero, Carlos Lorenzo, Asier Gómez-Olivencia, Adrián Pablos, Laura Rodríguez, Rebeca García-González, Alejandro Bonmatí, Rolf M. Quam, Ana Pantoja-Pérez, Ignacio Martínez, Arantza Aranburu, Ana Gracia-Téllez, Eva Poza-Rey, Nohemi Sala, Nuria García, Almudena Alcázar de Velasco, Gloria Cuenca-Bescós, José María Bermúdez de Castro, and Eudald Carbonell (2015) Postcranial morphology of the Middle Pleistocene humans from Sima de los Huesos, Spain. *Proceedings of the National Academy of Sciences* 112(37), 11524–11529.

Ascenzi, Antonio, and Aldo G. Segre (1971) A new Neandertal child mandible from an Upper Pleistocene site in Southern Italy. *Nature* 233(5317), 280–283.

Ascher, R. (1961) Analogy in archaeological interpretation. *Southwestern Journal of Anthropology* 17(4), 317–325.

Aubert, Maxime, Rustan Lebe, Adhi Agus Oktaviana, Muhammad Tang, Basran Burhan, Hamrullah, Andi Jusdi, Abdullah, Budianto Hakim, Jian-xin Zhao, I. Made Geria, Priyatno Hadi Sulistyarto, Ratno Sardi, and Adam Brumm (2019) Earliest hunting scene in prehistoric art. *Nature* 576, 442–445.

Aujoulat, Norbert (2005) *The Splendor of Lascaux*. New York, Thames & Hudson.

Aujoulat, Norbert, Jean-Michel Geneste, Christian Arhambeau, Marc Delluc, Henri Duday, and Dominique Henry-Gambier (2002) La grotte ornée de Cussac-Le Buisson-de-Cadouin (Dordogne): premières observations. *Bulletin de la Société Préhistorique Française* 99(1), 129–137.

Austin, Christin, Tanya M. Smith, Asa Bradman, Katie Hinde, Renaud Joannes-Boyau, David Bishop, Dominic J. Hare, Philip Doble, Brenda Eskenazi, and Manish Arora (2013) Barium distributions in teeth reveal early-life dietary transitions in primates. *Nature* 498(7453), 216–219.

Avanzini, Marco, Paolo Citton, Paolo Mietto, Adolfo Panarello, Pasquale Raia, Marco Romano, and Isabella Salvador (2020) Human footprints from Italy: the state of the art. *Journal of Mediterranean Earth Sciences* 12, 31–50.

Azéma, Marc, and Florent Rivière (2012) Animation in Palaeolithic art: a pre-echo of cinema. *Antiquity* 86, 316–324.

Bahn, Paul G. (1986) No sex please, we're Aurignacians. *Rock Art Research* 3(2), 99–120.

Bahn, Paul G. (1995) The impact of direct dating on Palaeolithic cave art: Lascaux revisited. *Anthropologie* 33(3), 191–199.

Bahn, Paul G. (2006) Sex and violence in rock art: Are cave paintings really little more than the testosterone-fuelled scribblings of young men? Review of *The Nature of Paleolithic Art* by Dale R. Guthrie. *Nature* 441(7093), 575–576.

Bahn, Paul G. (2011) Religion and ritual in the Upper Palaeolithic. In Insoll, Timothy (ed.) *The Oxford Handbook of the Archaeology of Ritual and Religion*, 1–15. Oxford, Oxford University Press.

Bahn, Paul G. (2012) Religion and ritual in the Upper Palaeolithic. In Insoll, Timothy (ed.) *The Oxford Handbook of the Archaeology of Ritual and Religion*, 344-357. Oxford, Oxford University Press.

Bahn, Paul G. (2015) Children of the Ice Age. In Coşkunsu, Güner (ed.) *The Archaeology of Childhood: Interdisciplinary Perspectives on an Archaeological Enigma*, 167–188. Albany, State University of New York Press.

Bahn, Paul G. (2016) *Images of the Ice Age*. Oxford, Oxford University Press.

Bahn, Paul G., and Jean Vertut (1988) *Images of the Ice Age*. Oxford, Oxford University Press.

Bailey, Shara E., and Jean-Jacques Hublin (2006) Dental remains from the Grotte du Renne at Arcy-sur-Cure (Yonne). *Journal of Human Evolution* 50(5), 485–508.

Baker, Rosalie F., and Charles F. Baker III (2001) *Ancient Egyptians: People of the Pyramids*. Oxford, New York, Oxford University Press.

Balzeau, Antoine, Alain Turq, Sahra Talamo, Camille Daujeard, Guillaume Guérin, Frido Welker, Isabelle Crevecoeur, Helen Fewlass, Jean-Jacques Hublin, Christelle Lahaye, Bruno Maureille, Matthias Meyer, Catherine Schwab and Asier Gómez-Olivencia (2020) Pluridisciplinary evidence for burial for the La Ferrassie 8 Neandertal child. *Scientific Reports* 10(1), 1-10. https://doi.org/10.1038/s41598-020-77611-z.

Bamforth, Douglas B., and Nyree Finlay (2008) Introduction: archaeological approaches to lithic production, skill and craft learning. *Journal of Archaeological Method and Theory* 15, 1–27.

Bandi, Hans Georg (1988) Mise bas et non défécation. Nouvelle interprétation de trois propulseurs magdaléniens sur des bases zoologiques, éthologiques et symboliques. *Espacio, Tiempo y Forma, Prehistoria* 1, 133–147.

Bang-Andersen, S. (1976) Steinalderboplasser I Bykleheiene 1000 moh. *Fra Haug ok Heidni* 6(4), 92–100.

Bang-Andersen, S. (1979) Fra barnets munn til arkeologens hånd. *AmS-Småtrykk* 5, 25–27.

Barbot, Baptise, and Brianna Heuser (2017) Living a creative life. In Maciej Karwowski and James C. Kaufman (eds), *The Creative Self*, 88–98. New York, Academic Press.

Barras, Colin (2017) Neanderthals may have medicated with penicillin and painkillers. *New Scientist* 3116, published March 8, 2017. https://www.newscientist.com/article/2123669-neanderthals-may-have-medicated-with-penicillin-and-painkillers /.

Barrickman, Nancy, Meredith L. Bastian, Karin Isler, and Carel P. van Schaik (2008) Life history costs and benefits of encephalization: a comparative test using data from long-term studies of primates in the wild. *Journal of Human Evolution* 54(5), 568–590.

Barriel, Véronique, and Anne-Marie Tillier (2002) L'enfant de Mezmaiskaya (Caucase) examiné dans une double perspective paléogénétique et paléoanthropologique. *Bulletins et mémoires de la Société d'Anthropologie de Paris* 14(1–2), 2002.

Barrière, Claude (1975) La Grotte de Gargas (Hautes-Pyrénées). *Bulletin de l'Association Françaises pour l'Étude du Quarternaire* 12(3–4), 201–203.

Barrière, Claude (1982) L'art parietal de Rouffignac: la grotte aux cent mammouths. Paris, Picard.

Barrière, Claude, and A. Sahly (1964) Les empreintes humaines de Lascaux. *Miscelanea en homenaje a Abate H Breuil* 1, 173–180.

Bartucz, Lajos (1940) Der Urmensch der Mussolini-Höhle. In Bartucz, Lajos, János Dancza, Ferenc Hollendonner, Ottokár Kadic, Mária Mottl, Vidor Pataki, Ervin Palosi, József Szabo, and Aladár Vendl (eds) *Die Mussolini-Höhle (Subalyuk) bei Cserepfalu*, 47–105. Hungarica, Spelaologische monographie, Geologici Hungarica 14.

Bateson, Patrick (2005) The role of play in the evolution of the great apes and humans. In Pellegrini, Anthony, and Peter K. Smith (eds) *The Nature of Play*, 13–26. New York, Guilford Press.

Bayle Priscilla, José Braga, Arnaud Mazurier, and Roberto Macchiarelli (2009a) Dental developmental pattern of the Neanderthal child from Roc de Marsal: a high-resolution 3D analysis. *Journal of Human Evolution* 56(1), 66–75.

Bayle Priscilla, José Braga, Arnaud Mazurier, and Roberto Macchiarelli (2009b) High-resolution comparative analysis of the dental development in the late Paleolithic child from La Madeleine. *American Journal of Physical Anthropology* 138, 493–498.

Bayle, Priscilla, Roberto Macchiarelli, Erik Trinkaus, Cidália Duarte, Arnaud Mazurier, and José Zilhão (2010) Dental maturational sequence and dental tissue proportions in the early Upper Paleolithic child from Abrigo do Lagar Velho, Portugal. *Proceedings of the National Academy of Sciences* 107(4), 1338–1342.

Baxter, Jane Eva (2005a) *The Archaeology of Childhood. Children, Gender, and Material Culture.* Walnut Creek, Altamira Press.

Baxter, Jane Eva (2005b) Making space for children in archaeological interpretations. *Archaeological Papers of the American Anthropological Association* 15(1), 77–88.

Baxter, Jane Eva (2008) Archaeology of childhood. *Annual Review of Anthropology* 37, 159–175.

Baxter, Jane Eva (2016) Adult nostalgia and children's toys past and present. *International Journal of Play* 5(3), 230–243.

Baxter, Jane Eva (2019a) *The Archaeology of American Childhood and Adolescence.* Gainsville, University Press of Florida.

Baxter, Jane Eva (2019b) How to die a good death: teaching young children about mortality in nineteenth century America. *Childhood in the Past* 12(1), 35–49.

Becam, Gael, and Tony Chevalier (2019) Neandertal features of the deciduous and permanent teeth from Portel-Ouest Cave (Ariège, France). *American Journal of Physical Anthropology* 168(1), 45–69.

Becerra-Valdivia, Lorena, Michael R. Waters, Thomas W. Stafford Jr., Sarah L. Anzick, Daniel Comeskey, Thibaut Devièse, and Thomas Higham (2018) Reassessing the chronology of the archaeological site of Anzick. *Proceedings of the National Academy of Sciences* 115(27), 7000-7003.

Beck, Margaret (2000) Female figurines in the European Upper Paleolithic: politics and bias in archaeological interpretation. In Rautman, Alison E. (ed.) *Reading the Body: Representations and Remains in the Archaeological Record*, 202–214. Philadelphia, University of Pennsylvania Press.

Bednarik, Robert G. (1998) The archaeological significance of beads and pendants. *Man and Environment* 23(2), 87-99.

Bednarik, Robert G. (2019) The significance of the earliest beads. Posted March 8th, 2019. *Brewminate, a bold blend of news and ideas.* https://brewminate.com/the-significance-of-the-earliest-beads/.

Bednarik, Robert. G., David Lewis-Williams, and Thomas A. Dowson (1990) On neuropsychology and shamanism in rock art. *Current Anthropology* 31(1), 77–84.

Bégouën, Henri, and Henri-Victor Vallois (1927) Étude des empreintes de pieds humains du Tuc d'Audoubert, de Cabrerets et de Ganties. In *Congrès International d'Anthropologie et d'Archéologie Préhistoriques*, 323–337. Amsterdam, Institut international d'Anthropologie.

Bégouën, Robert, Carole Fritz, Gilles Tosello, Jean Clottes, Andreas Pastoors, and François Faist (2009) *Le sanctuaire secret des bisons: Il y a 14 000 ans dans la caverne du Tuc d'Audoubert.* Paris, Somogy editions d'art.

Bello, Silvia M., Edward Blinkhorn, Andrew Needham, Martin Bates, Sarah Duffy, Aimée Little, Matt Pope, Beccy Scott, Andrew Shaw, Mark D. Welch, Tim Kinnaird, Lisa Millar, Ruth Robinson, and Chantal Conneller (2020) Artists on the edge of the world: an integrated approach to the study of Magdalenian engraved stone plaquettes from Jersey (Channel Islands). *PLoS ONE* 15(8), e0236875. https://doi.org/10.1371/journal.pone.0236875.

Bennett, Matthew R., John Harris, Brian Richmond, David Braun, Emma Mbua, Purity Kiura, Daniel Olago, Mzalendo Kibunjia, Christine Omuombo, Anna Behrensmeyer, David Huddart, and Silvia Gonzalez, Silvia (2009) Early Hominin foot morphology based on 1.5-million-year-old footprints from Ileret, Kenya. *Science* 323(5918), 1197–1201. do10.1126/science.1168132.

Bennett, Mathew R., and Sally C. Reynolds (2020) Fossil footprints: the fascinating story behind the longest known prehistoric journey. *The Conversation* https://theconversation.com/fossil-footprints-the-fascinating-story-behind-the-longest-known-prehistoric-journey-147520.

Bennet, Matthew R., David Bustos, Daniel Odess, Tommy M. Urban, Jens N. Lallensack, Marcin Budka, Vincent L. Santucci, Patrick Martinez, Ashleigh L.A. Wiseman, and Sally C. Reynolds (2020) Walking in mud: remarkable Pleistocene human trackways from White Sands National Park (New Mexico). *Quaternary Science Reviews* 249, 106610.

Bennison-Chapman, Lucy E., and Lori D. Hager (2018) Tracking the division of labour through handprints: applying Reflectance Transformation Imaging (RTI) to clay 'tokens' in Neolithic West Asia. *Journal of Archaeological Science* 99, 112–123.

Berge Christine, and Dionysis Goularas (2010) A new reconstruction of Sts 14 pelvis (Australopithecus africanus) from computed tomography and three-dimensional modeling techniques. *Journal of Human Evolution* 58(3), 262–72. doi: 10.1016/j.jhevol.2009.11.006. PMID: 20138331.

Berger, Lee R., John Hawks, Darryl J. de Ruiter, Steven E. Churchill, Peter Schmid, Lucas K. Delezene, Tracy L. Kivell, Heather M. Garvin, Scott A. Williams, Jeremy DeSilva, Matthew M. Skinner, Charles M. Musiba, Noel Cameron, Trenton W. Holliday, William Harcourt-Smith, Rebecca R. Ackermann, Markus Bastir, Barry Bogin, Debra Bolter, Juliet Brophy, Zachary D. Cofran, Kimberly A. Congdon, Andrew S. Deane, Mana Dembo, Michelle Drapeau, Marina C. Elliott, Elen M. Feuerriegel, Daniel Garcia-Martinez, David J. Green, Alia Gurtov, Joel D. Irish, Ashley Kruger, Myra F. Laird, Damiano Marchi, Marc R. Meyer, Shahed Nalla, Enquye W. Negash, ECaley M. Orr, Davorka Radovcic, Lauren Schroeder, Jill E. Scott, Zachary Throckmorton, Matthew W. Tocheri, Caroline VanSickle, Christopher S. Walker, Pianpian Wei, and Bermhard Zipfel (2015) *Homo naledi*, a new species of the genus *Homo* from the Dinaledi Chamber, South Africa. *eLife* (4), e09560. https://doi.org/10.7554/eLife.09560.

Bergfjord, C., Sabine Karg, Antoinette Rast-Eicher, M.L. Nosch, Ulla Mannering, Robin Allaby, B. Murphy, and Bodil Holst (2010) Comment on '30,000-Year-Old Wild Flax Fibers'. *Science* 328(5986), 1634–1634. 10.1126/science.1186345.

Bergman, Christopher A., and Christopher B. Stringer (1989) Fifty years after: Egbert, an early upper Palaeolithic juvenile from Ksar Akil, Lebanon. *Paléorient* 15(2), 99–111.

Bergström, Anders, and Chris Tyler-Smith (2017) Paleolithic networking: genomes reveal patterns of genetic and social interactions in Neandertal and Paleolithic hunter-gatherer groups. *Science* 358(6363), 586–587.

Bermúdez de Castro, José M., and Pilar Julia Pérez (1995) Enamel hypoplasia in the Middle Pleistocene hominids from Atapuerca (Spain). *American Journal of Physical Anthropology* 96(3), 310–314.

Bermúdez de Castro, José M., Juan Luis Arsuaga, Eudald Carbonell, Antonio Rosas, I. Martınez, and Marina Mosquera (1997) A hominid from the Lower Pleistocene of Atapuerca, Spain: possible ancestor to Neandertals and modern humans. *Science* 276(5317), 1392–1395.

Bermúdez de Castro, José M., and María Elena Nicolás (1997) Palaeodemography of the Atapuerca-SH Middle Pleistocene hominid sample. *Journal of Human Evolution* 33(2–3), 333–355.

Bermúdez de Castro, José M., Marina Martínez de Pinillos, Lucía López-Polín, Laura Martín-Francés, Cecilia García-Campos, Mario Modesto-Mata, Jordi Rosell, and María Martinón-Torres (2020) A descriptive and comparative study of two Early Pleistocene immature scapulae from the TD6.2 level of the Gran Dolina cave site (Sierra de Atapuerca, Spain). *Journal of Human Evolution* 139, 102689.

Berna, Francesco, Paul Goldberg, Liora Kolska Horwitz, James Brink, Sharon Holt, Marion Bamford, and Michael Chazan (2012) Microstratigraphic evidence of in situ fire in the Acheulean strata of Wonderwerk Cave, Northern Cape province, South Africa. *Proceedings of the National Academy of Sciences* 109(20), E1215–E1220. https://doi.org/10.1073/pnas.1117620109.

Bietti, Amilcare, and Cristina Molari (1994) The Upper Pleistocene deposit of the Arene Candide Cave (Savona, Italy): general introduction and stratigraphy. *Quaternaria Nova* 4, 9–27.

Binford, Lewis R. (1978) *Nunamiut Ethnoarchaeology*. New York, Academic Press.

Binford, Lewis, R. (1980) Willow smoke and dogs' tails: hunter-gatherer settlement systems and archaeological site formation. *American Antiquity* 45(1), 4–20.

Binford, Lewis R. (1981) Behavioral archaeology and the 'Pompeii Premise'. *Journal of Anthropological Research* 37(3), 195–208.

Bird, Caroline F.M. (1993) Woman the toolmaker: evidence for women's use and manufacture of flaked stone tools in Australia and New Guinea. In du Cros, Hilary and Laurajane Smith (eds) *Women and Archaeology: A Feminist Critique*, 22–30. Canberra, Australian National University.

Bird, Douglas, and Rebecca Bliege Bird (2000) The ethnoarchaeology of juvenile foragers: shell-fishing strategies among Meriam children. *Journal of Anthropological Archaeology* 19(4), 461–476.

Blakemore, Sarah-Jayne (2018) *Inventing ourselves: The secret life of the teenage brain*. New York, PublicAffairs.

Blanc, A.C. (1960) La palline di argilla della Grotta della Bàsura. *Rivista di Studi Liguri* 26, 9–24.

Blood, Anne J., and Robert J. Zatorre (2001) Intensely pleasurable responses to music correlate with activity in brain regions implicated in reward and emotion. *Proceedings of the National Academy of Sciences* 98(20), 11818–11823. https://doi.org/10.1073/pnas.191355898.

Bocherens, Hervé, Daniel Billiou, André Mariotti, Michel Toussaint, Marylène Patou-Mathis, Dominique Bonjean, and Marcel Otte (2001) New isotopic evidence for dietary habits of Neanderthals from Belgium. *Journal of Human Evolution* 40(6), 497–505.

Bocquet-Appel, Jean-Pierre, Pierre-Yves Demars, Lorette Noiret, and Dmitry Dobrowsky (2005) Estimates of Upper Palaeolithic meta-population size in Europe from archaeological data. *Journal of Archaeological Science* 32(11), 1656-1668.

Bodu, Pierre, Claudine Karlin, and Sylvie Ploux (1990) Who's who? The Magdalenian flintknappers of Pincevent, France. In Cziesla, E., S. Eickhoff, Nico Arts, and Doris Winter (eds) *The Big Puzzle. International Symposium on Refitting Stone Artefacts, Monrepos, 1987*, 143–163. Bonn, Holos Verlag.

Boëda, Eric, Jean-Michel Geneste, and Liliane Meignen (1990) Identification de chaînes opératoires lithiques du Paléolithique ancien et moyen. *Paléo, Revue d'Archéologie Préhistorique* 2(1), 43–80.

Boesch, Christophe, and Hedwig Boesch-Achermann (2000) *The Chimpanzees of the Tai Forest*. New York, Oxford University Press.

Bogin, Barry (1997) Evolutionary hypotheses for human childhood. *American Journal of Physical Anthropology* 104(S25), 63–89.

Bogin, Barry (2003) The human pattern of growth and development in paleontological perspective. In Thompson, Jennifer Louise, Gail E. Krovitz, and Andrew John Nelson (eds) *Patterns of Growth and Development in the Genus Homo*, 15–44. Cambridge, Cambridge University Press.

Bogin, Barry (2009) Childhood, adolescence, and longevity: a multilevel model of the evolution of reserve capacity in human life history. *American Journal of Human Biology* 21(4) 567–577.

Boivin, Nicole L., Melinda A. Zeder, Dorian Q. Fuller, Alison Crowther, Greger Larson, Jon M. Erlandson, Tim Denham, and Michael D. Petraglia (2016) Ecological consequences of human niche construction: Examining long-term anthropogenic shaping of global species distributions. *Proceedings of the National Academy of Sciences* 113(23), 6388–6396.

Bolter, Debra R., Marina C. Elliott, John Hawks, and Lee R. Berger (2020) Immature remains and the first partial skeleton of a juvenile *Homo naledi*, a late Middle Pleistocene hominin from South Africa. *PLoS ONE* 15(4), e0230440. https://doi.org/10.1371/journal.pone.0230440.

Bonmatí, Alejandro, Asier Gómez-Olivencia, Juan-Luis Arsuaga, José Miguel Carretero, Ana Gracia, Ignacio Martínez, Carlos Lorenzo, José María Bérmudez de Castro, and Eudald Carbonell (2010) Middle Pleistocene lower back and pelvis from an aged human individual from the Sima de los Huesos site, Spain. *Proceedings of the National Academy of Sciences* 107(43), 18386–18391.

Booth, Thomas J. (2016) An investigation into the relationship between bacterial bioerosion and funerary treatment in European archaeological human bone. *Archaeometry* 58(3), 484–499.

Booth, Thomas (2020) Using bone histology to identify stillborn infants in the archaeological record. In Gowland, Rebecca, and Siân Halcrow (eds) *The Mother-Infant Nexus in Anthropology: Small Beginnings, Significant Outcomes*, 193–209. Cham, Springer.

Booth, Thomas J., Rebecca C. Redfern, and Rebecca L. Gowland (2016) Immaculate conceptions: Micro-CT analysis of diagenesis of Romano-British infant skeletons. *Journal of Archaeological Science* 74, 124–134.

Borgel, Sarah, Bruce Latimer, Yvonne McDermott, Rachel Sarig, Ariel Pokhojaev, Talia Abulafia, Mae Goder-Goldberger, Omry Barzilai, and Hila May (In press) Early Upper Paleolithic human foot bones from Manot Cave, Israel. *Journal of Human Evolution*, 102668.

Boyd, Brian (2009) *On the Origin of Stories: Evolution, Cognition, and Fiction*. Cambridge, MA, Harvard University Press.

Boyd, Robert, Peter J. Richerson, and Joseph Henrich (2011) The cultural niche: why social learning is essential for human adaptation. *Proceedings of the National Academy of Sciences* 108(Supplement 2), 10918–10925. doi: 10.1073/pnas.1100290108.

Boyette, Adam Howell (2016) Children's play and the integration of social and individual learning: a cultural niche construction perspective. In Terashima, Hideaki, and Barry S. Hewlett (eds) *Social learning and innovation in contemporary Hunter-Gatherers: Evolutionary and ethnographic perspectives*, 159–169. Tokyo, Japan, Springer.

Boyette, Adam Howell (2018) Play in foraging societies. In Smith, Peter K., and Jaipaul L. Roopnarine (eds) *The Cambridge Handbook of Play*, 302–321. Cambridge, Cambridge University Press. https://doi-org.ezproxy.library.uvic.ca/10.1017/9781108131384.

Braga, José, John Francis Thackeray, Jean Dumoncel, Didier Descouens, Laurent Bruxelles, Jean-Michel Loubes, Jean-Luc Kahn, Marco Stamoanoni, Lunga Bam, Jakobus Hoffman, Frikkie de Beer, and Fred Spoor (2013) A new partial temporal bone of a juvenile hominin from the site of Kromdraai B (South Africa). *Journal of Human Evolution* 65(4), 447–456.

Braga, José, John Francis Thackeray, Laurent Bruxelles, Jean Dumoncel, and Jean-Baptiste Fourvel (2017) Stretching the time span of hominin evolution at Kromdraai (Gauteng, South Africa): recent discoveries. *Comptes Rendus Palevol* 16(1), 58–70.

Braga, José, Chafik Samir, Laurent Risser, Jean Dumoncel, Didier Descouens, John Francis Thackeray, Patricia Balaresque, Anna Oettlé, Jean-Michel Loubes, and A. Fradi (2019) Cochlear shape reveals that the human organ of hearing is sex-typed from birth. *Scientific Reports* 9(1), 10.1038/s41598-019-47433-9.

Breuil, Henri (1952) *Four Hundred Centuries of Cave Art*. Montignac, Dordogne, Centre d'Études et de Documentation Préhistoriques.

Bromage, Timothy G. (1987) The biological and chronological maturation of early hominids. *Journal of Human Evolution* 16(3), 257–272.

Bromage, Timothy G., and M. Christopher Dean (1985) Re-evaluation of the age at death of immature fossil hominids. *Nature* 317(6037), 525–527.

Burghardt, Gordon M. (2005) *The Genesis of Animal Play: Testing the Limits*. Cambridge, MA, MIT Press.

Burnett, Stephanie, and Sarah-Jayne Blakemore (2009) The development of adolescent social cognition. *Annals of the New York Academy of Sciences* 1167(1), 51–56.

Burton, Frances (2009) *Fire: The Spark that Ignited Human Evolution*. Albuquerque, University of New Mexico Press.

Buxton, L. H. Dudley (1928) Human remains. Excavation of a Mousterian rock-shelter at Devil's Tower, Gibraltar. *London, Royal Anthropological Institute of Great Britain and Ireland* 58, 57–91.

Capitan, Louis, and Jean Bouyssonie (1924) *Un atelier d'art préhistorique: Limeuil, son gisement à gravures sur pierres de l'âge du renne.* Publications de l'Institut International d'Anthropologie. Paris, Librairie Emile Nourry.

Carbonell, Eudald, José M. Bermúdez de Castro, Juan Luis Arsuaga, and Juan Carlos Diez (1995) Lower Pleistocene hominids and artifacts from Atapuerca-TD6 (Spain). *Science* 269(5225), 826–830.

Caron, François, Francesco d'Errico, Pierre Del Moral, Frédéric Santos, and João Zilhão (2011) The reality of Neandertal symbolic behavior at the Grotte du Renne, Arcy-sur-Cure, France. *PLoS ONE* 6(6), e21545.

Carroll, Maureen (2012) 'No part in earthly things': the death, burial and commemoration of newborn children and infants in Roman Italy. In Harlowe, Mary and Lena Larsson Lovén (eds) *Families in the Roman and Late Antique World*, 41–63. London, Continuum International Publishing Group.

Carroll, Sean T. (2016) *Tracking Flintknapper Skill Variation Through Debitage: An Experimental Approach.* Unpublished MA Thesis, University of Wyoming Department of Anthropology.

Carruthers, Peter (2002) Human creativity: its cognitive basis, its evolution and its connections with childhood pretense. *British Journal for the Philosophy of Science* 53(2), 225–249.

Carson, Linda (2012) *Drawing Accuracy, Quality and Expertise.* Unpublished dissertation, University of Waterloo, Ontario Canada.

Cartailhac, Emile, and Henri Breuil (1907) Les oeuvres d'art de la collection de Vibraye au Muséum National. *L'Anthropologie* 1–2(XVIII), 1–36.

Casey, B.J., Jay N. Giedd, and Kathleen M. Thomas (2000) Structural and functional brain development and its relation to cognitive development. *Biological Psychology* 54(1–3), 241–257.

Cataldo, Dana Michelle, Andrea Bamberg Migliano, and Lucio Vinicius (2018) Speech, stone tool-making and the evolution of language. *PLoS ONE* 13(1), e0191071. https://doi.org/10.1371/journal.pone.0191071.

Cave, Christine, and Marc Oxenham (2016) Identification of the archaeological 'invisible elderly': an approach illustrated with an Anglo-Saxon example. *International Journal of Osteoarchaeology* 26(1), 163–175. https://doi.org/10.1002/oa.2408.

Chakroun, Amel, Henry Baills, and Donato Coppola (2018) The site of Santa Maria di Agnano (Brindissi, Italy). *Global Journal of Archaeology and Anthropology* 4(2), 555632.

Chalmin, Emilie, Michel Menu, and Colette Vignaud (2003) Analysis of rock art painting and technology of Palaeolithic painters. *Measurement Science and Technology* 14(9), 1590–1597.

Changizi, Mark (2009) Why does music make us feel? *Scientific American*, 15 September. https://www.scientificamerican.com/article/why-does-music-make-us-fe /.

Chase, Philip G. (1990) Sifflets du Paléolthique moyen (?). Les implications d'un coprolithe de coyote actuel. *Bulletin de la Société Préhistorique Française* 87(6), 165–167.

Chase, Philip G. (2001) Punctured reindeer phalanges from the Mousterian of Combe Grenal (France). *Arheološki vestnik* 52, 17–23.

Chase, Philip G., and Harold L. Dibble (1987) Middle Paleolithic symbolism: a review of current evidence and interpretations. *Journal of Anthropological Archaeology* 6(3), 263–296.

Chazine, Jean-Michel (1999) Préhistoire: Découverte de grottes ornées à Bornéo. *Archéologie* 352, 12–19.

Chazine, Jean-Michel, and Luc-Henri Fage (1998) La Ligne de Wallace a-t-elle été franchie par les artistes des temps préhistoriques? Deux nouvelles grottes ornées à Bornéo. *Karstologia* 32(1), 39–46.

Chazine, Jean-Michel, and Luc-Henri Fage (1999) Deux nouvelles grottes ornées à Bornéo. *International Newsletter on Rock Art (INORA)* 23, 1–3.

Chazine Jean-Michel, and Arnaud Noury (2006) Identification sexuelle des empreintes de mains négatives du panneau de la grotte de Gua Masri II (Est-Kalimantan / Bornéo – Indonésie) / Sexual determination of hand stencils on the main panel of the Gua Masri II Cave (Est-Kalimantan / Borneo – Indonesia). *International Newsletter On Rock Art [INORA]*, 44, 21–26.

Chevalier, Tony (2019) Trauma in the upper limb of an Upper Paleolithic female from Caviglione Cave (Liguria, Italy): etiology and after-effects in bone biomechanical properties. *International Journal of Paleopathology* 24, 94–107.

Chiotti, Laurent, Roland Nespoulet, and Dominique Henry-Gambier (2015) Occupations and status of the Abri Pataud (Dordogne, France) during the Final Gravettian. *Quaternary International*, 359–360, 406–422.

Chiapella, Virginia G. (1952) Orsi e nomini preistorici nella grotta della 'Strega', (Genova). *Revista del Comune A* 29, 22–29.

Chintalapati, Manjusha, Michael Dannemann, and Kay Prüfer (2017) Using the Neandertal genome to study the evolution of small insertions and deletions in modern humans. BMC *Evolutionary Biology* 17, 179. https://doi.org/10.1186/s12862-017-1018-8.

Chirikure, Shadreck, and Abgail Joy Moffett (2018) Fluid spaces and fluid objects: nocturnal material culture in Sub-Saharan Africa with special reference to the Iron Age in Southern Africa. In Gonlin, Nancy and April Nowell (eds) *Archaeology of the Night: Life After Dark in the Ancient World*, 353–368. Boulder, University Press of Colorado.

Cho, Deung-Lyong, Ki-Hwa Park, Jae-Hwa Jin, and Wan Hong (2005) Age constraints on human footmarks in Hamori formation, Jeiu Island, Korea. *The Journal of the Petrological Society of Korea* 14(3), 149–156.

Citton, Paolo, Marco Romano, Isabella Salvador, and Marco Avanzini (2017) Reviewing the upper Pleistocene human footprints from the 'Sala dei Misteri' in the Grotta della Bàsura (Toirano, northern Italy) Cave: an integrated morphometric and morpho-classificatory approach. *Quaternary Science Reviews* 169, 50–64.

Clarke, Ronald J. (1979) Early hominid footprints from Tanzania. *South African Journal of Science* 75(4), 148–149.

Clottes, Jean (1975) Midi-Pyrénées. *Gallia préhistoire* 18(2), 613–650.

Clottes, Jean (1993) Paint analyses from several Magdalenian caves in the Ariège region of France. *Journal of Archaeological Science* 20(2), 223–235.

Clottes, Jean (1996) Thematic changes in Upper Palaeolithic art: a view from the Grotte Chauvet. *Antiquity* 70(268), 276–288.

Clottes, Jean (1997) Art of the light and art of the depths. In Conkey, Margaret, Olga Soffer, Deborah Stratmann, and Nina Jablonski (eds) *Beyond Art: Pleistocene Image and Symbol*, 203–216. San Francisco, Wattis Symposium Series in Anthropology, Memoirs of the California Academy of Science 23.

Clottes, Jean (2001) Paleolithic Europe. In Whitley, David S. (ed.) *Handbook of Rock Art Research*, 459–481. Walnut Creek, CA, AltaMira Press.

Clottes, Jean (2003) *Chauvet Cave: The Art of Earliest Times*. Salt Lake City, University of Utah Press.

Clottes, Jean (2010) *Cave Art*. New York, Phaidon.

Clottes, Jean (2013) Consequences of the discovery and study of the Chauvet Cave. In Sachs-Hombach, Klaus, and Jörg R.J. Schirra (eds) *Origins of Pictures*, 46–71. Köln, Herbert von Halem Verlag.

Clottes, Jean, and R. Simonnet (1974) Une datation radiocarbone dans la grotte ornée de Fontanet. *Bulletin de la Société Préhistorique Française* 71, 106–107.

Clottes, Jean, Hélène Valladas, Hélène Cachier, and Maurice Arnold (1992) Des dates pour Niaux et Gargas. *Bulletin de la Société Préhistorique Française* 89(9), 270–274.

Clottes, Jean, Jean Courtin, and Luc Vanrell (2005) *Cosquer Redécouvert*. Paris, Le Seuil.

Clutton-Brock, Juliet (2016) Origins of the dog: the archaeological evidence. In Serpell, James (ed.) *The Domestic Dog: Its Evolution, Behavior and Interactions with People*, 7–21. Cambridge, Cambridge University Press. doi:10.1017/9781139161800.002

Cofran, Zachary, and Jeremy M. DeSilva (2015) A neonatal perspective on Homo erectus brain growth. *Journal of Human Evolution* 81, 41–47.

Cohen, Jon (2012) Human brains wire up slowly but surely. *Science Now*, 1 February 2012. https://www.sciencemag.org/news/2012/02/human-brains-wire-slowly-surely.

Collard, Mark, Lia Tarle, Dennis Sandgathe and Alexander Allan (2016) Faunal evidence for a difference in clothing use between Neanderthals and early modern humans in Europe. *Journal of Anthropological Archaeology* 44, 235–246.

Conard, Nicholas J. (2011) The demise of the Neanderthal cultural niche and the beginning of the Upper Paleolithic, in southwestern Germany. In Conard, Nicholas J. and Jürgen Richter (eds) *Neanderthal Lifeways, Subsistence and Technology*, 223–240. Vertebrate Paleobiology and Paleoanthropology 19. New York, Springer.

Conard, Nicholas, Marina Malina, and Susanne Münzel (2009) New flutes document the earliest musical tradition in southwestern Germany. *Nature* 460(7256), 737–740.

Conkey, Margaret W. (1989) The structural analysis of Paleolithic art. In Lamberg-Karlovsky, Clifford Charles (ed.) *Archaeological Thought in America*, 135–154. Cambridge, Cambridge University Press.

Conkey, Margaret W. (1993) Humans as materialists and symbolists: image making in the Upper Paleolithic. In Rasmussen, D. Tab (ed.) *The Origin and Evolution of Humans and Humanness*, 95–118. Boston, Jones and Bartlett Learning.

Conkey, Margaret W. (1997) Beyond art and between the caves: thinking about context in the interpretive process. In Conkey, Margaret Wright, Olga Soffer, Deborah Stratmann and Nina Jablonski (eds) *Beyond Art: Pleistocene Image and Symbol*, 343–368. Memoirs of the California Academy of Sciences 23. San Francisco, University of California Press.

Conkey, Margaret W. (1999) A history of the interpretation of European Paleolithic art: magic, mythogram, and metaphors for modernity. In Lock, Andrew and Charles L. Peters (eds) *Handbook of Human Symbolic Evolution*, 288–349. Oxford, Oxford University Press.

Conkey, Margaret W. (2004) Making meanings: Paleolithic art and archaeological interpretation. *Lansdowne Lecture Series*. University of Victoria, Victoria, BC, October 19, 2004.

Conkey, Margaret W. (2007) Questioning theory: is there a gender of theory in archaeology? *Journal of Archaeological Method and Theory* 14(3), 285–310.

Conkey, Margaret W. (2010) Images without words: the construction of prehistoric imaginaries for definitions of 'us'. *Journal of Visual Culture* 9(3), 272–283.

Conkey, Margaret W. (2013) The future of gender in prehistoric archaeology. In Bolger, Diane (ed.) *A Companion to Gender Prehistory*, 108–120. Chichester, John Wiley and Sons.

Conkey, Margaret W. (2018) Afterword: a portal to a more imaginative archaeology. In Gonlin, Nancy and April Nowell (eds) *Archaeology of the Night: Life After Dark in the Ancient World*, 387–390. Boulder, University Press of Colorado.

Conkey, Margaret W. and Janet D. Spector (1984) Archaeology and the study of gender. *Advances in Archaeological Method and Theory* 7, 1–38.

Conkey, Margaret W., Olga Soffer, Deborah Stratmann and Nina Jablonski (1997) *Beyond Art: Pleistocene Image and Symbol*. Memoirs of the California Academy of Sciences 23. Oakland, CA, University of California Press.

Conroy, Glenn C., and Michael W. Vannier (1991) Dental development in South African australopithecines. Part II: dental stage assessment. *American Journal of Physical Anthropology* 86(2), 137–156.

Cooke, Amanda (2014) *Hands on Research: The Application of the 2D:4D Ratio to Children's Hand Stencils.* Unpublished Masters thesis, University of Victoria, Victoria, BC.

Cooney, Jessica (2018) Portrait of a Palaeolithic family: art, ornamentation, and children's relationship with their community. In Crawford, Sally, Dawn Hadley, and Gillian Shepherd (eds) *The Oxford Handbook of the Archaeology of Childhood*, 1–25. Oxford, Oxford University Press.

Copeland, Sandi R., Matt Sponheimer, Darryl J. de Ruiter, Julia A. Lee-Thorp, Daryl Codron, Petrus J. le Roux, Vaughan Grimes, and Michael P. Richards (2011) Strontium isotope evidence for landscape use by early hominins. *Nature* 474(7349), 76–78.

Coqueugniot, Hélene, Jean-Jacques Hublin, Francis Veillon, Francis Houët, and Teuku Jacob (2004) Early brain growth in *Homo erectus* and implications for cognitive ability. *Nature* 431(7006), 299–302.

Coqueugniot, Hélene, and Jean-Jacques Hublin (2007) Endocranial volume and brain growth in immature Neandertals. *Periodicum biologorum* 109(4), 379–385.

Coqueugniot, Hélene, and Jean-Jacques Hublin (2012) Age-related changes of digital endocranial volume during human ontogeny: results from an osteological reference collection. *American Journal of Physical Anthropology* 147(2), 312–318.

Coşkunsu, Güner (2015) *The Archaeology of Childhood: Interdisciplinary Perspectives on an Archaeological Enigma*. Albany, State University of New York Press.

Costall, Alan, and Ann Richards (2013) Canonical affordances; the psychology of everyday things. In Graves-Brown, Paul, Rodney Harrison and Angela Piccini (eds) *The Oxford Handbook of the Archaeology of the Contemporary World*, 82–93. Oxford, Oxford University Press.

Courtaud, Patrice, and Anne-Marie Tillier (2005) À propos de vestiges humains immatures inédits provenant des niveaux moustériens de Qafzeh. *Bulletins et mémoires de la Société d'Anthropologie de Paris* 17(1–2), 37–45.

Cowgill, Libby W., Erik Trinkaus, and Melinda A. Zeder (2007) Shanidar 10: a Middle Paleolithic immature distal lower limb from Shanidar Cave, Iraqi Kurdistan. *Journal of Human Evolution* 53(2), 213–223.

Cowgill, Libby W., M.B. Mednikova, A.P. Buzhilovs, and Erik Trinkaus (2015) The Sunghir 3 Upper Paleolithic Juvenile: pathology versus persistence in the Paleolithic. *International Journal of Osteoarchaeology* 25(2), 176–187.

Crabtree, Don E. (1972) An Introduction to Flintworking, Occasional Papers of the Idaho State Museum (no. 28). Pocatello, Idaho, Idaho State University Museum.

Craig-Atkinson, Elizabeth (2014) Eaves dropping on short lives: eaves-drip burial and the differential treatment of children one year of age and younger in early Christian cemeteries. In Hadley, Dawn M. and Katherine A. Hemer (eds) *Medieval Childhood: Archaeological Approaches*, 95–113. Oxford, Oxbow Books.

Crawford, Sally (2009) The archaeology of play things: theorising a toy stage in the 'biography' of objects. *Childhood Past* 2(1), 55–70.

Creanza, Nicole, Laurel Fogarty, and Marcus W. Feldman (2013) Exploring Cultural Niche Construction from the Paleolithic to Modern Hunter-Gatherers. In Akazawa, Takeru, Yoshihiro Nishiaki, and Kenichi Aoki (eds), *Dynamics of Learning in Neanderthals and Modern Humans Volume 1: Cultural Perspectives, Replacement of Neanderthals by Modern Humans Series*, 211–228. Tokyo, Japan, Springer.

Crevecoeur, Isabelle (2012) The Upper Paleolithic human remains of Nazlet Khater 2 (Egypt) and past modern human diversity. In Hublin, Jean-Jaques, and Shannon McPherron (eds) *Modern Origins. Vertebrate Paleobiology and Paleoanthropology*, 205–219. Dordrecht, Springer.

Crevecoeur, Isabelle, Priscilla Bayle, Hélène Rougier, Bruno Maureille, Thomas Higham, Johannes van der Plicht, Nora De Clerck, and Patrick Semal (2010) The Spy VI child: a newly discovered Neandertal infant. *Journal of Human Evolution* 59(6), 641–656.

Crompton, Richard H., Todd C. Pataky, Russell Savage, Kristiaan D'Août, Matthew R. Bennett, Michael H. Day, Karl Bates, Sarita Morse, and William I. Sellers (2011) Human-like external function of the foot, and fully upright gait, confirmed in the 3.66 million year old Laetoli hominin footprints by topographic statistics, experimental footprint-formation and computer simulation. *Journal of the Royal Society Interface* 9(69), 707–719.

Crown, Patricia L. (2001) Learning to make pottery in the Prehispanic American Southwest. *Journal of Anthropological Research* 57(4), 457–469.

Crown, Patricia L. (2007) Life histories of pots and potters: situating the individual in archaeology. *American Antiquity* 72(4), 677–690.

Culley, Elizabeth V. (2021) A comparison of 'scenes' in parietal and non-parietal Upper Paleolithic imagery: formal differences and ontological implications. In Davidson, Iain and April Nowell (eds) *Making Scenes: Global Perspectives on Scenes in Rock Art*, 179–193. New York, Berghahn Books.

Cunnane, Stephen C., and Michael A. Crawford (2014) Energetic and nutritional constraints on infant brain development: implications for brain expansion during human evolution. *Journal of Human Evolution* 77, 88–98.

Davenport, Demorest and Michael A. Jochim (1988) The scene in the Shaft at Lascaux. *Antiquity* 62(236), 558–562.

David, Francine, Nelly Connet, Michel Girard, Vincent Lhomme, Jean-Claude Miskovsky, and Annie Roblin-Jouve (2001) Le Châtelperronien de la grotte du Renne à Arcy-sur-Cure (Yonne). Données

sédimentologiques et chronostratigraphiques. *Bulletin de la Société préhistorique française* 98(2), 207–230.
David, Nicholas and Carol Kramer (2001) *Ethnoarchaeology in Action*. Cambridge, Cambridge University Press.
Dávid-Barrett, Tamás, and Robin I.M. Dunbar (2016) Bipedality and hair loss in human evolution revisited: the impact of altitude and activity scheduling. *Journal of Human Evolution* 94, 72–82.
Davidson, Iain (2013) Origins of pictures: an argument for transformation of signs. In Sachs-Hombach, Klaus and Jörg R.J. Schirra (eds) *Origins of Pictures: Anthropological Discourses in Image Science*, 16–46. Cologne, Herbert von Halem.
Davidson, Iain (2021) Scenes and non-scenes in rock art. In Davidson, Iain and April Nowell (eds) *Making Scenes: Global Perspectives on Scenes in Rock Art*, 16–31. New York, Berghahn Books.
Davidson, Iain and April Nowell (2021) Introduction. Behind the scenes – did scenes in rock art create new ways of seeing the world? In Davidson, Iain and April Nowell (eds) *Making Scenes: Global Perspectives on Scenes in Rock Art*, 1–15. New York, Berghahn Books.
Day, Felix R., Deborah J. Thompson, Hannes Helgason, Daniel I. Chasman, Hilary Finucane, Patrick Sulem, Katherine S. Ruth, *et al.* (2017) Genomic analyses identify hundreds of variants associated with age at menarche and support a role for puberty timing in cancer risk. *Nature Genetics* 49(6), 834–841.
De Angelis, M. (2009) Riscontri archivistici sull'origine del toponimo 'Ciampate del diavolo'. Unpublished report presented at the study conference *'Ciampate del diavolo: mezzo passo nella leggenda. Un passo nella storia'*. Tora e Piccilli (Volume 17).
De Beaune, Sophie A. (1987) Paleolithic lamps and their specialization: a hypothesis. *Current Anthropology* 28(4), 569–577. https://doi.org/10.1086/203565.
De Beaune, Sophie A., and Randall White (1993) Ice Age lamps. *Scientific American* 266(3), 108–113. https://doi.org/10.1038/scientificamerican0393-108.
de Lumley, Henry, and Giuseppe Vicino (1984) New data concerning the dating and interpretation of human footprints present in the 'Grotta della Basura' at Toirano (Savona, Northern Italy). Results of an international round table. *Journal of Human Evolution* 13(6), 537–540.
Dean, M. Christopher (1987) The dental developmental status of six East African juvenile fossil hominids. *Journal of Human Evolution* 16(2), 197–213.
Dean, M. Christopher, Christopher B. Stringer, and Timothy G. Bromage (1986) Age at death of the Neanderthal child from Devil's Tower, Gibraltar and the implications for studies of general growth and development in Neanderthals. *American Journal of Physical Anthropology* 70(3), 301–309.
Dean, M. Christopher, Meave G. Leakey, Donald Reid, Friedemann Schrenk, Gary T. Schwartz, Christopher B. Stringer, and Alan Walker (2001) Growth processes in teeth distinguish modern humans from *Homo erectus* and earlier hominins. *Nature* 414(6864), 628–631.
Dean, M. Christopher, and B. Holly Smith (2009) Growth and development of the Nariokotome youth, KNM-WT 15000. In Grine, Frederick E., John G. Fleagle, and Richard E. Leakey (eds) *The First Humans: Origin and Early Evolution of the Genus Homo*, 101–120. New York, Springer.
Dean, M. Christopher, and Helen M. Liversidge (2015) Age estimation in fossil hominins: comparing dental development in early *Homo* with modern humans. *Annals of Human Biology* 42(4), 415–429.
Debénath, André, and Harold L. Dibble (1993) *Handbook of Paleolithic Typology: Lower and Middle Paleolithic of Europe*. Philadelphia, University of Pennsylvania Museum of Archaeology and Anthropology.
Defleur, Alban (1993) *Les Sepultures Mousteriennes*. Paris, Centre National de la Recherche Scientifique.
Degioanni, Anna, Christophe Bonenfant, Sandrine Cabut, Silvana Condemi (2019) Living on the edge: was demographic weakness the cause of Neanderthal demise? *PLoS ONE* 14(5), e0216742. https://doi.org/10.1371/journal.pone.0216742.
Delporte, Henri (1984) L'art Mobilier et ses Rapports avec La Faune Paléolithique. In Bandi, Hans-Georg, Walter W. Huber, Marc-Roland Sauter, and Beat Sitter (eds) *La Contribution de la Zoologie et de L'ethologie à L'interprétation de L'art des Peuples Chasseurs Préhistoriques*, 111–142. Numero 3 Colloque de la Société Suisse des Sciences Humaines. Fribourg, Editions Universitaires Fribourg Suisse.

Delteil, J., P. Durbas, and L. Wahl (1971) Présentation de la galerie ornée de Fontanet (Ornolac-Ussat-les-Bains, Ariège). *Bulletin de la Société Préhistorique de l'Ariège* 27, 1–10.

Demuru, Elisa, Pier Francesco Ferraril, and Elisabetta Palagi (2018) Is birth attendance a uniquely human feature? New evidence suggests that Bonobo females protect and support the parturient. *Evolution and Human Behavior* 39(5), 502–510.

Denzil, Justin (1988) *Boy of the Painted Cave*. New York, Philomel Books.

Derev'anko, Anatoliy P. (1998) A short history of discoveries and the development of ideas in the Paleolithic of Siberia. In Derev'anko, Anatoliy P. (ed.) *The Paleolithic of Siberia*, 5–13. Urbana, University of Illinois Press.

d'Errico, Francesco (1994) L'art gravé azilien. De la technique à la signification. *31e supplément à Gallia Préhistoire*. Paris, Éditions du Centre National de la Recherche Scientifique.

d'Errico, Francesco (2009) The oldest representation of childbirth. In Bahn, Paul G. (ed.) *An Enquiring Mind. Studies in Honor of Alexander Marshack*, 99–109. American School of Prehistoric Research Monograph series. Oxford, Oxbow Books.

d'Errico, Francesco, and Marian Vanhaeren (2016) Upper Palaeolithic mortuary practices: reflections of ethnic affiliation, social complexity and cultural turnover. In Renfrew, Colin, Michael J. Boyd and Iain Morley (eds) *Death Rituals, Social Order and the Archaeology of Immortality in the Ancient World*, 45–61. Cambridge, Cambridge University Press.

d'Errico, Francesco, Christopher Henshilwood, Graeme Lawson, Marian Vanhaeren, Anne-Marie Tillie, Marie Soressi, Françoise Bresson, Bruno Maureille, April Nowell, Joseba Lakarra, Lucinda Backwell, and Michèle Julien (2003) Archaeological evidence for the emergence of language, art and symbolism and music: an alternative multidisciplinary perspective. *Journal of World Prehistory* 17(1), 1–70.

DeSilva, Jeremy M. (2011) A shift toward birthing relatively large infants early in human evolution. *Proceedings of the National Academy of Sciences* 108(3), 1022–1027.

DeSilva, Jeremy M., Bernhard Zipfel, Adam P. Van Arsdale, and Matthew W. Tocheri (2010) The Olduvai Hominid 8 foot: adult or subadult? *Journal of Human Evolution* 58(5), 418–423.

DeSilva, Jeremy M., Corey M. Gill, Thomas C. Prang, Miriam A. Bredella, and Zeresenay Alemseged (2018) A nearly complete foot from Dikika, Ethiopia and its implications for the ontogeny and function of Australopithecus afarensis. *Science Advances* 4(7), eaar7723. DOI: 10.1126/sciadv.aar7723.

DeVries, Kelly (1999) *Joan of Arc: A Military Leader*. Stroud, Sutton Publishing.

Di Leo, Joseph H. (1970) *Young Children and their Drawings*. New York, Brunner/Mazel

Díaz-Andreu, Margarita and Tommaso Matiolli (2015) Archaeoacoustics of rock art: quantitative approaches to the acoustics and soundscape of rock art. In Campana, Stefano, Roberto Scopigno, Gabriella Carpentiero, and Marianna Cirillo (eds) *Proceedings of the 43rd Annual Conference on Computer Applications and Quantitative Methods in Archaeology* 1, 1049–1058. Oxford, Archaeopress.

Díaz-Guardamino, Marta, Leonardo García Sanjuán, David Wheatley, Víctor Rodríguez Zamora (2015) RTI and the study of engraved rock art: a re-examination of the Iberian south-western stelae of Setefilla and Almadén de la Plata 2 (Seville, Spain). *Digital Applications in Archaeology and Cultural Heritage* 2(2–3), 41–54.

Dibble, Harold L., and Andrew W. Pelcin (1995) The effect of hammer mass and velocity on flake mass. *Journal of Archaeological Science* 22(3), 429–439. https://doi.org/10.1006/jasc.1995.0042.

Dibble, Harold L., Philip G. Chase, Shannon P. McPherron, and Alain Tuffreau (1997) Testing the reality of a 'living floor' with archaeological data. *American Antiquity* 62(4), 629–651.

Dillehay, Tom D. (1989) Monte Verde. *Science* 245(4925), 1436.

Dillehay, Tom D., Carlos Ramirez, Mario Pino, Michael B. Collins, Jack Rossen, and J.D. Pino-Navarro (2008) Monte Verde: seaweed, food, medicine, and the peopling of South America. *Science* 320(5877), 784–786.

Dingwall, Heather L., Kevin G. Hatala, Roshna E. Wunderlich, and Brian G. Richmond (2013) Hominin stature, body mass, and walking speed estimates based on 1.5 million-year-old fossil footprints at Ileret, Kenya. *Journal of Human Evolution* 64(6), 556–68. doi: 10.1016/j.jhevol.2013.02.004.

Dira, Samuel Jilo, and Barry S. Hewlett (2016) Learning to spear hunt among Ethiopian Chabu adolescent hunter–gatherers. In Terashima, Hideaki, and Barry S. Hewlett (eds) *Social learning and innovation in contemporary hunter-gatherers*, 71–81. Tokyo, Springer.

Dirks, Paul H., Eric M. Roberts, Hannah Hilbert-Wolf, Jan D. Kramers, John Hawks, Anthony Dosseto, Mathieu Duval, Marina Elliott, Mary Evans, Rainer Grün, John Hellstrom, Andy I.R. Herries, Renaud Joannes-Boyau, Tebogo V. Makhubela, Christa J. Placzek, Jessie Robbins, Carl Spandler, Jelle Wiersma, Jon Woodhead, and Lee R. Berger (2017) The age of *Homo naledi* and associated sediments in the Rising Star Cave, South Africa. *eLife* 6, e24231.

Dobres, Marcia-Anne (2001) Meaning in the making: agency and the social embodiment of technology and art. In Schiffer, Michael B. (ed.) *Anthropological Perspectives on Technology*, 47–76. Albuquerque, University of New Mexico Press.

Dobrovolskaya, Maria, MichaelRichards, and Erik Trinkaus (2012) Direct radiocarbon dates for the Mid Upper Paleolithic (eastern Gravettian) burials from Sunghir, Russia. *Bulletins et Mémoires de la Société d'Anthropologie de Paris* 24(1–2), 96–102.

Doe, Danielle M., Josefina Rascón Pérez, Oscar Cambra-Moo, Manuel Campo Martín, and Armando González Martin (2019) Assessing pubertal stage in adolescent remains: an investigation of the San Nicolás Maqbara burial site (Murcia, Spain). *Archaeological and Anthropological Sciences* 11(2), 541–554.

Donahue, Rudolph E., and Anders Fischer (2015) A Late Glacial family at Trollesgave, Denmark. *Journal of Archaeological Science* 54, 313–324.

Douka, Katerina, Viviane Slon, Zenobia Jacobs, Christopher Bronk Ramsey, Michael V. Shunkov, Anatoly P. Derevianko, Fabrizio Mafessoni, Maxim B. Kozlikin, Bo Li, Rainer Grün, Daniel Comeskey, Thibaut Devièse, Samantha Brown, Bence Viola, Leslie Kinsley, Michael Buckley, Matthias Meyer, Richard G. Roberts, Svante Pääbo, Janet Kelso, and Tom Higham (2019) Age estimates for hominin fossils and the onset of the Upper Palaeolithic at Denisova Cave. *Nature* 565(7741), 640–644.

Druzhkovka, Anna S., Olaf Thalmann, Vladimir A. Trifonov, Jennifer A. Leonard, Nadezhda V. Vorobieva, Nikolai D. Ovodov, Alexander S. Graphodatsky, and Robert K. Wayne (2013) Ancient DNA analysis affirms the canid from Altai as a primitive dog. *PLoS ONE* 8(3), e57754.

Duday, Henri, and Michel A. Garcia (1983) Les empreintes de l'Homme préhistorique. La grotte du Pech-Merle à Cabrerets (Lot): une relecture significative des traces de pieds humains. *Bulletin de la Société Préhistorique Française* 80(7), 208–215.

Duhard Jean-Pierre (1992) Les humains ithyphalliques dans l'art paléolithique. *Bulletin de la Société Préhistoire Ariègeoise* 47, 133–159.

Dunbar, Robin I.M. (1992) Neocrotex size as a constraint on group size in primates. *Journal of Human Evolution* 22(6), 469–493.

Dunbar, Robin I.M. (1998) *Grooming, Gossip, and the Evolution of Language*. Cambridge, Harvard University Press.

Dunbar, Robin I.M. (2014) How conversations around campfires came to be. *Proceedings of the National Academy of Sciences* 111(39), 14013–14014.

Dunne, Julie, Katharina Rebay-Salisbury, Roderick B. Salisbury, Alexander Frisch, Caitlin Walton-Doyle, and Richard P. Evershed (2019) Milk of ruminants in ceramic baby bottles from prehistoric child graves. *Nature* 574(7777), 246–248. https://doi.org/10.1038/s41586-019-1572-x.

Dunnsworth, Holly (2018) There is no 'obstetrical dilemma': Towards a braver medicine with fewer childbirth interventions. *Perspectives in Biology and Medicine* 61(2), 249-263. http://dx.doi.org/10.1353/pbm.2018.0040.

Dunsworth, Holly, and Leah Eccleston (2015) The evolution of difficult childbirth and helpless hominin infants. *Annual Review of Anthropology* 44, 55–69. https://doi.org/10.1146/annurev-anthro-102214-013918.

Duveau, Jérémy, Gilles Berillon, Christine Verna, Gilles Laisné, and Dominique Cliquet (2019) The composition of a Neandertal social group revealed by the hominin footprints at Le Rozel (Normandy, France). *Proceedings of the National Academy of Sciences* 116(39), 19409–19414.

Eaton-Krauss, Marianne (2015) *The Unknown Tutankhamun*. London, Bloomsbury Publishing.
Edwards, Betty (2012) *Drawing on the Right Side of the Brain*, 4th Edition. New York, TarcherPerigee.
Efremov, J.A. (1940) Taphonomy: a new branch of paleontology. *Pan-American Geologist* 74, 81–93.
Einwögerer, Thomas, Herwig Friesinger, Marc Händel, Christine Neugebauer-Maresch, Ulrich Simon, and Maria Teschler-Nicola (2006) Upper Paleolithic infant burials. *Nature* 444(7117), 285.
Einwögerer, Thomas, Marc Händel, Christine Neugebauer-Maresch, Ulrich Simon, Peter Steier, Maria Teschler-Nicola, and Eva Maria Wild (2009) 14C dating of the Upper Paleolithic site at Krems-Wachtberg, Austria. *Radiocarbon* 51(2), 847–855.
Eisner, Will, and P. Poplaski (2008) *Expressive Anatomy for Comics and Narrative: Principles and Practices from the Legendary Cartoonist*. New York, W.W. Norton and Company.
Emmanuel, Mickey, and Brooke R. Bokor (2020) *Tanner Stages*. StatPearls Publishing, Treasure Island, FL, LLC.
Emons Joyce, Andrei S. Chagin, Lars Sävendahl, Marcel Karperien, and Jan M. Wit (2011) Mechanisms of growth plate maturation and epiphyseal fusion. *Hormone Research in Paediatrics* 75(6), 383–391. doi:10.1159/000327788.
Ericsson, K. Anders (2006) The influence of expertise and deliberate practice on the development of superior expert performance. In Ericsson, K. Anders, Neil Charness, Paul J. Feltovich and Robert R. Hoffman (eds) *The Cambridge Handbook of Expertise and Expert Performance*, 683–703. Cambridge, Cambridge University Press.
Estalrrich, Almudena, and Antonio Rosas (2015) Division of labor by sex and age in Neandertals: an approach through the study of activity-related dental wear. *Journal of Human Evolution* 80, 51–63.
Faerman, Marina, Uri Zilberman, Patricia Smith, Vitaliy M. Kharitonov, and V. Batsevitz (1994) A Neanderthal infant from the Barakai Cave, western Caucasus. *Journal of Human Evolution* 27(5), 405–415.
Farbstein, Rebecca (2010) Beyond Venus figurines: technical production and social practice in Pavlovian portable art. In Gheorghiu, Dragos, and Ann Cyphers (eds) *Anthropomorphic and Zoomorphic Miniature Figures in Eurasia, Africa and Mesoamerica: Morphology, Materiality, Technology, Function and Context*, 9–16. British Archaeology Reports, 2138. Oxford, Archaeopress.
Farbstein, Rebecca (2011a) Technologies of art: a critical reassessment of Pavlovian art and society, using chaîne opératoire method and theory. *Current Anthropology* 52(3), 401–432.
Farbstein, Rebecca (2011b) The significance of social gestures and technologies of embellishment in Paleolithic portable art. *Journal of Archaeological Method and Theory* 18(2), 125–146.
Farbstein, Rebecca, and Wiliam Davies (2017) Palaeolithic ceramic technology: the artistic origins and impacts of a technological innovation. *Quaternary International* 441, 3–11.
Ferguson, Jeffrey R. (2003) An experimental test of the conservation of raw material in flintknapping skill acquisition. *Lithic Technology* 28(2), 113–131.
Ferguson, Jeffrey R. (2008) The when, where, and how of novices in craft production. *Journal of Archaeological Method and Theory* 15(1), 51–67.
Fewlass, Helen, Sahra Talamo, Bernd Kromer, Edouard Bard, Thibaut Tuna, Yoann Fagault, Matt Sponheimer, Christina Ryder, Jean-Jacques Hublin, Angela Perri, Sandra Sázelová, and Jiří Svoboda (2019) Direct radiocarbon dates of mid Upper Palaeolithic human remains from Dolní Věstonice II and Pavlov I, Czech Republic. *Journal of Archaeological Science: Reports* 27, 102000. https://doi.org/10.1016/j.jasrep.2019.102000.
Fiedel, Stuart J. (2017) The Anzick genome proves Clovis is first, after all. *Quaternary International* 444, 4–9.
Filippov, A.K. (2005) *Khaos i garmoniya v iskusstve paleolita*. St Petersburg, Nestor-Istoriya, Russia.
Finlay, Nyree (2015) Kid-knapped knowledge: changing perspectives on the child in lithic studies. *Childhood in the Past* 8(2), 104–112.
Fischer, Anders (1990a) A late Palaeolithic 'school' of flint-knapping at Trollesgave, Denmark. Results from refitting. *Acta Archaeologica* 60, 33–49.

Fischer, Anders (1990b) On being a pupil of a flintknapper of 11,000 years ago. A preliminary analysis of settlement organization and flint technology based on conjoined flint artefacts from the Trollesgave site. In *The Big Puzzle: Proceedings of the International Symposium on Refitting Stone Artefacts*, 447–464. Bonn, Holos.

Flynn, Emma G., Kevin N. Laland, Rachel L. Kendal, and Jeremy R. Kendal (2013) Developmental niche construction. *Developmental Science* 16(2), 296–313.

Foley, Robert, and Clive Gamble (2009) The ecology of social transitions in human evolution. *Philosophical Transactions of the Royal Society B: Biological Sciences* 364(1533), 3267–3279. doi:10.1098/rstb.2009.01.

Formicola, Vincenzo (1988) The male and the female in the Upper Paleolithic burials from Grimaldi Caves (Liguria, Italy). *Bulletin du Musée d'Anthropologie Préhistorique de Monaco* 31, 41–48.

Formicola, Vincenzo (2007) From the Sunghir children to the Romito dwarf: aspects of the Upper Paleolithic funerary landscape. *Current Anthropology* 48(3), 446–453.

Formicola, Vincenzo, and Alexandra Buzhilova (2004) Double child burial from Sunghir (Russia): pathology and inferences for Upper Paleolithic funerary practices. *American Journal of Physical Anthropology* 124(3), 189–198.

Formicola, Vincenzo, Paul B. Pettitt, Roberto Maggi, and Robert Hedges (2005) Tempo and mode of formation of the Late Epigravettian necropolis of Arene Candide Cave (Italy): direct radiocarbon evidence. *Journal of Archaeological Science* 32(11), 1598–1602.

Formicola, Vincenzo, and Brigitte M. Holt (2015) Tall guys and fat ladies: Grimaldi's Upper Paleolithic burials and figurines in an historical perspective. *Journal of Anthropological Sciences* 93, 71–88.

Formicola, Vincenzo, Antonella Pontrandolfi, and Jiří Svoboda (2001) The Upper Paleolithic Triple Burial of Dolní Věstonice: pathology and funerary behavior. *American Journal of Physical Anthropology* 115(4), 372–379.

Foucher, Pascal, Cristina San Juan-Foucher, Dominique Henry-Gambier, Carole Vercoutère, and Catherine Ferrier (2012) Discovery of the mandible of a young child in a Gravettian level of Gargas Cave (Hautes-Pyrenees, France). *PALEO. Revue d'archéologie préhistorique* 23, 323–336.

Franklin, Nathalie R., and Phillip J. Habgood (2009) Finger markings and the Willandra Lakes Footprint site, South-Eastern Australia. *Rock Art Research* 26(2), 199–203.

Frayer, David W., William A. Horton, Roberto Macchiarelli, Margherita Mussi (1987) Dwarfism in an adolescent from the Italian late Upper Palaeolithic. *Nature* 330(6143), 60–62.

Frayer, David W., R. Macchiarelli, and M. Mussi (1988) A case of chondrodystrophic dwarfism in the Italian Late Upper Paleolithic. *American Journal of Physical Anthropology* A5(4), 549–65. doi: 10.1002/ajpa.1330750412.

Frayer, David W., Jan Jelínek, Martin Oliva, and Milford H. Wolpoff (2006) Aurignacian male crania, jaws and teeth from the Mladeč Caves, Moravia, Czech Republic. In Teschler-Nicola, Maria (ed.) *Early Modern Humans at the Moravian Gate*, 185–272. Vienna, Springer.

Freedman, Adam H., and Robert K. Wayne (2017) Deciphering the origin of dogs: from fossils to genomes. *Annual Review of Animal Biosciences* 5(1), 281–307.

Freeman, Leslie G. (2009) *Anthropology Without Informants: Collected Works in Paleoanthropology*. Boulder, University Press of Colorado.

Freeman, Leslie G., F. Bernaldo de Quiros, and J. Ogden (1987) Animals, faces and space at Altamira: a restudy of the final gallery ('Cola de Caballo'). In Freeman, Leslie G. (ed.) *Altamira Revisited and other Essays on Early Art*, 179–247. Chicago and Santander, Institute for Prehistoric Investigations.

French, Jennifer C. (2015) The demography of the Upper Palaeolithic hunter-gatherers of Southwestern France: a multi-proxy approach using archaeological data. *Journal of Anthropological Archaeology* 39, 193–209.

French, Jennifer C. (In press) *Palaeolithic Europe: A Demographic and Social Prehistory*. Cambridge, Cambridge University Press.

French, Jennifer C., and Christina M. Collins (2015) Upper Palaeolithic population histories of Southwestern France: a comparison of the demographic signatures of 14C date distributions and archaeological site counts. *Journal of Archaeological Science* 55, 122–134.

Friedman, Sarah L., and Marguerite B. Stevenson (1980) Perception of movement in pictures. In Hagen, Margaret (ed.) *The Perception of Pictures Vol 1. Albert's Window: The Projective Model of Pictorial Information*, 225–255. New York, Academic Press.

Frink, Lisa, and Kathryn Weedman (2005) *Gender and Hide Production*. Walnut Creek, AltaMira Press.

Fritz, Carole (1997) Hacia una reconstitución de los procedimientos artistícos magdalenienses: contribución del analisis microscopico en el campo del arte mueble. *Trabajos de Prehistoria* 54(2), 43–59.

Fritz, Carole (1999a) La gravure dans l'art mobilier magdalénien, du geste à la représentation: contribution de l'analyse microscopique. *Documents d'Archéologie Française* 75. Paris, Maison des Sciences de l'Homme.

Fritz, Carole (1999b) Towards a rebuilding of the Magdalenian artistic processes: the use of microscopic analysis in the field of miniature art. *Cambridge Archaeological Journal* 9(2), 189–208.

Fritz, Carole, and Gilles Tosello (2007) The hidden meaning of forms: methods of recording Paleolithic parietal art. *Journal of Archaeological Method and Theory* 14(1), 48–80.

Fritz, Carole, Gilles Tosello, and Margaret W. Conkey (2016) Reflections on the identities and roles of the artists in European Paleolithic Societies. *Journal of Archaeological Method and Theory* 23(4), 1307–1332. DOI 10.1007/s10816-015-9265-8.

Fritz, Carole, Gilles Tosello, G. Fleury, E. Kasarhérou, Ph. Walter, F. Duranthon, P. Gaillard, J. Tardieu (2021) First record of the sound produced by the oldest Upper Paleolithic seashell horn. *Science Advances* 7, 1–6. eabe9510.

Fu, Qiaomei, Cosimo Posth, Mateja Hajdinjak, Martin Petr, Swapan Mallick, Daniel Fernandes, Anja Furtwängler, Wolfgang Haak, Matthias Meyer, Alissa Mittnik, Birgit Nickel, Alexander Peltzer, Nadin Rohland, Viviane Slon, Sahra Talamo, Iosif Lazaridis, Mark Lipson, Iain Mathieson, Stephan Schiffels, Pontus Skoglund, Anatoly P. Derevianko, Nikolai Drozdov, Vyacheslav Slavinsky, Alexander Tsybankov, Renata Grifoni Cremonesi, Francesco Mallegni, Bernard Gély, Eligio Vacca, Manuel R. González Morales, Lawrence G. Straus, Christine Neugebauer-Maresch, Maria Teschler-Nicola, Silviu Constantin, Oana Teodora Moldovan, Stefano Benazzi, Marco Peresani, Donato Coppola, Martina Lari, Stefano Ricci, Annamaria Ronchitelli, Frédérique Valentin, Corinne Thevenet, Kurt Wehrberger, Dan Grigorescu, Hélène Rougier, Isabelle Crevecoeur, Damien Flas, Patrick Semal, Marcello A. Mannino, Christophe Cupillard, Hervé Bocherens, Nicholas J. Conard, Katerina Harvati, Vyacheslav Moiseyev, Dorothée G. Drucker, Jiří Svoboda, Michael P. Richards, David Caramelli, Ron Pinhasi, Janet Kelso, Nick Patterson, Johannes Krause, Svante Pääbo, and David Reich (2016) The genetic history of Ice Age Europe. *Nature* 53(7606), 200–205.

Fukui, Hajime, and Kumiko Toyoshima (2014) Chill-inducing music enhances altruism in humans. *Frontiers in Psychology* 5, 1215. https://doi.org/10.3389/fpsyg.2014.01215.

Galván, Adriana (2020) The need for sleep in the adolescent brain. *Trends in Cognitive Sciences* 24(1), 79–89.

Gambier, Dominique (2000) Aurignacian children and mortuary practice in western Europe. *Anthropologie* 38(1), 5–21.

García-Diez, Marcos, Dirk L. Hoffman, João Zlihão, Carmen de las Heras, José A. Lasheras, Ramón Montes, and Alistair W.G. Pike (2013) Uranium series dating reveals a long sequence of rock art at Altamira Cave (Santillana del Mar, Cantabria). *Journal of Archaeological Science* 40, 4098–4106.

Garcia, Michel-Alain (2001) Les empreintes et les traces humaines et animales. In Clottes, Jean (ed.) *La Grotte Chauvet. L'Art des Origines*, 34–43. Paris, Le Seuil.

Garcia, Michel-Alain (2005) Ichnologie générale de la grotte Chauvet. *Bulletin de la société préhistorique française* 102(1), 103–108.

García-Martínez, Daniel, Markus Bastir, Asier Gómez-Olivencia, Bruno Maureille, Liubov Golovanova, Vladimir Doronichev, Takeru Akazawa, Osamu Kondo, Hajime Ishida, Dominic Gascho, Christoph P.E. Zollikofer, Marcia Ponce de León, and Yann Heuzé (2020) Early development of the Neanderthal ribcage reveals a different body shape at birth compared to modern humans. *Scientific Advances* 6(41), eabb4377.

Gärdenfors, Peter, and Anders Högberg (2017) The archaeology of teaching and the evolution of homo docens. *Current Anthropology* 58(2), 188–201.

Garfield, Zachary H., Melissa J. Garfield, and Barry S. Hewlett (2016). A cross-cultural analysis of hunter–gatherer social learning. In Terashima, Hideaki, and Barry S. Hewlett (eds) *Social learning and innovation in contemporary hunter-gatherers*, 19–34. Tokyo, Springer.

Gargett, Robert (1989) Grave Shortcomings: the evidence for Neandertal burial. *Current Anthropology* 30(2), 157–190.

Gargett, Robert (1999) Middle Palaeolithic burial is not a dead issue: the view from Qafzeh, Saint-Césaire, Kebara, Amud, and Dederiyeh. *Journal of Human Evolution* 37(1), 27–90.

Garralda, Maria-Dolorès, Giacomo Giacobini, and Bernard Vandermeersch (2005) Neanderthal cutmarks: Combe-Grenal and Marillac (France). A SEM analysis. *Anthropologie* 43(2–3), 189–198.

Garralda, Maria-Dolorès, and Bernard Vandermeersch (2000) Les Néandertaliens de la grotte de Combe-Grenal (Domme, Dordogne, France)/The Neanderthals from Combe-Grenal Cave (Domme, Dordogne, France). *PALEO Revue d'Archéologie Préhistorique* 12(1), 213–259.

Gazzoni, Valentina (2011) Contributo alla ricostruzione delle identità regionali e della differenziazione sociale presso i gruppi di cacciatori-raccoglitori paleo-mesolitici. Studio della ritualità funeraria in Italia e Francia e analisi degli isotopi stabili sul campione umano del versante alpino sud-orientale. Doctoral dissertation, Università degli Studi di Ferrara.

Gazzoni, Valentina, and Frederica Fontana (2011) Quelle mort? Quelle vie? Pratiques funéraires et organisation sociale des chasseurs-cueilleurs de la péninsule italienne. *Bulletins et mémoires de la Société d'anthropologie de Paris* 23(1), 52–69.

Gergely, György, and Gergely Csibra (2006) Sylvia's recipe: The role of imitation and pedagogy in the transmission of cultural knowledge. In Levinson, Stephen C., and Nicholas Enfield (eds) *Roots of human sociality; Culture, cognition and interaction*, 229- 255. Oxford, UK, Berg Publishers.

Gero, Joan (1991) Genderlithics: women's roles in stone tool production. In Gero, Joan and Margaret Conkey (eds) *Engendering Archaeology: Women and Prehistory*, 163–193. Oxford, Basil Blackwell Publishers.

Gero, Joan, and Margaret W. Conkey (1991) *Engendering Archaeology: Women and Prehistory*. Oxford: Basil Blackwell Publishers.

Giacobini, Giacomo (2006) Les sépultures du Paléolithique supérieur: la documentation italienne. *Comptes Rendus Palevol* 5(1–2), 169–176.

Giacobini, Giacomo (2007) Richness and diversity of burial rituals in the Upper Paleolithic. *Diogenes* 54(2), 19–39.

Giacobini, Giacomo, Marie-Antoinette de Lumley, Yuji Yokoyama, and Huu-Van Nguyen (1984) Neanderthal child and adult remains from a Mousterian deposit in Northern Italy (Caverna delle fate, finale ligure). *Journal of Human Evolution* 13(8), 687–707.

Gibson, James J. (1979) *The Ecological Approach to Visual Perception*. Boston, Houghton Mifflin.

Gilligan, Ian (2010) The prehistoric development of clothing: archaeological implications of a thermal model. *Journal of Archaeological Method and Theory* 17(1), 15–80.

Golovanova, Liubov V., John F. Hoffecker, V.M. Kharitonov, and G.P. Romanova (1999) Mezmaiskaya Cave: a Neanderthal occupation in the northern Caucasus. *Current Anthropology* 40(1), 77–86.

Goodnow, Jaqueline J. (1978) *Children's Drawings*. London, Open Books.

Gómez-Olivencia, Asier, María Dolores Garralda, Bernard Vandermeersch, Stéphane Madelaine, Juan-Luis Arsuaga, and Bruno Maureille (2013) Two newly identified Mousterian human rib fragments from Combe-Grenal (Domme, France). *PALEO. Revue d'archéologie préhistorique* 24, 229–234.

Gómez-Olivencia, Asier, Isabelle Crevecoeur, and Antoine Balzeau (2015) La Ferrassie 8 Neandertal child reloaded: New remains and re-assessment of the original collection. *Journal of Human Evolution* 82, 107–126.

Gómez-Olivencia, Asier, and Daniel García-Martínez (2019) New postcranial remains from the Roc de Marsal Neandertal child. *PALEO. Revue d'archéologie préhistorique* 30(1), 164–169. https://doi.org/10.4000/paleo.4631.

Gonlin, Nancy, and Christine C. Dixon (2018) Classic Maya Nights at Copan, Honduras, and El Cerén, El Salvador. In Gonlin, Nancy and April Nowell (eds) *Archaeology of the Night: Life After Dark in the Ancient World*, 45–76. Boulder, University Press of Colorado.

Gonlin, Nancy and April Nowell (2018a) *Archaeology of the Night: Life After Dark in the Ancient World*. Boulder, University Press of Colorado.

Gonlin, Nancy, and April Nowell (2018b) Introduction to the archaeology of the night. In Gonlin, Nancy, and April Nowell (eds) *Archaeology of the Night: Life After Dark in the Ancient World*, 5–26. Boulder, University Press of Colorado.

Gonzales-Morales, M.R. (1997) When the beasts go marching out! The end of Pleistocene art in Cantabrian Spain. In Conkey, Margaret W., Olga Soffer, Deborah Stratmann and Nina G. Jablonski (eds) *Beyond Art: Pleistocene Image and Symbol*, 189–199. Berkley, University of California Press.

Gosden, Chris, and Yvonne Marshall (1999) Cultural biography of objects. *World Archaeology* 31(2), 169–178.

Gowland, Rebecca L. (2006) Ageing the past: examining age identity from funerary evidence. In Gowland, Rebecca L., and Christopher Knüsel (eds) *Social Archaeology of Funerary Remains*, 143–154. Oxford, Oxbow Books.

Gowland, Rebecca, Nicolas Stewart, Kayla Crowder, Claire Hodson, Heidi Shaw, Kurt Gron, and Janet Montgomery (2021) Sex determination of teeth at different developmental stages using dimorphic enamel peptide analysis. *American Journal of Physical Anthropology* 2021, 1-11 https://doi.org/10.1002/ajpa.24231

Germonpré, Mietje, Martina Lázničková-Galetová, and Mikhail V. Sablin (2012) Palaeolithic dog skulls at the Gravettian Předmostí site, the Czech Republic. *Journal of Archaeological Science* 39(1), 184–202.

Gracia, Ana, Juan Luis Arsuaga, Ignacio Martínez, Carlos Lorenzo, José Miguel Carretero, José Maria Bermúdez de Castro, and Eudald Carbonell (2009) Craniosynostosis in the Middle Pleistocene human cranium 14 from the Sima de los Huesos, Atapuerca, Spain. *Proceedings of the National Academy of Sciences* 106(16), 6573–6578.

Granat, Jean, and Jean-Louis Heim (2003) Nouvelle methode d'estimation de l'age dentaire des Neandertaliens. *L'Anthropologie* 107(2), 171–202.

GRAPP (Groupe de Réflexion sur l'Art Pariétal Paléolithique) (1993) *l'Art Pariétal Paléolithique: Techniques et méthodes d'étude*. Paris, Comité des travaux historiques et scientifiques (CTHS).

Gray, Peter B. (2013) Evolution and human sexuality. *Yearbook of Physical Anthropology* 152(S57), 94–118.

Greer, Mavis, and John Greer (1999) Handprints in Montana rock art. *The Plains Anthropologist* 44(167), 59–71.

Grimm, Linda (2000) Apprentice flintknapping: relating material culture and social practice in the Upper Paleolithic. In Sofaer Derevenski, Joanna (ed.) *Children and Material Culture*, 53–71. London, Routledge.

Grine, Frederick E. (1982) A new juvenile hominid (Mammalia: Primates) from Member 3, Kromdraai Formation, Transvaal, South Africa. *Annals of the Transvaal Museum* 33(11), 165–239.

Groenen, Marc (1988) Les representations de mains negatives dans les grottes de Gargas et de Tibiran (Hautes-Pyrénées). Approche méthodologique. *Bulletin de la Société royale belge d'Anthropologie et de Préhistoire* 99, 81–113.

Grove, Matt (2013) Evolution of Hominin Social Systems. *Evolution of Hominin Social Systems. eLS*. DOI: 10.1002/9780470015902.a0024.

Gruber, Thibaud, Zanna Clay, and Klaus Zuberbühler (2010) A comparison of bonobo and chimpanzee tool use: evidence for a female bias in the Pan lineage. *Animal Behaviour* 80(6), 1023–1033.

Gunz, Philipp, Simon Neubauer, Dean Falk, Paul Tafforeau, Adeline Le Cabec, Tanya M. Smith, William H. Kimbel, Fred Spoor, and Zeresenay Alemseged (2020) *Australopithecus afarensis* endocasts suggest ape-like brain organization and prolonged brain growth. *Science Advances* 6(14), eaaz4729. DOI: 10.1126/sciadv.aaz4729.

Gustavsen, Jenifer (2014) *Developing a Method for Assessing the Skillfulness and Practice Time for Upper Palaeolithic Artists*. Unpublished Masters thesis, Simon Fraser University, Burnaby, British Columbia, Canada.

Guthrie, R. Dale (2005) *The Nature of Paleolithic Art*. Chicago, University of Chicago Press.

Halcrow, Siân E. (2020) Infants in the bioarchaeological past: who cares? In Gowland, Rebecca, and Siân E. Halcrow (eds) *The Mother-Infant Nexus in Anthropology: Small Beginnings, Significant Outcomes*, 19–38. Swtizerland, Springer. DOI: 10.1007/978-3-030-27393-4_2.

Halcrow, Siân E., and Nancy Tayles (2008) The bioarchaeological investigation of childhood and social age: problems and prospects. *Journal of Archaeological Method and Theory* 15(2), 190–215.

Halcrow, Siân E, Ruth Warren, Geoff Kushnick, and April Nowell (2020) Care of infants in the past: bridging paleoanthropological and bioarchaeological approaches. *Evolutionary Human Sciences* 2, e47.

Halffman, Carrin M., Ben A. Potter, Holly J. McKinney, Bruce P. Finney, Antonia T. Rodrigues, Dongya Y. Yang, and Brian M. Kemp (2015) Early human use of anadromous salmon in North America at 11,500 y ago. *Proceedings of the National Academy of Sciences* 112(40), 12344–12348.

Halstad McGuire, Erin (2019) 'Whim rules the child': the archaeology of childhood in Scandinavian Scotland. Journal of the North Atlantic 11(sp1), 13–27.

Halverson, John (1992) Paleolithic art and cognition. *The Journal of Psychology* 126(3), 221–236.

Hammond, Ashley S., Sergio Almécija, Yosief Libsekal, Lorenzo Rook, and Roberto Macchiarelli (2018) A partial *Homo* pelvis from the Early Pleistocene of Eritrea. *Journal of Human Evolution* 123, 109–128.

Hammond, Gawain, and Norman Hammond (1981) Child's play: a distorting factor in archaeological distribution. *American Antiquity* 46(3), 634–636.

Händel, Marc, Thomas Einwögerer, and Ulrich Simon (2008) Krems-Wachtberg–a Gravettian settlement site in the Middle Danube region. *Wissenschaftliche Mitteilungen aus dem Niederösterreichischen Landesmuseum* 19, 91–108.

Handpas Project. http://handpas.juntaex.es/.

Harmand, Sonia, Jason E. Lewis, Craig S. Feibel, Christopher J. Lepre, Sandrine Prat, Arnaud Lenoble, Xavier Boës, Rhonda L. Quinn, Michel Brenet, Adrian Arroyo, Nicholas Taylor, Sophie Clément, Guillaume Daver, Jean-Philip Brugal, Louise Leakey, Richard A. Mortlock, James D. Wright, Sammy Lokorodi, Christopher Kirwa, Dennis V. Kent, and Hélène Roche (2015) 3.3-million-year-old stone tools from Lomekwi 3, West Turkana, Kenya. *Nature* 521(7552), 310–315. doi.org/10.1038/nature14464.

Harrington, Spencer P.M. (1999) Human footprints at Chauvet Cave. *Archaeology* 52(5), 18.

Harvey, Paul H., and Timothy H. Clutton-Brock (1985) Life history variation in primates. *Evolution* 39(3), 559–581.

Hatala, Kevin G., Neil T. Roach, Kelly R. Ostrofsky, Roshna E. Wunderlich, Heather L. Dingwall, Brian A. Villmoare, David J. Green, John W.K. Harris, David R. Braun, and Brian G. Richmond (2016) Footprints reveal direct evidence of group behavior and locomotion in *Homo erectus*. *Scientific Reports* 6, 28766. DOI: 10.1038/srep28766.

Hatala, Kevin G., William E.H. Harcourt-Smith, Adam D. Gordon, Brian W. Zimmer, Brian G. Richmond, Briana L. Pobiner, David J. Green, Adam Metallo, Vince Rossi, and Cynthia M. Liutkus-Pierce (2020) Snapshots of human anatomy, locomotion, and behavior from Late Pleistocene footprints at Engare Sero, Tanzania. *Scientific Reports* 10(1), 7740. https://doi.org/10.1038/s41598-020-64095-0.

Hawcroft, Jennie, and Robin Dennell (2000) Neanderthal cognitive life history and its implications for material culture. In Sofaer Derevenski, Joanna (ed.) *Children and Material Culture*, 89–99. London, Routledge.

Hawkes, Kristen, and Nicholas Blurton Jones (2005) Human age structures, paleodemography, and the grandmother hypothesis. In Voland, Eckart, Athanasios Chasiotis, and Wulf Schiefenhovel (eds) *Grandmotherhood: The Evolutionary Significance of the Second Half of Female Life*, 118–140. New Brunswick, NJ, Rutgers University Press.

Hawkes, Kristen, James F. O'Connell, and Nicholas J. Blurton-Jones (2003) Human life histories: primate trade-offs, grandmothering socioecology, and the fossil record. In Kappeler, Peter M., and Michael E. Pereira (eds) *Primate Life Histories and Socioecology*, 204–231. Chicago, University of Chicago Press.

Hawks, John, Marina Elliott, Peter Schmid, Steven E. Churchill, Darryl J. de Ruiter, Eric M. Roberts, Hannah Hilbert-Wolf, Heather M. Garvin, Scott A. Williams, Lucas K. Delezene, Elen M. Feuerriegel, Patrick Randolph-Quinney, Tracy L. Kivell, Myra F. Laird, Gaokgatlhe Tawane, Jeremy M. DeSilva, Shara E. Bailey, Juliet K. Brophy, Marc R. Meyer, Matthew M. Skinner, Matthew W. Tocheri, Caroline VanSickle, Christopher S. Walker, Timothy L. Campbell, Brian Kuhn, Ashley Kruger, Steven Tucker, Alia Gurtov, Nompumelelo Hlophe, Rick Hunter, Hannah Morris, Becca Peixotto, Maropeng Ramalepa, Dirk van Rooyen, Mathabela Tsikoane, Pedro Boshoff, Paul H.G.M. Dirks, and Lee R. Berger (2017) New fossil remains of *Homo naledi* from the Lesedi Chamber, South Africa. *ELife* 6, e24232.

Haidle, Miriam Noël, Michael Bolus, Mark Collard, Nicholas J. Conard, Duilio Garofoli, Marlize Lombard, April Nowell, Claudio Tennie, and Andrew Whiten (2015) The nature of culture: an eight-grade model for the evolution and expansion of cultural capacities in hominins and other animals. *Journal of Anthropological Sciences* 93, 43–70. https://doi.org/10.4436/jass.93011.

Hardy, Bruce L., M.-H. Moncel, Céline Kerfant, Matthieu Lebon, Ludovic Bellot-Gurlet, and Nicolas Mélard (2020) Direct evidence of Neanderthal fibre technology and its cognitive and behavioral implications. *Scientific Reports* 10(1), 1–9.

Hayden, Brian (2012) Neandertal social structure? *Oxford Journal of Archaeology* 31(1), 1–26.

Hays-Gilpin, Kelley A. (2003) *Ambiguous Images: Gender and Rock Art*. Walnut Creek, AltaMira.

Hedges, Robert E.M., Rupert A. Housley, Christopher Bronk Ramsey, and Gert.Jaap Van Klinken (1993) Radiocarbon dates from the Oxford AMS system: archaeometry datelist 16. *Archaeometry* 35(1), 147–167.

Henry-Gambier, Dominique (2008a) Comportement des populations d'Europe au Gravettien: pratiques funéraires et interprétations. *PALEO. Revue d'archéologie préhistorique* 20, 399–438.

Henry-Gambier, Dominique (2008b) Les sujets juvéniles du Paléolithique supérieur d'Europe à travers l'analyse de sépultures primaires: l'exemple de la culture gravettienne. In *Nasciturus, infans, puerulus vobis mater terra: la muerte en la infancia*, 331–364. Servei d'Investigacions Arqueològiques i Prehistòriques.

Henry-Gambier, Dominique, Roland Nespoulet, Laurent Chiotti, Dorothée Drucker, and Arnaud Lenoble (2005) Datations. In Newpoulet, Roland, Laurent Chiottie, and Dominique Henry-Gambier (eds) *Le Gravettien final de l'abri Pataud (Dordogne, France). Fouilles et études 2005-2009*, 43–50. Oxford, Archaeopress.

Henry-Gambier, Dominique, Cédric Beauval, Jean Airvaux, Norbert Aujoulat, J.F. Baratin, and J. Buisson-Catil (2007) New hominid remains associated with gravettian parietal art (Les Garennes, Vilhonneur, France). *Journal of Human Evolution* 53(6), 747–750.

Henry-Gambier, Dominique, and Dominique Sacchi (2008) La Crouzade V-VI (Aude, France): un des plus anciens fossiles d'anatomie moderne en Europe occidentale. *Bulletins et Mémoires de la Société d'Anthropologie de Paris* 20(1–2).

Henry-Gambier, Dominique, Roland Nespoulet, and Laurent Chiotti (2013) An Early Gravettian cultural attribution for the human fossils from the Cro-Magnon rock shelter (Les Eyzies-de-Tayac, Dordogne). *PALEO. Revue d'archéologie préhistorique* 24, 121–138.

Herries, Andy I.R., Jesse M. Martin, A.B. Leece, Justin W. Adams, Giovanni Boschian, Renaud Joannes-Boyau, Tara R. Edwards, Tom Mallet, Jason Massey, Ashleigh Murszewski, Simon Neubauer,

Robyn Pickering, David S. Strait, Brian J. Armstrong, Stephanie Baker, Matthew V. Caruana, Tim Denham, John Hellstrom, Jacopo Moggi-Cecchi, Simon Mokobane, Paul Penzo-Kajewski, Douglass S. Rovinsky, Gary T. Schwartz, Rhiannon C. Stammers, Coen Wilson, Jon Woodhead, and Colin Menter (2020) Contemporaneity of *Australopithecus*, *Paranthropus*, and early *Homo erectus* in South Africa. *Science* 368(6486), eaaw7293. DOI: 10.1126/science.aaw7293.

Hershkovitz, Israel, Gerhard W. Weber, Rolf Quam, Mathieu Duval, Rainer Grün, Leslie Kinsley, Avner Ayalon, Miryam Bar Matthews, Helene Valladas, Norbert Mercier, Juan Luis Arsuaga, María Martinón-Torres, José María Bermúdez de Castro, Cinzia Fornai, Laura Martín-Francés, Rachel Sarig, Hila May, Viktoria A. Krenn, Viviane Slon, Laura Rodríguez, Rebeca García, Carlos Lorenzo, Jose Miguel Carretero, Amos Frumkin, Ruth Shahack-Gross, Daniella E. Bar-Yosef Mayer, Yaming Cui, Xinzhi Wu, Natan Peled, Iris Groman-Yaroslavski, Lior Weissbrod, Reuven Yeshurun, Alexander Tsatskin, Yossi Zaidner, and Mina Weinstein-Evron (2018) The earliest modern humans outside Africa. *Science* 359(6374), 456–459. DOI: 10.1126/science.aap8369.

Hewlett, Barry S. (2017) Hunter–gatherer childhoods in the Congo Basin. In Hewlett, Barry S. (ed.) *Hunter-gatherers of the Congo Basin: Cultures, histories and biology of African pygmies*, 275–306. Routledge.

Hewlett, Bonnie L., and Barry S. Hewlett (2012) Hunter–gatherer adolescence. In Bonnie L. Hewlett (ed.) *Adolescent identity: Evolutionary, cultural, and developmental perspectives*, 73–101. Routledge.

Hewlett, Barry S., and Casey J. Roulette (2016) Teaching in hunter-gatherer infancy. *Royal Society Open Science* 3(1), 150403.

Higham, Thomas, Roger Jacobi, Michèle Julien, Francine David, Laura Basell, Rachel Wood, William Davies, and Christopher Bronk Ramsey (2010) Chronology of the Grotte du Renne (France) and implications for the context of ornaments and human remains within the Châtelperronian. *Proceedings of the National Academy of Sciences* 107(47), 20234–20239.

Hildebrand, Jennifer (2012) Children in archaeological lithic analysis. *Nebraska Anthropologist* 27(176), 25–42.

Hillson, Simon W., R.G. Franciscus, T.W. Holliday, and Erik Trinkaus (2006) The ages-at-death. In Trinkaus, Erik and Jirí Svoboda (eds) *Early Modern Human Evolution in Central Europe: The People of Dolní Věstonice and Pavlov*, 31–45. New York, Oxford University Press.

Hirata, Satoshi, Koki Fuwa, Keiko Sugama, Kiyo Kusunoki, and Hideko Takeshita (2011) Mechanism of birth in chimpanzees: humans are not unique among primates. *Biology Letters* 7(5), 686–688. doi:10.1098/rsbl.2011.0214.

Hochberg, Ze'ev, and Melvin Konner (2020) Emerging adulthood, a pre-adult life history stage. *Frontiers in Endocrinology* 10, 918.

Högberg, Anders (1999) Child and adult at a knapping area: a technological flake analysis of the manufacture of a Neolithic square sectioned axe and a child's flint knapping activities on an assemblage excavated as part of the Öresund Fixed Link Project. *Acta Archaeologica* 70, 79–106.

Högberg, Anders (2008) Playing with flint: tracing a child's imitation of adult work in a lithic assemblage. *Journal of Archaeological Method and Theory* 15(1), 112–131.

Högberg, Anders (2018) Approaches to children's knapping in lithic technology studies. *Revista de Arqueologia* 31(2), 58–74.

Högberg, Anders, and Peter Gärdenfors (2015) Children, teaching and the evolution of humankind. *Childhood in the Past: An International Journal* 8(2), 113–121.

Horvath, Gabor, Etelka Farkas, Ildiko Boncz, Miklos Blaho and Gyorgy Kriska (2012) Cavemen were better at depicting quadruped walking than modern artists: erroneous walking illustrations in the fine arts from prehistory to today. *PLoS ONE* 7(12), e49786. doi:10.1371/journal.pone.0049786.

Hosfield, R. (2016) Walking in a winter wonderland? Strategies for Early and Middle Pleistocene survival in Midlatitude Europe. *Current Anthropology* 57(5), 653–683.

Hovers, Erella, Yoel Rak, Ron Lavi, and William H. Kimbel (1995) Hominid remains from Amud Cave in the context of the Levantine Middle Paleolithic. *Paléorient* 21(2), 47–61.

Howell, Nancy (2010) *Life Histories of the Dobe !Kung. Food, Fatness, and Well-Being Over the Life Span*. Berkeley, University of California Press.

Hrdy, Sarah Blaffer (2011) *Mothers and Others: The Evolutionary Origins of Mutual Understanding*. Cambridge, MA, Belknap Press.

Hublin, Jean-Jacques, Fred Spoor, Marc Braun, Frans Zonneveld, and Silvana Condemi (1996) A late Neanderthal associated with Upper Palaeolithic artefacts. *Nature* 381(6579), 224–226.

Hublin, Jean-Jaques, Simon Neubauer, and Philipp Gunz (2015) Brain ontogeny and life history in Pleistocene hominins. *Philosophical transactions of the Royal Society of London. Series B: Biological Sciences* 370(1663), 20140062.

Hublin, Jean-Jacques, Abdelouahed Ben-Ncer, Shara E. Bailey, Sarah E. Freidline, Simon Neubauer, Matthew M. Skinner, Inga Bergmann, Adeline Le Cabec, Stefano Benazzi, Katerina Harvati, and Philipp Gunz (2017) New Fossils From Jebel Irhoud, Morocco and the Pan-African Origin of *Homo sapiens*. *Nature* 546(7657), 289–292. DOI: 10.1038/nature22336.

Huffman, O. Frank (2001) Geologic context and age of the Perning/Mojokerto *Homo erectus*, East Java. *Journal of Human Evolution* 40(4), 353–362.

Humphrey, Louise T. (2010) Weaning behaviour in human evolution. *Seminars in Cell and Developmental Biology* 21(4), 453–461.

Humphrey, Louise T., M. Christopher Dean, Teresa E. Jeffries, and Malcolm Penn (2008) Unlocking evidence of early diet from tooth enamel. *Proceedings of the National Academy of Sciences* 105(19), 6834–6839.

Huntley, Katherine V. (2010) Identifying children's graffiti in Roman Campania: a developmental psychological approach. In Baird, Jennifer and Claire Taylor (eds) *Ancient Graffiti in Context*, 69–89. London, Routledge.

Huntley, Katherine V. (2016) The writing on the wall: age, agency, and material culture in Roman Campania. In Laes, Christian and Ville Vuolanto (eds) *Children and Everyday Life in the Roman and Late Antique World*, 137–154. London, Ashgate.

Huntley, Katherine V. (2018) Children's Graffiti in Roman Pompeii and Herculaneum. In Crawford, Sally, Dawn M. Hadley, and Gillian Shepherd (eds) *The Oxford Handbook of the Archaeology of Childhood*, 376–387. Oxford, Oxford University Press. DOI: 10.1093/oxfordhb/9780199670697.013.20.

Hurcombe, Linda M. (2014) *Perishable Material Culture in Prehistory: Investigating the Missing Majority*. New York, Routledge.

Huyge, Dirk (1991) The 'Venus' of Laussel in the light of ethnomusicology. *Archaeologie in Vlaanderen* 1, 11–18.

Hyodo, Masayuki, Naotune Watanabe, Wahyu Sunata, Eko Edi Susanto, and Hendro Wahyono (1993) Magnetostratigraphy of hominid fossil bearing formations in Sangiran and Mojokerto, Java. *Anthropological Science* 101(2), 157–186.

Hyodo, Masayuki (1998) The Sangiran geomagnetic excursion and its chronological contribution to the Quaternary geology in Java. In Simanjuntak, Truman, David Bulbeck, Bagyo Prasetyo, and Retno Handini (eds) *Sangiran: Man, Culture and Environment in Pleistocene, Solo, Indonesia, September, 1998*, 320–335. The National Research Centre of Archaeology, Jakarta, Indonesia.

Hyodo, Masayuki, Hideo Nakaya, Atsushi Urabe, Haruo Saegusa, Xue Shunrong, Yin Jiyun, and Ji Xuepin (2002) Paleomagnetic dates of hominid remains from Yuanmou, China, and other Asian sites. *Journal of Human Evolution* 43(1), 27–41.

Ibáñez, Juan José, Jesús Salius, Ignacio Clemente-Conte, and Narcís Soler (2015) Use and Sonority of a 23,000-Year-Old Bone Aerophone from Davant Pau Cave (NE of the Iberian Peninsula). *Current Anthropology* 56(2), 282–289.

Ingold, Tim (1993) The temporality of the landscape. *World Archaeology* 25(2), 152–174. DOI: 10.1080/00438243.1993.9980235.

Ingold, Tim (2000) *The perception of the environment*. London, Routledge.
Irish, Joel D., Bodil Bratlund, Romuald Schild, Else Kolstrup, Halina Królik, Dagmara Mańka, and Tomasz Boroń (2008) A late Magdalenian perinatal human skeleton from Wilczyce, Poland. *Journal of Human Evolution* 55(4), 736–740.
Isler, Karin, and Carel P. van Schaik (2012) Allomaternal care, life history and brain size evolution in mammals. *Journal of Human Evolution* 63(1), 52–63.
Isler, Karin, and Carel P. van Schaik (2014) How humans evolved large brains: Comparative evidence. *Evolutionary Anthropology* 23(2), 65–75.
Jacobi, Roger M., and Thomas F.G. Higham (2008) The 'Red Lady' ages gracefully: new ultrafiltration AMS determinations from Paviland. *Journal of Human Evolution* 55(5), 898–907.
Jalbert, Catherine L. (2011) A Lesson in Stone: Examining Patterns of Lithic Resources Use and Craft-learning in the Minas Basin Region of Nova Scotia. Masters thesis, Memorial University of Newfoundland.
Janssens, Luc, Liane Giemsch, Ralf Schmitz, Martin Street, Stefan Van Dongen, and Philippe Crombé (2018) A new look at an old dog: Bonn-Oberkassel reconsidered. *Journal of Archaeological Science* 92, 126–138.
Jazwa, Christopher S., Geoffrey M. Smith, Richard L. Rosencrance, Daron G. Duke, and Dan Stueber (2021) Reassessing the radiocarbon date from the Buhl burial from South-Central Idaho and its relevance to the Western Stemmed Tradition-Clovis debate in the Intermountain West. *American Antiquity* 86(1), 173–82.
Jodry, Margaret A., and Douglas W. Owsley (2014) A new look at the double burial from Horn Shelter No. 2. In Owsley, Douglas W., and Richard L. Jantz (eds) *Kennewick Man: The Scientific Investigation of an Ancient American Skeleton*, 549–604. College Station, Texas A&M University Press.
Johansen, Lykke and Dick Stapert (2004) *Oldeholtwolde. A Hamburgian Family Encampment around a Hearth*. Exton, PA, A.A. Balkema Publishers.
Johansen, Lykke and Dick Stapert (2008) Stone Age kids and their stones. In Sørensen, Mikkel and Pierre Desrosiers (eds) *Technology in Archaeology: Proceedings of the SILA Workshop* (Volume 14), 15–39. Copenhagen, The National Museum of Denmark.
Johanson, Donald C., and Maurice Taieb (1976) Plio-pleistocene hominid discoveries in Hadar, Ethiopia. *Nature* 260(5549), 293–297.
Johanson, Donald C., C. Owen Lovejoy, William H. Kimbel, Tim D. White, Steven C. Ward, Michael E. Bush, Bruce M. Latimer, and Yves Coppens (1982a) Morphology of the Pliocene partial hominid skeleton (AL 288-1) from the Hadar formation, Ethiopia. *American Journal of Physical Anthropology* 57(4), 403–451.
Johanson, Donald C., Tim D. White, and Yves Coppens (1982b) Dental remains from the Hadar Formation, Ethiopia: 1974–1977 collections. *American Journal of Physical Anthropology* 57(4), 545–603.
Johnson, Mathew (2020) *Archaeological Theory: An Introduction*, 3rd Edition. Oxford, Wiley-Blackwell.
Jonaitis, Aldona (2007) Art, adolescence, and testosterone in the Paleolithic. *The Quarterly Review of Biology* 82(2), 127–130.
Joyce, Rosemary A. (2000) Girling the girl and boying the boy: the production of adulthood in ancient Mesoamerica. *World Archaeology* 31(3), 473–483.
Joyce, Rosemary A., Linda Cordell, and Judith Habicht-Mauche (2012) Thinking about pottery production as community practice. In Cordell, Linda S., and Judith A. Habicht-Mauche (eds) *Potters and Communities of Practice: Glaze Paint and Polychrome Pottery in the American Southwest, AD 1250–1700*, 149–154. Anthropological Papers of the University of Arizona, University of Arizona Press.
Kahlenberg, Sonya M., and Richard W. Wrangham (2010) Sex differences in chimpanzees' use of sticks as play objects resemble those of children. *Current Biology* 20(24), R1067–R1068.
Kamp, Kathryn A. (2001a) Prehistoric children working and playing: a southwestern case study in learning ceramics. *Journal of Anthropological Research* 57(4), 427–450.

Kamp, Kathryn A. (2001b) Where have all the children gone? The archaeology of childhood. *Journal of Archaeological Method and Theory* 8(1), 1–34.

Kamp, Kathryn A. (2006) Dominant discourses; lived experiences: studying the archaeology of children and childhood. *Archaeological Papers of the American Anthropological Association* 15(1), 115–122.

Kaplan, Hillard S. (2002) Human life histories. In Pagel, Mark D. (ed.) *Encyclopedia of evolution (Vol. 2)*, 627–631. Oxford, Oxford University Press.

Karlin, Claudine and Michele Julien (1994) Prehistoric technology: a cognitive science? In Renfrew, Colin Autor and Ezra B.W. Zubrow (eds) *The Ancient Mind: Elements of Cognitive Archaeology*, 152–164. Cambridge, Cambridge University Press.

Keeley, Lawrence H. (1980) *Experimental Determination of Stone Tool Uses: A Microwear Analysis*. Chicago, University of Chicago Press.

Keller, Charles and Janet Dixon Keller (1996) *Cognition and Tool Use: The Blacksmith at Work*. Cambridge, Cambridge University Press.

Kelley, Jay, and Tanya M. Smith (2003) Age at first molar emergence in early Miocene *Afropithecus turkanensis* and life-history evolution in the Hominoidea. *Journal of Human Evolution* 44(3), 307–329.

Kellogg, Rhoda (1969) *Analyzing Children's Art*. Palo Alto, National Press Books.

Kerry, Kristopher W., and Donald O. Henry (2000) Conceptual domains, competence, and chaîne opératoire in the Levantine Mousterian. In Stager, Laurence E. and Joseph A. Greene (eds) *The Archaeology of Jordan and Beyond: Essays in Honor of James A. Sauer*, 238–254. Cambridge, Semitic Museum of Harvard University.

Khundrakpam, Budhachandra S., John D. Lewis, Lu Zhao, François Chouinard-Decorte, Alan C. Evans (2016) Brain connectivity in normally developing children and adolescents. *NeuroImage* 134, 192–203.

Kim, Cheong Bin, Jeong Yul Kim, Kyung Soo Kim, and Hyoun Soo Lim (2010) New age constraints for hominid footprints found on Jeju Island, South Korea. *Journal of Archaeological Science* 37(12), 3338–3343.

Kim, Jeong Yul, Kyung Soo Kim, Chang Zin Lee, and Jong Deock Lim (2004) Occurrence of hominid and other vertebrate footprints of Jeju Island, Korea, In Kim, Jeong Yul, Kyung Soo Kim, S.I. Park, and M.-K. Shin (eds) *Proceedings of International Symposium on the Quaternary Footprints of Hominids and Other Vertebrates*, 1–26. Namjejugun, Jeju, Korea.

Kim, Kyung Soo, Jeong Yul Kim, Sam Hyang Kim, Chang Zin Lee, and Jeong Deock Lim (2009) Preliminary report on hominid and other vertebrate footprints from the late Quaternary strata of Jeju Island, Korea. *Ichnos* 16(1–2), 1–11.

Kim, Peter S., James E. Coxworth, and Kristen Hawkes (2012) Increased longevity evolves from grandmothering. *Proceedings of the Royal Society B: Biological Sciences* 279(1749), 4880–4884. doi:10.1098/rspb.2012.1751.

Kirrilov, I., and Anatoli P. Derev'anko (1998) The Paleolithic of the Trans-Baikal. In Derev'anko, Anatoli P. (ed.) *The Paleolithic of Siberia: New Discoveries and Interpretations*, 137–273. Urbana, University of Illinois Press.

Khaleeq, Natasha (2016) Iceman Ötzi rocks the bear-fur hat and goat-leather coat look. *New Scientist* 3088, published 27 August 2016. https://www.newscientist.com/article/2101621-iceman-otzi-rocks-the-bear-fur-hat-and-goat-leather-coat-look/#ixzz6YRRBH6zU.

Klíma, Bohuslav (1991) Das paläolithische Massengrab von Předmostí, Versuch einer Rekonstruktion. *Quartär: Jahrbuch für Erforschung des Eiszeitalters und der Steinzeit* 41, 187–194.

Knappett, Carl (2004) The affordances of things: a post-Gibsonian perspective on the relationality of mind and matter. In DeMarrais, Elizabeth, Chris Gosden and Colin Renfrew (eds) *Rethinking Materiality: The Engagement of Mind with the Material World*, 43–51. Cambridge, McDonald Institute Monographs.

Koehler, Nicole, Leigh W. Simmons and Gillian Rhodes (2004) How well does second-to-fourth digit ratio in hands correlate with other indications of masculinity in males? *Proceedings of the Royal Society of London B* 271(Supplement 5), S296–S298.

Kohn, Marek and Steven Mithen (1999) Handaxes: products of sexual selection? *Antiquity* 73, 518–526.

Kohut, Betsy, M. (2011) Buried with children: reinterpreting Ancient Maya 'Toys'. *Childhood in the Past* 4(1), 146–161.

Konner, Melvin (2010) *Evolution of Childhood: Relationships, Emotion, Mind.* Cambridge, MA, Belknap Press of Harvard University Press.

Kosut, Mary (2015) Tattoos and body modification. *International Encyclopedia of the Social & Behavioral Sciences*, Second Edition 24, 32–38.

Králik, Miroslav, Vladimir Novotny and Martin Oliva (2002) Fingerprint on the Venus of Dolní Věstonice I. *Anthropologie* 40(2), 107–113.

Kramer, Karen L., and Erik Otárola-Castillo (2015) When mothers need others: the impact of hominin life history evolution on cooperative breeding. *Journal of Human Evolution* 84, 16–24.

Krause, Johannes, Qiaomei Fu, Jeffrey M. Good, Bence Viola, Michael V. Shunkov, Anatoli P. Derevianko, and Svante Pääbo (2010) The complete mitochondrial DNA genome of an unknown hominin from southern Siberia. *Nature* 464(7290), 894–897 (Suppl.).

Kretschmer, Inga (2015) Demographische Untersuchungen zu Bevölkerungsdichten, Mobilität und Landnutzung im späten Jungpaläolithikum. *Kölner Studien zur Prähistorischen Archäologie 6.* Verlag Marie Leidorf.

Krovitz, Gail E., Jennifer L. Thompson, and Andrew J. Nelson (2003) Hominid growth and development from australopithecines to Middle Pleistocene *Homo.* In Thompson, Jennifer L., Gail E. Krovitz, and Andrew J. Nelson (eds) *Patterns of Growth and Development in the Genus Homo (Volume 37)*, 271–294. Cambridge, Cambridge University Press.

Kubicka, Anna Maria, Rebecca Wragg-Sykes, April Nowell and Emma Nelson (forthcoming) Neanderthal sexual behaviour. In Shackelford, Todd K. (ed.) *The Cambridge Handbook of Evolutionary Perspectives on Sexual Psychology, Volume 4*, Cambridge, Cambridge University Press.

Kuhlwilm, Martin, and Cedric Boeckx (2019) A catalog of single nucleotide changes distinguishing modern humans from archaic hominins. *Scientific Reports* 9, 8463. https://doi.org/10.1038/s41598-019-44877-x.

Kuhn, Steven L., and Mary C. Stiner (2006) What's a mother to do? The division of labor among Neandertals and modern humans in Eurasia. *Current Anthropology* 47(6), 953–981.

Kvavadze, Eliso, Ofer Bar-Yosef, Anna Belfer-Cohen, Elisabetta Boaretto, Nino Jakeli, Zinovi Matskevich, and Tengiz Meshveliani (2009) 30,000 year-old wild flax fiber. *Science* 325(5946), 1359.

LaCruz, Rodrigo S., Fernando Ramirez Rozzi, and Timothy G. Bromage (2005) Dental enamel hypoplasia, age at death, and weaning in the Taung child. *South African Journal of Science* 101(11), 567–569.

Laland, Kevin N., and Kim Sterelny (2006) Perspective: Seven Reasons (Not) to Neglect Niche Construction. *Evolution* 60(9), 1751–1762.

Laland Kevin N., Tobias Uller, Marcus W. Feldman, Kim Sterelny, Gerd B. Müller, Armin Moczek, Eva Jablonka, and John Odling-Smee (2015) The extended evolutionary synthesis: its structure, assumptions and predictions. *Proceedings of the Royal Society B: Biological Sciences* 282(1813), 20151019.

Lally, Mike, and Traci Ardren (2009) Little artefacts: rethinking the constitution of the archaeological infant. *Childhood in the Past* 1(1), 62–77.

Lalueza-Fox, Carles (1995) Restos humanos del nivel Solutrense de la Cueva de Nerja (Málaga). *Zephyrus* 48, 289–297.

Lalueza-Fox, Carles, Antonio Rosas, Almudena Estalrrich, Elena Gigli, Paula F. Campos, Antonio García-Tabernero, Samuel García-Vargas, Federico Sánchez-Quinto, Oscar Ramírez, Sergi Civit, Markus Bastir, Rosa Huguet, David Santamaría, M. Thomas P. Gilbert, Eske Willerslev, and Marco de la Rasilla (2011) Genetic evidence for patrilocal mating behavior among Neandertal groups. *Proceedings of the National Academy of Sciences* 108(1), 250–253.

Lancaster, Jane B. (1986) Human adolescence and reproduction: an evolutionary perspective. In Lancaster, Jane B., and Beatrix A. Hamberg (eds) *School-age Pregnancy and Parenthood: Biosocial Dimensions*, 17–37. New Brunswick, Aldine de Gruyter.

Lancy, David F. (2010) Learning 'from nobody': the limited role of teaching in folk models of children's development. *Childhood in the Past* 3(1), 79–106. doi: 10.1179/cip.2010.3.1.79.

Lancy, David F. (2017) *Homo faber juvenalis*: a multidisciplinary survey of children as tool makers/users. *Childhood in the Past* 10(1), 72–90.

Langley, Michelle (2018) Magdalenian children: projectile points, portable art and playthings. *Oxford Journal of Archaeology* 37(1), 3–24.

Langley, Michelle L. (2020) Space to play: identifying children's sites in the Pleistocene archaeological record. *Evolutionary Human Sciences* 2(e41), 1–16. doi:10.1017/ehs.2020.29.

Laudicina, Natalie M., Frankee Rodriguez, Jeremy M. DeSilva (2019) Reconstructing birth in *Australopithecus sediba*. *PLoS ONE* 14(9), e0221871. https://doi.org/10.1371/journal.pone.0221871.

Lave, Jean, and Etienne Wenger (1991) *Situated Learning: Legitimate Peripheral Participation*. Cambridge, University of Cambridge Press.

Lawson, Graeme, and Francesco d'Errico (2002) Microscopic, experimental and theoretical reassessment of Upper Paleolithic bird-bone pipes from Istiritz, France: ergonomics of design, systems of notation and the origins of musical traditions. In Hickman, Ellen, and Ricardo Eichman (eds) *The Archaeology of Early Sound: Origin and Organization*, 119–142. 2nd Symposium of the Study Group on Music Archaeology. Berlin, Orient-Archäologie 12.

Layton, Robert, and Sean O'Hara (2010) Human social evolution: a comparison of hunter-gatherer and chimpanzee social organization. In Dunbar, Robin, Clive Gamble, and John Gowlett (eds) *Social Brain, Distributed Mind*, 1–27. British Academy Scholarship Online.

Lbova, Lyudmila, V., Darya Kozhevnikova, Pavel V. Volkov (2013) Musical instruments in Siberia (early stage of the Upper Paleolithic). In *Pleistocene Art of the World: Proceedings of the IFRAO Congress (September 2010)*, 1899–1904. Tarasçon-Sur-Ariège, Société Préhistorique Ariège-Pyrénées.

Lbova, Lyudmila V., and Pavel V. Volkov (2015) Microscopic analysis of the anthropomorphic figurines from Malta (Technology of Formation, Detalization and Decoration). *Stratum Plus Journal* 1, 161–168.

Lbova, Lyudmila V., and Pavel V. Volkov (2017) Pigment decoration of Palaeolithic anthropomorphous figurines from Siberia. *Rock Art Research* 34(2), 169–178.

Lbova, Lyudmila V., Pavel V. Volkov, E.N. Bocharova, Vasiliy S. Kovalev, and N.A. Khaykunova (2017) The techniques of modeling and decorating Upper Paleolithic anthropomorphic figurines from Malta, Eastern Siberia. *Archaeology, Ethnology & Anthropology of Eurasia* 45(3), 48–55.

Leigh, Steven R. (2004) Brain growth, life history, and cognition in primate and human evolution. *American Journal of Primatology* 62(3), 139–164.

Leigh, Steven R. (2012) Brain size growth and life history in human evolution. *Evolutionary Biology* 39(4), 587–599.

Lepper, Bradley T. (2014) The people who peopled America. In Owsley, Douglas W., and Richard L. Jantz (eds) *Kennewick Man: The Scientific Investigation of an Ancient American Skeleton*. College Station, Texas A&M University Press.

Leroi-Gourhan, André (1967) *Treasures of Prehistoric Art*. New York, Abrams.

Leroi-Gourhan, André and Michelson, Annette (1986) The hands of Gargas: towards a general Study. *October* 37: 19–34.

Lew-Levy, Sheina, Rachel Reckin, Noa Lavi, Jurgi Cristóbal-Azkarate, and Kate Ellis-Davies (2017) How do hunter–gatherer children learn subsistence skills? A meta-ethnographic review. *Human Nature* 28(4), 367–394.

Lew-Levy, Sheina, Noa Lavi, Rachel Reckin, Jurgi Cristóbal-Azkarate and Kate Ellis-Davies (2018) How do hunter-gatherer children learn social and gender norms? A meta-ethnographic review. *Cross-Cultural Research* 52(2), 213–255.

Lewis, Jerome (2016) Play, music, and taboo in the reproduction of an egalitarian society. In Terashima, Hideaki and Barry S. Hewlett (eds) *Social Learning and Innovation in Contemporary Hunter-Gatherers*, 147–158. Tokyo, Springer Japan.

Lewis, Mary E. (2007) *The Bioarchaeology of Children: Perspectives from Biological and Forensic Anthropology*. Cambridge, Cambridge University Press.

Lewis, Mary E. (2017) *Paleopathology of Children: Identification of Pathological Conditions in the Human Skeletal Remains of Non-Adults*. London, Academic Press.

Lewis, Mary, Fiona Shapland, and Rebecca Watts (2016) On the threshold of adulthood: A new approach for the use of maturation indicators to assess puberty in adolescents from Medieval England. *American Journal of Human Biology* 28(1), 48–56.

Lewontin, Richard C. (1983) Gene, organism, and environment. In Bendall, Derek S. (ed.) *Evolution from molecules to men*, 273–285. Cambridge, Cambridge University Press.

Lillehammer, Grete (1989) A child is born: the child's world in an archaeological perspective. *Norwegian Archaeological Review* 22(2), 89–105.

Lillehammer, Grete (2000) The world of children. In Sofaer Derevenski, Joanna (ed.) *Children and Material Cultures*, 17–26. London, Routledge.

Lillehammer, Grete (2011) The children in the bog. In Lally, Mike, and Alison Moore (eds) *(Re)Thinking the Little Ancestor: New Perspectives on the Archaeology of Infancy and Childhood*, 47–62. British Archaeological Reports S2271. Oxford, Archaeopress.

Liu, Xiling, Mehmet Somel, Lin Tang, Zheng Yan, Xi Jiang, Song Guo, Yuan Yuan, Liu He, Anna Oleksiak, Yan Zhang, Na Li, Yuhui Hu, Wei Chen, Zilong qiu, Svante Pääbo, and Philipp Khaitovich (2012) Extension of cortical synaptic development distinguishes humans from chimpanzees and macaques. *Genome Research* 22(4), 611–622.

Lockley, Martin, Gordon Roberts, and Jeong Yul Kim (2008) In the footprints of our ancestors: an overview of the hominid track record. *Ichnos* 15(3–4), 106–125. 10.1080/10420940802467835.

Logeswaran, Nidhya and Joydeep Bhattacharya (2009) Crossmodal transfer of emotion by music. *Neuroscience Letters* 455(2), 129–133. https://doi.org/10.1016/j.neulet.2009.03.044.

Lohse, Jon (2011) Step by step. *Lithic Technology* 36(2), 97–108.

Lombard, Marlize (2015) Hunting and hunting technologies as proxy for teaching and learning during the stone age of Southern Africa. *Cambridge archaeological Journal* 25(4), 877–887.

López-Ortega, Esther, Juan Ignacio Morales, Andreu Ollé, and Xosé Pedro Rodríguez-Álvarez (2020) Avoiding the blue and black/white and gold argument: an automated colour reference system applied to lithic refit processes. *Journal of Archaeological Method Theory* 27(2), 245–270. https://doi.org/10.1007/s10816-019-09426-w.

Lorenzi, Rossella (2014) Stonehenge intricate treasures made by children. *Seeker* https://www.seeker.com/stonehenge-intricate-treasures-made-by-children-1769096325.html.

Lovejoy, C. Owen, Donald C. Johanson, and Yves Coppens (1982) Hominid lower limb bones recovered from the Hadar Formation: 1974–1977 collections. *American Journal of Physical Anthropology* 57(4), 679–700.

Lovejoy, C. Owen, Gen Suwa, Linda Spurlock, Berhane Asfaw, and Tim D. White (2009) The pelvis and femur of *Ardipithecus ramidus*: the emergence of upright walking. *Science* 326(5949), 71–71e6.

Livingstone, Margaret (2014) *Vision and Art: The Biology of Seeing*. New York, Harry N. Abrams.

Lyons, Derek E., Andrew G. Young, and Frank C. Keil (2007) The hidden structure of overimitation. *Proceedings of the National Academy of Sciences* 104(50), 19751–19756. https://doi.org/10.1073/pnas.0704452104.

Macchiarelli, Roberto, Luca Bondioli, André Debénath, Arnaud Mazurier, Jean-François Tournepiche, Wendy Birch, and M. Christopher Dean (2006) How Neanderthal molar teeth grew. *Nature* 444(7120), 748–751.

MacDonald, Douglas H., and Barry S. Hewlett (1999) Reproductive interests and forager mobility. *Current Anthropology* 40(4), 501–523.

MacDonald, Katharine (2007) Cross-cultural comparison of learning in human hunting. *Human Nature* 18(4), 386–402.

Madre-Dupouy, Martine (1992) L'enfant du Roc-de-Marsal, Étude Analytique et Comparative. *Cahiers de Paléo- anthropologie*. Paris, Centre National de la Recherche Scientifique.

Maestripieri, Dario (2005) Early experience affects the intergenerational transmission of infant abuse in rhesus monkeys. *Proceedings of the National Academy of Sciences* 102(27), 9726–9729. DOI: 10.1073/pnas.0504122102O.

Marfart, Bertrand, Gaspard Guipert, Camille Alliez-Philip, and Jean-Jacques Brau (2007) Virtual reconstitution and new palaeopathological study of the Magdalenian child's skull of Rochereil. *Comptes Rendus Palevol* 6(8), 569–579.

Maier, Andreas, and Andreas Zimmerman (2017) Populations headed south? The Gravettian from a palaeodemographic point of view. *Antiquity* 91(357), 573–588.

Malafouris, Lambros (2013) *How Things Shape the Mind: A Theory of Material Engagement*. Cambridge, MIT Press.

Mallegni, Francesco (1992) Quelques restes humains immatures, des niveaux moustériens de la grotte du Fossellone (Monte Circeo, Italie): Fossellone 3 (Olim Circeo IV). *Bulletins et Mémoires de la Société d'Anthropologie de Paris* 4(1), 21–32.

Mallegni, Francesco, and R. Parenti (1973) Studio antro-pologico di uno scheletro giovanile d'epoca gravettiana raccolto nella grotta Paglicci (Rignano Garganico). *Rivista di Antropologia* 58, 317–342.

Mallegni, Francesco, and Annamaria Ronchitelli (1987) Découverte d'une mandibule néander-talienne à l'abri du Molare près de Scario (Salerno-Italie): observations stratigraphiques et palethnologiques, étude anthropologique. *L'Anthropologie* 91(1), 163–173.

Mallegni, Francesco, and Annamaria Ronchitelli (1989) Deciduous teeth of the Neandertal mandible from molare shelter, near Scario (Salerno, Italy). *American Journal of Physical Anthropology* 79(4), 475–482.

Mallegni, Francesco, and Erik Trinkaus (1997) A reconsideration of the Archi 1 Neandertal mandible. *Journal of Human Evolution* 33(6), 651–668.

Mann, Alan E. (1975) *Some Paleodemographic Aspects of the South African Australopithecines* (No. 1). Philadelphia, University of Pennsylvania publications in Anthropology.

Manning, John T., Diane Scutt, James Wilson, and D. Iwan Lewis-Jones (1998) The ratio of 2nd to 4th digit length: a predictor of sperm numbers and concentrations of testosterone, luteinizing hormone and estrogen. *Human Reproduction* 13(11), 3000–3004.

Manning, John T., Antony Stewart, Peter E. Bundred, and Robert L. Trivers (2004) Sex and ethnic differences in 2nd to 4th digit ratio of children. *Early Human Development* 80(2), 161–168.

Manolis, Sotiris, Leslie Aiello, R. Henessy, and Nina Kyparissi-Apostolika (2000) The Middle Palaeolithic footprints from Theopetra Cave (Thessaly, Greece), 87–93. In Kyparissi-Apostolika, Nina (ed.) *Theopetra Cave. Twelve Years of Excavation and Research 1987-1998*. Athens, Greek Ministry of Culture and Institute for Aegean Prehistory.

Marin, Manuela M., and Joydeep Bhattacharya (2009) Music induced emotions: some current issues and cross-modal comparisons. In Hermida, Joao, and Mariana Ferrero (eds) *Music Education*, 1–38. Hauppauge, NY, Nova Science.

Marlowe, Frank W. (2005) Hunter–gatherers and human evolution. *Evolutionary Anthropology: Issues, News, and Reviews* 14(2), 54–67.

Marom, Anat, James S. McCullagh, Thomas F. Higham, Andrey A. Sinitsyn, and Robert E. Hedges (2012) Single amino acid radiocarbon dating of Upper Paleolithic modern humans. *Proceedings of the National Academy of Sciences* 109(18), 6878–6881.

Marshack, Alexander (1975) Exploring the mind of Ice Age man. *National Geographic* 147(1), 64–89.

Masao, Fidelis T., Elgidius B. Ichumbaki, Marco Cherin, Angelo Barili, Giovanni Boschian, Dawid A. Iurino, Sofia Menconero, Jacopo Moggi-Cecchi, and Giorgio Manzi (2016) New footprints from Laetoli (Tanzania) provide evidence for marked body size variation in early hominins. *Elife* 5, e19568.

Matić, Uroš (2016) (De)queering Hatshepsut: binary bind in archaeology of Egypt and kingship beyond the corporeal. *Journal of Archaeological Method and Theory* 23(3), 810–831.

Maureille, Bruno (2002) Lost Neanderthal neonate found. *Nature* 419(6902), 33–34.

Maureille, Bruno, and Dominique Bar (1999) The premaxilla in Neandertal and early modern children: ontogeny and morphology. *Journal of Human Evolution* 37(2), 137–152.

Maureille, Bruno, and Marie Soressi (2000) A propos de la position chronostratigraphique de l'enfant du Pech-de-l'Azé I (commune de Carsac, Dordogne): la résurrection du fantôme/On the chrono-stratigraphic position of the Pech-de-l'Azé I child (Carsac, Dordogne): the ghost resurrection. *PALEO. Revue d'Archéologie Préhistorique* 12(1), 339–352.

Maureille, Bruno, María Dolores Garralda, Stéphane Madelaine, Alain Turq, and Bernard Vandermeersch (2011) Le plus ancien enfant d'Aquitaine: Combe-grenal 31 (Domme, France). *PALEO. Revue d'archéologie préhistorique* 21, 189–202.

Mauss, Marcel (1934) Les techniques du corps. *Journal de Psychologie* 32(3-4), 271-293.

McDougall, Ian, Francis H. Brown, and John G. Fleagle (2005) Stratigraphic placement and age of modern humans from Kibish, Ethiopia. *Nature* 433(7027), 733–736.

McKie, Robin (2020) Take a tusk, drill holes, weave a rope – and change the course of history. The Guardian https://www.theguardian.com/science/2020/aug/01/mammoth-tusk-drill-holes-make-rope-change-history-stone-age.

McKell, Sheila M. (1993) An axe to grind: more ripping yarns from Australian prehistory. In du Cros, Hilary, and Laurajane Smith (eds) *Women in Archaeology: A Feminist Critique*, 115–120. Canberra, Australian National University.

McLaren, Duncan, Daryl Fedje, Angela Dyck, Quentin Mackie, Alisha Gauvreau, and Jenny Cohen (2018) Terminal Pleistocene epoch human footprints from the Pacific coast of Canada. *PLoS ONE* 13(3), e0193522.

Medvedev, G.I. (1998) Art from central Siberian sites. In Derev'anko, Anatoliy P. (ed.) *The Paleolithic of Siberia: New Discoveries and Interpretations*, 132–136. Urbana, University of Illinois Press.

Medina-Alcaide, Mª Ángeles, Diego Garate-Maidagan, Aitor Ruiz-Redondo, and José Luis Sanchidrián-Torti (2018) Beyond art: the internal archaeological context in Paleolithic decorated caves. *Journal of Anthropological Archaeology* 49, 114–128.

Medina-Alcaide, Mª Ángeles, Luisa Mª Cabalín, Javier Laserna, José L. Sanchidrián, Antonio J. Torres, Iñaki Intxaurbe, Sonia Cosano, and Antonio Romero (2019) Multianalytical and multiproxy approach to the characterization of a Paleolithic lamp. An example in Nerja Cave (Southern Iberian Peninsula). *Journal of Archaeological Science: Reports* 28, 102021.

Mellars, Paul, and Jennifer C. French (2011) Tenfold population increase in western Europe at the Neandertal–to–modern human transition. *Science* 333(6042), 623–627. DOI: 10.1126/science.1206930.

Meltzer, David J. (1997) On the Pleistocene antiquity of Monte Verde, southern Chile. *American Antiquity* 62(4), 659–663.

Mercier, Norbert, Loïc Martin, Sebastian Kreutzer, Virginie Moineau, and Dominique Cliquet (2019) Dating the Palaeolithic footprints of 'Le Rozel' (Normandy, France). *Quaternary Geochronology* 49, 271–277.

Mesoudi, Alex, and Alex Thornton (2018) What is cumulative cultural evolution? *Proceedings of the Royal Society B* 285(1880), 20180712.

Mietto, Paolo, Marco Avanzinim, and Giuseppe Rolandim (2003) Human footprints in Pleistocene volcanic ash. *Nature* 422(6928), 133.

Milner, Emily J., Michael Gurven, Hillard Kaplan, and Steven J.C. Gaulin (2014) Sex difference in travel is concentrated in adolescence and tracks reproductive interests. *Proceedings of the Royal Society B: Biological Sciences* 281(1796), 20141476.

Minugh-Purvis, Nancy (1988) *Patterns of Craniofacial Growth and Development in Upper Pleistocene Hominids*. Ph.D. Dissertation, University of Pennsylvania.

Mittnik Alissa, Chuan-Chao Wang, Jirí Svoboda, and Johannes Krause (2016) A molecular approach to the sexing of the triple burial at the Upper Paleolithic Site of Dolní Věstonice. *PLoS ONE* 11(10), e0163019. https://doi-org.ezproxy.library.uvic.ca/10.1371/journal.pone.0163019.

Mohen, Jean-Pierre (2002) *Prehistoric Art: The Mythical Birth of Humanity*. Paris, Éditions Pierre Terrail.

Moore, Deborah (2015) The teacher doesn't know what it is, but she knows where we are: young children's secret places in early childhood outdoor environments. *International Journal of Play* 4(1), 20–31.

Morey, Darcy F., and Rujana Jeger (2015) Paleolithic dogs: why sustained domestication then? *Journal of Archaeological Science* 3, 420–428. https://doi.org/10.1016/j.jasrep.2015.06.031.

Morgan, Thomas J.H., Natalie T. Uomini, Luke E. Rendell, Laura Chouinard-Thuly, Sally E. Street, Hannah Lewis, Catherine P. Cross, C. Evans, R. Kearney, I. Torre, A. Whiten, and Kevin N. Laland (2015) Experimental evidence for the co-evolution of hominin tool-making teaching and language. *Nature Communications* 6, 7029. 10.1038/ncomms7029.

Morley, Iain (2013) *The Prehistory of Music: Human Evolution, Archaeology and the Origins of Musicality*. Oxford, Oxford University Press. https://doi.org/10.1093/acprof:osobl/9780199234080.001.0001.

Morrow, Toby M. (1996) Lithic refitting and archaeological site formation processes: a case study from the Twin Ditch site, Greene County, Illinois. In Odell, George H. (ed.) *Stone Tools: Theoretical Insights into Human Prehistory*, 345–376. New York, London, Plenum.

Morton, Helen (1996) *Becoming Tongan: An Ethnography of Childhood*. Honolulu, University of Hawai'i Press.

Moure, A., C. Gonzalez Sainz, F. Bernaldo de Quiros, and Victoria Cabrera Valdés (1996) Dataciones absolutas de pigmentos en cuevas cantábricas: Altamira, El Castillo, Chimeneas y Las Monedas. In Moure Romanillo, A. (ed.) *'El Hombre Fósil' 80 Años Después*, 259–324. Santander, Universidad de Cantabria, Servicio de Publicaciones.

Müller, Gerd B. (2017) Why an extended evolutionary synthesis is necessary. *Interface Focus* 7(5), 20170015. http://dx.doi.org/10.1098/rsfs.2017.0015.

Munion, Ascher K., Jeanine K. Stefanucci, Ericka Rovira, Peter Squire, and Michael Hendricks (2019) Gender differences in spatial navigation: Characterizing wayfinding behaviors. *Psychonomic Bulletin & Review* 26(6), 1933–1940.

Murdock, George P., and Caterina Provost (1973) Factors in the division of labor by sex: a cross-cultural analysis. *Ethnology* 12(2), 203–225.

Murdock, Andy (2017) Teens. OMG. What on earth is going on inside their brains to make them act so, well, like crazy teenagers? https://medicalxpress.com/news/2017-12-evolutionary-advantage-teenage-brain.html.

Murphy, Eileen (2011) Children's burial grounds in Ireland (Cilliní) and parental emotions toward infant death. *International Journal of Historical Archaeology* 15(3), 409–428.

Musgrave, Stephanie, Elizabeth Lonsdorf, David Morgan, Madison Prestipino, Laura Bernstein-Kurtycz, Roger Mundry, and Crickette Sanz (2020) Teaching varies with task complexity in wild chimpanzees. *Proceedings of the National Academy of Science* 117(2), 969–976.

Mussi, Margherita (2007) Women of the middle latitudes: the earliest peopling of Europe from a female perspective. In Roebroeks, Wil (ed.) *Guts and Brains: An Integrative Approach to the Hominin Record*, 165–184. Leiden, Leiden University Press.

Nathan, Smiti (2018) Midnight at the Oasis: past and present agricultural activities in Oman. In Gonlin, Nancy, and April Nowell (eds) *Archaeology of the Night: Life After Dark in the Ancient World*, 333–352. Boulder, University Press of Colorado.

Nava, Alessia, Alfredo Coppa, Donato Coppola, Lucia Mancini, Diego Dreossi, Franco Zanini, Federico Bernardini, Claudio Tuniz, and Luca Bondioli (2017) Virtual histological assessment of the prenatal life history and age at death of the Upper Paleolithic fetus from Ostuni (Italy). *Scientific Reports* 7, 9427.

Nava, Alessia, Federico Lugli, Matteo Romandini, Federica Badino, David Evans, Angela H. Helbling, Gregorio Oxilia, Simona Arrighi, Eugenio Bortolini, Davide Delpiano, Rossella Duches, Carla

Figus, Alessandra Livraghi, Giulia Marciani, Sara Silvestrini, Anna Cipriani, Tommaso Giovanardi, Roberta Pini, Claudio Tuniz, Federico Bernardin, Irene Dori, Alfredo Coppa, Emanuela Cristiani, Christopher Dean, Luca Bondioli, Marco Peresani, Wolfgang Müllerg, and Stefano Benazzi (2020) Early life of Neanderthals. *Proceedings of the National Academy of Sciences* 117(46), 28719–28726. DOI: 10.1073/pnas.2011765117.

Nelson, Emma C., John T. Manning, and Anthony G.M. Sinclair (2006) News: using the length of the 2nd to 4th digit ratio (2D:4D) to sex cave art hand stencils: factors to consider. *Before Farming* 1, 1–7.

Nelson, Emma C., Jason Hall, Patrick Randolph-Quinney, and Anthony Sinclair (2017) Beyond size: the potential of a geometric morphometric analysis of shape and form for the assessment of sex in hand stencils in rock art. *Journal of Archaeological Science* 78, 202–213.

Nelson, Sarah M. (2004) *Gender in Archaeology: Analyzing Power and Prestige*, 2nd Edition. Walnut Creek, AltaMira.

Neubauer, Simon, and Jean-Jacques Hublin (2012) The evolution of human brain development. *Evolutionary Biology* 39(4), 568–586.

Nespoulet, Roland, L. Chiotti, Dominique Henry-Gambier, Safia Agsous, Arnaud Lenoble, André Morala, Patricia Guillermin, and Carole Vercoutère (2006) L'occupation humain de l'abri Pataud (Les Eyzies-de-Tayac, Dordogne) il y a a 22 000 ans: problématique et résultats préliminaires des fouilles du niveau 2. *Mémoire de la Société Préhistorique Française* XLVII, 325–334.

Nowell, April (2000) The Archaeology of Mind: A Study of Symmetry and Standardization in Lithic Artifacts and Their Implications for the Evolution of the Human Mind. Unpublished doctoral dissertation. University of Pennsylvania.

Nowell, April (2006) From a Paleolithic art to Pleistocene visual cultures. *Journal of Archaeological Method and Theory* 13(4), 239–249.

Nowell, April (2010) Working memory and the speed of life. *Current Anthropology* 51(S1), S121–S133.

Nowell, April (2015a) Children, metaphorical thinking and Upper Paleolithic visual cultures. *Childhood in the Past* 8(2), 122–132.

Nowell, April (2015b) Learning to see and seeing to learn: children, communities of practice and Pleistocene visual cultures. *Cambridge Archaeology Journal* 25(4), 889–899.

Nowell, April (2016) Childhood, play and the evolution of cultural capacity in Neandertals. In Haidle, Miriam N., Nicholas J. Conard, and Michael Bolus (2011) *The Nature of Culture*, Vertebrate Paleobiology and Paleoanthropology Series, 87–97. New York, Springer.

Nowell, April (2017) Visual cultures in the Upper Paleolithic. *Cambridge Archaeological Journal* 27(4), 599–606.

Nowell, April (2018) Paleolithic soundscapes and the emotional resonance of nighttime. In Gonlin, Nancy, and April Nowell (eds) *Archaeology of the Night: Life After Dark in the Ancient World*, 27–44. Boulder, CO, University Press of Colorado.

Nowell, April (2020) Reconsidering the personhood of infants in the Gravettian. *Journal of Anthropological Research* 76(2), 232–250.

Nowell, April, and Melanie L. Chang (2009) The case against sexual selection as an explanation of handaxe morphology. *PaleoAnthropology*, 77–88.

Nowell, April, and Mark White (2010) Growing up in the Middle Pleistocene: life history strategies and their relationship to Acheulian industries. In Nowell, April, and Iain Davidson (eds) *Stone Tools and the Evolution of Human Cognition*, 67–82. Boulder, CO, University Press of Colorado.

Nowell, April, and Melanie L. Chang (2014) Science, the media, and interpretations of Upper Paleolithic figurines. *American Anthropologist* 116(3), 562–577.

Nowell, April, Cameron Walker, Carlos E. Cordova, Christopher J.H. Ames, James T. Pokines, Daniel Stueber, and Amer S.A. al-Asuliman (2016) Middle Pleistocene subsistence in the Azraq Oasis, Jordan: Protein residue and other proxies. *Journal of Archaeological Science* 73, 36–44.

Nowell, April and Jennifer French (2020) Adolescence and innovation in the European Upper Palaeolithic. *Evolutionary Human Sciences* 2(e36), 1–24.

Nowell, April, and Nancy Gonlin (2020) Affordances of the night: work after dark in the ancient world. In Edensor, Timothy, and Nick Dunn (eds) *Rethinking Darkness: Histories, Cultures and Practices*, 27–37. New York, Routledge.

Nowell, April, and Helen Kurki (2020) Moving beyond the obstetrical dilemma hypothesis: birth, weaning and infant care in the Plio-Pleistocene. In Gowland, Rebecca, and Siân Halcrow (eds) *The Mother-Infant Nexus in Anthropology: Small Beginnings, Significant Outcomes*, 173–190. New York, Springer.

Nowell, April, Michelle C. Langley, and Felix Riede (2020) Children and innovation: a Wenner-Gren workshop. *Evolutionary Anthropology: Issues, News, and Reviews* 29(1), 6–8. https://doi.org/10.1002/evan.21816.

Nowell, April, and Leslie Van Gelder (2020) Disentangled: the role of finger flutings in the study of the lived lives of Upper Paleolithic Peoples. *Journal of Archaeological Method and Theory* 27(3), 585–606.

Nowell, April, and Amanda Cooke (forthcoming) Culturing the body: adornment and ornamentation. In Lock, Andrew, Chris Sinha, and Nathalie Gontier (eds) *Oxford Handbook of Human Symbolic Evolution*. Oxford: Oxford University Press.

Nowell, April, Helen Kurki, and Lisa M. Mitchell (forthcoming) Conceiving reproduction in archaeology. In Han, Sallie, and Cecelia Tomori (eds) *Routledge Handbook on Anthropology and Reproduction*, London, Routledge.

Nowell, April and Aurora Skala (forthcoming) The well-dressed hominin: textiles and textile-production in the Pleistocene. In Collins, Benjamin R., and April Nowell (eds) *Culturing the Body*. New York, Berghahn Books.

Nunn, Charles L., and David R. Samson (2018) Sleep in a comparative context: investigating how human sleep differs from sleep in other primates. *American Journal of Physical Anthropology* 166(3), 601–612.

Odling-Smee, F. John, Kevin N. Laland, and Marcus W. Feldman (2003) *Niche construction: The neglected process in evolution*. Princeton, NJ, Princeton University Press.

Olgilvie, Marsha D., Bryan K. Curran, and Erik Trinkaus (1989) Incidence and patterning of enamel hypoplasia in the Neanderthals. *American Journal of Physical Anthropology* 79(1), 25–41.

Oliva, Martin (2006) The Upper Paleolithic finds from the Mladec Cave. In Teschler-Nicola, Maria (ed.) *Early Modern Humans at the Moravian Gate*. Vienna, Springer.

Olive, Monique (1988) Une habitation magdalénienne d'Étiolles. L'unité P15. *Mémoires de la Société préhistorique française* 20.

Olive, Monique (1992) En marge des unités d'habitations d'Étoiles: les foyers d'activité satellites. *Gallia préhistoire* 34(1), 85–140.

Olive, Monique, Nicole Pigeot, and Olivier Bignon-Lau (2019) Un campement magdalénien à Étiolles (Essonne). Des activités à la microsociologie d'un habitat. *Gallia Préhistoire* 59, 47–108. https://doi-org.ezproxy.library.uvic.ca/10.4000/galliap.1492.

Onoratini, Gérard, Almudena Arellano, Angiolo Del Lucchese, Pierre Elie Moullé, and Frédéric Serre (2012) The Barma Grande Cave (Grimaldi, Vintimiglia, Italy): from Neandertal, hunter of 'Elephas antiquus', to Sapiens with ornaments of mammoth ivory. *Quaternary international* 255, 141–157.

O'Reilly, Dougald, Louise Shewan, Kate Domett, Siân Halcrow, and Thonglith Luangkhoth (2019) Excavating among the megaliths: recent research at the 'Plain of Jars' site 1 in Laos. *Antiquity* 93(370), 970–989. doi:10.15184/aqy.2019.102.

O'Rourke, Suzanne, Heather Whalley, Sarah Janes, Niamh MacSweeney, Asaly Skrenes, Suzy Crowson, Laura MacLean, and Matthias Schwannauer (2020) The Development of Cognitive and Emotional Maturity in Adolescents and its Relevance in Judicial Contexts. Literature Review Prepared for the Consideration of the Scottish Sentencing Council. http://www.scottishsentencingcouncil.org.uk/.

Ovodov, Nikolai D., Susan J. Crockford, Yaroslav V. Kuzmin, Thomas F.G. Higham, Gregory W.L. Hodgins, and Johannes van der Plicht (2011) A 33,000-year-old incipient dog from the Altai

Mountains of Siberia: evidence of the earliest domestication disrupted by the Last Glacial Maximum. *PLoS ONE* 6(7), e22821.

Owens, D'ann, and Brian Hayden (1997) Prehistoric rites of passage: a comparative study of transegalitarian hunter-gatherers. *Journal of Anthropological Archaeology* 16(2), 121–61.

Owsley, Douglas W., David R. Hunt, Ian G. Macintyre and M. Amelia Logan (2001) Clovis and Early Archaic Crania from the Anzick Site (24PA506), Park County, Montana. *Plains Anthropologist* 46(176), 115–124.

Owsley, Douglas W., Margaret A. Jodry, Thomas W. Stafford Jr., C. Vance Haynes Jr., and Dennis J. Stanford (2010) *Arch Lake Woman: Physical Anthropology and Geoarchaeology*. College Station, Texas A&M University Press.

Pales, Léon (1954) Les empreintes de pieds humains de la 'Tana della Bàsura' (Toirano). *Rivista di studi liguri* 20, 5–12.

Pales, Léon (1960) Les empreintes de pieds humains de la 'grotta della Basura'. *Rivista di studi liguri* 26, 25–90.

Pales, Léon (1976) Les Empreintes de Pieds Humains dans les Cavernes. Les Empreintes du Réseau Clastres de la Caverne de Niaux (Ariège). *Archives de L'Institut de Paléontologie Humaine (36)*. Paris, Masson.

Pales, Léon, and M.T. De Saint-Péreuse (1976) Les empreintes de pieds humains dans les cavernes: Les empreintes du réseau nord de la caverne de Niaux (Ariège). Paris, Masson.

Palmquist, Aunchalee (2020) Cooperative lactation and the mother-infant nexus. In Gowland, Rebecca, and Siân Halcrow (eds) *The Mother-infant Nexus in Anthropology: Small Beginnings, Significant Outcomes*, 125–124. Cham, Springer.

Panarello, Adolfo (2005) Le impronte umane fossili di 'Foresta': Per una lettura storica del sito e una corretta interpretazione della scoperta scientifica. Vairano Scalo, Intergraphica.

Panarello, Aldofo, Maria Rita Palombo, Italo Biddittu, Mauro Antonio Di Vito, Gennaro Farinaro, and Paolo Mietto (2020) On the devil tracks: unexpected news from Foresta ichnosite (Roccamonfina volcano, central Italy). *Journal of Quaternary Science* 35(3), 444–456.

Pany-Kucera, Doris, Anton Kern, and Hans Reschreiter (2019) Children in the mines? Tracing potential childhood labour in salt mines from the Early Iron Age in Hallstatt, Austria. *Childhood in the Past* 12(2), 67–80. doi: 10.1080/17585716.2019.1638554.

Pares, Josep M., and Alfredo Perez-Gonzalez (1995) Paleomagnetic age for hominid fossils at Atapuerca archaeological site, Spain. *Science* 269(5225), 830–832.

Pargeter, Justin, Nada Khreisheh, and Dietrich Stout (2019) Understanding stone tool-making skill acquisition: experimental methods and evolutionary implications. *Journal of Human Evolution* 133, 146–166.

Park, Robert W. (2005) Growing up north: exploring the archaeology of childhood in the Thule and Dorset cultures of Arctic Canada. *Archaeological Papers of the American Anthropological Association* 15(1), 53–64.

Partiot, Caroline, Erik Trinkhaus, Christopher J. Knüsel, and Sébastie Villotte (2020) The Cro-Magnon babies: Morphology and mortuary implications of the Cro-Magnon immature remains. *Journal of Archaeological Science* 30, 102257.

Pastoors, Andreas, Tilman Lenssen-Erz, Tsamkxao Ciqae, Ui Kxunta, Thui Thao, Robert Bégouën, Megan Biesele, and Jean Clottes (2015) Tracking in caves: experience based reading of Pleistocene human footprints in French caves. *Cambridge Archaeological Journal* 25(3), 551–564. https://doi.org/10.1017/S0959774315000050.

Pastoors, Andreas, Tilman Lenssen-Erz, Bernd Breuckmann, Tsamkxao Ciquae, Ui Kxunta, Dirk Rieke-Zapp, and Thui Thao (2017) Experience based reading of Pleistocene human footprints in Pech-Merle. *Quaternary International* 430, 155–162.

Peignaux, Coralie, Sacha Kacki, Pierre Guyomarc'h, Eline M. Schotsmans, and Sébastien Villotte (2019) New anthropological data from Cussac Cave (Gravettian, Dordogne, France): in situ and virtual analyses of Locus 3. *Comptes Rendus Palevol* 18(4), 455–464.

Pelcin, Andrew W. (1997a) The effect of core surface morphology on flake attributes: evidence from a controlled experiment. *Journal of Archaeological Science* 24(8), 749–756. https://doi.org/10.1006/jasc.1996.0156.

Pelcin, Andrew W. (1997b) The formation of flakes: the role of platform thickness and exterior platform angle in the production of flake initiations and terminations. *Journal of Archaeological Science* 24(12), 1107–1113. https://doi.org/10.1006/jasc.1996.0190.

Pellegrini, Anthony D., Danielle Dupuis, and Peter K. Smith (2007) Play in evolution and development. *Developmental Review* 27(2), 261–276.

Pellis, Sergio, and Vivien Pellis (2009) *The Playful Brain: Venturing to the Limits of Neuroscience.* Oxford, Oneworld Publications.

Perper, Marina, Adam S. Aldahan, John P. Tsatalis, and Kevin Nouri (2017) Modifications of body surface: piercings, tattoos, and scarification. *International Journal of Dermatology* 56(3), 351–353.

Petraglia, Michael D., Ceri Shipton, and K. Paddyya (2005) Life and mind in the Acheulian: a case study from India. In Gamble, Clive, and Martin Porr (eds) *The Hominid Individual in Context: Archaeological Investigations of Lower and Middle Paleolithic Landscapes, Locales and Artifacts,* 197–219. London, Routledge.

Pettitt, Paul (2002) The Neanderthal dead: exploring mortuary variability in Middle Palaeolithic Eurasia. *Before Farming* 1, 1–26.

Pettitt, Paul (2010) *Palaeolithic Origin of Burial.* New York, Routledge

Pettitt, Paul (2018) Hominin evolutionary thanatology from the mortuary to funerary realm: the palaeoanthropological bridge between chemistry and culture. *Philosophical Transactions of the Royal Society B: Biological Sciences* 373(1754), 20180212. http://doi.org/10.1098/rstb.2018.0212.

Pettitt, Paul, and Nicolai O. Bader (2000) Direct AMS radiocarbon dates for the Sungir mid Upper Palaeolithic burials. *Antiquity* 74(284), 269–270.

Pettitt, Paul, M.P. Richards, Roberto Maggi, and Vincenzo Formicola (2003) The Gravettian burial known as the Prince ('Il Principe'): new evidence for his age and diet. *Antiquity* 77(295), 15–19.

Pfeiffer, John E. (1982) *The Creative Explosion: An Inquiry into the Origins of Art and Religion.* New York, Harper and Row.

Pfeiffer, Susan, L. Elizabeth Doyle, Helen K. Kurki, Lesley Harrington, Jaime K. Ginter, and Catherine E. Merritt (2014) Discernment of mortality risk associated with childbirth in archaeologically derived forager skeletons. *International Journal of Paleopathology* 7, 15–24.

Pigeot, Nicole (1987) Magdaléniens d'étiolles: Économie de débitage et organisation sociale. *Éditions du Centre National de la Recherche Scientifique, Gallia Préhistoire* Supplément 25.

Pigeot, Nicole (1990) Technical and social actors. Flintknapping specialists and apprentices at Magdalenian Etiolles. *Archaeological Review from Cambridge* 9(1), 126–141.

Pike, Alistair W., Dirk L. Hoffman, Marco García-Diez, Paul B. Pettitt, José. Alcolea, Rodrigo De Balbín, César Gonzalez-Sainz, Carmen de las Heras, José.A. Lasheras, Ramón Montes, and João Zilhão (2012) U-series dating of Paleolithic art in 11 caves in Spain. *Science* 336, 1409–1413.

Pinhasi, Ron, and Patrick Semal (2000) The position of the Nazlet Khater specimen among prehistoric and modern African and Levantine populations. *Journal of Human Evolution* 39(3), 269–288.

Plassard, Jean (1999) *Rouffignac: le sanctuaire des mammouths.* Paris, Seuil.

Pokines, James T., and Jade S. De La Paz (2016) Recovery rates of human fetal skeletal remains using varying mesh sizes. *Journal of Forensic Sciences* 61(S1), S184–S189.

Porter, Samantha T., Nadine Huber, Christian Hoyer, and Harald Floss (2016) Portable and low-cost solutions to the imaging of Paleolithic art objects: a comparison of photogrammetry and reflectance transformation imaging. *Journal of Archaeological Science: Reports* 10, 859–863.

Ponce de León, Marcia S., Lubov Golovanova, Vladimir Doronichev, Galina Romanova, Takeru Akazawa, Osamu Kondo, Hajime Ishida, and Christoph P.E. Zollikofer (2008) Neanderthal brain size at birth provides insights into the evolution of human life history. *Proceedings of the National Academy of Sciences* 105(37), 13764–13768.

Ponce de León, Marcia S., Thibaut Bienvenu, Takeru Akazawa, and Christoph P. Zollikofer (2016) Brain development is similar in Neanderthals and modern humans. *Current Biololgy* 26(14), R665–R666.

Potter, Ben A., Joel D. Irish, Joshua D. Reuther, Carol Gelvin-Reymiller, and Vance T. Holliday (2011) A terminal Pleistocene child cremation and residential structure from Eastern Beringia. *Science* 331(6020), 1058-1062.

Potter, Ben A., Joel D. Irish, Joshua D. Reuther, and Holly J. McKinney (2014) New insights into Eastern Beringian mortuary behavior: A terminal Pleistocene double infant burial at Upward Sun River. *Proceedings of the National Academy of Sciences* 111(48), 17060–17065.

Powell, Joseph F. (2005) *The first Americans: race, evolution, and the origin of Native Americans.* Cambridge, Cambridge University Press.

Prassack, Kari A., Josephine DuBois, Martina Láznicková-Galetová, M. Mietje Germonpré, and Peter S. Ungar (2020) Dental microwear as a behavioral proxy for distinguishing between canids at the Upper Paleolithic (Gravettian) site of Predmostí, Czech Republic. *Journal of Archaeological Science* 115, 105092. https://doi.org/10.1016/j.jas.2020.105092.

Prince-Buitenhuys, Julia R., and Eric J. Bartelink (2020) Niche Construction Theory in Bioarchaeology. In Cheverko, Colleen M., Julia R. Prince-Buitenhuys, and Mark Hubbe (eds) *Theoretical Approaches in Bioarchaeology*, 93–112. London, Routledge.

Prine, Elizabeth (2000) Searching for third genders: towards a prehistory of domestic space in Middle Missouri Villages. In Schmidt, Robert A., and Barbara L. Voss (eds) *Archaeology of Sexualities*, 197–219. London, Routledge.

Prüfer, Kay, Fernando Racimo, Nick Patterson, Flora Jay, Sriram Sankararaman, Susanna Sawyer, Anja Heinze, Gabriel Renaud, Peter H. Sudmant, Cesare de Filippo, Heng Li, Swapan Mallick, Michael Dannemann, Qiaomei Fu, Martin Kircher, Martin Kuhlwilm, Michael Lachmann, Matthias Meyer, Matthias Ongyerth, Michael Siebauer, Christoph Theunert, Arti Tandon, Priya Moorjani, Joseph Pickrell, James C. Mullikin, Samuel H. Vohr, Richard E. Green, Ines Hellmann, Philip L.F. Johnson, Hélène Blanche, Howard Cann, Jacob O. Kitzman, Jay Shendure, Evan E. Eichler, Ed S. Lein, Trygve E. Bakken, Liubov V. Golovanova, Vladimir B. Doronichev, Michael V. Shunkov, Anatoli P. Derevianko, Bence Viola, Montgomery Slatkin, David Reich, Janet Kelso, and Svante Pääbo (2014) The complete genome sequence of a Neanderthal from the Altai Mountains. *Nature* 505, 43–49.

Prüfer, Kay, Cesare de Filippo, Steffi Grote, Fabrizio Mafessoni, Petra Korlevic, Mateja Hajdinjak, Benjamin Vernot, Laurits Skov, Pinghsun Hsieh, Stéphane Peyrégne, David Reher, Charlotte Hopfe, Sarah Nagel, Tomislav Maricic, Qiaomei Fu, Christoph Theunert, Rebekah Rogers, Pontus Skoglund, Manjusha Chintalapati, Michael Dannemann, Bradley J. Nelson, Felix M. Key, Pavao Rudan, Željko Kucan, Ivan Gušic, Liubov V. Golovanova, Vladimir B. Doronichev, Nick Patterson, David Reich, Evan E. Eichler, Montgomery Slatkin, Mikkel H. Schierup, Aida M. Andrés, Janet Kelso, Matthias Meyer, and Svante Pääbo (2017) A high-coverage Neandertal genome from Vindija Cave in Croatia. *Science* 358(6363), 655–658.

Putt, Shelby S., Alexander D. Woods, and Robert G. Franciscus (2014) The role of verbal interaction during experimental bifacial stone tool manufacture. *Lithic Technology* 39(2), 96–112.

Quiles, Anita, Hélène Valladas, Hervé Bocherens, Emmanuelle Delqué-Kolic, Evelyne Kaltnecker, Johannes van der Plicht, Jean-Jacques Delannoy, Valérie Feruglio, Carole Fritz, Julien Monney, Michel Philippe, Gilles Tosello, Jean Clottes, and Jean-Michel Geneste (2016) A high-precision chronological model for the decorated Upper Paleolithic cave of Chauvet-Pont d'Arc, Ardèche, France. *Proceedings of the National Academy of Sciences of the United States of America* 113(17), 4670–4675. https://doi.org/10.1073/pnas.1523158113.

Radovcic, Jakov, Fred H. Smith, Eric Trinkaus, and Milford Wolpoff (1988) *The Krapina Hominids, An Illustrated Catalog.* Mladost, Zagreb.

Ragir, Sonia, and Sue Savage-Rumbaugh (2009) Playing with meaning: normative function and structure in play. In Botha, Rudolf, and Chris Knight (eds) *The Prehistory of Language*, 122–141. Oxford, Oxford University Press.

Rajendran, P., R. Bharath Kumar and B. Vijaya Bhanu (2003) Fossilized hominid baby skull from the ferricrete at Odai, Bommayarpalayam, Villupuram District, Tamil Nadu, South India. *Current Science* 84(6), 754–756.

Rajendran, P., Peter Koshy, and Santha Sadasivan (2006) *Homo sapiens* (archaic) baby fossil of the Middle Pleistocene. *Ancient Asia* 1, 7–13.

Rak, Yoel, and Baruch Arensburg (1987) Kebara 2 Neanderthal pelvis: first look at a complete inlet. *American Journal of Physical Anthropology* 73(2), 227–231.

Ramirez Rozzi, Fernando, Francesco d'Errico, Marian Vanhaeren, Pieter M. Grootes, Bertrand Kerautret, and Véronique Dujardin (2009) Cutmarked human remains bearing Neandertal features and modern human remains associated with the Aurignacian at Les Rois. *Journal of Anthropological Sciences* 87, 153–185.

Rasmussen, Morten, Sarah L. Anzick, Michael R. Waters, Pontus Skoglund, Michael DeGiorgio, Thomas W. Stafford, Simon Rasmussen, Ida Moltke, Anders Albrechtsen, Shane M. Doyle, G. David Poznik, Valborg Gudmundsdottir, Rachita Yadav, Anna-Sapfo Malaspinas, Samuel Stockton White V, Morten E. Allentoft, Omar E. Cornejo, Kristiina Tambets, Anders Eriksson, Peter D. Heintzman, Monika Karmin, Thorfinn Sand Korneliussen, David J. Meltzer, Tracey L. Pierre, Jesper Stenderup, Lauri Saag, Vera M. Warmuth, Margarida C. Lopes, Ripan S. Malhi, Søren Brunak, Thomas Sicheritz-Ponten, Ian Barnes, Matthew Collins, Ludovic Orlando, Francois Balloux, Andrea Manica, Ramneek Gupta, Mait Metspalu, Carlos D. Bustamante, Mattias Jakobsson, Rasmus Nielsen, and Eske Willerslev (2014) The genome of a Late Pleistocene human from a Clovis burial site in Western Montana. *Nature* 506, 225–29.

Reynolds, Natasha, Rob Dinnis, Alexander A. Bessudnov, Thibaut Devièse, and Thomas Higham (2017) The Kostënki 18 child burial and the cultural and funerary landscape of Mid Upper Palaeolithic European Russia. *Antiquity* 91(360), 1435–1450.

Riede, Felix, Niels N. Johannsen, Anders Högberg, April Nowell, and Marlize Lombard (2018) The role of play objects and object play in human cognitive evolution and domain-specific innovation: a niche construction perspective. *Evolutionary Anthropology: Issues, News, and Reviews* 27(1), 46–59.

Riede, Felix, Matthew J. Walsh, April Nowell, Michelle Langley, and Niels N. Johannsen (2021) Constructing the niches of and for innovation. Play objects and object play from a niche construction perspective. *Evolutionary Human Sciences*, 1-47. https://doi.org/10.1017/ehs.2021.7

Riel-Salvatore, Julien and Geoffrey A. Clark (2001) Middle and Early Upper Paleolithic burials and the use of chronotypology in contemporary Paleolithic research. *Current Anthropology* 42(4), 449–479.

Riel-Salvatore, Julien, and Claudine Gravel-Miguel (2013) Upper Palaeolithic mortuary practices in Eurasia. In Tarlow Sarah, and Liv Nilsson Stutz (eds) *Oxford Handbook of the Archaeology of Death and Burial.* Oxford, Oxford University Press. DOI:10.1093/oxfordhb/9780199569069.013.0017.

Riga, Alessandro, Tommaso Mori, Travis Rayne Pickering, Jacopo Moggi-Cecchi, and Colin G. Menter (2019) Ages-at-death distribution of the early Pleistocene hominin fossil assemblage from Drimolen (South Africa). *American Journal of Physical Anthropology* 168(3), 632–636.

Rivero, Olivia (2016) Master and apprentice: evidence for learning in Palaeolithic portable art. *Journal of Archaeological Science* 75, 89–100.

Robb, John (2017) 'Art' in archaeology and anthropology: an overview of the concept. *Cambridge Archaeological Journal* 27(4), 587–597. doi:10.1017/S0959774317000725.

Robson, Shannen L., and Dernard Wood (2008) Hominin life history: reconstruction and evolution. *Journal of Anatomy* 212(4), 394–425.

Roebroeks, Wil, and Paola Villa (2011) On the earliest evidence for habitual use of fire in Europe. *Proceedings of the National Academy of Sciences* 108(13), 5209–5214. https://doi.org/10.1073/pnas.1018116108.

Roenneberg, T., T. Kuehnle, P.P. Pramstaller, J. Ricken, M. Havel, A. Guth, and M. Merrow (2004) A marker for the end of adolescence. *Current Biology* 14(24), R1038–R1039.

Rogoff, Barbara (2003) *The Cultural Nature of Human Development.* Oxford, Oxford University Press.

Roldán Garcia, Clodoaldo, Valentín Villaverde Bonilla, Isabel Ródenas Marín, and Sonia Murcia Mascarós (2016) A unique collection of Palaeolithic painted portable art: characterization of red and yellow pigments from the Parpalló Cave (Spain). *PLoS ONE* 11(10), e0163565. https://doi.org/10.1371/journal.pone.0163565.

Romano, Marco, Paolo Citton, Isabella Salvador, Daniele Arobba, Ivano Rellini, Marco Firpo, Fabio Negrino, Marta Zunino, Elisabetta Starnini, and Marco Avanzini (2019) A multidisciplinary approach to a unique palaeolithic human ichnological record from Italy (Bàsura Cave). *eLife* 8, e45204. DOI: 10.7554/eLife.45204.

Romer, Daniel, Valerie F. Reyna, Theodore D. Satterthwaite (2017) Beyond stereotypes of adolescent risk taking: placing the adolescent brain in developmental context. *Developmental Cognitive Neuroscience* 27, 19–34.

Ronchitelli, Annamaria, Sonia Mugnaini, Simona Arrighi, Andrea Atrei, Giulia Capecchi, Marco Giamello, Laura Longo, Nadia Marchettini, Cecilia Viti, and Adriana Moroni (2015) When technology joins symbolic behaviour: The Gravettian burials at Grotta Paglicci (Rignano Garganico–Foggia–Southern Italy). *Quaternary International* 359, 423–441.

Roosevelt, Anna C. (2002) Gender in human evolution: sociobiology revisited and revised. In Nelson, Sarah Milledge, and Myriam Rosen-Ayalon (eds) *Pursuit of Gender: Worldwide Archaeological Approaches*, 355–376. Walnut Creek, AltaMira Press.

Rosas, Antonio, Cayetana Martínez-Maza, Markus Bastir, Antonio García-Tabernero, Carles Lalueza-Fox, Rosa Huguet, José Eugenio Ortiz, Ramón Julià, Vicente Soler, Trinidad de Torres, Enrique Martínez, Juan Carlos Cañaveras, Sergio Sánchez-Moral, Soledad Cuezva, Javier Lario, David Santamaría, Marco de la Rasilla, and Javier Fortea (2006) Paleobiology and comparative morphology of a late Neandertal sample from El Sidrón, Asturias, Spain. *Proceedings of the National Academy of Sciences* 103(51), 19266–19271. https://doi.org/10.1073/pnas.0609662104.

Rosas, Antonio, Luis Ríos, Almudena Estalrrich, Helen Liversidge, Antonio García-Tabernero, Rosa Huguet, Hugo Cardoso, Markus Bastir, Carles Lalueza-Fox, Marco de la Rasilla, and Christopher Dean (2017) The growth pattern of Neandertals, reconstructed from a juvenile skeleton from El Sidrón (Spain). *Science* 357(6357), 1282–1287.

Rothschild, Nan A. (2002) Introduction. In Kamp, Kathryn Ann (ed.) *Children in the Prehistoric Puebloan Southwest*, 1–13. Salt Lake City, The University of Utah Press.

Roveland, Blythe (2000) Footprints in the clay: Upper Palaeolithic children in ritual and secular contexts. In Sofaer Derevenski, Joanna (ed.) *Children and Material Culture*, 29–38. London, Routledge.

Ruff, Christopher B. (2010) Body size and body shape in early hominins - implications of the Gona pelvis. *Journal of Human Evolution* 58, 166–178.

Russell, Pamela (1989) Who and why in Palaeolithic art. *Oxford Journal of Archaeology* 8(3), 237–249.

Russell, Pamela (1991) Men only? The myths about European Paleolithic artists. In Willows, Noreen D., and Dale Walde (eds) *The Archaeology of Gender*, 346–351. Calgary, Chacmool Archaeological Association of the University of Calgary.

Salmon, Fabien, Catherine Ferrier, Delphine Lacanette, Jean-Christophe Mindeguia, Jean-Claude Leblanc, Carole Fritz, and Colette Sirieux (in press) Numerical reconstruction of Paleolithic fires in the Chauvet-pont D'Arc, Cave (Ardèch, France). *Journal of Archaeological Method and Theory*, 1–13. doi:10.1007/s10816-020-09484-5.

Samson, David R., Alyssa N. Crittenden, Ibrahim A. Mabulla, Audax Z.P. Mabulla, and Charles L. Nunn (2017) Chronotype variation drives nighttime sentinel-like behaviour in hunter–gatherers. *Proceedings of the Royal Society B: Biological Sciences* 284(1858), 20170967. http://dx.doi.org/10.1098/rspb.2017.0967.

San Juan-Foucher, Cristina (2005) Industrie osseuse décorée du Gravettien des Pyrénées. *Munibe Antropologia-Arkeologia* 57(3), 95–111.

Sandgathe, Dennis M., Harold L. Dibble, Paul Goldberg, and Shannon P. McPherron (2011) The Roc de Marsal Neandertal child: a reassessment of its status as a deliberate burial. *Journal of Human Evolution* 61(3), 243–253.

Saos, Thibaud, Sophie Grégoire, Jean-Jacques Bahain, Thomas Higham, Anne-Marie Moigne, Agnès Testu, Nicolas Boulbes, Manon Bachellerie, Tony Chevalier, Gaël Becam, Jean-Pierre Duran, Alex Alladio, Maria Illuminada Ortega, Thibaut Devièse, and Quigfeng Shao (2020) The Middle and Upper Palaeolithic at La Crouzade Cave (Gruissan, Aude, France): new excavations and a chronostratigraphic framework. *Quaternary International* 551, 85–104.

Savage-Rumbaugh, E. Sue, Nicholas Toth, and Kathy Schick (2007) Kanzi learns to knap stone tools. In Washburn, David A. (ed.) *Primate Perspectives on Behavior and Cognition*, 279–291. Washington, DC, American Psychological Association.

Sawyer, Susan M., Peter S. Azzopardi, Dakshitha Wickremarathne, and George C. Patton (2018) The age of adolescence. *The Lancet Child and Adolescent Health* 2(3), 233–238.

Sayers, Kent, and C. Owen Lovejoy (2008) The chimpanzee has no clothes: a critical examination of pan troglodytes in models of human evolution. *Current Anthropology* 49(1), 87–114. DOI: 10.1086/523675.

Schick, Kathy D., Nicholas Toth, Gary Garufi, E. Sue Savage-Rumbaugh, Duane Rumbaugh, and Rose Sevcik (1999) Continuing investigations into the stone tool-making and tool-using capabilities of a Bonobo (*Pan paniscus*). *Journal of Archaeological Science* 26(7), 821–832.

Schiffer, Michael B. (1975) Archaeology as behavioral science. *American Anthropologist* 77(4), 836–848.

Schiffer, Michael B. (2010) *Behavioral Archaeology: Practices and Principles*. New York, Routledge.

Schillinger, Kerstin, Alex Mesoudi, and Stephen J. Lycett (2016) Copying error, evolution, and phylogenetic signal in artifactual traditions: an experimental approach using 'model artifacts'. *Journal of Archaeological Science* 70, 23–34.

Schlanger, Nathan (1994) Mindful technology: unleashing the chaîne opératoire for an archaeology of mind. In Renfrew, Colin Autor, and Ezra B.W. Zubrow (eds) *The Ancient Mind: Elements of Cognitive Archaeology*, 143–151. Cambridge, Cambridge University Press.

Schlegel, Alice, and Herbert L. Barry (1991) *Adolescence: An anthropological inquiry*. New York, Free Press.

Schmidt, Isabell V. (2010) The 'Malta Realism': on interpreting Siberian anthropomorphic figurines from the Upper Paleolithic. *Archaeology, Ethnology and Anthropology of Eurasia* 38(3), 50–57.

Schmidt, Isabell V., and Andreas Zimmermann (2019) Population dynamics and socio-spatial organization of the Aurignacian: scalable quantitative demographic data for western and central Europe. *PLoS ONE* 14(2), e0211562.

Schofield, Roger, and Edward Anthony Wrigley (1979) Infant and child mortality in England in the late Tudor and early Stuart period. In Webster, Charles (ed.) *Health, Medicine and Mortality in the Sixteenth Century*, 61–95. Cambridge, Cambridge University Press.

Schwarcz, Henry P., Rainer Grün, Bernard Vandermeersch, Ofer Bar-Yosef, Hélène Valladas, and Eitan Tchernov (1988) ESR dates for the hominid burial site of Qafzeh in Israel. *Journal of Human Evolution* 17(8), 733–737.

Scott, Jeremiah E., and Curtis W. Marean (2009) Paleolithic hominin remains from Eshkaft-e Gavi (southern Zagros Mountains, Iran): description, affinities, and evidence for butchery. *Journal of Human Evolution* 57(3), 248–259.

Séguy, Isabelle, and Luc Buchet (2013) *Handbook of Palaeodemography*. Dordrecht, Springer.

Shackelford, Laura L, Ashley Stinespring Harris, and Lyle W. Konigsberg (2012) Estimating the distribution of probable age-at-death from dental remains of immature human fossils. *American Journal of Physical Anthropology* 147(2), 227–253.

Shapland, Fiona, and Mary E. Lewis (2013) Brief communication: a proposed osteological method for the estimation of pubertal stage in human skeletal remains. *American Journal of Physical Anthropology* 151(2), 302–310. DOI: 10.1002/ajpa.22268.

Shapland, Fiona, and Mary E. Lewis (2014) Brief communication: a proposed method for the assessment of pubertal stage in human skeletal remains using cervical vertebral maturation. *American Journal of Physical Anthropology* 153(1), 144–153. DOI: 10.1002/ajpa.22416.

Sharpe, Kevin, and Leslie Van Gelder (2004) Children and Paleolithic art: indications from Rouffignac Cave, France. *International Newsletter on Rock Art* 3, 9–17.
Sharpe, Kevin, and Leslie Van Gelder (2005) Techniques for studying finger flutings. *Society of Primitive Technology Bulletin* 30, 68–74.
Sharpe, Kevin, and Leslie Van Gelder (2006a) Evidence of cave marking by Paleolithic children. *Antiquity* 80(310), 937–947.
Sharpe, Kevin, and Leslie Van Gelder (2006b) The study of finger flutings. *Cambridge Archaeological Journal* 16(3), 281–295.
Sharpe, Kevin, and Leslie Van Gelder (2006c) Finger flutings in Chamber A1 of Rouffignac Cave, France. *Rock Art Research* 23(2), 179–198.
Shea, John J. (2006) Child's play: reflections on the invisibility of children in the Paleolithic record. *Evolutionary Anthropology* 15(6), 212–216.
Shelley, Phillip H. (1990) Variation in lithic assemblages: an experiment. *Journal of Field Archaeology* 17(2), 187–193. DOI: 10.1179/009346990791548349.
Shennan, Stephen J., and James Steele (1999) Cultural learning in hominids: a behavioral ecological approach. In Box, Hilary O., and Kathleen R. Gibson (eds) *Mammalian Social Learning*, 367–388. New York, Cambridge University Press.
Shipman, Pat (2020) What the dingo says about dog domestication. *The Anatomical Record* 2020, 1–12. DOI: 10.1002/ar.24517.
Shipton, Ceri, and Mark Nielsen (2018) The acquisition of biface knapping skill in the Acheulean. In Di Paolo, Laura Desirèe, Fabio Di Vincenzo, and Francesca De Petrillo (eds) *The Evolution of Primate Social Cognition*, 283–297. Heidelberg, DE, Springer.
Sikora, Martin, Andaine Seguin-Orlando, Vitor C. Sousa, Anders Albrechtsen, Thorfinn Korneliussen, Amy Ko, Simon Rasmussen, Isabelle Dupanloup, Philip R. Nigst, Marjolein D. Bosch, Gabriel Renaud, Morten E. Allentoft, Ashot Margaryan, Sergey V. Vasilyev, Elizaveta V. Veselovskaya, Svetlana B. Borutskaya, Thibaut Deviese, Dan Comeskey, Tom Higham, Andrea Manica, Robert Foley, David J. Meltzer, Rasmus Nielsen, Laurent Excoffier, Marta Mirazon Lahr, Ludovic Orlando, and Eske Willerslev (2017) Ancient genomes show social and reproductive behavior of early Upper Paleolithic foragers. *Science* 358(6363), 659–662. doi:10.1126/science.aao1807. PMID 28982795.
Simon, Ulrich, Marc Händel, Thomas Einwögerer, and Christine Neugebauer-Maresch (2014) The archaeological record of the Gravettian open air site Krems-Wachtberg. *Quaternary International* 351, 5–13.
Simpson, Scott W., Jay Quade, Naomi E. Levin, Robert Butler, Guillaume Dupont-Nivet, Melanie Everett, and Sileshi Semaw (2008) A female *Homo erectus* pelvis from Gona, Ethiopia. Science, 322(5904), 1089–1092.
Skinner, Mark (1997a) Age at death of Gibraltar 2. *Journal of Human Evolution* 32(5), 469–470.
Skinner, Mark (1997b) Dental wear in immature Late Pleistocene European hominines. *Journal of Archaeological Science* 24(8), 677–700.
Skinner, Mark F., and Geoffrey H. Sperber (1982) *Atlas of Radiographs of Early Man*. New York, Liss.
Skoglund, Pontus, Erik Ersmark, Eleftheria Palkopoulou, and Love Dalén (2015) Ancient wolf genome reveals an early divergence of domestic dog ancestors and admixture into high-latitude breeds. *Current Biology* 25(11), 1515–1519.
Slon, Viviane, Bence Viola, Gabriel Renaud, Marie-Theres Gansauge, Stefano Benazzi, Susanna Sawyer, Jean-Jacques Hublin, Michael V. Shunkov, Anatoly P. Derevianko, Janet Kelso, Kay Prüfer, Matthias Meyer, and Svante Pääbo (2017) A fourth Denisovan individual. *Science Advances* 3(7), e1700186.
Smith, B. Holly (1986) Dental development in *Australopithecus* and early *Homo*. *Nature* 323(6086), 327–330.
Smith, B. Holly (1991) Standards of human tooth formation and dental age assessment. In Kelley, Larsen, Mark A. Kelley, and Clark Spencer Larsen (eds) *Advances in Dental Anthropology*, 143–168. New York, Wiley-Liss.

Smith, B. Holly (1994) Patterns of dental development in *Homo, Australopithecus, Pan* and *Gorilla*. American Journal of Physical Anthropology 94(3), 307–325.

Smith, B. Holly, and Robert L. Tompkins (1995) Towards a life history of the Hominidae. *Annual Review of Anthropology* 24(1), 257–279.

Smith, Daniel, Philip Schlaepfer, Katie Major, Mark Dyble, Abigail E. Page, James Thompson, Nikhil Chaudhary, Gul Deniz Salali, Ruth Mace, Leonora Astete, Marilyn Ngales, Lucio Vinicius, and Andrea Bamberg Migliano (2017) Cooperation and the evolution of hunter-gatherer storytelling. *Nature Communications* 8(1), 1853. DOI: 10.1038/s41467-017-02036-8.

Smith, Kiona (2019) 14,000-year-old footprints record an underground Stone Age family outing. *Ars Technica* May 29, 2019. https://arstechnica.com/science/2019/05/14000-year-old-footprints-record-an-underground-stone-age-family-outing/.

Smith, Peter K. (2010) *Children and Play: Understanding Children's Worlds*. Malden, MA, Wiley-Blackwell.

Smith, Patricia E. (2005) Children and ceramic innovation: a study in the archaeology of children. *Archaeological Papers of American Anthropological Association* 15(1), 65–76.

Smith, Tanya M., Michel Toussaint, Donald J. Reid, Anthony J. Olejniczak, and Jean-Jacques Hublin (2007a) Rapid dental development in a middle Paleolithic Belgian Neanderthal. *Proceedings of the National Academy of Sciences* 104(51), 20220–20225.

Smith, Tanya M., Paul Tafforeau, Donald J. Reid, Rainer Grün, Stephen Eggins, Mohamed Boutakiout, and Jean-Jacques Hublin (2007b) Earliest evidence of modern human life history in North African early *Homo sapiens*. *Proceedings of the National Academy of Sciences* 104(15), 6128–6133.

Smith, Tanya M., Paul Tafforeau, Donald J. Reid, Joane Pouech, Vincent Lazzari, John P. Zermeno, Debbie Guatelli-Steinberg, Anthony J. Olejniczak, Almut Hoffman, Jakov Radovčić, Masrour Makaremi, Michel Toussaint, Chris Stringer, and Jean-Jacques Hublin (2010) Dental evidence for ontogenetic differences between modern humans and Neanderthals. *Proceedings of the National Academy of Sciences* 107(49), 20923–20928.

Smith, Tanya M., Zarin Machanda, Andrew B. Bernard, Ronan M. Donovan, Amanda M. Papakyrikos, Martin N. Muller, and Richard Wrangham (2013) First molar eruption, weaning, and life history in living wild chimpanzees. *Proceedings of the National Academy of Sciences* 110(8), 2787–2791.

Smith, Tanya M., Christine Austin, Daniel R. Green, Renaud Joannes-Boyau, Shara Bailey, Dani Dumitriu, Steward Fallon, Rainer Grün, Hannah F. James, Marie-Hélène Moncel, Ian S. Williams, Rachel Wood, and Manish Arora (2018) Wintertime stress, nursing, and lead exposure in Neanderthal children. *Science Advances* 4(10), eaau9483.

Snow, Dean R. (2006) Sexual dimorphism in Upper Paleolithic hand stencils. *Antiquity* 80(308), 390–404.

Snow, Dean R. (2013) Sexual dimorphism in European Upper Paleolithic cave art. *American Antiquity* 78(4), 746–761.

Sobel, David (1993) *Children's Special Places: Exploring the Role of Forts, Dens, and Bush Houses in Middle Childhood*. Tucson, Zephr Press.

Sofaer Derevenski, Joanna (2000a) *Children and Material Culture*. London, Routledge.

Sofaer Derevenski, Joanna (2000b) Material culture shock: confronting expectations in the material culture of children. In Sofaer Derevenski, Joanna (ed.) *Children and Material Culture*, 3–16. London, Routledge.

Sofaer, Joanna R. (2006) *The Body as Material Culture: A Theoretical Osteoarchaeology*. Cambridge, Cambridge University Press.

Sofaer, Joanna R. (2015) Bodies and encounters: seeing invisible children in archaeology. In Coşkunsu, Güner (ed.) *The Archaeology of Childhood: Interdisciplinary Perspectives on an Archaeological Enigma*, 73–90. New York, State University of New York Press.

Soffer, Olga (1985) *The Upper Paleolithic of the Central Russian Plain*. Orlando, Academic Press.

Soffer, Olga (2004) Recovering perishable technologies through use wear on tools: preliminary evidence for Upper Paleolithic weaving and net making. *Current Anthropology* 45(3), 407–413.

Soffer, Olga, James M. Adovasio, and David C. Hyland (2000a) The 'Venus' figurines: textiles, basketry, gender, and status in the Upper Paleolithic. *Current Anthropology* 41(4), 511–537.

Soffer, Olga, James M. Adovasio, and David C. Hyland (2000b) The well dressed 'Venus': women's wear ca. 27,000 BP. *Archaeology, Ethnology and Anthropology of Eurasia* 1, 37–47.

Soffer, Olga, and Margaret W. Conkey (1997) Studying ancient visual cultures. In Conkey, Margaret W., Olga Soffer, Deborah Stratmann, and Nina G. Jablonski (eds) *Beyond Art: Pleistocene Image and Symbol*, 1–16. Oakland, CA, University of California Press.

Soffer, Olga, James M. Adovasio, and David C. Hyland (2002) Perishable technologies and invisible people: nets, baskets, and 'Venus' wear ca. 26,000 BP. In Purdy, Barbara A. (ed.) *Enduring Records: The Environmental and Cultural Heritage of Wetlands*, 233–245. Oxford, Oxbow Books.

Soffer, Olga, and James M. Adovasio (2010) The role of perishable technologies in Upper Paleolithic Lives. In Zubrow, Ezra, Françoise Audouze, and James G. Enloe (eds) *The Magdalenian Household: Unraveling Domesticity*, 235–244. Albany, Suny Press.

Sohn, Young Kwan, Woo-seok Yoon, U.S. Ahn, Gi-bom Kim, Jeong-Hyun Lee, Choon-kil Ryu, Yongmun Jeon, and C.H. Kang (2015) Stratigraphy and age of the human footprints-bearing strata in Jeju Island, Korea: controversies and new findings. *Journal of Archaeological Science: Reports* 4, 264–275.

Sommer, Maria, and Dion Sommer (2015) *Care, Socialization and Play in Ancient Attica: A Developmental Childhood Archaeological Approach*. Milton Park, Taylor and Francis.

Somerville, Kyle (2015) 'A place for everything and everything in its place': the cultural context of late Victoria toys. In Coşkunsu, Güüner (ed.) *The Archaeology of Childhood: Interdisciplinary Perspectives on an Archaeological Enigma*, 275–294. New York, State University of New York Press.

Soriano, Sylvain, Paola Villa, and Lyn Wadley (2007) Blade technology and tool forms in the Middle Stone Age of South Africa: the Howiesons Poort and post-Howiesons Poort at Rose Cottage Cave. *Journal of Archaeological Science* 34(5), 681–703.

Soressi, Marie, Heather L. Jones, William Jack Rink, Bruno Maureille, and Anne-Marie Tillier (2007) The Pech-de-l'Azé I Neandertal child: ESR, uranium-series, and AMS 14C dating of its MTA type B context. *Journal of Human Evolution* 52(4), 455–466.

Southwell-Wright, William (2013) Past perspectives: what can archaeology offer disability studies? In Wappett, Matthew, and Katrina Arndt (eds) *Emerging Perspectives on Disability Studies*, 67–95. New York, Palgrave Macmillan.

Sparacello, Vitale Stefano, Stefano Rossi, Paul Pettitt, C.A. Roberts, Julien Riel-Salvatore, and Vincenzo Formicola (2018) New insights on Final Epigravettian funerary behavior at Arene Candide Cave (Western Liguria, Italy). *Journal of Anthropological Sciences* 96, 1–24.

Spikins, Penny, Gail Hitchens, Andy Needham, and Holly Rutherford (2014) The cradle of thought: growth, learning, play and attachment in Neanderthal children. *Oxford Journal of Archaeology* 33(2), 111–134.

Spitery, Éliane (1980) L'enfant de Starocelje et sa pathologie. *Bulletins et Mémoires de la Société d'anthropologie de Paris* 7(1), 65–73.

Spoor, Fred, Philipp Gunz, Simon Neubauer, Stefanie Stelzer, Nadia Scott, Amandus Kwekason, and M. Christopher Dean (2015) Reconstructed *Homo habilis* type OH 7 suggests deep-rooted species diversity in early *Homo*. *Nature* 519(7541), 83–86.

Stapert, Dick (2007a) Neanderthal children and their flints. *PalArch's Journal of Archaeology of Northwest Europe* 1(2), 16–39.

Stapert, Dick (2007b) Youngsters knapping flint near the campfire: an alternative view of Site K at Maastricht-Belvédère (The Netherlands). *Archäologisches Korrespondenzblatt* 37(1), 19–35.

Stearns, Stephen C. (1992) *The Evolution of Life Histories*. Oxford, Oxford University Press.

Steeves, Paulette F. (2019) Indigenous method and theory in archaeology. In Smith, Claire (eds) *Encyclopedia of Global Archaeology*, 1–10. Cham, Springer. https://doi.org/10.1007/978-3-319-51726-1_2736-1.

Stefanović, Sofija, Bojan Petrović, Marko Porčić, Kristina Penezić, Jugoslav Pendić, Andrej Starović, and Tamara Blagojević (2019) Bone spoons for prehistoric babies: detection of human teeth marks on the Neolithic artefacts from the site Grad-Starčevo (Serbia). *PLoS ONE* 14(12), e0225713.

Stewart, Nicolas Andre, Raquel Fernanda Gerlach, Rebecca L. Gowland, Kurt J. Gron, and Janet Montgomery (2017) Sex determination of human remains from peptides in tooth enamel. *Proceedings of the National Academy of Sciences* 114(52), 13649–13654.

Storbeck, Justin, and Gerald L. Clore (2005) With sadness comes accuracy; with happiness, false-memory: mood and the false memory effect. *Psychological Science* 16(10), 785–791.

Storey, Glenn Reed (2018) All Rome is at my bedside: nightlife in the Roman Empire. In Gonlin, Nancy, and April Nowell (eds) *Archaeology of the Night: Life After Dark in the Ancient World,* 307–332. Boulder, University Press of Colorado.

Storm, Paul (1994) De morfologie van Homo modjokertensis. *Cranium* 11(2), 97–102.

Stotz Karola (2017) Why developmental niche construction is not selective niche construction: and why it matters. *Interface Focus* 7(5), 20160157. doi:10.1098/rsfs.2016.0157.

Stout, Dietrich (2002) Skill and cognition in stone tool production: an ethnographic case study from Irian Jaya. *Current Anthropology* 43(5), 693–722.

Stout, Dietrich, and Thierry Chaminade (2007) The evolutionary neuroscience of tool making. *Neuropsychologia* 45(5), 1091–1100.

Stout, Dietrich, Nicholas Toth, Kathy Schick, and Thierry Chaminade (2008) Neural correlates of Early Stone Age toolmaking: technology, language and cognition in human evolution. *Philosophical Transactions of the Royal Socociety B: Biological Sciences* 363(1499), 1939–1949. http://doi.org/10.1098/rstb.2008.0001.

Sternke, Farine, and Mikkel Sørensen (2009) The identification of children's flint knapping products in Mesolithic Scandinavia. In McCartan, Sinéad Rick Schulting, Graeme Warren, and Peter C. Woodman (eds) *Mesolithic Horizons: Papers Presented at the Seventh International Conference on the Mesolithic in Europe Belfast 2005,* 722–729. Oxford, Oxbow Books.

Street, Martin, Thomas Terberger, and Jörg Orschiedt (2006) A critical review of the German Paleolithic hominin record. *Journal of Human Evolution* 51(6), 551–579.

Street, Sally E., Ana F. Navarrete, Simon M. Reader, and Kevin N, Laland (2017) Coevolution of cultural intelligence, extended life history, sociality, and brain size in primates. *Proceedings of the National Academy of Sciences* 114(30), 7908–2914. https://doi.org/10.1073/pnas.1620734114.

Stringer, Christopher B., M. Christopher Dean, and Robert D. Martin (1990) A comparative study of cranial and dental development within a recent British sample and among Neandertals. In DeRousseau, C. Jean (ed.) *Primate Life History and Evolution,* 115–152. New York, Wiley-Liss.

Stringer, C.B., and M. Christopher Dean (1997) Age at death of Gibraltar 2 a reply. *Journal of Human Evolution* 32(5), 471–472.

Sugiyama, Michelle Scalise (2001) Food, foragers and folklore: the role of narrative in human subsistence. *Evolution and Human Behavior* 22(4), 221–240.

Sugiyama, Michelle Scalise (2017) Oral Storytelling as evidence of pedagogy in forager societies. *Frontiers in Psychology* 8, 471. https://doi.org/10.3389/fpsyg.2017.00471.

Sutikna, Thomas, Matthew W. Tocheri, Michael J. Morwood, E. Wahyu Saptomo, Jatmiko, Rokus Due Awe, Sri Wasisto, Kira E. Westaway, Maxime Aubert, Bo Li, Jian-xin Zhao, Michael Storey, Brent V. Alloway, Mike W. Morley, Hanneke J.M. Meijer, Gerrit D. van den Bergh, Rainer Grün, Anthony Dosseto, Adam Brumm, William L. Jungers, and Richard G. Roberts (2016) Revised stratigraphy and chronology for *Homo floresiensis* at Liang Bua in Indonesia. *Nature* 532(7599), 366–369. https://doi.org/10.1038/nature17179.

Svoboda, Jiří (2006a) The burials: ritual and taphonomy. In Trinkaus, Erik, and Jiří Svoboda (eds) *Early Modern Human Evolution in Central Europe: The People of Dolní Věstonice and Pavlov,* 15–26. New York, Oxford University Press.

Svoboda, Jiří (2006b) The structure of the cave, stratigraphy, and depositional context. In Teschler-Nicola, Maria (ed.) *Early Modern Humans at the Moravian Gate,* 27–40. Vienna, Springer.

Svoboda, Jirí (2007) The Gravettian on the middle Danube. *PALEO. Revue d'archéologie préhistorique* 19, 203–220.

Svoboda, Jirí (2008) The Upper Paleolithic burial area at Předmostí: ritual and taphonomy. *Journal of Human Evolution* 54(1), 15–33.

Svoboda, Jirí, Martin Novák, Sandra Sázelová, and Jaromír Demek (2016) Pavlov I: a large Gravettian site in space and time. *Quaternary International* 406, 95–105.

Swisher, Carl C. III, Garniss H. Curtis, Teuku Jacob, A.G. Getty, A. Suprijo, and Widiasmoro (1994) Age of the earliest known hominids in Java, Indonesia. *Science* 263(5150), 1118–1121.

Taborin, Yvette (2004) *Langage Sans Parole: La Parure aux Temps Préhistoriques*. Paris, La Maison des Roches.

Tacail, Théo, Jeremy E. Martin, Florent Arnaud-Godet, J. Francis Thackeray, Thure E. Cerling, José Braga, and Vincent Balter (2019) Calcium isotopic patterns in enamel reflect different nursing behaviors among South African early hominins. *Science Advances* 5(8), eaax3250 DOI: 10.1126/sciadv.aax3250.

Tackney, Justin C., Ben A. Potter, Jennifer Raff, Michael Powers, W. Scott Watkins, Derek Warner, Joshua D. Reuther, Joel D. Irish, and Dennis H. O'Rourke (2015) Two contemporaneous mitogenomes from terminal Pleistocene burials in eastern Beringia. *Proceedings of the National Academy of Sciences* 112(45), 13833–13838.

Takakura, Jun (2013) Using lithic refitting to investigate the skill learning process: lessons from Upper Paleolithic assemblages at the Shirataki Sites in Hokkaido, Northern Japan. In Akazawa, Takeru, Yoshihiro Nichiaki, and Kenichi Aoki (eds) *Dynamics of Learning in Neanderthals and Modern Humans Volume 1: Cultural Perspectives*, 151–171. Springer, Japan.

Tardieu, Christine (1998) Short adolescence in early hominids: infantile and adolescent growth of the human femur. *American Journal of Physical Anthropology* 197, 163–178.

Taylor, R.E., L.A. Payen, C.A. Prior, P.J. Slota, Jr., R. Gillespie, J.A.J. Gowlett, R.E.M. Hedges, A.J.T. Jull, T.H. Zabel, D.J. Donahue and R. Berger (1985) Major Revisions in the Pleistocene Age Assignments for North American Human Skeletons by C-14 Accelerator Mass Spectrometry: None Older Than 11,000 C-14 Years B.P. *American Antiquity* 50(1), 136–140.

Tennie, Claudio, Josep Call, and Michael Tomasello (2009) Ratcheting up the ratchet: on the evolution of cumulative culture. *Philosophical Transactions of the Royal Society B: Biological Sciences* 364(1528), 2405–2415.

Teschler-Nicola, Maria, Walpurga Antl-Weiser, and Hermann Prossinger (2004) Two Gravettian human deciduous teeth from Grub/Kranawetberg, lower Austria. *Homo* 54(3), 229–239.

Teschler-Nicola, Maria, Christian Czerny, Martin Oliva, Doris Schamall, and Michael Schultz (2006) Pathological alterations and traumas in the human skeletal remains from Mladec. In Teschler-Nicola, Maria (ed.) *Early Modern Humans at the Moravian Gate*, 473–489. Vienna, Springer.

Teschler-Nicola, Maria, Daniel Fernandes, Marc Händel, Thomas Einwögerer, Ulrich Simon, Christine Neugebauer-Maresch, Stefan Tangl, Patrick Heimel, Toni Dobsak, Anika Retzmann, Thomas Prohaska, Johanna Irrgeher, Douglas J. Kennett, Iñigo Olalde, David Reich, and Ron Pinhasi (2020) Ancient DNA reveals monozygotic newborn twins from the Upper Palaeolithic. *Communications Biology* 3(1), 650. https://doi.org/10.1038/s42003-020-01372-8.

Testart, Alain (2012) *Avant l'histoire: L'évolution des sociétés, de Lascaux à Carnac*. Paris, Éditions Gallimard.

Tillier, Anne-Marie (1979) La dentition de l'enfant moustérien Chateauneuf 2 découvert à l'abri de Hauteroche (Charente). *L'Anthropologie* 83(3), 417–438.

Tillier, Anne-Marie (1983a) L'enfant néandertalien du Roc de Marsal (Campagne-du-Bugue, Dordogne). Le squelette facial. *Annales de Paléontologie* 69(2), 137–149.

Tillier, Anne-Marie (1983b) Le crâne d'enfant d'Engis 2: un exemple de distribution des caractères juvéniles, primitifs et néandertaliens. *Bulletin de la Societe Royale Belge d'Anthropologie Préhistoire* 94, 51–75.

Tillier, Anne-Marie (1984) L'enfant *Homo* 11 de Qafzeh (Israël) et son apport à la compréhension des modalités de la croissance des squelettes moustériens. *Paléorient* 10(1), 7–48.

Tillier, Anne-Marie (1988) A propos de séquences phylogéniques et ontogéniques chez les Néandertaliens. In Trinkaus, Erik (ed.) *L'Homme de Néandertal: L'Anatomie*, 3, 125–136. Liège, ERAUL 30.

Tillier, Anne-Marie (1995) Paléoanthropologie et pratiques funéraires au Levant méditerranéen durant le Paléolithique moyen: le cas des sujets non-adultes. *Paléorient* 21(2), 63–76.

Tillier, Anne-Marie (2008) Early child deliberate burials. Bioarchaeological insights from the near Eastern Mediterranean. In Djindjian, François, and Luiz Oosterbeek (eds) *Proceedings of the XV World Congress (Lisbon, 4-9 September 2006)*, 3–14. Oxford, Archaeopress.

Tillier, Anne-Marie (2011) Facts and ideas in Paleolithic growth studies (paleoauxology). In Condemi, Silvana, and Gerd-Christian Weniger (eds) *Continuity and Discontinuity in the Peopling of Europe*, 139–153. Netherlands, Springer.

Tillier, Anne-Marie, and E. Genet-Varcin (1980) La plus ancienne mandibule d'enfant découverte en France dans le gisement de La Chaise de Vouthon (Abri Suard) en Charente. *Zeitschrift für Morphologie und Anthropologie* 71(2), 196–214.

Tillier, Anne-Marie, Baruch Arensburg, Henri Duday, and Bernard Vandermeersch (2001) Brief communication: an early case of hydrocephalus: the Middle Paleolithic Qafzeh 12 child (Israel). *American Journal of Physical Anthropology* 114(2), 166–170.

Tillier, Anne-Marie, Bernard Vandermeersch, Baruch Arensburg, and Mario Chech (2003) New human remains from Kebara Cave (Mount Carmel). The place of the Kebara hominids in the Levantine Mousterian fossil record. *Paléorient* 29(2), 35–62.

Tillier, Anne-Marie, Zsolt Mester, Herve Bocherens, Dominique Henry-Gambier, and Ildiko Pap (2009) Direct dating of the 'Gravettian' Balla child's skeleton from Bükk Mountains (Hungary): unexpected results. *Journal of Human Evolution* 56(2), 209–212.

Tillier, Anne-Marie, Baruch Arensburg, Anna Belfer-Cohen, and Bernard Vandermeersh (2011) Early hominid remains from Hayonim Cave (Israel) in the context of the Late Middle and Upper Pleistocene record from the Near East. *Paléorient* 37(2), 47–63.

Tillier, Anne-Marie, Nikolay Sirakov, Aleta Guadelli, Philippe Fernandez, Svobooda Sirakova, Irean Dimitrova, Catherine Ferrier, Guillaume Guérin, Maryam Heidari, Ivailo Krunov, Jean-Claude Leblanc, Viviana Miteva, Vasil Popov, Stanimira Taneva, and Jean-Luc Guadelli (2017) Evidence of Neanderthals in the Balkans: the infant radius from Kozarnika Cave (Bulgaria). *Journal of Human Evolution* 111, 54–62.

Tilley, Lorna (2015) Accommodating difference in the prehistoric past: revisiting the case of Romito 2 from a bioarchaeology of care perspective. *International Journal of Paleopathology* 8, 64–74.

Thompson, Jennifer L., and Andrew J. Nelson (2011) Middle childhood and modern human origins. *Human Nature* 22(3), 249–280.

Thompson, Jenifer L., Marta P. Alfonso-Durruty, and John J. Crandall (2014) *Tracing Childhood: Bioarchaeological Investigations of Early Lives in Antiquity*. Gainsville, University Press of Florida.

Tobias, Philip V. (1991) *The Skulls, Endocasts and Teeth of* Homo habilis. Olduvai George Vol. 4. New York, Cambridge University Press.

Tomasello, Michael (1999) *The Cultural Origins of Human Cognition*. Cambridge, Harvard University Press.

Tomasello, Michael (2014) *A Natural History of Human Thinking*. Cambridge, MA, Harvard University Press.

Tompkins, Robert L. (1996) Relative dental development of Upper Pleistocene hominids compared to human population variation. *American Journal of Physical Anthropology* 99(1), 103–118.

Torrence, Robin (2001) Hunter-gatherer technology: Macro- and microscale approaches. In Panter-Brick, Catherine, Robert H. Layton, and Peter Rowley-Conwy (eds) *Hunter-Gatherers: Interdisciplinary Perspectives*, 73–98. Cambridge, Cambridge University Press.

Toth, Nicholas, Kathy D. Schick, E. Sue Savage-Rumbaugh, Rose A. Sevcik, and Duane M. Rumbaugh (1993) Pan the Tool-maker: investigations into the stone tool-making and tool-using capabilities of a Bonobo (*Pan paniscus*). *Journal of Archaeological Science* 20(1), 81–91.

Toth, Nicholas, and Kathy Schick (2009) The Oldowan: the tool making of early hominins and chimpanzees compared. *Annual Review of Anthropology* 38, 289–305.

Toups, Melissa A., Andrew Kitchen, Jessica E. Light, and David L. Reed (2010) Origin of clothing lice indicates early clothing use by anatomically modern humans in Africa. *Molecular Biology and Evolution* 28(1), 29–32. doi:10.1093/molbev/msq234.

Trevathan, Wenda (2015) Primate pelvic anatomy and implications for birth. *Philosophical Transactions of the Royal Society B: Biological Sciences* 370(1663), 20140065. http://dx.doi.org/10.1098/rstb.2014.0065.

Tringham, Ruth, and Margaret Conkey (1998) Rethinking figurines: a critical view from archaeology of Gimbutas, the 'goddess' and popular culture. In Goodison, Lucy and Christine Morris (eds) *Ancient Goddesses: The Myths and the Evidence*, 22–45. Madison, University of Wisconsin Press.

Trinkaus, Erik (1995) Neanderthal mortality patterns. *Journal of Archaeological Science* 22(1), 121–142.

Trinkaus, Erik (2005) Anatomical evidence for the antiquity of human footwear use. *Journal of Archaeological Science* 32(10), 1515–1526.

Trinkaus, Erik (2014) *The Shanidar Neandertals*. New York, Academic Press.

Trinkaus, Erik (2018) An abundance of developmental anomalies and abnormalities in Pleistocene people. *Proceedings of the National Academy of Sciences* 115(47), 11941–41196.

Trinkaus, Erik, and Christopher B. Ruff (1996) Early modern human remains from eastern Asia: the Yamashita-cho 1 immature postcrania. *Journal of Human Evolution* 30(4), 299–314.

Trinkaus, Erik, Jiří Svoboda, Dixie L. West, Vladimir Sládek, Simon W. Hillson, Eva Drozdová, and Miriam Fišáková (2000) Human remains from the Moravian Gravettian: morphology and taphonomy of isolated elements from the Dolní Věstonice II site. *Journal of Archaeological Science* 27(12), 1115–1132.

Trinkaus, Erik, Vincenzo Formicola, Jiří Svoboda, Simon W. Hillson, and Trenton W. Holliday (2001) Dolní Vestonice 15: pathology and persistence in the Pavlovian. *Journal of Archaeological Science* 28(12), 1291–1308.

Trinkaus, Erik, and Hong Shang (2008) Anatomical evidence for the antiquity of human footwear: Tianyuan and Sunghir. *Journal of Archaeological Science* 35(7), 1928–1933.

Trinkaus, Erik, Jiří Svoboda, Piotr Wojtal, M. Nyvltova Fišákova, and J. Wilczyński (2010) Human remains from the Moravian Gravettian: morphology and taphonomy of additional elements from Dolní Věstonice II and Pavlov I. *International Journal of Osteoarchaeology* 20(6), 645–669.

Trinkaus, Erik, Alexandra P. Buzhilova, Maria B. Mednikova, and Maria V. Dobrovolskaya (2014) *The People of Sunghir: Burials, Bodies, and Behavior in the Earlier Upper Paleolithic*. New York, Oxford University Press.

Trinkaus, Erik, Maria B. Mednikova, and Libby W. Cowgill (2016) The appendicular remains of the Kiik-Koba 2 Neandertal infant. *PaleoAnthropology* 2016, 185-210. doi:10.4207/PA.2016.ART103.

Trinkaus, Erik, and Alexandra P. Buzhilova (2018) Diversity and differential disposal of the dead at Sunghir. *Antiquity* 92(361), 7–21.

Trujillo, Cleber A., Edward S. Rice, Nathan K. Schaefer, Isaac A. Chaim, Emily C. Wheeler, Assael A. Madrigal, Justin Buchanan, Sebastian Preiss, Allen Wang, Priscilla D. Negraes, Ryan A. Szeto1, Roberto H. Herai, Alik Huseynov, Mariana S. A. Ferraz, Fernando S. Borges, Alexandre H. Kihara, Ashley Byrne, Maximillian Marin, Christopher Vollmers, Angela N. Brooks, Jonathan D. Lautz, Katerina Semendeferi, Beth Shapiro, Gene W. Yeo, Stephen E. P. Smith, Richard E. Green, and Alysson R. Muotri (2021) Reintroduction of the archaic variant of *NOVA*1 in cortical organoids alters neurodevelopment. *Science* 371(6530), eaax2537 DOI: 10.1126/science.aax2537

Tsirk, Ari (2014) *Fractures in Knapping*. Oxford, Archaeopress.

Turq, Alain, Harold L. Dibble, Paul Goldberg, Shannon P. Mcpherron, Dennis Sandgathe, Heather Jones, Kerry Maddison, Bruno Maureille, Susan Mentzer, Jack Rink, and Alexandre Steenhuyse (2004) Les Fouilles Récentes du Pech de l'Azé IV (Dordogne). *Gallia Préhistoire* 53(1), 1–58. 10.3406/galip.2011.2486.

Tyrberg, T. (1998) *Pleistocene Birds of the Palearctic: A Catalogue*. Cambridge, MA, Nuttall Ornithological Club.

Ucko, Peter, and Andrée Rosenfeld (1967) *Palaeolithic Cave Art*. London.
Ullrich, Herbert (1996) Předmostí – an alternative model interpreting burial rites. *Anthropologie* 34(3), 299–306.
Uomini, Natalie, Joanna Fairlie, Russell D. Gray, and Michael Griesser (2020) Extended parenting and the evolution of cognition. *Philosophical Transactions of the Royal Society B: Biological Sciences*, 375(1803), 20190495. https://doi.org/10.1098/rstb.2019.0495
Utrilla, Pilar, Vincente Baldellou, Manuel Bea, and Ramon Viñas (2012) La Cueva de la Fuente del Trucho (Asque-Colungo, Huesca). Una Cueva mayor del arte gravetiense. In de las Heras, C., J.A. Lasheras, Á. Arrizabalaga, and M. de la Rasilla (eds) *Pensando el Gravetiense: nuevos datos para la region cantábrica en su context peninsular y pirenaico. Monografías del Museo Nacional y Centro de Investigación de Altamire, no. 23*, 526–537. Spain, Ministerio de Educación, Cultura y Deporte & Museo de Altamira.
Utrilla, Pilar, and Manuel Bea (2015) Fuente del Trucho, Huesca (Spain): Reading Interaction in Palaeolithic Art. In Primitiva Bueno-Ramirez and Paul Bahn (eds) *Prehistoric Art as Prehistoric Culture: Studies in Honour of Professor Rodrigo de Balbín Behrmann*, 69–78. Oxford, Archaeopress.
Utrilla, Pilar, Carlos Mazo, Rafael Domingo, and Manuel Martínez-Bea (2021) Maps in Prehistoric Art. In Davidson, Iain, and April Nowell (eds) *Making Scenes: Global Perspective on Scenes in Rock Art*, 207–222. New York, Berghahn Books.
Valladas, Hélène, Hélène Cachier, P. Maurice, M. Arnold, F.B. de Quiros, Jean Clottes, V.C. Valdes, and P. Uzquiano (1992) Direct radiocarbon dates for prehistoric paintings at the Altamira, El Castillo and Niaux caves. *Nature* 357(6373), 68–70.
Valladas, Hélène, Norbert Mercier, Laurence Froget, Erella Hovers, J-L. Joron, William H. Kimbel, and Yoel Rak (1999) TL dates for the Neanderthal site of the Amud Cave, Israel. *Journal of Archaeological Science* 26(3), 259–268.
Valladas, Helene, Norbert Mercier, Laurence Froget, Jean-Louis Joron, Jean-Louis Reyss, Panajotis Karkanas, Eleni Panagopoulou, and Nina Kyparissi-Apostolika (2007) TL age-estimates for the Middle Palaeolithic layers at Theopetra Cave (Greece). *Quaternary Geochronology* 2(1–4), 303–308.
Vallois, Henri-V. (1971) Le crâne trépané magdalénien de Rochereil. *Bulletin de la Société préhistorique française. Études et travaux* 66(2), 485–495.
Van der Leeuw, S.E. (2000) Making tools from stone and clay. *Australian Archaeologist: Collected Papers in Honour of Jim Allen*, 69–88.
Van Gelder, Leslie (2010a) New methods and approaches in the study of finger flutings. *Proceedings from the IFRAO Conference: Pleistocene Art of the World. September 6-11, 2010*, 1207–1220.
Van Gelder, Leslie (2010b) Ten years in Rouffignac Cave, France: a collective report on a decade of finger flutings research. *Proceedings from the IFRAO Conference: Pleistocene Art of the World. September 6-11, 2010*, 377–388
Van Gelder, Leslie (2012) Rouffignac rock art: finger fluting and the cave children of France. *Current World Archaeology* 5(2), 28–30.
Van Gelder, Leslie (2015a) *Cave Art and Enduring Kindness*. TEDx, Queenstown, New Zealand, April 19, 2015. https://www.youtube.com/watch?v=BYGPc0hf5Ss.
Van Gelder, Leslie (2015b) Counting the children: the role of children in the production of finger flutings in four Upper Paleolithic caves. *Oxford Journal of Archaeology* 34(2), 120–131.
Van Gelder, Leslie (2015c) The role of children in the creation of finger flutings in Koonalda Cave, South Australia. *Childhood in the Past: An International Journal* 8(2), 149–160.
Van Gelder, Leslie and Nowell, April (2021) Scene makers: finger fluters in Upper Paleolithic caves. In Davidson, Iain, and April Nowell (eds) *Making Scenes: Scenes in Global Rock Art*, 194–206. New York, Berghahn Books.
Van Gelder, Leslie, and Kevin Sharpe (2009) Women and girls as Upper Paleolithic cave 'artists': deciphering the sexes of finger fluters in Rouffignac Cave. *Oxford Journal of Archaeology* 28(4), 323–333.

Van Gilder, Cynthia L. (2018) In the sea of night: ancient Polynesia and the dark. In Gonlin, Nancy and April Nowell (eds) *Archaeology of the Night: Life After Dark in the Ancient World*, 155–178. Boulder, University Press of Colorado.

Vandermeersh, Bernard (1969) Les nouveaux squelettes moustériens découverts à Qafzeh (Israel) et leur signification. *Comptes rendus de l'Académie des sciences* 268(21), 2562–2565.

Vandiver, Pamela B., Olga Soffer, Bohuslav Klima, and Jiři Svoboda (1989) The origins of ceramic technology at Dolní Věstonice, Czechoslovakia. *Science* 246(4933), 1002–1008.

Vanhaeren, Marian, and Francesco d'Errico (2001) La Parure de L'Enfant de la Madeleine (Fouilles Peyrony): Un Nouveau Regard sur L'Enfance au Paléolithique Supérieur. *Paléo* 13, 201–240.

Vanhaeren, Marian, and Francesco d'Errico (2002) The body ornaments associated with the burial. In Zilhão, João, and Erik Trinkaus (eds) *Portrait of the Artist as a Child. The Gravettian Human Skeleton from the Abrigo do Lagar Velho and its Archaeological Context*, 154–186. Lisboa, Instituto Português de Arqueologia.

Vanhaeren, Marian, and Francesco d'Errico (2003) Childhood in the Epipaleolithic. What do personal ornaments associated to burials tell us? In Larsson, Lars, Hans Kindgren, Kjel Knutsson, David Loeffler, and Agneta Åkerlund (eds) *Mesolithic on the Move: Papers Presented at the 6th International Conference on the Mesolithic in Europe, Stockholm, September 2000*, 494–505. Oxford, Oxbow Books.

Vanharen, Marian, and Francesco d'Errico (2006) Aurignacian ethno-linguistic geography of Europe revealed by personal ornaments. *Journal of Archaeological Science* 33(8), 1105–1128. DOI: 10.1016/j.jas.2005.11.017.

Vermeersch, Pierre (2002) Two Upper Palaeolithic burials at Nazlet Khater. In Vermeersch, Pierre (ed.) *Palaeolithic Quarrying Sites in Upper and Middle Egypt*, 273–282. Leuven, Leuven University Press.

Verna, Christine, Véronique Dujardin, and Erik Trinkaus (2012) The Early Aurignacian human remains from La Quina-Aval (France). *Journal of Human Evolution* 62(5), 605–617.

Villotte, Sébastien (2018) Unexpected discovery of more elements from the prehistoric immature skeleton from Baousso da Torre (Bausu da Ture) (Liguria, Italy). Inventory, age-at-death estimation, and probable sex assessment of BT3. *Bulletins et Memoires de la Société d'anthropologie de Paris* 30(3), 162–168.

Villotte, Sébastien, Christopher J. Knüsel, Piers D. Mitchell, and Dominique Henry-Gambier (2011) Probable carpometacarpal and tarsal coalition from Baousso da Torre Cave (Italy): implications for burial selection during the Gravettian. *Journal of Human Evolution* 61(1), 117.

Villotte, Sébastien, Mathilde Samsel, and Vitale Sparacello (2017) The paleobiology of two adult skeletons from Baousso da Torre (Bausu da Ture) (Liguria, Italy): implications for Gravettian lifestyle. *Comptes Rendus Palevol* 16(4), 462–473.

Villotte, Sébastien, A.R. Ogden, and Erik Trinkaus (2018) Dental abnormalities and Oral pathology of the Pataud 1 upper Paleolithic human. *Bulletins et Mémoires de la Société d'Anthropologie de Paris* 30(3–4), 153–161.

Vlak, Dejana, Mirjana Roksandic, and Michael A. Schillaci (2008) Greater Sciatic Notch as a sex indicator in juveniles. *American Journal of Physical Anthropology* 137(3), 309–315.

Vlček, E. (1975) Morphology of the first metacarpal of Neandertal individuals from the Crimea. *Bulletins et Mémoires de la Société d'Anthropologie de Paris* 2(3), 257–276.

Von Petzinger, Genevieve (2017) *The First Signs: Unlocking the Mysteries of the World's Oldest Symbols*. New York, Atria.

Voss, Barbara L. (2008) Sexuality studies in archaeology. *Annual Review of Anthropology* 37, 317–336.

Vygotsky, Lev Semenovich (1978) *Mind in society: The Development of Higher Psychological Processes*. Cambridge, MA, Harvard University Press.

Wachtel, Edward (1993) The first picture show: cinematic aspects of cave art. *Leonardo* 26(2), 135–140. https://doi.org/10.2307/1575898.

Wales, Nathan (2012) Modeling Neanderthal clothing using ethnographic analogues. *Journal of Human Evolution* 63(6), 781–795.

Wall-Scheffler, Cara M., Janelle Wagnild, and Emily Wagler (2015) Human footprint variation while performing load bearing tasks. *PLoS ONE* 10(3), e0118619. https://doi.org/10.1371/journal.pone.0118619.

Wall-Scheffler, Cara M., Helen Kurki, and Benjamin M. Auerbach (Forthcoming). *The Evolutionary Biology of the Human Pelvis: An Integrative Approach*. Cambridge, Cambridge University Press.

Wang, James Z., Weina Ge, Dean R. Snow, Prasenjit Mitra, and C. Lee Giles (2010) Determining the sexual identities of prehistoric cave artists using digitized handprints: a machine learning approach. In *Proceedings of the ACM International Conference on Multimedia*, 1325–1332. New York, ACM.

Ward, Carol V., William H. Kimbel, Elizabether H. Harmon, and Donald C. Johanson (2012) New postcranial fossils of *Australopithecus afarensis* from Hadar, Ethiopia (1990–2007). *Journal of Human Evolution* 63(1), 1–51.

Warren, Matthew (2018) Mum's a Neanderthal, dad's a Denisovan: first discovery of an ancient-human hybrid. *Nature* 560(7719), 417-419. Gale OneFile: CPI.Q, link.gale.com/apps/doc/A572819389/CPI?u=uvictoria&sid=CPI&xid=50da3ba0.

Washburn, Sherwood L. (1960) Tools and human evolution. *Scientific American* 203(3), 63–75.

Watkins, Joe (2000) *Indigenous Archaeology: American Indian Values and Scientific Practice*. Walnut Creek, CA, Altamira Press.

Watkins, Joe (2016) Research, representation, redemption and repatriation: archaeology and community relationships in 21st Century America. In Coleman, Simon, Susan B. Hyatt, and Ann Kingsolver (eds) *The Routledge Companion to Contemporary Anthropology*, 264–282. New York, Routledge.

Weaver, Timothy D., and Jean-Jaques Hublin (2009) Neandertal birth canal shape and the evolution of human childbirth. *Proceedings of the National Academy of Sciences* 106(20), 8151–8156.

Weaver, Timothy D., Hélène Coqueugniot, Liubov V. Golovanova, Vladimir B. Doronichev, Bruno Maureille, and Jean-Jacques Hublin (2016) Neonatal postcrania from Mezmaiskaya, Russia, and Le Moustier, France, and the development of Neanderthal body form. *Proceedings of the National Academy of Science* 113(23), 6472–6477. https://doi.org/10.1073/pnas.1523677113pmid:27217565.

Weedman, Kathryn (2005) Gender and stone-tools: an ethnographic study of Konso and Gamo hideworkers of Southern Ethiopia. In Frink, Lisa, and Kathryn Weedman (eds) *Gender and Hide Production*, 175–196. Walnut Creek, AltaMira Press.

Weedman, Kathryn (2006a) An ethnoarchaeological study of hafting and stone tool diversity among the Gamo of Ethiopia. *Journal of Archaeological Science* 13(3), 188–237.

Weedman, Kathryn (2006b) Gender and ethnoarchaeology. In Nelson, Sarah M. (ed.) *Handbook of Gender in Archaeology*, 247–294. Lanham, MD, AltaMira Press.

Weisner, Thomas S. (1987) Socialization for parenthood in sibling caretaking societies. In Lancaster, Jane Beckman, Jeanne Altmann, Lonnie R. Sherrod, and Alice Rossi (eds) *Parenting across the Life Span: Biosocial Dimensions*, 237–270. New York, Aldine de Gruyter.

Welker, Frido, Mateja Hajdinjak, Sahra Talamo, Klervia Jaouen, Michael Dannemann, Francine David, Michèle Julien, Matthias Meyer, Janet Kelso, Ian Barnes, Selena Brace, Pepijn Kamminga, Roman Fischer, Benedikt M. Kessler, John R. Stewart, Svante Paabo, Matthew J. Collins, and Jean-Jacques Hublin (2016) Palaeoproteomic evidence identifies archaic hominins associated with the Châtelperronian at the Grotte du Renne. *Proceedings of the National Academy of Sciences* 113(40), 11162–11167.

Weyrich, Laura, Sebastian Duchene, Julien Soubrier, Luis Arriola, Bastien Llamas, James Breen, Alan G. Morris, Kurt W. Alt, David Caramelli, Veit Dresely, Milly Farrell, Andrew G. Farrer, Michael Francken, Neville Gully, Wolfgang Haak, Karen Hardy, Katerina Harvati, Petra Held, Edward C. Holmes, John Kaidonis, Carles Lalueza-Fox, Marco de la Rasilla, Antonio Rosas, Patrick Semal, Arkadiusz Soltysiak, Grant Townsend, Donatella Usai, Joachim Wahl, Daniel H. Huson, Keith Dobney, and Alan Cooper (2017) Neanderthal behaviour, diet, and disease inferred from ancient DNA in dental calculus. *Nature* 544(7564), 357–361. https://doi.org/10.1038/nature21674.

Wheeler, Michael, and Andy Clark (2008) Culture, embodiment and genes: unravelling the triple helix. *Philosophical Transactions of the Royal Society B: Biological Sciences* 363(1509) 3563–3575.

White, Randall (2003) *Prehistoric Art: The Symbolic Journey of Humankind*. New York, Harry N. Abrams.

White, Randall (2007) Systems of personal ornamentation in the Early Upper Paleolithic: methodological challenges and new observations. In Mellars, Parul, Katie Boyle, Ofer Bar-Yosef, and Christopher Stringer (eds) *Rethinking the Human Revolution: New Behavioural and Biological Perspectives on the Origin and Dispersal of Modern Humans*, 287–302. Cambridge, McDonald Institute.

White, Tim D., and Gen Suwa (1987) Hominid footprints at Laetoli: facts and interpretations. *American Journal of Physical Anthropology* 72(4), 485–514.

White, Tim D., Berhane Asfaw, Yonas Beyene, Yohannes Haile-Selassie, C. Owen Lovejoy, Gen Suwa, and Giday Wolde Gabriel (2009) *Ardipithecus ramidus* and the paleobiology of early hominids. *Science* 326(5949), 64–86.

White, Tim D., Michael T. Black, and Pieter A. Folkens (2012) *Human Osteology*, 3rd Edition. Amsterdam, Elsevier.

Whiten, Andrew (2020) Wild chimpanzees scaffold youngsters' learning in a high-tech community. *Proceedings of the National Academy of Sciences* 117(2), 802–804.

Whiten, Andrew, Jane Goodall, William Mcgrew, Toshida Nishida, Vernon Reynolds, Yukimaru Sugiyama, Caroline Tutin, Richard Wrangham, and Christophe Boesch (1999) Cultures in Chimpanzees. *Nature* 399(6737), 682–685. 10.1038/21415.

Whiten, Andrew, Nicola McGuigan, Sarah Marshall-Pescini, and Lydia M. Hopper (2009) Emulation, imitation, over-imitation and the scope of culture for child and chimpanzee. *Philosophical Transactions of the Royal Society B: Biological Sciences* 364(1528), 2417–2428. doi:10.1098/rstb.2009.0069.

Whitley, David S. (2008) *Cave Paintings and the Human Spirit: The Origin of Creativity and Belief*. Amherst, Prometheus.

Whittaker, John C. (1994) *Flintknapping: Making and Understanding Stone Tools*. Austin, TX, University of Texas Press.

Wiessner, Polly W. (2014) Embers of society: firelight talk among the Ju/'hoansi Bushmen. *Proceedings of the National Academy of Sciences of the United States of America* 111(39), 14027–14035. https://doi.org/10.1073/pnas.1404212111.

Wilczyński, Jarosaw, Micha Wojenka, Piotr Wojtal, Anita Szczepanek, and Dobrawa Sobieraj (2012) Human occupation of the Borsuka Cave (southern Poland) – from Upper Palaeolithic to the post medieval period. *Eurasian Prehistory* 9(1–2) 77–91.

Wilczyński, Jarosaw, Anita Szczepanek, Piotr Wojtal, M. Diakowski, Micha Wojenka, and Dobrawa Sobieraj (2016) A mid Upper Palaeolithic child burial from Borsuka Cave (southern Poland). *International Journal of Osteoarchaeology* 26(1), 151–162.

Wild, Eva M., Maria Teschler-Nicola, Walter Kutschera, Peter Steier, and Wolfgang Wanek (2006) 14C Dating of Early Upper Palaeolithic Human and Faunal Remains from Mladeč. In Teschler-Nicola, Maria (ed.) *Early Modern Humans at the Moravian Gate*, 149–158. Vienna, Springer.

Wileman, Julie (2005) *Hide and Seek: The Archaeology of Childhood*. Oxford, Tempus.

Wilke, L.A. (1994) Childhood in the quarters: playtime at Oakley and Riverlake plantations. *Louisiana Folklife* 18, 13–20.

Wilkie, Laurie (2000) Not merely child's play: creating a historical archaeology of children and childhood. In Sofaer Derevenski, Joanna (ed.) *Children and Material Culture*, 100–113. London, Routledge.

Wilkie, Laurie A. (2003) *The Archaeology of Mothering: An African American Midwife's Tale*. New York, Routledge.

Williams, Frank L'Engle, Jessica L. Droke, Christopher W. Schmidt, John C. Willman, Gaël Becam, and Marie-Antoinette de Lumley (2018) Dental microwear texture analysis of Neandertals from Hortus Cave, France. *Comptes Rendus Palevol* 17(8), 545–556.

Williams, Justin H.G., K.D. Greenhalgh, and John T. Manning (2003) Second to fourth finger ratio and possible precursors of developmental psychopathology in preschool children. *Early Human Development* 72(1), 57–65.

Wilson, Laura A., Norman MacLeod and Louise T. Humphrey (2008) Morphometric criteria for sexing juvenile human skeletons using the ilium. *Journal of Forensic Sciences* 53(2), 269–278. https://doi.org/10.1111/j.1556-4029.2008.00656.x.

Wood, David J., Heather Wood, and David Middleton (1978) An experimental evaluation of four face-to-face teaching strategies. *International Journal of Behavioral Development* 1(2), 131–147.

Wood, James W. (1994) *Dynamics of Human Reproduction: Biology, Biometry and Reproduction*. New York, Aldine de Gruyter.

Wragg Sykes, Rebecca (2020) *Kindred*. London, Bloomsbury Sigma.

Wrangham, Richard (2017) Control of fire in the Paleolithic: evaluating the cooking hypothesis. *Current Anthropology* 58(S16), S303–S313.

Young, Diane, Suzanne Patrick, and D. Gentry Steele (1987) An analysis of the Paleoindian double burial from Horn Shelter No. 2, in Central Texas. *Plains Anthropologist* 32(117), 275–298.

Zeller, Anne C. (1987) A role for children in hominid evolution. *Man* 22(3), 528–557.

Zihlman, Adrienne (2012) Engendering human evolution. In Bolger, Diane (ed.) *A Companion to Gender Prehistory*, 23–44. Hoboken, NJ, John Wiley & Sons.

Zilhão, João, and Francisco Almeida (2002) The archaeological framework. In Zilhão, João, and Erik Trinkaus (eds) *Portrait of the Artist as a Child. The Gravettian Human Skeleton from the Abrigo do Lagar Velho and its Archaeological Context*, 29–57. Lisboa, Instituto Português de Arqueologia.

Zilhão, João, and Erik Trinkaus (2002) *Portrait of the Artist as a Child. The Gravettian Human Skeleton from the Abrigo do Lagar Velho and Its Archeological Context*. Lisbon, Instituto Português de Arqueologia.

Zilhão, João (2005) Burial evidence for the social differentiation of age classes in the early Upper Paleolithic. In Vialou, Denis, Josette Renault-Miskovsky, and Marylène Patou-Mathis (eds) *Comportements des hommes du Paléolithique moyen et supérieur en Europe: Territoires et milieux*, 231–241. Actes du Colloque de Groupement de Recherche 1945 du Centre National de la Recherche Scientifique.

Zilhão, João (2006) Chronostratigraphy of the Middle-to-Upper Paleolithic transition in the Iberian penninsula. *Pyrenae* 37(1), 7–84.

Zimmermann, Elke, and Ute Radespiel (2007) Primate life histories. In Henke, Winifried, and Ian Tattersall (eds) *Handbook of Paleoanthropology, vol 1: Principles, Methods and Approaches*, 1163–1205. Berlin, Springer.

Index

Page numbers in italics indicate figures or tables

Abri du Poisson (France), 135
Abri Pataud (France), 148, 157, *225–226*, *286–287*
Abris du Maras (France), 142
adolescents/adolescence, 14–15, *69*
    archaeology and, 146
    biological markers of, 146–151
    brain development, 151–152
    burials, 157–160, 163n1
    cognitive markers of, 151–153
    dogs as companions, 160–163
    emotional development, 152–153
    evolution and, 146, 152–153, 168
    growth spurt, 146–147
    images of, 57
    innovation and, 155, 169
    learning and, 101
    as life history stage, 23
    maturity of, 147–151
    mortality, in Paleolithic, 148
    puberty, 15, 17, 18, 19, 147, 150, 152
    risk taking behavior, 152
    shifting sleep patterns, 150
    social markers of, among foragers, 153–156
    stresses of, in Paleolithic, 156–157
    teenage years, 150–151
    See also age; biological age; Neandertals; puberty
adults
    as agents, 7
    archaeology of, 1, 6, 7
affordances
    definition, 99
    relationality, 100
    sociality, 100
    transparency, 100–101
ageing (assignment of age), 15–17
    of fossil hominin subadults, 19
    of subadults, 19
age, of humans
    chronological age, 17–18

reproductive age, 21
social age, 17–18, 78, 153
See also biological age; life history
Aldène (France), 118
Altamira (Spain), 74, *75*, 111, *112*, 125
Amud (Israel), 59, *174–176*
animal materials, as grave goods, *185*, *191*, *215*, *248–249*, *259*, *261*
    aurochs, 160, *180*, *294*
    badger, *255*
    bovine, 159, *253*, *311*
    coyote, *270*
    Cyclope sp., 142, *192–193*, *214*, *224*, *256*, *265*, *281*; deer, 60–61, 159, *176*, *214*, *225*, *231*, *251*, *254–256*, *265*, *281–282*, *284–285*, *294*
    Dentalium sp., 140, *141*, *247*
    elk, 159, *180*, *251*
    fish, 159, *214*, *253–255*
    fox, 62, 158, *189*, *214*, *245*, *250*, *260–261*, *309–310*
    hare, *293*
    horse, *224*
    Littorina obtusata, 61, *215*, *247*
    mammoth ivory/bone, 62–63, 139–140, 158, 159, *189*, *211*, *245*, *251*, *259–261*, *271*, *286*, *291–293*, *309–310*
    mollusk, 62
    reindeer, 158
    rhinoceros, *204*
    shell, 63, 148, 159, *202*, *214*, *225*, *247*, *251*, *254–255*, *259*, *270*, *281–282*, *286*
    Siberian ibex, 60
    steppe wisent, *180*
    tortoise/turtle, *185*, *270*
    ungulate, *180*, *209*, *224*, *281*, *284–285*
    wolf, 158
Anthropocene, 166
archaeology
    agency of individual and, 7
    as anthropological, 46
    archaeological subject, changes in, 14

communities of practice and, 98
ethnoarchaeological studies, 84–85, 92, 93
excavator bias, 3
handprint study, 135, 156
inorganic materials in archaeological record, 144
of intimacy, 87
lithics/stone tools identification, 79–81
of nighttime activities, 13, 105
of novice flintknappers, 82–85
of Paleolithic, 19
periodization, 20n1, *172*
plants/organic materials in archaeological record, 143–144, 157, *185*
social structure determination and, 39–40
textiles, 139
toolmaker identification, 89–90
See also artifacts; context; demographics; ethnography
archaeology of children, 46, 164
adolescents, 146
vs. archaeology of adults, 7
archaeological record vs. living populations, 1–4, 44
dance and, 114–115
distortion of archaeology record and, 4–7
excavation/screening techniques of, 4
flintknapping and, 79–82, 85–89
footprints, 67–74, 120, 145n6
lithics/stone tools and, 78–79
marginalization of, 13–14
material culture and, 7
music and, 115–116
Paleolithic, 19, 170–171
publications on, 13, 14
secret spaces, 65–66
small spaces, 66–67
toys and games and, 48–49
See also children as producers of art; children as producers of goods
Ardipithecus sp., 20n2
Ardipithecus kadabba, *172*
Ardipithecus ramidus, 25, *172*
birth process, 25–26
Infant to Mother Mass Ratio, 33
Arene Candide (Italy), 64, *251–252*
artifacts
transposition of, 5–6
See also fiber technologies; lamps; limestone; lithics/stone tools; music/musical instruments; personal ornaments; portable art objects; tools; toys and games; weapons
art of Paleolithic, 59
ceramics production errors, 127–128
communities of practice, 123–125
definition, 123, 144n3
engraving errors, 126–127
image quality errors, 128–131
interpretation of, 117
lack of images of humans in, 55, 112
novices, identification of, 126–131
practice and, 126
raw materials errors, 128
scenes in, 113–114
sex and, 133
study of, 125
varying levels of skill in, 132
visual play in, 111
See also children as producers of art; parietal art; portable art objects
Ascher, Robert, 5
Atapuerca (Spain), *252*
Sima de los Huesos, 27, 58, *236–238*, *295–307*
Australopithecus sp., 20n2, *219*, *221–222*, *244–245*, *247*, *280*, *309*
Au. afarensis, 24, 26, 29, 30, 41, 67, 69, *172–174*, *219*, *235*, *251*, *311*
Au. africanus, 25, 26, 30, 35–36, 40, 41, *172*, *244–245*
Au. anamensis, *172*
Au. garhi, *172*
Au. sediba, 19, 26, *172*, *235*
birth process, 25–26
brain size, 29
burials, *235*
childhood, 41
family/social structure, 40–41
footprints, 67
infant care, 34, 167
Infant to Mother Mass Ratio, 33
infants, 29–30, 33
Grandmother Hypothesis and, 38–39
Hadar specimen, 29
Lucy, 26, 29
Selam/Dikika baby/ Lucy's Child, 29, 30, 33, *235*
Taung child, 30, *246*
weaning and teeth analysis, 35–36

baby
    definition of, 15
    Selam/Dikika baby/Lucy's Child, 29, *30*, 33, *235*
Barma Grande (Italy), 158–159, *180*, *253–255*
Baxter, Jane, 5, 11–12, 14
Bédeilhac (France), 49, 67, *76*, 118
Bernifal (France), 135
Binford, Lewis, 5–7
biological age, 18, 153
    sex and, 16
    skeletal development and, 16–17
    teeth and, 16, 17
birth process, of hominins, 23–28
    birth canal, 17, 23–26, 27, 28, 41
    delivery assistance, 25
    Obstetrical Dilemma (OD), 23, 26, 28
    rotated birth, 25, 27
    See also fetus; neonates; reproduction
Boncuklu Höyük (Turkey), 132
bones/bone structure, of hominins
    cranium/skull, 17, 18, 24–25, 31
    foot, 33
    pelvis, 18, 24–27
    preservation of, 3
    See also skeletons
Bonn-Oberkassel (Germany), 162
brain, of hominins
    energy needs, 34
    growth/development of, 28–29, 151–153
    of infant Australopithecines, 29
    of infant hominins, 23, 29
    of Neandertals, 31–32
    plasticity of, 100, 152, 168
    play and development of, 47, 48
    vs. primate brains, 28–29
    reproduction and, *22*, 23, 26
    social structure and, 40, 152
    See also cognitive processes
Breuil, Abbé Henri, 133
Bronze Age, 9, *10*, 133
Buret' (Siberia), 55, 57, 139
Bush Barrow (UK), 9, *10*

Calvert Island (Canada), *68*
Cerén (El Salvador), 5, 6
Chauvet (France), *68*, 72, 107, *108*, 109–111, 113, 114, 118, 129
childhood, 15, 18
    of Australopithecines, 41
    of hominins, 19, 23, 101
    of *Homo* sp., 41
    modern/Western conceptions of, 7–9
children/offspring
    as active learners, 167–168
    bones, 3
    agency of, 7–13, 47, 164, 169–170
    as caregivers, 9
    child-rearing practices, 11
    definitions of/terminology, 14–15
    as distorters of archaeological record, 4–7
    evolution and, 164, 169–170
    as food providers, 9
    images/representations of, 55–57
    mortality rates, 3
    Nariokotome/Turkana boy, 26, *27*, *223*
    oral storytelling and, 103–106, 167
    Paleolithic archaeology and, 1, 19, 46, 57–58
    percentage of prehistoric population, 1, 3
    plants and, 143, 157
    in political/military sphere, 10, 52
    in religious sphere, 10, 52
    space and, in Paleolithic, 64–77
    in work force, 9
    See also adolescents; age; archaeology of children; baby; biological age; funerary practices; infants; neonates; play; subadults; toys
children as producers of art
    age and apprenticeship, 131–133
    communities of practice and, 124–125, 170
    development stages, 132
    engagement, 120–123
    figurative/non-figurative images, 118–120
    finger flutings by, 67, 119–122, 131, 145n7, 155–156
    in general, 117–118
    handprints/hand stencils, 72, 74–77, 114, 121, 134, 156
    initiation rites and, 115, 155–156
    parietal art, 156
    sex of, 133–138
children as producers of goods, 9–10, 71
    age and, 90–92
    communities of practice of, 97–99, 170
    as novices, 79, 85–89
    scaffolding and, 85, 87, 90, 95
    skill acquisition/apprenticeship, 96–97, 101–103
Ciampate de Diavolo (Italy), *68*

cognition, of hominins
  development in adolescents, 151–153
  distributed cognition, 169, 170
  embodied cognition, 99–101, 125
  extended cognition, 100
  See also brain
Combe-Capelle (France), 83
Combe Grenal (France), 53, *181, 256–257*
communities of practice
  archaeology and, 98, 170
  embedded learning, 98, 101
  ethnography of, 97
  innovation and, 170
  legitimate peripheral engagement, 99
  in Paleolithic, 97, 102–103, 123–125, 170
  scaffolding, 85, 87, 90, 95
  situated learning, 99, 169–170
  Zone of Proximal Development, 168
Conkey, Margaret, 13–14
context, of artifacts
  archaeological vs. systemic, 5
  primary, 5–6
  secondary, 5
cooperative breeding, in hominins, 37–39
  alloparenting, 37–39, 41
  Grandmother Hypothesis/grandmothering, *22, 23,* 38–39, 41
  See also infant care
Cosquer Cave (France), 74, *75,* 77, 107, *109,* 118
Cougnac (France), 110
Covalanas (Spain), 111
Cro-Magnon (France), 32, *184*
Cueva del Niño (Spain), 113
cupules, 59

dance, 114–115
death, 2
  age at, 15
  associated pathologies, 57, 63, 64, 157–158
  mortality of adolescents in Paleolithic, 148
  mortality rates, 3
  toys and, 12
  See also funerary practices
demographics, and archaeology
  analysable population, 2, 3
  archaeological population, 1, *2*
  buried population, *2*
  burying population, 2
  deceased population, 2

  exhumed population, *2,* 3
  living population, 1–3
dogs, 72, 74, 160–163
Dolní Věstonice I/II (Czech Republic), 19, 51, 132, 139, 157–158, *188–189, 258–262*
Drimolen (South Africa), 3, 30

Egypt (ancient), 2, 9, 10
El Castillo (Spain), *75,* 111, 118, 133, 135, *189*
El Sidrón (Spain), 35, 156, *189–190, 263*
Engare Sero (Tanzania), 42
Ericsson, Anders, 96
ethnography, 62, 89, 106, 114, 115, 116, 139, 151
  of craft learning, 90, 97, 131
  ethnoarchaeology, 84–85, 93
  taphonomy and, 85
Étiolles (France), 65–66, 87, 88
evolution, of hominins, 45n5
  activity theory, 167–168
  children/adolescents and, 146, 152–153, 164, 168–170
  cultural transmission and, 170
  cumulative culture/ratchet effect and, 169
  Developmental Niche Construction, 166, 167–171
  direct teaching and, 168
  distributed cognition, 168, 170
  environmental change and, 166, 169
  Extended Evolutionary Synthesis, 165
  genetics and, 164–166
  Modern Synthesis, 164–165, 166
  natural pedagogy, 167
  natural selection, 21, 164–165
  Niche Construction Theory, 165–166, 171n1
  oblique teaching and, 155, 168, 169
  play and, 46–49, 168
  Selective Niche Construction, 166
  situated learning and, 169–170
  storytelling and, 167–168, 169

family
  grandmothering, *22, 23,* 38–39, 41
  social learning, 23, 97, 105–106
family, in Paleolithic, 21, 39, 73–74
family structure
  of *Australopithecus* sp., 40–41
  of *Homo* sp., 40–42, 44–45
  of Neandertals, 42
  in Paleolithic, 39–40

fetus, 18
  of hominins, 17, 24, 148, *211, 213, 223, 231, 248, 250*
  images of, 55
  See also baby; birth process; infants; neonates
fiber technologies
  clothing, 138–143
  cordage, 142–143
  footwear, 139
  taskscape, 143–144
  textile production, 139
finger flutings, 67, 115
  age/sex determination of makers, 120, 132, 133–134
  by children, 74, *75–76, 118*, 119, 121–122, 131, 133–134, 145n7, 155–156
  communities of practice and, 97
fire, 104, 107, 116–117, 144n1
  hearths, 110
  See also lamps
flintknapping, 79–82
  affordances and, 100–101, 168–169
  age and, 90–92
  chaîne opératoire and, 83–84, 125, 144
  communities of practice, 99, 102–103, 170
  errors in, 81–82, 85–86
  ethnoarchaeological studies and, 84–85, 92, 93
  location on a site, 86–87
  non-productivity, 86
  by novices, 82–89
  raw material quality, 87–88
  recycled materials, 88
  refitting studies and, 83–84, 125
  replication studies and, 82–83, 92, 125
  sex and, 92–95
  size, 88–89
  skill acquisition/apprenticeship, 95–97, 101–103
  strategies, 88
Fontanet (France), 54–55, *68*, 72, *76*, 118
Font-de-Gaume (France), 113, 118, 135, *190*
foragers/hunter-gatherers, 2, 52, 85, 89, 93, 143
  adolescence of, 148, 151, 153–156
  contemporary vs. Paleolithic, 153
  creativity of adolescents, 155
  dance and, 114
  demographics, 153–154

  empathy and, 152
  initiation rites, 155–156
  intimacy and autonomy, 153–154
  music and, 115–116
  oral storytelling and, 105–106, 117
  sexual freedom/exploration, 154–155
  sleep patterns, 150
  teaching by, 95
Fronsac (France), 67
Fuente del Salín (Spain), *76*
Fuente del Trucho (Spain), *76*, 77n6
funerary practices
  adolescents and, 157–160, 163n1
  burial grounds/cemeteries, 2, 3, 64
  burials, defined, 57–58
  children's clothing and, 139–140
  cillini, 4
  double burials, 148–149, 157, 163n1, *178, 192–193, 211, 231, 245, 247, 265, 270, 285, 293*
  funerary caching, 31, 58, 63
  grave goods, 4, 60–62, 64, *191*
  hematite and, *283–284*
  manganese oxide, *282*
  of modern humans, 60–64
  of Neandertals, 31, 43, 58–61, 63–64
  oligist and, *254–256*
  in Paleolithic, 15, 57–64
  stones and, *204, 214–215, 217, 231, 234, 250, 259–260, 265, 275, 286–287, 311*
  triple burials, 157, *248–249, 254, 259–260, 309–310*
  variation in and archaeological record, 2, 4
  See also animal materials; death; taphonomy *and under Homo* sp.; limestone; lithics/ stone tools; Neandertals; ochre; personal ornaments; portable art objects; tools

Gargas Cave (France), *75*, 77, *118*, 121, 135, *191*
Geißenklösterle (Germany), 116
gender
  and archaeology, 13
  toys and, 12
genetics
  biological age and, 17
  evolution and, 164–166
  exogamy of hominins and, 44
  genotype, 21, 171n1
  of Neandertals, 43, 44
  phenotype, 21, 166, 171n1
  sexing of subadults and, 19

Gibson, James, 99
Gombore (Ethiopia), 67, *68*, 71
Gönnersdorf (Germany), 55, 139
Gorham's Cave (Gibraltar), *76*
Gramsbergen (Netherlands), 101
Grotta della Bàsura (Italy), *68*, 73–74, 162
    Tana della Bàsura, *70*
Grotte de Enfants (Italy), 63, 140, 142, *192*
Gua Masri (Borneo), 135

Hattoridai (Japan), 84, 86, 87, 98
Hohle Fels (Germany), 116, 142
hominins, 3–4, 20n1
    anatomical evolution, 24
    bipedalism of, 23, 24, 26, 29, 33, 41, *69*
    chondrodystrophic dwarf, 159–160
    definition, 20n2
    fire/artificial light and, 104–105, 107–108, 116–117, 144n1
    fossil, 19, 29, 30, 33, 151
    periodization, 20n1, *172*
    plants and, 143
    play and, 47
    See also Ardipithecus sp.; *Australopithecus* sp.; cooperative breeding; evolution; *Homo* sp.; life history; Neandertals; *Paranthropus* sp.
Homo sp., 3, 19, 20n2, *184*, *187*, *204–208*, *241*, *258*
    Afropithecus turkanensis, 174
    birth process, 26–28
    Buia specimen, 26
    burials, 60–64, 140, 148–149, 157–159, *176–178*, *180*, *185*, *189*, *191–193*, *211*, *214–215*, *217*, *221*, *224*, *231*, *233–234*, *243*, *245*, *247–256*, *259–261*, *264–265*, *270–271*, *280–287*, *291*, *293–294*, *309–311*
    childhood, 31, 41
    cranial growth, 30
    family/social structure, 40–42
    Gona specimen, 26
    Grandmother Hypothesis and, 39
    H. denisova, *258*
    H. erectus, 19, 26, 30–32, 34, 36, 39, 41–42, 147, *172*, *222–223*, *235*
    H. floresiensis, 27, *172*
    H. habilis, *172*, *224*
    H. heidelbergensis, 27, 67, *68*, *172*, *191*, *238*
    H. naledi, 19, 27, *172*, *200–201*
    H. rudolfensis, *172*
    H. sapiens, 24, 25, 32, 42, 44–45, 58, 64, 68–70, 75–76, 166, *172*, *176–181*, *184*, *188–193*, *203–204*, *208–212*, *214–227*, *229–235*, *243–256*, *258–265*, *270–273*, *275–280*, *282–289*, *291–294*, *309*, *311*
    infant/juvenile specimens, 30–32
    Infant to Mother Mass Ratio, 33
    Kenyanthropus platyops, *172*
    Mojokerto infant, 30, 31, *222*
    Nariokotome/Turkana boy, 26, *27*, *223*
    Orrorin tugenensis, *172*
    Sahelanthropus tchadensis, *172*
    weaning and teeth analysis, 35–36
    See also Neandertals
hunter-gatherers. *See* foragers

Il Principe (Italy), 159
infant care, 149
    breastfeeding and weaning, 34–38, 41
    diet and, 34, 41
    evolution of, 33–39
    infant carrying, 33–34, 167
    play mothering, 48
    See also cooperative breeding; Neandertals
infants, of hominins, 1, 3, 4, 11, 18
    Australopithecine, 29–30, 33
    brains of, 26
    burials, 59, 62–63, 148, *176*, *179*, *185*, *204*, *215*, *217*, *248*
    definition of, 14–15
    fossil record of, 44, *173–175*, *192*, *196*, *202*, *212*, *229*, *231*, *250*
    hand stencil, 77
    H. specimens, 30–32
    images of, 55
    Infant to Mother Mass Ratio, 33
    intentionality and, 34, 167
    Selam/Dikika baby/Lucy's Child, 29, *30*, 33, *235*
    nutritional needs of, 34
    vulnerability of, 33
    See also baby; Neandertals; neonates
Inuit people, 11, 89
    Thule, 11
Isturitz (France), 116, *203*

Jebel Irhoud (Morocco), 45n7, *204*
Jeju Island (South Korea), *69*

Kamishirataki 2 (Japan), 99
Knappett, Carl, 99–101

Koonalda (Australia), 67, 118
Kostenki I/II (Russia), 51, 139, *271*
Krems-Wachtberg (Austria), 62–63, *210–211, 272*

Laetoli (Tanzania), 67, *69*, 215
La Ferrassie (France), 59–60, *212–213*, 274
Lagar Velho (Portugal), 61, *215*
Lagrave (France), 113
La Lastrilla (Spain), *76*
La Madeleine (France), 140, *141*, 214
La Marche (France), 55, *56*
Lamarck, Jean-Baptiste, 166
lamps/torches, 108–110. *See also* fire
La Pasiega (Spain), 67
Lascaux (France), *69*, 107, *109–110*, 112, 113–114
Las Chimeneas (Spain), 67, *76*, 118
latrine, 6
La Vergre (France), 64
Laugerie-Basse (France), 49, *50*, 215–216, *275*
Leang Bulu' Sipong 4 (Sulawesi), 113
Le Mas d'Azil (France), 49, *50*, 51, *221*
Le Moustier (France), 59, 147, *217*, *275*
Le Mouthe (France), 110
Le Rozel (France), *69*, 71
Les Combarelles (France), 67, 135
Les Trois Frères (France), 112
Lewis, Mary, 16
life history, of hominins, 41, 153
    definition, 21–22
    derived features, *22*
    K-strategy features, 22–23
    r-strategy features, 22–23
    stages, 15
Lillehammer, Grete, 1, 46
limestone, 108
    in burials, 59, 60, 140, *186*, *213*, *221*, *233, 291–293*
lithics/stone tools, 65–66, 84, 103n1, *190, 193–202, 209, 213, 222, 263, 270*
    flints/flint tools, 101–102, *233*
    as grave goods, 60, 65, 158, 159, *185–186, 191, 247–249, 251, 253–254, 256, 259–261, 265, 270, 281–282*
    identification of makers of, 89–95
    making of, 79, 101–103
    microlithics, 88–89
    Paleolithic subadults and, 78–79
    study of, 125
    See also flintknapping

Maastricht-Belvédère (Netherlands), 83, 88
Mal'ta (Siberia), 50, 55, *56*, 57, 62, 139, *220*
material culture, and children, 11–13, 65
Mayan culture, 5, 9, 10, 13
Mezin (Ukraine), 53
Mezirich (Ukraine), 53
Mezmaiskaya (Russia), 59, *221*
Montespan (France), 118
Monte Verde (Chile), *69*
Murphy, Eileen, 4
music/musical instruments, 115–116
    bullroarers, 52, *54*
    flutes, 116
    percussive instruments, 53, *54*, 116
    whistles, 53–54, 116

Neandertals (*H. neanderthalensis*), 70, 71, 142, 163n2, *172, 174–175, 177, 179, 181, 187, 189–197, 199, 202–203, 209–210, 212, 214, 216–217, 222, 224, 227–228, 230, 232, 235–238, 244–246, 249, 252, 256–258, 262–264, 266–278, 280, 289–291, 295–307, 309*
    adolescent development, 32, 147, 149
    adolescents, 157
    birth process, 27
    bone development, 32
    burials, 31, 43, 58–60, 63, *176, 182–186, 198, 200, 203, 213, 221, 231, 233, 243, 311*
    brain size/development, 31–32
    breastfeeding, 36–37
    clothing, 138–139
    extinction, 43, 44, 139
    family/social structure, 42–44, 69
    genetic mutations, 44
    grave goods, 60–61
    infant mortality, 44
    infant specimens, 31
    pregnancy, 36, 37
    Roc de Marsal child, *31, 32*, 59, *233*
    sexual maturity, 147
    subadult specimens, 31
    weaning, 35, 36–37, 43
neonates, of hominins, 4, *208, 223*
    Ardipithecus sp., 25
    Australopithecus sp., 41
    birth process and, 23–25
    Homo sp., 32, *185, 225–226, 229*
    Neandertal, 31–32, *187, 198, 213, 221, 231*
    underdevelopment of human, 28
    See also baby; fetus; infants

Nerja Cave (Spain), 108, *223*
Niaux (France), *69, 72, 73*, 118, 132

ochre
  in burials, 61, 62, 63, 148, 157–158, *185, 189, 211, 214–215, 224–225, 245, 247–249, 251–256, 259–261, 270, 281–285, 287, 310–311*
  in parietal art, 114
  red, 60, 159, *189, 211, 215, 224–225, 245, 248–249, 251–256, 281–282, 285, 310*
  yellow, 159, *252*
Ohalo II (Israel), 142
Ojo Guareña (Spain), 118
Oldeholtwode (Netherlands), 87, 88, 99, 101
Ostuni (Italy), 148–149, 157, *224, 281–282*
Ozette (USA), 5, 6

Pair-Non-Pair (France), 111
Paleolithic
  periodization, 20n1, *172*
Paranthropus sp., 20n2, *239–243, 247–248*, 280, *308–309, 311*
  family/social structure, 40–41
  Infant to Mother Mass Ratio, 33
  P. aethiopicus, 172
  P. boisei, 33, *172, 207, 224*
  P. robustus, 3, 33, 35–36, 40, 41, *172, 204, 239–242, 308*
  weaning and teeth analysis, 35–36
parietal art, in Paleolithic, 97, 125
  animal images in, 107–114, 120, 122, 123, 129–130
  ceramic, 124–125
  children and, 117–118
  communities of practice and, 123
  dance and, 114–115
  engravings, 117, 123–124, 128
  figurative/non-figurative images, 118–120
  handprints/hand stencils, 72, 74–77, 114, 121, 134–138, 156
  image quality, 128–131
  narrative in, 113–114
  painting/drawing, 111, 117, 123, 128
  storytelling in, 107, *109*, 112–114, 117
  tectiforms, *118*, 119–120, 122
  therianthropic figures, 112–113
  three dimensionality in, 110–112, 130
  traditions in, 123
  visual play in, 111–112
  See also art of Paleolithic; children as producers of art; portable art objects
Pavlov (Czech Republic), 51, 139, *226–227, 287–289*
Pech Merle (France), *70, 75*, 110, 118, 133, 135
personal ornaments, 97, 138
  beads, 60, 62, 139–142, 158, *193–200*, 211, 245, *267, 286*
  as grave goods, 62, 64, 157–159, *185, 202*, 211, *214*, 245, *251, 253–255, 259–260, 270, 286–287, 309–310*
personhood, of children, 4, 43, 64
Pincevent (France), 84, 88, 90, 99, 101
play, 4–5, 72–73
  evolution and, 46–49
  fantasy play, 48
  in general, 46–47
  learning and, 89, 90, 101–103
  in parietal art, 111
  playhouses/secret spaces, 65–66
  social play, 46–47
  visual play/humor, 49–50
  See also children; toys and games
Pompeii, 6, 132
'Pompeii premise', 5
portable art objects, in Paleolithic, 97
  animal figurines, 51–52, 62, 115, 128
  anthropomorphic figurines, 51–52, 62, 128, 132, 139
  ceramics, 127–128, 145n9
  child images/representations, 55–57
  communities of practice and, 123–125
  engraving of, 126–128
  image quality, 128–131
  as grave goods, *259–260, 294, 309–311*
  plaquettes, 55, 124
  rondelles/thaumatropes, 49–51, 139
  spearthrowers/atlatls, 49
  See also art of Paleolithic; children as producers of art; parietal art
Předmostí (Czech Republic), 51, 162, *229–230, 291–293*
primates
  alloparenting, 37
  birth process, 25
  bonobos (*Pan paniscus*), 25, 91, 93, 94
  brain growth/development of, 28–29
  chimpanzees (*Pan troglodytes*), 24, 25, 28, 29, 30, 40, 93–95
  fecundity vs. life span, 38

fetuses/infants of, 24, 25, 28, 33, 34, 35, 149
Great Apes, 23
vs. humans, 23, 24, 28–29, 33–35, 45n5, 105, 147, 167
life history of, 22
macaques, 28
play of, 48
scaffolding by, 93–95
sex and tool use, 93, 95
social structure, 40, 42

Qafzeh (Israel), 60, 163n1, *230–232*, *293–294*

reproduction
gestation, in hominins, 22, 23, 28
Grandmother Hypothesis and, 22, 23, 38–39
K-strategists, 22–23, 47
pregnancy, in Paleolithic, 36, 37, 148
reproductive age, 21
r-strategists, 22
See also adolescence; birth process; infant care
Réseau Clastres (France), 72, 118
Rome/Romans (ancient), 5, 9, 13
Romito Cave (Italy), 159–160, *294*
Rouffignac (France), *75*, 107, 111, *112*, 118–122, 133, 144n2

Schiffer, Michael, 5–6
Schöningen (Germany), 52
sex
biological sex, 18
child producers of art and, 133–138
communities of practice and, 97
definition, 20n6
sexual division of labor, 42, 44, 92, 132
tool making/use and, 92–95
sexing
aDNA and, 18–19
of fossil hominin subadults, 16, 19
of subadults generally, 18–19
skeletons, of hominins
assignment of biological age and, 16–17
assignment of sex and, 18–19
growth of, 151
of Paleolithic subadults, 27, 59–61, 77n3
puberty and, 147
See also bones/bone structure
Skhul (Israel), 60

skill acquisition, by Paleolithic subadults, 95–97, 101–103
social structure
of *H. erectus*, 42
of *H. sapiens*, 44–45
of Neandertals, 42, 44
in Paleolithic, 40, 44
Sofaer Derevenski, Joanna, 7–8
Solvieux (France), 85–87, 99
space, use by children
footprints, 67–74, 115
in general, 64
handprints/hand stencils, 72, 74–77, 145n6
secret spaces, in Paleolithic, 65–66
small spaces, in Paleolithic, 66–67
See also finger flutings
Stone Age
in Africa, 88, 98, 148
periodization, 20n1
storytelling
as direct teaching, 105–106
evolution and, 167–169
as oblique teaching, 168
in Paleolithic, 107, 116–117
parietal art as, 107–109, 112–114
subadults, of hominins, 37
ageing of, 15–18
Au. sp., 41
definition of, 15
fossil, 19, 30
H. sp., 41, 42
learning and, 23
Neandertal, 31, 37, 42, 59
percentage of 'analysable population', 3–4
Roc de Marsal child, 31, 32, 59
sexing of, 18–19
skill acquisition/apprenticeship, in Paleolithic, 78
See also adolescents/adolescence; baby; children; infants; neonates
Sunghir 1/2/3 (Russia), 19, 139–140, *245*, *309–310*

taphonomy, 145n9
archaeology and, 3–4
C-transforms, 5–6
ethnography and, 62, 85
flintknapping refitting studies and, 84
N-transforms, 5, *233*

teeth
    biological age and, 16, 17
    dental development, 16
    life history of humans and, 15
    neonatal line, 16, 37
    sex and, 16
    weaning and analysis of, 35–37
Teshik-Tesh (Uzbekistan), 60, *246*, *311*
Theopetra (Greece), *70*
Tianyuan (China), 139
Tito Bustillo (Spain), 111
Tobias, Phillip, 21
Toirano (Italy), 54–55
tools
    communities of practice, 97
    as grave goods, 59, 62, 158, 159, *176*, *251*, *255*, *259–261*, *265*, *282*, *284–285*, *287*
    handaxes, 52, 58, 89
    instruction in making of, 95
    sex and making/use of, 92–95
    standardized production/traditions of, 98
    story knives, 106
    as toys, 52
    See also flintknapping; lithics/stone tools
torches. *See* lamps/torches
toys and games, 4
    animal figurines, 51–52
    anthropomorphic figurines, 51–52
    clay pellets, 54–55
    as embodying/transmitting societal values, 11–12
    musical instruments as, 52–54
    overview, 48–49
    as pedagogical devices, 11–12
    repurposing of toys by children, 12
    rondelles, 49–51
    thaumatropes, 49–50
    tools as, 52, 66
    weapons as, 11, 52, 89
    See also children; play
Trollesgave (Denmark), 99, 101
Tuc d'Audoubert (France), *69*, 72–73, 115, 118

Vela Spila Cave (Croatia), 51
Venus of Laussel, 53, *54*
Vogelherd (Germany), 116

weaning, 16, *22*, 34–38
    chemical analysis of teeth and, 35–36
    H. erectus and, 41
    Neandertals and, 43
weapons
    daggers, 9, *10*
    spears, 52
    spearthrowers/atlatls, 49
    as toys, 11, 52, 89
White Sands (USA), *70*, 71
Whitley, David, 125–126
Willandra Lakes Region (Australia), 71
wolves, 160–162
women
    as archaeological subjects, 14
    as producers of Paleolithic art, 133

Zaraisk (Russia), 139